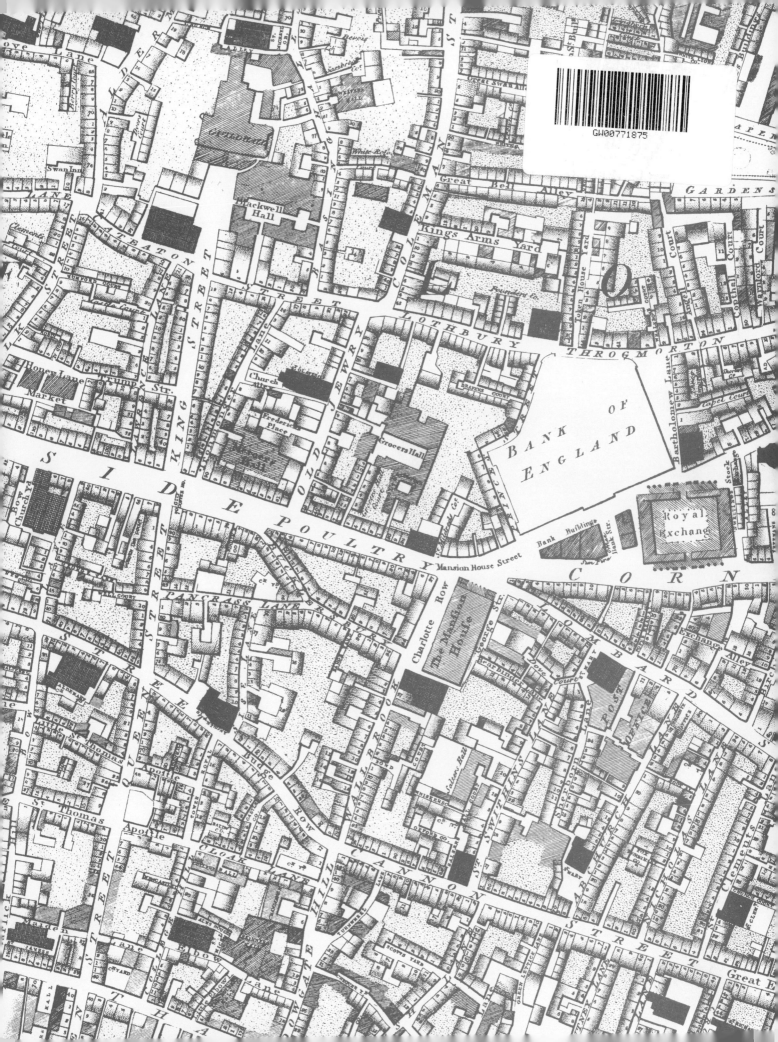

The

ROYAL EXCHANGE

Sir Thomas Gresham aged 26. Painted in Antwerp by an unknown artist,
possibly William Scrots, in 1544, at the time of his marriage.

By kind permission of the Mercers' Company

The
ROYAL EXCHANGE

Edited by
ANN SAUNDERS

The London Topographical Society
Publication No. 152
1997

© London Topographical Society
Publication No. 152 of the London Topographical Society
3 Meadway Gate, London NW11 7LA
ISBN 0 902 087 38 X

PRINTED IN GREAT BRITAIN BY
W. S. MANEY & SON, HUDSON ROAD, LEEDS

CONTENTS

LIST OF COLOUR PLATES

PREFACE

THE GENESIS OF THIS BOOK lay in a telephone call, made late in the summer of 1990, from John Watts of Guardian Royal Exchange to the present editor. He asked for a substantial book about the Royal Exchange, to be researched, written and printed in time to give to Her Majesty The Queen on 23 October 1991 when she would come to re-open the restored and enlarged building. A small, well illustrated booklet was written for Her Majesty and was duly presented, but during its preparation I realised what a wealth existed of scarcely known archival material, and that several other people were working in related fields. Jean Imray, former Archivist to the Mercers' Company, had written an account of the acquisition of land for the Exchange; Robert Thompson had made a special study of tokens which depicted the building; Clare Willsdon had devoted a substantial section of her doctoral thesis to the nineteenth- and twentieth-century paintings around its walls. Earlier accounts of the Exchange, the best of them written by Charles Welch in 1913, were brief but the material for a large book was there, and the London Topographical Society undertook its publication. Before long, a team of thirty enthusiasts was assembled — historians, archaeologists, architects, numismatists, actuaries, insurance specialists and museum curators — and the chapters began to be written. Gatherings and workshops were held at the editor's home, at University College London, and at the Institute of Historical Research. Somehow, everything came together on time.

We have not attempted to write a coherent, comprehensive history, taken from a single viewpoint, of the Exchange, nor, where full studies are already in print, have we included matters covered elsewhere. Burgon's *Life of Sir Thomas Gresham* (1839), though perhaps old-fashioned and inclined to hero-worship, is still invaluable; Professor Barry Supple's excellent *The Royal Exchange Assurance* (1970) is still in print; David Kynaston's studies of finance are readily available in *The City of London* (1994, 1995). Rather, we have concentrated on the Royal Exchange as a social and topographical magnet to which all men were drawn and which provided London with a focal point, a fulcrum, perhaps even a heart. News and information — possibly the most valuable commodities of all — were traded there; buildings, particular to related crafts, trades and professions, clustered around it. It would not be too much to say that the Royal Exchange became London's own mascot, its icon.

In achieving this volume, we have received help and support from a number of individuals and institutions. Dr Anne Sutton, FSA, Archivist to the Mercers' Company, gave it her blessing, and Ursula Carlyle, the Assistant Archivist, received and made welcome every one of the contributors; without her help, the volume would never have been completed. The staff of the Guildhall Library — Ralph Hyde, FSA, John Fisher, Jeremy Smith and Lynne MacNab in Prints and Maps, Irene Gilchrist in Books, and Stephen Freeth and Judith Etherton in Manuscripts — gave help beyond the call of duty, as did James Sewell, Vivienne Aldous, Juliet Bankes and Larry Francis in the Corporation of London Record Office, while Robert Pulham tackled the bulk of the photography there. Veronica Stokes, FSA, former Archivist to Coutts' Bank, and Henry Cobb, CBE, former Clerk of the Records at the House of Lords, gave comfort and support with the more difficult palaeography; Dr Nigel Ramsey, FSA, generously made available the manuscript of his late father's edition of Sir Thomas Gresham's letters, the publication of which is eagerly awaited. Betty Masters, former Archivist to the Corporation of London, gave kindly encouragement and good advice.

At Hatfield, Robin Harcourt-Williams guided me among the Salisbury papers and in Antwerp Dr Meewis and Mme Degueldre patiently helped me to trace Hendryck van Paesschen among the well-ordered archives of that amiable city. Livia Visser-Fuchs translated the substantial entry from the Antwerp Certificatie-boek and Dr N. Maddens of Kortrijk advised on other entries. Dr Lorne Campbell of the National Gallery has discussed the portraits of Thomas Gresham. Pamela Clabburn gave advice and hospitality when the Bacon Papers were being consulted in the University of East Anglia.

Her Majesty The Queen has graciously permitted the reproduction of two items from the Royal collection; the Earl of Jersey has most kindly allowed us to use a hitherto unpublished painting of Gresham from his collection, and the Marquis of Salisbury has permitted the reproduction of the original plan for the Exchange. The bulk of the other illustrations are from the collections of the Corporation of London, of Guardian Royal Exchange and of the Mercers' Company. The British Museum and the Museum of London have been most helpful.

I owe a personal debt of gratitude to the whole team who, though scattered throughout England, Scotland and Wales, have worked as a unit, with rhythm, precision and punctuality; special thanks are due to John Watts, to Professor Michael Port and to Professor Ian Blanchard for advice in editorial dilemmas. Anthea Hanhart has typed, patiently and skilfully, a large proportion of the text; my husband, Bruce Saunders, has proof-read doggedly; Dr Hana Sambrook has tackled the Index.

The archaeology of the site was originally to be described by Dr Ralph Merrifield but when, to all our sorrow, he died early on in the undertaking, the work was taken over by Dr Peter Marsden and Dr Jenny Hall at very short notice.

University College London made me an Honorary Research Fellow. The Nuffield Foundation made me an award under the Social Sciences Small Grants Scheme. The Corporation of London and the Mercers' Company gave invaluable assistance at the start of the project. The Corporation gave further welcome assistance as the work approached completion. Guardian Royal Exchange has contributed towards the cost of the colour illustrations; the London International Financial Futures Exchange has supported the undertaking most generously. The publication has been made possible by a grant from the Scouloudi Foundation in association with the Institute of Historical Research. Further generous encouragement came from an individual benefactor, who prefers to remain anonymous, from the Kenneth Hargreaves Charitable Trust, from the Marc Fitch and the Titsey Foundations, the Worshipful Company of Ironmongers, and from Gonville and Caius College, Cambridge — Sir Thomas Gresham's own place of study. The London Topographical Society is deeply grateful to them all.

Finally, thanks must go to the individual members of the Society whose support has made the enterprise possible, and to Graham Maney, Linda Fish and Jackie Maidment of Messrs Maney of Leeds who have dealt with a complicated text with patience, courtesy, good humour and unfailing professionalism.

ANN SAUNDERS

ABBREVIATIONS

APC	*Acts of the Privy Council of England*, ed. J. R. Daseur (new series, vols. 1–7) (London, 1890–93).
BL	British Library
BM	British Museum
Burgon, *Gresham*	J. W. Burgon, *The Life and Times of Sir Thomas Gresham*, 2 vols. (London, 1839).
CLRO	Corporation of London Record Office
DNB	*Dictionary of National Biography*
GL	Guildhall Library
GR	Gresham Repertories
GRE	Guardian Royal Exchange
L & PD	*Letters and Papers, Domestic Series*
L & PF	*Letters and Papers, Foreign Series*
L & P Henry VIII	*Letters and Papers, Foreign and Domestic of the Reign of Henry VIII*, ed. J. Gardner (London, 1890–1907).
MC	Mercers' Company
PRO	Public Record Office
RCHM	Royal Commision on Historic Monuments
SPD	*State Papers, Domestic*
SPF	*State Papers, Foreign*
Ward, *Lives*	John Ward, *Lives of the Professors of Gresham College* (1740).
Welch, *Royal Exchange*	Charles Welch, *Illustrated Account of the Royal Exchange and the pictures therein* (1913).

BIBLIOGRAPHY

BINDOFF, S. T.
   The Fame of Sir Thomas Gresham (Neale Lecture in English History, 1973).

BURGON, JOHN WILLIAM
   The Life and Times of Sir Thomas Gresham, 2 vols (1839).

DOOLITTLE, IAN
   The Mercers' Company, 1579–1959 (1994).

FEATHERSTONE, ERNEST
   Sir Thomas Gresham and his Trusts (1952).

IMRAY, JEAN
   The Mercers' Hall (1991).

WELCH, CHARLES
   Illustrated Account of the Royal Exchange and the pictures therein (1913).

WHITE, J. G.
   History of the Three Royal Exchanges, the Gresham Lectures and Gresham Almshouses (1896).

NOTES ON CONTRIBUTORS

JENNY HALL
Curator of Roman Collections in the Department of Early London History and collections in the Museum of London.

JEAN IMRAY, BA, FSA
Archivist to the Mercers' Company, 1962–1981.

IAN BLANCHARD
Professor of Medieval Economic History at the University of Edinburgh and Central European University, Budapest. Research interests are in the workings of the international economy 410–1836 and Post-Petrine Russian economic history.

ANN SAUNDERS, PhD, FSA
Hon. Editor, London Topographical Society, 1975–   . Fellow of University College London. Liveryman of the Horners' Company. Author of *Art and Architecture of London*.

DAVID MITCHELL
David Mitchell (Centre for Metropolitan History, University of London) has written widely on the design, production and distribution of damask and diaper napery, its use in the setting of tables and the ceremonies of dining.

DIANA SCARISBRICK, FSA
Has lectured on jewellery at seminars on both sides of the Atlantic, and has contributed to many exhibition catalogues. Her most recent books are *Jewellery in Britain 1066–1837* (Norwich, 1994) and *Chaumet* (Paris, 1995).

KAY STANILAND
Curator (Costume and Textiles), Department of Later London History and collections, Museum of London.

CHRISTOPHER CHALLIS
Reader in Modern History at the University of Leeds and sometime President of the British Numismatic Society; author of *The Tudor Coinage* (Manchester, 1978) and editor of *A New History of the Royal Mint* (Cambridge, 1992).

PETER RAMSEY
Professor of History, Aberdeen University (1966–93). Author of *Tudor Economic Problems* (1963) and articles on sixteenth-century accountancy and trade.

TREVOR SIBBETT
Senior actuary working mainly on international life assurance matters in the Royal Exchange. He holds a number of appointments in insurance organisations. He was a founder member of the Royal Exchange Archives Committee in 1980. In addition to editing the ten-volume *History of Actuarial Science* with Professor Steven Haberman (William Pickering, 1995), he has written extensively on actuarial history for publications of the Institute of Actuaries and the Staple Inn Actuarial Society and has also contributed papers to the congresses of the International Actuarial Association.

JULIA GASPER, PhD
Author of *The Dragon and the Dove: The Plays of Thomas Dekker* (OUP, *Oxford English Monographs*, 1990). She teaches English Literature for the Open University.

HAZEL FORSYTH
Curator, Post-Medieval Department of Early London History and Collections.

SIR HOWARD COLVIN, FBA

Emeritus Fellow of St John's College, Oxford, and was formerly Reader in Architectural History at Oxford. He is the author of *A Biographical Dictionary of British Architects 1600–1840* (3rd edn, 1995), *Unbuilt Oxford* (1983) and *Architecture and the After-Life* (1991), and was editor of the collaborative *History of the King's Works* (1963–82).

KATHARINE GIBSON

Registered at the Courtauld Institute of Art in London where she has nearly completed her doctoral thesis on 'The Iconography of Charles II'.

INGRID ROSCOE, PhD

Her doctoral thesis, 'Peter Scheemakers and Classical Sculpture in Early Hanoverian England' (Leeds, 1990), has been the starting point for a number of articles and for a Catalogue Raisonné, scheduled for publication by the Walpole Society in 1999. She co-edits the Church Monuments Society *Journal*.

MICHAEL HARRIS, PhD

Senior Lecturer in History at Birkbeck College. He has written extensively on the newspaper press and the book trade in London, and is founder and co-editor of the annual *Studies in Newspaper and Periodical History*.

NATASHA GLAISYER

PhD student at the University of Cambridge. She is undertaking research on the culture of commerce in late seventeenth- and early eighteenth-century England.

LAURENCE WORMS, BA

Has run Ash Rare Books, 25 Royal Exchange, since 1971. General bookseller with small but varied stock — mainly first edition literature, travel, maps, atlases and early London material. Writes on publishing and cartographic history, and is compiling a dictionary of British map engravers. Currently writing on early English atlases for the Cambridge University *History of the Book*. Also working on a number of 'lives' for the revision of the *DNB*. Recently elected to the Council of the Bibliographical Society. Represents the Antiquarian Booksellers' Association on the National Book Committee and the (DTI) Art Trade Steering Group.

GLORIA CLIFTON, PhD

Curator of navigational instruments at the National Maritime Museum, Greenwich, London. She was compiler of the recently published reference work, *Directory of British Scientific Instrument Makers 1550–1851* (London, 1995).

ROBERT THOMPSON, FSA, ALA

Librarian. Fellow of the Royal Numismatic Society and successively Hon. Librarian and then Director of the British Numismatic Society. He has published five volumes on tokens in the British Academy's *Syllogie of Coins of the British Isles*, and many papers and bibliographies.

DEREK KEENE, PhD

Director of the Centre for Metropolitan History at the Institute of Historical Research. He has published extensively on the history, archaeology, and topography of English cities from the early medieval period onwards.

PETER MARSDEN, PhD

Field archaeologist, Guildhall Museum, 1960–72, thereafter Senior Archaeologist, Museum of London. Has a special interest in marine archaeology, London being the premier port of Roman Britain. Now Director of the Shipwreck Heritage Centre in Hastings.

MICHAEL PORT, PhD, FSA

Architectural historian and Emeritus Professor of Modern History, Queen Mary and Westfield College, University of London.

CLARE WILLSDON, PhD
> Graduate of Cambridge University, where she studied Modern Languages and History of Art. Her doctoral thesis for Cambridge was on 'Aspects of Mural Painting in London 1890–1930'. She is a Fellow of the Royal Society of Arts and lectures in History of Art at the University of Glasgow. She has conducted the first major research project on British murals 1840–1940, which is to be published by OUP; has researched mural art on the Continent and published 'European Mural Painting *c*. 1810–1930' in the Macmillan's *Dictionary of Art*; and has a special interest in the mural paintings of Brangwyn and the Austrian artist Gustav Klimt.

IAN LEITH
> Curator at the Royal Commission on the Historical Monuments of England, and was one of the founders of the Public Monuments and Sculpture Association.

CHRISTOPHER EIMER, MPhil
> Medal dealer and historian.

PETER JACKSON, FSA
> Chairman, London Topographical Society. Author of *John Tallis's London Street Views, 1938–40* (1969), *George Scharf's London* (1987), and co-author of *London, 2000 Years of a City and its People* (1974).

PETER JEFFERSON SMITH
> Read history at Cambridge University and is a former Deputy Chairman of HM Customs and Excise. He lives in Clapham, where his study of local architectural history led him to the work of Edward I'Anson and Son. He is currently researching the history of the firm from 1800 to 1912.

JOHN WATTS
> Curator for The Royal Exchange and has been employed in its upkeep for the past forty years. He was a founder member of the GRE Archives Committee and later its chairman. He was also a founder member of the Donizetti Society, the second chairman and, as editor, contributed articles to the Society's first three journals.

COLIN CHRISTMAS
> Colin Christmas commenced his career with Sir Giles Gilbert Scott, following which he joined the Fitzroy Robinson Partnership. As a partner in the practice he was responsible for the design concept, and detailing of the Royal Exchange project. He is currently engaged by Guardian Properties as architectural and historic consultant for Covent Garden Market and the Royal Exchange.

PART ONE
THE FIRST EXCHANGE

1566–1666

CHAPTER I

The Site of the Royal Exchange in the Roman Period

By JENNY HALL

THE SITE OF the Royal Exchange was excavated in 1840–41, prior to building the new Exchange, and the surviving remains were described by the antiquarian Charles Roach Smith in a letter published in 1842, and by William Tite, the architect for the new Royal Exchange, in a catalogue published in 1848. Unfortunately the level of recording has made it difficult to determine the true nature of Roman occupation on the Royal Exchange site. It is possible, however, to view the descriptions of the site together with those objects found and to compare them with the evidence from surrounding sites in order to surmise the possible nature of occupation of the site and its relation to the rest of Roman London.

THE FINDS FROM THE ROYAL EXCHANGE

In 1842 Charles Roach Smith published a letter to Sir Henry Ellis in *Archaeologia* describing the foundations of Roman buildings which were found in the central part of the site as having 'well constructed walls running in a diagonal direction from N.E. to N.W.'. To the west, there were other foundations with a mass of masonry consisting of tiles and mortar. Some wallplaster still remained, pink in colour with painted or moulded decoration. He recorded that there was a layer of gravel (2 feet thick) that overlaid a gravel pit (some 40 × 50 feet and 19 feet deep). The pit which lay below these substantial foundations was filled with 'refuse from adjacent shops and houses'. In addition, a shaft was sunk in front of the Exchange, and a Roman wall (7 feet wide) was found standing to a height of 14 feet, 20 feet down below street level.

However, according to Roach Smith, he was prevented by 'regulations' from making more detailed

observations of the excavations[1] and a bitter rift ensued between him and Tite.[2]

William Tite, the architect of the third Royal Exchange, produced a detailed descriptive catalogue of the antiquities from the site (Tite, 1848). He recorded that the eastern part of the site revealed 'very few relics of antiquity' but that the middle and western part of the site had considerable archaeological strata, already disturbed by the earlier building of the old Exchange. The western wall of the old Exchange had been partly erected on the remains of a Roman building and a mass of masonry still had plaster adhering, yellow-ochre in colour. The gravel pit, as described by Roach Smith above, had a layer of gravel (over 1 foot thick) above it, which was thought at the time to be natural, and above that Roman rubble foundations to a height of over 3 feet. It was this area of the site that yielded a greater quantity of artefacts. Most of these finds came from the gravel pit, described by Tite as 'filled with hardened mud', and included such faunal remains as oyster shells and animal bones, as well as pottery, leather fragments, glass, lamps, brooches, general artefacts and Roman coins.

Tite's catalogue indicated that the finds were held in the museum of the Corporation of London. This was later to become the Guildhall Museum, one of the predecessor museums of the Museum of London. It is now impossible to identify all those artefacts in the present collections of the Museum of London. Of those items still attributable to the Royal Exchange, few are closely identifiable except for the Roman coins. The records of the early Guildhall Museum were scant, the only information being that published

[1] Roach Smith, *Archaeologia*, XXIX, p. 272.
[2] See *infra*, pp. 3, 272–78.

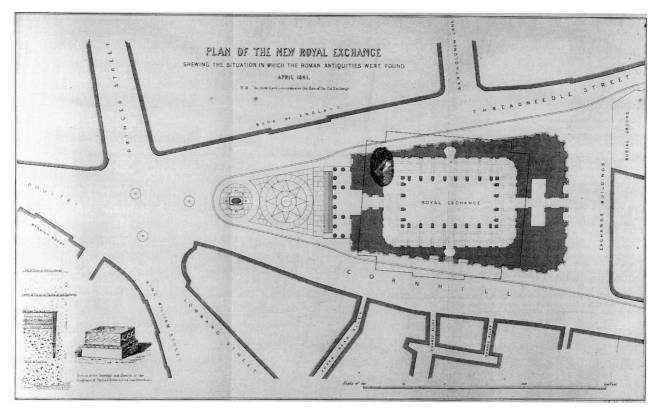

FIG. 1.   The site of the new Royal Exchange, as published in Tite's *Catalogue* of 1848, indicating the locations where antiquities were found.

in the Guildhall Museum Catalogue in 1908, some sixty years after the excavations. In addition, more recent detailed cataloguing of the museum's collections have meant that some items have been re-identified and are no longer deemed to be Roman in date. The British Museum also holds Roman material from the site, collected at the time by Roach Smith who looked over the spoil heaps of earth cleared from the site 'and disposed of many miles from the place of exhumation in an open unfenced situation accessible to all' (Roach Smith papers, Museum of London).

Tite singled out certain items as worthy of special mention. Building material included a flat building tile (*tegula*) with a circular maker's mark, two curved roof tiles (*imbrices*) and fragments of other building tiles. The pottery consisted of sherds of at least two amphorae, a mortarium (stamped CRACIUS F), other sherds of pottery mortaria and stone mortars and numerous sherds of various beakers. Fragments of lamps are listed but one volute picture lamp is described as having 'the head of an empress with a

crescent moon' on the discus. This is now identified as a lamp with the goddess Luna (MOL Accession No. 1405). The Roman red glossy tableware, samian, is listed in profusion and the catalogue of potters' stamps (Tite, 1848, pp. 18–22) seems to consist of potters from southern Gaul (for example, Aquila, Alius, Calvus, Carus, Crestio, Firo, Montanus, Primulus, Roppus, Sabinus, Severus, Virilis and Vitalis). Samian was produced in the area of modern-day Millau in southern France, the main sites being La Graufesenque, Montans and Bannassac. Those potters listed above were producing their pottery in the first century, especially in the mid to late first century.

The descriptions of the Roman glass show representational samples of first- and second-century glass comprising fragments from square bottles, round flasks and pillar-moulded bowls. The catalogue also records wooden writing tablets and at least twenty-five iron or copper-alloy styli. Tite then included a miscellaneous category which included copper-alloy military fittings, studs and mounts; brooches; a strigil;

wooden comb and spindles; iron tongs; a fragment of weighing beam (steelyard) and various iron tools comprising gouges, a saw, an auger, knives, nails and linch pins. A variety of leather was also recorded, consisting of the soles and insoles of typical styles of Roman shoes as well as offcuts indicating leather-working as well as discarded shoes. Roach Smith elected for special mention the shoes (Roach Smith, 1842, p. 269) and also recorded two iron knives, stamped with the makers' names, Olondus (RIB II 2428.14) and P Basilius (RIB II 2428.6). These knives are now in the British Museum.

Tite goes on to describe in detail some forty-nine Roman coins. The coins were of the emperors Augustus, Tiberius, Nero, Vespasian (9), Domitian (11), Nerva, Trajan (2), Hadrian, Antoninus Pius (2), Faustina the Elder (2), Marcus Aurelius (3), Faustina the Younger and Septimius Severus. The majority of these coins were recorded as being found from the gravel pit and date to the first to early third centuries. Coins of emperors of the later third and fourth centuries (Valerian, Victorinus, Carausius, Constantine I, Valens and Gratian) were found elsewhere on site. Of the forty-nine coins described by Tite, forty-seven can be now be closely identified in the Museum of London collection as of the emperors Augustus, Claudius (2), Nero, Galba, Vespasian (7), Domitian (16), Nerva, Trajan, Hadrian (3), Antoninus Pius, Faustina the Elder, Marcus Aurelius (3), Faustina the Younger, Septimius Severus, Valerian, Victorinus, Carausius, Constantine I, Valens and Gratian (2). Further information can be obtained from the Early London Department at the Museum of London.

THE AREA SURROUNDING THE ROYAL EXCHANGE

By comparing the scanty records of the buildings found on the site with those sites that surround the Royal Exchange, it may be possible to postulate the significance of the Royal Exchange site during the Roman period. To the north lies the site of the Bank of England in Threadneedle Street. The Bank site yielded a wealth of Roman material but little in the way of structural information. To the west lay the Walbrook stream valley, its course underlying sites at the junction at the Bank, the National Safe Deposit Company, No. 1 Poultry and Queen Victoria Street. To the south, the route of the main east to west Roman road (the *Via Decumana*) ran parallel to the Royal Exchange, cutting across modern-day King William Street. To the east, in the Gracechurch Street and Leadenhall area, lay the Roman forum and basilica, the main centre of administration and commerce. The site of the Royal Exchange, therefore, lay just north of the heart of Roman London.

Excavations in this defined area were conducted as early as 1785. Objects from it formed a large part of Charles Roach Smith's collection that went to the British Museum in 1851. Other objects from the Bank of England and National Safe Deposit Company were collected by the then Guildhall Museum and the British Museum. References contained in the following review of surrounding sites recorded prior to 1965 are drawn from Ralph Merrifield's *Gazetteer of City sites* (Merrifield, 1965). Information about the site records and objects from more recent excavations is held at the Museum of London and the Museum of London Archaeological Service.

SITES TO THE NORTH

The northern and western boundaries of the review area are bounded by the Walbrook stream. A site in Threadneedle Street (Merrifield, no. 182) and Bartholomew Lane (Merrifield, no. 181) revealed buildings, the former with a shallow rectangular bath, plastered walls and a floor made of crushed tile and mortar (*opus signinum*), the latter with a black and white tessellated pavement depicting a scroll of ivy leaves. Further to the north at Austin Friars (Molas, 1989, pp. 14–15) a silted-up tributary of the Walbrook crossed the site. The ground surface had been consolidated by large-scale dumping to provide a platform for building. The area was then redeveloped with impressive stone-built houses, one with a small courtyard overlooking the Walbrook. Tessellated floors were laid throughout the main building. In time, these masonry buildings were abandoned and the building material re-used for a final, less substantial building.

The excavations for the present Bank of England building were conducted between 1926 and 1936.

FIG. 2.   Roman coins from the gravel pit at the Royal Exchange, now in the Museum of London.

Other discoveries had been made previously. Merrifield recorded that a patterned mosaic floor was found in 1805 (Merrifield, no. 167) which is now in the British Museum. The pattern of acanthus leaves in a roundel is dated to the third century. In 1927 (Merrifield, no. 169) Roman floors of *opus signinum* were found with an associated timber-lined drain. To the north lay a timber-framed structure. Higher occupation levels contained fragments of first-century leather and pottery. In 1933–34 (Merrifield, no. 168), the stream-bed of the Walbrook was observed running across the site. From it came a great quantity of leather, iron- and bronze-work. In the same year (Merrifield, no. 171), a square tessellated floor with a circular central panel was found. Underlying pottery

was of the early second century and the floor itself has been dated to the second century. Another tessellated floor was also found, second to third century in date. However, no associated walls were recorded to be able to determine the size and nature of the buildings.

The interpretation of the Bank of England excavations is assisted by more recent excavations. At Lothbury (Molas, 1988, pp. 22–23), for example, north of the Bank of England, excavation of a circular ventilation shaft for the Docklands Light Railway in 1987 revealed a large masonry building constructed soon after A.D. 200. It was probably a large townhouse with interconnecting rooms ranged around a central courtyard. The house incorporated an underfloor

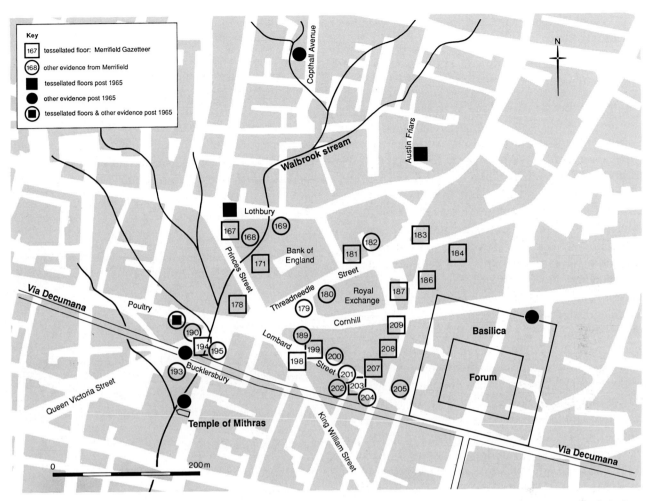

FIG. 3.   The area around the site of the Royal Exchange in the Roman period. The numbers within squares and circles
refer to Merrifield's *Gazetteer*.

heating system, tessellated floors and painted wall-plaster. It was abandoned in the late fourth century.

Wilmott reviewed a number of sites excavated in the middle Walbrook valley including the Bank of England (Wilmott, 1991). He concluded that this part of the Walbrook valley in the first to mid-second century had been characterised by a gradual attempt to raise the ground level in the stream valley and to drain the upper Walbrook basin. During this period, the area had been devoted to industry and dumping (Wilmott, 1991, p. 180) with the main stream acting as an outlet for the major drainage scheme to the north in the upper Walbrook. The stream continued to be maintained from *c.* A.D. 160 well into the third century. On cessation of this programme, the industrial activity in the lower Walbrook valley ceased and

the upper and middle Walbrook became a place to build fine townhouses. It is inconceivable that such structures would have been erected here if there was any danger of flooding. Professor Grimes found evidence from the excavations of the Temple of Mithras on the eastern bank of the Walbrook (Shepherd, forthcoming) that between the late second century and when the temple was constructed, *c.* A.D. 240–250, the Walbrook channel did not appear to be as well maintained. Occupation on both banks continued until the end of the Roman period. The work at Copthall Avenue to the north provided additional evidence that the systematic maintenance of the drainage programme broke down in the late third or fourth century (Maloney, 1990, pp. 119–23) when the upper Walbrook began to revert to marsh.

It is probable that a similar reversion also began in the lower valley.

SITES TO THE WEST

In 1867 at the corner of Princes Street, a portion of mosaic floor was found with its underfloor heating system (Merrifield, no. 178). In addition, sites in Queen Victoria Street have again indicated that the Walbrook valley was well maintained in the first and second centuries and that stone buildings were constructed in the third century. Excavations in Queen Victoria Street in 1869 revealed walls with a tessellated floor with a mortar skirting (Merrifield, no. 193). Elsewhere, a very fine mosaic floor, known as the Bucklersbury Pavement, was found with its underfloor heating system intact, surrounded by walls of chalk and ragstone (Merrifield, no. 194). The floor is dated to the third century. Elsewhere in Queen Victoria Street (Merrifield, nos. 190 and 195) the Walbrook stream-bed was found to contain quantities of pottery, metal artefacts and coins, and the stream's banks had substantial wooden piles for revetments and foundations for buildings. The level of preservation of both objects and wooden structures was excellent due to the waterlogged nature of the sites. At Bucklersbury, for example, during excavations for the Docklands Light Railway (Molas, 1988, pp. 22–23) the waterlogged conditions had preserved a sequence of Roman timber buildings. Dumps of earth used to level the ground surface contained a huge quantity of smashed and burnt samian pottery of the early second century. Although broken, the vessels were unused and may have come from a nearby warehouse or shop that had been destroyed by the early second-century fire that devastated a large part of Roman London.

The site at No. 1 Poultry (Molas, 1996, pp. 22–25) revealed the western side of the Walbrook valley, near where the main road crossed the stream. A length of the main east to west Roman road was excavated, dating to c. A.D. 50. To the north of the main road, the earliest buildings, of clay and timber, were destroyed by fire during the Boudican rebellion of A.D. 60/61. They were rapidly rebuilt as narrow-fronted strip buildings and were a mix of residential, commercial and industrial premises. They too had

been destroyed by the second-century fire, as at Bucklersbury. These buildings were rebuilt but less densely, and towards the end of the second century were replaced by stone buildings. During the third and fourth centuries, many of the roadside properties were cleared of timber buildings and were replaced by yards or open areas between the main road and northern range of stone buildings. The stone buildings had tessellated floors and remained in use until the late fourth or early fifth centuries.

SITES TO THE SOUTH

The designated area for the purposes of this review is bounded to the south by the main Roman road (the *Via Decumana*). To the north of this road and to the south of the Royal Exchange site, Merrifield records nine sites (Merrifield, nos. 189, 198–205) in the Lombard Street area. All the records show evidence of ragstone walls, or ragstone with chalk and flint, some with tile courses. Many of the buildings had plain red tessellated floors. A site in Lombard Street in 1785 also recorded a pavement of red, black and white tesserae (Merrifield, no. 199).

SITES TO THE EAST

Sites excavated to the immediate east of the Royal Exchange are less numerous and Roman buildings in that area must have been affected by the development of the forum and basilica in the Gracechurch Street and Leadenhall area. However, sites in Threadneedle Street (Merrifield, nos. 182–84), Finch Lane (Merrifield, nos. 186, 187) and Birchin Lane (Merrifield, nos. 207–09) have revealed evidence of walls and wallplaster, plain red tessellated pavements and fine patterned mosaics of both second- and fourth-century date. Two mosaic floors from Threadneedle Street are now in the British Museum, other fragments of mosaics from Finch Lane and Birchin Lane are now in the Museum of London.

A review of the pottery of the early Roman period (Davies in Milne and Wardle, 1993, pp. 137–38) has shown that by c. A.D. 50 there was 'a restricted core east of the Walbrook stream south of Cornhill, in the area of modern Gracechurch Street, with subsequent development along the east–west Roman road. It is not until the A.D. 70s that the town expanded to encompass the Leadenhall area'. Excavations at Leadenhall Court in 1983 produced much information about the development of the forum and basilica (Milne, 1992). Milne showed that by A.D. 60 and the Boudican rebellion, the area of occupation of London had not spread as far as the hill top to the east of the Walbrook stream valley. By this time, however, a large quarry had been dug to extract the natural brickearth for use in building. The hole resulting from the quarrying had been left open and slowly silted up. The ground had been prepared for building by the dumping of refuse material. In the last quarter of the first century, a radical redevelopment of the area produced the first forum, built c. A.D. 70–80 and strip buildings fronting on to the east to west main road. The area was later cleared ready for the construction of the second forum and basilica, built between A.D. 90–120. The new basilica was placed squarely on the highest point, Cornhill, in order to dominate the skyline. It is likely, therefore, that the area surrounding the prestigious forum attracted the finer shops and higher-class premises.

CONCLUSION

It is possible, therefore, to postulate certain phases of activity on the site of the Royal Exchange. The earliest activity in the area was the construction of the main east to west Roman road in c. A.D. 50, as demonstrated by the site at No. 1 Poultry. The road was constructed using layers of rammed gravel to provide a hard-wearing surface. Several gravel pits must have been opened at this time to provide the raw material, one of which may have been on the rising ground north of the road at the Royal Exchange. The gravel could also have been used for courtyards and make-up material to raise the level of floors. The pit either remained open for gravel extraction or, as at Leadenhall Court, was left to silt up prior to the dumping of refuse material. It would seem that there was little need for building in the area at this time and there is no evidence of structures on the site being destroyed in the two major fires, at the time of the Boudican rebellion in A.D. 60 and in c. A.D. 120–125. These fires formed distinct blackened layers in the archaeological strata, for which we have no record at the Royal Exchange. The

main area of development of the Roman town in the first and second centuries lay along this important main road, around the lower and middle Walbrook and along the waterfront.

The finds from the Walbrook valley sites as published by the Guildhall Museum (1955), Merrifield (1965), Wilmott (1991) and Shepherd (forthcoming) show a variety of small finds of copper-alloy and iron, organic leather and wood, all in a very good state of preservation. As indicated above, waterlogged conditions aided the preservation of the objects and the Walbrook stream provided suitable anaerobic conditions. The objects found in the gravel pit and described by William Tite are very similar in nature to those from the clearance programme in the Walbrook valley. They included objects of wood and leather which rarely survive unless waterlogged. There is no tributary of the Walbrook recorded in close proximity to the Royal Exchange. The question to consider, therefore, is how such material, and especially organic material, came to be found in a large gravel pit away from the stream. It is known that the maintenance of the Walbrook valley continued until the early third century (Shepherd, forthcoming) and that from the first century onwards the stream was regularly cleared of rubbish which was dumped on to the banks. Grimes believed that the material from the banks, full of organic debris, came from the cleaning of the stream and that the upcast had been dumped on nearby banks (Shepherd, forthcoming). Those banks were continuously being occupied and built on and there must have been times when the stream-bed was cleared and sites further afield used for dumping. At Leadenhall Court, we have seen that pits dug for the extraction of brickearth were infilled to provide solid platforms for building. The quarry pit at the Royal Exchange was also filled and the land levelled for building. The infill would appear to come from the clearing of the Walbrook stream. The final coin recorded from the pit was of Septimius Severus (dated to A.D. 209) and its early third-century date equates with the final phase of stream maintenance (Shepherd, pers. comm.). A note written by Roach Smith in the Museum of London records that Tite stated that the pit was filled with soft peaty earth, a description not unlike the dark silt of the stream. It would seem, therefore, that the site of the Royal Exchange remained undeveloped until the early third century when the gravel pit was filled ready for building and a layer of gravel laid down.

At that time, it is quite likely that stone buildings were built on the site — the well-constructed walls and wallplaster mentioned by Roach Smith. In the third and fourth centuries, the nature of the town was changing. The city wall had been constructed at the beginning of the third century and the close-set clay and timber buildings that had been so combustible in the two major fires had given way to spacious stone-built townhouses. This area of the town underwent a major redevelopment with numerous records of stone townhouses, discussed above. Many of these provide a record of mosaic floors of second- to fourth-century date. Unfortunately, although walls were found, no tessellated floors were found at the Royal Exchange to substantiate the evidence for townhouses. The layer of gravel and wall foundations may indicate open yards or courtyards or perimeter walls, although the presence of painted wallplaster does indicate internal decorations. In the fourth century, when the town was shrinking in size within the city wall boundary, many areas were no longer developed, but the south-eastern part of the town continued to be inhabited. Records show that buildings in this area of the town lasted into the fourth century and even into the early fifth, but we can only surmise that the structure or structures on the Royal Exchange site also lasted until that time. The last coin found on the site was of the Emperor Gratian of the late fourth century. On some sites, however, for example at Austin Friars, the masonry buildings were abandoned at an earlier date and the building materials re-used for less substantial buildings, or areas became open spaces used as yards as at No. 1 Poultry. This may have been the case at the Royal Exchange and accounts for the scant evidence since much of the building material would have been removed.

The Royal Exchange site, therefore, will always remain something of an enigma. The level of recording precludes it from being a truly informative site and it is unfortunate that it led to a long-running dispute between the two protagonists, Tite and Roach Smith. If Roach Smith, who recorded so much of London's archaeology during the Victorian redevelopment of the City, had been allowed on site to record the findings, a much more detailed picture would have emerged. With this proviso, it is now possible to provide only an outline sketch of how the site of the Royal Exchange may have been used in the four hundred years that the Romans remained in London.

BIBLIOGRAPHY

GUILDHALL MUSEUM *Small Finds from the Walbrook, 1954–1955*

MALONEY, C. *The upper Walbrook in the Roman period*, CBA Research Report (1990)

MERRIFIELD, R. *The Roman City of London* (1965)

MILNE, G. *From Roman Basilica to Medieval Market*, HMSO (1992)

MILNE, G. & WARDLE, A. 'Early Roman development at Leadenhall Court, London and related research' in *Trans* LAMAS, vol. 44 (1993), pp. 23–170

MOLAS (THE MUSEUM OF LONDON ARCHAEOLOGY SERVICE) *The Annual Review* (1988)

MOLAS *The Annual Review* (1989)

MOLAS *The Annual Review for 1995* (1996)

FRERE, S. S. & TOMLIN, R. S. O. (eds.) *The Roman Inscriptions of Britain*, vol. II, fasc. 3 (1991)

ROACH SMITH, C. 'Observations on further Roman Remains discovered in London' in *Archaeologia*, XXIX (1842), pp. 267–72

SHEPHERD, J. *The Temple of Mithras — Excavations by W. F. Grimes and A. Williams at the Walbrook*, English Heritage, forthcoming

SHEPPARD, F. *The Treasury of London's Past* (1991)

TITE, W. *A Descriptive Catalogue of the Antiquities found in the Excavations at the New Royal Exchange, preserved in the Museum of the Corporation of London* (1848)

WILMOTT, T. *Excavations in the Middle Walbrook Valley, City of London, 1927–1960*, LAMAS Special Paper No. 13 (1991)

CHAPTER II

Sir Thomas Gresham *c.* 1518–1579[*]

By IAN BLANCHARD

THOMAS WAS BORN in his father's house in Milk Lane, London in about 1518. He was the second and younger son of Richard Gresham, by his first wife Audrey, daughter of William Lynne of Southwick in Northampton, who bore him four children — John (*c.* 1517–60), Thomas, Christiana, and Elizabeth (d. 1552). Nothing is known of his childhood, save that he was deprived of a mother's care at the age of three or four; and that he was subsequently sent to Cambridge and admitted as a pensioner at Gonville College. On leaving Cambridge, Gresham was apprenticed by his father in *c.* 1535, at the age of seventeen, to his uncle John Gresham, in consequence of which he was some eight years later, in 1543, admitted a member of the Mercers' Company. As he himself later explained, this was a somewhat unusual course of events as 'I need not have bynne prentisse for that I was free by my Father's coppye: albeit my Father Sir Richard Gresham being a wyse man, although I was free by his coppye, it was to no purpos, except I was bound prentisse to the same; whereby to come by the experience and knowledge of all kinds of merchandise'.[1] Clearly following that mid-life crisis, which during the years 1531–35 had made Richard Gresham only too aware of the fragility of domestic happiness and public esteem, Thomas's father was not only plotting out a new career for himself but was also carefully grooming his sons for their future roles in life.

Sir Richard's efforts in the moulding of his elder son John's career were, at least as he perceived the results of his endeavours, less than successful. With regard to Thomas it was otherwise. As during the years 1535–47 Sir Richard withdrew from the management of that branch of the 'House of Gresham's' activities which was concerned with the pursuit of the traditional mercer's trade at the Netherlands marts, he set about grooming Thomas to take his place. By apprenticing Thomas to his uncle, John Gresham, in 1535 he hoped to give him 'the experience and knowledge of all kinds of merchandise' which would fit him for the mercer's craft. Perhaps as a direct result of his disappointment at the failure of his efforts to further his eldest son John's fortunes in the career that he had chosen for him, Richard also during the years of Thomas's apprenticeship (1535–43) began to reveal to his younger son the mysteries of exchange dealings, preparing him for a partnership in this branch of his father's business empire. To this full gamut of training in mercantile-financial skills Richard Gresham, moreover, now also added other elements. He augmented his now favoured younger son's existing knowledge of classical languages with a pragmatic education in contemporary tongues — French and Flemish. By securing Thomas's admission to Gray's Inn he provided him with at least a cursory knowledge of law. Nor did Thomas, like his elder brother, waste these opportunities which his father opened up for him. Indeed he proved himself a very adept pupil. Thus, having spent some time prior to the summer of 1538 in Paris,[2] where he obtained both a knowledge of the intricacies of his uncle John's French trading connections and of the French tongue, Thomas was soon able to put his seemingly excellent French to practical use. Returning to London in June he was rapidly embroiled by his father in the lavish hospitality which the latter, in his capacity as Lord Mayor, had arranged for the Lady of Montreuil and her train during their stay (22–28 August 1538) in the English capital.[3] It was Thomas, 'by reason of' his knowledge of 'the language', moreover, that he sent to accompany the ladies on their protracted five-day

---

[*] An extended version of this paper is to be published in the *New Dictionary of National Biography*.
[1] *SPF*, 1547–53, no. 655.

[2] *L&P Henry VIII*, XIII (1), no. 1186.
[3] *L&P Henry VIII*, XIII (2), nos. 2, 177, 201, 205, 209 and 226.

journey to Dover. He also saw fit to inform Cromwell of the fact and utilised the opportunity to bring the young man to his attention.[4]

Thereafter the young apprentice-mercer was employed by the Crown on various small errands in the Netherlands. On 25 February 1540, for instance, he was said to be with a Mr Parker and Mr Blunt, collectively described as 'Henry's servants', in Brussels on the King's business.[5] He departed from thence for England via Calais before 29 March and by 2 April Sir Thomas Wyatt, the unwisely amorous courtier who had been packed off to undertake diplomatic duties for a jealous king in the Netherlands, writes as though Gresham has by then returned to London and has probably already seen Cromwell.[6] His work seems to have sufficiently impressed Cromwell for the latter to note that he should 'remember Mr Gresham'.[7] Through his direct services for the Crown the young Thomas was beginning to impress. Acting on his father's behalf in the latter's exchange dealings he also seems to have attracted the attention of royal officials. Thus Wyatt, writing from Ghent to Cromwell at this time, not only asked the latter to thank Sir Richard Gresham for the letters of exchange he had despatched, but was also concerned that Cromwell should know of his treatment of Sir Richard's son, Thomas, who having delivered the bills of exchange had now returned to London, writing, 'I suppose his son (Thomas) will say I have done him some pleasure in these parts'.[8] At twenty-two Thomas was clearly marked out for further advancement in royal service.

As a merchant contemporaries also recognised his worth. By the time of his marriage to the widowed Anne Ferneley and his admittance to the freedom of the Mercers' Company in 1543, although still operating in the shadow of his father, he was already well on the way to becoming the de facto head of the Netherlands branch of the 'House of Gresham's' commercial operations. Before he could in 1546/7 assume the mantle fashioned for him by his father, however, he had one more obstacle to overcome. On

3 March 1545 Secretary Paget wrote from Brussels that Thomas, then trading in his own right, was one of the English merchants whose goods had been seized by order of Charles V. He also explained, in a section of his letter which is worth quoting in full, why the Greshams, because of their particular activities, were likely to survive this disastrous turn of events.

Some in dede shall win by it [the seizure]; as William Lok, Sir Richarde Gressam and his sonne [Thomas], and William Gressem, with such other for the most parte that occupie sylkes, who owe more than they have here. But Mr Warren, Mr Hill, Chestre, and dyverse others a greate nombre, ar like to have a greate swoope by it; having muche here, and owing nothing or little.[9]

And so it was. Thomas, like those other mercers who for 'the most parte ... occupie sylkes', had already received delivery of these goods in time for the Pasche (Easter) mart, and although their suppliers might dun them for payment, lacking alternative customers for their wares, they were unlikely to follow such a drastic course of action, particularly as these mercers had nothing at Antwerp on which to distrain. The Italian silk dealers knew that the money needed to pay for their wares would only be available when merchants like the Greshams had sold the cloths despatched to them at Antwerp and others had been able to honour their bills of exchange from the proceeds of their own cloth sales. Until that occurred they would simply have to grin and bear it. Thomas thus emerged out of the crisis virtually unscathed to assume in 1546/7 the headship of the Netherlands branch of the 'House of Gresham's' commercial operations.

MERCER AND MERCHANT ADVENTURER, 1543–1551[10]

In three short years following his admission to the freedom of the Mercers' Company in 1543, Thomas

---

[4] Ibid., no. 209.
[5] L&P Henry VIII, xv, no. 264.
[6] Ibid., nos. 507/4 and 539, 448.
[7] Ibid., no. 195.
[8] Ibid., no. 448.

[9] L&P Henry VIII, xx (1), no. 303.
[10] The following description of Thomas Gresham's career as a mercer and merchant adventurer is based on the London particular customs accounts — PRO, E122/81/32A (1544/5); 85/3 (1546/7); 167/1 (1547/8); 85/7, 11 (1548/9); 85/9 (1549/50); 84/8 (1550/1); 84/9 (1551/2); 84/12 (1552/3); 86/2–87/4 (1553/4); 86/6, 7 (1556/7) and E101/347/16 (1546/7) — and his own day book, 1546–51, preserved at the Mercers' Company. The data from this volume has been entered on an Ingres database system, developed at Edinburgh University with funding from the ESRC (grant R-000232851).

Gresham had fulfilled every aspiration that his father had of him. During this period he was entrusted by the Crown with increasingly delicate tasks on the Continent.[11] Also at this time he assumed headship of the Netherlands branch of the 'House of Gresham's' commercial operations. This involved him, as it had his father, in the 'normal' mercers' trade, buying silks such as velvet, satin, taffeta and sarsenet which together with fine woollen cloths and tapestries commanded a ready market in London. Also like his father his other speciality was the importation of armour and weaponry which was designated in his accounts as 'harness'. To pay for these wares he continued, moreover, to follow the time-honoured practice of either putting over the necessary moneys on the exchange or exporting English woollen cloth. In pursuing this trade by 1545, in spite of Paget's diplomatic use of a juvenile appelation in his description of him, Thomas had already become the leading force in the company's operations. Following the lifting of the restraint on the English merchants' goods at Antwerp on 6 April in that year[12] he was responsible for over 90 per cent of the company's goods shipped from the mart : four chests and a pack containing 50 pieces of velvet (1,117 yards) and 22 pieces of taffeta (873 yards); six sacks of cotton and six vats of 'harness', officially valued at £1,394. The transition to his *de jure* headship of the company's Netherlands operations in 1546/7 was thus accomplished with considerable ease. In that year he was again solely responsible for the company's purchases of mercery and 'harness' at the Netherlands marts and for the shipment of these wares to London. Most of the company's woollen cloths (1,025 'cloths' or 75 per cent of a total of 1,375 'cloths'), despatched from London to the Netherlands to provide cash for the purchase of this mercery, were also registered in his name. The older generation of Greshams now contributed only diminutive quantities of textiles — Sir Richard and William 100 'cloths' each and Sir John 150 — to the company's exports and received from Thomas's hands a correspondingly diminutive share in the company's mercery imports. Long groomed for the task, Thomas had now replaced his father as

head of the Netherlands branch of the 'House of Gresham' and was to continue in that position until his assumption of the post of Royal Agent in the Netherlands in 1551/2.

Yet his situation during the years 1546–51 was a very different one from that in which his father had found himself some twenty years earlier. Successive debasements of the English silver coinage by the profligate Henry VIII and his son had led to the emergence of a system of bi-metallic premiums on the Anglo-Netherlands exchanges which, in enhancing the cost of commercial credits, had resulted in the overpricing of English textiles at the Netherlands marts.[13] In response to this phenomenon, Thomas, like many of his peers, altered the composition of his company's commodity export mix, replacing traditional long and short cloths with the lightweight, and cheap, kersey. In 1546/7 kerseys made up almost half (635 'cloths' or 46 per cent) of the company's exports, only marginally ceding ground to the short cloths (661 'cloths' or 48 per cent), which remained the staple of the elder generation's trade, and completely displacing the luxurious longs (71 'cloths' or 6 per cent). Yet in spite of this initiative on his part, the company's woollen cloth exports during the years 1546–51 never attained a level amounting to more than 60 per cent of that achieved by the 'House of Gresham' in 1535. Thomas accordingly had to resort to other means to generate the necessary cash flow for the purchase of mercery and 'harness' at the Netherlands marts. Like other members of the family he dabbled in the monastic lead trade, the very low price of the base metal at this time ensuring its ready sale on continental European markets.[14] Moreover, when in 1548–49 the Mair-Fugger consortium was able to monopolise Bohemian tin production[15] and with the support of King Ferdinand was able to

[11] *L&P Henry VIII*, XVIII (1), nos. 731 and 743.
[12] *L&P Henry VIII*, XX (1), no. 494.

[13] On the operations of the Exchange at this time see the contribution of Christopher Challis, *infra*, pp. 68–72.
[14] I. Blanchard, *International Lead Production and Trade in the 'Age of the Saigerprozess' 1460–1560* (Stuttgart: Zeitschrift für Unternehmensgeschichte, Bd. 85, 1995), pp. 162–63, 167–74.
[15] On the activities of this consortium see H. Kellenbenz, 'Sächsisches und böhmisches Zinn auf dem europäischen Markt' in H. Kellenbenz and H. Pohl (eds.), *Historia Socialis et Oeconomica. Festschrift für Wolfgang Zorn zum 65. Geburtstag* (Stuttgart: Vierteljahrschrift für Sozial- und Wirtschaftsgeschichte, Beiheft 84, 1987), pp. 246–50.

exclude Saxon and English competition, thereby raising tin prices to a level some 40 per cent higher than those prevailing on the free market, he rapidly responded to the new situation. His servant John Elliot intensified his activity in Cornwall acquiring tin supplies which after their shipment to London were exported to the Continent, supporting a trade which for some eighteen months, before the collapse of the German consortium and resultant fall in tin prices, made a significant contribution to the company's coffers. He also performed during the years to 1549 small services for his uncle, Sir John, and father, Sir Richard, in their continuing operations for the Crown on the Anglo-Netherlands exchange.[16] By such means for some five years (1546–51) Thomas secured for the 'House of Gresham' a premiere place in Anglo-Netherlands commerce.

Then, by his own account, on securing the post of Royal Agent in the Netherlands during the winter of 1551/2, he closed the account book in which he had recorded all his business since 1546 and finally turned his back on his mercantile activities.[17] Like so many other such statements, written by Thomas in a spirit of self-advertisement, however, this was only a half-truth. The Flemish branch of the 'House of Gresham' continued to operate after the winter of 1551/2 much as it had before. Its members merely added a new range of activities to their old. Those factors and agents who had served him well as a merchant remained. The only exception was the replacement of Robert Berney by Richard Clough. Berney, who had served Gresham's father-in-law, William Reade, and then Thomas himself faithfully at Antwerp for at least ten years, in 1552 decided to establish his own mercantile house. Clough, on his departure to take up residence at Antwerp in 1552, thus became the new boy in a long-established network of factors and agents serving Thomas Gresham in his joint capacities as merchant and financial agent for the Crown. His counterpart at the opposite end of the Antwerp-London axis, which formed the main highway for the house's business transactions, was John Elliot, who

continued during the years 1552–57 to oversee the firm's business at its London office in Lombard Street in much the same way as he had previously conducted matters when the office had been located at Gresham's houses in Basinghall Street (1546–48) and Cheapside (1548–51). At this time both Clough and Elliot could avail themselves, moreover, of the services of other long-standing members of Thomas Gresham's team: Francis Tomazo, who from 1549–54 carried the company's despatches between the two commercial metropoli, and William Bindlowe and John Spritewell, who from 1547–54 and 1550-55 respectively were entrusted with the much more delicate task of accompanying supplies of bullion and armaments during their often illicit passage from Antwerp to London. Neither agent had much to do, however, with a secondary network which, super-imposed upon the first, serviced the requirements of the Spanish trade which, in this mercantile house as in others, during the years 1547–56 increased in importance in relation to the traditional Anglo-Netherlands connection. At the centre of this important sub-network was Edmund Hogan, who, from the company's office at Seville, managed not only Thomas Gresham's Spanish business but also that other important branch of the 'House of Gresham's' activities — Sir John Gresham's Levantine trade. For the first five years (1552–56) of his employment at the 'House of Gresham', therefore, Richard Clough served as a junior, but not unimportant, member of an extended team supporting Thomas Gresham in his joint capacities as merchant and financial agent for the Crown.

Then from 1557 changing circumstances served to increase the importance of his position within the firm. Against a background of major staff changes, which made him one of the longest serving members of the team, the temporary closure of the Seville office once more elevated the Anglo-Netherlands trade to the forefront of the firm's commercial activities. Nor was his position weakened by the subordination of that trade to Gresham's increasingly important financial business on behalf of the Crown. In the aftermath of the 1557 Imperial bankruptcy, Antwerp's money markets underwent a major transformation which allowed Clough's mercantile connections, developed in both his capacity as private

---

[16] *APC*, 1542–47, pp. 161, 224, 274, 329, 386, 415, 417, 423, 437, 453, 461, 501, 563. Ibid., 1547–50, pp. 10, 85, 170, 179.
[17] Memorial, 16 August 1553 quoted from BL Cotton MS Otho Ex, f. 43 by John William Burgon, I, pp. 115–20 and *SPF*, 1553–58, no. 105.

merchant and factor for the 'House of Gresham', to be exploited by his master in both his commercial and financial dealings. They could also be used and extended by Gresham's mentor, Sir William Cecil, as from 1558 he began to build an intelligence network to report on political conditions in the increasingly troubled Low Countries. Clough was rapidly becoming the central figure in a completely remodelled network. His counterpart at the opposite end of the Antwerp-London axis, along which now passed a flow of political intelligence as well as news of mercantile-financial transactions, was one Richard Candeler, a member of a respectable Norfolk family, who from 1557–66 acted as Gresham's factor in the English capital. The two men, moreover, continued to utilise the services of another of Thomas Gresham's servants, John Spritewell, who, with Francis Tomazo's elevation in December 1553 to the lucrative office of Queen's Post at Calais, became the company's carrier of despatches. Gresham thus had at the core of his business a formidable team headed by Clough, who were quite capable of handling not only his increasingly important financial business on behalf of the Crown but also his residual commercial activities at Antwerp. As the 'House of Gresham' also became a front for Cecil's intelligence operations, Clough also became a key figure in an extended network of agents scattered throughout the Low Countries.

During the years 1551–67 the Flemish branch of the 'House of Gresham', although acquiring new functions and being subject to significant staff-turnover, thus retained at its core a mercantile function which was clearly revealed during those periods (July–November 1553 and March 1556–December 1557) when, possibly as a consequence of the intrigues of the Lord Treasurer,[18] Thomas lost his post as Royal Agent and was consigned to the political wilderness. On each of these occasions he simply resumed his activities as a merchant. Thus having continued in the craft of mercer-merchant adventurer until 8 December 1551, when he received at London his last shipment of 'harness' from the Netherlands, Thomas then, as he himself declared, left 'my occupying and whole trade of living for the space of two

years'. Yet with his fall from grace in July 1553 he was able immediately to pick up his old trade, buying some 308 'cloths' that summer for shipment to the Netherlands at the Cold Mart.[19] Thomas's ability to resume, with such ease, the threads of his earlier life on this occasion belie the self-proclaimed discontinuity in his career associated with his assumption of the office of Royal Agent in December 1551. Indeed, it would be to impose an anachronistic functional division upon the activities of Thomas and his team to perceive them as uniquely merchants or financial agents. They were both. The 'House of Gresham' did not close its doors in December 1551. It merely underwent a metamorphosis as its head, Thomas, added a range of new activities to his old.

ROYAL AGENT IN THE NETHERLANDS, 1551–1564[20]

Thomas Gresham's appointment to the post of Royal Agent in the Netherlands in December 1551 came at a particularly critical juncture in the operations of the English Crown on the Antwerp money market. Ever since that fateful instruction in May 1544 when, amidst a myriad of fund-raising schemes,[21] the English Crown ordered the then Royal Agent, Stephen Vaughan, to raise a loan on the Antwerp Bourse,[22] the indebtedness of the English Crown to the great South German merchant-banking houses had increased. In 1548 the debt amounted to almost £240,000 sterling and increased to some £325,000 sterling in 1551. Thereafter it was steadily reduced in the years to 1564 when, in transformed conditions on the London market, the Crown resumed its practice of borrowing in England. Even at its height, however,

---

[18] *SPF*, 1560–61, no. 224.

[19] The Netherlands fairs began at the following times: Paasch Mart in the third week of April; Sinxen Mart, the second week of June; Bamus Mart, the third week of September and the Cold Mart in early November. In this latter instance, however, the official opening was largely irrelevant to the English, trading operations beginning in January.

[20] In order to set Thomas's activities as Royal Agent in context see I. Blanchard, 'English Royal Borrowing at Antwerp, 1544–1574' in Marc Boone and Walter Prevenier (eds.), *Finances publiques et finances privées au bas moyen âge. Actes du colloque tenu à Gand le 5–6 mai 1995* (Leuven & Apeldoorn: Studies in Urban Social, Economic and Political History of the Medieval and Modern Low Countries, no. 4, 1996), pp. 57–63.

[21] *L&P Henry VIII*, XIX (1), nos. 272/2–3.

[22] *L&P Henry VIII*, XIX (1), no. 578.

English royal indebtedness at Antwerp was tiny in comparison with that of the Habsburgs and, accordingly, successive royal agents were price-takers in a market dominated by the imperial authorities. Throughout the years 1544–64 the base-line rates of interest paid on loans raised for the English Crown shadowed those paid by the agents of Charles V and Philip II. Such rates were also subject, however, to marked fluctuations about this trend-line, which are largely explicable in terms of the personalities of those involved in the negotiations concerning the management of the English royal debt on the Continent.

Under Vaughan's guidance during the years 1545–47 this mounting indebtedness had been managed with some care — but only after he had been forced in 1544 to serve a hard apprenticeship, learning the intricacies of operations on the Bourse. Secure in the support of the King's Council, his primary objective during that year had been concerned with gaining some knowledge of the labyrinthine tactics of the denizens of the Antwerp Bourse — the South German merchant-banks, the brokers, and the underwriters — who, possibly under the orders of the emperor, for a year managed to manipulate the inexperienced agent, creating a major differential between the 'nominal' and 'real' interest rates on the loans he raised for the English Crown. Vaughan was an apt pupil, however, and from 1545 until he left his post as Royal Agent in the Netherlands in 1547 he was able to cut through this tangle of financial ploys, simplifying the basis for negotiations and establishing direct links with the Antwerp agents of the South German merchant-bankers. Thereby he was able to reduce transactions costs and the 'real' rate of interest paid by the English Crown. By the accession of the boy-king, Edward VI, the English Crown was able to borrow what it required at Antwerp at a discounted rate which shadowed that obtained by the Habsburgs on continental markets.

Neither of Vaughan's principal successors, William Dansell (1547–51) and Thomas Gresham (1551–64), however, were able to secure from their political masters the same unreserved support as had been enjoyed by their predecessor. Throughout their periods in office both political expediency and economic illiteracy on the part of Council members combined to plague relations between the Crown and its agents in the Netherlands which, at least until 1564, were reduced to a low ebb. Whenever money could be raised easily on the Continent, the agents were left to their own devices and the Crown obtained loans at heavily discounted rates. When rates rose, usually as a result of Habsburg intervention on these markets in 1549–52, 1554–55 and 1557–58, however, the members of the King's Council panicked, displaced their agent and either appointed others or took over direct negotiations with the bankers — with disastrous results.

For nearly the first three years of Dansell's term in office, from the Cold Mart of 1546/7 to 1549/50, when annual interest rates on the Antwerp Bourse fell from twelve to an all-time low of nine per cent, he was left very much to his own devices, successfully rolling over a debt of about £240,000 sterling at a cost which was usually no more than two per cent above base interest rates. Then, during two years, from the Cold Mart of 1549/50–1551/2, circumstances conspired against the Royal Agent. Habsburg intervention forced up the cost of finance on the Antwerp Bourse at a time when the Council was becoming very rate conscious as a result of the increasing cost of servicing royal debts arising from the contemporary crisis on the Anglo-Netherlands exchange. In this situation the Council took the unwise step of displacing its agent and undertaking, at the Bamus Marts of 1550 and 1551, direct negotiations with the bankers. The terms obtained were disastrous, and, as the total debt of the English crown at Antwerp rose to an all-time high of £325,000 sterling, relations between the Crown and its agent were reduced to a low ebb, as a welter of accusations and counter-accusations were exchanged, finally resulting in Dansell's dismissal on 29 December 1551 and the appointment of a new agent — Thomas Gresham.

The task facing Thomas at this critical juncture in the operations of the English Crown on the Antwerp money market was a formidable one, but at least the Gods now smiled upon him. Interest rates on the Bourse might continue to rise, attaining a level of sixteen per cent a year at the Sinxen Mart, 1552, but a developing crisis in central European silver production, in enhancing the price of that metal on Antwerp bullion markets, caused the exchange to rise. This increase in the value of sterling, from 16*s*. to 22*s*. Flemish, for which Gresham fancifully claimed full credit, goes a long way to explaining the success of his operations at this time. Able to deploy a part of the sterling balances reserved for scheduled payments at the lower exchange rate to the end of loan redemption he managed, within a mere nine months of taking office, to reduce the level of royal indebtness to £108,000 sterling. These remaining debts, renegotiated at the Cold Mart, 1551/2 and Sinxen Mart, 1552, moreover, might carry 'nominal' interest rates of fourteen and fifteen and a half per cent respectively but, at the enhanced exchange rate prevailing at the time of the latter mart, the service charges amounted to only £16,500 sterling or less than a third of the amount paid during the previous winter. As he had declared to Northumberland in the summer of 1552, moreover, he fully intended to clear totally the King's debts in one year or two.

In this course of action he was thwarted, however, by the death of the young King and the accession of Mary in July 1553. The politically unreliable Thomas was now removed from office and immediately resumed his old trade. For some four months the inexperienced Christopher Dawntsey acted in his stead — with disastrous results. In spite of monies being available for the English Crown at the Bamus Mart at the normal two per cent discount on the Habsburg rate of twelve per cent, the hapless individual took up on the 10 November some 200,000 guilders (or *c*. £128,300 sterling) from Lazarus Tucher at a 'nominal' thirteen per cent which the latter turned into a 'real' fourteen per cent by delaying delivery of the cash for a month. The Council's response on receipt of the bond for this transaction was immediate.[23] Letters were drafted removing Dawntsey from office and re-appointing Gresham as Royal Agent in the Netherlands. Thus, with his arrival at Antwerp on 17 November 1553, Thomas resumed the work abandoned some four months earlier, but not before he had repaired the serious damage done to the English Crown's credit in the interval.[24] In conditions of acute monetary disorder and exchange instability, and with the remembrance of Dawntsey's extravagant terms still fresh in

the bankers' minds, Thomas had to struggle long and hard during the Cold Mart of 1553/4 to conclude new loans at reasonable rates. By his efforts, however, he was able to re-establish the Queen's credit and obtain monies at rates (twelve per cent) which were again discounted (by two per cent) in relation to those secured by the Habsburgs before he sailed homeward on 3 March 1554. The financial strategy for the remainder of the decade was now established. The £100,000 sterling raised by Gresham at twelve per cent was not, as he probably hoped, used to pay off Tucher as part of a debt conversion operation but rather was spent, raising royal indebtedness once again to *c*. £230,000 sterling. Nor was any serious attempt made to reduce these debts before 1560. Gresham's task henceforth was to roll over existing debts on the most favourable terms available — a commission not always easy to accomplish as he was to find on his return to Antwerp on 12 May in time for the Sinxen Mart of 1554.

As he had already anticipated the previous November, the market was then in turmoil. Rates, already edging up at Easter, stood at fourteen and one sixth per cent at the opening of the new fair but before its close they had reached eighteen per cent. The time had come to move on and during the fortnight of his stay at Antwerp Gresham busied himself with putting together a deal, like the one first proposed to him by Genoese merchants the previous January, whereby he entered into contracts with Anton Fugger and nephews, Gaspar Schetz and brothers, John de Mantansa, John Lopez de Gallo, Antonio Spinola and Octavian Lomellini, which involved the delivery of bills of exchange to him for payments of 300,750 ducats (worth £97,878 15*s*. sterling) in Spain. Thus began the 'Spanish venture' which required him, from June 1554, to travel to Spain, collect the monies and ship them to England. By the end of the year this task had been accomplished and then, prudently perhaps, he disappeared, pursuing his commercial interests in Spain and leaving the job of rolling over the Crown's Flemish debts to his cousin, John, and Nicholas Holbourne.

By the time of his return to duty at Antwerp, in time for the Sinxen Mart of 1555, however, the market situation had eased considerably. Over the next two years he had little difficulty in securing

[23] *SPF*, 1553–58, nos. 69–70, 86.
[24] *SPF*, 1553–58, no. 77.

prolongations of the Queen's debts and, as interest rates fell from fourteen to twelve per cent, of reducing them from the post-crisis level of 1,357,446 florins (or *c.* £226,245 sterling) in 1555 to 506,769 florins (*c.* £98,785 sterling) in October 1556.

His further plans for English government debt redemption were again thwarted, however, when during 1556–57, in conditions of rapidly rising interest rates, the Antwerp Bourse was again thrown into turmoil as a result of the Imperial state bankruptcy. Old tensions reappeared between the Council and its financial agent in the Netherlands, and possibly as a consequence of the intrigues of the Lord Treasurer,[25] Gresham again from March 1556 to December 1557 lost his post as Royal Agent and was consigned to the political wilderness. How those negotiating loans for Mary fared during these months is uncertain but their legacy to the reinstated agent at the Cold Mart of 1557/8 is only too clear. To cover outstanding debts he had to negotiate in 1558 loans amounting, according to contemporary calculations, to £336,133 sterling. Mary's reign thus closed with the English Crown's debts at Antwerp again hovering about the third of a million pounds sterling mark.

Only under her successor, Elizabeth, was Gresham again able to resume the task which he had set himself some six years earlier, of reducing English royal indebtedness abroad. Under the tutelage of his friend Cecil and secure in the confidence of both Elizabeth and her Council, he was now able to operate, largely free from constraint, on an Antwerp market which, in the aftermath of the Imperial bankruptcy, had been transformed. No longer subject to the depredations of the Habsburgs, who henceforth secured their funds from dealings on the Sevillian-Genoese financial axis, the centre of gravity of that city's financial prosperity had shifted dramatically to the provision of commercial investments, and as from 1559–65 trade boomed, these could be funded at interest rates which fell rapidly from twelve to slightly more than nine per cent. In these circumstances Gresham could hardly fail, and by deploying a part of the sterling balances reserved for scheduled payments at the higher interest rates to the end of loan redemption, he henceforth reduced the level of royal indebtness to

c. £280,000 sterling in 1560 and a mere £20,000 in 1565,[26] some two years before he finally ceased his visits to the city on the Scheldt.

PUBLIC BENEFACTOR, 1564–1579

The years 1559–64 marked the high point of Gresham's career as a servant of the Crown. Knighted in the summer of 1559, preparatory to taking up a temporary appointment as ambassador to the court of the Duchess of Parma, Regent of the Netherlands, Thomas's career had thereafter gone from strength to strength. In his capacity as Royal Agent in the Netherlands, having all but eliminated the English Crown's debts to the Antwerp financiers, he stood high in Elizabeth's esteem and was increasingly involved by her in such wide-ranging schemes as the recoinage of 1560[27] or the reform of the London customs house in 1561–62. His successes in public office, moreover, brought with them public reward and, much to the delight of his social-climbing wife Anne, a complete change in life-style. This involved him in acquiring new country houses, convenient to London, at Mayfield in Sussex and Osterley in Middlesex, whose opulence may perhaps be gauged by the valuation of the former property's furnishings at some £7,550. In London he transformed his modest house in Lombard Street into business premises and took up occupancy in the grandiose Gresham House which he built a few years before 1566 in Bishopgate and furnished at a cost of some £1,128. Whether at Antwerp or his English properties, he dispensed, moreover, a lavish hospitality, of which all classes were glad to take advantage. Public recognition and esteem were also coupled at this time with domestic contentment. He enjoyed close relations with his wife, the Lady Anne, who revelled in her role as mistress of his opulent household, and when in London enjoyed the company of his now adult children and step-children, as well perhaps as the companionship of his cousins, Noel and Cecily, who, with her husband German Coill occupied the

[25] *SPF*, 1560–61, no. 224.

[26] O. De Smedt, *De Englelse natie te Antwerpen in de XVIe eeuw (1496–1582)* (Antwerp, 2 vols., 1950–54), I, p. 329 and II, p. 558.
[27] C. E. Challis, *The Tudor Coinage* (Manchester, 1978), pp. 120–21.

neighbouring Crosby Hall before the latter's bankruptcy in 1566. Looking back, Gresham must have later remembered these as the 'good' years.

Certainly from 1564 life was never to be the same again. Plagued since 1560 with a mis-set broken leg, the result of a riding accident, his health thereafter, in spite of the efforts of the surgeons, steadily deteriorated until in 1572, at the relatively young age of fifty-four, he declared himself to be both 'blynde and lame'. Far more significant in shaping his later life, however, was the psychological trauma occasioned by the death in 1564 of his only son, Richard. As in the case of his own father, some forty years earlier, domestic tragedy made Thomas only too aware of the fragility of familial happiness and public esteem and caused him to review his life. With his link to immortality through his son suddenly severed, he accordingly almost immediately set about recreating it — in stone. On 4 January 1565 accordingly he proposed to the Court of Aldermen of the City that a Bourse or Exchange should be built in London at his expense for the accommodation of merchants.[28] Thus began a project which was to occupy fully both Sir Thomas and his factor and friend Richard Clough for some three years. Initially, in March 1565 a subscription was opened which before its termination in October 1566 raised the £3,737 needed to buy properties upon Cornhill and to pay for clearing the site where the Bourse was to be built. Already by Christmas 1565 the necessary arrangements for the acquisition of the properties had been made and notice given to the tenants to vacate their dwellings. Such was the sense of urgency felt by Gresham, however, that within a fortnight of the last tenant being evicted from the Cornhill site, on 10 April, whilst the site was still being cleared, he requested Cecil's permission to visit Norfolk 'to take order for [the] free-stone' needed for the foundations of the structure. On 7 June 1566 he personally laid its foundation stone. Clearly nothing was going to be allowed to interfere with his attempt to enshrine his own immortality, and over the next two and a half years Gresham employed the full resources of his estates and business to complete the project.[29]

Yet even before the final touches were put to the edifice in December 1568 and commercial success ensured by Elizabeth's visit thereto in January 1571, the daemon which drove him ensured that he would continue in his new role as public benefactor. Thus were built the eight almshouses behind his mansion in Bishopsgate. It was probably also at about this time that he first conceived the idea of making an educational endowment, his first choice of recipient seemingly being his old university of Cambridge. When it came to making the necessary dispositions in 1575, however, it was not Cambridge that benefited. He ordained that Lady Gresham should enjoy his London house, as well as the rents from the Royal Exchange during her life, but that thereafter they would be vested in the hands of the Corporation of London and the Mercers' Company, who would conjointly nominate seven professors to lecture there successively, one in each day of the week, on the seven sciences. And so it was. Following the death of his widow, the Lady Anne, in November 1596 Gresham College was born, the first professors occupying their chambers in the Bishopgate property during March 1597 and lectures commencing the Trinity term following.

Gresham thus secured his place in history, but at a heavy cost. Watching the family fortunes dissipated in her husband's self-glorificatory projects, relations between Anne and Thomas rapidly deteriorated, reaching a particularly low ebb during the period from June 1569 to April 1572 when their enforced and protracted entertainment of the Lady Mary Grey put intolerable strains on their marriage. How much she actually resented her husband's profligate course of action was only revealed, however, after his death on 21 November 1579 when twice she tried to undo the complex arrangements surrounding his establishment of Gresham College. On both occasions her efforts were thwarted, but she perhaps had the last word, making arrangements so that she would be buried, on 14 December 1596, as she had always wanted to live, with great public display and heraldic pomp.

---

[28] On the labyrinthine negotiations concerning the acquisition of a site for the Royal Exchange, see the contribution of Jean Imray in this volume, pp. 20–35.

[29] Fully described in Ann Saunders' contribution in this volume, pp. 36–47.

CHAPTER III

The Origins of the Royal Exchange

By JEAN IMRAY

'THE EYE OF LONDON', 'Great Britain's Glory', 'a sun whence every ray expands life and spirit to the remotest corner of the metropolis',[1] these colourful descriptions refer to the Royal Exchange, a familiar landmark in the City of London for more than 400 years, and yet the history of this building and of its place in the life of the City has been surprisingly neglected. The printed sources for the history of the Royal Exchange are scant. Writers like John Stow, Samuel Pepys and Samuel Rolle, John Evelyn, Joseph Addison and Richard Steele described the Royal Exchange or chronicled events there in their own lifetimes. John Burgon, in his two-volume *Life and Times of Sir Thomas Gresham*, published in 1835, dealt both with the founding of the Royal Exchange and, briefly, with its later history, and in 1844 Effingham Wilson, a bookseller and publisher who had a shop at the south-east corner of the Royal Exchange, wrote an account of the then newly erected third Exchange. The only attempt at a full history of the Royal Exchange has been Charles Welch's *Illustrated Account of the Royal Exchange*, published in 1914. Competent though this is, it is far from complete.

Yet the amount of documentary material available for a full-scale study of the Royal Exchange, even in its earliest days, is considerable, so considerable that this essay will confine itself to the origins of the Royal Exchange, that is to say, to early, unsuccessful attempts to provide an exchange for the City, to Sir Thomas Gresham's agreement with the City to build an exchange, to the way in which the City fulfilled its part of that bargain and to the unsatisfactory nature of the arrangement between Gresham and the City. The account will end before so much as the foundation stone of the first Royal Exchange had been laid.

Before the building of the Royal Exchange the traditional meeting place for London merchants was Lombard Street. In 1564 the City declared that 'the burse of Lombard Street is of longer antiquity than any other burse is known to be of that is within all Europe'.[2] Not that it was a burse in any physical sense, for the merchants conducted their business in the open street. Stow describes how 'the merchants and tradesmen, as well English as strangers, for their general making of bargains, contracts and commerce . . . did usually meet twice every day . . . but their meetings were unpleasant and troublesome, by reason of walking and talking in an open narrow street . . . being there constrained either to endure all extremities of weather, viz. heat and cold, snow and rain: or else to shelter themselves in shops'.[3] The merchants were also at the mercy of passing traffic so that in 1527 the Court of Aldermen agreed that a chain should be drawn across the street to stop the passage of carts and carriages both morning and afternoon, while the merchants were meeting.[4]

Both Burgon and Welch credit Sir Richard Gresham, father of Sir Thomas Gresham, with first conceiving the idea of building a burse or exchange for the merchants of London. Burgon wrote '. . . with Sir Richard Gresham rests the honour of having originally projected the "goodly burse", which his own son was happily possessed of the means as well as the inclination, thirty years later, to construct', and Welch echoes him almost word for word.[5] They cite, as their evidence, the letter written by Richard Gresham, as Lord Mayor, to Thomas Cromwell, then Lord Privy seal, on 25 July 1538, mentioning 'a plan that was drawn out for to make a goodly burse in Lombard Street for merchants to repair unto'.[6]

---

[1] Hughson, *History of London* (1800), vol. II, p. 100.

[2] H. L. Hopkinson, *Ancient Records of the Merchant Taylors' Company* (1915), p. 61.
[3] Stow's *Chronicle* (1631 edn), p. 668.
[4] CLRO, Repertory 7, f. 222.
[5] John Burgon, vol. I, pp. 31–33. Welch, *Royal Exchange*, p. 13.
[6] BL Cotton MSS Otho. Ex., f. 45.

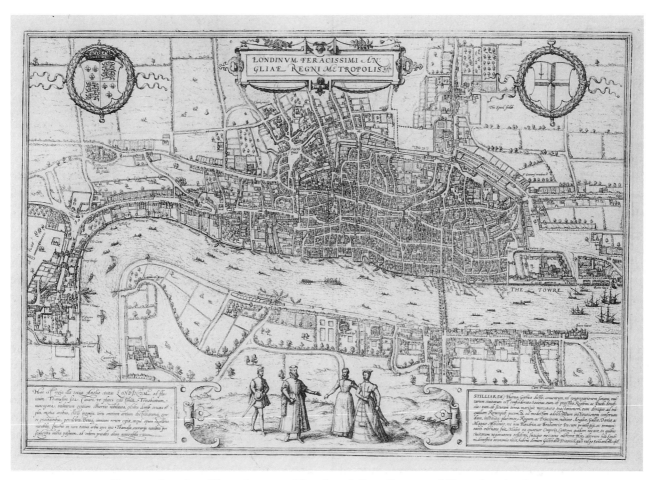

FIG. 4.   London, Westminster and Southwark from Braun and Hogenberg's atlas,
Civitates Orbis Terrarum, post-1574 edition.
Guildhall Library, Corporation of London

Both writers, however, contradict their own statements about Richard Gresham as the first conceiver of an exchange for London by referring to an occasion in 1534 when, they say, the King himself had proposed that Leadenhall should be used as a burse, but that the royal proposal had been turned down by the Court of Common Council, on a show of hands. It appears, however, that Leadenhall may have been considered as a possible exchange as early as 1521.

A few years before 1521, the future of Leadenhall was being discussed by the Corporation, who had received applications for a lease of Leadenhall from two sources.[7] One was from the Merchants of the Staple, who had had accommodation at Leadenhall since the fifteenth century, the other from a group of twenty-four unidentified merchants whose purpose was not immediately recorded. There was a good deal of hostility to the whole idea of leasing Leadenhall and on 28 September 1518[8] the Court of Common Council received a petition against the letting of Leadenhall, especially to any fellowship or body corporate, on the grounds that it was a convenient place for the citizens of London to assemble. The petitioners pointed out that Leadenhall housed the City's store of guns, ammunition and other weapons, as well as timber for the repair of the City's tenements. It was a useful place to prepare a triumph and it was the customary place for the doling out of largess to the poor. Moreover, it had been the intention of the

---

[7] CLRO, Repertory 5, ff. 83 and 105.

[8] CLRO, Journal 11, f. 362.

founder of Leadenhall that market men and women should have free standing there in wet weather. If Leadenhall were let to some corporate body, dissent was bound to arise and it should, therefore, be kept in the City's hands.

The application for a lease from the group of twenty-four merchants was referred to the Staplers for their comments on 5 April 1519.[9] This move seems reasonable in view of the fact that the Staplers had already had accommodation at Leadenhall, but does it also suggest that the interests of the two groups might have come into conflict and, if so, could the group of twenty-four have represented the Merchants Adventurers?

The only other reference to the proposed lease to the group of twenty-four is a slightly mysterious entry in the records of the Court of Aldermen, which suggests that the group may have been wanting Leadenhall for an exchange.[10] The entry is dated Tuesday, 19 February, but no year is given. However, it was probably 1521, since 19 February fell on a Tuesday in that year, and another entry on the same folio names John Kyme as Sheriff[11] and 1521 was the year in which he held that office. The entry reads: 'At this Court, Master York, one of the heralds brought in the King's letter concerning Leadenhall, to be appointed to merchants, there to have their communication as other merchants in other countries have, as by the said letter more plainly appeareth, whereupon it is agreed that diverse of every fellowship of merchants shall be sent for to know their minds'.

Turning now to the events of 1534 when, as Burgon and Welch state, the King lent support to the idea of using Leadenhall as an exchange, these two writers imply that it was the King himself who took the initiative. It can be shown, however, that the City had already begun discussions before the King took a hand. On 16 July 1534 the Court of Common Council passed a motion for 'a burse and a place meet and convenient for merchants to treat of their feat of merchandise, as is accustomed and used in other noble cities in other outward parts beyond the

sea'.[12] Four Aldermen and twelve commoners were appointed to meet at Leadenhall the following Thursday. The twelve commoners represented the twelve Great Livery Companies, so the Court was adopting the procedure which had been proposed in the King's letter of 1521. From the very earliest days, therefore, the Livery Companies were involved in the proposals to establish an exchange in London.

On 27 August 1534[13] this committee reported that Leadenhall would be a convenient place for an exchange, but a final decision was postponed until the first meeting of Common Council after Christmas. Perhaps opposition to Leadenhall as a site for an exchange was already making itself felt, because, on the same day 'eight commoners of this City that dwell westward' were to be added to the twelve appointed on 16 July. It was to become evident that there was a party in the City which wanted the burse to be in Lombard Street, the traditional home of exchange business, but it is difficult to see the choice of commoners dwelling 'westward' as necessarily representing their views.

The first mention of royal intervention occurs on 3 November 1534,[14] when the King's letter concerning the burse to be made at Leadenhall was read to the Court of Aldermen. The text of that letter cannot now be traced. Had the King sent a new letter, or was the Court looking again at the letter of 1521?

The first meeting of the Court of Common Council after Christmas was on 19 January 1535.[15] The eight additional commoners had still not been appointed, but there was another reference to the King's letter for the making of a new burse for the assembly of merchants at Leadenhall. It was agreed that it should be tried by show of hands whether the burse should be moved from Lombard Street or not, and the vote which followed was in favour of remaining in Lombard Street.

Clearly this entry forms the basis of the accounts given by Burgon and Welch, but the Corporation did not rely on a show of hands for its final decision. The matter was brought up again at the Court of Common

⁹ CLRO, Repertory 5, f. 112.
¹⁰ CLRO, Repertory 5, f. 181.
¹¹ Revd A. B. Beaven, *Aldermen of the City of London* (1913), Vol. II, p. 24.

¹² CLRO, Journal 13, f. 417.
¹³ CLRO, Repertory 9, f. 72.
¹⁴ As note 13.
¹⁵ CLRO, Journal 13, f. 435.

Council on 15 April 1535[16] and it was agreed that the two parties, presumably for and against the move from Lombard Street, should bring in their considerations, in writing, by the following Saturday, 18 April. The Journal lists the names of those in each of the two parties, but unfortunately does not say which favoured Lombard Street and which Leadenhall. Nevertheless, the two lists are of some interest. In particular it should be noticed that Richard Gresham's name does not appear in either list, whereas Richard Reynolds, Mercer, William Bowyer, Draper and Paul Withipoll, Merchant Taylor, who are named, all played a prominent part both in these negotiations and in the subsequent 1538 negotiations.

The writings called for on 15 April were actually produced on Friday, 17 April,[17] described as 'One book for establishing of a new burse to be made at Leadenhall, the other for the continuance of a burse to be kept still in Lombard Street'. Both books were read and signed by the two parties, to be delivered to the King by the Lord Mayor, who was to report 'that it is tried by the most voices in Common Council that Lombard Street shall be exercised for the assembly of merchants as it hath been heretofore accustomed and not to be translated to Leadenhall and the same to be most expedient for the commonwealth of this City'.

We now come to the events of 1537/8 and the so-called attempt by Sir Richard Gresham to establish a burse, which led Burgon and Welch to honour him as the pioneer. We have already seen that he played no prominent, if any, part in the earliest attempts to found an exchange. That is not to imply that he did not favour the idea of an exchange, but it seems more likely that it was because he held the office of Mayor in 1537/8 that he played a leading role in the events of that year, rather than because of any deep personal involvement.

In fact the first steps were taken before Gresham became Mayor and, at that stage his name is still missing from the records. On 3 July 1537[18] the Court of Aldermen passed a motion in support of a burse in Lombard Street to be built on the site of the Pope's Head, belonging to Mr Monnocks, Alderman. This was the same George Monnocks, Draper, who was probably among the group of twenty-four merchants who had tried to obtain a lease of Leadenhall in 1521. A committee was appointed to negotiate with Monnocks but, on 17 July, it was decided to postpone any further action, partly so that it could be discovered what financial support might be forthcoming to build an exchange.

The matter rested for a whole year, until 25 July 1538,[19] when Richard Gresham wrote his often quoted letter to Thomas Cromwell. After reminding Cromwell that he had previously shown him a plan for a burse in Lombard Street, he went on:

I do suppose it will cost £2,000 and more, which shall be very beautiful to the City and also for the honour of our sovereign Lord and King. But there is certain houses in the said street belonging to Sir George Monnocks and except we may purchase them, the said burse cannot be made. Wherefore it may please your good lordship to move the king's highness to have his most gracious letters directed to the said Sir George, willing and also commanding him to cause the said houses to be sold to the Mayor and Commonalty of the City of London, for such prices as he did purchase them for: and that he fault not, but to accomplish his gracious commandment. The letter must be sharply made, for he is of no gentle nature: and that he shall give further credence to the mayor, I will deliver the letter and handle him the best I can: and if I may obtain to have the said houses, I doubt not but to gather £1,000 toward the building, or I depart out of my office. There shall lack no good will in me.

The letters from Henry VIII, written to George Monnocks in response to Gresham's request, were copied in full into the Corporation's Journal. The first letter was dated at Chichester on 13 August 1538.[20]

[16] CLRO, Journal 13, f. 442.
[17] CLRO, Journal 13, f. 443.

[18] CLRO, Repertory 9, f. 255. Sir George Monnocks, whose name is commemorated in a more elegant form in Sir George Monoux's School in Walthamstow, was a notoriously stubborn gentleman: see George F. Bosworth, *George Monoux: the Story of a Walthamstow worthy*, WAS Monograph 3 (1916); and *George Monoux: the Man and his Work*, WAS Monograph 17 (1927). I am most grateful to Jo Parker of the Vestry House Museum, Waltham Forest, for her help.
[19] BL Cotton MSS Otho. Ex., f. 45.
[20] CLRO, Journal 14, f. 124. Copied into the Journal by the Court of Aldermen, 30 January 1538/9, Repertory 10, f. 42.

The King wrote that he understood that Sir George had certain houses and tenements about Lombard Street which were very meet for certain intended purposes to the weal and common furtherance of merchants and the intercourse of the same, which Sir Richard Gresham, the Mayor, and other brethren of the City could declare unto him, and

forasmuch as we tender much that their good mind and purpose in that behalf may take effect, and not doubting but being brought up there, ye have a good zeal and affection to the same, vouchsafe that you will at our intercession bestow on such a common weal, so much of housing as is necessary, freely and frankly, or at least with an agreement, undelayably, to be made between you and Gresham as they may have cause to think that ye want no good affection towards the said City, and also that ye have such good respect to our requisition, your gentle consent shall be thankfully accepted and remembered accordingly.

This was hardly the sharp letter that Gresham had asked for and, as we shall see, it proved ineffective. On 27 August[21] Gresham was authorised by the Court of Aldermen to make Monnocks an offer of £200 or a life annuity of £10 for the Lombard Street property. However, the same day the Court received a letter from Richard Rich, Chancellor of the Court of Augmentations, who apparently was Monnocks' intended executor, asking the Court to wait until after Michaelmas so that he could speak with the Lord Privy Seal (Thomas Cromwell) and his brethren to ensure that 'an honest recompense' was given for the property.

On 17 September[22] the Court arranged for a deputation headed by Gresham, still Mayor, to meet Monnocks at St Botulph's Church at eight o'clock the following Saturday morning, and, after talking with him, to report back to the Court. It was probably soon after this that the King wrote the second, undated letter, to Monnocks, though it could have been written as late as November, since, on 21 November, Gresham, now no longer Mayor, was again appointed to head a small deputation to ride to Sir George Monnocks with the King's letters for the obtaining of his houses in Lombard Street.[23]

The second royal letter was much more what Gresham had originally intended.[24] Henry wrote that he had been informed that Gresham and other citizens had lately been with Monnocks and that, at that time, the matter had been remitted to Sir Richard Rich. Gresham and his companions had agreed with Rich to pay a yearly rent of 20 marks for the houses

yet this notwithstanding through the evil council and dehortation of certain persons of froward disposition, which little regard our pleasures and your estimation, contrary to our expectation and less to the furtherance of the commonwealth of that our City, have disturbed the said good purpose to our no little marvel: we therefore much desiring the same to take effect, eftsoons desire & heartily require you that, pondering and weighing with yourself the benefit and commodity that shall ensue thereof to our commonwealth and to the beautifying of that our City and Chamber of London, to condescend to our desire and conclude the said grant accordingly without further delay, requiring you that, of your gentle conformity herein to be used on your behalf, the contrary whereof we nothing look for, ye well advertise us, with convenient diligence by this bringer, Sir Richard Gresham, to the intent that according to your proceedings herein we may give you our condigne thanks and also remember the same, when occasion shall serve, to your no little benefit.

This second letter quickly had the desired effect and on 25 November the King wrote again from Westminster[25] that he had heard from the Lord Privy Seal

how at the contemplation of our letters lately directed unto you . . . ye have like a loving subject conformed yourself unto the same and have of your own gentleness showed and declared more conformity unto their suit . . . So we assure you we shall have the same your towardness in the performing hereof in such remembrance as when occasion shall serve you in your lawful pursuits, the same shall redound unto your benefit accordingly.

It was the following February before there were any further developments. An entry in the Repertory dated 23 February 1539[26] suggests that a draft deed was then being drawn up, but the matter dragged on for the rest of the summer. Meanwhile Monnocks complained that he had been unkindly handled because the Corporation was already claiming rent

[21] CLRO, Repertory 10, f. 42.
[22] CLRO, Repertory 10, f. 46.
[23] CLRO, Repertory 10, f. 66.

[24] CLRO, Journal 14, f. 124. See also note 20.
[25] CLRO, Journal 14, f. 124.
[26] CLRO, Repertory 10, f. 81.

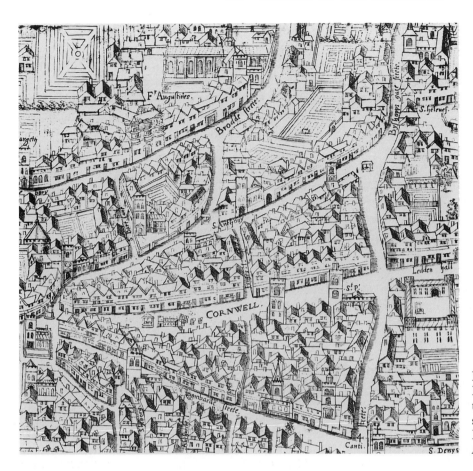

Fig. 5. Site of the Royal
Exchange. An enlarged detail of
the pre-1566 copperplate map
showing the future site of the
Exchange covered with houses.
Museum of London

from his tenants. Finally on 26 August[27] the Under-Chamberlain reported that Monnocks, while still protesting that the matter for the burse was but a communication and not a conclusion, had agreed that the necessary indentures should be drawn up and that the Corporation had the right to collect rent from his tenants.

On the face of it the way was now open for the building of an exchange in Lombard Street but, surprisingly, from this point on the records are completely silent on the matter. Why did the project peter out just when it looked poised for success? Monnocks must have been an old man by this time (he died in 1543) and his involvement in the negotiations for a lease of Leadenhall in 1521 suggests that he favoured a move away from Lombard Street, so that his prevarication may have been based on something more than just the protection of his own Lombard Street interests. By 1539 Gresham was no

longer Mayor and maybe the Corporation missed his drive and influence, particularly at Court. But perhaps it was simply that the Corporation realised the full financial implications of building an exchange themselves and let the matter drop.

The failure to pursue the acquisition of the Lombard Street site in 1539 resulted in the total eclipse of the proposals for an exchange for twenty years, except for a solitary glimmer of light in 1557. On 23 November[28] in that year the Court of Aldermen received a petition from the Merchant Adventurers for a burse to be made near Lombard Street. It was agreed that 'the same merchants shall have free liberty to travail with whom they will and to take the benevolence of all such persons as will willingly bestow any thing upon the making of the said burse, provided always that this house shall not in any wise be chargeable at any time hereafter towards the making of the said burse'. Clearly the City had no

[27] CLRO, Repertory 10, f. 116.

[28] CLRO, Repertory 13, no. 2, f. 567.

great enthusiasm for the proposal, but it is interesting that it should have come from the Merchant Adventurers. It lends weight to the theory that it was the Adventurers as a whole, with their experience of continental exchanges, who were keen to have an exchange in London.

Just how the Adventurers felt about the lack of such a facility in London was expressed by Richard Clough, Thomas Gresham's agent in Antwerp, in a letter written to his master in December 1561.[29] Clough castigated the City fathers in no uncertain terms: 'for indeed it is marvel that we have so good orders as we have, considering what rulers we have in the City of London: such a Company that do study for nothing else but their own profit. As for example, considering what a City London is, and that in so many years they have not found the means to make a burse, but must walk in the rain when it raineth, more like pedlars than merchants'. Clough expressed his willingness to take on the task himself: 'Indeed and if your business were done, and that I might have the leisure to go about it, and that you will be a means to Mr. Secretary to have his favour therein, I will not doubt but to make so fair a burse in London as the great burse is in Antwerp, without molesting of any man more than he should be well disposed to give'.

We do not know whether Clough's letter had any influence on Gresham. Burgon firmly linked Sir Thomas Gresham's decision to build an exchange at his own expense with the death of his only legitimate child, Richard, on 2 May 1563. He wrote: 'I cannot but think that this spiritual proposal was the result in a measure of the domestic calamity which its author had just before experienced: and that he sought by this means both to employ usefully a portion of the wealth which he must then have regarded as a superfluous acquisition: and to divert the melancholy which the bereavement itself was so naturally calculated to inspire'.[30] Almost immediately afterwards, on 11 May 1563, the Court of Aldermen appointed Sir Lionel Duckett 'to move Sir Thomas Gresham for and concerning his benevolence towards the making of a burse and understanding his pleasure therein'.[31]

Two years later, Gresham made his pleasure publicly known. It was on 4 January 1565 that Gresham's famous offer was made to and accepted by the City. The exact wording of the offer will be quoted in full because it is important to bear in mind just what was promised on that occasion. The entry[32] in the Repertory reads:

After the gentle and very friendly offer of the right worshipful Sir Thomas Gresham kt., made unto the Court here this day by Anthony Stringer, his servant, for the erecting and building at his only costs and charges of a comely burse for merchants to assemble upon, so that the City at their charges will provide and appoint a meet and apt place for the same, being well and ripely conceived and understood by the Court, it was finally granted and agreed by the same Court, that the City at their charges shall provide an apt and meet place for the said purpose.

The City lost no time in endeavouring to fulfil its part of the bargain. On the day that Gresham made his offer a committee of Aldermen and merchants was appointed to view possible sites, to decide which was the most suitable and to establish the purchase price. Four days later, on 8 January,[33] the day on which the City had undertaken to inform Gresham of their choice, the Court of Aldermen agreed that the burse should be built between Lombard Street and Cornhill on the site of certain houses belonging to the Merchant Taylors' Company. Both Burgon and Welch refer to the attempt to buy a site from the Merchant Taylors and state that it failed, but they give no reason for that failure and it seems unlikely that either of them read the detailed and entertaining account of the negotiations in the Merchant Taylors' own records.[34]

On 10 January 1565 Alderman Thomas Rowe, himself a Merchant Taylor and a kinsman to Gresham by marriage, warned the Merchant Taylors that the Corporation was going to apply for the Company's property in Lombard Street, which had been left to them by Sir John Percyvall, a former Mayor, subject to certain charitable trusts. There and then the Company examined Percyvall's will, decided that they would not part with the property and

[29] BL Lansdowne MSS V, art. 27. Quoted by Burgon, vol. I, p. 409.
[30] Burgon, *Gresham*, vol. II, p. 81.
[31] CLRO, Repertory 13, f. 237.

[32] CLRO, Repertory 15, f. 403.
[33] CLRO, Repertory 15, f. 406.
[34] Charles Clode, *Early History of the Merchant Taylors* (1888), p. 227, and Appendix 28, p. 396. Also Hopkinson, op. cit.

appointed a committee to draft a letter of refusal to the Corporation. This was all before any official approach had actually been made by the City.

The approach arrived in the form of a deputation on Friday, 12 January 1565. Sir William Chester, Draper, acted as its spokesman and his speech is reported in full in the Merchant Taylors' records. He declared that: 'Sir Thomas Gresham knight for the great good will and love he hath to this City was contented and had already promised unto the said Lord Mayor and Aldermen to build and plant within this City a burse to be more fair and costly builded in all points than is the burse of Antwerp', provided the City would supply a site. The offer had been accepted by the Lord Mayor and Aldermen who had already viewed various grounds in the City and 'could find none so fit for to build the same upon as was the ground belonging to this Company, adjoining upon Lombard Street and Cornhill'. The City had resolved to build there, provided the Merchant Taylors were willing to part with the property on such considerations as should content them, because 'the burse might thereby retain and keep the ancient name of Lombard Street, for that the policies that hath been made time out of mind between merchant and merchant in other foreign regions, had had relations to be of as good effect, to all respects, as the policies usually made in Lombard Street . . .'.

Although the Merchant Taylors had already made up their minds on the matter, they did not admit it. Their Master said that the Company would want time to consider the Corporation's request and so the delegation withdrew. In their absence the Company agreed that their answer, which was already in writing, should not be delivered until five or six o'clock that evening. The delegation were not, however, to be told this, only that the Company could not take a quick decision on such an important matter.

Chester and his companions were kept waiting for an hour. The Company then apologised for the delay, saying that they had not yet reached a decision, but that they would deliver their answer to the Corporation that evening, and so the delegation departed.

The reply of the Merchant Taylors also appears in full in their records. The substance of it was that Sir John Percyvall had acquired this property 'by his great industry and long travail' and had occupied one of the houses himself. He had bequeathed the property to the Company, putting them in trust of certain 'godly and charitable deeds'. If the property were sold its value as a memorial to Percyvall would be lost and, if the Company failed in its trust, they might be thought unworthy of fulfilling similar trusts. The present occupants were members of the Company and other good citizens and, if they were dispossessed, they would no longer have occasion 'to wish for the properous state and long continuance of the Company'. The Merchant Taylors said that they were as anxious as any to further the establishment of a burse and, if another suitable site could be found, they would be 'as willing and as liberally assisting thereto' as anyone else.

The letter was considered by the Court of Aldermen on the following day, Saturday, 13 January. The entry in the Repertory[35] merely records that the letter was referred back to the Wardens of the Merchant Taylors to be further considered on Thursday, 18 January. Again the Merchant Taylors' records supply the details of what happened on that Saturday. The Wardens reported to the Court of Assistants that they had been summoned to the Inner Chamber of Guildhall before the Lord Mayor and Aldermen who, by themselves, or through the Recorder, answered the objections raised by the Merchant Taylors.

The Court of Aldermen felt that the principal reason for the Merchant Taylors' refusal to part with the property was the breaking of a dead man's will, and the Recorder commented that the dead's will could just as well be performed out of other lands which the Company should receive in exchange. 'If the Company did strive so much upon the persuasion of their consenting, he doubted not but that the Bishop of London or the Dean of St. Paul's' would 'resolve them therein'.

The Wardens reported that they had remained steadfast: they could not part with the property without breach of Percyvall's will. To this the Recorder replied, somewhat tetchily, that it appeared to him that the Company refused to consent 'more of a will than any conscience, for', said he, 'a man may not take to himself a conscience, of that there is no conscience to be made of'.

[35] CLRO, Repertory 15, f. 410.

FIG. 6.   Gresham's Exchange, late 1560s. Detail from the woodcut map of London, ascribed to
Ralph Agas; it is probably the earliest representation of the Exchange. Note the grasshopper
atop the tower.

Guildhall Library, Corporation of London

The five days' grace granted to the Company by the Corporation made no difference. The Wardens brought the Company's final refusal to Guildhall on Thursday, 18 January, and the Corporation had to admit defeat and agree that they would have to deliberate further on the question of a site for the burse.[36]

On 30 January the City assured Gresham that they intended with all speed to prepare for the building of his burse and two days later the Court of Aldermen heard from Sir John White and a small committee appointed to help him that they had found 'a very apt place' on the north side of Cornhill. The Court instructed the committee to proceed with the purchase of the site 'with all convenient diligence'.[37]

The 'apt place' referred to consisted of thirteen tenements, a storehouse and a garden belonging to the Dean and Chapter of Canterbury and, during February and March 1565, Alderman Thomas Rowe was engaged in negotiations with the Dean and Chapter for its purchase. On 27 March[38] the Corporation received a letter from the Dean and Chapter setting out their terms, which were accepted by the Court of Aldermen. The Repertory does not indicate what the terms were, but they can be deduced from

an important record called 'The Book concerning the new Burse, which shall declare the charge that the City and Citizens thereof sustained and bare for the obtaining of the soil thereof'. This document was compiled by Thomas Rowe and completed on 14 September 1566. It was delivered by him to the Court of Aldermen on 22 October in the same year and the Court ordered it to be kept by the Town Clerk and entered among the City's records. The full text of the Book appears both in Journal 19 and in Letter Book V.[39]

The Book shows that the Canterbury property was valued at £25 a year. The City were to pay £600 for its purchase within six months of their giving notice to the Dean and Chapter to vacate the property. Meanwhile the City was to pay Canterbury an annual rent of £30. The Book also shows that the City had to pay a total of £444 9s. to buy out the interests of the tenants of this property.

Among the sundry charges for the purchase from the Dean and Chapter of Canterbury recorded in the Book was £10 9s. 6d. to Chancery men for licences procured under the Great Seal for the Church of Canterbury to pass the lands to the City and for writing the licences. The relevant Calendar to the Patent Rolls, 1563–66,[40] shows that Letters Patent

[36] CLRO, Repertory 15, f. 412.
[37] CLRO, Repertory 15, ff. 416 and 417.
[38] CLRO, Repertory 15, f. 433.
[39] CLRO, Journal 19, f. 12 and Letter Book V, f. 70.
[40] Calendar of Patent Rolls, 1563–66, 2185.

were granted on 3 April 1566 to enable the Dean and Chapter to alienate their property and the City to pay the rent of £30 and the purchase money of £600. Entries in the Corporation records also show that various deeds to effect the conveyance were drawn up and sealed.[41] To date, however, no trace of the original Letters Patent, nor of the deeds, has been found.

The Book concerning the new Burse also shows that, in addition to the property purchased from Canterbury, the City also bought other property adjoining it, comprising sixteen tenements and seven cottages belonging to private citizens and, in one case, to the parish of St Michael Cornhill. Negotiations for the purchase of this additional property probably took place late in 1565, though there are no references to such negotiations in the Corporation records.

On 28 March 1566[42] the Court of Aldermen gave instructions that the conveyances of these properties should be made to Sir Thomas White, Sir William Garrard, Sir William Chester, Sir John White, Alderman Rowe and Alderman Hayward. When, in October 1566, Thomas Rowe delivered his Book concerning the new Burse to the Court, he also delivered a 'new chest of all the writings and evidences concerning the soil purchased by the City for erecting the Burse' to the Chamberlain 'safely to be kept to the City's uses'. The writings and evidences have not survived but sundry charges in the Book included a payment of £7 11s. by the Chamberlain for deeds and indentures passed by divers sellers of land to be enrolled. A search in the appropriate Husting Roll revealed that, although deeds to Corporation property were not normally enrolled, these particular deeds, relating to the additional property purchased for the site of the exchange, were an exception, and they were all, save one, enrolled on 18 May 1566.[43]

The additional property purchased comprised:

In the parish of St Michael Cornhill:

1. A great messuage with shops, cellars, warehouses, yards, etc., lately occupied by Sampson Walkeden, and a tenement adjoining on the east: bought from Alderman Rowland Hayward on 9 April 1566 at a cost of £340, the materials of which were sold for £57 13s. 4d.

2. A house, previously occupied by Humfrey Parris, Barber; lying between the land and way belonging to John Traves leading into Swan Alley on the east, a house occupied by Edward Radley, Clothworker, on the west, Cornhill on the south and Swan Alley on the north, purchased from the parish of St Michael Cornhill on 13 April 1566 for a sum of £120. It cost £33 6s. 8d. to purchase Humfrey Parris's interest. The house measured 17 feet from east to west and 16 feet from south to north, and the materials were sold for £67 6s. 8d.[44]

3. A messuage comprising a cellar, a parlour and a chamber over the parlour lying between the tenement occupied by Sampson Walkeden on the north, south and east and the garden occupied by John Traves on the west: also six tenements on the west side of Swan Alley lately occupied by Humfry Parris, Richard Piggott, Thomas Bateman, John Holford, Elizabeth Kettlewell, widow, and George Kirby, together with the soil of Swan Alley to the middle of the gutter in the Alley, the current of which ran from north to south: and the western moiety of a messuage in Swan Alley, now occupied by William Brittane, lying near the tenement lately occupied by George Kirby and measuring 15 feet 6 inches from north to south and 14 feet from east to west. All these properties were purchased from John Traves, Merchant Taylor, on 18 April 1566, at a cost of £226 13s. 4d. The materials were sold for £31.

4. Three tenements lately occupied by John Traves and Robert Dunkyn, purchased from William Pawne, Esq., of Writtle, Essex, for £200. It cost an additional £360 to buy out John Traves and Robert Dunkyn. The materials were sold for £53 10s.

[41] CLRO, Repertory 16, ff. 38, 39, 59, 60.
[42] CLRO, Repertory 16, f. 35.
[43] CLRO, Repertory 16, f. 126, and CLRO, Hustings Roll 254, except deed no. 4: 1. 49 and 50; 2. 54; 3. 45 and 46; 4. Hustings Roll 255/3: this deed was not enrolled until 17 October 1566; 5. 51, 52 and 53; 6. 47 and 48; 7. 43 and 44.
[44] See also St Michael Cornhill Vestry Minutes, 1 November 1566 and 12 January 1566/7; Guildhall Library MSS 4072/1, concerning the use and receipt of the purchase money; and CLRO, Repertory 16, f. 81, concerning sealing of the deed by the Bishop of London.

In the parish of St Christopher Cornhill:

5. Two messuages with shops, cellars, etc., lately occupied by Henry Rushall, Merchant Taylor, and Anthony White, Haberdasher, purchased from William or John Solham, Merchant Taylor, and Walter Myers, Waxchandler, on 5 May 1566, at a cost of £205. It cost £120 to purchase the interests of Henry Rushall and Andrew White. The materials were sold for £67.

In the parish of St Bartholomew the Less:

6. A great messuage with shops, cellars, warehouses, yards, etc., in Brodestrete, and a tenement adjoining the great gate of the same messuage on the west, purchased from Richard Springham, Mercer, on 31 March 1566, ay a cost of £350, the materials of which were sold for £50.

7. Seven tenements in Black Alley occupied by William Pryme, Draper, Anthony Lamberson, Draper, John Pickering, Barber, John Clarke, Tiler, Thomas Lancaster, Clothworker, Ralph Seymour and Alice Spencer, widow, purchased from William Phillips, Merchant Taylor, on 10 April 1566, for £300. It cost £71 to buy out the tenants' interests and the materials sold for £28 13s. 4d.

    In order to complete the block the City agreed on 7 May 1566[45] with Elizabeth, widow of John Jacques, Merchant Taylor, that they would set aside a sum of 100 marks for the little old house in Cornhill that had been her husband's. She would demolish the house at her own cost and, in return, the City would pay her 5 marks a year during her lifetime. On her death the full sum of 100 marks would be paid to her heir.

    The site thus acquired by the City is described in full in the Book concerning the new Burse. The description is entitled: 'The Limits of the Ground taken in for the soil of the Burse intended' and reads as follows:

The parish of St. Michael in Cornhill	The length of the soil of that parish on the street side from the half or channel of the late alley called Swan Alley on the east part, unto the further most of the late alley called New Alley on the west part containeth feet of assize 115 foot. The breadth from the late Swan Alley abutting on the street on the south part, unto the ground late Richard Springham's on the north part, containeth the feet of assize 108 foot. And the breadth from the street at the late New Alley gate on the south part unto the grounds late of Christs Church in Canterbury on the north part, containeth 62 foot of assize.
The parish of St. Christopher	The length of the soil of that parish on the street side of Cornhill from the late New Alley gate on the east part, unto the house late John Jakes on the west part, containeth 66 foot and 6 inches of assize. The breadth from the said street on the south part unto the house whereon one Scother late dwelled, and the ground late of Christ Church in Canterbury on the north part containeth 73 foot and 6 inches of assize.
The parish of St. Bartholomew the Little in the Ward of Broad Street	The length of that parish on the street side from the house whereon Thomas Bates dwelleth on the east part, unto the house late of John Jakes on the west part, containeth 198 foot and 6 inches of assize. The breadth from the street on the north part of the said Bates his house, unto the grounds late John Traves on the south part, containeth 90 foot of assize. The breadth at Jakes his house from the street side on the north part unto the grounds late Walter Meares and William Sollames on the south part, containeth 76 foot of assize. The length of the soil of the intended Burse and buildings thereof in Cornhill side from the east to the west containeth a hundred three score and one foot six inches of assize, large measure. The length on the street side called Broad Street, east and west, containeth a hundred eighteen foot and six inches of assize. The breadth beginning at the late Swan Alley on the street side of Cornhill, unto the street called Broad Street south and north, containeth a

⁴⁵ CLRO, Repertory 16, f. 45.

hundred eighteen foot and six inches of assize.

The breadth from the late New Alley gate on the street of Cornhill unto the street called Broad Street, south and north, containeth a hundred forty nine foot and six inches of assize.

According to the Book concerning the new Burse, the sum spent on the purchase of freeholds was £2,208 6s. 8d. This, together with the amount spent on buying out the leases and 'men's interests of the tenements' and to gratify tenants at will, £1,222 14s., and 'charges necessarily spent and given in reward for the procurement of the purchase', such as fees, writing documents, travelling expenses, £101 16s. 6d., produced a grand total of £3,532 17s. 2d. This represented a large investment on the part of the City. How was the money raised?

The Corporation began to think about ways and means of raising money for the exchange in June 1565.[46] Six Aldermen, including Sir John White and Thomas Rowe, and representatives of the twelve Great Livery Companies and of the Leathersellers were to meet at Sir Martin Bowes' house to discuss the matter, and they held a further meeting at Alderman Rowe's house in July.

The first move was to persuade individual liverymen to subscribe towards the cost of purchasing a site for the exchange. The way in which two of the Great Twelve Companies, the Mercers and the Goldsmiths, set about this task is recorded in their minutes. On 23 July the Renterwarden and several Assistants of the Mercers' Company[47] assembled in the parlour at Mercers' Hall and 'weighing the commission directed from the Lord Mayor and Aldermen to this fellowship for the free liberality of this Company', they 'commanded Leverich Forster, their Clerk, to write in a book the names of 128 persons of this fellowship, and John Ramridge, the Company's officer, to present the same to Alderman Thomas Rowe'. The Goldsmiths[48] met on the same day and agreed on a list of 59 names of such of the Company as were thought meet to be sent to the commissioners for the burse to be delivered by the Beadle to Alderman Rowe.

In August it was decided to involve some of the minor Companies and precepts were sent to the Leathersellers, Girdlers, Dyers, Cutlers, Scriveners, Tallowchandlers, Painterstainers and Pewterers to supply the commissioners with the names of such persons '. . . as are of ability and substance somewhat to contribute and give towards the setting forward of the said Burse'.[49]

At this stage the commissioners were provided only with lists of liverymen willing to contribute towards the cost of purchasing the site. On 13 December 1565[50] the Court of Aldermen ordered the Town Clerk to issue precepts to the Wardens of those Companies which had agreed to contribute, to appoint two collectors for each Company to receive the money promised and to pay it over to Alderman Edward Jackman by Lady Day 1566. A follow-up precept was delivered to the Companies on 1 March following, urging them to collect money from those who had not yet paid their contributions.[51]

Alderman Edward Jackman had been appointed Treasurer for the Burse on 13 December 1565 and on the same day Sir Thomas White, Sir William Garrard, Sir William Chester, Sir John White and Alderman Rowe had been appointed commissioners to act for the Corporation in all matters concerning the Burse. Their terms of appointment included authority for any three of them to approve expenditure.[52]

A complete list of the contributions from individual liverymen appears in the Book concerning the new Burse. The twelve Great Companies produced a total of £1,563 10s. This ranged from £23 10s. collected from seventeen Vintners, to £296 6s. 8d. collected from 83 Mercers (out of a list of 128) in sums ranging from £1 to £10. The minor Companies who had become involved in August 1565 contributed a total of £94 6s. 8d.

In December 1565 the Court of Aldermen[53] had also ordered that letters should be sent to the Governors of the Merchant Adventurers and of the Merchants of the Staple, asking for contributions.

[46] CLRO, Repertory 15, f. 445.
[47] MC, Acts of Court, 1560–90, f. 81.
[48] Goldsmiths' Company Archives, Book K, part 1.

[49] CLRO, Repertory 15, f. 461.
[50] CLRO, Repertory 15, f. 509.
[51] CLRO, Journal 18, f. 385.
[52] CLRO, Repertory 15, f. 509.
[53] As note 52.

The letter to the Adventurers written in January 1566 asked for 400 marks, that to the Staplers, written in May 1566, for 200 marks.[54] The letter to the Adventurers pointed out that the costs of purchasing the site for the exchange were so great 'that they do far surmount and exceed all the benevolence of all the merchants and other wealthy citizens of this City here residing and abiding, albeit that we have caused them to be very earnestly moved and travailed withall'. There is no evidence, however, that the City actually received any money either from the Adventurers or the Staplers.

By Lady Day 1566 it was apparent that individual contributions would fall short of the sum required. On 21 March[55] the Wardens of the twenty Companies who had already been involved were summoned to be at the Lord Mayor's house at noon on the following Saturday 'to prest for a season the several sums of money upon them here noted', namely from the Mercers, Grocers, Drapers and Merchant Taylors, £60 each, from the Goldsmiths, Fishmongers, Skinners and Haberdashers, £40 each, from the Ironmongers, Clothworkers, Salters and Leathersellers, £30 each, from the Vintners, Girdlers and Saddlers, £20 each, and from the Cutlers, Dyers, Pewterers and Tallowchandlers, £10 each. At this same meeting the Wardens of the Companies, with the exception of the Grocers and Dyers, acceded to these forced loans with a good grace and the Town Clerk was asked to issue precepts for the collection of the various sums of money within fourteen days. At the same time he was to make out bills for the repayment of the loans in 1568.

The Mercers again showed their enthusiasm for the Burse, either that, or their wish to placate their powerful liveryman, Thomas Gresham, by agreeing to lend not £60, but £70, at a Court of Assistants held on 1 April.[56] The Court of the Goldsmiths[57] also agreed to their loan on the same day as the Mercers, but with a good deal less enthusiasm. They agreed to lend the £40 asked for by the Corporation only 'if the superior companies that are afore this Company do

likewise lend for that purpose such sums as of them are required — or else not'. The Grocers[58] were not represented at the meeting on 23 March, nor did they agree initially to make a loan. At their Court of Assistants on 29 March they discussed the Lord Mayor's precept, but 'the Company aforesaid not in good part receiving the same or to grant his request, examining the state of this House and charges future' asked the Master and Wardens to see the Lord Mayor 'and declare the state of this Company, with all circumstances as they shall think best, meet and convenient, desiring that the house therefore may be unburdened'. Their protest was in vain, however, for on 9 April the Wardens reported that, as a result of their talk with the Lord Mayor and Aldermen, they were fully persuaded 'since there is no remedy' that they must lend the £60 asked for. Assuming that the Dyers, who also refused to make a loan at first, received similar treatment, the sum lent to the City by the Livery Companies was £620.

The City also raised money by selling the materials from the houses demolished on the site of the exchange. On 13 December 1565[59] two committees were appointed, one to give notice to the tenants of the houses to vacate them by 25 March 1566, the other 'to sell by their sad discretions all the said houses that . . . are to be taken down, to the City's most commodity and benefit'. The first of these two committees wasted no time. On 18 December[60] they were already being thanked 'for their gentle pains already taken' in talking with tenants and persuading them 'quietly to avoid out of the same'.

Demolition had been completed by May 1566[61] for the Chamberlain was then instructed to pay for cleaning out all the privies on the void ground in Cornhill where the new Burse was to be erected. The sum received from the sale of materials was £478 3s. 4d. The Book concerning the new Burse gives details of the sums received for each house and, by comparing these with the purchase price, it is possible to gain some idea of the condition of these houses at the time of their sale to the City. For

[54] CLRO, Journal 18, f. 381 (Merchant Adventurers), and Repertory 16, f. 43 (Staplers).
[55] CLRO, Repertory 16, f. 31.
[56] MC, Acts of Court, 1560–90, f. 85.
[57] Goldsmiths' Company Archives, Book K, part 1.

[58] Grocers' Company Archives, Calendar of Minute Book, 1556–69, Guildhall Library MSS S.L. 37–G873.
[59] CLRO, Repertory 15, f. 509.
[60] CLRO, Repertory 15, f. 511.
[61] CLRO, Repertory 16, f. 46.

instance, the sum for the materials from the house belonging to the parish of St Michael Cornhill equalled half its purchase price. By contrast, the materials from six houses and tenements and the moiety of another, formerly belonging to John Traves, fetched little more than one-seventh of the purchase price.

If we add together the various sums of money raised by all these means, that is contributions from individual liverymen, forced loans from the Companies, sale of the materials from the demolished houses, and include also two other small sums of £5 6s. 6d. contributed by 'foreign men' and £23 6s. 8d. by way of benevolence from the Salters, Skinners, Leathersellers, Pewterers, Dyers and Glaziers, we achieve a figure of £2,690 6s. 8d. The Book concerning the new Burse also puts on the credit side an additional sum of £203 3s. 4d. which included contributions promised by liverymen not yet received. Even if all this money was eventually paid to the Corporation, the total receipts were still only £2,894 9s. 10d., that is, £638 7s. 4d. short of the amount the City had to pay for the purchase of the site of the exchange. How that deficit was made good, the records do not reveal.

Lastly, let us look at the promises made by Gresham up to this time, that is, to May 1566, and to the documentation, or rather lack of it, of the terms of the arrangement between Gresham and the City.

We know that an agreement between Gresham and the Corporation was drawn up and that the Corporation's copy, at least, was sealed. On 13 December 1565[62] it was agreed that the Recorder, Mr Bromley and Mr Wilbraham should join with the commissioners appointed on the same day 'for devising the conveyance of such assurance and writings as they shall thank meet and expedient to be made by Sir Thomas Gresham for and concerning the Burse and the inheritance of the same to the City', and on 7 January 1566[63] Alderman Garrard exhibited to the Court of Aldermen certain articles for their ratification. The Court approved the site chosen for the burse and agreed that it should be 55 yards in length and 45 yards in breadth, and they directed that the houses should be vacated and, presumably, demolished, by the following May so that workmen could 'fall in' with the foundations. Alderman Garrard also reported that Gresham wanted permission to make cellars and vaults in the exchange and 'when they are made to have little estate, as is already agreed upon in the pawns (i.e. the shops) . . . without any condition to him and his heirs for ever'. The Court gave its conditional consent to this request. 'If it may, by order of law [that] whole walk of Burse [i.e. the central courtyard] indented may be assured to the City, the vaults and passages being left to Thomas Gresham, then we are content that the vaults shall be made, so the doors be in the street side'.

On 5 March 1566[64] the Recorder, Bromley and Wilbraham were instructed to join with 'such other learned men as it shall please Sir Thomas Gresham to name and appoint for him in and for making up of books and writings that are to be devised and drawn between the City and him concerning the Burse'. Two days later the commissioners for the Burse were told to meet with the Recorder, Bromley and Wilbraham on the following Saturday (9 March) to 'consider and set out in articles such covenants and conditions as they shall think meet'.[65] On 4 April,[66] Sir William Garrard and Alderman Rowe reported to the Court of Aldermen that the indenture of covenants devised by Mr Recorder and Mr Bromley for the City and by counsel learned in the law for Sir Thomas Gresham, concerning the Burse, to be built by Gresham at his own costs and charges within a certain time expressed in the said indenture, was now drawn and ready to be engrossed in parchment. Unfortunately the full text of the draft indenture is not included in the Repertory but the record does state that, among other things, it had been agreed that the soil on which the Burse was to be erected should stand bound for the performance, presumably by the City, of the covenants in the indenture and that Gresham would enter into an recognisance for £5,000 for the same purpose. The Court approved the draft indenture and ordered it to be engrossed.

62 CLRO, Repertory 15, f. 509.
63 CLRO, Repertory 15, f. 511.

64 CLRO, Repertory 16, f. 25.
65 CLRO, Repertory 16, f. 27.
66 CLRO, Repertory 16, f. 37.

On 14 May 1566[67] the Court of Common Council authorised the sealing of the counterpart of the indentures made between the City and Sir Thomas Gresham, and the document was sealed 'in sight of the said commons'. The Court ordered the counterpart to be delivered to Gresham as the City's deed, on receipt of the other part from him. It is clear, therefore, that a formal, legal document, embodying the terms of the arrangement between Gresham and the City, was prepared and this was, no doubt, the 'great book between the City and Sir Thomas Gresham, knight', for which, according to the Book concerning the Burse, a payment of £3 13s. 4d. was made to 'Mr Recorder his clerks' for its engrossing.

What is less certain is that this document was ever finally executed, that is to say, whether the exchange of counterparts between Gresham and the City ever actually took place. It is remarkable that all traces of this key document for the foundation of the Royal Exchange have disappeared. The City took very great care that all actions relating to the foundation were recorded in the Book concerning the new Burse, compiled in September 1566, and it seems most unlikely that they would have omitted this agreement, apparently sealed in the previous May, without good reason. Can we conclude, therefore, that something went wrong at the last moment and that the agreement was cancelled?

When on 4 April 1566,[68] Sir William Garrard and Alderman Rowe had reported to the Court of Aldermen that Gresham would enter into a recognisance for £5,000 for the performance of the covenants in the agreement, they had added 'that other or further assurances he will none make'. Is there a hint here that Gresham was loath to commit himself and that the City had begun to doubt his intentions? Was it because Gresham was proving somewhat difficult that two days earlier, on 2 April,[69] Alderman Hayward and Robert Christopher, Secondary of the Compter, were asked to move Secretary Cecil in the City's favour in the preferment of the Book concerning the Burse to the Queen's Majesty? We do not have to look very far to find a possible reason for the City's apparent unease at this time, and perhaps also

for the abandonment of the agreement. On 9 February 1566[70] Gresham had made a characteristically extravagant gesture, recorded in the Book concerning the new Burse and quoted by both Burgon and Welch as evidence of Gresham's generosity. Set in its proper context, however, it may be seen in a somewhat different light.

The entry in the Book is entitled: 'The copy of the Bill mentioning the promise made by Sir Thomas Gresham to the City, over and besides the bargain made by the said Sir Thomas, included in the great book, whereunto Sir William Garrard, Sir William Chester, Mr. Lionel Ducket, Alderman, and divers other are witnesses'. It describes how, at the house of Alderman John Rivers, Gresham promised that

within one month next after the building and fully finishing of the Burse and Burse pawns and other buildings intended, he would assure to the City . . . the moiety all other within the circuit of the Burse, as without: the profits thereof to come to the City . . . after the decease of the said Sir Thomas Gresham and of his wife, so that it happen that the said Sir Thomas do die without issue of his body lawfully begotten: and the other moiety he hath likewise promised to leave to the Mercery, with like estate and like condition as aforesaid. And for the sure performance of the premises, the said Sir Thomas . . . did give his hand to Sir William Garrard and drank a carouse to Thomas Rowe, the day and year aforesaid.

This would appear to be the first occasion on which Gresham intimated that the City was not to have the burse to itself, as it might have supposed, but was going to have to share it with the Mercers' Company. The new promise, to give assurances to the City and the Mercers' Company, within one month of the completion of the building was not, in fact, fulfilled until Gresham made his will in 1575, by which time his gift to the City had also become encumbered with a number of expensive trusts. It seems significant that the promise of 9 February 1566 was scrupulously recorded in the Book concerning the new Burse, while the agreement sealed on 14 May following was not, surely reflecting the changes which were taking place in Gresham's own mind. The failure to secure a proper agreement in 1566 was only the first of a number of disappointments the City and later the Mercers were to suffer with regard to Gresham's

[67] CLRO, Journal 18, f. 398.
[68] CLRO, Repertory 16, f. 37.
[69] CLRO, Repertory 16, f. 36.

[70] CLRO, Journal 19, f. 12, and Letter Book V, f. 70.

original 'friendly offer', disappointments which led the Mercers, when they and the Corporation finally gained possession of the Royal Exchange following the death of Gresham's widow in 1596,[71] to comment:

'. . . sure we are that neither the City nor the Company of Mercers shall be any gainer by Sir Thomas Gresham's will, but take upon them charge without profit', a rather different, but more realistic view than that expressed by more recent writers.

[71] MC, Acts of Court, 1595–1629, f. 14.

CHAPTER IV

The Building of the Exchange

By ANN SAUNDERS

WE SHALL NEVER KNOW exactly why Thomas Gresham was driven to establish his Exchange. He would have been nineteen in 1538, the year in which his father held office as Lord Mayor; by then he would have been apprenticed to his uncle, Sir John Gresham, and must have heard family discussion about the establishment of a Bourse in London. He might already have visited Antwerp and seen the two Exchanges there; at all events, within a few years, he was living in the adjacent Nieuwe Lange Straat and visiting the Nieuwe Beurs almost daily.

At that time, Antwerp was at the height of its prosperity. Flooding had widened the Scheldt and the easier access helped the city to become the chief port of Flanders. Throughout the fifteenth century, the English wool trade through Calais had slackened, while Antwerp handled an ever-increasing amount of raw wool and cloth. The four great annual fairs drew merchants there from all over Europe. But it was not only textiles that changed hands. Merchants met to exchange credit, to arrange transport and cargo space, to negotiate loans on behalf of their governments and to receive and pass on information. In 1515, the Oude Beurs was established just off the Grote Markt. It was an open, arcaded courtyard with a tower in one corner housing a bell to announce the hours of trading. It proved too small for the throng of merchants, and in 1531 the Nieuwe Beurs was constructed. It can be seen clearly on Virgilius Bononiensis' map of 1565 (Col. Pl. IIB) and is engraved magnificently in Guicciardini's *Descrittione di Tutti i Paese Bassi* of 1588. By the 1540s, Gresham was living within 300 yards of it. He, and the factors who worked for him — Richard Clough, Henry Cobham, John Conyers, Edmund Hogan and others beside — knew what a nerve centre the Antwerp Bourse was, so much so that in 1560, Clough wrote to his master in London urging him to provide the

same facility for the English capital. Gresham, perhaps understandably in view of the likely expense, made no immediate response.

Then personal tragedy intervened. An exchange of letters between Henry Cobham and John Conyers in Antwerp to Sir Thomas Challoner, ambassador in Madrid, carried the bad news.[1] Conyers wrote on 20 May 1563:

But as heavie news as maie be for my m[aster]s partte wherein the wyll of God must be fulfilled. As the first of this present my m[aster]s sonne fell sicke of the plorissie and was presentlie lett bludde for the same x onzone togeyther. So that at the second of the present he departtid this worlde of whousse Soyll God have marssie. I Asseure y[r] honnour y[t] was no Smalle greaffe unto my m[aste]r and to my Laddie for that they had no moy children. But now thanks be to Gode they are all sattisfied for the wyll of Gode must be fulfilled.[2]

Whatever slight evidence survives, points to Gresham as having been devoted to his family. The superb portrait — the first full-length representation of an English commoner — which hangs today in the Mercers' Hall was probably painted to celebrate his marriage in 1544 to Anne Ferneley, the widow of another Mercer, William Reade (frontispiece). When she became pregnant, three different doctors were paid for their attendance at and after the birth in March 1547.[3] That child, their sole offspring, was the Richard, named for his grandfather, who was to die so untimely. In later years, Gresham was to see his illegitimate daughter Anne well settled. Her mother, whose maiden name is unknown but who was said to have been from Bruges, was married, either before or after the child's birth, to Thomas Dutton, another of

---

[1] PRO, SP 70/57/673, 676, 702.
[2] The youth may have died of pleurisy, as Conyers' letter says, but it should be remembered that consumption was very frequent at that time.
[3] I am indebted to Professor Ian Blanchard for this information.

Gresham's factors. Dutton was eventually to own a small estate at Isleworth, near to Gresham's own handsome country house at Osterley. Anne herself was brought up, at least in part, in Gresham's own household and was married in 1569 to Nathaniel Bacon, half-brother to Sir Francis Bacon;[4] later, the couple were to build Stiffkey Hall in North Norfolk. It would be reasonable to claim that Gresham cared about his family; certainly, the perpetuation of his family name was a matter of intense — almost obsessional — importance to him.

The Court of Aldermen met on 11 May 1563, nine days after the boy's death. Lionel Duckett, later to be Gresham's own executor, was instructed to move Sir Thomas towards founding a Bourse.[5] We cannot know, but it may have been that Gresham clutched at the suggestion, eager for anything that would draw his mind away from his grief. The memory of the dead boy and the idea of the Exchange may have become inextricably linked in his thoughts; the one may have driven him to devote the more energy and determination to the other. Such an association might also explain Lady Gresham's later exploitation of the Exchange.

One scrap of evidence remains to give an indication of Gresham's desolation of spirit. Writing on 2 March 1564, less than a year after his boy's death, to Sir William Cecil, he addresses the letter 'from my powre dowffe howse at Oystreley'.[6] The word 'dowffe' is unexpected, being Scots, or at least northern English, rather than East Anglian, and meaning sad, melancholy, listless. Grief was still heavy on the writer.

We know, however, from his factors' letters that the Greshams had moved up to Norfolk during the summer of 1563, but by September Clough was writing to Challoner that Sir Thomas was expected in Flanders within a day or two,[7] and it was in Antwerp that the fabric of the Exchange was to have its beginnings.

In Antwerp there lived a mason, Hendryck van Paesschen.[8] He was associated with the architect Cornelis Floris, and may have been his pupil. Hendryck had had a part in the building of the Town Hall (Stadhuis) in Antwerp, and from the Aldermen's Registers (Schepenregisters) in the City Archives there, would appear to have been a man of substance, active in all manner of land and building business. A search of those Registers between 1540 and 1580 reveals repeated references to him engaging in a variety of property deals, both large and small. By 1564, his name is prefixed with Mr — Magister — an indication of his increasing social and professional status. Hendryck van Paesschen was the man to whom Gresham intended entrusting the realisation of London's first Exchange.

On 4 January 1564, Gresham made his offer to the City to build a Bourse at his own expense, on condition that the City would provide the necessary land. The entry in the Repertory continues:

And it was also graunted and agreed that he shall have lycense to sett such straungers on worke on and about the makyinge of the same burse as to him shall be thought requisite and useful to be hadde for the accomplishment.[9]

Cleary, Gresham knew exactly what he intended to do, and how he was going to do it. The City authorities appointed a committee to select a site and to obtain an approximate estimate of the cost, which they were to deliver 'on Sunday nexte at 8 of the clock at the chapel in Paul's Church where in they do usually assemble before the sermon time'.

There is one further piece of evidence that Gresham had planned everything well before he made his

---

[4] Gresham settled the manors of Langham and Morston, North Norfolk, on the young couple in 1572 but — characteristically — leased out the land afresh just before surrendering it, so that Nathaniel had only the rent and not immediate full control of the property. The letters, published in *The Papers of Nathaniel Bacon of Stiffkey*, ed. A. Hassell Smith (University of East Anglia, 1979), give the impression that Nathaniel was a critical and pedantic husband, and that Lady Gresham may have been a not overkindly stepmother.

[5] CLRO, Repertory 15, f. 237b.

[6] PRO, SP 70/69/164.

[7] PRO, SP 70/74/569.

[8] The name appears in a variety of forms — Henrick, Hendryk or Hendryck; Paesschen becomes Van den Passe. Fuller information may be found in 'Foreign Artists of the Reformed Religion working in London, 1560–1660' by Lionel Cust in *Proceedings of the Huguenot Society* (1903), Vol. VII, pp. 45–82; in 'L'Architecte Henri van Paesschen et l'ancienne bourse de Londres' by Henri Hymans in *Bulletin de l'Academie Royale d'Archéologie de Belgique* (Brussels, 1908), pp. 343–54, in Robert Hedicke, *Cornelis Floris und die Florisdekoration* (Berlin, 1913), and in J. F. Millar, *Classical Architecture in Renaissance Europe, 1419–1585* (1992), published Thirteen Colonies Press, Williamsburg, Virginia.

[9] CLRO, Repertory 15, f. 406v.

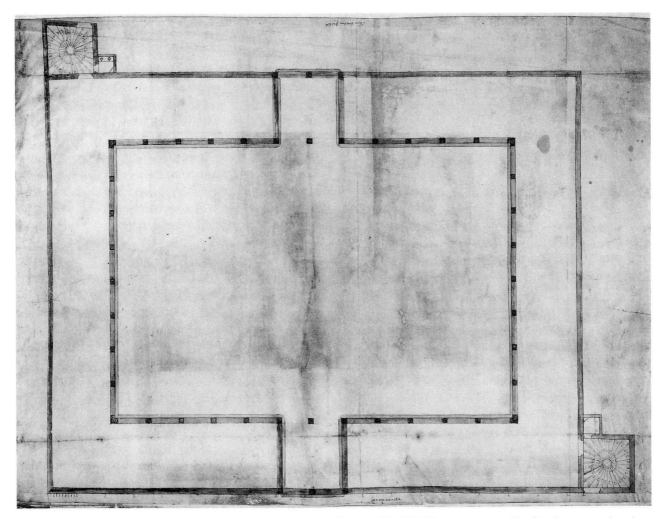

FIG. 7.   Ground plan of the Exchange. This is among the archives at Hatfield House; presumably Gresham sent the plan
to his patron, Lord Burghley.

By kind permission of the Marquess of Salisbury

formal offer to the City. His patron was Sir William
Cecil, later Lord Burghley, and among the papers
now at Hatfield House there is a plan for the proposed
Bourse (Fig. 7). It is on a large sheet of vellum
measuring $29\frac{1}{2}$ by $20\frac{3}{4}$ inches and is executed in pen
and colour wash.[10] The outer walls and the two inside
staircases are delineated in a soft pink, the inner
courtyard with its entrances is in green. No orienta-
tion is given, but in the left-hand margin is written
'Lombartt Street' and on the right 'Cornywalle',
presumably Cornhill; an additional note refers to 'Sir
Martyn Bues . . .'. This plan must predate the

negotiations for the site of the Exchange for, as we
have seen, the Merchant Taylors refused to part with
their cherished land. It does, however, correspond
with later representations and we can assume that the
design was transferred to the new site, once that was
agreed. The Sir Martyn named on the plan was Sir
Martin Bowes, goldsmith, Alderman and formerly
Lord Mayor in 1545, who had owned a substantial
mansion on Lombard Street.

The site was cleared by May 1566 and work began
immediately. Stow's account in his *Survey of London*
tells the story best:

he [Gresham] on the seventh of June laying the first stone
of the foundation, being Bricke, accompanied with some

[10] Hatfield House, CPMII I.9. The diagram seems to be an
exceptionally early example of a scaled plan.

Aldermen, every one of them laid a piece of Golde, which the workmen tooke up, and forthwith followed upon the same with such diligence, that by the month of November, in the yeare, 1569, the same was covered with slate, and shortly after fully finished.[11]

But this propitious account tells only half the story. The workmen fortunate enough to gather up the gold pieces were presumably Flemings, brought over by van Paesschen; notwithstanding Gresham's licence to employ 'straungers', the bricklayers of the City were — literally — up in arms and Gresham had a lively industrial dispute on his hands. The Court of Aldermen dealt with it summarily; on 13 June 1566:

After the longe and deliberate debatement of the matter concerning the Bursse wᵗʰ the Brickelayers of this Citie and their misdemeanours therein towards Sʳ Thomas Gresham and the hole City both in wordes and also in deedes . . . It was fynally and upon their humble submission and suite here presently in right earnest wise made . . . agreed that the said Mr Gresham shall be specially moved in their favour as well by some of this Court as by Mr John Gresham, mercer . . . that they may have his favour and parcel of his work at the said Bursse.[12]

Gresham, or perhaps his brother, presumably made an agreement with the Bricklayers' Company that their men should have a fair share of the work, though he continued to import the ornamental stonework from Antwerp. The bricklayers' ring-leader, however, did not escape without rebuke, for on the same day the Warden of the Company was charged

to bring one William Crow, one of his Company, before my Lord Mayor, so that his Lordship may send him to ward for his very lewd demeanour towards Henrick the said Sir Thomas Gresham's chief workman there.

We may guess that there had been picketing and a near riot, but that the authorities had contained it, though later in the year an unknown hand defaced the Gresham coat of arms.[13] The culprit was not caught, but otherwise matters went on smoothly enough.

We can trace the progress of the work in the letters that passed between Antwerp and London. On 22 July 1566, Richard Clough wrote:

Towching the steves and other thynges you wryte for, they are in hand, and shall be sent you as soone as they are done; beyng glad that you do so well lyke Henryke, and that your works go so well forwards. So that, when he comyth over, I wyll follow your order for the rest.[14]

In August Gresham himself travelled up to his house at Ringshall in Suffolk, to view timber intended for the Bourse, as he informed Cecil.[15] On 24 November 1566, Clough again reassured his master that matters were in hand: 'And as touching your things belonging to the Burse, according to your last, they shall be provyded here, and sent away as soon as they shall be ready'.[16] In December, the busy factor sent to Amsterdam to buy a substantial amount of wainscoting, some small part of which was to be for the Earl of Ormonde. Transport was a problem, however:

Notwythstanding, I doubt there wyll no ship depart for those parts before March; but and if there do, and that I can by any meanes gett so much fraight in them, they shall be sent with the first, whereof have you no doubt.[17]

In the spring of the following year, 1567, Clough being in Wales on a personal quest, John Morrall, another of Gresham's agents, wrote:

. . . Richard Backar your worships man and his fellowes who be hear readie to passe this nyxt shipes for London. Whearfor I mayen to send them in one of the shippes layden with stones for the Bourse for the whiche there ys 3 shipes readie to departte from hence as to morowe yf the wynde serves them.[18]

[14] Burgon, *Gresham*, II, pp. 115–16.
[15] PRO, SP 70/85/52. Burgon tells us that the indentations of sawpits were still visible when he was writing (1839) but I could find no sign of anything when I went over the ground in 1996.
[16] Burgon, *Gresham*, II, p. 117.
[17] Ibid. Wholesale shipping of building materials was going on between the Low Countries and London. The Gresham correspondence reveals regular anxieties over materials required for Cecil's mansions, Theobalds in Hertfordshire and Burghley at Stamford in Lincolnshire — paving stones (20 October 1566), 15,000 slates and 3,000 feet of board (13 September 1568), pillars of marble (13 October 1570) — while in the summer of 1565 the *Christopher* had brought from Antwerp, on Gresham's orders: '1 galarye of stone for my Lord of Arundell c̄tyn other stone for . . . makynge of hys galarye & gate' [PRO, Customs Accounts, E.190.312]. In the same ship Richard Clough had imported 'ij cayses of pattrons for framing of a howsse, ij cayses wythe locks & hyndges for dorrs and wyndowes . . . wᵗ viij peces of lether for the hangings of a chamber', as well as three feather beds, a bolster and six pairs of sheets. Was he already hoping to get married? Burgon tells the romantic story of his courtship, *Gresham*, II, pp. 211–15.
[18] PRO, SP 70/89/1137.

[11] John Stow, *A Survey of London*, ed. C. L. Kingsford (1908), I, pp. 192–93.
[12] CLRO, Repertory 16, f. 61v.
[13] CLRO, Journal 19, f. 150v.

By 17 August Clough, now a married man, was trying to provide ornamentation for the Bourse: 'I have received the pictures you wryte of, whereof I will cause the Queenes Majestie's to be made, and wyll send you the rest back againe with that, as soone as yt ys done'.[19]

By the autumn, the carcass of the building was complete and ready for roofing. The slates came from Flanders, too. On 14 September Clough wrote:

And as touching that you woulde have sayd to Henryke, I have so done; and he wyll make his provysion thereafter, and wyll come with all along seas: for he sayeth he wyll nott go over and leve the stones beynd him. And for the slates they shall be bought and sent you with the rest of the stuff.[20]

A fortnight later, the slates had not arrived. Clough wrote again:

I do perceive by your letters, that the slates were not come from Dort, where of I have marvell: so that I wyll send away the other that you wrote for, hoping that Henryk ys arrived with you long past, and all such stones as was lacking for the Bourse.[21]

Through all this, van Paesschen was travelling to and fro between Antwerp and London; confirmation of this is to be found in the Stadsarchief of Antwerp where it is recorded that, on 19 October 1568, Marie, daughter of Jan of Delft and lawfully wedded wife of Hendryck van Paesschen, sworn surveyor of that same city, appeared before the magistrates in her husband's stead, he of necessity being in England making and building there the Bourse of the merchants of London, to swear that money was owing to them for work undertaken and completed for the deceased Lord Anthony van Stralen.[22]

Gresham's own new mansion was being built in Bishopsgate just before work began on the Exchange. He had moved there from Lombard Street by the autumn of 1566, when his letters began to be addressed from Gresham House. It was a substantial, old-fashioned property with a range of buildings around a courtyard, covering almost an acre but, though van Paesschen may have had a hand in the

designing or building, there is no evidence for so believing.

Although no trace remains of Gresham's Bourse, the entire building having been swept away by the Great Fire of 1666, it is still possible, from engravings and from contemporary descriptions, to have a reasonably clear idea of what it looked like. In addition to the Hatfield plan, there are two engravings of the façade and of the interior of the Exchange. Executed about 1569 or 1570, they were the work of Franz Hogenberg, at that time a refugee in this country from religious persecution in the Netherlands, and are the earliest known topographical engravings of any English building.[23]

The exterior view presents the Exchange from the south, that is, from Cornhill. It is shown as a four-storey building, the ground floor probably of stone, possibly reticulated, and with shutters which could be opened up to give light to the shops and doors, of which we can only see half, leading down to the basement area. Above are two storeys with generous window space to light the booths within, while in the steeply pitched roof are dormers topped with grass-hoppers. The entrance is under a double archway, the wall above it divided into three compartments, the broad central space filled with the royal arms, and Gresham's own arms to the left. In the right-hand section is a lozenge-shaped shield, the dexter side with Gresham's arms again, the sinister left blank, though presumably intended for Lady Gresham's maiden bearing, the arms of her father, the Mercer William Ferneley.

The engraving is not easy to interpret, but it would seem that substantial blocks of building projected on either side of the entrance, that on the east being, possibly, the Tendring House. Its function is nowhere specified, but it would seem to have housed the day-to-day administration of the Exchange and, from its name, to have been where deals, once agreed, could be recorded, though no ledger has survived. The front, turned to Cornhill, shows a handsome classical double entrance approached by steps, with the two doors set at right angles to each other, flanked by Doric columns, and surmounted by an entablature

[19] *SPF*, 1566–67, item 1603.
[20] Burgon, *Gresham*, II, p. 119.
[21] Ibid., II, p. 120.
[22] Stadsarchief, Antwerp, Certificatieboek 28 (1568), f. 34r.

[23] I am most grateful to Professor Michael Port for his help in interpreting these engravings.

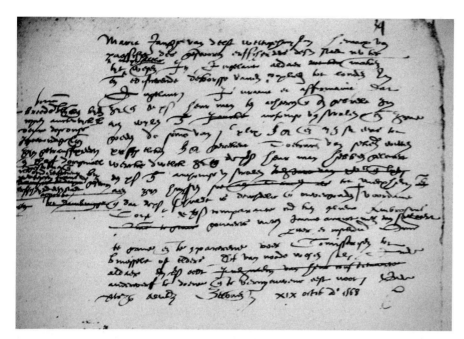

FIG. 8. Extract from the Certificatieboek 28 (1568), in which Marie van Paesschen tells of her husband's absence in England where he is busy building the Exchange.

By kind permission of the Stadsarchiel, Antwerp

matching the order of the internal arcade. These additions show a development of the Hatfield plan.

From the roof of the Tendring House rises a bell tower, from which the hours for meeting were rung out. Half-way up, a balcony runs round the tower with another above it, crowned in turn by a belfry stage; between the two a clock is shown, though we may doubt whether the clock was anything more than an intention at this stage. The balconies served to accommodate the City Waites who performed their music there on Sundays. The tower was topped by four ogee-shaped buttresses and above them Gresham's own crest, a triumphant grasshopper, an insect which had been his family's crest since the previous century.[24] Smaller grasshoppers are shown on chimneys and dormers, though whether they were ever really executed may be in doubt.

The internal view gives even more detail. It shows the open courtyard, paved with Turkey stones, with a

dozen groups of people, talking in two and threes, and a dog frisking. Around the walls runs the arcade, the sheltered walks within paved in black and white marble, and a bench set against the wall. The arcade of Doric columns, surmounted by semicircular arches with a plain keystone set in each, is crowned by an entablature. If we look carefully within the arcade, we can see what appears to be a carved frieze of reclining figures running round the wall; these figures may be the 'stones for the Bourse' which John Morrall, writing from Antwerp on 27 April 1567, assured Gresham were on their way in three ships, or they could have been fashioned from the alabaster which Gresham seems to have shipped to Antwerp in October 1570, for which transaction he needed a special licence. The upper storey is composed of an almost continuous range of niches, separated by Ionic pilasters and containing life-sized figures. This internal façade is a classical composition which would have been unique in the City in 1566 and for many years to come and, save for Somerset House, with few comparisons in London as a whole.

Unfortunately, it is difficult to say to what extent Hogenberg's views represent reality. The slender lofty Corinthian column, topped with the mightiest grasshopper of all, rearing itself above the roof on the northern, Threadneedle Street side, probably never

[24] The first recorded instance of its use is on a seal to a letter of 16 October 1456 by James Gresham among the Paston Letters in the British Museum (Add. MSS 43488, f. 10). When Gresham's step-mother died in the Spring of 1565, she left him a 'counter-point of fine imagery, with grasshoppers'. When Faneuil Hall was built in Boston, Massachusetts, in 1742, Peter Faneuil commissioned Shem Drowne to make a grasshopper weather-vane which still swings aloft. I am most grateful to Professor John Manning for this information.

FIGS. 9 and 10 (*above and right*).   The exterior and interior of the Royal Exchange, *c.* 1569, by Frans Hogenberg, re-issued
by Robert Wilkinson, 1810. Hogenberg's engravings are the earliest topographical prints to be produced in England.
Crace collection, XXII, 34 and 35.
By courtesy of the Trustees of the British Museum

existed; it is certainly not visible in Hollar's engraving of Winter (see Fig. 18). The clock was not, in fact, added till 1599 (see p. 92), and Hollar's etching of 1644 (Fig. 17) depicts the arcade somewhat differently, with no keystones to the arches but their spandrels decorated and surmounted by a frieze of foliage swags; the sculptures under the arcade differ and the dormers, too, are of a different form. The statues of the English monarchs, though an essential feature of Gresham's original design, were not realised till the next century, almost a generation after his death.

In each corner of the top halves of the two engravings nestles a cartouche. Each bears a text, in French and Dutch on the external view, in Latin and English for the interior. The latter reads:

Sʳ Thomas Gresham Knight at his own costs and charges to the ornament and publike use of this Royall citie of London caused this place from the foundacion to be erected the VII of June Anno MDLXVI And is ended Anᵒ MDLXIX.

Between the cartouches are the royal arms and, below them, Gresham's arms and his motto — *Fortun A My*. The French and Dutch inscriptions are surmounted by seated figures with emblems of trade and commerce; below them hang packages, weighing scales and swags of exotic fruit. From the Latin and

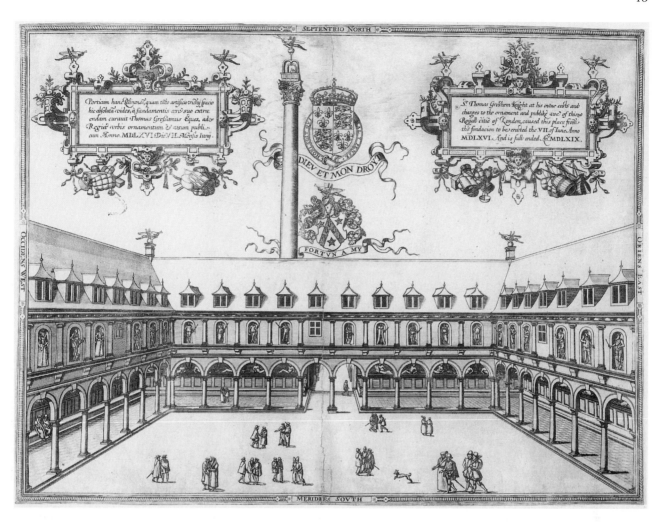

English texts dangle bundles, trunks and barrels; grasshoppers balance on any convenient perch.

Map-makers, too, took notice of the new building. Hogenberg amended his 1572 map of London to show the Royal Exchange on the 1574 edition, and the woodcut map, traditionally ascribed to Ralph Agas, shows the building and emphasises the grasshopper on top of the tower. Indeed, there was nothing in all London like the great courtyard with the arcade around it and the shops above. The Flemish-inspired structure had a cosmopolitan air, it spoke of a sophisticated Europe beyond the experience of the less travelled London citizens, it opened up new possibilities which an enterprising merchant might seek and grasp, if only he were sufficiently adventurous and sufficiently lucky.

For English commerce, the Exchange opened at the right moment. The revolt against Philip II of Spain had already broken out in the Netherlands in 1558, the new religion was spreading throughout the Low Countries and in 1566 religious zealots were rioting in Antwerp, with the treasures in the cathedral, Onze Lieve Vrouw, the particular targets of their iconoclasm. Ten years later, Antwerp was sacked in what became known as the Spanish Fury, when 7,000 citizens were butchered in a single night and the Stadhuis, on which van Paesschen had served his apprenticeship, was partly destroyed. The citizens doggedly rebuilt it but Antwerp's economic decline had begun, to reach its nadir in 1648 when the Peace of Munster closed the Scheldt, ruining Antwerp as a port for a century and a half.

It is just possible that the Hogenberg engravings were issued in connection with the most romantic incident in the history of the Exchange — the visit made to it, on 23 January 1571, by Queen Elizabeth. Gresham's relationship with the Court was close. The Queen would have known that the building had reached completion, would have expressed interest and would, graciously, have accepted Gresham's invitation to dine at his house and to view his achievement. We do not know what they ate and drank at Gresham House in Bishopsgate, but the damask tablecloth from Flanders (Fig. 13) and the generously large napkins survive to whet the imagination for what the celebration must have been. Gresham was determined to make a brave show, but comparatively few of the shops about the Pawn, as the upper floor was called, were as yet tenanted. Stow tells us in his *Chronicle* that Gresham went

twice in one day round the upper Pawn, and besought those few shopkeepers then present that they would furnish and adorn with wares and wax-lights as many shops as they either could or would, and they should have all those shops so furnished rent-free that year, which otherwise at that time was forty shillings a shop by the year.[25]

On the day appointed, Her Majesty came; again, it is Stow who describes the occasion for us:

In the yeare 1570 [1571], on the 23. of Januarie, the Queenes Maiestie, attended with her Nobilitie, came from her house at the Strand called Sommerset house, and entered the citie by Temple Barre, through Fleetstreete, Cheape, and so by the North side of the Bursse through Threeneedle [*sic*] streete, to sir *Thomas Greshams* in Bishopsgate streete, where she dined. After dinner, her Maiestie returning through Cornehill, entered the Bursse on the southside, and after that she had viewed euery part thereof aboue the ground, especially the Pawne, which was richly furnished with all sorts of the finest wares in the Citie: shee caused the same Bursse by an Herauld and a Trumpet, to be proclamed the *Royal Exchange*, and so to be called from thenceforth, and not otherwise.[26]

In bestowing such an honour, the Queen inadvertently defeated Gresham's intention of perpetuating his own name by linking it to the Exchange.

Sir James Dyer of the Middle Temple noted the occasion:

Memorandum que le primer jour de cest terme le quenes majestie ove grand companie et solemnitie rode de Somerset Place at Stronde throught the citie of London to Sir Thomas Gressams house in Bishopgate Streete, and there dined, and after dinner viewed the bursse, and soe returned to Somerset Place at 7 of the clock at night, the Frenche embasador beinge there, and the cardinall, and the

[25] John Stow, *Chronicle* (1604), p. 296.

[26] John Stow, *A Survey of London*, ed. C. L. Kingsford (1908), 1, p. 193.

Cardinall Chatillon. And the name of the bursse turned by the quene and called le Royall Eschange.[27]

One wonders whether Dyer watched the torchlit procession making its way back from the City, along Fleet Street and the Strand. The French ambassador was Bertrand de Salignac de la Mothe Fénélon, recently arrived in England to conduct the complicated negotiations centred on the Duc d'Anjou's courtship of the Queen. Cardinal Châtillon was Odet de Coligny, brother to Admiral de Coligny who, eighteen months later, would be a victim of the St Bartholomew's Day Massacre in Paris. In spite of his high position in the Catholic Church, the cardinal had much sympathy for the Huguenots and had already spent some time as Gresham's guest, both at the Bishopsgate house and at Osterley, in the autumn of 1568.

The royal visit had an immediate effect on the fortunes of the Exchange; fashionable London thronged the Pawn and soon all the shops were let

and within two yeres after, hee [Gresham] raysed that rent unto foure marks a yeere; and within a while after that, hee raised his rent of every shoppe unto foure pounds tenne shillings a yeere, and then all shoppes were well furnished according to that time; for then the milliners or haberdashers in that place solde mousetrappes, bird-cages, shooing-horns, lanthorns, and Jewes-trumpes, &c. There was also at that time that kept shoppes in the upper pawne of the Royall Exchange, armorours that sold both olde and new armor, apothecaries, booke-sellers, goldsmiths, and glassesellers; although now it is as plenteously stored with all kinde of rich wares and fine commodities, as any particular place in Europe. Unto which place many forraine Princes dayly send, to be served of the best sort.[28]

The Exchange was certainly a landmark to foreign visitors. The first to leave a record was a French Protestant, L. Grenade, who came in 1576; we give a translation in full of his long and lively description on pages 48 to 49. Paul Hentzner, coming in 1598 from Germany, marvelled at it as a 'public ornament . . . [for] the convenience of merchants' and did not know whether to admire more 'the stateliness of the building, the assemblage of different nations, or the

quantities of merchandise'.[29] Thomas Platter, also from Germany, came in the following year and recorded his impressions:

The exchange is a great square place like the one in Antwerp a little smaller though, and with only two entrances and only one passage running through it, where all kinds of fine goods are on show; and since the city is very large and extensive, merchants having to deal with one another agree to meet together in this place, where several hundred may be found assembled twice daily, before lunch at eleven, and again after their meal at six o'clock, buying, selling, bearing news, and doing business generally.[30]

In the summer of 1600, Baron Waldstein came from Bohemia and he too made particular mention of the Exchange in his diary.[31]

But in spite of all this, there is a great deal we do not know. The City's expenditure on land is recorded, but not what Gresham's costs were on the building. Correspondence yields tantalising fragments about its structure, its engravings allow us a peep but without assurance that what is shown is what really existed. We do not know how Gresham ran the building, how lettings were organised or how rents were collected. His Day Book, covering his business transactions from 1546 to 1552, ends too early to help us. Documentary evidence for the first quarter-century of the existence of the Exchange seems to be lacking.

Gresham himself did not have long in which to enjoy his good fortune and honourable position in the City. In October 1560, on one of his frequent journeys between London and Antwerp, he had fallen from his horse and broken his leg. It mended ill and continued to plague him. In May 1567, writing to Cecil, he mentions 'my wrenched legge'. In March 1572, he was at his house at Mayfield in Sussex and wrote that he had sent home Derrick the surgeon who 'has brought his leg to some good pass'.[32] In November 1575, he wrote to Walsingham that he could no longer deal with foreign loans 'being 62 yeres of ayge,

[27] Reports from the lost *Notebooks of Sir James Dyer*, ed. J. H. Baker, vol. 1 (Selden Society, vol. 109, 1994), p. 195. I am most grateful to Professor John Baker for this reference.
[28] Charles Knight, *The Life of Sir Thomas Gresham* (1845), p. 193.

[29] Paul Hentzner, *A Journey into England* (1757), p. 40.
[30] Thomas Platter, *Travels in England*, ed. Clare Williams (1937), p. 157.
[31] Zdenek Waldstein, *The Diary of Baron Waldstein*, ed. G. W. Groos (1981).
[32] PRO, SP 12/85/65.

and blynde and lame',[33] and recommended a fellow Mercer and his former factor, Edmund Hogan, for the transaction. He still had an eye for business matters within England, however, and we may note that when, in December 1577, the merchant and traveller Michael Lok wrote to Sir Francis Walsingham about setting up mills on the river Thames, he recommended that Sebastian, the Dutch millwright, and Hendryck the mason be sent for at once,[34] so we may deduce that Gresham's former employee was still in England and possibly in touch with his old patron.

On the evening of Saturday, 21 November 1579, Gresham fell down in his own kitchen with a stroke or seizure, and was dead almost immediately. He was buried in the vault beneath St Helen's Bishopsgate, beside the son whom he had so mourned; a fine table tomb was set up in the nave, its alabaster sides carved with his coat of arms, the crest surmounted by his faithful grasshopper (Fig. 11).

*   *   *

There had for some time been doubts and suspicions about the conditions of Gresham's Will. Rumours had begun to circulate as early as 1575 that Sir Thomas wished to set up a college that would perpetuate his name. First it was to be in Cambridge, where he himself had been a student, but then his mind veered towards London — his house in Bishopsgate was large enough for the purpose and his fellow citizens were in need of instruction in the new sciences. He had never given the Corporation any written guarantee of his intentions; when his Will was read, the City's worst fears were confirmed. Whereas the City Fathers had assumed in 1564, when they had agreed to provide the land for the building, that on Sir Thomas's death, the Exchange would belong to them absolutely, subject to Lady Gresham's life interest, they now found that it was left jointly to the Corporation and to the Company of Mercers and that — worse still — the profits from it were to be encumbered in perpetuity with provision of an income for a new institution of learning, Gresham College, and with other charges. The City was to pay

£50 a year to each of four lecturers in Divinity, Astronomy, Music and Geometry, while the Mercers were to support Law, Physic and Rhetoric. Eight almsmen were to be pensioned and annual payments were to be made to hospitals and to prisons; a small sop was that the Mercers were allowed £100 a year towards the cost of Company dinners. In short, what should have been a profitable legacy, well worth the City's earlier investment in land, was now encumbered with annual outgoings of £603 6s. 8d. — almost half the annual income.[35]

But the person probably the most angered was Lady Gresham herself. Young Richard Gresham might be dead but she had had other sons by her previous marriage, of whom one, William Reade, had survived and had been brought up in the Gresham household in Bishopsgate. From the published Will, it would seem that no provision had been made for him, and that Gresham's heir apparent had been his only niece, Elizabeth, daughter of his elder brother John and wife of Sir Henry Nevill of Billingbere, Berkshire, who had pre-deceased her uncle. Lady Gresham herself was left well provided with an annual income of £2,388 10s. 6½d. in all, £751 5s. from the Exchange itself and the rest from land distributed over London, Wales and ten counties besides, and she determined to leave as much as possible to William. For the remaining seventeen years of her life — and they must have seemed a long seventeen years to the City and to the Mercers — she did all she could to overturn her late husband's Will, and as little as possible to keep the Exchange in good repair.[36]

The year after Gresham's death, the City and the Mercers asked his widow for an 'assurance' of their interest in the Exchange. She agreed, provided Edmund Hogan, of whom we have already heard, was given a lease, which was duly granted for the sake of peace. A year later, the lady was at loggerheads with Elizabeth Gresham's widower, Sir Henry Nevill, and was also in dispute over her own late husband's debts. An Act of Parliament was needed to make a

---

[33] PRO, SP 12/105/69.
[34] SPD, vol. CXIX, item 12.

[35] The clearest and most accessible account of the troubles over Gresham's Will and the setting up of the College is to be found in Ward, *Lives* (1740).
[36] Guildhall Archives, Cornhill Inquest book. For Lady Gresham's immense wealth, see Ward, *Lives*, Appendix IV.

settlement, into which the City and Company contrived to have a clause inserted protecting their interests in the Exchange. Thereafter the redoubtable widow neglected the necessary repairs to the Exchange until pulled up by the Privy Council — 'The Queen will take great offence if so beautiful a monument is suffered to decay'. In 1593, Lady Gresham tried again, petitioning the Privy Council for an Act of Parliament to grant leases on the Exchange for twenty-one years or three lives, the fines therefrom to be for her enjoyment or that of her heirs, which would have left the City and Company with a scant income from the rents. The City replied forcefully:

... her demand is utterly against both the last will and testament of Sir Thomas Gresham, her late husband, as also expressly against an Act of Parliament made in the twenty-third year of her Majesty's reign [1581]. Unto which Act the said Lady Gresham was privy, and her counsel was heard, what they could say, before the said Act passed. And they say also, the same request of the said Lady Gresham is against all reason and equity: for that the citizens of the City of London purchased in fee simple, in the name of divers feoffees, the soil whereupon the Royal Exchange is builded, and paid for the same above four thousand pounds; and in the eighth year of her Majesty's reign [1566] conveyed the same to Sir Thomas Gresham, upon condition to have reassurance made according to certain covenants, which was not done. And albeit the citizens might lawfully have entered for breach of the said condition, and presently taken the rents and profits of the whole, yet they have contented themselves to accept of the same according to the last will and Act of Parliament and

have suffered the said Lady Gresham to take the whole profits. And yet they have been at great charges in defending of title made to some part of the same, and in paying of quit rents, tithes and widows' dowers, which they still continue to this day.

Touching the employment of the profits of the Exchange, according to the purport of the testament of Sir Thomas Gresham, it is thereunto answered that it is meant, and so it shall be performed, that the same, after the death of Lady Gresham, shall be employed justly and truly according to the trust and confidence in them reposed. Which if they should break, there are Courts of Equity that can take order for the remedy thereof. But for as much as the said Lady Gresham is to have the same during her life and the employments are not to be made until after her death, therefore this complaint is now made before any injury be offered.[37]

Thereafter, Lady Gresham made no public agitation but chance played into her hands. As her death drew near, a number of the original Exchange leases fell in, and she renewed them on favourable terms but with substantial fines. There was nothing anyone could do about it, and we may guess that the money went to William Reade. When Lady Gresham died on 23 November 1596, he may have mourned his mother,[38] but the Corporation and the Mercers must have been thankful.

[37] Ward, *Lives*, pp. 30–31.
[38] She was buried with considerable pomp at St Helen's Bishopgate — The Wardens' Register (Guildhall MS 6836, f. 58) shows an entry for £5 for 'the ground and knill of Ladye Anne Gresham'. The entry for her husband (f. 29) was less exalted: 'For the grave and knele of Mr Thom. Gresham xvs. ood'.

CHAPTER V

L. Grenade, *Les Singularitéz de Londres, 1576*

From VATICAN LIBRARY. REG. LAT. 672

THIS SUMPTUOUS EDIFICE is called the Royal Exchange, which name was given to it by Her Majesty Queen Elizabeth at present reigning, who took the trouble of coming in person to see the noble edifice — may the Lord God preserve Her Majesty against all her enemies! Amen.

The Royal Exchange, then, which the French usually call the Bourse, is situated right in the middle of the City and here, twice a day, the merchants who buy and sell all over Europe meet together in different sections according to nationality, from 11 to 12 in the morning and from 5 to 6 in the evening. Each nation has its own quarter, so that those who have business with them can find them more easily. The English occupy about half the Exchange, and the French have their particular station too, as do the Flemish and the Walloons, the Italians and the Spanish. However, they are all at liberty to go hither and thither through the Exchange according to their need. Their letters can reach them there, and letter-carriers deliver [messages] to those to whom they are addressed. Here also one regularly hears the news of other countries and regions, which is a great convenience for those who traffick in merchandise across the seas.

As for the form and shape of the Exchange: it is a quadrangle surrounded by three great walks or galleries one above the other. The lowest one is subterranean; here and there in that one are several stalls to sell merchandise and here drapers and cloth-merchants lay out their wares, but I think it is rather a dark and solitary place for it only gets a view through certain gratings which correspond with the central aisle. This undercroft is called New Venice. The central aisle is where the merchants retire and shelter when it rains; it is six or seven paces wide and paved with black and white blocks — a fine work! Around this alley are 36 great stone columns [de pierre bize], each 12 feet high, set four paces apart.

The heart of the Exchange is the quadrangle, large enough to hold 4,000 merchants aside from the central walk; it is cobbled and is 80 paces long and 60 wide. Here the merchants stroll in fine weather and talk business at the times aforesaid. High on the façade, on the inner walls, all about the Exchange, are 36 columns of Jasper marble, set at 10 feet apart, and between them niches in the façade in which to place figures of the Kings and Queens of England, those who have reigned since William the Conqueror, which are to be of bronze; above the columns are to be painted, flat, the arms and names of the Kings, Princes and Lords of those times.

You enter the Exchange by two great portals or doorways, one on the South side, the other on the North. These portals are flanked on either side with a huge column of fine Jasper marble; each must be 14 feet high, and in the middle of the aforesaid entrances is a similar column which divides them in two. The threshold of the aforesaid portals is of the same marble as the columns. Above the portals, in front of the Exchange, is a bas-relief with the arms and devices of England — very fine work. The first device is *Honi soit qui mal y pense* and the second *Dieu et mon droit*.

The third walk is a gallery, which is above the others and is excellent, beautiful and rich. You climb to it by 25 or 30 steps which are arranged in flights of seven. That gallery has all around it 150 stalls of rich merchandise, most notably of all sorts of mercery.

The Exchange is covered all around with fine slates and right above the entrance on the South side is a brave little tower, upstanding and well built, and in the upper storey is a bell with a double purpose: first, it is rung when trading time is over, that is at 12 in the morning or at 6 in the evening; secondly, it serves as a clock to alert the merchants to the times of the Exchange. Around the said tower are two galleries, one above the other, very well built, where the

Pourtraict d'vne nouuelle Bourse pour la nation Angloise
A bastir deuant le refectoir des Cordeliers.

FIG. 12.   The Royal Exchange. An anonymous, undated engraving; the inscription mis-identifies the site of the building, placing it near the Franciscan (Greyfriars) monastery on Newgate Street.
Guardian Royal Exchange collection

musicians of the City perform marvels of sound, on Sundays at 4 o'clock in the afternoon, when the days are long, to the great contentment of all who hear, and their number is very large.

However much the aforesaid Bourse or Exchange is magnificent and wonderful in all its parts, so that they astonish all those who contemplate them carefully, how much more should one marvel and find strange that it was one man, one single Merchant, who undertook and completed so sumptuous a building at his own sole cost? He undertook it and achieved it, as you see it today, to his honour and renown. It was Sir Thomas Gresham who by his worthiness was raised to the honourable rank of knighthood by Her Majesty Queen Elizabeth, whom God preserve. However, I have omitted several things belonging to the Exchange, like the houses which adjoin it, and which are part of the same enterprise, and the cellars and caves underground, by reason of brevity. Only, I venture to say in a word, that in all Europe you will not find as fine an edifice for the purpose to which it is dedicated and the man who could say differently is not yet born. So Sir Thomas Gresham has won praise which will last longer than his undertaking. Opposite the Exchange, on the Cornhill side is a beautiful fountain which gives water through several conduits. It was built at the expense of the Citizens of London, in the year 1400.

The importance of the manuscript was recognised by DEREK KEENE; *it was translated by* GILL HEALEY *and* ANN SAUNDERS

CHAPTER VI

Table Linen Associated with Queen Elizabeth's Visit to Gresham's Exchange

By DAVID MITCHELL

LOT 901 A very fine damask Elizabethan table cloth (92 in. by 84 in.). Patterns of the Royal Arms, heads of Queen Elizabeth, and St George and the Dragon, especially woven to the order of Sir Thomas Gresham, Founder of the Royal Exchange, and used at a Banquet attended by Queen Elizabeth at the Guildhall, in commemoration of the opening of the Exchange in 1571.

LOT 903 Ten damask dinner napkins (26 in. by 39 in.) *en suite*, and specially woven and used on the same occasion.

ON 13 JUNE 1923, the Royal Exchange Assurance purchased two lots of fine table linen with apparent Gresham connections at the auction of the estate of A. F. G. Leveson Gower, Esq.[1] The purchase was reported in *The City Press* on 30 June under the headline 'Gresham Relic Secured By Royal Exchange Assurance'.[2] This article corrected the venue where the Queen dined to Bishopsgate Street and added that 'it appears that the heiress of Gresham married a Gower'. In fact, the descent to Leveson Gower was not through the heiress, but the family of the heir male, Sir Thomas's cousin once removed, Sir William Gresham of Titsey.[3] Nevertheless, it is possible that this cloth was used at Gresham's house in Bishopsgate Street when he entertained the Queen on 23 January 1570/71. However, was it especially woven to his order and were the napkins which depict the story of Susanna and the Elders used on the same occasion?

The tablecloth has four horizontal registers: a portrait of the Queen; a falcon badge; a royal coat of arms; and St George and the Dragon (Fig. 13). Elizabeth is depicted in half-length, wearing a French hood and resting her arms upon a tasselled cushion. The pose and the attire are very similar to an engraving published in Antwerp in 1559 by Hieronymous Cock, possibly after a drawing by Frans Huys or Pieter van der Heyden (Fig. 14). There is a full-length variant published by Hans Liefrinck in Antwerp at about the same time whose authorship is also uncertain.[4] The damask portrait is entitled above and below, 'QVENE ELIZABETH' and 'GOD SAVE THE QVENE'. The second register has the falcon badge of Anne Boleyn, a device that was used by her daughter Elizabeth, notably on the bindings of a number of her books.[5] The third register has crowned royal Tudor arms impaled with those of Boleyn with the leopard and griffin supporters used by Queen Anne.[6] Along the top of this register are the cross of St George, the Prince of Wales' feathers issuing from a crown, and

---

[1] 'Hadleigh House' & 'Clifford Lodge', Windsor, 11 to 14 June 1923, *Catalogue of the Valuable Antique and Modern Contents*. Messrs James M. Richardson & Pierce, The Great Hall, Tunbridge Wells, p. 39.

[2] *The City Press*, 20 June 1923, p. 13.

[3] For descent of the Leveson Gowers from Gresham, see Burgon, *Gresham*, Pedigree of the Gresham Family. Also see *Burke's Extinct & Dormant Baronetcies* (London, 1838).

[4] These engravings are discussed and illustrated in F. M. O'Donoghue, *A Descriptive and Classified Catalogue of Portraits of Queen Elizabeth* (London, 1894), E10 & 11; A. M. Hind, *Engravings in England in the sixteenth and seventeenth centuries*, 'Part I The Tudor Period' (Cambridge, 1952), plates 41(a) & (c); R. C. Strong, *Portraits of Elizabeth I* (Oxford, 1963), E1 & 2; Harold Barkley, *Likenesses in Line. An Anthology of Tudor and Stuart England Portraits* (London, 1982), p. 19.

[5] J. H. & R. V. Pinches, *The Royal Heraldry of England* (London, 1974), p. 146; 'a silver falcon crowned gold, holding a gold sceptre in its right talon, standing upon a golden trunck out of which sprouted both red and white roses'. For illustration of binding see Charles Hasler, *The Royal Arms. Its graphic and decorative development* (London, 1980), p. 148.

[6] Pinches, *Royal Heraldry*, illus. 138 and p. 145. Anne Boleyn's copy of *The Ecclesiaste* has a fine example of her arms on its cover. See Eric Ives, *Anne Boleyn* (Oxford, 1986), illus. 34.

FIG. 13.   Linen damask tablecloth with portrait of Queen Elizabeth (Pattern A), Kortrijk, *c.* 1560.
London, Royal Exchange Assurance

the Tudor rose. The fourth register shows St George about to deliver the *coup de grâce* to the dragon snarling beneath his horse's hoofs.

There are several surviving examples of this pattern, as well as others of a very similar one which omits the whole of the fourth register of St George

FIG. 14.   Engraving with portrait of Queen Elizabeth,
published in Antwerp by Hieronymous Cock, 1559.
London, Victoria & Albert Museum, E.2584–1960

and the Dragon, as well as the Prince of Wales'
feathers (Fig. 15).[7] The details of the portrait busts
also have differences in detail. Nevertheless they both
present the same problem by portraying Queen
Elizabeth with the arms of her mother, Anne Boleyn.
As monarch, Elizabeth always used the arms of her
father and grandfather, but apparently did not bear

[7] Examples of damasks with the fourth register of St George
and the Dragon (Pattern A) include: Victoria & Albert Museum
857–1907, napkin 54 in. by 43 in.; V&A, T119–1927, tablecloth
6 ft 10 in. by 6 ft 11½ in.; Sotheby's, London, December 1920,
Lot 73, napkin; Christie's, South Kensington, 15 June 1982,
Lot 106, tablecloth (purchased by Rijksmuseum, Amsterdam).
In addition, a napkin was submitted to the V&A for their
opinion in 1953, and a tablecloth and napkins in 1958 (notes in
V&A, Linen Damask handlist).
   Examples of the alternative design without the fourth register
(Pattern B) include: V&A, T200–1960, napkin 44 in. by 27 in.;
V&A, T214–1963, tablecloth 10 ft by 6 ft 9 in.; V&A,
T215–1963, napkin 44½ in. by 27½ in.; Royal Scottish Museum,
Edinburgh, 1962–1015, napkin; Christie's, South Kensington,
12 May 1987, Lot 129, napkin 46½ in. by 27½ in.

FIG. 15.   Linen damask tablecloth with portrait of
Queen Elizabeth (Pattern B), Kortrijk, c. 1560.
Edinburgh, Royal Scottish Museum A1962.1015

any personal arms as a princess.[8] This is perhaps not
surprising in view of her mother's execution and her
own often precarious position.
   Dr van Ysselsteyn suggested that these pieces with
the Queen's portrait were woven at Haarlem about
1600, a view subsequently endorsed by Marguerite

[8] R. B. McKerrow, *Printers & Publishers Devices*, Bibliographical
Soc. Illustrated Monograph 16 (London, 1913), p. 154.

Prinet.[9] Apart from early details such as the half-repeat single border on some of the tablecloths and the horizontal bands of tracery and knotwork between the registers, it is surely inconceivable that an image of 1559 would be re-used in 1600, particularly as several later engravings after Isaac Oliver, Nicholas Hillard and others were widely available. Indeed, as early as 1563 attempts had been made by the Crown to control and standardise the Queen's image.[10] Thus the portrait of the 1559 engraving would not only have been anathema to the Queen in 1600, but the French hood and puffed sleeves would also have struck her wealthy and discerning subjects, who were the potential customers for fine napery, as outrageously old-fashioned.

As the portraits on both damask patterns bear such a resemblance to the engraving of 1559 and both incorrectly incorporate Anne Boleyn's rather than the Tudor arms used by Elizabeth, it seems that they were first woven immediately after Elizabeth's accession to the throne. Further, as there are more examples of these two patterns than any others surviving from the sixteenth century, they must have been stock patterns woven for the English market.[11] If the design had been especially commissioned by Gresham, it is likely to have incorporated his own arms and the grasshopper device that was so prominently displayed on the Royal Exchange. Such bespoke damasks were ordered during the sixteenth century by Englishmen, for example at the beginning of the century the Duke of Buckingham had napery strewn with his badges surrounded by Stafford knots, and during Elizabeth's reign the Earl of Leicester had a tablecloth 'of fine Damaske, wth sondrie scutchions of yor L. Armes in it'.[12]

If these patterns with the Queen's portrait were indeed first produced about 1559, they would have been woven in Kortrijk in the Spanish Netherlands, which by this time had become the centre of the trade.[13] However, their specification and design probably originated with a merchant or factor in Antwerp.[14] The confusion over the Queen's arms may have arisen by the specifier assuming that Elizabeth would use her mother's arms. Alternatively an order may have been placed in Kortrijk about 1535 for a parcel of table linen for Queen Anne which was cancelled on her fall.[15] Such an order would have been entirely appropriate as the royal household was divided into a King's side and Queen's side, each with their own every officers and supplies of linen. Further, Anne had served as a *fille d'honneur* in the brilliant Burgundian Court of Margaret of Austria at Mechelen and would have seen the finest damask napery.[16]

It is unlikely that the napkins with the story of Susanna and the Elders belonged to Gresham as the type of drum-shaped farthingale worn by Susanna is not thought to be earlier than 1585 (Fig. 16). This suggests that the ownership marks in white linen cross stitch of 'T' and possibly a Gothic 'G' may have been embroidered when the napkins were purchased by a descendant of Sir Thomas Gresham who bore the same name.[17] Even if the napkins had belonged to the first Sir Thomas, they were not *en suite* with the tablecloth and it is unlikely that they would have been used for the Queen's service.

Both the tablecloth and napkins are piece goods, having side but neither top nor bottom borders.

[9] G. T. van Ysselsteyn, *White Figurated Linen Damask* (The Hague, 1962), p. 35; Marguerite Prinet, *Le Damas de Lin Historié* (Berne, 1982), p. 88.
[10] For discussion of the Queen's image see Roy Strong, *Gloriana* (London, 1987).
[11] The weaver in Kortrijk presumably either saw a drawing or the half-length engraving, as the full-length engraving included the correctly drawn royal arms.
[12] On his attainder in 1521 much of Buckingham's damask entered the royal household. In Henry VIII's inventory of 1547, it is detailed in the Old Jewel House at Westminster. BL Harley 1419B; V&A, MS 86 CC 35, An Inventorie ... Earle of Leicester, 1583.

[13] A second centre was established at Haarlem in the United Provinces by refugees from Kortrijk about 1582.
[14] Etienne Sabbe, *De Belgische Vlasnijverheid* (Kortrijk, 1975), pp. 185–89.
[15] Bespoke napery took a considerable time to design, weave and bleach. A parcel 'given' by the Burgomasters of Haarlem in 1660 to the Princess Royal was delivered during 1663.
[16] Ives, *Anne Boleyn*. Anne's sojourn of 1513 in Brabant had a lasting effect; for example, at Christmas 1530 she emblazoned her servants' liveries with the motto '*Ainsi sera, groigne qui groigne*' ['Thus it will be, grudge who grudges'], an adaptation of Margaret's '*Groigne qui groigne et vive Bourgoigne*', pp. 173–75.
[17] Unfortunately, the descent from Sir Thomas Gresham to Leveson Gower passed through Sir William Gresham to his younger brother, also named Sir Thomas. The author is very grateful to Janet Arnold for her advice as to the dates of the costumes.

FIG. 16.   Linen damask napkin with the story of Susanna
and the Elders, Kortrijk, *c.* 1585.
London, Royal Exchange Assurance

indicating where they were to be cut. It was usual for the wealthy to buy three pieces of new napery: one piece each of tabling, napkining and towelling, all of the same pattern. For example, Henry VIII's inventory of 1547 had fifteen such sets. The pieces were converted within the household by cutting into the required lengths, hemming and marking them. Towels had important functions in the dining ceremonies of the sixteenth century and in the presence of the sovereign were endowed with quasi-liturgical significance. Before sitting at the start of the meal, perfumed water was poured from a ewer over the sovereign's hands into a basin held beneath. A short towel, which had been formerly kissed and laid on the shoulder of the principal nobleman or gentleman of the highest status, was then offered to dry the royal hands. Within the Court, the towel was then carried from the chamber accompanied by sergeants-at-arms. After the sovereign had been seated and two courses had been served, the table was cleared and the top damask tablecloth removed, revealing a plain tablecloth beneath. A long towel of the same length and pattern of the damask tablecloth was stretched by the Gentleman Usher using his wand, along the table to receive the basin for the final washing of hands.

Although dining ceremonies changed during the sixteenth century, it seems that, as in her father's reign, the edge of the tablecloth was lifted and placed in Elizabeth's lap when she was seated at table. Thus a napkin was only given to the Queen when required. Her sewer had two napkins, one on his arm for the Queen and his own over his left shoulder.[18] At this period, apart from at events such as Coronation and Garter feasts and Livery Company dinners, there were few diners at the principal table, although within noblemen's households it was normal to have a second table within the dining chamber for the

Damask napery was woven in Kortrijk in pieces of not less than $44\frac{1}{2}$ Kortrijk ells (some 33 yards) in length, and for tabling not more than $47\frac{1}{2}$ ells, and napkining and towelling not more than $50\frac{1}{2}$ ells. At this period only the very finest were woven with top and bottom borders with narrow plain strips between

[18] There are a number of household books and other documents that describe dining ceremonies including: John Nichols (ed.), *Ordinances and Regulations of the Royal Household*, Society of Antiquaries (London, 1790); W. H. St J. Hope, *Cowdray and Easebourne Priory* (London, 1919), Appendix II, Viscount Montague's Household Book, 1595; BL Sloane 1494. Also see D. M. Mitchell, ' "By Your Leave My Masters": British Taste in Table Linen in the Fifteenth and Sixteenth Centuries' in *Textile History*, vol. 20, no. 1 (Spring, 1989), pp. 49–77.

principal gentlemen servants.[19] It is possible that the second tablecloth in the Leveson Gower sale was used for such a table at Bishopsgate Street.

Doubtless Gresham's dinner for the Queen was less formal than her dining in state at Court, but it would have been hedged about with considerable ceremony. It is likely that after two multi-dish courses had been served by a procession of servants, tables were cleared, hands washed and Gresham, the Queen and the other diners at his table would have moved to another chamber for the banquet. This was a course of comfits and sweetmeats washed down with sweetened wine and distilled 'waters'.[20] In great houses this was served in comparative privacy in a small banqueting house. These took several forms such as the turret rooms at Longleat, the triangular lodge at Rushton and the 'herbour in the little parke of Windesore' of Elizabeth of York.[21]

Although the house in Bishopsgate Street may not have had a banqueting house, it appears that Gresham had special linen for the banquet. The Leveson Gower sale included three similar cloths that were described as 'exceedingly fine damask table cloths (50 in. by 41 in.), decorated with the Royal Coat of Arms in centre'.[22] Despite the auction description, these seem to have had the same pattern as the tablecloth with the portrait of Queen Elizabeth, as in the letter to the Royal Exchange Assurance, Victoria Leveson Gower wrote,

There is a facsimile of this table cloth [that purchased in 1923 by the Royal Exchange Assurance] in the possession of the Victoria & Albert (53″ by 42″) . . . My father was in possession of 4 other similar tablecloths. These were all sold after his death.[23]

Although these cloths were larger than standard napkins, they were much too small to be tablecloths. They measure approximately two Kortrijk ells in length by one and a half ells in width. In 1605 damasks of this size were described in a Haarlem weaver's bill for napery to be presented to the Prince of Wales by the States General, as 'banquet napkins or cradle sheets'.[24] At Holyrood House in 1561, Mary Queen of Scots had 'sex serviettis for banquettis', although unfortunately their size was not noted.[25]

The surviving examples of both of the patterns with portraits of the Queen have the same weaving structure: bindings of satin of five and unbalanced weaves with warp densities between 32 and 38 threads per centimetre and finer, denser wefts between 48 and 55 threads per centimetre. The Royal Exchange tablecloth is one of the finer examples with warp and weft densities of 38 and 50 threads per centimetre respectively. Quality was defined in the ordinances of the Guild of St Catherine in Kortrijk in terms of warp threads per ell.[26] Thus a density of 32 threads per centimetre, which seems to have become the most frequently woven quality by the end of the sixteenth century, corresponds to twenty-two hundred per ell (22^c), whereas the Royal Exchange cloth's 38 threads per centimetre is equivalent to twenty-seven hundreds per ell (27^c). The latter was not, however, the finest quality for the ordinances of 1605

[19] Unless it has been reduced in size, the tablecloth in Lot 901 which is 92 in. by 84 in. would only fit a modest table some 4 ft 8 in. long by 4 ft wide (allowing for 18 in. drop of the tablecloth).
[20] C. A. Wilson (ed.), 'Banqueting Stuffe'. The fare and social background of the Tudor and Stuart banquet (Edinburgh, 1991).
[21] For general discussion of the banquet and banqueting houses see Mark Girouard, Life in the English Country House (London, 1978); for Windsor example see N. H. Nicolas, Privy Purse Expenses of Elizabeth of York (London, 1830), p. 31.
[22] Catalogue, Messrs Richardson & Pierce, Lots 904–06.
[23] GRE, Letter of 1 February 1952. The cloth referred to at the V&A is 857–1907, which had been bought by the Museum in 1907.

[24] C. A. Burgers, 'Some notes on Western European Table Linen from the 16th through the 18th Centuries', in E. S. Cooke, jun. (ed.), Upholstery in America & Europe from the Seventeenth Century to World War I (New York, 1956), p. 155.
[25] A Collection of Inventories and other records of the Royal Wardrobe and Jewelhouse; and of the Artillery and Munitioun in some of the Royal Castles, 1488–1606 (Edinburgh, 1815), p. 150.
[26] The first ordinances were promulgated in 1496 followed by regular reissues and revisions. Although those of 1496 have not survived, the ordinances of 1545, 1605 and 1663 are extant. See Isabelle de Jaegere, 'De Nering van Sint-Catharina in Kortrijk', in De Leiegouw, vol. 28, nos. 3–4 (December 1986), pp. 183–92. The warp consists of the longitudinal threads on a loom which pass through the reed to keep them evenly spaced and aligned. To increase the density of the warp, and thus the quality of the finished cloth, a finer reed is used. The different qualities, as defined in Kortrijk, in hundreds of warp threads per ell, would have been woven by simply fitting the appropriate reed to the loom.

specified in addition thirty, thirty-six and forty hundreds per ell respectively.[27] However, it seems that the qualities above thirty hundreds were rarely woven as no examples appear to have survived.

There are precedents for patterns with the royal arms and devices, some of which appear to be bespoke designs ordered by the Crown, and others woven for the general English market. There is a tablecloth in an inventory of 1495 with 'Roses and sonnes', which probably refer to Edward IV's badge of the 'rose en soleil', and pieces with portcullises and roses in Margaret Beaufort's inventory of 1509.[28] A detailed description of the Garter Feast at Windsor in 1519 describes the tablecloth covering the King's board as 'the armes of England, the portcullice, the rose & the pomegranade w^t many other thinges of pleaso^r wch was woven in the said cloath'.[29] This was also said to be as fine 'as could be made' and was almost certainly woven to royal commission, as were the pieces in Henry VIII's 1547 inventory with 'the Kinges Armes Crowned in a garter'.[30] There is a splendid napkin in the Victoria & Albert Museum which possibly originates from this later source.[31]

The Museum also has two pieces with royal arms and badges which appear from their design and structure to date from Henry VIII's and Edward VI's reigns respectively.[32] Two wealthy London merchants, Austen Hynde and Sir Ralph Warren, owned damasks with the royal arms at their deaths, in the same year, 1554. Their inventories valued these pieces at similar rates to stock patterns such as 'of the prodygall Son' and 'of Imagery', which suggests that they were probably of the same type as the repeat patterns in the Museum.[33]

To summarise, the Royal Exchange tablecloth purchased in 1923 may well have belonged to Sir Thomas Gresham and have been used at the dinner given for Elizabeth in 1571. It is likely to have been part of a large set of napery which also included towels and both table and banquet napkins. It was of good quality but of a stock pattern that was probably bought for Sir Thomas's household in the early 1560s. The napkins also purchased in 1923 from the Leveson Gower estate with the story of Susanna and the Elders were probably woven after Sir Thomas Gresham's death in 1579. Sadly it seems they did not grace the tables at the dinner at Bishopsgate Street during the visit to the 'bursse turned by the quene and called le Royall Eschange'.[34]

---

[27] Conversion of thread counts of bleached damasks to unbleached qualities is taken from an unpublished manuscript of Isabelle de Jaegere, *Kortrijkse Damastwevers* (Kortrijk, 1984).

[28] PRO, PCC Prob. 2/99 [?] oclby, 1495 (part of the name is missing). For Beaufort see Cambridge, St John's College D 91.5.

[29] BL Sloane 1494, f. 62v. The author is grateful to Lisa Monnas for drawing his attention to this document.

[30] BL Harley 1419B, Westminster — Received of Sr Anthony Denys, f. 130v.

[31] V&A 169–1869. Illustrated in Mitchell, *Textile History* (Spring, 1989), p. 67.

[32] V&A 56–1890 & 1162–1893. Both illustrated in J. Six, 'Zestiende-Eeuwsch Damast' in *Het Huis oud en nieuw* (1913), Plates XLVI & XLVII.

[33] PRO, PCC Prob 2/257, Austen Hynde, & Prob 2/256, Sir Ralph Warren.

[34] J. H. Baker, *The Reports of Sir James Dyer omitted from the previous Editions*, vol. 1, Selden Soc. (1994), p. 195.

PLATE I

Portrait of a young man, thought to be Thomas Gresham. Originally attributed to Holbein, it now seems more likely that it is the work of William Key who was busy in Antwerp by the early 1540s.

By courtesy of the Earl of Jersey

PLATE II

A. *The Bourse at Antwerp,
30 May 1842.* Wash drawing by
the Rt Revd Walter John Trower,
Bishop of Gibraltar.
Private collection

B. Virgilius Bononiensis' map of Antwerp in
1565. This detail shows the Bourse and a stretch
of the Lange Nieuwstraat on which Gresham
made his home.
By kind permission of the Plantin Moretus Museum, Antwerp

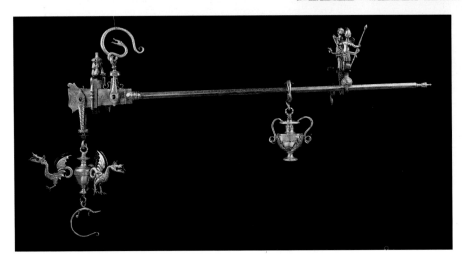

C. The so-called 'Gresham'
steelyard in the collection of the
Museum of London.
By kind permission of the Museum of London

PLATE III

A, B.   Gold ring with the arms of Sir Robert Taylor, one of the Tellers to the Exchequer, in enamel covered with crystal, and Gresham's grasshopper on the back of the bezel.

Private collection

C.   *Sir Thomas Gresham's Gift of the Royal Exchange to the City of London and the Mercers' Company,* by Edward Henry Wehnert (1813–68); watercolour, signed and dated 1851.

Guardian Royal Exchange collection

PLATE IV

A. The courtyard of the Royal Exchange with Spiller's copy of Grinling Gibbons' statue of Charles II, presumably viewed from an upper window. Watercolour by Robert Blemmel Schnebbelie, 4 May 1818.
Private collection

B. Model of Edward III attributed to Caius Gabriel Cibber (1667)
Skinners' Hall. Photo: N. K. Gibson

C. Model of Edward IV attributed to Caius Gabriel Cibber (1667).
Ironmongers' Hall. Photo: N. K. Gibson

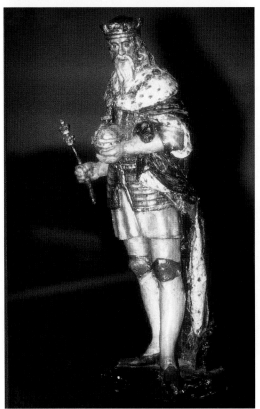

CHAPTER VII

Sir Thomas Gresham and the 'Grasshopper' Rings

By DIANA SCARISBRICK

NO CITIZEN OF THE TUDOR PERIOD has more rings associated with his name than the great Mercer and financier, Sir Thomas Gresham. His signet is mentioned by Thomas Heywood in the play, *If You Know Not Me, You Know No Bodie* (1606) when, as the principal character, away from home and in sudden need of funds, he sends his servant John to his factor, Timothy. When John says, 'Here's his seal ring: I hope a warrant sufficient', Timothy replies, 'Upon so good a security, John, I'll fit me to deliver it', and promptly hands over the required sum. A gold signet with the initials TG and a merchant mark, believed to be his, was found during the building of London Bridge in 1842[1] and his fine wedding ring of 1544 still belongs to the Titsey Place Foundation.[2] In addition there is a famous group of seven heraldic signets which, according to tradition, were gifts from him to the various owners. The tradition rests on the presence of a green grasshopper enamelled at the back of each bezel. This insect was a canting device for Gresham, derived from the Anglo-Saxon words GRAES and HAM for grass and farm, and adopted as a family badge. It was used for titles, for seals and proudly surmounted each tower and corner of the Royal Exchange.

The rings are of plain design with convex hoops expanding to an oval or round bezel set with a crystal intaglio of the owner's arms, the tinctures painted on foil below. This type of signet was a great status symbol from the 1540s, and both Archbishop Cranmer[3] and Sir Nicholas Bacon[4] were portrayed wearing them on the left index finger, ready to seal private and business correspondence. Whereas the heraldry was usually engraved directly on a metal or cornelian bezel, these foiled crystal intaglios were much more decorative, being executed in colour, and protected by the crystal from damage by the hot wax. No ring proclaimed a gentleman's place in society so well, and it is significant that in 1588, when the poor but ambitious Robert Boyle, future Earl of Cork, arrived to seek his fortune in Dublin, all he possessed was a sword and a foiled crystal signet for his finger.[5]

Who were the owners of the 'grasshopper' rings? The first recorded was exhibited at the Society of Antiquaries in 1742. Dated 1557, it bore the arms of Sir Henry Woodhouse, son-in-law of William Gresham, and it was found on the Gresham estate of Budesdale in Suffolk.[6] It has not been seen since, nor has the second, engraved with the arms of Tremayne, also exhibited at the Society of Antiquaries by Dr Hildburgh, and subsequently deposited in Martin's Bank.[7] The third, which is in the Victoria and Albert Museum, bears the arms and crest granted Sir Robert Lee in 1554: Per chevron Or and Gules, in chief two lions combattant Sable; Crest: an arm in armour embowed holding a sword Argent hilt Or with fire from the blade: the arms borne quarterly with those of Chute and Newbury. Exceptionally, the motto 'FLAME ET FAME' is inscribed on the back with the grasshopper.[8] Another achievement is engraved on the ring of Jacques Wingfield of Ireland: Argent on a bend Gules cotised Sable three pairs of wings Silver: Crest an eagle's head Or armed Gules between two wings displayed Argent: the arms borne quarterly with those of Bovill, Goussell, Fitzalan quartering Warrenne, Wiltshire and Legrand.[9] The fifth ring,

---

[1] *Proceedings of the Society of Antiquaries*, 2nd series, vol. 15 (1893–95), pp. 239–40, exhibited by Charles Welch, 22 November 1894.

[2] D. Scarisbrick, *Tudor and Jacobean Jewellery* (1995), p. 33.

[3] Ibid., p. 25.

[4] National Portrait Gallery Collection.

[5] D. Scarisbrick, *Jewellery in Britain* (1994), p. 150 and note.

[6] BL MS Egerton 1041, f. 513.

[7] *Antiquaries Journal*, x (1930), p. 304.

[8] Victoria and Albert Museum. Inv. M 249–1928.

[9] Sold Christie's, 19 December 1977, lot 1, now private collection.

originally owned by Gabriel Goodman, bears the arms granted him in 1573, 'partie per pale ermyn and sable an eagle with two necks displayed gold on a Canton azure a martlet gold'.[10] The sixth has a shield with the arms of Sir William Fleetwood: Party nebuly Or and Azure six martlets in pairs countercoloured.[11] The seventh, which is dated 1575, bears the arms of Robert Taylor: Or a chevron between in chief two griffins and in base an annulet Sable (Taylor?) impaling Argent on a fess between three hawks rising Sable, a leopard's face and two molets Or (Stonehouse).[12]

All are prominent people. The Tremayne ring was probably that of Edmund Tremayne (d. 1582), appointed Clerk of the Privy Council in 1571; Sir Robert Lee of Sopwell (d. 1575) was a neighbour of Chancellor Bacon at Gorhambury and received his grant of arms in recognition of his services as a military engineer at Boulogne; Jacques Wingfield (d. 1587) was Master of the Ordnance in Ireland; Sir William Fleetwood (d. 1594) was a Commissioner of Customs, appointed Recorder of London in 1571 and returned to Parliament as member for the City in 1572; while Robert Taylor, one of the Tellers of the Exchequer himself, was son-in-law to George Stonehouse of Peckham, Clerk to the Green Cloth to Queen Elizabeth. Gabriel Goodman (1529–1601), Doctor of Divinity, was for many years chaplain to Lord Burghley and in 1561 was appointed Dean of

Westminster. In his will which lists all the rings in his collection, Gabriel Goodman bequeaths to his nephew and namesake 'a ring of gold with mine arms engraven and a grasshopper thereon'. In 1925 it was still in the family home at Coed Coch in Denbighshire.[13]

While some of them were linked with Sir Thomas Gresham by marriage, all must have had contact with him through his hugely successful activities as a businessman and agent of the Crown. As he is known to have bribed the Flemish customs with costly presents, it is also likely that he might have rewarded the English officials who helped him with the purchase and distribution of military supplies. According to the *Dictionary of National Biography*, 'he incurred little or no risk as a government financier, that his profits were very large and that his conduct open to serious misconstruction', and at the time of his retirement in 1574 his immensely complicated accounts had not been audited for eleven years. In these circumstances he must have needed the assistance of his friends, particularly those in the Exchequer such as Robert Taylor. Covering as they do the period 1557 to 1575, the grasshopper rings would seem to have been gifts by which Sir Thomas Gresham acknowledged services from those officials helpful to his business interests until the final endorsement of his accounts by the Treasury commissioners. Since the grasshopper was hidden, only the wearer knew it was there, reminding him of his membership of the exclusive club presided over by the greatest merchant of the day.

[10] W. Hemp, 'The Goodman and Other Grasshopper Rings', *Antiquaries Journal*, v (1925), pp. 403–08.
[11] British Museum.
[12] A. Somers Cocks (ed.), *Princely Magnificence* (1980), no. 30.

[13] Hemp, op. cit., p. 404.

CHAPTER VIII

Thomas Deane's Shop in the Royal Exchange

By KAY STANILAND

ONE OF THE FIRST OCCUPANTS of the small shops in the Pawn in the newly-built Royal Exchange was Thomas Deane, a fletcher by Livery affiliation but seemingly trading as a haberdasher at the end of his life. He died, in January 1572, only six months after first renting this shop. When a first assessment of his property was considered undervalued and incomplete the subsequent inventories of his possessions, both in his home and in the Royal Exchange shop, were lodged in the records of the Mayor's Court at Guildhall.[1] Like all old inventories these transport the reader directly into Deane's home and shop, revealing the minutiae of his private life as well as his final trading venture.

The house inventory yields no clue to its location. It was a modestly-sized and well furnished property, almost certainly within the City boundaries. John Stow, writing in 1598, commented that 'Grubstreete of late yeares [was] inhabited for the most part by bowyers, fletchers, bowstring makers, and such like' as it was convenient for the archery butts in Finsbury Fields. But perhaps Deane had already abandoned the locality for one more suited to the sale of haberdashery. In 1572 Richard Bletcher, Warden of the Fletchers' Company, is known to have lived in Fleet Street.[2] The property Thomas Deane leased possessed a hall, a parlour, three bedchambers, kitchen, wash-house, counting house, and shop.[3] This shop contained no stock when the inventory was made and throws no light on Deane's activities before his tenancy of the shop in the Royal Exchange: its sole contents were a 'table with frame' and an old chest. Deane's counting house appears to have had no furniture beyond a 'small old chest' but was the repository of an interesting assortment of goods, presumably stored in the chest. These do not give the impression of shop stock, but appear to be a deposit of more valuable personal possessions: two 'pointed' diamonds, several rings set with precious stones, twenty silver spoons with gilt heads, a gilt salt with cover, two parcel gilt bowls, a silver whistle, stoneware pots with silver covers, a mazer, trenchers, knives, daggers, a Bible and four other books, the lease of the house, purses, boots, a satin night cap, and various other small items. Only nine 'steales of shaftes' and an unspecified quantity of bow-strings point to Thomas Deane's 'official' trade as a fletcher, a maker of arrows; stored in his hall were 'two shootinge bowes with a quyver and 24 shaftes and the bowe cases' valued at $13\frac{3}{4}d$. This is not the stock of an active fletcher. It is merely speculation, but had Deane switched to selling haberdashery earlier in his career when archery declined and the use of firearms increased or, indeed, had he ever actually practised as a fletcher?

His personal possessions suggest modest affluence and a comfortable, pleasurable lifestyle. Was this the result of inheritance or years of successful, and diverse, trading? The contents of his hall included a pair of virginals and two 'playing tables' as well as a painted cloth hanging, a table, three chairs and nine stools. The parlour below was similarly well furnished and appears to have contained a fireplace. Quantities of clothing and bedlinen were stored in the bedchambers, some of very good quality: a gown faced with taffeta and welted with velvet, a satin doublet with pinked sleeves, gowns faced with damask, taffeta or lambskin, a cloak with a velvet cape, ruffs, handkerchiefs with blackwork ·and gold lace, tablecloths, napkins, and so on. His own bedchamber Deane had comfortably furnished with cushions of

[1] CLRO, MS Mayor's Court Original Bills 1/4 B, m. 14,15–19. In my transcription of this inventory I have extended contractions for 'dozen' and 'gross'.

[2] J. Stow, *A Survey of London*, ed. C. L. Kingsford (Oxford, 1908), II, p. 79; J. E. Oxley, *The Fletchers and Longbowstringmakers of London* (London, 1968), p. 20.

[3] J. Schofield, *Medieval London Houses* (New Haven & London, 1994), pp. 71–74.

needlework (embroidery) or painted leather, tapestry and needlework carpets, and a needlework valance.

Who was Thomas Deane? Such records of the Fletchers' Company as now survive show Thomas 'Dene' as freeman 1542–60, warden 1566, and assistant 1572.[4] This seems to be the Thomas Deane of the inventories, but the records fail to reveal whether he was admitted to the Company as the result of apprenticeship or patrimony. It can reasonably be deduced that he may have been between fifty and sixty years old at his death. Records of the City parishes reveal a number of men named Thomas Deane, none of whom can be associated with certainty with the Thomas Deane of the Royal Exchange. The surviving documents reveal virtually nothing about his family and relatives. His house inventory includes a list of 'Deanes firste wyves apparell' — three cassocks and 'one kirtell which she hathe made fitt for her sence he died' — valued at only £3 16s. 8d., whilst in his 'bedde chamber' a 'mantell for a childe' and a 'cradell clothe', apparently stored amongst table linen and furnishing textiles, suggest a dead infant. That Deane left a widow is apparent from references to debts which had been paid to her after his death. Meanwhile stored in 'the Maids Chamber' was the feather bed and bolster 'in the shoppe that Deane died upon'. This suggests that Deane may already have been ill and confined to a bed on the ground floor of his house in the days or weeks before his death.

A number of names are mentioned in the inventories and these reflect the two aspects of Deane's professional activities already referred to. The same 'Maids Chamber' also contained an old feather bed which had been lent to the late John Early, fletcher (Liveryman 1566–71), whilst two bowyers, Albon Chiseldon and – Preston of London, were included in the list of Deane's 'desperate debts'. Deane was owed a considerable amount of money, some £435 17s. 6d. in good, doubtful and desperate debts, and £260 of this was owed by Roger Hodges, haberdasher. Hodges is the only known haberdasher to have owed money to Deane, whose other debtors

(owing between £40 and £1 each) embraced an innholder, a 'carier', a joiner, a 'bromeman', Thomas Burton 'pointmaker' and two gentlemen.[5] Burton may well have been the supplier of the points stocked in the Royal Exchange shop, lent money to continue his craft. Deane himself had few debts, presumably an indication of the prudent financial management which had helped him build up his comfortable home. At his death he owed only 9s. 9d. for house rent, 45s. to the tailor Edward Osborne, and £5 to Alderman Barnham. The latter must have been the draper Francis Barnham (d. 1579), alderman of Farringdon without since 1568 and sheriff in 1570, at this point in his second term as Master of the Drapers' Company; he was the father of Benedict Barnham (1559–98) who was one of those who became involved in administering the Royal Exchange on the death of Lady Gresham in 1596.[6] Of 'redy money' found in Deane's house there was £20, whilst the fate of one of Deane's gowns 'pawned for 15s.' is intriguing and suggests unstable fluctuating finances.

Only a few of those who 'perused and praysed' Thomas Deane's goods can now be identified with any certainty. John Catcher was a resident of Breadstreet ward, and Thomas Pennyton (Pennyngton) of All Hallows in the Wall. Peter Daunsere may have been related to Thomas Dauncer, a girdler who had become heavily involved in the importation of haberdashery.[7] It seems probable that Thomas Deane transferred all his stock from the shop in his house to that at the Royal Exchange in 1571/2, and thereafter concentrated upon this new, and potentially highly remunerative, trading outlet. The shops in the Exchange were very small, only 2.28 metres by 1.52

---

[4] Guildhall Library, MS 21030, Index to the Freemen of the Fletchers, 1519–1602. Note that 'Mrs. Earley' owed 2s. 8d. to Deane's Royal Exchange shop, presumably for goods taken but not paid for.

[5] Deane's debtors were: Good debts: Roger Hodges (haberdasher), Robert Johnson ('carier'), Hugh Richards (innholder), Thomas Burton (pointmaker), Edward Randall, Thomas Harman, Richard Frando, Robert Lyons, John With. Doubtful debt: Mr. Smythe. Desperate debts: Edmond Grete, Albon Chiseldon ('bowier'), Mr. Graye (gentleman), Preston of London ('bowier'), Henry Browne (joiner), Thomas Jeve of Bickleworth, Peter Wood ('bromeman').

[6] Supra, p. 85; DNB (Oxford, 1908), entry for Benedict Barnham; The Aldermen of the City of London, ed. A. B. Beaven, I, pp. 200, 48. Benedict Barnham was not made alderman until 1591.

[7] Beaven, op.cit., II, p. 43. John Catcher (d. 1602), pewterer, Master of Pewterers' Company 1585, alderman and sheriff 1587–88. I. W. Archer, The History of the Haberdashers' Company (Chichester, 1991), p. 25.

metres, much the size of small platform kiosks on the London Underground. The inventory of Deane's stock, the only one for any of the Exchange shops, is long and consequently gives the impression of a very packed space. However, these are all small and compact haberdashery wares which would easily have fitted into a medium-sized chest, although such overnight storage is not included in the inventory. The inclusion of a 'staull cloth' in the inventory suggests that Deane was able to lay out his wares on the stallboard of his shop when open for trading. The lock included with this may well have been used to secure the board over the shop aperture at night, a construction typical of medieval and Tudor shops. Clearly the form of the new Exchange's shops was traditional, any novelty lying in the bringing together of such a large and varied assemblage of retailing outlets under a single roof in a building dedicated to trading.[8]

The wares with which Thomas Deane stocked his Exchange shop are typical of those found in numerous contemporary inventories of haberdashers' goods. With only a few exceptions they concentrate upon the small necessities constantly needed for clothing — trimmings and fastenings — which would have been sought by the merchants, their clerks, and others frequenting Gresham's new building. It is not known whether any other haberdashers were renting shops in the Royal Exchange in the first year that it was operational. The range of goods offered by Thomas Deane appears to have been limited. His stock as inventoried did not include paper, pens and ink, ink horns, money boxes, small chests, pouches, girdles, gloves, caps, spectacles, razors, looking-glasses, combs, brushes, toothpicks, earpicks, toys, pins and needles, bodkins, thimbles, shears, knives, hawks' bells and so on.[9] It is impossible to know whether Deane had already sold out of a lot of his original stock and had not renewed it, perhaps as the result of his ill health. He may have been approaching

the potential trade of the Exchange with caution. Could there even have been an agreement with other Exhange haberdashers to specialise in certain goods? Within a very few years there would be competition for leases for the shops in the Pawn, but when the Exchange first opened in 1569 few shops were occupied and Gresham, so John Stow relates, induced these shopkeepers to spread their wares into unoccupied shops to make his venture appear more prosperous when Queen Elizabeth visited it in January 1571 (*supra*, p. 44). No doubt these earliest traders, Thomas Deane amongst them, were uncertain of the success of the venture and had stocked their shops with caution.

So what did Thomas Deane's stock consist of? Of writing materials he merely maintained a small quantity of French 'parchement', in two qualities, and 'tabelletes' (writing tablets), small, smooth inflexible leaves of bone, ivory or horn, usually hinged in pairs, with inside a coating of wax to act as the writing surface; they formed handy notebooks for ephemeral jottings or reckonings and would therefore have appealed to the merchants and clerks frequenting the Exchange.[10] It is just possible that neither of these items were related to writing. Parchment had a great many other uses, as a wrapping material, for instance, and to seal the tops of jars and other containers for cooks and pharmacists, whilst the term 'tabelletes' might instead refer to the pierced tablets which control the warp threads in the ancient braid-making technique known as tablet weaving. The inventory includes only one item assuredly for a child, a purse. Did Deane perhaps not expect to attract much sale in the Exchange for such objects? Is it perhaps modern fancy that such a small purse would make an excellent gift for a merchant's child? The silk purse, valued at 2s. 4d., was presumably intended for an adult. Another 'trifel' in Deane's stock were pomanders, the moulded, dried mixture of aromatic substances believed to ward off ills like the plague: precious gums and resins, myrrh, spikenard and ambergris are listed in contemporary recipes, with fixatives of benzoin, storax, civet, and musk. Or does the entry simply refer to the hollow pierced metal spheres used to hold

[8] J. Bennell, 'Shop and Office in Medieval and Tudor London', *Transactions of the London and Middlesex Archaeological Society*, 40 (1989), pp. 189–206 (pp. 199–200). D. Keene, 'Shops and Shopping in Medieval London', in *Medieval Art, Architecture and Archaeology in London*, The British Archaeological Association, Conference Transactions for the year 1984 (Leeds, 1990), pp. 29–46 (p. 37).

[9] Archer, op. cit., p. 21.

[10] *The Oxford English Dictionary* (1971) defines a 'tabellet' as 'a small smooth inflexible or stiff-sheet or leaf for writing upon; usually one of a pair or set hinged or otherwise fastened together'.

these perfumed balls? These were worn suspended by a chain from the neck or waist, and very ornate forms are often to be seen in Tudor and Elizabethan portraits. It is tempting to associate with these pomanders the necklaces and bracelets which Deane lists, for just such perfumed adornments were also very popular, the aromatic mixtures being formed into beads which were strung whilst still hot.[11] However there is no indication that Deane's necklaces and bracelets necessarily took this attractive form and an alternative possibility is discussed below.

More practical household and clothing necessities in fact formed the major part of Deane's stock. Several forms of thread were probably of linen, for firm stitching of clothing seams or for finer work on household or personal linen. Black 'pyssinge' thread was presumably an import from Pisa and perhaps only sold slowly, for a large quantity remained in stock at Deane's death. There were smaller quantities of 'vetnall' thread (not identified so far), whilst 'Sisters' thread appears to have been a bleached white thread. These linen threads were naturally very much cheaper than the silk threads which Deane stocked in some quantity. Ferret silk, 8–12s. per pound, is thought to have been an untwisted (floss) thread, and would probably have been suitable for embroidery, especially the counted threadwork so often used to adorn fine linen. Deane owned such work himself, 'handkirchers' ornamented with blue- or black-work and a 'face clothe wrought with silke vearye good'. 'Bridges' (?Bruges) silk, 16s. per pound, may have been a spun or even plied thread whose strength made it suitable for sewing or decorative work on clothing and household textiles. The most expensive silk thread, 24s. per pound, was almost certainly very finely spun. Presumably the silk for which Adam Willson and Goodman Tyddy were in debt to Deane's shop was in the form of thread rather than woven cloth, and it is tempting to wonder whether both were perhaps local tailors or embroiderers?[12] There appears to have been a short length of woven silk, only five yards, which if the inventory is correct was the only piece of cloth Deane stocked;

it may have been a fine plain or tabby weave silk, perhaps of the kind used for linings or facings, for which Deane had found a demand.

Plain tapes and ribbons formed a very small part of Deane's stock. It would be surprising at this date not to find inkell, a plain linen tape used for many domestic purposes — apron strings, girdles, bindings, and in embroidery — which was always found in the packs of chapmen and pedlars in the seventeenth and eighteenth centuries; it is still in use today as the red tape which ties up legal documents.[13] This appears to have been the only linen tape stocked by Deane. Of ribbons, presumably all woven in silk, he had quite a variety, mostly sold by weight. Ribbon the width of two English pennies inexplicably was cheaper than ribbon the width of one penny (12d. per oz. and 13d. per oz.), and it can only be assumed that quality of weave, decoration or dye necessitated the higher price. Were these ribbons woven in London? By inference the 'Spanyishe' and 'gyne' (?Genoa) ribbons were imported and consequently much more expensive (21d. and 22d. per oz.).

Fastenings were an important part of Deane's stock, especially those which might be urgently needed to replace those lost from or damaged on clothing. Since the fourteenth century or earlier laces of plaited silk or linen, or of ribbon, tape or leather, had been used to fasten the form-fitting clothing and armour just then coming into fashion. The ends of these, like modern shoelaces, were protected by a tapering metal tag or chape, usually refered to as 'points' in Thomas Deane's time. He stocked large quantities of silk or thread (linen) 'poynts' in his Royal Exchange shop, no doubt anticipating a lively trade in these practical items.[14] They were much used in men's clothing to attach the waist edges of breeches to doublets, by means of a narrow band worked with corresponding eyelets which was attached to an inner waistband in the doublet; this arrangement was usually hidden from sight by the ornamental tabs suspended from the waist of the doublet. Personal preference, and purse, was provided for in Deane's

---

[11] J. Hériteau, *Pot Pourris and Other Fragrant Delights* (Harmondsworth, 1978), p. 103. J. Arnold, *Queen Elizabeth's Wardrobe Unlock'd* (Leeds, 1988), p. 369.

[12] *Oxford English Dictionary.*

[13] M. C. Linthicum, *Costume in the Drama of Shakespeare and his Contemporaries* (Oxford, 1936), p. 99.

[14] See G. Egan and F. Pritchard, *Medieval Finds from Excavations in London: Dress Accessories* (London, 1991), pp. 281–90, for medieval examples.

varied stock: 'poynts' of plaited silk and of silk 'ryband', 'rownde silk poyntes' (probably made from a circular plaited braid, like 'hollowe lace'), and the much cheaper 'thred poyntes'. The slightly earlier clothing accounts of Thomasine Petre, a younger daughter of William Petre, a Principal Secretary to Henry VIII and succeeding monarchs, included pointing ribbon as well as 'holowe' lace for fastening (presumably lacing) her kirtles.[15]

The use of the word lace ('lase') in the inventory is confusing and reveals that already a parallel use of the term had emerged which referred to an apparently different textile trimming; this dual use of the term causes much confusion. The earlier use referred to the plait or braid — or even strip of leather — which tied or bound (i.e. laced) two edges together, as in the modern shoelace. 'Poynts' apart, there are several entries in Deane's shop inventory which may refer to rather longer narrow laces of the kind used to lace up a woman's dress, or perhaps even a man's doublet on occasion; the 'hollowe lase' described above may reasonably be taken to refer to a piece of tube-like handplaiting used for lacing garments. Lengths of lace or tape were also slotted through the round shanks of early buttons, down the back of the centre front edge, to hold them in place; this ingenious method enabled sets of valuable decorative buttons to be changed frequently on rich fashionable clothing. Some of the narrow laces listed in the inventory may rather have been used as decorative edgings. 'Sherte lases' were very fine hand-worked ties used in pairs to fasten the necks of men's shirts; portraits of the second half of the sixteenth century reveal that sometimes two or even three pairs of these laces were used on the upstanding band collars fashionable at the time. These laces must frequently have broken and their inclusion in a haberdasher's shop stock underlines the point that the skills to make them were not necessarily available in every household. These must certainly have been made in London by that group of women who were particularly skilled in spinning, dyeing,

plaiting and weaving silk and linen thread into plaits, braids, tapes and ribbons.[16]

The term 'lace' had also come to be applied to decorative braids, and some of the narrow laces listed in Deane's stock may in fact have been used as decorative edgings on clothing. These could be made of silk enriched with silver or gold threads, plaited or woven. A number of these decorative braids seem to feature in Deane's stock: 'Copper lase' at 2s. 8d. per ounce, for instance, and 'lace of Silke and golde'. 'Porele lase' (presumably the same as 'purled lace') is thought to be a braid with edgings of purls, minute twisted loops, whilst 'chene lace' is currently defined as a braid ornmented with a design resembling a chain.[17] Of all these decorative trimmings the one most closely associated with the term 'lace' is 'bone lace' which was worked on a special lacemaking pillow using fine linen thread wound on turned bone bobbins. A piece of parchment bearing the desired design was attached to the pillow and over this the threads were woven and plaited in a variety of patterns, solid and netlike, to suit the requirements of the design; meanwhile pins held the newly worked lace in position until the whole section had been completed and all threads were securely held in place. Essentially bone lace was descended from braid weaving. Its origins are uncertain and the term only begins to appear in English documents in the middle years of the sixteenth century; much of this early bone lace seems to have been composed of metal threads, like that of black silk and gold used on a partlet for Thomasine Petre in 1557 which cost 3s. 4d. Several bone laces appear in Deane's shop inventory but none of the entries indicate whether it was composed of linen or metal thread. Perhaps the 'v yardes of Bone lase' which altogether cost only 2½d. might reasonably be construed as a narrow thread lace of the kind much used on shirts, chemises and

[16] See E. Crowfoot, F. Pritchard and K. Staniland, *Medieval Finds from Excavations in London: Textiles and Clothing* (London, 1992), pp. 138–42, for medieval examples. K. Lacey, 'The Production of "Narrow Ware" by Silkwomen in Fourteenth and Fifteenth Century England', *Textile History*, 18 (2), (1987), pp. 187–204.

[17] *Oxford English Dictionary*. Arnold, op. cit., p. 362; Buck, op. cit., p. 32 defines 'Chayned lace' as 'a needlepoint lace worked in chain stitch' and refers to S. M. Levey, *Lace: A History* (Leeds, 1983), fig. 392.

[15] A. Buck, 'The Clothes of Thomasine Petre, 1555–59', *Costume* 24 (1990), p. 23.

ruffs?[18] Comparison with other haberdashers' inventories, as well as with wardrobe accounts and household inventories, might throw more light on the
pricing and form of these laces and help a little more
to differentiate the bone laces of metal threads from
those of linen thread.

A further lace in the inventory which is not yet
satisfactorily defined is the 'Silke byllament lace'
costing 20s. per pound; another entry is for 'narydge
Bellament' at 14d. the dozen (?yards). Although the
Oxford English Dictionary defines this as an ornamental
lace used for trimming in the sixteenth century more
recent writers, working from the evidence of contemporary documents, suggest otherwise. In her glossary
to the Thomasine Petre extracts, Anne Buck defines
a billament as a 'border worn as part of a hood or as
a separate headdress', whilst Janet Arnold, drawing
on the wardrobe accounts of Elizabeth I, Thomas
Deane's own sovereign, and contemporary dictionaries, similarly connects billament with women's
headdresses. She suggests that it was probably a form
of braid particularly used on headdresses but also
found it used as a binding on jacket slits as well as an
ornament on buttons in the Queen's accounts.
Thomas Deane himself owned 'a cassocke of grog-
rayne laid on with bilament lace and frindged with
silke frindges'.[19] Fringes were also included in the
shop stock. Crewel fringe was composed of the fine
two–ply worsted thread much associated with
embroidery and was probably intended mainly for
use on such household furnishings as cushions, val-
ances or curtains. It only cost 3d. or 4d. a yard and
could well have been of London manufacture. But
the fringe costing 17d. a yard was almost certainly
made of silk and may have been imported; certainly
this must have been the case with the even more
expensive 'jane [?Genoa] frindge' (22d. per yard).
These silk fringes were used on household furnishings,
like cushions, as well as on clothing. Little is known of
their forms or manufacture.

The inventory includes quite a number of entries
for buttons which need to be sifted carefully because
the term was used rather more broadly at the time,
indicating a knop or tassle as well as the familiar
fastener. We are therefore faced with the dilemma of
deciding whether 'buttons for clokes' at 5d. each
actually held a cloak together or were merely decorative. And what was the purpose of the more expensive
'button', priced at 7d.? Listed together with the cloak
buttons, can one assume it served a similar purpose?
These were costly buttons. Infinitely less expensive
were the buttons at 18d., 20d. and 2s. 4d. the gross
(144), and the crewel buttons at 2s. per gross. Were
these fastenings or were they again perhaps destined
for ornamental use? The crewel buttons were probably made using a turned wooden core which was
then covered with thread in a decorative manner;
these may therefore have had an ornamental application. Buttons used for fastenings were made of all
kinds of materials, from humble bone, horn and
wood through to gold and silver; the latter, often set
with precious or semi-precious stones, were supplied
in sets by goldsmiths which were stored with jewellery
so that they could be used on different garments. The
buttons on Deane's own clothing is never mentioned
and they must have been purely utilitarian.

Two of the Exchange inventory entries refer to
buttons for handkerchiefs and these were the knops
or tassles which often ornamented (garnished) the
corners, sometimes short like acorns and sometimes
longer drops or tassles. The antiquarian John Stow
noted in his *Annales* for 1580 that 'Maydes and
gentlewomen gave their favourites, as tokens of their
love, little handkerchiefs of about three or four inches
square, wrought round about with a tassel at each
corner'.[20] Is this perhaps how Thomas Deane
acquired his highly decorative handkerchiefs? The
entries are too brief to mention any buttons or tassles,
but their high value demonstrates what precious and
cherished possessions they were: '8 handkirchers
bleweworke, 6s. 8d.; 3 blacke worke handkirchers
with golde lace, 15s.'. By stocking 'garnishe bottons'
Deane quite clearly demonstrates the level he aimed
at or expected in his shop, for handkerchiefs were the
accessories of the refined in society: his customers
were likely to make or refurbish such elegant
possessions.

---

[18] Buck, op. cit., p. 23, where mention is also made of a narrow
bone lace costing 1d. per yard purchased to 'egge handkerchiefs'.
Levey, op. cit., pp. 15–16 and figs. 73–75.

[19] Buck, op. cit., pp. 22, 31; Arnold, op. cit., pp. 252, 276, 360.

[20] J. Levillier, 'The Handkerchief in History', *Connoisseur*, 96
(1935), pp. 274–78; M. Braun-Ronsdorf, *The History of the Handkerchief* (Leigh-on-Sea, 1967), p. 20.

Knitted sleeves in the later sixteenth century might be viewed as practical possessions. The inclusion of five 'paier of garnesey sleves at 16d. the paier' is one of the most interesting entries in the inventory not, so far as I know, noted in any other contemporary listing of shop goods. Examples of such knitted sleeves have been excavated in London. They covered the lower arm only and were worked in stocking stitch in what was probably a soft white wool. None are known to appear in portraits of the time. Were they therefore worn underneath sleeves or were they used to replace sleeves when, for instance, their owner was engaged in some more practical pursuit in cold weather? Pairs of knitted sleeves were sold to the Petre family at 6d. and 7d. per pair just over a decade earlier, specifically for use by the ladies of the household the entries suggest, rather than for their female servants; they were apparently knitted by women living close to the family's country house at Ingatestone in Essex. Fragments of knitting have now been excavated from late fourteenth-century London sites, whilst the considerable collection of sixteenth-century examples found unstratified earlier this century on a number of London sites reveals the skills and productivity of the London knitting industry. Once again Deane's stock underlines the fact that such practical skills were not always common to all households, to such an extent that it was worth his while to stock a small quantity of these knitted sleeves to tempt the otherwise busy or less skilled amongst his female customers.[21]

He similarly stocked a variety of cauls, hair nets, which had been much used long since the thirteenth century at least. A complete fourteenth-century specimen and some fragmentary hair nets were excavated in London in 1972; these have fine hand-knotted meshes of imported silk and were presumably made in the city; no examples of hair nets survive amongst the mid-sixteenth-century excavated textiles. In the fifteenth century these cauls became ornate fashionable accessories, worked in gold thread and sometimes enriched with precious and semi-precious stones. They are often shown on the heads of women in tomb effigies, and then again in portraits of the Tudor and Elizabethan nobility; cauls were included in the various rich hair coverings and headdresses

acquired for Queen Elizabeth herself. How, then, are we to judge the various cauls stocked by Thomas Deane? The values quoted suggest some variation in quality — from 12d. through 10d., 9d., 6d., and 1½d. Fineness and colouring of the thread used would be one consideration — silk presumably, but maybe also wool — and so too would be the quality of the knotted mesh. The cheapest ones were indeed very cheap and presumably were workmanlike but coarse, perhaps of wool. Was there a size variant too which should be taken into account? Or embellishments or ornaments not indicated by those compiling the inventory?[22]

Finally we should return to the necklaces and bracelets in the shop stock. At only 3d. or so each these may have been composed of something like silk or linen thread, perhaps plaited or made like a decorative braid or even bobbin lace. Very occasionally such ornaments can be spotted in fifteenth- and sixteenth-century portraits, although none are known to survive. Braids to which jewels or imitation jewels were once attached have been found in medieval excavations in London and it is likely that this method of producing cheap jewellery continued. Other excavated finds reveal that there was an extensive production of cheap metal jewellery in medieval and Tudor London, employing lead and copper alloys in place of gold and silver, which allowed less affluent citizens to indulge in personal adornment on a far greater scale than has been realised. Deane's small stock of necklaces and bracelets might even have taken this form.[23]

Thomas Deane's shop inventory is the only one known for the Royal Exchange. Although by no means unique as a record of a haberdasher's stock — other either earlier or more extensive inventories are known — it nevertheless provides a valuable insight into one small business venture and the commodities offered to its customers. Ian Archer has shown in his history of the Haberdashers' Company that exploration of existing inventories can throw up much valuable information about the trading activities of these merchants, the growth in imports and the general expansion of their markets. Presumably

---

[21] Buck, op. cit., p. 21. Crowfoot *et al.*, op. cit., pp. 72–75.

[22] Ibid., pp. 145–49. Arnold, op. cit., p. 362.
[23] Ibid., pp. 132, 136 (fig. 106). T. Murdoch (ed.), *Treasures and Trinkets: Jewellery in London from pre-Roman Times to the 1930s* (London, 1991), p. 110.

Thomas Deane represents many who moved into this expanding area when their own craft was ailing or was failing to meet their financial goals; the potential it offered to those with drive and enterprise was considerable, as the careers of the more eminent and wealthy haberdashers demonstrate. From the research necessary for this study of Deane's shop, it is clear that there still remains a great deal of work to be carried out on the goods traded by haberdashers. Terminology is one area which cries out for more attention. Another aspect is the provenance of their goods. The inclusion of items from Italy, Spain and Flanders in Deane's small stock, for example, is entirely in accord with the great incursion of imported goods described by Ian Archer which were seen as such a threat to the livelihoods of many London citizens. Yet they often filled a void in the market until local goods began to be produced. A further interesting aspect for research might involve the identification of changing fashions, which surely must be reflected in the changing stocks of the haberdashers.

It is one of the great values of an inventory like Deane's that we can gain an insight into the lives of ordinary citizens of London, of the merchants, clerks, and others who habituated the Royal Exchange and sought very ordinary, and generally inexpensive, necessities of life like sewing threads, tapes or points. Inventories from noble households reflect only one scale of living, at the top of the social and economic ladder; although often far less rich in detail, inventories from less affluent households, struggling to maintain a living or perhaps gradually making their way up the social ladder, have much to reveal about the broader urban community in London. This community has left behind it a valuable record of clothing and textile skills in London archaeological deposits, evidence rarely preserved elsewhere, and often not found in contemporary portraits. Inventories like Deane's are also valuable for demonstrating the provision of ready-made goods like cauls and knitted sleeves, unremarkable items in themselves, but part of the process of clothing a large urban community where practical skills like netting and knitting had already been drawn into the industrial superstructure. Numerous other inventories of the goods of London traders of the fifteenth and sixteenth centuries still survive, and it is hoped that this account of Thomas Deane's modest stock will convince others of the value of examining and publishing this very neglected source for London history.

APPENDIX

The inventory of all such goods, householde stuff plate and Jewells as were — Thomas Deanes Citizen and fletcher of London perused and praysed by Christopher Bumpsted, Thomas Cobbe, James Dodson, Thomas Pennyton, John Catcher, Richard Netmaker, and Peter Daunsere (beinge thereunto appoynted) seen the 29th day of January in the foureteenth yere of the Reign of our soueraign lady Elizabeth by the grace of God Quene of England, France and Ireland, defender of the faith, etc.

The Shoppe in the Ryall exchange cast over the 21th [sic] *of July 1571 amountes as followeth*

Item lace of Silke and golde x dossen vij yardes at vd. the dossen	xiijs. vjd.
Item frenche parchement of divers collers xiij dossen at xvd. the dossen Amountes	xvjs. iijd.
Item frenche parchement ix dossen at xxd. the dossen	xvs.
Item Smale Naridge lase xi dossen ix yardes at ivd. the dossen	iijs. xjd.
Item smale Narydge lase xxviij dossen iij yardes ijs. viijd. the gross	vjs. viijd.
Item ij lb. ij oz. silke at xvjs. the lb.	xxivs.
Item j lb. v oz. $\frac{1}{2}$ fyne silke at xxivs. the lb. amountes	xxxijs. iijd.
Item ij papers of silke weyenge iv lb. at xxijs. the lb.	iv li. viijs.
Item j lb. $\frac{1}{2}$ of redd ferret silke at xijs the lb.	xviijs.
Item j lb. xv oz. of blacke feryt silke at viijs. the lb.	xvs.
Item j lb. ix oz. of blacke bridges silke at xvjs. the lb.	xxvs. vjd.
Item ij lb. ij oz. of narroe Inckell at iijs the lb.	vjs. vd.
Item vj oz. $\frac{1}{4}$ of Redd crewell fringe at vjs. viijd. the lb.	ijs. ivd.
Item vj oz. $\frac{1}{2}$ of blacke crewell frindge at iijd. the oz.	xixd.
Item vij oz. of Blacke frindge at ivd. the oz.	ijs. ivd.
Item xxviij gross $\frac{1}{2}$ of Sylke poyntes at ijs. viijd. the gross	iij li. xvjs.
Item ix gross of rownde silke poyntes at ivs. viijd. the gross	ij li. ivs. ivd.
Item v dossen of poyntes at xvijd. the dossen	vijs. jd.

Item x dossen of silke poyntes at xjd. the dossen   ixs. ijd.

Item iv dossen of Ryband silke poyntes at   js. viijd.

Item j gross vij dossen of thred poyntes at ijs. ivd.
the gross   iijs. viijd.

Item xj oz. of Silke byllament lace at xxs. the lb.   xiijs. ixd.

Item $\frac{1}{2}$ gross porele lace at vjs. the gross   iijs.

Item v oz.$\frac{1}{2}$ Silke ijd. Brede at xijd. the oz.   vs. iijd.

Item xiij oz.$\frac{1}{2}$ chene lace at xxivs. the lb.   xxs. iijd.

Item xx oz. of gyne Ribband at xxijjd. the oz.   xviijs. ivd.

Item xv oz.$\frac{1}{2}$ of Spaynishe Ryband at xxjd.
the oz.   xxvijs. ijd.

Item ij oz. jd. brede xiijd. the oz. amo[u]ntes to   ijs. ijd.

Item xx lb. xi oz. of Blacke pyssinge thrid at xxd.
the lb. Amo[u]ntes to   xlis. ivd.ob.

Item xiij yardes of silke Rybande ijd. ob. the
yarde   ijs. viijd.ob.

Item v dossen vij yardes of lase at xvjd.
the dossen   vijs. vd.ob

Item x dossen vij yardes of lase at xiijd. the
dossen   xjs. vjd.

Item xxvij yardes lase at xivd. the dossen   ijs. viijd.

Item iij oz. of lase at xviijd. the oz. amo[u]ntes to   ivs. vjd.

Item vj buttons for clokes at vd. the button   ijs. vjd.

Item 1 button   vjd.

Item xiij knottyd Cawles at xijd. the pece   xiijs.

Item v Cawles at vjd. the pese   ijs. vjd.

Item v Cawles at xd. the pese   ivs. ijd.

Item iv Cawles at jd. ob. the pese   vjd.

Item ij oz. of grenadowe silke at xxiijd. the oz.   iijs. xd.

Item j Silke purse at   ijs. ivd.

Item xi necklases at iijs. ijd. the dossen   iijs.

Item vj braslettes at iijd. the pese   xviijd.

Item ij oz. of hollowe lase at xd. the oz.   xxd.

Item ij oz.$\frac{3}{4}$ of Copper lase at ijs. viijd. the oz.   vijs. ivd.

Item v yardes of Bone lase at   ijd.ob.

Item v paier of garnesey sleves at xvjd. the paier   vjs. viijd.

Item one childes purse at   ivd.

Item ix dossen ij yardes naridge at xijd. the
dossen   ixs. ijd.

Item vj dossen naridge lase at xivd. the dossen   vijs.

Item viij dossen narydge lase at xiijd.
the dossen   viijs. viijd.

Item xiv yardes of narydge lase at xivd. the
dossen   xvijd.

Item xiv yardes of narydge lase at xvd. the dossen   xviijd.

Item vj dossen of thrid lase at vjd. the dossen   iijs.

Item vij yardes of Coppar golde at ijs. ivd. the
dossen   xvjd.ob.

Item xv yardes of parchement at vjd. the dossen   viijd

Item iij yardes of Sylke at   vd.

Item v dossen of narydge Bellament xivd. the
dossen   vs. xd.

Item j Cawle at   ixd.

Item iij dossen of sherte lases at xijd. the dossen   iijs.

Item j gross of lace at   vijs.

Item ij dossen of Sherte lases   xijd.

Item xviij gross of Buttons at xviijd. the gross   xxvijs.

Item vj gross of Buttons at xxd. the gross   xs.

Item xxviij dossen Buttons at ijs.ivd. the gross   vs. vd.

Item xj oz.$\frac{3}{4}$ frindge at xvijd. the oz.   xvjs. vijd.

Item iij oz.$\frac{3}{4}$ Jane fryndge at xxijd. the oz.   vjs. xd.

Item viij oz.$\frac{1}{2}\frac{1}{4}$ chene lase at xviij s. the lb.   viijs.

Item v oz.$\frac{1}{4}$ Sisters thrid at iijd. the oz.   xvjd.

Item ij oz. of vetnall thrid at   ivd.

Item xxxvj yardes of Porell lase at vjd. the dossen   xviijd.

Item xxvij yardes purled lase at   xjd.

Item vij yardes $\frac{3}{4}$ of bone lase at iijs. viijd. the
dossen   ijs. ixd.

Item viij dossen and viij Buttons for
handkirchuises   ijs.

Item xxj tabelletes at xivd. the dossen   ijs.

Item ij garnishe bottons for handkirchuses   ijs.

Item v yardes of lase at   vijd.

Item j $\frac{1}{2}$ dossen Bone lase at   iijs. ijd.

Item ij oz. of silver at vs.ivd. the oz.   xs. viijd.

Item iij Bugels   iijs.

Item in penny Brede lasses xvj yardes   xivd.

Item in Pomaunders and other trifels   ivd.

Item viij dossen and ix longe buttons at xjd. the
dossen   viijs. jd.

Item j gross ix dossen longe Cruell buttons ijs. the
gross   iijs. vjd.

Item viij dossen Rownde Poyntes at ivs. viijd. the
gross   iijs.

Item iij peses of narydge lase   js. vjd.

Item in money in the Shopp amountes to   iv li. iijs. ivd.

Item in Wares taken out by my Sister and is by
her to paye   iij li. xvijs.

Item in Wares taken out by me & is for me to
paye   viijs.

Item Mrs Eareley   ijs. viijd.

Item Mrs Dutton owethe Brydge othes   iijs. viijd.

Item Mrs Byston owethe   xxd.

Item Addam Willson owethe for silke   iijs. jd.

Item goodman Tyddy owethe for silke   vjs.

Item certen od lases   ixd.

Item the Costes of thinges as locke, staull clothe
and other chardges amountes   xxijs. vjd.

Some totalis   Lij li. ixs. vjd.

CHAPTER IX

Currency and the Bill of Exchange in Gresham's England

By C. E. CHALLIS and P. H. RAMSEY

Currency

By C. E. CHALLIS

THROUGHOUT THE PERIOD when Thomas Gresham was Royal Agent — 1551 to 1574 — the English coinage was full bodied, being made from either gold or silver. There were no English coins of copper or bronze and there was no general circulation of paper money. The world in which this coinage circulated and in which Gresham moved was influenced by a number of important monetary considerations, of which the first was instability, caused by the circulation of fiat money produced in the course of the great debasement. Then there was the seemingly constant lack of fine money; that is to say, coin which was made at full standard according to well established conventions and which consequently was readily acceptable both at home and abroad. Thirdly, there were the complications raised by the injection of foreign coins into the English circulating medium. And, finally, there was the question of the rehabilitation of the English silver standard in the early years of Elizabeth I's reign and the effects which this had.

Let us turn first to instability. Under normal circumstances the face value of full-bodied coins is equal to their intrinsic value (i.e. the current market value of their precious metal content), plus a small charge for coinage. From this it follows that so long as this relationship obtains coins will be more valuable as coins than as bullion and will remain in circulation. On the other hand, if bullion prices rise on the open market, thereby causing the intrinsic value of coins to rise above their face values, coins become vulnerable and are culled (or removed from circulation) to be consigned either to hoards or to the melting pot. In practice this potential danger could be removed in one of two ways: either by altering the weight and/or

the fineness (i.e. the purity) of coins, for it was indeed weight and fineness which determined intrinsic values; or by enhancing face values so that once again they exceeded intrinsic values. Leaving on one side those times in the Tudor period when currency was exploited for fiscal purposes, it was, with only one exception, the process of enhancement which was used to establish stability in the gold coinage; the upshot being that the gold sovereign of 240 gr. introduced by Henry VII in 1489 at a value of 20*s.* was retariffed at 22*s.* 6*d.* in 1526 and at 30*s.* in 1551,[1] at which value it was to remain for each of the subsequent issues in the next half century.[2] For silver the maintenance of stability was achieved by adjustments of weight, purity being maintained at 11 oz.

---

[1] Contemporaries reckoned coinage weights according to the Troy pound which was subdivided as follows:

1 Troy pound (lb.) = 12 ounces (oz.)
1 oz. = 20 pennyweights (dwt)
1 dwt = 24 grains (gr.)

While the Troy pound was used to define the purity of silver, 12 oz. being regarded as absolute purity, as far as gold was concerned calculations were done in terms of carats (car.), 24 of which gave a perfect standard. Each carat was divided into either 4 large grains (gr.) or 12 small grains (gr.), so that, for example, a standard defined as 23 car. $3\frac{1}{2}$ gr. was in reality the same as one given as 23 car. $10\frac{1}{2}$ gr.

Today, fineness is given on a millesimal scale, 1000 being regarded as absolute purity. At that time face value was reckoned in terms of the £ sterling, which contained 20 shillings (*s.*), each of 12 pence (*d.*).

[2] The exception came in the indenture of 1601 which marginally increased the value of gold whilst at the same time maintaining the existing face values of the denominations. The upshot was that an angel of 80 gr. which had been valued in 1485 at 6*s.* 8*d.*, in 1526 at 7*s.* 6*d.* and from 1551 at 10*s.* 0*d.* was now reduced to 78.9 gr. C. E. Challis, *The Tudor Coinage* (Manchester, 1978), appendix III.

2 dwt (or 925 parts in 1000). Thus, the 12 gr. penny of 1464 was reduced in 1526 to 10.66 gr., in 1551 to 8 gr. and in 1601 to 7.7 gr. Irrespective of the route pursued, it is important to remember that in doing what it did government was acting honestly in the interests of the economy at large and purely in response to market forces beyond its control.

In contrast to this process of currency depreciation, currency debasement was carried out for one purpose and one purpose alone: the fiscal advantage of the Crown, and its timing and extent were dictated solely by the Crown. Debasement worked by divorcing the face and intrinsic values of coins, the gap between the two (having taken coinage charges into account) representing the Crown's profit, and could continue just so long as bullion could be brought, or forced, into the mints and there was still some intrinsic value left in the coins to extract. In practice, the process, which began secretly in 1542 and effectively ended so far as England was concerned in 1551, damaged the silver coin more seriously than the gold, the fineness of the former falling from 925 to 250 parts per 1000, and of the latter from 994.8 to 833.3. Coins in both metals suffered weight reductions. Overall, the £ sterling finished up containing only 73 per cent of the gold and 17 per cent of the silver it had had before debasement began.[3] The overall profit to the Crown was £1.27 millions.[4]

Consisting of coins of differing standards but all alike in being fiat money, that is to say, coins which took their value simply from government edict rather than from intrinsic value, the circulating medium which debasement created was inherently unstable and it was to help remedy this that in 1549 government carried out two manipulations. At that time silver was being struck at 48s. per lb. (which meant that 12d. would weigh 120 gr.), but so low was the silver content (4 oz. or 333) that coins took on a coppery appearance and suffered a loss in confidence accordingly. In February a new issue appeared at twice (8 oz. or 666) the existing standard and gave the appearance of being reasonable silver but since

government could not really afford such a reform it neutralised the effect of doubling the fineness by halving the weight, so that 12d. now only weighed 60 gr. Unsurprisingly, at this shrunken size the new coin — or 'pretty little shilling', as Hugh Latimer called it — proved to be unacceptable and in April it was replaced by a further issue. Once again the government was in no position to afford a true reform and once again it adopted the solution of counter-balancing improvement in fineness by reduction in weight. This time, however, the stratagem worked because at 6 oz. fine (500) the new coins avoided the hues of the old 4 oz. (333) issues and at 72s. per lb. (12d. now weighed 80 gr.) were of a more acceptable size. Something had been achieved but nothing of the order required if confidence was to be fully restored.[5]

In 1551 government acted again: first, by calling down all silver coin by 50 per cent, so that a shilling now became 6d.; and, second, by announcing new coins of both gold and silver at fine standards. Unfortunately, neither measure proved entirely successful. Quite apart from being badly bungled by virtue of being accomplished in two stages during which speculation and uncertainty was increased, the devaluation did not reduce the silver coins to as low a face value as their silver content warranted nor was it accompanied by a plan for a comprehensive withdrawal. Bad, overvalued coin remained in circulation with the ability not only to drive out the good but also to breed instability.[6]

Over and besides the difficulties it faced through the operation of 'Gresham's Law', the new silver coin which issued from the mints from October 1551 suffered from being, at 60s. per lb., undertariffed, which meant that it proved difficult for the mint to

---

[3] C. E. Challis, *Currency and the Economy in Tudor and early Stuart England.* The Historical Association, New Appreciations in History, 4 (1989).

[4] C. E. Challis, 'The Debasement of the Coinage, 1542–1551', *Economic History Review*, 2nd ser. xx (1967), 441–66.

[5] *The Tudor Coinage*, pp. 98–99. A further manoeuvre which may well have had a stabilising effect was the conversion of testoons, or pieces of 12d., ordered in 1548. Issued in quantity from the start of open debasement in 1544 and therefore synonymous with the fraud, these coins were recalled as a source of bullion from which further debased issues could be made. J. D. Gould, *The Great Debasement: Currency and the Economy in Mid-Tudor England* (Oxford, 1970), pp. 187–98; C. E. Challis, 'The Conversion of Testoons: A Restatement', *British Numismatic Journal*, L (1980), 67–80; C. E. Challis, 'The Circulating Medium and the Movement of Prices in Mid-Tudor England', in *The Price Revolution in Sixteenth-Century England*, edited by P. H. Ramsey (1971), p. 143.

[6] *The Tudor Coinage*, pp. 105–06.

attract bullion in any quantity. According to a contemporary estimate no more than £124,179 was struck before Edward VI's death in July 1553.[7] Why the new valuation was fixed at this unattractive level is unclear, as also is the reason for the purity of the new coins being set at a quite unusually high level. At first sight the latter statement may appear to be incorrect for traditionally it has been said that at 11 oz. 1 dwt (920.8) Edward VI's fine coinage was under sterling standard (11 oz. 2 dwt, or 925), just as subsequently was that of his sister Mary (11 oz., or 916.6 fine). It was only with the restoration of the silver coinage by Elizabeth that sterling once again reigned supreme. To explain why this traditional interpretation is incorrect it is necessary to consider the operation of assaying silver by fire, in which silver is wrapped in a known quantity of lead and then heated to melting point in a bone ash cupel. As a result of this process the impurities in the silver drain away with the lead into the cupel but so too at the same time does 2 dwt of silver (8.33 parts per 1000). This inadvertent loss means that at the report of the assay, out of the fire, as contemporaries put it, the silver will appear to be 2 dwt worse than it actually is. And by the same token, if the fineness of coin is expressed as 'out of the fire', this means that the fineness will be 2 dwt worse than it would be if expressed at the 'comixture', or point when the metal and alloy were put together before melting. In October 1551 the commission ordering the new silver coinage did indeed employ the former formulation, thereby creating a standard the equivalent of 11 oz. 3 dwt at the comixture, something quite unique in England's coinage history.[8]

The explanation for this new departure is as obscure as is that for its abandonment at the accession of Queen Mary who, in specifying the silver standard as 11 oz. 'out of the fire', effectively restored it to the old sterling standard of 11 oz. 2 dwt (925). Once again mint output remained low, amounting in the first two years to only £216,459.[9]

In addition to the fine issues of Edward VI and Mary the circulating medium of mid-Tudor England contained foreign coins which received comprehensive official tariffing in 1554. In silver there was the Spanish real ($6\frac{1}{2}d.$), its double and half and in gold French and Imperial crowns (6s. 4d.), the Spanish ducat (6s. 8d.) and its double, crusadoes (6s. 8d. or 6s. 4d.) and pistolets (6s. 2d.). This was not the first time, of course, that foreign coin had circulated here but there are grounds for believing, first, that it now did so in greater quantity than ever before and, second, that it was because of the confusion and loss which this brought that in 1561 the government decided to ban all foreign coins other than the French crown and the Flemish or Burgundian crown.[10] Although in subsequent years this was to remain the official position it is clear that in practice the case was quite different. William Harrison recalled the existence in his day of ducats, crusadoes and portagues while pleadings before the Exchequer court in respect of the illegal export of coin reveal a whole range of other coins in both gold and silver, prominent amongst them being pistolets, reals of plate, and daalders.[11]

At the same time as it regulated the circulation of foreign coins the government carried through the great recoinage of debased silver. According to Burgon, Thomas Gresham may well have been 'the originator of the whole scheme' and certainly can be seen as one of the 'earliest of its promoters' because it was he who was responsible for recommending Daniel Ulstate & Co. to do the refining.[12] Now, that the Germans did do most of the work is true, for they engrossed into their hands no less than 83 per cent of the whole enterprise, but to begin the story of the Elizabethan recoinage with this achievement is to neglect the importance of what had gone on in the preceding years.[13] Serious discussions about what should be done to restore confidence in the coinage had begun in the later years of Edward VI and the

[7] C. E. Challis and C. J. Harrison, 'A contemporary estimate of the production of silver and gold coinage in England, 1542–1556', *English Historical Review*, LXXXVIII (1973), 834.

[8] *A New History of the Royal Mint*, edited by C. E. Challis (Cambridge, 1992), pp. 251–66.

[9] Challis and Harrison, p. 834.

[10] *Tudor Royal Proclamations*, edited by P. L. Hughes and J. F. Larkin (New Haven and London, 1964–69), II, nos. 408, 412, 487.

[11] *The Tudor Coinage*, p. 218. See, for example, PRO, E159/362 Rec.Eas.11d; 363 Rec.Mich.13, 235; 371 Rec.Mich.280; 372 Rec.Eas.8.

[12] J. W. Burgon, 'On the Amelioration of the Coinage A.D. 1560', *Numismatic Chronicle*, II (1840), 12–17.

[13] *The Tudor Coinage*, pp. 126–27.

upshot had been the devaluation of silver by 50 per cent already referred to. Initially, it seems also to have been the intention to follow devaluation by the withdrawal and recoinage of the debased coin, as appears from a 'Deliberation touching the coin' recorded by King Edward in his *Chronicle* in September 1551.

Memor. that there were divers standards — 9 ounces fine a few; 8 ounces fine as ill as four, because although that that [*sic*] was fine, yet a shilling was reckoned for two shillings; 6 ounces, very many; 4 ounces, many also; 3 ounces £130,000 now of late. Whereupon agreed that the teston being called to sixpence, 4 with help of 6 should make ten fine, 8 fine with help of nine, being fewer than those of eight, should make ten ounces fine; the two ounces of alloy should quit the charges of minting; and those of threepence being but few, should be turned to [the stan]dard of 4, of farthings and halfpence and pence for to serve for the poor people.[14]

Here the king goes beyond stating the basic prerequisite of devaluation and lets us know that at this stage the new standard to be aimed at was, for the principal coins, 10 oz., and, for the smaller ones, 4 oz. Although the precise arithmetic which lay behind his words is missing — something which long ago led Ruding to conclude that this was indeed a 'very obscure passage' — Edward does reveal the broad thrust of an argument which suggested that, taking into account the various finenesses of the silver coins in existence, the quantities of each then in circulation and the effect of a 50 per cent devaluation, the debased coins might yield sufficient fine silver to permit a recoinage at 10 oz. fine, without loss to the government. That this was simply a theoretical calculation is suggested by a subsequent entry in the *Chronicle* alluding to 'a letter directed to the Lord Treasurer, the Lord Great Master, and the Master of the Horse, to meet at London for the ordering of my coin and the payment of my debts; which done, to return and make report of their proceedings'. One week later Edward was able to write that, 'having

tried all kinds of stamping, both of the fineness of nine, eight, six, four, and three', this committee had 'proved that without loss but sufferable the coin might be brought to eleven [nine *crossed out*] ounces fine. For whereas it was thought before that the teston was through ill officers and ministers corrupted, it was tried that it had the valuation just, by eight sundry kinds of melting; and four hundred pounds of sterling money, a teston being but sixpence, made four hundred pounds 11 ounces fine of money sterling'.[15]

In the event, therefore, practical experiment had shown that some of the debased coins were not as bad as had originally been thought and, in view of this, a reformed standard of 11 oz., rather than 10 oz., might be achieved. As the proclamation of 30 October 1551 announcing the new fine issue made plain, the government still cherished the hope that conversion of the old moneys would take place 'with all possible expedition'. However, since no mechanism for withdrawal, other than its own ability to send coin to the mint and the individual's desire to exchange fine coin for base, was ever formalised, full scale conversion did not take place and it was not until Mary's reign that the whole issue was rehearsed again. In June 1556 a committee was appointed to determine how best the coinage might be reformed and in the months which followed silver coin was tested by melting and assaying and an estimate prepared of the quantity of base coin which had been minted. By the summer of 1557 revaluation and, possibly, recoinage of debased silver coins seemed a distinct likelihood, but then King Philip left England, Mary's adviser, William Paget, left London for health reasons and Mary lacked the resolve to carry the matter through.[16]

When reform finally did come, in 1560–61, it was preceded by further calculations of the quantity of debased silver in circulation, the establishment of a second mint in the Tower to speed up recoinage, and another devaluation. This time the better kind of sterling, which had been reduced in 1551 to 6d., was to pass for 4½d. and the poorer sort at only half this rate. To enable the distinction to be made (and this

[14] *The Chronicle and Political Papers of King Edward VI*, edited by W. K. Jordan (1966), p. 80. For a rebuttal of the view that King Edward was merely a 'bright pathetic lad (who) was in fact the manipulated one, more the parrot of Northumberland's plans than the Renaissance prodigy of legend', see C. E. Challis, 'Presidential Address (on Edward VI and his fine coinage)', *British Numismatic Journal*, 63 (1993), 172–77.

[15] R. Ruding, *Annals of the Coinage* (3rd edn, 1840), I, 322; *Chronicle and Political Papers*, pp. 81–82.
[16] Challis and Harrison, pp. 821–26; *Tudor Royal Proclamations*, I, no. 382.

tells us a great deal about the assertion still commonly made that contemporaries could distinguish clearly between one coin and another and adjust prices accordingly) puncheons were distributed in London and the provinces so that the better pieces might be identified with a portcullis countermark and the poorer with a greyhound. Subsequently, demonetised, this coin was forced back to the mints where it was made into new sterling worth £764,418. Since this sum replaced £1,084,000 of debased silver in circulation on the eve of recoinage, the circulating medium was significantly reduced and it was to be some years before the deficiency was made good. How great was the social and economic dislocation caused is difficult to judge, but it does seem clear that, as far as government was concerned, the great silver recoinage was a significant success; for not only had a profit of some £50,000 been produced but the young queen had clearly stamped her mark on the new reign with a most prestigious achievement, something which Camden believed 'turned to her greater, yea greatest glory'.[17]

[17] *The Tudor Coinage*, pp. 118–27; *A New History of the Royal Mint*, p. 248.

Credit Instruments

By P. H. RAMSEY

COIN OF THE REALM was not the only means of payment available to Tudor merchants, though it was far the most common, and ultimately indispensable. A number of devices were available to them that delayed or even occasionally avoided the need for cash settlement, though these were less numerous and sophisticated than those available to Mediterranean merchants of the period. The major Italian and Spanish firms were ahead of their English counterparts in developing the use of bills of exchange and giro payments through banker-cashiers at the great fairs (like that of Medina del Campo), and sixteenth-century London lacked the facilities of contemporary Antwerp or even fifteenth-century Bruges. This deficiency was due in part to the delay affecting the travel of advanced southern techniques to northern Europe — double-entry bookkeeping was similarly slow to be adopted in the north — and in part simply to lack of any urgent need for them in the England of the time. London merchant firms were relatively small in scale compared to the great Italian multinationals, and were usually one-man concerns operated with a few apprentices and perhaps an overseas factor. Partnerships were rare; even the powerful Gresham clan in the 1540s traded as individuals, not as a family business. Moreover, the trade consisted overwhelmingly of the export of woollen cloths to nearby Antwerp and the import of miscellaneous goods from that trade centre, and such a limited bilateral trade did not call for complicated and advanced techniques. For the time being, at least, the Londoners could get along without them.[1]

By far the most common financial document in use was the simple obligation (or IOU). The great majority of trade transactions were on credit, or partly so, the most common among many variations being a down payment of half the sum due with the balance payable in two instalments at three-month intervals (at Antwerp at the two next fairs, similarly spaced).[2] An obligation would be given to the creditor, to be cancelled upon full payment of the instalments. If these obligations had been freely transferable among merchants, whether at a discount

[1] Similarly they did not immediately need the facilities of the Antwerp Bourse, founded in 1531 to the great satisfaction of the merchant community, which was to be the inspiration for the later Royal Exchange.
[2] This is clear from both the accounts of Sir Thomas Kitson (Cambridge University Library, Hengrave Hall Deposit, 78 (i–iv)) and the Day Book of Thomas Gresham covering the years 1546–52, at Mercers' Hall, London.

or at face value, they might have formed a supplementary paper money that would have obviated the need for cash payments. In Antwerp such transfers were not unknown, and in the accounts of Thomas Kitson there is a clear instance of his agent Thomas Washington disposing of a discounted bill at the Sinksen Mart of 1536. The same Washington subsequently declared in evidence before an Antwerp court that this was normal practice for the London merchants at the end of the quarterly Antwerp fairs. However, his own accounts (and the Day Book of Thomas Gresham) do not support the idea that this was common practice, even in Antwerp, though it is possible that (as he suggested) English merchants were regularly prepared to honour bills signed by their fellows when presented by foreigners for payment.[3] In England the Common Law did not encourage the transfer of obligations, and the legal status of transferred bills was uncertain. This need not have precluded the London merchants from the practice, operating as they were in a quite narrow circle of mutual acquaintance, but they do not seem to have adopted it at all commonly. The Gresham accounts show his debtors (and Gresham himself) overwhelmingly settling in hard cash, albeit frequently late and by instalments that do not at all correspond to the original agreement. It is true that debasement of the currency greatly increased the supply of coin in precisely the years covered by Gresham's Day Book (1546–52)[4] but the inference remains strong that in London obligations were still a means of delaying cash payment, not of substituting for it. They were not paper money.

Sixteenth-century London did not enjoy the amenity of banker/cashiers who could effect giro transfers between the accounts of their clients — another possible way of minimising cash transactions. This had to wait till the next century. In principle a substantial merchant like Thomas Gresham might have performed a similar function, but in practice his suppliers (the clothiers) and his customers (fellow-dealers in imported textiles and retailers) fell into two distinct groups, and the possibility of transfer rarely arose. The few instances that do occur mainly concern members of his family. Once again cash settlement is the normal order of the day.

One essential financial instrument was the bill of exchange, without which, merchants claimed, they could no more exist than ships without water. Its prime and normal purpose was to move money where it was needed without incurring the risks and expenses of shipping coin, commonly forbidden by governments and always at danger from pirates and robbers. In principle its use involved four parties: the original buyer and seller of the bill (the 'deliverer' and 'taker' in contemporary parlance) at one trade centre, and their agents at another. The bill was an instruction from the buyer to his agent, requiring him to reimburse the agent of the seller for value received, at a stipulated rate of exchange agreed by buyer and seller. The rate would be expressed at both centres as a variable number of coins of the one currency against a fixed unit of the other; as between London and Antwerp the rate was given as a variable number of shillings and groats Flemish against the pound sterling. In English usage the form of the document changed in the first half of the century from a rather loose and verbose missive, more akin to an obligation than a bill and not always including the exchange-rate, to the Italian style of a terse instruction to the agent to make repayment at the stated rate of exchange. It was normal to send two copies of the bill by separate post, so as to avoid loss and delay.

In the communications system of the early modern period every bill was a time bill as well as an exchange bill, since a period must necessarily elapse during its sea and land transmission. The period was standardised for any two centres as the 'usance' current for them; between London and Antwerp usance was fixed at one month. It was, however, possible to stipulate 'double usance', half-usance or 'sight', though even sight involved a delay of at least a week. Since every bill thus unavoidably involved a short-term loan from buyer to seller, it is not surprising that interest was charged on the transaction, though the interest-rate was concealed within the stated exchange-rate on the bill and not made explicit. Thus

---

[3] Antwerp City Archives, 'Engelse Natie', III, 17 March 1537.
[4] The Day Book of Thomas Gresham, owned by the Mercers' Company of London, is a detailed account of Gresham's London transactions in these years, 6,572 entries in all. It was a part of a double-entry system, of which the ledger unfortunately does not survive. It is hoped that a reconstruction of the ledger, based on the Day Book entries, will be published by the London Record Society.

in London the exchange-rate for a bill at double-usance would be higher than for one at usance. It is possible from Gresham's accounts to estimate approximately the interest-rate at the time. It in fact hovered about 15 per cent, significantly above the 10 per cent legally allowed for interest on loans in England at this time.

The exchange-rate at any one time was basically determined by the mint par of the two currencies involved, that is, their respective precious metal content. Debasement of the currency by either government had a rapid effect on the rate; the Tudor debasement brought the rate down from 23/24s. Flemish to 12s. 8d. Flemish in a few years, though the issue is complicated by the differing rates of debasement for gold and silver coins. Apart from the mint par, the rate might be affected by the balance of trade or payments in general, and by temporary surpluses or shortages of cash in particular. When the Merchant Adventurers had sold their woollen cloths at the Antwerp fairs, their need to repatriate their takings would drive up the cost of bills (by lowering the exchange-rate in Antwerp). A further disturbing factor might be the raising or repayment of loans by European princes. In reasonably stable conditions, however, in spite of all these variables, the buyer of a bill of exchange could expect a profit, this arising from the concealed rate of interest. Hence arose two variants of the 'merchant' bill of exchange, both of some concern to theologians and moralists, these being 'dry' exchange and fictitious exchange.

In dry exchange the original transaction in London would be immediately reversed in Antwerp by a bill agreed by the two agents of the originators. The effect was that the original seller would recompense the original buyer for the initial sum plus the implicit interest on both bills. The one had thus made a two-month loan at interest to the other (assuming the bills were at usance), and at a higher rate of interest than was legally permissible on a straight loan not involving exchange. This was essentially fraudulent, since no bona fide transfer of funds had taken place, and moreover the interest charges had been concealed from view. However, the second bill would be based on the current market exchange-rate at Antwerp, and in theory fluctuations of the market between the first and second bill might expose the original seller to a

loss on the operation. This was a very unlikely outcome, but the bare possibility of a loss made it just possible for some moralists to defend the practice.

Quite indefensible was fictitious exchange, basically similar in its working to dry exchange, but with the difference that the exchange-rates for both bills were agreed at the outset. In this case market fluctuations were excluded, and profit was guaranteed. This was simply concealed usury.

There seems little or no clear evidence that English merchants of the early sixteenth century practised either dry or fictitious exchange. It was possible to play the exchanges without resort to either device, and Gresham may have done this to a modest extent, though in the absence of details of his transactions in Antwerp it is difficult to know this for certain.[5] Such speculation would depend on maintaining an agent in Antwerp for all or most of the year, and probably few merchants would choose to do this.[6] The great majority probably used bills of exchange for their legitimate purposes only — the risk-free transfer of resources to finance their trade. How vital this was to them can be measured by their indignation in 1576 when a three-man commission was appointed for the direction of exchange dealings; their furious protests ensured that the commission endured only for some eight months.

There is likewise little to suggest that in England, at least, bills of exchange circulated freely from hand to hand, though in Antwerp the 'payable to bearer' clause was generally accepted by the middle of the century, and even bills without it could be transferred before a notary. Even some Italian merchants became disturbed by the extent of this development, possibly because the practice of sending duplicate bills made them dangerously open to fraud in such a situation. Still less had the regular endorsing or discounting of bills become normal English practice.

[5] The Day Book records numerous exchange transactions between London and Antwerp, in both directions, though it does not quote the actual texts of the bills. It is not possible to calculate from it Gresham's credit situation at Antwerp at any particular date, and this makes it difficult to know whether any exchange transaction was a speculation or a necessary movement of funds.
[6] Gresham's Antwerp factor Robert Berney seems to have been more or less permanently in residence there. On the other hand Kitson's agent in the 1520s, Thomas Washington, seems normally to have attended only the four annual marts at Antwerp and Bergen-op-Zoom.

In general it seems that sixteenth-century English merchants increasingly enjoyed, to a modest extent, the growing freedom of Antwerp in the use of credit instruments as a supplementary currency. But the new practices were slow to impinge on the home market. It was not until the next century that English merchants enjoyed the banking facilities and the legal safety to transfer bills among themselves that had long been available to their foreign counterparts.

CHAPTER X

Early Insurance and the Royal Exchange

By TREVOR SIBBETT

THE BACKGROUND

POPE'S HEAD ALLEY leads into Cornhill by the front entrance of the present Royal Exchange. As I write, Pope's Head Alley must be the dreariest alley in the City of London. The land here was granted to rich Florentine merchants in Papal service in the year 1318. The alley itself was named after a tavern, *The Pope's Head*, which is first mentioned nearly a century later in 1425.[1] The alley is mentioned in another chapter of this book and has its place in history. Down the centre of the alley, it is still possible to see the line of the old medieval gutter, which has been covered with tarmac and badly repaired in places.

Along both sides of Pope's Head Alley, the freeholders of the surrounding buildings have insisted on their old property rights underneath the alley and glass lights are set in the tarmac as far as their property boundaries. The result is that the old medieval street width is still discernible and it is possible, with some stretching, to stand just off one side of the old alley and shake hands with a person standing just off the other side. In 1769, New Lloyd's Coffee House was established at No. 5 Pope's Head Alley by a group of dissatisfied customers from Lloyd's Coffee House, then located in Lombard Street. It is from New Lloyd's Coffee House that the insurance market known today as Lloyd's owes its descent. In 1774, New Lloyd's underwriters moved into the Royal Exchange and stayed there until 1928, apart from a brief sojourn elsewhere, mainly at the London Tavern, after the Royal Exchange was burnt down by fire in 1838 until the reopening in 1844.

The other end of the Pope's Head Alley runs into Lombard Street. This street is the site of the wool market held by Lombardy merchants who bought wool from the English from the thirteenth century onwards.[2] Tradition has it that merchants gathered in the street and did their deals. Lombard Street is the historical centre[3] of an area of insurance stretching from St Bartholomew's Lane in the north, to King William Street in the west, Eastcheap in the south and the City of London boundary in the east. In the sixteenth century, and perhaps earlier, life and marine insurance deals were concluded in this street and the policy terms set a standard for others.

Birchin Lane, which runs from Lombard Street up to the rear of the Royal Exchange, was the home of John Graunt who, in the middle of the seventeenth century, started the study of bills of mortality[4] and produced a hypothetical mortality table. This led to the study of mortality generally and eventually to scientific life assurance, sickness insurance, pension funds, mortality tables from census data and to other work in the area of the contingencies of human life.[5] In Nicholas Lane, which runs off Lombard Street, scientific life assurance was transacted for the first time in 1762. In 1755, James Dodson, who was once a master at the Royal Mathematical School in Christ's Hospital, worked out the mathematics for calculating level age-related premiums for risks which varied in size from year to year. Sadly, Dodson did not live to 1762 to see his ideas put into practice.

Change Alley (an abbreviation for Royal Exchange Alley), which runs from Lombard Street to the old entrance of the Royal Exchange in Cornhill, was the scene of the 1720 South Sea Bubble speculations and

---

[1] S. Fairfield, *The Streets of London* (Macmillan, London, 1983).

[2] Op. cit.

[3] In the seventeenth century, trade in London moved gradually westward, except for some retained by the Royal Exchange. The insurance centre remained, though. Source: John Graunt, *Natural and Political Observations Mentioned in a following Index and made upon the Bills of Mortality* (London, 1662).

[4] John Graunt, op. cit.

[5] Detailed information in this area is available in *The History of Actuarial Science*, 10 vols., Steven Haberman and Trevor A. Sibbett, William Pickering (London, 1995).

the formal meeting place of the stockbrokers in Jonathan's Coffee House, which later evolved into the London Stock Exchange.

EARLY INSURANCE

Just who the sixteenth-century merchants were who stood in Lombard Street and transacted life assurance as well as the circumstances which gave rise to these deals is knowledge not available to us. Underwriting as a profession was unknown and the early under-writers accepting risks were men whose wealth had accumulated in other fields. Underwriting risks was only one of the forms of business undertaken by them. We can surmise that some policies were on the lives of ships' captains and lasted for the duration of a voyage. We do know for certain that after the opening of the Royal Exchange in 1569, long before Lloyd's existed, the underwriters did their deals in the courtyard of the building.

Normally, marine insurances (assurance was the word frequently used in the sixteenth century where we now would use the word insurance) were upon ships to be laden with goods at one port and bound from one place to another or were placed upon the goods themselves. Trade was national and international in character and insurance likewise. Insurance could be on ships from Lisbon to Brazil, Portugal to the East Indies, Santo Domingo, Peru and other places. Communication was poor in these times and ships could make additional journeys during their voyages unknown to the underwriters. Departing ships were often many months away and news of them was frequently scant until the voyage finished. There was scope for fraud on the insurers and this included insuring rotten and unsaleable ships as if they were sound, and the ships being deliberately lost at sea. Insurance was also made on the transport of goods by land from, for example, London to Venice or Frankfurt. Goods were often marked for identification purposes which made the insurance easier to obtain.

Life assurance was also effected for many purposes. Some men enjoyed their estates for life only, the estate passing to others on their deaths. There was a wish to pass on some benefit of the estate to children or friends. The lives could be valued for insurance

purposes at so many hundred pounds for one or more years and life assurances were effected at a rate of 5, 6, 10 per cent (of the sum assured) or more. Sir Richard Martin, Master of the Mint, had his life insured for £300 at the age of 90 for a premium of 25 per cent of the sum insured (i.e. £75) for a year. He died within the year and the insurers paid up.[6] (It is not clear if this is the same Richard Martin who was involved in the 1583 life assurance case below, but it may well have been.)

Mr Kiddermaster purchased the office of the six Clerks of the Chancery[7] with money taken up of others (presumably a loan). His life was insured for a sum of £2,000 at a premium rate of £4 per cent and £5 per cent of the sum insured for many years until he had repaid the money. A traveller voyaging to Jerusalem or Babylon, due to pay money on his return, would assure a sum of money on his life either in order to make it easier for him to raise money for the journey or so that he could leave money to friends if he died and did not return.

THE OFFICE OF ASSURANCES IN THE ROYAL EXCHANGE

During the second half of the sixteenth century, the Privy Council dealt with a number of marine insurance matters and did so in a way which increased the reputation of insurance in the City of London.[8] Often disputes over insurance matters were referred to the

[6] Gerard Malynes, *Consuetudo, vel, Lex Mercatoria; or, the Ancient Law-Merchant*, vol. 1, 3rd edn (London, 1685/6), p. 107. Facsimile reprint by Professional Books Ltd, Abingdon, England.

[7] Richard Hayes, *An Estimate of Places for Life: shewing how many years purchase a place for life is worth* (W. Meadows, London, 1728) gives extensive financial information on the sale of places. The duties of the six Clerks of Chancery are outlined on p. 94. In general, the sale of offices, or places, was extensive not only in Great Britain but also in Europe. The offices held a fixed annual income and were sold by the King, the Pope for Vatican offices, etc., and until the offices were resold by a new incoming King, Pope, etc., were freely transferable by the incumbent to others.

[8] Harold E. Raynes, *A History of British Insurance*, 2nd edn (Pitman, 1964). This work is very informative on the early insurance scene and I have drawn extensively from it. Raynes mentions no less than 21 recorded minutes in the Privy Council on marine insurance matters between 1571 and 1577. Also, Professor John Baker of St Catherine's College, Cambridge, has kindly drawn attention to an early marine insurance law case where the Royal Exchange was mentioned (1571 CUL MS 2.9, f. 23r).

Lord Mayor of London and City merchants for arbitration. In order to add some transparency to insurance deals and to help detect fraud, the Office of Assurances was formed.

In February 1576, the Privy Council granted a Patent[9] to Richard Candler (or Candeler — there were also other ways of spelling this name) to set up and run the Office (or Chamber[10]) of Assurances in the Royal Exchange. Candler was a member of the Mercers' Company and the agent of Sir Thomas Gresham in London. He must have been aged about twenty when appointed by Thomas Gresham as his factor. Candler was related to the Gresham family through Susan, first daughter of William Chaundler or Candeler of Walsingham, Norfolk.[11] Susan was first cousin to Sir Richard Gresham and Sir John Gresham, who were uncles of Sir Thomas Gresham. There is a magnificent tomb of Richard Candeler (d. 1602), and his wife in Tottenham Church, together with his daughter, Ann, and her husband, Sir Ferdinando Heybourne. Heybourne was appointed jointly to the office of Registrar together with C. Candler in 1605.

The purpose of the Office of Assurances was to make and to register all insurances of any kind. Richard Candler was the first registrar. Underwriters were then able to see the terms on which policies were effected and check that there was no insurance for excessive sums (often the first sign of an attempted fraud). Assurers (underwriters) were compared to orphans because they could endure much wrong but not commit any. An incidental effect of policies being drawn up mainly in one office was that a standard form of policy document evolved, part of which lasted for a *very* long time.[12]

Independent commissioners were appointed to determine fees payable to the registrar and, *inter alia*, to resolve disputes. The commissioners also acted as arbitrators in cases of dispute and were a court of inquiry, too. One of the first commissioners was Dr Lewis, a judge of the Admiralty Court. The insurers were subject to judgments of commissioners and had to perform their promises or be committed to prison for a limited time or until they had satisfied the judgment.

The setting up of the Office of Assurances in 1576 was not without some controversy. Prior to the formation of this office, policies were drawn up by brokers and notaries. The office took away some of their work. In addition, Richard Candler was not satisfied with the amount of the fees drawn up by the commissioners under whose control he operated. The fees paid in Antwerp were higher. Although the registration of assurances became compulsory, it appears that in practice not all policies were registered and the commissioners were turning a blind eye to any problem. In their scale of fees, they referred to Candler having 12*d.* for 'making every policy that shall be brought to him to be made and that it shall be lawful for the said Richard Candler to make intimations as other notaries may and not otherwise'. Sir Francis Walsingham (Secretary of State) commented that the Office of Assurances had been set up so that certain deceits could be redressed and as long as others could make policies this would not happen.

Despite Richard Candler's dissatisfaction with the scale of fees, it appears that the office was adequately remunerated, as there was no shortage of applicants each time it fell vacant, despite there being a charge for rent of £400 or £450 per annum. In addition to fees, the registrar or his assistant could claim commission for placing assurances where no insurance broker was employed. The earliest surviving insurance broker's account is for a period from 16 October 1654 to 19 December 1655.[13]

The Privy Council required the Office of Assurances to set down the basis on which the office was to be run. In July 1576 they reminded the Lord Mayor that 'the books and orders of assurances which his

[9] H. E. Raynes, op. cit.
[10] Chambers of Insurance were established very early in a number of European cities. Cornelius Walford, *The Insurance Cyclopaedia* (1871), vol. I, p. 485, mentions the twelfth century as the start, although the earliest date ascertainable is 1310 for the Chamber of Bruges.
[11] John Chandler, 'Richard Chandeler of Tottenham', article from the *Home Counties Magazine*, vol. III (1900), pp. 301–04.
[12] H. E. Raynes, op. cit., comments that Lloyd's marine policies at the time he was writing contained the words 'and it is agreed by us the insurers that this policy or writing of assurance shall be of as much force and effect as the surest writing or policy of assurance heretofore made in Lombard Street or in the Royal Exchange or elsewhere in London'.

[13] Quoted by Raynes as being in the Rawlinson MS, A 21, p. 26, Bodleian.

Lordship hath so often been written unto for may be finished with expedition . . .'. In January 1577 two Aldermen had made substantial headway in completing the work. 'A Booke of Orders of Assurances within the Royall Exchange London'[14] consists of some 126 articles. Lewin[15] has given brief notes on the content of each of the 126 articles and discussed the life assurance content. The greater part of the manuscript is devoted to marine insurance, articles 113–19 only being specific to life assurance. These seven articles cover in detail, with reasons, the following points:

(113)   Policies can only be issued for a period up to a year.

(114)   Each policy issued to a person on his own life must have some justification, for example, he was entitled to a lump sum (pension, rent, annuity or money owing) which was lost if he died before a certain day. This has to be proved at death otherwise the policy is void. Also the life assured had to be 'in health' at the time the policy was effected or, at least, survive 40 days.

(115)   An assurance taken out on the life of another person also has to be justified.

(116)   Details the declarations to be made if the assurances are on the lives of people due to make voyages or long journeys. This is stated to be the most common reason for effecting a policy.

(117)   Procedures to be followed to make a claim.

(118)   The maximum sum assured on any life is £1,000. Also, insurances on the life of another are restricted so that the underwriters bear only 80 per cent of the loss occasioned by the death.

(119)   If the assured is missing three years after the expiry of the policy, the assurer shall pay.

There is evidence that the orders were not always followed. Mr Kiddermaster's policy referred to above was in excess of the maximum amount permitted and another policyholder is recorded as having effected a two-year policy.

It is clear from these orders that life policies were regarded as policies providing indemnity for losses only, so that it was not possible for the owner of the policy to make a profit from it. This was the position for other insurances, too, and remains the situation for policies which are not life assurance today. Only after the Office of Assurances ceased functioning were life assurance gambling policies in vogue and that led to the Life Insurance Act 1774 which prohibited any life policy unless an insurable interest could be shown. By legal interpretation, a person since then has an unlimited insurable interest in his own life. However, these later developments are outside the scope and time-frame of this chapter.

THE FIRST RECORDED BRITISH LIFE ASSURANCE POLICY

On 18 June 1583 Richard Martin, a citizen and Alderman of London, effected a life policy on the life of William Gibbons, a salter of London. Payment was to be made 'if it hapen (as God defend) the said William Gibbons to dye or decase out of this p'sent world by any wayes or meanes whatsoevere', so that death by duelling and suicide were amongst the risks covered. The price was £8 per £100 of sum assured and the policy term was twelve months. The cost of the policy looks high when judged against policies issued about forty years later. However, we do not know the age of William Gibbons and, although the relationship between death rates and age had not been established at this time, it is still conceivable that this was at least suspected and taken into account by individual underwriters. A few months earlier, on 24 February 1583, another twelve months' policy had been granted on the life of William Gibbons and the price had, perhaps, taken into account both sums which would be paid on death before the first twelve months had expired. Two of the sixteen underwriters were at risk on both policies.

The policy also recited that

It is to be vnderstanded that this p'sent writing is and shall bee asmuch force, strength and effect, as the best hath bene eu' heretofore vsed to be made upon the life of any pson in Lumbard Street, or nowe within the Roill Exchange in London. yeven in the office of assurance within the Royall Exchange aforesaid the xviijth day of June 1583.

[14] BL Harleian MS 5103, ff. 154–85. This MS is clearly Elizabethan as there are references to 'the Queen's Majesty', but is undated.
[15] C. G. Lewin, in *FIASCO, The Magazine of the Staple Inn Actuarial Society*, April 1988, and *The Actuary*, March and November 1991 issues.

This statement is part of the evidence that policies on lives were common in Lombard Street before the Royal Exchange was built and afterwards moved to the Royal Exchange.

The reasons for effecting this and the earlier policy are not given. As the policy was issued not to William Gibbons, but another party, it seems likely that it was part of a commercial transaction which would have been frustrated on William Gibbons's death. Marine policies issued at this time were of a similar character. One very well known and respected German insurance historian, the late Heinrich Braun, suggested that the policy was a gambling policy (Wettvertrag),[16] but there is no evidence whatsoever to support this as far as the writer of this chapter can determine.

Also notable is that there is no recitation of the state of health of Gibbons. However, the policy ends with the exhortation 'God send the said William Gibbons helth and long lief', so we can presume that his health was known to be good. One of the health hazards of this time was the plague, which struck in great force in some years and was quiescent or subject to minor outbreaks in other years. In 1562, Bills of Mortality, that is lists of deaths giving plague deaths separately, were published weekly in manuscript form. Later, Bills of Mortality were published by the Fraternity of St Nicholas (Parish Clerks) whenever the plague was rife and it seems that records were kept even in years when there was no publication.[17] 1583, the year when William Gibbons's life was insured, had an excessively hot and dry summer and various dysenteries (mainly bloody fluxes) were common. This year is not recorded as a year in which a major plague epidemic occurred. In major plague years, we can speculate that underwriters would not be willing to write life policies on lives resident in London.

William Gibbons (or Gybbons — the policy used both forms of spelling) died on 29 May 1584 and the sixteen underwriters refused to pay the sum assured of £383 6s. 8d. The grounds for the refusal were that twelve months, counting a month as 28 days, had already expired.

The refusal to pay was disputed and led to a case in the Court of Admiralty. The life policy wording[18] is found in the report of this court case. The case was not immediately easy to decide, as the normal law of the realm for transactions between man and man being not merchants was to count a month as 28 days. The underwriters were not acting as merchants when they accepted the case. Richard Martin swore that the contract meant that the assurance was for a whole year. Merchants and foreigners swore that the custom in Lombard Street and the Royal Exchange was that months were accounted according to the calendar and not as 28 days to the month. Further, Richard Candler, who had drawn up and penned the contract, and others, also swore the true meaning of twelve months was a whole year. John Stokes and Henry Clitheroe, who were underwriters on the February 1583 policy as well as the policy under dispute, had issued a receipt on 6 March 1583 which made it clear that in the earlier policy twelve months meant a full calendar year. Judgment was given against the underwriters and they had to pay before the feast of the Annunciation of the Virgin Mary next ensuing.[19]

Another life policy issued in the Royal Exchange in May 1596 is given by West.[20] The policy paid its sum assured on death within five months and the rate of premium was 5 per cent for this period. The life assured was TB, 'Which TB is now in health and well and meaneth not to travel out of England'. In the seventeenth century life insurers took into account whether the persons being assured were young or old, sober in their diet and behaviour, much travelled abroad or staying at home, subject to sickness and the like.[21] In the sixteenth century the practices were similar, as the Book of Orders mentioned above makes clear.

[16] Heinrich Braun, *Geschichte der Lebensversicherung und der Lebensversicherungstechnik* (Carl Koch, Nuremberg, 1925), p. 61.
[17] Dr William Ogle, 'An Inquiry into the Trustworthiness of the Old Bills of Mortality', *Journal of the Royal Statistical Society*, vol. LV (1892).
[18] J. Lefort, *Traité Théoretique et Pratique du Contrat d'Assurance sur la Vie* (Paris, Thorin & Fils, 1894), vol. 1, gives on pp. 35–36 some Latin text from Genoese records (Archiv. not. de Gènes) of life contracts effected in the years 1427–28.
[19] BL Lansdowne MS no. 170, f. 123.
[20] William West, *Symboleography* (1598), section 664.
[21] Gerard Malynes, op. cit., p. 247.

LATER DEVELOPMENTS AND THE END OF THE OFFICE OF ASSURANCES

One of the common contracts containing an element of insurance was that of *bottomry* and there was much law on the subject. The first use of the word was in 1593, but the practice is very much older. The word derived from the Dutch word for the bottom of a ship. The financial background in the period we are considering lies in the legal prohibition of taking interest over and above amounts prescribed by law. At this time, the word usury signified the taking of interest on a loan and did not have the sense of excessive interest which it has now. From 31 January 1545, the maximum interest rate permitted was 10 per cent per annum. This was reduced to 8 per cent per annum from 24 June 1625, 6 per cent per annum from 29 September 1660 and 5 per cent per annum from 29 September 1714.[22]

Some ingenuity was exercised on finding a way to exceed the legal rates of interest and this could be achieved by combining an element of risk with a financial transaction such as involving the hazards of human life. Malynes[23] gives a number of examples. Bottomry consisted of making a loan at a high rate of interest to finance a ship's voyage and the purchase of the cargo. This was one of the forms of marine insurance registered in the Royal Exchange. With a normal loan, the lender can expect his money back in all circumstances. With bottomry, the loan is repaid *only* if the ship successfully completes its voyage. Effectively, the lender was placing his money on the bottom of the ship and the terms were such that he took a share of the profits.

Bottomry was not popular with sea captains and was often taken only in times of necessity. The risks of failure for the lender were real enough and, if a voyage were successful, the lender would enjoy 30 per cent or more on his money. The lender was sometimes subject to fraud, when the borrower took more loans on bottomry than his ship and cargo were worth and the ship then was 'lost' at sea.

In 1601, the City merchants were not satisfied with the use of the Office of Assurances, particularly as

some persons would not 'conform themselves to the order of the Commissioners'. These persons were using Her Majesty's Courts to settle disputes rather than using the commissioners. This led to much expense and delays. A petition to the Privy Council was quickly followed by an act, 43 Eliz. cap. XII, part of the preamble of which is often quoted since it gives a good description of the principles of insurance:

And whereas it hath been Time out of Mind an Usage amongst Merchants both of this Realm and of foreign Nations, when they make any great Adventure (especially into remote Parts) to give some Consideration of Money to other Persons (which commonly are in no small Number) to have from them assurance made of their Goods, Merchandizes, Ships and things adventured, or some Part thereof, at such Rates and in such Sort as the Parties Assurers and the Parties assured can agree; which Course of dealing is commonly termed a Policy of assurance; by means of which Policies of Assurance it cometh to pass, upon the Loss or perishing of any Ship there followeth not the undoing of any Man, but the Loss lighteth rather easily upon many than heavily upon few, and rather upon them that adventure not than those that so adventure, whereby all Merchants, especially of the younger Sort, are allured to venture more willingly and more freely.

The act set up a new commission, with increased powers, which effectively made it a Court of Law, to determine disputes. The new commissioners, to be renewed yearly at the least, were the Judge of the Admiralty, the Recorder of London, two Doctors of Civil Law, two common lawyers, and eight discreet merchants, any five of which acting together had full powers. However, this new act had weaknesses. It only applied to policies entered within the Office of Assurances. The act 'did not exclude others from making Insurances in whose Policies was inserted, that they should be as of as much force as those heretofore made in Lombard-Street, at the Royal Exchange, or any where else'.[24]

The commissioners were not paid for their trouble and it was alleged that they were tempted to neglect their duties. They could not summon witnesses from abroad and their only sanction was imprisonment without bail. Their decrees did not allow the commissioners to make orders affecting the property of the

[22] Information on interest rates from John Smart, *Tables of Interest, Discount and Annuities* (London, 1726).
[23] Op. cit., pp. 243–44 for what is and is not legal. Also information on bottomry, pp. 122–23.

[24] Wyndham Beawes, *Lex Mercatoria Rediviva: or, the Merchant's Directory* (John Moore, London, 1752), p. 262, and sold by Edmund Comyns at the South Gate of the Royal Exchange.

underwriters. For these reasons, Beawes says that the continuance of the act was not of long duration. He quotes the office as being 'kept on the West Side of the Royal-Exchange'. This is possibly the only information we have on its location. The records of the Mercers' Company and the City of London give no information.

There seems to have been another act[25] in the reign of Charles I in 1627 'for the sole making and registering of all manner of assurances, intimations, and renunciations, made upon any ship or ships, goods or merchandise, in the Royal Exchange, or other places within the City of London'.

A later act of 1662, 14 Car II, c. 23, revived the commission. It reduced the quorum from five to three and strengthened the commissioners by giving powers to examine witnesses beyond the seas and to proceed to execution against a party's goods as well as his person. However, recovery of losses on policies not entered at the Office of Assurances was easy at common law. Further, the commissioners practised some partiality and an appeal against their determination was granted at the Court of Chancery. As a result, the business of this court soon diminished and the granting of commissions was discontinued.[26]

The Great Fire of London destroyed much of the City of London and its records. The Revd Samuel Rolle, describing the fire at the Royal Exchange says, 'Though there was in that place an insurance-office, which undertook for those ships and goods that were hazarded at sea, either by boisterous winds or dangerous enemies, yet it could not secure itself, when sin, like Sampson, took hold of the pillars of it, and went about to pull it down'.

Despite the problems of the Court allied with the Office of Assurances, the Office of Assurances was accommodated once more in the Royal Exchange after the Great Fire of London in 1666. Molloy[27] has a chapter on Policies of Assurance in which he notes that private assurances are ones where the assured keeps it secret and the contracts are never entered in the Office of Assurances. Public Assurances are entered and the information about them is public knowledge. He continues by saying at common law both have the same validity 'as in reference to obtain satisfaction from the Ensurer if loss or damage should happen to the adventure'. Only policies entered in the Office of Assurances can be sued upon or determined there.

It is not clear precisely when the Office of Assurances fell into complete disuse. The last appointment of Registrar was granted by Charles II to Sir Allen Broderick for his own life and the life of William Broderick and thirty years after. In Leybourne's *Panarithmologia* of 1693, there is a description of the process of insuring goods which includes the words 'This policy of ensurance ought to be copied in the Office of Ensurance in a book kept there for that purpose, and for which you pay a certain sum unto the clerk or clerks sitting at the time'. It is also apparent from Leybourne that the registrar, or his clerk, could act as a broker. This was referred to in a proclamation by James II.[28] There is no subsequent contemporary reference to the Office of Assurances.

We can, with a knowledge of human nature, make an educated guess at what happened. The Office of Assurance was probably performing a useful function without its associated court, since the details of registered policies provided one means of detecting the signs of possible frauds. Further, the Office of Assurances in the Royal Exchange must have been a place where information over the whereabouts of ships and the state of risks was made available as it became known.

Over the years, the registrar probably became more interested in making money out of his post and crossed the thin line between receiving commission when there was no broker involved in setting up an insurance contract and insurance broking. Brokers and their policyholders would then regard the registrar as a competitor and would not wish to register policies as this would be giving confidential information to a business competitor. Coffee houses kept longer hours than the Royal Exchange and became a useful place for brokers to exchange information. Also, common law was just as good, if not better, for

25 Effingham Wilson, *Wilson's Description of the New Royal Exchange* (1844), p. 57.
26 Wyndham Beawes, op. cit.
27 Charles Molloy, *De Jure Maritimo Et Navali: or, a Treatise of Affairs Maritimo and of Commerce, in three Books*, 3rd edn (1682), pp. 166–77.

28 Tudor and Royal Proclamations, Vol. III, 13 April 1686.

settling insurance contract disputes. The Office of Assurances had no particular advantages left and became completely defunct.

FIRE INSURANCE

The development of fire insurance in England commenced with a scheme devised by Nicholas Barbon, nicknamed Bare Bones, in 1680. The Fire Office was located at the back of the Royal Exchange and was a proprietary, or partnership, venture with a trust fund vested in trustees as security for payment of claims. References to its operations are few. However, on Sunday, 19 November 1682 a careless, idle fellow caused a fire in Cinamon-Lane, Wapping. A strong south-west wind defeated strenuous efforts to contain the fire and it consumed several hundred houses. It was not extinguished until Monday night.

The fire policies on houses had a clause permitting the underwriters to defer paying the claims for a time, perhaps inserted to allow the underwriters time to raise the cash required. Nevertheless, the underwriters of the Fire Office were willing to pay the Wapping claims promptly at a discount. They placed an advertisement in the *London Gazette*,[29]

These are to give notice to those Persons whose Houses were burnt down or demolished in the late Fire in Wapping, which were Insured at the Office on the Backside of the Royal Exchange, That although there is some time allowed by their policy for the Payment of the Money, yet if they have occasion for their Money in the interim, they may receive it at the Office upon discount of the Interest for the time it shall be paid before it is due.

Prompt payment of claims is an important feature of insurance today as well as in the past.

FINAL DEVELOPMENTS UP TO 1720

There are other references to offices where insurance is transacted after the Great Fire of London in 1666, but these are brokers' offices. Boyer[30] refers to these and differentiates between private insurers and insurance made with a company acting under a charter granted for Mines Royal and Battery Works. Since insuring with this company became possible, very few policies were made by private individuals. He goes on to say that only merchants make insurances and they risk their fortunes with private insurers. Some 150[31] private insurers were operating, but the major part of these were rarely writing insurance policies. He continues, 'A diffidence must ever attend making insurances with private people; especially, when I have occasion to make an insurance, I must go to their office, where an Office-Keeper only attends, who can't certainly inform me who shall subscribe to my policy, but I must leave directions with him to procure me one for such a sum'. This is clearly not the old Office of Assurances still operating, as the only function described is that of an insurance broker.

The dissatisfaction with private underwriters led to the formation of the two charter companies during the South Sea Bubble period. Lord Onslow's bubble was the Royal Exchange Assurance and Lord Chetwynd's bubble was the London Assurance. The very first parliamentary report on insurances[32] details the controversy surrounding the events leading up the formation of both. The history of these two companies after their formation is very well documented.[33]

There are additional references to insurance office-keepers in the Royal Exchange in the Special Report[34] of 1720 but these, too, are clearly insurance brokers' offices.

---

[29] Issue no. 1775 covering the news from Monday, 20 November to Thursday, 23 November 1682. This issue also contains a report of the fire.

[30] A. Boyer, *The Political State of Great Britain*, vol. XIX (London, 1720), pp. 534–38.

[31] Case Billingsley said that 486 merchants had effected insurances with the Mines Royal company from 8 March then last (i.e. 1718) — reported in a communication by Nicholas Lechmere, the Attorney General, to the King dated 3 March 1720, given on p. 43 of 'The Special Report from the Committee appointed to Inquire into, and Examine the several Subscriptions for Fisheries, Insurances, Annuities for Lives &c., Jacob Tonson &c.' (1720). On the same page, Mr Joseph Paice reported that 33 private underwriters had, to his knowledge, failed and lost him and his principals large sums of money.

[32] Ibid.

[33] See e.g. Barry Supple, *The Royal Exchange Assurance* (Cambridge University Press, 1970).

[34] E.g. pp. 21, 25, 29, 30 (with an unambiguous description), 33, 40 and 41. There is also a reference on p. 48 by Nicholas Lechmere (the Attorney General) to two acts of Parliament still being in force, viz. 43 Eliz. C. 12. and 14 Car. 3. C 23., but the language used and the complete absence of any submission of evidence by, or reference to, the Office of Assurances is plain evidence that it no longer existed.

Cornelius Walford[35] refers to the *London Gazette* for 2 to 6 February 1720: 'Public Assurance Office on the Royal Exchange, Feb. 6 1719 [old style[36]]: Whereas information has been given that there have been illegal and fraudulent practices committed to the prejudice of this Office, Notice is hereby given to all persons who can make any such discoveries, that they shall meet with suitable encouragement from the

Office.' Walford says underwriters assembled there for the purpose of undertaking any manner of insurance risk which offered but there is no mention of policies being registered or of the existence of a court.

Walford believed that the constitution of the Office of Assurance was defective in that it appeared to have no control over the underwriters who frequented it and undertook risks apparently under the shadow of its authority. Lloyd's instituted a system of membership in the course of time, and so obtained at least some control over the action of its members.

An anonymous article in the *Baltimore Underwriter* of 16 October 1873, titled 'Historical Notes and Memoranda. A Court of Insurance', says that the Court of Insurance has long since been discontinued, although the statutes concerning it of Elizabeth and Charles II are still in force. Perhaps they are still.

[35] Cornelius Walford, *The Insurance Cyclopaedia*, vol. 1 (C. & E. Layton, London, 1871), pp. 485–87. This publication did not get past vol. 6, finishing alphabetically at 'Her'. Walford's incomplete MS notes for the remainder are deposited in the library of the Chartered Insurance Institute in London. The article on 'Politics of Assurance, Court of' has a small amount of additional information. Walford's extensive library of insurance texts was acquired by the Equitable Life Assurance Society of the United States, New York, but unfortunately was destroyed by fire, except for a few minor items, in 1912.

[36] Unless otherwise indicated all dates are quoted on the new style (Gregorian) calendar.

CHAPTER XI

The Organisation of the Exchange

By ANN SAUNDERS

ONCE LADY GRESHAM was dead, the City Corporation and the Mercers' Company were at last able to lay hands on their inheritance. Power of Attorney was acquired that Gresham's Will might be performed and that the shops in the Exchange might be let out on twelve-year leases.[1] A committee was set up to manage the Exchange and the College; the first meeting, in Gresham House, was held on 17 March 1597; all the appointed members were there.[2]

The City was represented by three Aldermen, Stephen Soame, Nicholas Mosseley and Benedict Barneham, supported by Thomas Wylford, the Chamberlain of London, and by Thomas Campbell, ironmonger, Thomas Bramley, haberdasher, Andrew Palmer, goldsmith, and William Cobb, painter-stainer. For the Mercers' side, there were Aldermen Thomas Bennett and Henry Rowe, Baudwyn Denham the master warden, the three other wardens William Quarles, Baptist Hickes and David Holliland, and two liverymen, Thomas Cordell and Edmond Hogan, who had once been Gresham's factor in Antwerp. The choice of these men demonstrates that the City and Company were in no doubt about the importance of the Gresham legacy. Soame, Moseley, Campbell, Bennett and Rowe were all knighted, while Baptist Hickes was made a baronet in 1620 and then Viscount Campden in 1628. The first four all served as Lord Mayor, Soame in 1598–99 and Moseley in the following year, so from almost the very start of the City and Company takeover of the Exchange, London's chief citizen was on the Committee. Soame, Barnham and Hickes were all, at various times, Members of Parliament; the first two lived long enough for each to become the Father of the City, while Campbell, Bennett, Rowe, Quarles and Cordell all become Masters of their respective

Companies at least once. They brought useful personal connections, too — Rowe was a grandson of Sir John Gresham, Sir Thomas's elder brother, and one of Barneham's daughters married Francis Bacon. Altogether, they made up a pretty formidable team. Later, dignitaries such as Sir Lionel Cranfield, Sir William Craven and Sir Hugh Myddleton were to join them.[3]

From the beginning, minutes were kept which survive in the volumes known as the Gresham Repertories, running from 1597 to the present day. They are a tantalising record, at first examination almost overwhelmingly complete, crammed with names and dates and facts and leases, but time and again the end of a particular episode is omitted and the student realises that the matter must have been settled out of court, by voices now silent and lost forever. Nevertheless, a careful examination enables us to build up a reasonably clear picture of England's first shopping mall, of the men and women who peopled it, and of the Committee which worked steadily, carefully, with patient thoroughness, at its administration.[4]

At the first meeting on 17 March 1597, the subjects discussed were the issuing of leases to the tenants of the shops — not an easy matter for, as we have noticed, in a number of cases Lady Gresham, just before her death, had granted new leases at very low rents on the payment of substantial fines which, we may assume, had remained with her. It was two years before the Committee succeeded in properly asserting its authority, but on 16 December 1597 the rents were laid down as £7 for a shop on the north side, £8

---

[1] CLRO, Journal 24, ff. 173, 197.
[2] MC, GR, I, p. 1.

[3] A. A. Beaven, *The Aldermen of the City of London* (1908), is particularly useful.
[4] All subsequent details, unless otherwise ascribed, are taken from MC, GR, vols. I and II. I am most grateful to the Deputy Archivist, Ursula Carlyle, for her support and patience over six years of research.

for those on the east and west, and £10 (later reduced to £9) for the favoured side, the south, lying along Cornhill. No man was to be allowed to hold more than two shops — though many schemed and strove to do so; before long, leases for 21 years were the rule.

At their second meeting, on 31 March 1597, the Committee allocated rooms in Gresham House to the professors whom they were about to appoint, and discussed, as they were to do with regularity, what repairs were needed to Gresham House and to the Royal Exchange. A month later, on 20 May, they agreed on a weekly meeting, to be held each Wednesday. This proved too onerous, but in the first year there were 21 meetings, in the second 12, in the third 16, in the fourth 13, and in 1601, the fifth year, there were 12. Thereafter a quarterly meeting became the pattern, with perhaps extra meetings close together in any one month if there were much business to settle, though in 1610–13 the gaps were much longer, one meeting only being held in each year. The members attended conscientiously — it was rare for there not to be a quorum — and we can feel confident that, even though the duties might sometimes be vexing, yet it was accounted an honour to serve on the Committee of the Exchange and men of importance were generous with their time and attention.

Through the summer of 1597, apart from the issuing and settling of leases, there were two matters which aroused particular concern — the ejection of William Reade from what had been his mother's and stepfather's house, and the selection of lecturers for Gresham College. On 30 July, Reade was still firmly lodged in various galleries and rooms, refusing to remove his furniture and belongings and so vacate them for the use of the professors.[5] On 3 August, orders were given that the rooms should be broken into if necessary; the threat of force was presumably sufficient to persuade Reade to clear his goods but — perhaps understandably — he cherished his resentment and brought a suit against the City later. Letters were written to Oxford and to Cambridge, asking for guidance in the selection of lecturers; Oxford responded helpfully with suggestions but Cambridge, angered perhaps that one who had studied at Gronville and Caius College for however short a time

should leave his largess to another foundation, wrote to Lord Burghley, their Chancellor, asking for his instructions lest the College 'be greatly prejudiciall to our University'.[6]

Throughout the first two years the Board struggled with those tenants who had paid heavily to renew their leases at low rents with Lady Gresham. Now the Committee were demanding substantially higher rents. The tenants appealed to Lord Egerton, the Lord Keeper, and then to members of the Privy Council, Sir John Fortescue, the Chancellor of the Exchequer and second cousin to the Queen herself, and Sir William Knollys, later the Earl of Banbury but at this time Comptroller of the royal household. They continued to mediate to try to effect a settlement but the course of the negotiations was difficult and contentious.

As a result, during the summer of 1598 the Committee drew up accounts to make clear their true position and to establish what return there might be on their investment in providing the land for the Exchange.[7] On 2 May, they calculated that the 120 shops around the Pawn, as the upper storeys were called, were bringing in an income of £819 10s. which, with the rental from the vaults and from adjacent buildings, produced a total of £998 6s. 8d. But against this had to be set the 'payments yeerly appointed by the Wills' — £50 apiece to each of the seven lecturers, 20 nobles to each of the eight almsmen, £10 a year to the inmates of each of the ten prisons and hospitals in and around the City, and £100 a year to the Mercers' Company for feasting — amounting to £603 6s. 8d. in all. And there were other charges besides, which Sir Thomas had forgotten or could not have foreseen — quit rents to the Queen for 'Certain Tenements wheer the Exchange standeth', the tithes due on that building and on Gresham House, charges for maintaining a clock and for providing candles in winter, wages and payments to the custodians of both the Exchange and College, to the clerk, to the scavengers and to the rent-collectors, as well as repairs to the buildings and such largess as £12 a year to the City Waites for their music and £10 every other year to provide the eight

[5] MC, GR, I, pp. 14, 16.

[6] Ward, *Lives*, p. 38. Burghley was Chancellor of Cambridge.
[7] MC, GR, I, pp. 46–47, 76–78.

almsmen with a new gown apiece, and with a pewter badge adorned with a Gresham grasshopper, no example of which is known to survive.[8]

By this time, the near £1,000 worth of income was heavily reduced — 'thear remaynith 121^li the year' — and worse was to come. There would be charges in acquiring the licence in mortmain, so that the City and Company could hold the Exchange in perpetuity — Sir Henry Montague, who acted for them, had to be 'gratified' with £55 'for the great paynes he hath taken' — and a lawsuit with John Jacques over buildings on the Exchange site sold by his father had cost £700. Altogether, the Gresham legacy was beginning to look like a liability rather than an asset.

Gloomy accounts were again cast towards the end of July, when the Committee totalled up what they had already paid out since building had begun in 1566.[9] There were annuities to the Dean and Chapter of Canterbury (£45), to Robert Dunkyn, merchant taylor (£20), to Elizabeth Hill (£1 11s.), to the Jacques orphans (who were now suing them) and to Helen Barton, later the wife of Stephen Rumford (£3 6s. 8d.), with occasional payments to James Balson, Robert Bingham and Thomas Palson besides. The suit brought by John and Martin Jacques had cost a further £188 1s. 4d. in legal expenses, and £100 19s. 11½d. had had to be laid out in building repairs. In 1593, there had been £1 in payment to the celebrated Surveyor Ralph Treswell to make a plan, now lost, of the Exchange, and in 1598 it had cost £2 in 'charges in defence of a sute presented against Mr Chamberlain & others for a supposed Riote made in Gresham House'; we may guess that William Reade was the instigator of the trouble. All in all, the Corporation and the Mercers calculated they were £1,765 10s. 4d. out of pocket; they must have felt it was high time that the Royal Exchange began to provide at least some income, and preferably some profit for them.

That profit was going to come, if at all, from the shops around the upper storeys of the Exchange, but before we begin to examine the shops and their tenants, let us look at the use of the building as a whole. From the first, it had a dual function. The Exchange provided, free of charge, a public meeting place where merchants could gather to transact business, but the walls of the courtyard housed two tiers of shops, the (main) Pawn and the Upper Pawn; these, let out for rent, were intended to produce a good income, first for the Greshams and then for the City and the Mercers.

Wenceslas Hollar's engraving of 1644 (Fig. 17) gives a lively impression of how the courtyard must have looked at trading times. He shows it thronged with several hundred people, thus confirming Platter's estimate in 1599 of the crowds gathered there. In the left foreground we can see two Dutch merchants in fur hats and padded breeches with a woman selling news-sheets or ballads nearby, while two Turks can just be distinguished in the front rank of the central crowd. The artist catches the life, the bustle, the excitement of the scene. This was the place where deals were to be done, fortunes made or lost, and money raised with which to send out 'tall ships of the City of London' on the perilous voyages which Richard Hakluyt described so well.

Though the open courtyard provided the meeting place for merchants to exchange news and to arrange deals with each other, they were not at liberty to do so at any time of the day, a bell being rung at eleven o'clock in the morning and at five o'clock in the afternoon in winter or six o'clock in summer, so that trading might continue for an hour thereafter. On 17 August 1630, Common Council passed a regulation that trading must be restricted to a bare hour on each occasion since meetings were going on for too long and 'merchants are hindered from other business'. The bell was to be rung again at noon, for a full quarter of an hour, to make it quite obvious that trading must cease; presumably the incessant ringing would have hindered conversation. 'If any offer or presume to tarry', he was to be fined sixpence, half to go to the Keepers of the Exchange and half to the parish poor; the regulations were re-enacted at intervals through the seventeenth century, the fine rising with inflation to 5s. for an ordinary trader but 50s. for brokers — they must have been regarded as excessively wealthy.[10]

---

[8] MC, GR, I, p. 23. The City Waites were soon debarred from practising in Gresham House since they disturbed the Professors.

[9] MC, GR., I, pp. 76–78.

[10] CLRO, Journal 35, f. 228; 47, ff. 33, 74, 94.

FIG. 17.   Interior of the Royal Exchange by Wenceslas Hollar, 1644.
Guardian Royal Exchange collection

The courtyard itself, with its Turkey stone paving, was to be swept regularly. On 20 April 1598, it was found that Jack Cade

hath and doth neglect his office and dutie in keepinge clean off the Roial Exchange appoynting the same to A deputie. [He] supporteth the place to lie foule and children do play there contynually to the great disturbance of merchants and others resorting thither.

Thomas Crosier was appointed to take over his place at £8 a year. A watchman was chosen in October 1599 and, in the summer of 1601, it was decreed that the Exchange Keepers should be provided with long staves 'tipped with silver and the Arms of the Citty and Company of Mercers engraved thereon'.

It was frequently a problem to keep good order in the courtyard. On 23 January 1639, the Committee received

A complaint in writing being presented to this Court of divers abuses daily committed in the Roiall Exchange by idle boyes, beggars, cheaters and other people of base quality, the Keepers were nowe called in, and warning given them from the Board to be more diligent in theire places for the p~venting of the like abuses for the future.[11]

The two Almsmen, Robert Thompson and Bernard Newdigate, elected at this meeting assured the Committee that they would reinforce the Keeper's efforts to preserve order.

[11] MC, GR, i, p. 70.

One of the Committee's first decisions was to convert 'the vaults under the fowre walkinge places of the Roiall Exchange' from shops to storage purposes. It is clear from Grenade's comments that this was the only purpose for which they were fit.

We can now look at the shops on the upper floor of the Exchange which was called the Pawn. The word derives from the Dutch *pandt* or the German *bahn*, a street or passageway, and must refer to the corridor which led round the rectangle, probably running along the inner wall so that the shops might benefit from whatever light came through the windows. The shops themselves were tiny, 5 feet wide, 7½ feet deep.[12] A man's outstretched arms would span the width, three paces would carry him from the entrance to the back wall and shelves. One wonders how Thomas Deane (see pp. 59–67) ever managed to cram such a multiplicity of fancy goods into so small a space.

No register of shop leases appears to have survived, giving details of the nature of the individual wares and callings of each. The only record is what is to be found in the Gresham Repertories. Every so often, the clerk enters a man's company against his name so, though we cannot be certain that a grocer was going to fill his shop with groceries or that a haberdasher would inevitably trade in ribbons and laces, yet it is a fair assumption that there was a relationship between a man's company and the nature of the goods sold in his shop. Counting up the trades mentioned in the first volume of the Repertories, we find 55 haberdashers, 25 mercers, 21 painter-stainers, 17 merchant taylors, 12 grocers, ten each of leathersellers, clothworkers and stationers, nine girdlers, seven drapers, six goldsmiths and six vintners, five each of barber-surgeons, scriveners, notaries and merchants pure and simple, three embroiderers, two milliners, two upholders — that is, upholsterers — and two smiths, and single listings for a bookseller, an ironmonger, a pewterer, an armourer, a joiner, a sadler, a salter, a barber and a doctor of physic. We can scarcely hope that this gives the full range but it does give a pretty fair idea of what one could have bought around the Pawn in the

first half of the sixteenth century, and literary references only reinforce our findings that small articles of clothing, fancy goods, pins and needles, textiles and leather goods were what were stocked on the shelves in those narrow little kiosks. The number of painter-stainers is particularly interesting; it bears out the belief that portraits of important personages and of one's own family were valued in the late sixteenth and early seventeenth centuries, and that they proliferated. The two milliners, Joseph Atkinson and Walter Gorstellow, considered themselves as particularly valuable tenants. They were anxious to have two adjacent shops and were represented at the meeting in January 1639 by Mr Ball, the Queen's Attorney, who declared that they were Her Majesty's own milliners and that it would show disrespect to Henrietta Maria 'if her Matie repair in p⁻son divers times to the shops' only to find them cramped and inconveniently separated. They got their two shops on the south side, at the accepted rent of £8, though they paid £100 fine for the privilege. One wonders what Mr Ball charged for his legal advice; with the civil war so soon to break out, it seems doubtful whether the milliners got good return for their money.[13]

Summer or winter, the Pawn must have been a gay place in which to saunter, very much as the Burlington Arcade is today. Since not everyone could read, each shop would have had its sign hanging out into the corridor. Since also there was such proliferation, such a multitude of haberdashers, mercers, merchant taylors and drapers, a goods-related sign would only have been confusing and all the signs recorded are of animals or birds.[14] We do not know whose idea this was — whether Sir Thomas remembered his country childhood, or whether Lady Gresham loved animals, or whether — more prosaically — the shopkeepers calculated that there were sufficient living creatures to give clear individuality to each of the 120 shops. But the result was that on the favoured south side we have Robert Stratford, haberdasher, holding two and a half shops, the Squirrel, and the Bull, with John Hill, described simply as a merchant, at the Catt and Mouse, Ralphe Conyeus, a 'gouldsmith', at the Blewe

[12] Ward, *Lives*, p. 12.

[13] MC, GR, II, p. 69.
[14] The bulk of the names are given in MC, GR, I, pp. 90–124.

Boare, and George Grave, a grocer, at the Broode Henne and the Buck. Sampson Clarke, a stationer, was at the Owle, his widow Hellen continuing to trade for a while after his death, while Edward Erby, grocer, held the Unicorne, and Thomas Parsons, merchant taylor, had the Camellion and the Cockatrice. On the west side, George Gosling, a goldsmith, sold his wares at the sign of the Wolf, Thomas Boxe, haberdasher, died and his widow Mabel took over at the Lapwinge, whilst Thomas Robinson managed the Cony and Phesant. Opposite, on the east, Lawrence Callwell, a blacksmith, had the White Bull and the Spredd Eagle, John Rixman, clothworker, passed the fferitt and Nitingale to Christopher Porter of the same company, and George Carleton, painter-stainer, moved to and fro from the Marten, which he took over from William Jarvis, clothworker, to the Pleasant Lyon and then to the Male Griffin, whilst Richard Crashaw, goldsmith, and namesake and godfather to the poet, remained steadily at the White Boare. On the north Christopher Potkin, painter-stainer, occupied the Marmoset and — Gresham's own crest — the Grasshopper. William ffiringe, barber-surgeon, was at the Black Raven and Green Dragon, Francis Lodg, haberdasher, at the Half Moone, another painter-stainer, Thomas Heron, at the Turkey Henne, with Anthony Clowes, a saddler, at the Lyonesse. Mary Coates, widow, took over her deceased husband's ironmongery at the Popinjay, while another widow, Lyria White, plied an unspecified trade at a stall, the Black Boare. This raises the question of whether there were free-standing stalls besides the well defined shops. It is difficult to be certain, though since we have both terms, shop and stall, applied to the same premises, it seems probable that they were synonymous.

Although, when the Exchange opened in 1569, the shops had been slow to let and Gresham had had to cajole tenants to adorn untenanted booths when the Queen came on her all-important visit in 1571 (see p. 41), yet by 1597 there seems to have been a waiting list for accommodation. Applicants were being told that they should have the next vacancy, implying that every outlet was already occupied. And possession — or non-possession — of a shop was something worth several years of lawsuit with the attendant fees. The most celebrated — or notorious — case was between

Paul Hill and Jeffrey Lodge.[15] It would seem that Lodge, a haberdasher, had been granted a lease of two shops by Lady Gresham for which he undoubtedly would have paid a heavy fine. The Committee did not recognise the lease and let one of the shops to Paul Hill, of the same company, who had previously been in arrears with his rent but who had amended his ways. Lodge was incensed; he appealed to the Lord Mayor and, when that did not produce immediate results, to Sir William Knollys, then Comptroller of the royal household and a Privy Councillor, to Sir John Fortescue the Chancellor of the Exchequer, to Sir Thomas Egerton the Lord Chancellor, to Thomas Buckhurst, soon to become Lord Treasurer and later Earl of Dorset, to Lord Nottingham, to Lord North, and to Robert Cecil, Secretary of State and later the 1st Earl of Salisbury. They responded. Letters went back and forth. Knollys and Fortescue demanded to know why the Exchange authorities had questioned the legality of Lodge's lease, on what grounds did they 'make doubt of that wch by credible report of an honest gentle woman and other good testimonie?' The City and Mercers humbly besought their lordships to be patient. They only wanted to do what was right, but the Gresham lease had never been set down in writing and they doubted its existence. Perhaps their Lordships would consider the matter on 'yor next comynge into the Cittie of London about the subsidie for her Matie'? In the end, their Lordships agreed that the whole affair should be left in the hands of the Committee. Lodge was at least partially pacified, and on 28 November 1600 it was agreed that he should have a 16-year lease of one shop at a rent of £6 a year without fine on entry, and that Hill should have a similar lease for which he should pay £20 as fine but £10 of it should be

given to Lodge of the free gifte and benevolence of the Cittie and Compaine of Mercers in respect of his Antiquitie in the exchaunge and great charge of children. To be reported to Sir Wm Knollys and Sir John Fortescue.

What is amazing about this incident is not that there should be a disagreement about a lease or that two shopkeepers should fall out, but that such appeals should be made to the highest dignitaries in the land,

[15] MC, GR, I, pp. 17, 28, 35, 73, 83, 89, 102, 105, 107, 115, 136–39, 145–51, 157.

and that they should respond immediately. Clearly, the smooth and honourable running of the Exchange was seen as a matter of national importance.

This was not the only occasion when the great and the good were invoked. In March 1600,[16] Sir William Knollys received a letter from Thomas Price, servant to the Countess of Warwick, who alleged that he had leased a vault from Lady Gresham and now had been thrown into prison for eight days along with his workmen and '200^{li} demanded and nowe it is worse by 300^{li}'. The Committee replied in indignation that the letter was 'altogether slanderous', that it was nothing to do with a Gresham lease but that Price had been committed to prison 'having very outrageously beaten a poore man in such sorte that he was in greate danger of his liefe'. Furthermore, 'the annoyance and smoake coming through the grates [of the vault] and the noise of . . . other idle companie frequenting the same vaults which they were used to victualling was so intolerable that . . . others could not abide the usual meeting place of the Roiall Exchange, whereupon they were inforced to remove him and other [?tiplers] having no leases or other interest herrein'. The Committee added that

the complainant undermined the the main walls [of the Exchange] in such sorte that no^t onlie by opinion of workmen one of the corners of the Exchange was thereby greatlie endangered to fall. But also he [set] some ovens so neare into the wainscott of the Exchange that the whole house was in danger to be fired thereby. Wherefore the Citie and the Mercers foreseeing such p[er]ils caused the same undermyninge to be made up firme as it was before the comp$^{l[ainant]}$ coming thither. Touchinge the mortgaging and sale of the lease of his house, they were not privie thereunto. But long after the Comp^l[ainant] had sould away the same, to one Ffrythe, they upon the said ffrythe's earnest request and surrender of his terme to come, and such other considerations as were agreed upon, did make him a lease for 21 yeares, so that if the comp^l[ainant] were damnified therebie, it was onlie through his owne follie and negligence. And therefore they praie y^r Lo^{shps} to forbear to credditt him such unjust clamor against them.

No more is heard of Thomas Price so presumably the authorities accepted the City's and Mercers' explanation.

It is worth noting that a number of the leaseholders were women, occupying shops in their own right.

The first to be recorded was Gertrude Watkin; the Minute for 12 April 1598 tells us that Christopher Watkin leased the shop in the north-eastern corner and that his daughter was to have a lease in her own right on the south side.[17] Sometimes we can almost hear their voices. The widowed Mrs de la Fountaine, summoned several times over to pay her arrears, arrived before the court on 3 December 1628 and 'after much speech with her son and another Agent was ordered to pay in the Lx^{li} she oweth tomorrow, and then she may be a suiter at the next court for a new lease'.[18] On 30 January 1652 Mrs Mary Shaw had fallen out with her landlady, Mrs Roberta Streete, another widow.

The Committee sent for the said Roberta Streete, who was appearing before them they did mediate with her that the said Mary Shawe might injoy that part of a shop she holdeth from Mrs Streete for some terme. Whereupon the said Mrs Streete did now promise to lett her the said under tenante to have a lease for that parte of a shop for — years at the rent of xviij per annum. And the said Mary Shawe did now pay xij^d to the said Roberta Streete.[19]

That must have been a stormy day for the Committee. No sooner had the two ladies, now reconciled, left the room than Richard Chase and George Touch, his sub-tenant in a half-shop on the west side, were called in.

This Court did mediate with the said Chase to lett the said George Touch to have some considerable terme in the same, but the said Chase did desire to be left to doo what he shall think fitt to of his owne account in that behalfe.[20]

By September of that year, Touch had got a whole shop of his own on the west side, paying £90 fine for it and donating 5s. to the Poor Box.

Sometimes romance flourished on the Exchange. Widows remarried; Mrs Alice Smith brought the lease of a shop, the Black Greyhound on the west side, as an asset to a second union with Frederick Powell, and in 1636, Mrs Katherine Allen similarly enriched her second husband, Richard Story, with 1½ shops.[21]

[16] MC, GR, I, pp. 112, 128, 130–32.

[17] MC, GR, I, p. 38.
[18] MC, GR, II, p. 13.
[19] MC, GR, II, p. 126.
[20] MC, GR, II, p. 126.
[21] MC, GR, II, pp. 18, 44.

As the seventeenth century went on, the number of women holding shops increased. Most of them were widows, like Philadelphia Uphill, but there were enterprising spinsters like Helen Youth, and two sisters, Mary and Dorothy Hill, who took over their deceased father's lease and seem to have made a success of it.

The Committee, though invariably businesslike, did realise how hard it could be for a widow with young children to survive at all. In April 1654, Mary Southwarke appealed to them

praying that she may pay but one fine of Alienation for a shop and a halfe . . . The Court did not think fitt to breake their ordinary rule in this behalfe, and therefore Directed that she shall pay for the severall fines of Alienation of the same, yet in regard she hath a charge of children, they ordered that she shall have all the said ffynes of Alienation, save one, returned unto her againe.[22]

The Court were also tender towards Widow Christian Tripp who had a house on Cornhill. On 25 February 1636 Samuel Lynaker came to the Committee and assured them that he would give her board and lodging for her life. 'He will admit the saide widow to his Table for her dyett gratis during his and her ioynt lives in such sort as he hath done of late'. Lynaker presumably wanted the house but by June of the following year had done nothing to confirm or to pay for his lease, and Jeremy East and Edward Stroud petitioned for it, East agreeing 'to give her dyett and viijli per annum'. In March and July 1639 they applied again, and presumably acquired the house, but the old lady was becoming frail and needing more nursing. In the January of 1645, the City awarded her 20s. relief and the Mercers gave 40s. more with an additional 40s. in May. In September 1646, she was being nursed by Elizabeth Sorocold who was given £4 towards her expenses, Mrs Tripp being 'an antient Tenant of this City and Compie'. She is not mentioned again so we may assume that she died soon after.[23]

We should notice that the Exchange Committee was regular in its payment of tithes to St Peter-le-Poer, to St Michael's Cornhill and to St Bartholomew the Great, and it was generous to the almsmen,

bestowing coal in winter, having a water supply laid on from the New River Company and being regular in the provision of new gowns. Unsuccessful applicants for places in the almshouses seldom went away empty-handed — the contents of the Poor Box would be divided between them or tips from general funds, ranging from 3s. 4d. (half a mark) to 10s., would be handed out. When, in cold February 1625, the inappositely named Richard Money, an unelected supplicant, somehow crept into an almshouse and was found there, bedridden, they let him stay till he died, and presumably provided other accommodation for the rightful claimant.[24]

Widows and almsmen were not the only recipients of the Committee's charity:

. . . [17 March 1656] Thomas Brasior (a Madman as doth appear by his distempered carriage) doth not only frequently abuse the Exchange and the Persons walking therein, but doth also endainger many mens lives by running after them with a drawne knife and swearing that he will kill them. vli from poore box to Mr Depty Gethin, Treasurer of Bedlam (where Thomas Braisor now is) to pay for him at 3s a week.[25]

These early Repertories give a general impression that London was still small enough for men to feel responsibility for fellow beings and that the early seventeenth-century Committee was a reasonably humanitarian body of men.

The Committee members had regularly to concern themselves with the physical condition of both the Exchange and the College installed in Gresham House in Bishopsgate where their meetings were normally held. Within six months of taking over their responsibilities, Kirwin and Walton, masons, were required to repair the turret of the Exchange in stone at 12d. per foot, and there were further repairs to it in February 1601. The vaults, as we have observed, were remodelled and let out at £30 a year in all, and more windows were to be made — the lighting of the shops was a constant problem. In March 1599 they were concerned with the provision of a clock and examined Mr Stape's estimate:

I will make an artificiall and a good clock wth two very faire Jacks to smyte the qters wth a fyne chyme of eight bells to

22 MC, GR, ii, p. 144.
23 MC, GR, ii, pp. 39, 51, 56.
24 MC, GR, ii, pp. 264–65.
25 MC, GR, ii, p. 177.

chyme viij, foure and xij and to mayntaine the same during my liefe for 4 nobles the yeere, and will make all this for 24ˡⁱ. Item, I will do this, make alarum upon the clock bell that all the citie shall understand when thexchange begyneth; and this alarum shall goe at the howers of xj and five.[26]

A second estimate was needed, however, and Mr Randolfe Bull supplied one. For £20 down and another £15 to follow, he would provide

a verry strong & substantiall clock so great as the tower of the royal Exchaunge in London will conteyne and two faire large Jacks of foure foote being all guilt that shall strike the quarter upon twoo good tunable bells to be made of the best bell mettall and to be of the compasse of the bells of St. Peters church of Westmynster with a new quarter shall according to the modell hereunto annexed with a penthouse to be made over the Jacks to defend them from the rayne.

The chimes were to ring out at noon and at six o'clock in the evening — the hours when trading was to finish — and the clock was to have four faces. Bull undertook to complete it by 24 August 1600, got the job, completed it, possibly on time, and was paid the £15 due to him in June 1601, with an additional £15 to express the Committee's satisfaction with the work. He continued in charge of the clock until July 1606 when he retired, since he lived too far away, and the City and Company awarded him £3 6s. 8d. in gratitute for his good services.

The clock continued to be an object of great pride; when in February 1636 George Farmer was appointed its keeper he was 'admitted for a trial of 6 moneths and hath undertaken to keepe it soe that it shall not vary from ye Sunne above one quarter of an hower'.

Then there was the bell for announcing the morning and afternoon gatherings of merchants. An 'ould bell' is mentioned in passing in June 1601 and five years later on 2 May 1606 later we find a sub-committee appointed to view the condition of the north side of the Exchange and

to cause a modell to be drawne for a convenient steeple to be there erected if the ffoundacions be sufficient to beare the same that the bell may be hunge up there again accordinge as it was used in Sir Tho Greshams lief tyme.

Plans were certainly made since the entry for Mid-summer's Day reads:

²⁶ MC, GR, I, pp. 100, 127, 135, 153.

Mr Reeve the bridghouse carpenter shall have iijˡⁱ for his 3 modles and Mr Edmonde and Mr Smith shall have xxˢ a peece for their modles. The modles of Mr Reeve being 80ᵗʸ foote and the other two modles one of stone an other of tymbre 60ᵗʸ fete a peece.[27]

We do not know whether this steeple was ever erected but it seems unlikely.

The worst problem was sanitation — or rather the lack of it — which produced constant complaints. A water supply was laid on by the New River Company — Sir Hugh Myddleton served on the Court of Committee from 1623 to 1629 — and scavengers were employed, but the need for 'funnels of leade to the house of office' was a regular subject for the Committee's consideration. In September 1646, Ralph Smith was

dealt withall to make a funnel to his house of office in regard some of the tenants on the upper pawne . . . are annoyed thereby, but he alledging he is not able at p⁻sent to be at that charge this committee did agree that there should be such a funnel of leade made to the said house of office,[28]

with Smith paying half the cost and the City and Mercers dividing the rest between them. The same Committee meeting had to deal with smoke abatement as well:

Whereas divers p⁻sons (whose Chimney or top of the Exchange) some of them appeared and some not . . . [they are now] warned . . . to reduce their chimneys to be lower than the Exchange, those that will not confirm to be warned to a Court of Aldermen.[29]

There were two regular complaints from the tenants — the restriction of the booths and the poor lighting. In November 1599 Thomas Twigge sought a reduction in rent since the space was 'so little that a man of reasonable bignesse cannot turne himselfe'.[30] The inner corner shops were particularly cramped and as early as 1601 it was agreed that their rentals were to be reduced by half; one of the tenants who benefited was the goldsmith Richard Crashaw, whom we have met before, renting the White Boare on the east side.

²⁷ MC, GR, I, p. 177.
²⁸ MC, GR, II, p. 143.
²⁹ MC, GR, II, p. 101.
³⁰ MC, GR, I, p. 112.

The lighting was a constant problem, though some shopkeepers clearly found that there were advantages in the gloaming. In June 1637 the Chamberlain of London and the Mercers' renter-warden

are entreated to admonish the Tenants in the Exchange that darken their lights with canvas, blinds or anything & to pull down the same and they that refuse are to be presented at the next Court.[31]

But the opposite was true for other tenants. In January 1624, the Viewing Committee went to inspect Edward Wadeson's stall to see 'how a light may be contrived for the benefit of the same'. All sorts of contraptions likely to increase the risk of fire must have been rigged up. When the days grew shorter and darker in the November of 1627, the Committee were alert:

The false lights are again to be taken down by Mr Leate and Mr Bishop, and Southorne [an Exchange Keeper] shall looke that they continue downe, and he to give notice to the saide Committee.[32]

The same problems of space, light and sanitation troubled a rival Exchange, one which came into being only too soon for the City's comfort.

In the early 1600s, Sir Robert Cecil, Lord Burghley's second son and intellectual heir, acquired land along the Strand frontage of Durham House, adjacent to his own residence, Salisbury House, and on it built the New Exchange, or Britain's Burse as James I called it when he declared it open on 10 April 1609. At the first rumour of the new undertaking, in February 1608, the Committee and shopkeepers had reacted with alarm; a petition was presented, objecting that 'a house of trade in the Strand' was being constructed 'by great means and great p⁻son-ages to allure trading and com⁻erce to the place aforesaid'; there was 'nothing more pregnant for the goode and advancement of the one, nor anie thinge more dangerous to detract and suppress the other' and they feared the newcomer would lower and ruin the City Exchange.[33] The Lord Mayor wrote in protest too, but Cecil, replying tactfully, pressed ahead with his venture. A first elegant design for it was produced by Inigo Jones; a more prosaic building was constructed by Simon Basil, Surveyor of the King's Works; it went up with impressive speed, being completed within ten months. Unlike Gresham's Bourse, the raw materials were chiefly home-provided, though the fine carving for the Strand frontage was the work of John de Beeke and Garret Christmas, both from the Low Countries but now resident in England. In all, the building cost £10,760 in construction charges, besides the money laid out in acquisition of land.[34]

There were about a hundred shops in the New Exchange; Cecil found — as Gresham had done — that they were slow to let. The rents were substantial — £10 a year for an 11-year lease with a £30 fine at each renewal. Six months after the spring opening, only 27 shops were occupied. One gets the impression that the goods offered were slightly upmarket compared with the Royal Exchange; certainly, the shop signs were more fanciful. Though there were plenty of animals — a clothworker at the Falcon, a milliner at the Blue Boar, a perfumer at the Phoenix and a merchant taylor at the Henne and Chickens — others were more poetical — The Bird in Hand (a tallow chandler), the Spanish Gypsy (a milliner), the Flower de Luce and the Meremaiden (both haberdashers), the Manne in the Moone (a cutler), and the Hart and Garland (a fishmonger), while Mary Blackman, spinster, and Katherine Bryers, widow, sold unspecified wares at the Halfe-Moon and Seven Stars, and at the Sheaf of Arrows. But trade continued to be slack and in 1627 the shops were ripped out of the upper floor and 16 small flats were inserted into the space. Business picked up ten years later, the tenants were turned out and the shops re-instated. They continued to prosper in spite of the Civil War — indeed, the New Exchange in the Strand was to be one of Samuel Pepys' favourite haunts — but the westwards drift of the town in the later years of the century dampened affairs once again, and in 1737 the New Exchange was pulled down and is forgotten today. The Royal Exchange had a stronger constitution.

---

[31] MC, GR, II, p. 50.
[32] MC, GR, II, p. 7.
[33] MC, GR, I, p. 188.

[34] The archival evidence is among the Salisbury Papers at Hatfield House. The fullest account so far is by Lawrence Stone, *Family and Fortune* (1973), pp. 95–109, and also in 'Inigo Jones and the New Exchange', *Archaeological Journal*, CXIV (1959), pp. 108–11.

The cold, not cruelty makes her weare
In Winter, furrs and Wild beastshaire   **Winter**   For a smoother skinn at night,
                                                       Embraceth her with more delight.

FIG. 18. *Winter*, one of a set of engravings of the Four Seasons by Wenceslas Hollar, 1643–44. The masked fur-clad lady stands with her back to Cornhill, the tower of the Royal Exchange, and the Tun, as the prison for night vagrants was called, visible to the right; she faces towards Cheapside, in the direction of the Mercers' Hall.

The Royal Collection, © 1993: Her Majesty The Queen

Throughout the 1630s the Gresham Repertories keep up their steady meeting-to-meeting flow of details of daily arrangements and particularities — one might almost say trivialities; there is little direct reference to the impending disturbances though it is clear that the Committee were only too aware of what was going on. When on 23 January 1640 John Charles asked for a new lease of a house in Cornhill, wherein he had been undertenant for seventeen years, it was agreed for £10 in rent and £120 in fine, but a new clause was added to his lease, that he 'stowe not Turpentine, Gunpowder, or any other Dangerous combustible stuff therein',[35] and the same guarantee was required of the East India Company in March 1642 when they sought to the rent the vaults. Matters were worse by April of the next year, when prisoners were temporarily lodged in Gresham College, and in November 1643 it was decided that a thrifty store of corn and other victuals should be stowed away there, wherever room could be found.[36] Even the Gresham professors were viewed with a new caution; Benjamin

[35] MC, GR, II, p. 68.
[36] MC, GR, II, p. 92.

Thornton, Professor of Civil Law, petitioning on 20 August 1645 for arrears of pay due to him, was told that he would receive his money, 'provided that he first bring a certificate that he had taken the National Covenant'.[37]

Rather more leniency was shown to Exchange tenants a little behind with their rents; the number of women admitted as shopkeepers increased and they too were treated very fairly. The number of applicants swelled for each deceased almsman's place — 12 on 22 October 1647, 13 in June 1648, 19 in March 1649 — and by October 1651, it had become usual to admit a man's wife with him, though the poor soul was to be forced to leave within 20 days should she become a widow. In August 1654 and in July 1656, relief was sent to Susan Gresham, Sir John Gresham's unmarried daughter in Norwich, in grants of £10 on each occasion.[38]

But there is no mention anywhere in the Minutes of the symbolic events when an Order was given by the Council of State on 31 July 1650, that the statue of the late King standing at the Exchange was to be demolished by having the head taken off and the sceptre out of his hand, and 'this inscription to be written

Exit Tyrannus Regum Ultimus
Anno primo restituae libertatis Angliae

and this to be done between this and Saturday next'.[39] No other statue was mutilated; the citizens remained as proud of their Exchange as ever — as indeed did those in exile, such as John Evelyn who had discreetly gone abroad. Staying in Amsterdam in 1641, he wrote: 'The building is not comparable to that of London, built by that worthy citizen, Sir Thomas Gresham'. In Paris in February 1644 he recorded:

I went to the Exchange; the late addition to the building is noble, but the gallarys where they sell their petty merchandize are nothing so stately as ours in London, no more than the place they walk below, being only a low vault.[40]

While in Venice the following summer he observed, 'I went to their Exchange, a place like ours frequented by merchants, but nothing so magnificent'.

Though the Minutes ignore the King's death, the Committee knew they were confronted by a changing world. On 15 October 1649, Gresham professors and shopkeepers were petitioning alike that they might be 'eased in their taxes' and begging that a sub-committee be appointed 'to repair to the Assessors and Commissioners for Assessment . . . to mediate with them to carry a gentle hand in rating those shops'.[41] The tenants felt that they were particularly hard used, since they had already paid charges to the Parliamentary Government for their main properties in the City. The Minutes carry no report of the sub-committee's success or failure.

The uneasy atmosphere continued. In March 1652, it was decided that all property should be viewed and revalued, and in August 1652 and December 1656 the new charges were set out: each shop in the main Pawn on the south side was to pay £24 rent a year and each in the Upper Pawn £22; the east and west sides were valued at £22 and £20 respectively and the north at £20 and £15. Leases were to be renewed on a fine of six times the annual rent. There is no mention of a stipulated length for a lease, and the shopkeepers seem to have accepted the increases as inevitable.[42] In June and August 1654, the Clerk was warned that he should enquire into the estate of each applicant for a lease, and in the following months each person's company or calling was carefully set down, haberdashers, girdlers, leathersellers, mercers, painter-stainers, and grocers making up the assembly.

Other entries are a little more sinister. In July 1652, Dr William Petty, installed as professor of music though he was later to win a title, fame and fortune as a doctor, a land surveyor and a political economist, was complaining of the misdemeanours of John Harnscombe the porter and saying that he feared 'some dangers about the Colledge by people that lurke therein'.[43] Enquiries were made and Harnscombe was told 'to shut up and bolt the back door of the colledge by eight of the clock every night'

[37] MC, GR, II, p. 100.
[38] MC, GR, II pp. 158, 166.
[39] SPD, 1650 (1876), p. 261.
[40] John Evelyn, Diary, ed. E. S. de Beer, vol. II, pp. 46, 98.

[41] MC, GR, II, p. 114.
[42] MC, GR, II, pp. 135, 169.
[43] MC, GR, II, p. 131.

and to check on the inmates and in the stables. The same Committee was also warned that the recently widowered Sir Kenelm Digby was staying in the College and that he had with him his servant John Lee who lodged there without permission.[44] A sub-committee was appointed to go with a constable to search 'his chamber for letters and other writings of evil consequence to the State', but there is no record of any doubtful matter being found. In October 1653, John Metcalfe and Francis Walcott, the Keepers of the Exchange, were admonished for slack supervision and were threatened with dismissal if they did not attend the Exchange

from Eleavon of the clock to one of the clock daily, the one on the one side the other on the other side with their staves, and to suffer none to carry any burthens, nor to sell books nor bandstrings therupon.[45]

They were, however, given the encouragement of 40s. a year for the daily shutting and opening of the gates. On 11 August 1654, it was agreed that Capt. Stanion and Joseph Kinsman, plaisterers, should have £30 for whitening the Upper Pawn, and on 19 December 1656 Michael Darby, painter-stainer, was to have £4 a year for 'brushing, washing and clensing the statues and walls of the Royal Exchange at times convenient'.[46] Clearly, save for that of the late executed monarch, the statues were intact and were being treated with care and respect.

On 25 August 1654, there was a suggestion that the Commissioners should hold their meetings in Gresham College but the Committee firmly rebuffed it, though they were forced to accept the married Dr Thomas Horton as divinity professor when he presented a letter from Oliver Cromwell himself;[47] the appointment was soon revoked at the Restoration. Possibly Monck's soldiers had been billeted at the College, for on 10 August 1660, the young King Charles II now being safely back on his father's throne, the Committee decided to reward Francis Draper, porter of the College,[48] for

his greate care and diligence in the looking to the Colledge and in preserving the leades, wainscotts, and other materials of the house during the time the souldiers quartered here, and of the Paines and charge he hath bin at in clensing the same from time to time, did thereupon graunt him a benevolence of xli as a gratification for his former care and for incouragement of his future diligence.

Once again the Minutes stay discreetly silent about the restoration of the headless royal statue but Pepys' *Diary* tells us what happened:

16 March 1660. Tonight, I am told that yesterday, about 5 o'clock in the afternoon, one came with a ladder to the great Exchange and wiped with a brush the Inscripcion that was upon King Charles, and that there was a great bonefire made in the Exchange and people cried out 'God bless King Charles the Second!'[49]

The atmosphere in London must, in those days, have been like that in Berlin when the Wall was broken down; Pepys sums it up: 'Indeed, it was past imagination, both the greatness and suddenness of it'.

The City celebrated by setting up triumphal arches, one of them adorned with a painting of the Exchange. Later, in the summer of 1662, there was a celebratory pageant, about which the residents of Gresham College complained and were rebuked; it had been 'in honour of that Government which spends its time to serve the complainants . . . [it] could not be offensive'.[50]

By the end of May, the young Charles II was back in Whitehall and petitions were pouring in from all those who felt they had suffered in his father's cause. Among them were an orphaned brother and sister, Robert and Margaret Lendall, whose father had 'hazarded his life for his loyalty' and now was dead at Flushing in the Low Countries, along with their mother. We do not know what was done for Robert, but Margaret was provided with a seven-year apprenticeship in the lace business, in the Royal Exchange. In another undated petition of about 1670, she asked for further help to set up in business on her own account.[51]

The Gresham Committee continued with its work as usual. King Charles's statue was quietly restored

---

[44] Ibid. But see also *SPD, 1649–1650* (1867), p. 381, which shows John Lee still in residence at the college, when his master had gone to Calais.
[45] MC, GR, II, p. 140.
[46] MC, GR, II, pp. 160, 170.
[47] MC, GR, II, pp. 162, 165, 207.
[48] MC, GR, II, p. 193.

[49] Samuel Pepys, *Diary*, ed. R. Latham and W. Matthews, vol. I, p. 89. A footnote there tells us that the man with the paintbrush was Michael Darby, 'now painter to the Company of Mercers'.
[50] MC, GR, II, pp. 211–12.
[51] *SPD, 1670* (1895), p. 621.

and appears intact when Hollar's engraving of the courtyard was re-issued in 1668, this time with an additional royal figure, Charles II. The usual applications were made for renewals of leases; the usual complaints poured in, too — the shops were too small, too dark, some tenants encroached on the space allotted to others. Adjacent buildings made the lack of light still worse. In August 1660, Mr Thomas Bostock on the north side of the Exchange was 'to be dealt effectively with all, to pull down those rails and banisters on the top of his house which obstruct the lights from the shops of Mr Lazenby, Mr Minshaw and Mr Spiry'.[52]

Other tenants were singing the same tune: 'An antient and continued complaint' came from Widow Hulse, James Windess and Widow Wainer for want of light on the south side. 'Though their shops have the name to stand best being on the south and dearest side of the Exchange, yet customers generally avoyd them, because they want competent light'.[53] The Committee inspected the problem and agreed that 'they may make a window or inlarge an old one or two to their best advantage'. That autumn, Mr Pate and Mr Hilliard, with shops on the east side, asked for permission to sue Mr Burroughs 'the looking glasse maker in Cornhill' 'who by a new building hath much darkened the lights of that parte of the Exchange, and will not reduce the same to its former condition by any faire means'.[54] At the same time, other tenants had cut trap-doors out on to the leads and Peter Cole 'hath made a jetty out of his garet which becomes malicious as well as in the example, as in prejudice to the Exchange'.[55] The Committee and tenants could not know that the Great Fire, which would sweep away all these problems, was only six years into the future.

[52] MC, GR, II, p. 197.

[53] Ibid.
[54] MC, GR, II, p. 200.
[55] MC, GR, II, p. 201.

Extract from London and the Countrey Carbonadoed and Quartered into several Characters
By DONALD LUPTON

1632

... THE MERCHANTS are men generally of good habite, their words are usually better than their consciences; their discourse ordinarily begins in water, but ends in wine. The frequenting the walkes twice a day and a careless laughter argues that they are sound; if they visit not once a day, 'tis suspected they are cracking or broken. Their countenance is ordinarily shap'd by their successe at sea, either merry, sad, or desperate; they are like ships at sea, top-gallant this day, to-morrow sincking. The sea is a tennis-court, their states are bals, the winde is the racket, and doth strike many for lost under line, and many in the hazard ... Conscience is sold here for nought, because it is as old sermons, a dead commodity. They will dissemble with and cozen one another, though all the kings that ever were since the Conquest overlooked them. Here are usually more coaches attendant than at church doores. The merchants should keep their wives from visiting the upper roomes too often, lest they tire their purses by attyring themselves. Rough seas, rockes and pyrats, treacherous factors, and leaking ships affright them. They are strange politicians, for they bring Turkey and Spaine into London, and carry London thither. . .

CHAPTER XII

The Literary Legend of Sir Thomas Gresham

By JULIA GASPER

WHEN SIR THOMAS GRESHAM died, in 1579, he was already one of the most illustrious citizens London had ever seen. His foundations of the Royal Exchange and Gresham College established him as a benefactor of mythical status, and this myth soon found expression in the drama and literature of the next generation. Even in his own lifetime, Gresham was made the subject of a Latin play by one J. Rickets, entitled *Byrsa Basilica sive Regale Excambicum in honorem Thomae Greshami*. It is dated 1570, and is preserved in the Bodleian Library: it was probably written for performance at one of the colleges or possibly the Inns of Court. At the height of the Elizabethan period, many vernacular writers mentioned Gresham or his Exchange: Ben Jonson, Thomas Middleton, Thomas Dekker and Thomas Heywood, who actually made Gresham into the hero of a full-length play.

In Jonson's early comedy *Every Man in His Humour* (1598) the merchant Kitely arranges to meet one Master Lvcar on the Exchange, to deal in 'siluer stuffes' and 'grograns'. Later when he enquires the time, his clerk, Cash, replies 'Exchange time, sir'. Worried that Cash might betray him, Kitely fears being ruined: 'Lost i' my fame forever, talke for th'Exchange'. So the Exchange is not just a commercial centre, but a hub of every City activity, a microcosm of the City itself. In the same play, Captain Bobadil says that he has been accosted by swordsmen there wishing to test his skill.[1]

In *Every Man Out of His Humour*, Fastidius Briske, the foppish courtier, arranges to meet Signior Puntavarlo 'at a *Notaries*, by the *Exchange*, presently . . .'. The Exchange, being such a conspicuous landmark in the crowded old medieval city, made a convenient rendezvous for all manner of purposes. Puntavarlo and the others have a long wait, throughout three scenes,

until Briske eventually turns up, apologising for his lateness by saying that he was banqueting with a 'beuie of ladies'. He also tells us that his pearl-embroidered 'Italian cut-worke band . . . cost me three pound in the exchange, but three daies before'.[2] The shops inside the Exchange were famous for their fine draperies and haberdasheries, which attracted a fashionable clientele. This sort of reputation is apparent from the passage in Jonson's later comedy, *Bartholomew Fair*, in which the citizen Master Littlewit praises his wife's fine clothes: 'I challenge all *Cheapside*, to shew such another: Morefields, *Pimlico* path, or the *Exchange*, in a summer evening . . .'.[3] She later falls into the hands of a bawd, and her own husband does not recognise her when she turns up, masked, at Bartholomew Fair.

In some other plays, activities of a shady kind are associated with the Exchange. In *The Devil Is An Ass* (1616) the sinister dealer Meercraft makes an assignation with one Master Woodcock there: 'Tell Master Woodcock I'll not fail to meet him Upon th' Exchange at night. Pray him to have the writings there, and we'll dispatch it.' The names suggest that Woodcock is to be the victim of some double-dealing.[4]

In Jonson's satire *The Staple of News*, performed in 1626 by the King's Men, the barber, Thomas, announces that they will need four emissaries for the news office, placed in the four 'Cardinall Quarters' of London, which are 'the *Court*, Sir, *Pauls*, *Exchange*, and *Westminster-Hall*'. So the Exchange is one of the principal organs of the City, its commercial heart which also has something of the function of an ear since foreigners arriving to do business might also bring news. The emissary stationed at the Exchange will be 'Froy *Hans Buz*; A Dutch-man'.[5] England did

---

[1] *The Dramatic Works of Ben Jonson*, ed. Herford and Simpson (OUP, 1933), vols. I–II, pp. 323, 347, 350. This is the revised version of the play.

[2] Ibid., vol. III, pp. 533–35, 546, 549.

[3] Ibid., vol. VI, p. 20.

[4] Ibid., vol. VI, p. 187.

[5] Ibid., vol. VI, p. 287.

a lot of trade with the Dutch at this time, and so there were a lot of them to be found in the City. The choice of nationality probably has a political point, too: the City's appetite for news at this time was being stimulated by the religious wars on the Continent, in which the Dutch were hoping England would prove their ally. Jonson did not approve of this trade in 'news', regarding it as a dangerous innovation.

In Thomas Middleton's comedy *A Chaste Maid in Cheapside* (1613) some of the more dubious ideas sometimes associated with the Exchange are apparent. Allwit, a citizen, is recounting how his wife, lying-in for childbirth, decks herself out in finery: 'there's her embossings, Embroid'rings, spanglings, and I know not what, As if she lay with all the gaudy-shops In Gresham's Burse about her . . .'.[6] But Allwit suspects he is not the father of the child, and it is her lover who pays for all this meretricious show.

There are two allusions to the Exchange in *Westward Ho!*, a comedy of 1607 by Dekker and Webster. Master Tenterhooke, a citizen and money-lender, reports that he has heard about another merchant's bankruptcy there: 'Maister *Iustiniano* the Italian . . . Yea sooth, I was offered forty yesterday vpon the Exchange, to assure a hundred.' Listening to the talk at the Exchange served the same sort of purpose as reading the *Financial Times* today. Later in the same scene, Mistress Honeysuckle offers rather a nasty slur, gossiping that Master Monopoly only loves women when they are 'as stale as a Countrey Ostes, an Exchange Sempster, or a Court Landresse'.[7] This is not typical of Dekker's allusions to the Exchange, most of which express a citizen's pride in this still new institution.

In one of the finest passages of his satirical prose work, *The Gull's Horn-book*, Dekker compares the theatres of Elizabethan London to the Royal Exchange:

The theatre is your poets' Royal Exchange, upon which their muses, that are now turned to merchants, meeting, barter away that light commodity of words for a lighter ware than words — plaudities, and the breath of the great

FIG. 19.   In the gardens at Stowe, Buckinghamshire, is a screen, designed by William Kent, *c.* 1740, with busts of English Worthies; Gresham holds pole position, perpetuating the legend.

beast; which, like the threatenings of two cowards, vanish all into air. Players are their factors, who put away the stuff, and make the best of it they possibly can, as indeed 'tis their parts so to do. Your gallant, your courtier and your captain had wont to be the soundest paymasters, and, I think, are still the surest chapmen: and these, by means that their heads are well stocked, deal upon this comical freight by the gross . . .[8]

There is drama in commerce, as well as business in art.

In his late plague pamphlet, *The Black Rod and the White Rod* (1630), Dekker went a step further and took the Royal Exchange for a metaphor of the whole world, a microcosm of human society:

[6] *A Chaste Maid in Cheapside*, ed. R. B. Parker, Revels Plays (Methuen, 1969), Act I scene ii.
[7] *The Dramatic Works of Thomas Dekker*, ed. Fredson Bowers (CUP, 1953–61), vol. II, pp. 326, 328.

[8] R. B. McKerrow (ed.), *The De La More Press* (London, 1904), p. 49.

This world is a Royall Exchange, where all sorts of Men are Merchants: Kings hold Commerce with Kings, and their Voyages are vpon high Negotiations: As, the deare buying of anothers Countrey, with their own Subiects Bloud: The Purchasing of new Crownes, and new Sceptres, not satisfied with the old.

And, as Kings, so Princes, Dukes, Earles, Lords, Clergymen, Iudges, Souldiers, haue their Trading in particular Marchandizes, and walke euery day for that purpose vpon this Old Royall Exchange.

They talke in seuerall Languages, And (like the murmuring fall of Waters) in the Hum of seuerall businesses: insomuch that the place seemes Babell, (a Confusion of Tongues.)

The best, (yet most incertaine) Commodity, which all these Merchants striue for, is Life: if Health be got into the Bargaine, He is a Made man, into whose hands it comes. Yet when these two inestimable Treasures are shipped in one Bottome, together; There are Winds, and Waues, and Woes, which still fill the Sayles, and hang vpon the Tacklings.

> What's the end of this Voyage?
> *Currit Mercator ad Indos.*
> To heape vp Gold,
> The Merchants Name i'th Indies, is inroll'd.

'Nay, though he casts a Girdle about the World, yet, Anchor he must in one Harbour or another, to come to shore, and Proclaime his lading on this Ryalta, this Burse, or this Royall Exchange, and when the Exchange-Bell rings, (his passing-Bell tolles) That's the warning-Peece to tell him hee must go off, he must for that time talke there no more of his Transitorie Commodities, the Exchange of this world with him is then done, and Home does he hasten to dine with Wormes.'[9]

Dekker is in a sombre mood here, mindful of mortality because of the impact of the Plague on London, and that of the Thirty Years War on the Continent. Since the Habsburg invasion of Bohemia, much of Germany had been devastated by the long and bitter war. He himself was in his old age (probably nearing sixty) when he wrote this. The passage continues with the same metaphor of the Exchange:

The sum, vpshot and cloze of all, is this: That, as many Men as that walke on that Royall Exchange, and seeme rich, doe often breake and are lay'd in Prison: So in this World; when we appear neuer so strong in Body, neuer so stirring in minde; yet, if health turnes Banquerupt once,

and that the Sergeant with the Blacke Rod, (Sicknesse) Arrests vs; if eyther Casualties, by Sea or Land, if losses, vexations, misfortunes or miseries, breake our hearts, whether then are we carried! To our euerlasting Prison the Graue.

The conclusion exhorts Londoners to repent in time, so that they may become citizens of the heavenly Jerusalem.[10]

No author wrote more frequently about the Royal Exchange, or presented it in a more laudatory fashion, than Thomas Heywood. His play *If You Know Not Me You Know Nobody* (Part II), performed by the Queen's Men in 1606, not only features the Exchange, but also Gresham himself who is given a very prominent role. The first part of this chronicle play concerns the young Princess Elizabeth: towards the end of the second part she reappears, as a great and gracious Queen, whom Gresham has the honour to entertain at his house in Bishopgate Street, in the heart of the City of London. Gresham was one of the very few figures of such recent history who were deemed worthy of being the protagonist of a history play: when contemporary personages were represented on the stage, it tended to be in a satirical light. But Gresham's portrayal is far from satirical and his appearance alongside monarchs shows that Elizabethans regarded him as a historical figure of the first rank.

In the opening scene of this play, one of Gresham's 'factors', that is, assistants, is discussing his master's business with a Barbary merchant, and this gives the opportunity for some praise of Gresham: 'He is a man of heedful prouidence', says the merchant, 'and one that by innatiue courtesie Winnes loue from strangers.' The factor agrees: 'He is a Merchant of good estimate: Care how to get, and forecast to encrease (If so they be accounted) be his faults.' 'They are especiall vertues', the merchant replies, 'being clear from auarice and base extortion.'[11] The question raised in this bit of dialogue does open an interesting line of enquiry into the ethics of the business world, which runs through the entire play. Gresham is presented largely as a hero — but a few

---

[9] *Dekker's Plague Pamphlets*, ed. F. P. Wilson (Clarendon Press, 1925), pp. 199–200.

[10] Ibid., p. 201.
[11] *The Dramatic Works of Thomas Heywood*, ed. anon. (John Pearson, London, 1874), vol. I, p. 251.

questions are asked so that his heroic status will not be accepted too complacently. In the first scene, Gresham buys a sugar-monopoly from the Barbary King for the considerable sum of £60,000. The monopoly will last only during the present King's lifetime, but the factor tells Gresham that by general opinion

Tis held your credit and your countries honor, That being but a Merchant of the City, And taken in a manner vnprouided. You should vpon a meere presumption And naked promise, part with so much Cash, Which the best merchants both in Spaine and France Denied to venture on . . . London will yield you partners enow.[12]

Perhaps Gresham is unwise to be swayed by such considerations, because half-way through the play he loses a tremendous amount of money in the Barbary trade.

A prominent part in the play is taken by Gresham's nephew, John, a character for whom the historical basis is not very clear: he does not figure in the chronicles. Gresham in the play calls him 'Cosin', but reprimands the young man about his dissolute life:

I haue tane note of your bad husbandry,
Carelesse respect, and prodigal expence,
And out of my experience counsell you.[13]

John excuses himself boldly of such faults as adultery and bestowing a gown on a strumpet, bringing biblical quotes in his own defence, but says he is ready to adopt 'a more conformable and strict course of life'.[14] On this understanding, Gresham pays for John's new clothes and sends him as an assistant to another merchant, Master Hobson. John offers to do any menial work, but Gresham insists:

Your education challenges more respect.
The factor dealt for him in France is dead.[15]

So John is given a good position representing Hobson's business interests in France. But when Gresham is out of the room, John expresses no gratitude to his uncle: on the contrary, he is resentful because he claims that Gresham has already cheated him out of an inheritance: 'Ile giue you leaue to call me Cut, and

cozen me of my patrimony, as you haue done.'[16] It is an intriguing accusation, but Gresham in the play never has a chance to defend himself against it as John never says it to his face.

When Gresham soon after trusts John with £100, John absconds with the money, but Gresham is still indulgent towards him, calling him 'mad *Jack*' and saying that a bit of wildness is a family trait. When Jack goes to France he takes up with a courtesan and, being caught at it by Hobson, has the cheek to call up his fellow factors (disguised as civic officers) and pretends to get Hobson arrested for frequenting a bawdy-house. Hobson is alarmed and makes a pact with John:

conceale this from my wife,
And Ile keep all thy knauery from thine vncle.[17]

Jack Gresham's impudence is as great as ever when, on returning to England, he proposes to the rich widow, Lady Ramsey. She refuses him, but does agree to pay all his debts. It seems implausible that the Gresham of the play, who is presented as a man of undoubted probity, should have cheated his nephew out of a patrimony, but it creates a stimulating uncertainty. Perhaps the playwright does not put our minds at rest because a mind at rest is a bored mind, and anyway life is just not like that.

The historical Gresham did, according to Stanley Bindoff, have a cousin called Sir John Gresham, an MP who got himself into debt and eventually forfeited his house, Mayfield in Sussex, to Sir Thomas as a result.[18] And according to Burgon's nineteenth-century biography of Gresham, there was an assistant by the name of John Gresham working for him in his Antwerp office in 1554.[19] Was he the model for the 'nephew' of the play? Could he have been a son of Sir John who felt diddled out of his inheritance because of the transaction with his father? Even if he existed,

[12] Ibid., p. 254.
[13] Ibid., p. 254.
[14] Ibid., p. 255.
[15] Ibid., p. 256.

[16] Ibid., p. 256.
[17] Ibid., pp. 282, 315.
[18] Stanley T. Bindoff, *The Fame of Sir Thomas Gresham*, Neale Lecture in English History 1973, delivered at University College, London (Jonathan Cape, 1973), p. 20.
[19] John William Burgon, *The Life and Times of Sir Thomas Gresham*, (London, 1839), vol. I, p. 179. The family tree in the back of this book says that the Sir John who owned Mayfield and had a son John Gresham was Sir Thomas's uncle, not cousin (vol. II, appendix).

this would not resolve the problem in the play because of course the characters in Heywood are not the historical personages themselves, but only representations of them. No nephew features in the chronicle sources, and Heywood may have been relying on oral tradition for his story or he may just have invented it.

Oral tradition may have provided many of the details of the account given in the play of how Gresham comes to found the Royal Exchange. It starts by showing Gresham having a meeting with one Sir Thomas Ramsey, with whom he has been involved in a lawsuit for seven years. The meeting is arranged by Dr Nowell, Dean of St Paul's, at the desire of Lady Ramsey, and Dr Nowell mediates between the two men:

> My Lady *Ramsy*, I haue heard ere this,
> Of their contentions, their long suit in law;
> How by good friends they haue been persuaded both,
> Yet both but deafe to faire persuasion.[20]

The two opponents, together with Dr Nowell, Lady Ramsey and Master Hobson, meet in Lombard Street, 'on the Lumbard' as it was called, because at that time this was the usual meeting place for merchants in London. Their quarrel began when Gresham gazumped Ramsey for a property, Osterley manor; as Lady Ramsey recounts:

> There is a lordship called *Osterley*
> That M. Gresham hath both bought and built upon.
> Gresh: And tis a goodly manour, M. Deane.
> Lady R: Which *Osterley*, before he dealt therein,
> Sir *Thomas*, my husband here, did thinke to buy,
> And had giuen earnest for it.[21]

Hobson points out how much money this quarrel has poured into the pockets of lawyers over seven years:

> I will not haue a couple of such men
> Make cackling lawyers rich, and themselues fooles.[22]

Doctor Nowell suggests a compromise:

> Thus it shall be: because that Sir *Thomas Ramsie*
> Had earnest giuen before you bought the land,
> Though you were not acquainted with so much,
> I do award he haue an hundred pounds
> Towards his charges; and that for you

Haue both paid for the land and built vpon it,
It shall continue yours.[23]

Both men accept this, admitting they have already spent £500 on legal fees, and they shake hands. Then it begins to rain heavily, and Gresham says that what London needs is a covered meeting place:

> Now, passion-a-me, Sir *Thomas*, a cruel storm;
> And we stay long, we shall be wet to th' skin.
> I do not lik't: nay it angers me,
> That such a famous city as this is,
> Wherein so many gallant merchants are,
> Haue not a place to meet in, but in this,
> Where euery showre of raine must trouble them.
> I cannot tell, but if I liue: lets step into the Popes-head;
> We shall be dropping dry [*sic*] if we stay here.
> Ils haue a roofe built, and such a roofe,
> That merchants and their wiues, friends, and their friends,
> Shall walk vnderneath it, as now in Powles . . .
>
> Ile raise a worke shall make our merchants say,
> Twas a good showre that fell vpon that day.[24]

Heywood may have heard some of these details from Dr Nowell himself, because Alexander Nowell, who was Dean of St Paul's from 1561 (five years before the Exchange was built) was, according to the *Dictionary of National Biography*, 'a great composer of private quarrels'.[25] Nowell's portrait still hangs in the Bodleian Library, and Heywood may have known him and heard the story from him personally since Nowell lived to be ninety-five, only dying in 1602. He was also a benefactor of Emmanuel College, Cambridge, where Heywood is thought to have studied, so they could have met there if not in London. Sir Thomas Ramsey likewise has a historical basis: he is listed in Fuller's *Worthies* as being Sheriff of London in 1568.[26]

Gresham's philanthropic plans are encouraged by Dr Nowell in the play when he invites Gresham, Hobson and Lady Ramsey to view a gallery in his house where the portraits of famous benefactors of the City and realm are displayed. One distinguished example is 'Sir *Richard Whittington*', whose bequests provided:

---

[20] Heywood, p. 263.
[21] Heywood, p. 265.
[22] Heywood, p. 266.

[23] Heywood, p. 267.
[24] Heywood, pp. 268–69.
[25] *DNB* under Nowel or Noel.
[26] Thomas Fuller, *The History of the Worthies of England*, ed. Nichols (1811), vol. II, p. 97.

Whittington Colledge, thirteen Alms-houses for poor men,
Repair'd S. *Bartholomewes*, in Smithfield,
Glased the Guildhall, and built Newgate.[27]

The others include two women, in whose charitable foundations Lady Ramsey takes a particularly close interest. Both she and Gresham are inspired to emulate the examples Nowell shows them:

Lady R.: Why should not I liue so, that being dead,
          My name should haue a register with theirs.
Gresham: Why should not all of vs being wealthy men,
          And by Gods blessing onely raised, but
          Cast in our minds how we might them exceed
          In godly workes, helping of them that need.[28]

Nowell urges them to start the work in their lifetime, and not leave it to heirs or executors who may be negligent or greedy. And Gresham certainly loses no time, for a couple of scenes later we see him getting permission from the Corporation of London to erect his new building:

          Now when this worke is rais'd
          It shall be in the pleasure of my life
          To come and meet the merchants at their houre,
          And see them, in the greatest storme that is,
          Walke dry, and in a worke I rais'd for them;
          Or fetch a turn within my vpper walke,
          Within which square I haue ordered shops shall be
          Of neat, but necessariest trades in London.[29]

Sir Thomas Ramsey, who is now Lord Mayor, tells Gresham that the site in Cornhill has been bought by the City so that Gresham can build a 'Burse' on it. Straight away Gresham takes some workmen, along with Hobson and Dr Nowell, to lay the first brick, under which he buries a sovereign. Nowell admires the plans, and Gresham explains that the design is to resemble a cloister so that people will be neither stifled by summer's heat nor frozen in winter, but will get plenty of light.

Shortly afterwards, we see the completed Exchange, now being admired by a group of lords, who declare it to be finer than any comparable building in Christendom:

2 Lord: I might say, all the world has not his fellow.
         I haue been in Turkies great Constantinople;
         The merchants there meet in a goodly temple,
         But haue no common Burse: in Rome, but Rome's
         Built after the manner of *Frankford* and *Embden*:
Ramsey: I think you haue not seene a goodlier frame.
2 Lord: Not in my life; yet I haue beene in *Venice*,
         In the *Realto* there, called S. *Marks*;
         Tis but a bable, if compard to this.
         The nearest that which most resembles this,
         Is the great Burse in *Antwerp*, yet not comparable
         Either in height or wideness, the fair cellerage,
         Or goodly shops aboue. Oh, my Lord Maior,
         This *Gresham* hath much graced your city, *London*:
         His fame will long outliue him.[30]

However, at this point in the play, Gresham suffers a series of misfortunes. First, a comet is seen in the sky, and Dr Nowell explains that it is a bad omen. Then Gresham's factor brings him news that the King of Barbary has been killed at the battle of Alcazar. At first, Gresham hopes that the new King will honour the monopoly agreement or return his money. He hosts a banquet at his house for the Lord Mayor and the Russian ambassador, but while it is going on a mariner enters and tells Gresham that one of his ships has sunk, bearing all the statues of monarchs which were going to adorn his new Exchange building. Then a factor enters and brings a message from the new King of Barbary, who refuses either to maintain the sugar monopoly or to return Gresham's premium. So Gresham loses £60,000 without having made a penny out of the contract. All the King sends him is a rather insulting present, consisting of a pair of slippers and a dagger. Gresham responds with calm dignity, and indeed some display of insouciance: he puts on the slippers, saying 'he had the just length of my foot', then drinks a toast to Queen Elizabeth in a draught of wine containing a valuable pearl.[31]

We may well ask why Heywood chose to present Sir Thomas Gresham in such a situation, apparently the victim of immense bad luck. Did it just provide an opportunity to show the audience the hero's splendid fortitude and resignation in adversity, and such moral qualities? That is one aspect of it. T. S. Eliot complained, in his very patronising and inaccurate essay on Heywood, that Heywood is not 'moral' enough.[32] Well, it is a useful rule of thumb to follow

---

[27] Heywood, p. 277.
[28] Ibid., p. 279.
[29] Ibid., p. 288.
[30] Ibid., p. 295.
[31] Ibid., pp. 299–301.
[32] T. S. Eliot, *Selected Essays* (Faber and Faber, 1932, rpt 1972), pp. 177–79, 180.

in life, that whatever T. S. Eliot said about anything is always wrong. Of course Heywood has a serious moral purpose throughout this play, for instance in the scenes concerning the poor man Tawneycoat, and even in the parts about Mad Jack who is not just a comic figure: Heywood surely intends to compare, in a serious way, the bourgeois ethos with the aristocratic one. If Gresham had been a peer, instead of just a wealthy commoner, he would probably have had to leave all his wealth to his nephew regardless of that nephew's wild and dissolute behaviour. As it is, he can leave all he has to charitable causes that benefit the City instead. But that does not account for everything in the play, and there are other ways of interpreting what happens to Gresham in the banquet scene, for instance as symbolism. To understand why, first of all we have to understand that there was something very odd about Queen Elizabeth visiting Gresham's Burse, as it was first called, and honouring it with the title of the Royal Exchange.

The Burse had been modelled on the one at Antwerp, where Gresham had spent so much of his career as the financial agent of the Crown. In Antwerp, the trade in bills of exchange was unregulated by the government, but in England the Crown had long claimed a prerogative of controlling currency exchange and regulating the rates. This control, like any arbitrary control, could be highly unwelcome to those trying to operate in an open, international market. The title of 'Royal Exchange' or 'Cambium Regis' was given by Tudor monarchs to the minister whose job it was to exercise this control. Yet Elizabeth did, in 1571, bestow the very same title on Gresham's Exchange, where merchants from all over Europe were doing free-trade business. But what could Elizabeth do to stop them? In 1576, her government issued a new proclamation which again said 'that by the laws and statutes of this realm no man ought to make any exchange or rechange of money but such as her majesty shall authorize', and vested this authority in three London merchants.[33] This Act, like the numerous Tudor statutes against usury, seems to have been completely ignored in practice. How could it have been enforced, unless all the merchants in the Exchange, English and foreign alike, had been put in gaol, together with the Corporation of London?

Surely Elizabeth had to be realistic and, by visiting the Exchange and giving it her blessing in 1571, was in fact bowing to necessity though passing it off as royal favour. She needed the city merchants to go on lending her money on a regular basis, and so did everybody else. In Heywood's play, Queen Elizabeth is actually shown borrowing money from Gresham's friend Hobson, and this has sound historical foundation although Hobson is a representative figure. The setting up of Gresham's Burse was actually a triumph for the powers of the City and of market forces against the claims of the Crown and of arbitrary control. And when we look at it in this light, the scene in which Gresham hears of his ship being sunk can start to appear quite different, as a piece of symbolism (witting or unwitting). The shop was carrying a cargo of statues of past monarchs, to adorn the newly built Exchange, but those symbols of royal authority will not be needed. It is not just the statues, but one aspect of the royal prerogative, that is being dumped.

In the case of the King of Barbary, who treats Gresham in such a callous (and costly) fashion, Gresham is the loser. He makes light of it, and putting on the slippers tells his guests, 'A London merchant thus treads on a king's present'. To prove that his generosity is not dimmed by these losses, he goes on to mention his new 'schoole of the seuen learned liberal sciences, Which I haue founded here near *Bishops gate* . . . I will make it, Lords, An Vniuersity within itselfe, And giue't from my reuenues maintenance'.[34] He means, of course, Gresham College. Clearly the citizen hero is very admirable, and the Barbary King is very dishonourable and deplorable, but the Barbary King is still boss, and he has trodden Gresham underfoot like a pair of slippers. Perhaps we should bear in mind that it was the monarch, or at least his representative, who imposed censorship of the stage in 1606, not the Corporation or citizens of London. One could say what one liked about Gresham, but one could not say what one liked about a king — unless it was a king of a very distant and heathen country, such as the Barbary Coast.

[33] Bindoff, pp. 18–19.

[34] Heywood, ibid., p. 301.

Tudor and Stuart monarchs regularly exacted forced loans, and increasing rates of tax (often through import duties) from the merchant class of London, and if Heywood wanted to show where his sympathies lay, he might have been using the Barbary King as a means of doing it. Why does the King send a dagger? What could Gresham do with it? Perhaps the slippers and the dagger are symbolic, representing the choice that must be made when people push one around. Either one must get very tough indeed, or otherwise choose the slippers and be, like them, downtrodden. The time for a showdown had not come in Gresham's generation, but the establishment of the Exchange — unadorned by any monarch's statue — was a sign that the power of the City was, in the long term, growing. Towards the end of the play, Queen Elizabeth's visit to the Exchange and to Gresham's house is dramatised:

Queen: Our leasure now serues to suruey your Burse,
          A goodly frame, a rare proportion.
          This city our great chamber cannot show vs,
          To add vnto our fame a monument
          Of greater beauty

But her minister the Earl of Sussex, admits that it will win fame for Gresham rather than for Elizabeth:

          This *Greshams* work of stone
          Will liue to him when I am dead and gone.[35]

So great was Heywood's admiration of the Royal Exchange, that he wrote one other play which is almost entirely set within it, *The Fayre Mayde of the Exchange*. This was printed in 1607, so was probably written to follow up the success of *If You Know Not Me* in 1606. It is a pleasant comedy whose heroine, Phillis Flower, the fair maid of the title, is the daughter of a draper and moneylender who has a shop in the Exchange. She is loved and wooed by three brothers, Ferdinand, Anthony and Frank Goulding. Her father wants her to marry Ferdinand. Her mother wants her to marry Anthony. But Phillis rejects them all in favour of a cripple, Master Drawer, whom she loves and esteems because he once rescued her and her friend Ursula from a pair of muggers and rapists when they were delivering linen to Mile End on a dark evening. She does not realise that the stranger who helped the cripple and beat off the attackers a second time was Frank Goulding. Phillis makes her love known to Master Drawer by the modest means of an embroidered handkerchief, but he, though flattered, thinks that handsome young Frank is a better match for her: he gets Frank to woo her in disguise and she eventually yields to their joint persuasion. Another maiden who lives in the Exchange, Mall Berry, has a leading role and proves that shopkeepers' daughters can be witty and spirited in managing their unwanted suitors, as well as pretty and chaste. Heywood gives Master Drawer a speech which strongly defends the womenfolk of the Exchange from the sort of nasty slights that were sometimes aimed at them:

O thou art one of those, that if an honest Maid be sent to thy chamber with her Mistris goods, and returne as honest and chast as the Moone: Sirra, you are one of those that will slaunder the poore wenches, by speaking liberally of their pronenesse to love; and withall, bragge how cheape you have bought their ware metaphorically, when indeed they depart as honest as they came thither . . .[36]

It is typical of the way that Heywood was always quick to champion the honour and reputation of the City of London, of which the Royal Exchange was such a proud and visible symbol.

Gresham's foundation was recalled again in Beaumont and Fletcher's *The Knight of the Burning Pestle* (1613). In the comic Introduction to this play, a Citizen of London leaps on stage and interrupts the speaker of the Prologue, saying that he can have no good meaning in calling a play 'The London Merchant' because 'I have observed it, you still have girds at citizens'. The Citizen admits that he is a Freeman of the City and member of the Grocer's Company. The Speaker denies any satirical intent, but the Citizen carries on,

No, sir! yes, sir: if you were not resolved to play the jacks, what need you study for new subjects, purposely to abuse your betters? why could you not be contented as well as others, with 'The legend of Whittington,' or, 'The Life and Death of Sir Thomas Gresham, with the building of the

---

[35] Ibid., p. 317.

[36] Heywood, vol. II, p. 26.

Royal Exchange,' or, 'The story of Queen Eleanor, with the rearing of London Bridge upon woolsacks?'

The first two items in this list are surely references to Heywood's works (he also wrote a pamphlet about Dick Whittington). The citizen's pride in his heritage is being sent up, but it is genial humour, and it shows

what a deep impression Gresham had made on the imagination of Londoners.[37]

[37] *Select Plays of Beaumont and Fletcher*, Everyman's Library no. 506, ed. G. P. Baker (J. M. Dent and Sons Ltd, London, 1911, rpt 1946), p. 7.

CHAPTER XIII

'Weighed in the Balances and Found Wanting . . .'[1] An Analysis of a Steelyard or Unequal Armed Balance in the Museum of London's Collection

By HAZEL FORSYTH

INTRODUCTION

IN 1912, THE LONDON MUSEUM acquired an unequal armed balance or steelyard,[2] with an inscription to Thomas Gresham on one of the weights; and on the left supporting bracket, escutcheons bearing the Gresham arms and TG cipher (Figs. 22, 23). Although it was recognised that some of the ornamentation was of a later period, a misreading of the date on the beam as 157[2] led to the mistaken belief that the steelyard had been made for use in the 1571 Royal Exchange. The steelyard is on display in the Tudor Gallery at the Museum of London.

It hardly seemed likely that there could be anything new to say on this object, beyond a simple catalogue description; but for the purposes of this volume, a detailed study has been undertaken which throws serious doubt on the steelyard, its association with Gresham and thereby the Royal Exchange.

What is a steelyard? In essence, a steelyard consists of an unequal armed horizontal rod or beam, marked along most of its length with a graduated scale. The short, wide arm is unmarked and of sufficient weight to hold the beam in equilibrium from its vertical pivot point. A load is suspended from the short arm of the beam, and balanced by moving a counterpoise along the scale, against which the weight of the goods can be read. The overall size of the beam corresponds to the weight it is designed to support and measure.

THE 'GRESHAM' STEELYARD

What then can we say of the functional application of the so-called 'Gresham' steelyard? The beam is

745 mm long, with a scale of diamond section, engraved on the two upper faces with 12 × 38 (456) equal divisions. There are no numbers, but a series of circles and oblique lines which do not conform to any standard calibration and are quite unlike the conventional scale markings for steelyards. Steelyard beams are either completely unmarked, or more usually numbered to facilitate use and rapid calculation.

The scale divisions came to an abrupt and rather curious stop at each end. At the point furthest from the fulcrum the rod has been cut through a division point and a brass urn has been soldered in place as a decorative terminal. This urn is of neo-classical 1790s style and may well have come from a clock or piece of furniture. At the other end of the beam the scale stops part way through a division.

There is a decorative section at the junction of the scale and short arm, which appears to have been hand-turned, since the rings vary in depth and circumference. The construction of this section is intriguing. It looks as if the circular section covers a join in the iron bar; but if so, how is it held together, and would this be likely at the very point of maximum stress and downward force?

The short beam arm of the rectangular section is 170 mm long. A rod of iron extends from the upper face to mark the pivot point and centre of verticality. There are two transverse holes for the knife edges (wedges of steel which enable the beam to oscillate). The short beam arm seems to have been constructed from part of another object, a lock plate, perhaps. The outline is oddly shaped, and the back edge has been deliberately cut down, leaving an irregular, unfinished surface, and there are three holes in the longitudinal axis with internal threads, suggestive of

---

[1] *The Bible*, Daniel 5 v. 27.
[2] Museum of London Accession number A6483.

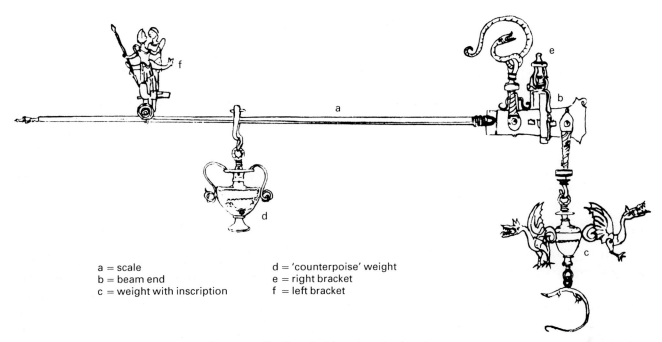

a = scale
b = beam end
c = weight with inscription

d = 'counterpoise' weight
e = right bracket
f = left bracket

FIG. 20. Steelyard with supporting brackets.

additional attachments. Moreover, the short beam arm is of insufficient weight to provide equilibrium. This fact is of crucial significance. As it stands, the steelyard is of no functional use, and would probably require something in the region of 7–8 lb. extra weight on the end of the beam to balance. Furthermore, it is clear that the end of the beam was cut after the decoration had been applied, since the engraved border of a bird's foot trefoil design and the large decorative swag have been dissected. The engraved decoration is very characteristic of eighteenth-century ornamentation.

In addition to the bird's foot trefoil engraved border and swag, the short beam arm bears the date, 1579 (the year of Gresham's death) and not 1572 as was previously supposed. The last number is partially formed, but the loop is clear and the downward curve just visible through a binocular microscope. Between the etched and divided date 15 and 79 a brass escutcheon 'spade' shield of the nineteenth century has been crudely recessed and brazed into the surface (Fig. 21). The shield is evidently an addition, and in all probability conceals an earlier armorial device. (Since copper is denser than iron, we cannot investigate this tantalising problem further. But even if we

could prize off the escutcheon, it is likely that any device underneath would have been erased.)

There are two 'stirrups' or clamps, which pass around the short beam arm, one serving to suspend the steelyard from its pivot point and the other to take the weight and hook. These components are made of cast and wrought iron and much care has been lavished on their manufacture, even down to the small screws clustered around the knife edges. Given this attention to detail, it is surprising that the design on these 'stirrups' is different to those on the rest of the beam. Indeed, the design detail is not unlike Nuremberg work on nest weight covers of the early 1500s.

The steelyard hangs from a suspension ring through which the gordian body of a wrought iron serpent entwines, the tail recurving to form a hook. Although decorative, the hook was not constructed to be load bearing and for this reason the steelyard is supported by brackets.

THE WEIGHTS

After the beam, the second most important part of a steelyard is the weight (Fig. 22). Steelyards only

Fig. 21.

Fig. 22.

Fig. 23.

Fig. 24.

Fig. 25.

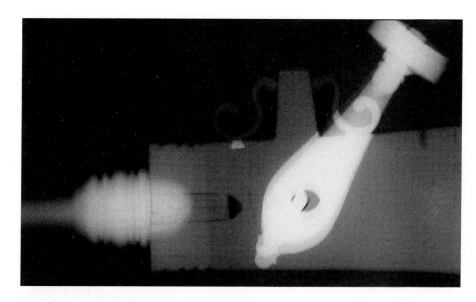

FIG. 26. X-ray film of the beam showing screw thread join.

require *one* weight as a counterpoise, but the 'Gresham' steelyard has two weights and they are both quite different from each other.

Under the short arm there is a hook on to which a cast and turned brass urn is suspended, filled with lead. The urn is 90 mm × 45 mm and weighs 634.36 g. The shape is interesting in that, of the surviving steelyard weights in museum collections, none resemble it in form apart from Chinese examples in the Science Museum dating from A.D. 960–1368. This weight and its embellishments serve no practical purpose on the steelyard, and a weight at this point is entirely superfluous. On the shoulder of the urn-shaped weight, and cast into it, is the inscription THOMAS . GRESHAMUS . Ɛ . F . LOND. There is no doubt that the inscription was cast into the brass since the characteristic stipple marks of the greensand mould can be seen. The inscription is only very slightly raised, and fairly clear with the exception of the two letters between Greshamus and Lond. The letter immediately after Greshamus is particularly intriguing. Its shape suggests a partially closed 'O' with a lateral tick through the left half, thus ; 'Ɛ' ; perhaps a 'C' for *Civis* (citizen) so this part of the inscription might then read . . . *civis fecit*. But this

makes little sense in relation to Gresham, unless one infers that a citizen of London made this item for Gresham. An alternative, and more convincing explanation, could be that the 'Ɛ' shape is an E for *Eques* (Sir), and the F for *Fundator* (Founder). That is, Sir Thomas Gresham, founder, London; by implication founder of the 1571 Royal Exchange. If so, the letter E is quite different from the E in Greshamus. Different punches have also been used for the letters 'H' and 'S'. The style of the lettering is not inappropriate for the late sixteenth century, but could easily have been copied at a later date.[3]

Attached to this weight are three dragons of wrought iron, and hanging below the urn a suspension ring is attached to a hook in the form of a salamander. Made from six pieces, the dragons are all constructed in the same way, but vary in minor detail and weight — 206.27 g.; 223.67 g. and 240.74 g. This weight variation is entirely consistent with hand-crafted work. The heaviest is the most elaborately chased, with scales extending almost to the tip of the tail. The barbed tongues (one missing) are screwed into place, and the dragons are secured to the urn by screws through their tails. With one exception, all the screws are hand cut. The overall dimension, 21 mm × 17 mm, is standard, but the

FIGS. 21–25. Steelyard: (21) detail of etched date and brass shield escutcheon; (22) detail of brass 'inscribed' weight; (23) the left bracket; (24) detail of left bracket; (25) the right bracket.

[3] I am indebted to James Mosely of the St Bride's Printing Library and John Cherry of the British Museum for their help and suggestions here.

heads vary in angle and there are a few areas of restoration on the wings and neck.

Two of the dragons, those with the least chasing, conform very well to the woodcut engraving[4] which accompanies the Revd Edward Topsell's *Historie of Serpents*, first published in 1607 (Fig. 27). Topsell wrote the first volume of natural history in the English language and much of his source material and inspiration came from Swiss naturalist Konrad von Gesner's monumental four-volume *Historia Animalium* published between 1551 and 1587.

Topsell devotes fifteen pages in his *Historie of Serpents* to the 'divers forts of Dragons, diftinguished partly by their Countries, partly by their quantity and magnitude and partly by the different form of their external parts'.[5] The 'external parts' of the steelyard dragons could well have been derived from Topsell; his work was much used, and illustrations copied in succeeding centuries. But why choose dragons? Although used as supporters of the City of London arms, dragons have an unpleasant symbolic association. Randle Holme,[6] however, suggests that dragons are a 'fit bearing for vigilent and ftrenuous Heroes, that will take hold of any opportunity & occafion'. Whilst one might look hard for any trace of the heroic in Gresham's character, there is no doubt that he was quick to grasp both opportunity and occasion. That said, the Gresham crest is a grasshopper, and this would have been a more obvious and appropriate choice, and no more difficult to construct. Furthermore, as Topsell reminds us, grasshoppers are noble creatures:

> Although I am an Infect very fmall,
> Yet with great virtue am endow'd with all.[7]

A salamander of wrought iron with recurving tail hangs below the urn weight, as a hook. It is clear that the salamander hook could support very little weight, perhaps a few ounces, and certainly not the possible 56 lb. or so suggested by the length of the graduated scale. Furthermore, the suspension ring holding the salamander is held by an internal screw thread into the base of the urn. This screw thread is crude with a

FIG. 27.   A dragon from Topsell's *Historie of Serpents*, p. 701.

fairly large pitch for its diameter, and it has been sunk into lead, which suggests either a bodged repair to a worn thread or the need to reduce a larger hole to fit a new thread. Either way, this results in weakness, and raises questions about its position and function.

Why choose salamanders? Topsell writes: 'But the greateft matter in the salamander to be enquired after, is whether it can live and be nourifhed by and in the fire, or whether it can paffe through the fire without any harm, or quench and put out the fame.'[8] The origin of this rather curious statement may stem from the simple fact that salamanders prefer to live in forests, but near water. When obliged to forsake their natural environment, log piles outside houses offer a perfect place to hibernate and rest. Hence 'the sight of bright yellow and black salamanders fleeing from piles of burning logs gave rise to the belief that they lived in fire'.[9] This association may also explain why the Ironmongers chose salamanders for supporters on their grant of armorial bearing, and why salamanders in iron appear on the steelyard. It is intriguing in this connection to note that Thomas Gresham had particular interests in the iron industry of the Weald, acquiring Mayfield furnace in 1570 and obtaining a licence to export ordnance to Denmark in 1574.[10]

---

[4] Topsell, 1607, Ch. 17, Bk 1, fig. p. 701.
[5] Topsell, ibid., Ch. 17, Bk 1, p. 703.
[6] Holme, 1688, Bk II, Ch. 10 (on the significance of beasts used in armoury), p. 217.
[7] Topsell, ibid., Ch. 17, Bk 1, p. 995.

[8] Topsell, ibid., Ch. 17, Bk 1, p. 748.
[9] Clarke, 1993, p. 46.
[10] PRO, SP12 95/62 and PRO, C24/41, pt 1.

The weight serving as an apparent counterpoise weight which looks suspiciously like a bed knob, is made from fifteen different components and weighs a total of 1524.41 g. This weight is held by a suspension ring and screw thread to a wrought iron salamander whose tail encircles the ring. The body of the salamander (its back legs are missing) curls around a crescent which in turn hangs from the beam, marking a position on the scale. Unfortunately the knife edge of the crescent does not rest securely on the scale to effect a really good reading, and for this reason steelyards usually have some notched surface from which the counterpoise is suspended. The 'counterpoise' weight, like the inscribed weight, is also of cast brass with a lead core and urn shape. However, the shape of the 'counterpoise' urn is quite different. The lead core extends from top to bottom, and has been plugged at the base, which is a little odd and perhaps suggests that the brass urn originally served another purpose, possibly as a finial. Two wrought iron slow worms or possibly smooth snakes form 'handles', and these are secured by screws with their heads resting in the neck flange of the urn. Their combined weight is 73 g.

There are many parallels for urns with snake handles, particularly amongst the work of the Kleinmeister engravers of southern Germany in the second quarter of the sixteenth century. Nuremberg craftsman Peter Flotner (1458–1546) produced engravings of vases and urns, some with snake handles, in an architectural treatise published some time before 1546, and this work and others of its kind provided ample source material for craftsmen wishing to replicate Renaissance classical designs.

The counterpoise weight is further embellished by applied cast iron festoons, one on either side, and held in place by screws which, with one exception, support rather than pierce the design. Two central flower heads are flanked by, on one side, oak leaves and acorns with rosettes, and on the reverse, tulips and foliage. The urn has also been chased with small annular and crescent punches. The crescent chasing has been executed in a rather bizarre fashion, stopping and starting around the festoon decoration, which suggests that the chasing may have been applied as an afterthought, perhaps in an attempt to match decoration elsewhere.

THE BRACKETS

We must now turn our attention to the two brackets, which have no bearing on the 'functional' use of the steelyard, and serve only to display the beam and support it in a horizontal position (Figs. 23–24). The socket ends of the brackets have different profiles, and were clearly not made of a piece. The right-hand bracket consists of three pieces of wrought iron, all of quite different composition and

has attached to it part of the steel hilt of a small-sword of about 1700. This consists of a portion of the sleeve and the guards it supports; the knuckle-guard, the rear quillon and the arms of the hilt. It is secured to the underside of the frame by means of a rivet passing through the hole for the tang of the blade.[11]

The end of the knuckle-guard has been welded to the bracket. Joined to this small-sword hilt are two copper alloy openwork mounts, probably taken from a piece of furniture and dating to the eighteenth century.

The left-hand bracket is an extraordinary assemblage of metalwork. Three wrought iron scrolls support two iron escutcheon shields of baroque design, one bearing the Gresham arms: Argent, a chevron Ermines between three mullets pierced of the field Sable, the other depicts an entwined TG cipher of baroque design. It is not the cipher used by Thomas Gresham on his will,[12] which is of simple merchant's mark form with the letters TG interposed. Neither does the cipher design match any ciphers used by Gresham's descendants who bore his initials. Above the escutcheons are components from the hilts of two different swords. The first, of cast steel, is from the hilt of a small-sword of about 1680–1710 which is fitted to the bracket as if the blade was pointing upwards. It consists of a complete sleeve framed by rows of small dots in relief with military trophies on each face in moderate relief. The sleeve supports the

[11] I am indebted to A. V. B. Norman for this, and the following notes on the sword hilts (pers. comm.): 'There is a small-sword with a comparable hilt in the Royal Armouries (Inv. No. IX.1362) and another with a silver hilt in a private collection. The second bears no hall-mark, but has a maker's mark DH, which is thought to be English. This hilt is very like one illustrated in a portrait of Sir John St Aubyn, the 2nd Bt, by D. Short, dated 1703 (private collection). A somewhat comparable hilt of brass was found in a wreck said to be of a vessel which went down off the Kent coast in 1703.'

[12] Burgon, *Gresham*, vol. I, p. vii.

arms of the hilt and the stumps of either a knuckle-guard and rear quillon or a pair of quillons. It is not clear whether the oval washer is an integral part of the sleeve. The roots of the arms and the end of the sleeve towards the grip are clasped by acanthus calyxes.[13]

Immediately above and placed at right-angles is a dragon/serpent which appears to have been part of the guard from a mid-seventeenth-century parade sword. This animal, in iron with gold leaf, is punched and incised with a mixture of scales and foliate decoration. The dragon's head, or rear quillon, originally faced the blade. What at first appears to be a bifurcated tail are two broken stumps; the shorter with foliate design originally formed part of the knuckle-guard, whilst the larger scrolled branch which seems to represent the wing tips was presumably the forward quillon. Swords with dragon guards formed in this way are rare. Seated on the dragon's back is a naked infant of indeterminate gender with arms raised, and hair swept back from the forehead. The crown of the head has been flattened in manufacture. The child is made from cast iron.[14]

On either side are three-dimensional male and female figures in Roman military garb, which were almost certainly manufactured in the nineteenth century. They are both made from cast and wrought iron with brass 'aprons', and hold shields of iron depicting trophies of arms in niello. The shields, which seem to be a pair, are half of the shell from the hilt of a small-sword. The male figure (height 118 mm) holds a lance, the lower end of which has been restored in this century to fifteenth-century calvary lance shape. The female figure (height 114 mm) has lost her weapon. Both figures face each other, but the female figure stares out to the middle distance, and it looks as though she needs to be rotated through 45 degrees to stand at the correct position. Both of the figures' heads have been cast separately; their long necks probably secured to the trunk with internal rivets.

Although both figures are engraved with *lorica segmentata* on the front of the torso, when viewed from the back they seem to be wearing a plain cuirass. Both figures wear ornamented 'aprons' and calf-length sandals, but there are subtle differences in costume detail. The male figure has a helmet of bizarre design, a sort of Roman/Renaissance *casque de parade* with an additional chin strap. He also sports a curling moustache. In contrast, the female figure has wavy longish locks covered by a coil of textile, plait of hair, or snake, which winds around the crown of the head and forehead. The neck line and sleeves of the tunics are also different, the female tunic is shaped and more elaborate, and her apron has additional repoussé studs. The sandal shapes for both figures follow quite different patterns.

Taken together, the figures on the left bracket form a very eccentric grouping indeed. Are they a random assortment put together for convenience and amusement, or is there an underlying symbolic significance in their juxtaposition? It has been proposed[15] that the adult figures represent the mythical giants Gog and Magog; but the apparent difference in gender would immediately suggest otherwise. Even if both figures are taken to be male, the Gog Magog legend does not fit happily with their appearance.

One version of the legend describes the story thus:[16] Diocletian, an Eastern potentate, had thirty-three daughters. After much difficulty he married them off, but the daughters collectively decided to murder their husbands. This they proceeded to do. Diocletian was most displeased and sent his daughters away in disgrace on a six-month voyage, which ended when they eventually landed on the island of Albion. When Brutus arrived in Britain, he engaged the giant descendants of Diocletian's daughters in battle, two of whom, Gog and Magog, were taken captive and

---

[13] Norman, pers. comm. 'The date is probably around 1680–1710, but . . . we do not have enough evidence [to assign a nationality] to such a hilt.'

[14] Norman, pers. comm. 'There are two swords [with Dragon guards of this type] in the Danish Royal Collection and a third with guards formed as serpents. One of each type, both of enamelled gold, belonged to Christian "the King Elect" (1603–47) A. Hoff, H. D. Schepelern & G. Boesen, *Royal Arms at Rosenborg* Copenhagen 1956, Cat. Nos. 17 and 16 respectively. A carved ivory hilt with a dragon forming its guard in the British Royal Collection is thought to be of Dutch workmanship of the middle of the seventeenth century. (Exhibited *Carlton House* The Queen's Gallery 1991, Cat. No. 134.) A sword hilt of this type is illustrated in van Dyck's portrait of a man in armour with a red scarf, painted about 1627 (Dresden, Staatliche Kunstsammlung *Catalogue* 1989, No. 1026).'

[15] London Museum, 1937.
[16] Boreman, 1741, and Fairholt, 1859.

tied to the City gates. Effigies were made in their memory after death.

The second version[17] suggests that Brutus's brother Corineus fought a single giant called Gogmagog and triumphed; hence the depiction of a giant in Roman military costume and a giant of somewhat barbarian appearance, as represented by the Guildhall figures.

If the figures are not Gog and Magog, perhaps they are supposed to represent the warlike Ares (Mars) and his twin sister Eris (Bellona). The female figure does not have dishevelled hair, although a snake may be coiled in her locks. Or are the figures Ares and Pallas-Athene (Minerva)?

Although the method of manufacture, treatment of the costume and general appearance suggests that the figures were made in the nineteenth century, similar statuettes in bronze were made in Nuremberg in the sixteenth century (Van Marle, *Iconographie de l'Art Profane*, Vol. 1, p. 299, fig. 291 for comparanda). In the Untermeyer *Catalogue*[18] a comparable figure in latten, of sixteenth-century date and of roughly the same size as the steelyard statuettes but with a hollow centre, seems to have been part of a hanging candelabrum. Were the bracket figures taken from another object?

How do these figures relate, if at all, with the infant and dragon? Are we looking at a chance juxtaposition, or should we try to look for a plausible explanation? It is possible that the infant was removed from a small shrine or statuette of the Madonna and Child. Was it associated with the quillon dragon, to represent the triumph of good over evil? But equally, the child and dragon could be taken to represent Harpocrates or even the infant Dionysus! Are we simply tempted to read more into this curious grouping than was ever intended? Before trying to address these issues, what do we know of the provenance of the 'Gresham' steelyard?

THE PROVENANCE

The London Museum acquired the steelyard in 1912 from Mr G. Hubbard, who, although evidence is lacking, seems to have purchased the object from the Thurlow family. Lady Thurlow, in 1912 correspondence with the Museum,[19] believed that the steelyard had belonged to Edward Thurlow[20] (1781–1829), a minor poet and antiquarian, and that this gentleman had displayed the steelyard together with a portrait of Gresham in the dining room of his home at Baynards, Surrey, in the early 1800s. Edward Thurlow also had a collection of pictures and 'other things of chiefly Tudor times'. His effects passed to his son, who sold much of the collection, but took the pictures and steelyard to London. In 1904 there were two sales at Christie's[21] sold by order of the Executors of T. L. Thurlow, late of Baynard's Park. On 9 July, the second of these, a portrait of Sir Thomas Gresham by Sir Antonio More was sold. The steelyard was not put up for sale in either auction, and there is no record of any other Thurlow sale in the *Repertoire des Catalogue de Ventes*.[22]

CONCLUSION

Thus far I have done little more than examine the steelyard and its anomalies, adding a string of questions to the descriptive analysis. All of these questions demand answers, but we are confronted by a fascinating enigma; an assembly of attractive metalwork which makes little sense. A steelyard beam of no functional use, which does not balance, seemingly made from two pieces of steel, and joined at the point of greatest mechanical weakness; inscribed with a late sixteenth-century date and decorated with eighteenth-century engraving. The whole smothered in a vast repertoire of ornament; with two weights instead of one, and both different. The weight with the inscription hangs in a totally inappropriate place, and there are useless, if decorative, hooks, with two extraordinary brackets. All apparent nonsense which we must try to turn into sense.

There is a temptation when confronted by a strange object which stretches the bounds of probability, to doubt part and then all. The more you think, the queerer it becomes, and the less likely you are to believe any of it. But we should be cautious in our

---

[17] Boreman, 1741, and Fairholt, 1859.
[18] Untermeyer, *Catalogue*, vol. v (London, 1962), fig. 143.

[19] Lady Thurlow, correspondence 10 January 1908.
[20] *DNB*, entry Thurlow, afterwards Hovell-Thurlow, Edward, 2nd Baron Thurlow, p. 829.
[21] Lot 29.
[22] Lught, 1987.

judgement. Is it possible that the date etched into the beam, 1579, is correct, and that it was originally longer and complete? Perhaps it had belonged to someone quite unconnected with Gresham and the Exchange; which might explain why a nineteenth-century shield has been interposed between the two parts of the date. Was the length reduced and function altered in a deliberate attempt to mislead?

What do genuine sixteenth-century steelyards look like? There are very few extant examples, and these are mostly continental, published in a variety of unhelpful antiquarian catalogues. Provenance information is usually lacking and the dating insecure; the beam ends vary in design although most have a rectangular profile. The most helpful evidence comes from the late sixteenth-century woodcut of mills by Galle,[23] which shows two steelyards, one in use and the other hanging from the withers of a pack horse. Both of the beam ends are rectangular.

Was the 'Gresham' steelyard made as an ornament, copying the style of a late sixteenth-century unequal armed balance? One could argue that the excessive ornament and exaggerated detail was employed for emphasis and impact, hence the lack of functionality and the idiosyncratic scale markings. But, if so, one would have expected the steelyard to have been smothered in grasshoppers rather than dragons and serpents.

All the disparate elements of the steelyard are well made, giving a general impression of technical accomplishment, which suggests a considered approach to its construction. It is therefore all the more surprising that the ornament is so various and the steelyard non-functioning.

There are no references to a steelyard amongst the Gresham or Royal Exchange archives, and why select a steelyard to adorn the buildings of the Royal Exchange, when an equal armed balance, the symbol of justice and impartiality, would have carried far more symbolic weight? The provenance of the steelyard is uncertain, and we have little more to go on than recollected family history taking us back to the early 1800s, and thereafter a lacuna until 1579. It is hardly conceivable that a steelyard was made as a commemorative piece for Gresham and the Royal Exchange when the use of unequal armed weighing instruments were actively discouraged in the City of London. Although steelyards can be highly accurate, it is not difficult to modify the weight of the detachable counterpoise, and thus operate the balance fraudulently. Documents such as the *Liber Albus* refer to the widespread nature of the problem: 'whereas merchants do feel aggrieved, by reason that the weights in the hostels and in the selds of citizen-merchants of London, by which they sell, do not agree with the weight by which they buy'.[24] These grievances led to new regulations, restricting use of the steelyard and enforcing standards of weight and measure. Furthermore, is it not curious that the weights of brass have no mark or stamp of authorisation, in direct contravention of mensural legislation? Statute II, Henry VII, c. 4 of 1495, contains a very clear enactment in this regard: that no person within any city or market town buy or sell, with any weight or measure, *except it be marked*, signed, or printed. This practice continued, with frequent legislative support, until 1908.

What are the facts? The evidence suggests that the beam is made from two pieces of wrought iron, cut to shape to approximate a steelyard of sixteenth-century date. The metal bar forming the end of the beam was evidently cut to size after the eighteenth-century decorative engraving had been applied. The date 1597 may have been added to give credence to the Gresham connection.

Thus far, I have only looked at the steelyard from a technical and art-historical perspective, but what of its metallurgical and physical structure? A complete evaluation is impossible without recourse to scientific analysis. Although the beam looks as if it is made from two pieces of steel, is that actually so? Brian Gilmour, Archaeo-metallurgist for the Royal Armouries, has obtained an X-radiograph of the beam (Fig. 26); and this proves beyond doubt that it is made up from two pieces, held together by a short threaded pin; the pin is screwed into an internally threaded aperture at the end of the long arm. The two sections of beam fit well together. Screw dimensions can provide helpful dating evidence, and the

23 P. Galle (1537–1612), engraving of water and floating mills, origin uncertain, but possibly from German book of *c.* 1617.

24 Carta Mercatoria, 1 February 1303: grant to foreign merchants in return for new custom.

screwed joint of the steelyard beam deserves close attention. If the date of the screw thread can be determined, this will suggest an approximate date for the construction of the beam. For this reason, the screw thread was examined by Michael Wright, Curator of Mechanical Engineering, Science Museum, and although it is impossible to obtain precise dimensions from an X-ray, the screw appears to be about $\frac{7}{16}$ inch diameter, with approximately 12 threads to the inch, and thread profiles of about 75 to 80 degrees. Wright suggests that the observed thread form, proportions and tapering of the screws, are consistent with early mechanical practice which, while common enough into the early nineteenth century, would have seemed primitive by the middle of that century. On the basis of what we see in the radiographs this joint is likely to have been made before the middle of the nineteenth century — but this would not, of course, preclude — a later crafts-man from employing an old-fashioned joint; although it is perhaps unlikely.

In addition, dispersive X-ray fluorescence (xrf) was undertaken, which identifies elements present in major or minor amounts in the surface of an object. Analysis of chemical composition can provide a very precise indication of the date of manufacture. Some of the copper alloys were analysed in an attempt to determine whether the composition was consistent with a late sixteenth-century date. The results show that 'a wide variety of brass or gunmetal (a ternary copper-zinc-tin) alloys were used', an unexpected combination 'for any genuine original working object unless there is evidence for repairs or restoration which is not the case here'. The conclusion drawn from the scientific analysis outlined above suggests that the steelyard cannot have been constructed much before the early nineteenth century.

The steelyard has undoubtedly been made up from parts of objects of various dates, and was almost certainly assembled in the late eighteenth or early nineteenth century. Mr Thurlow evidently had a collection of 'Tudor things'; he also had a portrait of Gresham, so perhaps his antiquarian proclivities and obvious interest in Gresham induced him to purchase a steelyard with apparent Gresham connections from an unscrupulous knick-knackitarian. But, if so, one must ask whether there was sufficient interest in

Gresham at this date to justify such an elaborate fabrication?

The brackets have a number of sword-hilt elements in their construction, which perhaps indicates that a nineteenth-century dealer in arms and armour had a hand in the fabrication. There is evidence of collusion between dealers and collectors to fabricate material history, and it is possible that Edward Thurlow asked a dealer to customise the steelyard for him with odds and ends from his personal collection.

All we know today is that this object is full of anomalies and has been constructed in such a way as to make the obvious conclusion of late eighteenth- or early nineteenth-century fake unavoidable. If nothing else, the steelyard points to a thriving interest in Sir Thomas Gresham in the early nineteenth century.

BIBLIOGRAPHY

ARNOLD, E. N. & BURTON, J. A. *A Field Guide to Reptiles and Amphibians of Britain and Europe* (Collins, 1978)

BARBER, R. & RICHES, A. *Dictionary of Fabulous Beasts* (Macmillan, 1971)

BINDOFF, S. T. *The Fame of Sir Thomas Gresham*, Fourth Neale Lecture in English History (Jonathan Cape, 1973)

BREWER, T. 'On the antiquity of marking and stamping weights and measures', *J. Brit. Archaeol. Assoc.*, VIII (1853), pp. 309–22

BURGON, J. W. *The Life and Times of Sir Thomas Gresham*, 2 vols. (London, 1839)

CLARKE, B. *Eyewitness Guides: Amphibians* (Dorling Kind-ersley, 1993)

CLEERE, H. & CROSSLEY, D. *The Iron Industry of the Weald*, 2nd edn (Merton Priory Press, 1995)

CONNOR, R. D. *The Weights and Measures of England*, Science Museum (HMSO, 1987)

D'ALLEMAGNE *Musée le Secq des Tournelles Ferroniere Ancienne* (Paris, 1924)

DU CERCEAU, A. *Manual for the Making of Vases*, MS French *c.* 1545–50 (Victoria and Albert Museum L9.-1982)

FAIRHOLT, F. W. *Gog and Magog the Giants in the Guildhall, with an Account of other Civic Giants at Home and Abroad* (London, 1859)

FLANAGAN, L. N. W. 'Steelyards and steelyard weights', *International Journal of Nautical Archaeology and Underwater Exploration*, XVI (1987), pp. 249–65

FLOTNER, P. *Architectural Treatise* (Nuremburg, before 1546)

FOX-DAVIES, A. C. *The Art of Heraldry: an encyclopaedia of armory* (London, 1904)

FRIEDLANDEN, M. J. *On Art and Connoisseurship*, trans. Tancred Borenius (London, 1943)

FURFIELD D. R. & DE ROOVER, R. 'On the authorship and dating of *For the Understanding of the Exchange*', *Economic History Review*, 2nd series, XX (1967), pp. 145–52

GESNER, K. *Curious Woodcuts of Fanciful and Real Beasts: A selection of 190 sixteenth-century woodcuts from Gesner and Topsell's natural histories* (Dover, New York, 1971)

GOMBRICH, E. H. *Symbolic Images* (London, 1972, reprinted 1985)

HADLEY, G. *Citizens and Founders: a history of the Worshipful Company of Founders, London 1365–1975* (London, 1976)

HOFF, A. *et al.*, *Royal Arms at Rosenborg* (Copenhagen, 1956)

HOLME, R. *The Academy of Armory; or, a storehouse of armory and blazon* (1688)

JEWELL, B. *Veteran Scales and Balances* (Midas Books, 1978)

KISCH, B. *Scales and Weights: A historical outline* (Yale University Press, 1965)

KULA, W. *Measures and Men*, trans. R. Szreter (Princeton University Press, 1986)

LAKING, G. *A Record of European Armour and Arms*, vols. 4 and 5 (London, 1921)

LAVAGNE, F. G. *Piles a godets*, notes on the Victoria and Albert Museum Collections (1972)

LEVESON-GOWER, G. W. G. *Genealogy of the Family of Gresham* (London, Mitchell & Hughes, 1883)

LUGT, F. *Repertoire des Catalogues de Ventes* (1901–25) (Paris, 1987)

MELLER, S. *Die Deutchen Bronzestatuetten der Renaissance* (K. Wolff, Munich, *c.* 1926)

PANOFSKY, E. *Meaning in the Visual Arts* (New York, 1957)
—— *Studies in Iconography* (New York, 1962)

PETRIE, F. *Measures and Weights* (London, 1934)

RENN, D. F. 'Steelyard Weights: A postscript', *Proc. Dorset Natural History and Archaeol. Soc.*, VIII (1959), pp. 148–49

RIJKSMUSEUM, KAMTE, G. M. *Descriptions of the Collections in the Rijksmuseum*, No. 7 in series (Nijmegen, 1973)

RILEY, H. T. (ed.) *Liber Albus*, vols. I & II (London, 1859)

ROTHWELL, H. (ed.) *English Historical Documents 1189–1327* (London, 1975)

SAXL, F. *A Heritage of Images* (London, 1970)

SKELTON, J. *Engraved Illustrations of Ancient Arms and Armour from the Collection at Goodrich Court, Herefordshire after the Drawings of Sir S. Rush Meyrick*, 2 vols. (London, 1854)

SMITH, M. *The New Naturalist: the British amphibians and reptiles* (Collins, 1951)

TOPSELL, E. 'The Historie of Serpents', *The Historie of Four-Footed Beasts* (London, 1658)

VAN DER VAAL, H. *Iconclass*, 9 vols. (Amsterdam, 1980, 1981)

VON GESNER, C. K. *Historiae Animalium Libri*, 1st edn, 5 vols. in 4 (Tiguri, 1551–87)

WAINWRIGHT, C. *The Romantic Interior: The British collector at home 1750–1850*, Paul Mellon Centre (Yale University Press, 1989)

WILKINS. J. *Mathematical Magick*, 4th edn (London, 1691)

WILLIAMS, G. A. *Medieval London from Commune to Capital*, University of London Historical Studies XI (1963)

ZADOKS, A. N. *et al.* *The Figural Bronzes* (Rijksmuseum, Nijmegen, 1973)

ZUPKO, R. E. *British Weights and Measures: A history from antiquity to the seventeenth century* (University of Wisconsin Press, 1977)

PART TWO
THE SECOND EXCHANGE

1669–1838

THE SECOND EXCHANGE

CHAPTER XIV

The Second Exchange

By ANN SAUNDERS

THE FIRE REACHED the Royal Exchange on its second day, during the afternoon of Monday, 3 September 1666. Thomas Vincent described the disaster:

When the Fire was entered, how quickly did it run around the galleries, filling them with flames; then descending the stairs compasseth the walks, giving forth flaming vollies, and filling the court with sheets of fire! By and by, the kings fell all down upon their faces, and the greater part of the stone building after them (the founder's statue alone remaining) with such a noise as was dreadful and astonishing.[1]

Others marvelled at the speed of the destruction, Samuel Rolle likening it to the collapse of a canvas tent:

How quickly was it taken down, as if it had been but a Sleight Tent, the Cords whereof are presently loosened and the Stakes soon removed . . .[2]

By Wednesday, 5 September, the heart of the City was desolate. Samuel Pepys, ever the first to venture and to record, viewed the destruction:

. . . I walked into the town and find Fanchurch Street, Gracious Street and Lumbard street all in dust. The Exchange a sad sight, nothing standing there of all the statues or pillars but Sir Tho. Gresham's picture in the corner. Walked into Moorfields (our feet ready to burn, walking through the town among the hot coles) . . . And I took up (which I keep by me) a piece of glass of Mercer's Chapel in the Street, where much more was, so melted and buckled with the heat of the fire, like parchment. I also did see a poor catt taken out of a hole in the chimney joyning to the wall of the Exchange, with the hair all burned off the body and yet alive . . .[3]

Two days later, John Evelyn set out on the same exploration:

I went this morning on foote from White-hall as far as London Bridge thro' the late Fleet Street, Ludgate Hill, by St. Paules, Cheapside, Exchange, Bishopsgate, Aldersgate, and out to Moorfields, thence through Cornehill etc. with extraordinary difficulty, clambering over heaps of yet smoking rubbish, and frequently mistaking where I was. The ground under my feet so hot, that it even burnt the soles of my shoes . . . Sir Tho. Gressham's statue, tho' fallen from its nich in the Royal Exchange, remain'd intire, when all those of the kings since were broken to pieces . . .[4]

Less than a week later, on 13 September, he put into the King's hands 'a plot of a new citty, with a discourse on it' and was examined thereon by Charles II and by the Duke of York, who had already received another design from Dr Christopher Wren. Other plans were received from Robert Hooke, Peter Mills and Richard Newcourt. Before we consider the very practical and down-to-earth reactions of the Gresham Committee, we should look at these plans, to see what emphasis, what importance, they laid upon the Royal Exchange.[5]

Wren recognised the importance of the Royal Exchange to the City and placed it, almost equal to St Paul's Cathedral, on the eastern high ground, where indeed it had stood, but with the streets around it realigned to isolate the commercial heart, so giving it proper pre-eminence. John Evelyn proposed that the Exchange should be moved south, to the riverside, and that a fountain should stand in its place. Robert Hooke's plan, which the City authorities preferred above that of their own surveyor Peter

---

[1] Thomas Vincent, *God's Terrible Voice in the City* (1667), pp. 61–62.
[2] Samuel Rolle, *The Burning of London* (1668), p. 49.
[3] Samuel Pepys, *Diary*, ed. R. Latham and W. Matthews (1972), vol. VII, pp. 276–77.

[4] John Evelyn, *Diary*, ed. E. S. de Beer (1955), vol. III, pp. 458–60.
[5] For Wren's plan, see C. Wren, *Parentalia* (1750); for Evelyn's see Walter Harrison, *History of London* (1775). The best histories of the Great Fire and the subsequent reconstruction of the capital are still George Bell, *The Great Fire of London* (n.d.), and T. F. Reddaway, *The Rebuilding of London after the Great Fire* (1940). For a discussion of the various ideal plans, see T. F. Reddaway in *Town Planning Review* (1937), vol. XVII, nos. 3 & 4; vol. XVIII, no. 3, deals with Newcourt's extraordinary design.

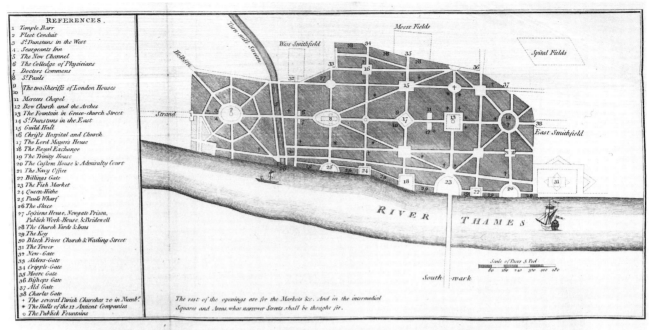

REFERENCES.
1 Temple Barr
2 Fleet Conduit
3 St Dunstans in the West
4 Seargeants Inn
5 The New Channel
6 The Colledge of Physicians
7 Doctors Commons
8 St Pauls
9 The two Sheriffs of London Houses
10
11 Mercers Chapel
12 Bow Church and the Arches
13 The Fountain in Grace-church Street
14 St Dunstans in the East
15 Guild Hall
16 Christs Hospital and Church
17 The Lord Mayors House
18 The Royal Exchange
19 The Trinity House
20 The Custom House & Admiralty Court
21 The Navy Office
22 Billings Gate
23 The Fish Market
24 Queen-Hithe
25 Pauls Wharf
26 The Sluce
27 Sessions House, Newgate Prison,
    Publick Work-House, & Bridewell
28 The Church Yards & Inns
29 The Key
30 Black Friers Church & Watling Street
31 The Tower
32 New-Gate
33 Alders-Gate
34 Cripple-Gate
35 Moore Gate
36 Bishops Gate
37 Ald Gate
38 Charles Gate
+ The several Parish Churches 20 in Numb?
* The Halls of the 12 Antient Companies
o The Publick Fountains

The rest of the openings are for the Markets &c. And in the intermedial
Squares and Areas, what narrower Streets shall be thought fit.

Mr John Evelyns Plan for Rebuilding the City of London after the Great Fire in 1666.

FIG. 28.   Evelyn's plan for the City, 1666. The Royal Exchange is by the Thames at No. 18.
Guildhall Library, Corporation of London

Mills, survives only in a curious little diagram in the corner of a 1667 Dutch engraving of the fire damage by Jacob Venckel which indicates a grid-iron pattern of streets imposed on the devastated city. Peter Mills' plans have vanished — perhaps they might have been more realistic — while Richard Newcourt the map-maker suggested dividing the city into almost self-contained squares, each sheltering a church or an important civic building, though he does not seem to indicate a specific place for the Exchange. All the surviving plans treat London as a *tabula rasa*, a blank sheet upon which any design, particularly an elegantly geometrical one, could be laid. What they ignored were the claims of the freeholders to the sites of their ruined homes and places of business, the impossibility of compensating them for their land, and the amount of time it would have taken to decide upon an ideal plan and to translate it into bricks and mortar.

The Joint Committee's approach to the reconstruction of the Royal Exchange was more mundane but much more realistic. The members assembled on 18 September in Gresham House which, being in the north-eastern corner of the City, was one of the few public buildings to have escaped the devastation. Nineteen of them were present, seven for the City, twelve for the Company. The name of Sir Thomas Bludworth, Lord Mayor, headed the City side, that of the Master, John Godden, the Company's. Men may have blamed Bludworth's over-cautiousness in the early hours of the Fire for the completeness of the destruction, but he took his proper place and continued with his duties. The entry for that meeting is short:

The Committee having taken into consideration how they may accomodate the publique concerne for the City and Company in the house [Gresham House] in this time of publique Calamity and how they may dispose of the residue thereof as well for the Accomodation and keeping together of the Exchange Tenants as for the raising of rents for supply of the uses of the founder . . .[6]

A sub-committee was appointed to allot spaces within Gresham House for the use of the City and

[6] MC, GR, II, p. 227.

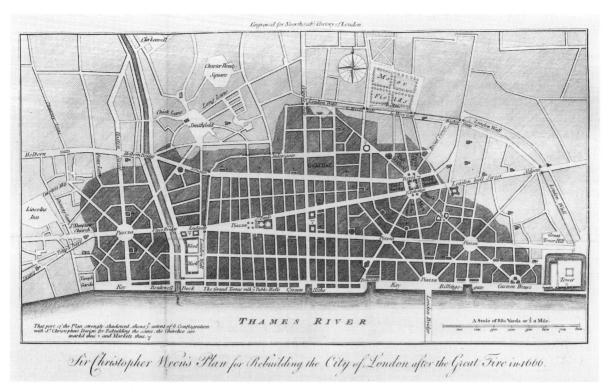

FIG. 29.   Wren's plan for the City, 1666, published by his son in 1750.
Guildhall Library, Corporation of London

Company dignitaries and officers. Sir John Lawrence, Sir George Smith and Deputy Cade were appointed for the City, Sir Richard Ford, Richard Clutterbuck and Rowland Wynne for the Mercers. A quorum of four — Smith, Cade, Clutterbuck and Wynne — assembled the next day and duly allocated the available space; Gresham House was large but it was going to be a tight fit to squeeze in the whole administration of the City and of the leading Company, as well as to provide shop space for all those tenants about the Pawns who were determined to continue trading. The Sub-Committee

viewed all the lecturers lodgings and the publique roomes, the warehouses, cellars, stables, haylofte, shedds & other buildings in and about Gresham College[7]

and they doled out the space as fairly as they could. The Lord Mayor got the Divinity Lecturer's lodging and the Chamberlain of London had the Gallery. The City Recorder was given two large Common

Rooms and Dr Horton's rooms and the Mercers' records could be stowed either in the four rooms of the Civil Law Lecturer or in the three belonging to Rhetoric. The Aldermen who had passed the Chair, 'respect being had to theire seniority', must manage in Dr Goddard's kitchen and two lavatories, sharing them with the Assurance Office, and being promised a public room when a Court was held; the Common Sergeant and four attorneys would have to squeeze in together. The main quadrangle could be divided into a hundred shops for the tenants of the Upper Pawn — we may guess that, at least at first, they set up stalls — and the covered walk 'in the centre next Bishopsgate' was divided into seven compartments for Thomas Culling, Esq., Rowland Worsopp, Mercer, Mr Henry Mosse, Major Wright, Notary Public, and presumably three others.

The stables and hayloft

if cleansed and fitted may serve for the Judicature if occasion shall require, and if not, then divided into shops and lodgings, and to be disposed of for rent, to the best Advantage,

[7] MC, GR, II, pp. 228–31.

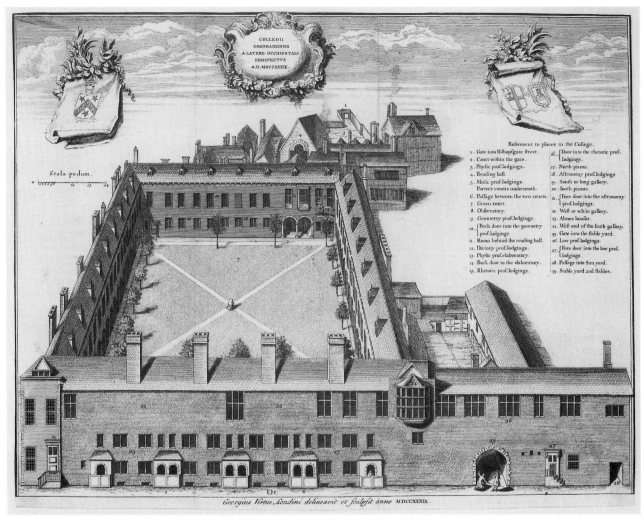

FIG. 30.   Gresham College, drawn and engraved by George Vertue, for Ward's *Lives of the Professors*, 1740.
Guildhall Library, Corporation of London

while

We conceive that the best profitt ought to be made of the Greate Warehouse and the severall cellars belonging to the house on condicion noo carte be suffered to come within the Gates.

No specific area was set aside as a public meeting place but perhaps, in such an emergency, it was felt that none would be needed. From later regulations, the main quadrangle seems to have served the purpose. It is amazing how swiftly some sort of order was imposed on the chaos.

The almsmen had their stipends raised to £10 a year but were told to find themselves lodgings so that their dwellings could be used to better advantage.

The only space left undistributed was the Astronomy Lodgings; they were to

bee left as now they are, in regard of the many curiosityes which remaine there and that the Royal Society may have accomodacion there for theire meetings.

Otherwise, every available corner was to be used to its fullest potential and any rents that could be raised needed to be gathered in; everyone realised that the rebuilding of the Exchange would cost an intolerable amount of money, but that it was unthinkable not to restore London's pride.

The Joint Committee reconvened two days later and made additions to the Sub-Committee — Mr Deputy Sexton and Mr Moss for the City,

FIG. 31.   The Royal Exchange, drawn and engraved by Robert White, 1671, and dedicated by Thomas
Cartwright to Sir Richard Ford, Lord Mayor.
Guildhall Library, Corporation of London

Wardens Knightly and Papillon for the Company. For the moment Sir John Lawrence and Sir Richard Ford were clearly too burdened with the City's and their own affairs to be able to give time to the Exchange. And it was going to take a lot of time and energy; between the first meeting (18 September 1666) and the last (2 August 1669), there would be 111 sessions in all, either of the Joint Committee or the Sub-Committee. Fifty-four names appear on the roll-call of those attending, though some came only to two or three meetings. Others attended regularly for some months, and then became too engrossed by other responsibilities. A few were present at almost

every gathering. Of these, the most faithful and persevering were Deputy Cade for the City and Rowland Wynne for the Mercers. As the work progressed, Sir George Smith and Sir John Lawrence, who had been a brave and steadfast Lord Mayor in Plague Year, gave generously of their time to the enterprise, as did Sir John Moore, Col. Thomas Neville and Deputy Fluellin for the City, and Samuel Moyer, Richard Clutterbuck and Mr Agge for the Mercers. Many of them were Aldermen, two of them, Sir John Lawrence and Sir John Moore, lived long enough to become Fathers of the City; Ford, Clutterbuck, Moyer, Papillon and Wynne all became

FIGS. 32, 33.   The exterior of the Royal Exchange. These remarkably fine pen and wash drawings, executed on vellum, are unusually early examples of such detailed perspective representations. The figures of William and Mary in their niche on the upper storey, with Anne beyond them, indicate a date between 1702 and 1714. Gresham's statue is visible in the lower arcade, under the first arch on the right.

Guardian Royal Exchange collection

Masters of the Mercers' Company, while Fluellin, Lawrence and Moore were respectively Masters of the Tallow Chandlers', Haberdashers' and Grocers' Companies. Of others, much less can be traced, their names appearing in the Minutes for this critical undertaking being their only memorial.

The Sub-Committee's next two meetings were taken up with readjustments of space and with calming the fears and demands of the merchants:

As to theire Dissatisfaction about the uncertainty of theire rents for the future years, they conceive yf the Comittees gentle dealing with them for the first ought to banish all Distrust for the future.[8]

The courtyard of Gresham House was paved over, probably fairly roughly, at a cost of £40, the carter 'who brought in the bricks and rubbish for paving ye Great Quadrangle for ye Meeting of the Merchants' being told to apply to the tenants, the 'Exchange men' for his charges; they were slow to pay. On 19 October, the City Surveyors, Mr Mills and Mr Jerman were called in

to give their Assistance and to Contrive a large passage out of the yard on Bishopsgate side into the place nowe used for Exchange Meetings.[9]

The congestion in Gresham House must have been intense — it must have seemed as though all London were camping out there. The Exchange Keepers were ordered

[8] MC, GR, II, p. 234.

[9] MC, GR, II, p. 250.

FIG. 33.

to stand att Doores in the Exchange time and a little before on Bishopsgate Street to direct people in theire Passage in and out . . . because of the narrowness.

They were also instructed to hang out lanterns, as had been done at the Exchange, ring a hand bell by eight o'clock and to lock Gresham House by nine o'clock at night. Then a vault had to be sunk to provide a house of office, much needed with such a crowd — complaints were already coming in about the 'noysome noyse' of the dung hill.

The Joint Committee, meeting on 26 October, began to prepare for the task of rebuilding 'that Greate Worke'. Labourers were to be employed at eighteen pence a day to clear the site, separating lead and useful materials from the rubbish, and to 'clear the cellars of bricks caused by the falling in of the arches'.[10] By 2 November, the Committee was able to report that it had full powers from the Common Council and the Company's Court to 'consult and

resolve' about the rebuilding: 'The first thing necessary is to know the charge that bothe sides may prepare to raise money.'[11] Accordingly Dr Robert Hooke, Gresham Professor of Geometry, and Peter Mills and Edward Jerman were asked to view the site and to prepare estimates.

These three were the Surveyors appointed by the City to deal with the rebuilding of London after the Fire. The royal appointees were Christopher Wren, Sir Roger Pratt, and Hugh May. Hooke we have already met (p. 121). Mills had served as Bricklayer to the City from 1643–60, as Master of the Tylers' and Bricklayers' Company in 1649–50 and 1659–60, and from 1644 as a Governor of St Bartholomew's Hospital. Jerman had been City Carpenter from 1633–57. The Gresham Committee were calling on the best advice available.

Jerman and Mills, the two professional builders, were chary of committing themselves to any firm

[10] MC, GR, II, pp. 253–54.

[11] MC, GR, II, p. 257.

estimate and asked for more time, but Hooke, ever zealous in anything concerned with the Gresham foundation, hastened to report:

Upon examining the foundation of the Royall Exchange, and considering the former structure of itt, as well as I canne recollect it from my memory, and by the helpe of the parts now standing, I doe finde, that by making a particular estimate of the several thinges to bee done in order to the rebuilding of itt anew, in the same forme as itt was of heretofore (abateing onely the statues of the kinges in the nieches, and the arched roofe of stone over the walke, which I thinke would be better if made a plastered seeleing, whereby all the crosse-irons might bee spared); to make the pillars, arches, architrave, freez, and cornice, and the borders of the nieches and the fower windowes, of *Portland* stone; and to pave the walkes with squared *Purbeck* stone, that the wholle charge will amount to betweene fower and five thousand pounds, supposeing all the matterialls weare to be new bought, but the paveing for the most parte seemes good. The pedestalls of all the pillars are very little damnifyed by the fyre; there are more than halfe bricks enough to rebuild it; there is a greate quantity of stone which may bee made use of for making the arches; the pillars and arches and fronts att both the entryes are little hurt, and there is a good quantity of lead, &c. which, lying yet confused, I cannot soe readily make an estimate of.[12]

The Joint Committee asked him to provide more detailed particulars, though no survey of the site by him appears to survive. During November, Jerman and Mills did prepare some figures and Hooke was asked to go over them but, understandably enough, no clear, firm estimate could be given.

By the turn of the year, the Committee were determined to drive the rebuilding on with all speed, even though the final cost was still beyond guessing.

11 February 1666. The Committee judging itt necessary to come to a Quick result about that affaire, as well for the Incouragement of others, and that the Season of the yeare may not bee lost, Ordered that the Right honourable the Lord Mayor bee desired forthwith to call the Grand Comitee togeather to resolve what is to be done for speedy raising of money, the onely Engine that can give vigorous motion to that greate and needful worke.[13]

Four days later, Mills and Jerman were requested to view the site, to supervise its clearance and preparation for rebuilding, and to ascertain who owned the

ground to the east and west of the Exchange. George Widmerpool was to set labourers to work sifting the debris,

and what thereof is grosse and unfitt for use they are to carry out into the Streete on Cornhill side where it may bee ready to bee taken away by carte.

The 'great Iron barrs' were to be stored in the vaults, and Mr Mills was asked to meet the Committee again on 'Munday morneing' with Mr Marshall and Mr Young the masons for further conference. On 25 February 1667, the masons informed them that Portland Stone cost 18s. 6d. per ton, that there would be a loading charge of 10s. a ton, and another 10s. for freight. The Committee resolved to petition the King for assistance, since the whole Isle of Portland was royal property.[14]

On 4 March, the Sub-Committee interviewed Mr Mills and Mr Jerman.

The Committee considering that the first thing necessary towards Reedifying the Exchange is to make choyse of some able p⁻son or p⁻sons for Surveyors and Directors of the same, and to that end Judging that none can bee more serviceable than Mr Mills and Mr German who have bin already imployed in the makeing of a generall estimate and they being now p⁻sent weare asked whether they could intend the business also. Mr Mills thereupon Declared his readinesse but Mr German makeing some Demurr, had time given him to resolve untill the Day Seavenight.

Mr Mills was asked to study the estimates delivered by the masons, Marshall and Young, and to see how their figures compared with his own computations.

The Sub-Committee reassembled on 11 March but Mr Jerman was still undecided. They 'took notice of the readinesse of Mr Mills to serve them and left the consent of Mr German to be taken after the next Com⁻on Councell'. They again considered the estimates for the masonry.

The Committee having received the prizes of diverse parcells of the stone worke to bee used in the Reedifying of the Exchange exhibited by Mr Marshall and Mr Young the Masons, and finding they have not given valuation of the charge of the Turret Staire also the ffrontispeeces because of the p⁻sent uncertainecy how the same shall be built, they therefore ordered Mr Mills to p⁻pare a Draught of what hee thinkes may bee most Ornamentall in the place of the Turret and whether a flat or sharpe roofe and how

[12] MC, GR, II, pp. 262–63.
[13] MC, GR, II, p. 277.

[14] MC, GR, II, p. 282.

the Staircases and ffrontispeeces, North, and South may bee best contrived that soo a certaine Estimate may bee p͞pared. And the Committee deferred the more Imediate Consideration of the p͞misses untill Munday morning next when also they appointed Mr Cartwright the Mason to attend with the prizes of the stoneworke according to the valuation.[15]

This is the first mention of Thomas Cartwright who, before the work was accomplished, would be the man in charge and who was, twice over, to be Master of the Masons' Company. A notice was put in the *Gazette* to all artificers that the Committee would assemble regularly each Monday morning at the end of the Long Gallery. The great rebuilding was able to begin.

Peter Mills was unable to attend the Sub-Committee on 18 March but Cartwright sent in his estimate. From the Minutes of 15 April, it is clear that there was some underlying friction.

The Com͞ittee formerly being sensible that an able Surveyor or Surveyors to devise withall upon the Emergent affaire of rebuilding the Royall Exchange was the first thing necessary. Did upon the ffourth Day of March last make an offer of that Service to mr Mills and Mr Jerman which the former accepted but the latter Declared that unless the City weare pleased to put him in the same capacity of a Surveyor with Mr Mills he could not attend the business but was otherwise ingaged to Intertaine such proffers as weare made him by private persons. And thereupon tyme was Given until the pleasure of the Com͞on Councell was knowne in that Case since which the Comittee have rec͞d noo absolute resolution but ensured have remained in suspense without having their Assistance in theire weekly meetings whereby much Tyme hath bin lost. And forasmuch as they cannot yet p͞ceed in that most necessary worke because they judge it fitt to have the Assistance of Mr Jerman a knowne Artist rather than any other that may bee comended to them and in whom they cannot have that satisfaction. Therefore (that noo more tyme may be lost) The Co͞mittee doo humbly returne the matter againe into the hands of the Grand Comittee to Advise and resolve who shall Survey and Direct the building.[16]

The Joint Committee met on 22 April 1667. They agreed that work on the new Exchange

hath bin thereto retarded for want of a settled Surveyor or Surveyors to attend the frequent Meetings of the Sub committee And y͞t such want hath Sprung from the

overmuch business of Mr Mills and from some Dissatisfaction in Mr Jerman, And that such small remoras [*sic*] may noo longer stopp the carrying on soe greate and soe considerable a worke as rebuilding the Royall Exchange,[17]

they agreed to meet again the next day to settle the matter. Mr Tanner the City Bricklayer, and Roger Jerman, later to be City Carpenter and Edward Jerman's younger brother, were also to attend.

Peter Mills was certainly very busy indeed. It was his duty, in company with Robert Hooke and John Oliver, to survey the ruined city and to stake out the lines of the new streets. His unwillingness to participate is entirely understandable. Why Jerman was so coy and so reluctant to commit himself is less clear. Perhaps he felt that he alone should have been consulted at the beginning; perhaps he was already in ailing health. Like Mills, the Fire had brought much work to him. Though he refused to join in the surveying of the devastated area, he was responsible for designing new halls for the Mercers', Haberdashers', Drapers', Fishmongers' and Wax Chandlers' Companies, but he did not live to see all the work completed.

In the event, the Committee met three days later on 25 April, the new Lord Mayor, Sir William Bolton, joining them for this crucial session. They noted:

as Mr Mills the City Surveyor hath declared that hee cannot p͞form that worke alone and the Comittee being very sensible of the greate burthen of Businesse lying upon him for the City att the time, And considering that Mr Jerman is the most able knowne Artist (besides him) that the City now hath Therefore the Comittee unanimously made choice of Mr Jerman to Assist the Comittee in the Agreement for Ordering and Directing of that worke, and having Declared the same unto him, Hee after much reluctancy and unwillingnesse (objecting itt might bee thought a intrenchment upon Mr Mills his right) at length accepted being assured first by the Lord Mayor and the Comittee that it was noo intrenchment and that the wholle Comittee att all times would acquit him from any scandall in that behalfe Then the Comittee Ordered the Clarke to acquaint Mr Jerman w͞th all the p͞ceedings of the Comittee about the said building.[18]

The Committee then proceeded to vote 'gratifications' of £20 apiece to Mills and Jerman, and £10 to Dr Hooke.

[15] MC, GR, II, p. 285.
[16] MC, GR, II, p. 287.
[17] MC, GR, II, p. 292.
[18] MC, GR, II, p. 293.

At the next meeting on 3 May, Jerman laid a series of questions before the Committee. Was the new building to follow exactly to the pattern of the old? Who should get the contracts for masonry, carpentry and brickwork? Where were the building materials to be found? (Full text in Appendix, pp. 416–28.) The Committee, having considered carefully, ordered that the new building should stand on the old foundations, and that

the number of the pillars and Arches, and the manner of the roofe be lefte to Mr Jerman to Modell according to the rules of Arte, for the best Advantage of the wholle Structure.

Thomas Cartwright got the masonry contract 'upon Condicion hee will Agree upon as easie Termes as other able men of that Trade' and all other agreements were left to Jerman. The entry closed triumphantly:

Memorand: That the Sixth Day of May Anno 1667 the workmen beganne the Worke of rebuilding the Royall Exchange.

At the next meeting on 10 May, Mr Jerman appeared and told the members that the walks must be enlarged but that it would cost nothing extra, so they agreed, and appointed a special sub-committee of four — Deputy Fluellin, Deputy Cade, Mr Clutterbuck and Mr Wynne — to deal with the workmen's bills as they came in. Special bricks would be needed for the arches and Mr Jerman was to procur them at the 'reasonablest rate he can'. Before the end of the month, the industrious surveyor had inspected quarries in the Isle of Portland, in Somerset and in Oxfordshire and, with the aid of a warrant from Sir John Denham, His Majesty's Surveyor-General, had made an agreement with Mr Switzer of Portland for 300 tons of stone to be delivered to the Port of London for £100, to be paid in advance.

The Comittee being satisfyed by Mr Jerman that he verily beleeved that the said payment maybee safely made and that the stone will be sent accordingly, they ordered that the said Hundred pounds shalbe paid.

The work went on steadily through the summer months but when the Joint Committee reassembled on 12 September, Jerman informed them that the whole site must be enlarged and that additional land would have to be purchased. The Committee bravely agreed and Jerman presented a draft at the next meeting on 20 September. It was shown to the King who, it was reported a week later, approved the design and the expansion of the site, provided that landowners were properly recompensed.[19]

As far as we know, Jerman's draft has not survived. It must have shown the Exchange with a colonnade on all four sides, freed from the humble buildings which clustered about it. Two handsome ink drawings on vellum are now in the collection of the Guardian Royal Exchange; they were formerly in the Gardner Collection to which they came from the Carpenters' Company, of which Jerman was a member. These, however, cannot be the working drafts laid first before the Committee and then the King. Like the Hogenbergs, they show a south, Cornhill façade and an internal view of the courtyard; there is no ground plan, no indication of a continuous surrounding colonnade, and the figures are clothed in the styles of 1720–30 rather than the 1660s. Jerman's draft is more likely to have been worn out on the site.

Another special sub-committee — Sir Thomas Bludworth and Deputies Fluewellyn, Cade and Rosewell for the City, Messrs Clutterbuck, Dawnay, Hilliard and Jones for the Company — was appointed to deal with the landowners and tenants over 'setting the Exchange free from contiguous buildings . . . desiring them . . . to surrender theire respective leases upon just satisfaction'. Those holding the desired area must have felt their fire-wrecked footage and ruins were turned to gold. William Cooper said that he 'could not parte with the Interest without Prejudice to himselfe' and Ralph Smith assured the Committee 'that noo satisfaction can be given him wholly to parte wth the ground in regard itt would bee the losse of his trade, and consequently of his Livelyhood', but that he would rebuild his premises as they directed him. John Webb , Robert Swift, Mrs Roberta Spense and Michael Mynot agreed unwillingly to co-operate upon compensation. The stumbling blocks were going to be Messrs Sweeting, Morris and Grice who held much of the land needed on the east and west sides, but for the moment all efforts were concentrated on the main quadrangle. Edward Jerman was in charge with Thomas Cartwright as chief mason,

[19] MC, GR, ii, pp. 301–04.

John Tanner as bricklayer and Roger Jerman, Edward's brother, as carpenter. Prices for masonry were agreed — £9 for each of the smaller pillars, 'Base, Body and Capitall', and £13 for 'each of the fower greate pillars at the fower Angles' with the mouldings carved at 6s. 6d. the foot and the ashlar niches, presumably for the statues, at 1s. the foot — while the brickwork was settled at £2 5s. the perch.[20] As far as we can tell from the Minutes, the Gresham Committee never received a clear, firm estimate; the times were such that no reliable set of figures could have been provided; the City and the Company, convinced of the over-riding importance of the work, could only struggle on in faith and hope.

After the September meeting, the work went on swiftly, the Minutes declaring triumphantly six weeks later:

Bee itt Remembered that the Kings Maty King Charles the second, came to the Royall Exchange on the Three and Twentythe Octobr aᵒ 1667 and there fixed the first pillar at the Reedifying thereof, which is that standing on the West side and North Entrance. He was entertained by the City and Company with a Chyne of beefe, Grand Dish of fowle, Gam͞ons of Bacon, Dryed Tongues Anchovees caviare etc and plenty of severall sorte of wyne. He gave xxˡⁱ in Gold to the workemen. The intertainment was in a Shedd built and adorned on purpose upon the Scottish Walke.

As might have been expected, Samuel Pepys managed to observe what was going on:

Thence Sir W. Pen and I back into London; and there saw the King with his kettle-drums and trumphets, going to the Exchange, to lay the first stone of the first pillar of the new building of the Exchange; which, the gates being shut, I could not get in to see: but, with Sir W. Pen, to Captain Cocke's to drink a dram of brandy, and so he to the Treasury office about Sir G. Carteret's accounts, and I took coach and back again towards Westminster; but in my way stopped at the Exchange, and got in, the King being newly gone; and there find the bottom of the first pillar laid. And here was a shed set up, and hung with tapestry, and a canopy of state, and some good victuals and wine, for the King, who, it seems, did it [i.e. laid the stone]; and so a great many people, as Tom Killigrew, and others of the Court there, and there I did eat a mouthful and drink a little, and to find Mr. Gawden in his gowne as Sheriffe, and understand that the King hath this morning knighted him upon the place, which I am mightily pleased with; and I think the other Sheriffe, who is Davis, the little

fellow, my schoolfellow, and bookseller, and now become Sheriffe; which is a strange turn, methinks. Here mighty merry (there being a good deal of good company) for a quarter of an hour, and so I away and to Westminster Hall, where I come just as the House rose.[21]

Once begun, the work continued with all possible speed; the Committee Minutes keep record:

Also His Royall Highnesse James Duke of York fixed the pillar on the west side that entrance, on the last day of October, 1667, and was interteyned by the City and Company in the same place.

His Highness Prince Rupert fixed the pillar on the east side and south entrance, on the eighteenth day of November 1667, and was interteyned by the City and Company in the same place.[22]

It was time for the Committee to show its appreciation of those who had worked so hard. On 9 December, rewards were handed out — £50 to Mr Jerman, £10 to John Godfrey the Committee Clerk, £4 to John Bassett who summoned members to the meetingas, and 40s. apiece to Francis Draper and Samuel Wright, the Exchange Keepers. There were bills, too — £200 due to Thomas Cartwright the mason, 'Mr Jerman having first satisfied the Committee that the worke done did require soo much money', and Deputy Dawnay and Mr Jerman were requested to view a

parcell of Eastland Bawkes [baulks] and to Bargain for them if they find them a pennyworth, in regard they may bee very usefull att the Exchange for Scaffolding and other Occasions.

The City Side spread its generosity still wider; one of the almsmen, John Boogey, 'almost One hundred yeares of age & soo weake', was granted an extra £3 6s. 8d. 'towarde his present Releife'. A week later, having fended off a letter from the Earl of Manchester recommending Caius Gabriel Cibber as sculptor for a new sequence of royal statues — 'the buisinesse of makeing the Statues is yett very remote from theire thoughts haveing the wholle Exchange to build first'[23] — the Committee remembered

how much trouble they have from tyme to tyme given Sr John Denham his Matⁱᵉˢ Surveyor General in . . . as well in

[20] MC, GR, II, p. 307.

[21] Pepys, *Diary*, ed. R. Latham and W. Matthews (1974), vol. VIII, pp. 496–97.
[22] MC, GR, II, pp. 308–09.
[23] MC, GR, II, p. 315.

his coming downe to view the Exchange and Streetes adjoyning as in furthering theire Addresse to his Majesty and giveing them full Warrants for Portland Stone, They therefore desired [the Sub-Committee] to make provision of Six to Eight dishes of meate att the Sun Taverne on Wednesday nexte to interteyne him withall att his comeing downe. And to p⁻sent him with Thirty Guineypeeces of Gold as a toaken of theire Gratitude.

The merry gathering presumably took place on 20 December 1667 when, earlier in the day, the main Committee had been joined by Sir John and by Hugh May, one of the King's Commissioners for the Rebuilding, and Sir John declared the King's enthusiasm for the grand design and assured them that, if the landowners and tenants refused reasonable compensation, and

presume to build in contradiction and hindrance of the works aforesaid, then His Majesty and Council will interpose theire authority to give a stop to theire proceedinges, until an Act of Parliament can bee obteyned.[24]

The work went on doggedly throughout 1668. Materials were dear and hard to obtain, the very street scavengers for the parishes of St Helen and St Peter-le-Poer were demanding £3 and over for their work whereas they had formerly been content with £1 or 10s., and the design of the Exchange was still under debate. Should there be porticoes only to the north and south, or should they surround the building? Should there be a double pawn of shops throughout, or rather fewer premises? Former lessees urged restricted numbers

praying the committee would not think of building a double pawne of shops, because it would bring ruine upon them and disreputation upon the place,

but the sub-tenants clamoured for expansion:

After a full debate of the arguments and reasons on both sides, the committee seemed to inclyne to the building of a double pawne, because itt will be more magnificent and pleasing to His Majesty, and because itt will better answeare the charge of building; yett they deferred the final resolution

until the cost of the additional land was settled. Mr Jerman the Surveyor was noticeable by his absence and the Comittee sent to him 'to know the reason . . . and to order and compose all differences,

that the building may goe cheerefully on'.[25] Jerman may have been a touchy individual but he was already a sick man, trying to shoulder an undertaking too heavy for his health. He was still working, measuring Mr Sweeting's ground, on 22 October but was probably dead before 11 November when

the chiefe workeman now appearing, and being demanded the reason why they have of late proceeded so slowly in the worke of the Royall Exchange, they alleaged the cause lay in the uncertainety of what should bee done. The Committee, to remove that inpediment, ordered that itt shall be built with porticos on all sides and a double pawne of shops.[26]

Fortunately, Mr Cartwright the mason 'declared himselfe master of the wholle designe intended for that building; whereupon the Committee desired him to proceed vigoerously in the worke', and asked him for a firm estimate for the porticoes and 'cupilo'.

The negotiations for additional land dragged on and on, with Morris and Sweeting being the most obdurate, each demanding at least £1,000. Appointments were made to measure up the ground but not kept; Mr Morris was 'composing a difference' with his mother-in-law, and could not answer the Committee. Mrs Saintlow asked £200 for her interest, was offered £120 and threw herself on the mercy of the Committee, 'praying they would consider her condicion having nothing else in the world to maintain her in her Old Age'. She settled for £20 a year for life. At last on 27 April 1669

Dr Wren, the surveyor-general of His Majestyes buildinges, happening to bee att Mr Hooke's lodgeings, [the Committee] desired his company; and, haveing declared how much they have indeavored the building of porticos on all sides of the Exchange, and how many difficultyes they have incountered in that affaire, and that it appears almost an impossibility to effect the matter on the east and west sides (the north and south being in hand) and hopeing His Majesty will not obleige them to proceed in a matter soe much to theire trouble and prejudice, they earnestly desired Doctor Wren (if His Majesty should happen to consult him in the matter) to represent the Committee's design (of carrying walls twenty-four foote from the east and west walls of the Exchange, to beare the outward pawne of shops without any portico) favourable to His Majesty.[27]

[24] MC, GR, II, p. 316.

[25] MC, GR, II, p. 335.
[26] MC, GR, II, p. 340.
[27] MC, GR, II, p. 380.

The King must have agreed and the eastern and western porticoes were omitted.

Suddenly, the end was in sight. A new sense of purposeful, almost triumphant, urgency enters the Minutes. On 30 April, the Committee

Ordered, that Mr [Roger] Jerman the carpenter doe goe on to finish the wholle tymberworke of the inner quadrangle . . . and he (being urged with all earnestnesse, to speede the same) faithfully promised to ymploy such a number of men, and such care and industry about the same, that noe other trades shall stay for him.[28]

On 10 July, orders were given for an inscription to be set up over the south entrance inside the quadrangle:

Ex Cambium Hoc anno 1666 in cineres reductum in plusquam antiquum splendorem, Praetore Will' mo Turnero, Equite, anno 1669, restitutum fuit.[29]

The courtyard was reopened for trading on 28 September 1669 by the Lord Mayor but without elaborate ceremony. The King was busy elsewhere, much to the disappointment of those involved. Thomas Jordan, creator of Lord Mayor's Pageants, had written one specially for the occasion, which was to have had a perspective scene of the Exchange in ruins painted by 'the ingenious Mr Streeter', to be viewed to 'a rich strain of grave Musick' by Mr Purcell. 'As HIS MAJESTY came not down according to hope and expectation . . . 'twas done with but small ceremony', he lamented, but in spite of his resentment he published the text.[30] The stationer, Nathaniel Brooke, working 'at the Angell in Cornehill', nostalgically reissued Hollar's engraving of Gresham's original Exchange, the Latin inscription replaced with the royal arms. A careful examination of the print shows a statue of Charles II inserted into the furthest right-hand niche. The figure may well have been engraved by Hollar himself; he had returned to England from the Continent but, in spite of Charles's favour, was desperately poor and glad of any work he could get.

The second Royal Exchange followed, more or less, the plan and arrangements of Gresham's original structure. Four arcades, their upper storeys lined once again with small shops, defined the central courtyard

for trading; if late seventeenth- and eighteenth-century engravings provide hard evidence, the pavement was still made up of the original 'Turkey stones' which had survived the Fire. The façades towards the main streets were, however, considerably more imposing. The south and north fronts facing Cornhill and Threadneedle Street now had thirteen bays, with porticoes set forward over the street before the central nine and the two at either end recessed a little behind their neighbours. The central bays formed a triumphal entrance with a large archway in the middle and smaller ones on either side. Above these doorways were statues of Charles I and Charles II, set in aedicules with broken pediments. Each doorway was flanked by giant Corinthian columns supporting semicircular pediments; the royal arms were in the middle. These bays provided the base for a three-storeyed tower, not unlike the steeples which Wren was designing for the City churches; it is, perhaps, worth noting that Cartwright was the contractor for St Mary-le-Bow. High aloft, Gresham's grasshopper swung proudly as a weather-vane.[31]

One last piece of equipment was needful for the Exchange, and that was a chiming clock, so that all men might know the hours of trading. The contract went to Edward Stanton, who had premises in Leadenhall Street and who was to become Master of the Clockmakers' Company in 1696. His instructions were precise; he was to

make and set up in the cupola of the Royall Exchange, a substantial workemanlike clock, *viz.* the bignesse upon the square to be five foote; the height about three foote; the barrell of iron to be three foot diameter, with six tunes, such as shall be liked of; the rest of the worke to be every way proportionable to the going thirty howers. That it shall strike the quarters upon fower bells; that it shall strike the hower; that it shall repeat at the halfe hour; that it shall have fower dials, with hands to shew the time, upon the fower sides of the cupilo; that he shall keep the said clock in good order for the first yeare, *viz*, from Lady-day 1671,

[28] MC, GR, II, p. 382.
[29] MC, GR, II, p. 395.
[30] Society of Antiquaries, Fairholt collection.

[31] This grasshopper, which survived the 1838 fire, still adorns the Exchange.

FIG. 34.   Trade card for the Royal Exchange
Assurance.
Guardian Royal Exchange collection

to our Lady-day 1672. For all which the city and company
are to pay him 120*l.*[32]

If the Rebuilding Committee were satisfied, there was
to be a further £10 gratuity at the end of three
months.

The whole undertaking had cost a breath-taking
£58,122 17*s.* 4*d.* — £51,456 7*s.* 4*d.* for the construction work, £6,666 10*s.* 0*d.* for additional land. It was
an amazing achievement, the City's declaration that
even a fire as overwhelming as that of 1666 could not
annihilate London's supremacy and ability to trade.
The cost was justified in as much as it restored the
confidence of Londoners in themselves and of foreign
merchants in the City but, while the Corporation was
sustained, at least in part, by subsidies from the Coal
Tax, the burden of debt upon the Mercers' Company
would bring it to the verge of bankruptcy by the
beginning of the next century.[33]

Though the courtyard was open for trading, it was
not until Lady Day 1671 that the shops were ready to
re-admit the tenants. Materials remained scarce and
skilled craftsmen were valuable prizes. On 4 November 1670, Sir Richard Ford had had to write to the
Navy Commissioners to entreat the discharge of four
carpenters

impressed from the Royal Exchange for service at
Chatham by which means the finishing of works of the
Exchange — which is of great advantage to the City and
for which His Majesty was taken particular care — are
retarded; also for an order that no workman may be
impressed from the public works of the City for the future.

The men were released four days later and the work
was pushed on with determination. Among the
miscellaneous charges, recorded faithfully by John
Godfrey, the industrious clerk, are items such as the
following:

For 14 labourers yt wrought all night ye 23 March above
in ye Exchange att 16*d.* a man . . . . 18*s.* 8*d.*

But at last all was done, the Exchange fully
reopened, and Gresham College free to spruce itself
up and to go back to its scholarly activities. Samuel
Purchas provided seventeen yards of 'stuf for curt-
inges for the cummitey rome' and the almsmen had
new gowns 'of sad coloured mixt cloath' with a
grasshopper embroidered on each in gold silk.[34]

On 1 December 1673, the Royal Society was
welcomed back to the premises and well entertained;
the company drank six quarts of each of canary, of
Rhenish wine and of claret, and were regaled with
four and a half pounds of fine cakes, two pounds of
small 'macheroones' and two pounds of small march-
panes, the whole bill, with porterage, coals and hire
of plate, totalling £2 17*s.* 9*d.*[35]

At first there were plenty who were eager to flock
back, and as late as 1711 and 1712 Addison and
Steele were writing enthusiastically in the *Spectator*
(see pp. 206–08) but the Gresham Account Books
begin to show a different situation. From the 1680s
shop after shop began to stand empty and the lists of
'Desperate Debts' grew larger each year. The income
from the shops, let at between £25 to £35 a year with
a modest renewal fine at ten-yearly intervals, was

---

[32] The sweetness of the four bells at the quarter-hour was such
that in 1763, when the Vestrymen of St Michael's Church,
Charles Town, South Carolina, were ordering a new clock from
the London Clockmaker, Ainsworth Thwaytes, they specified
that the chime should be as that of the Royal Exchange, London.
Those notes are still sounding. I am grateful to Mr George
Williams of North Carolina for this fascinating information.

[33] In giving this figure, I am following CLRO, Gresham Account
Book for 1674. Professor Reddaway accepted this, *Rebuilding*,
p. 269. Strype in his edition of Stow gives £80,000, but one
suspects exaggeration with passage of time. For the sad story of
the Mercers' troubles, see Ian Doolittle, *The Mercers' Company,
1579–1959* (1994), ch. VII.

[34] CLRO, R.Ex., misc. MSS 133.6 18*s.* 8*d.*
[35] CLRO, R.Ex., misc. MSS 135.31.

insufficient to cover the six per cent interest on the rebuilding debts, let alone repay the capital. The western outer pawn had to be shut up in 1684; what was needed was a new kind of corporate tenant, institutions rather than individuals.

The first to arrive was the Corporation of the Mines Royal and Mineral and Battery Works, moving in at midsummer 1719 to premises at the north-west corner for which it paid £120 rental. Two years later, it was joined by the Royal Exchange Assurance which

took up residence in the south pawn at a rent of £300. In 1774, Lloyd's became a 'tenant above stairs', occupying most of the north, east and west pawns. The Royal Exchange entered a fresh lease of life; the building had found a new purpose.[36]   [37]

[36] CLRO, R.Ex., misc. MSS 151.3.
[37] CLRO, R.E., Gresham Accounts. For the history of insurance in the Exchange see Barry Supple, *The Royal Exchange Assurance* (1970); for the use of the building by Lloyd's see Vanessa Harding and Priscilla Metcalf, *Lloyd's at Home* (1986).

CHAPTER XV

The North Front of the Royal Exchange

By HOWARD COLVIN

MANY VIEWS EXIST of the principal front of the Royal Exchange as rebuilt by Edward Jerman and Thomas Cartwright in 1667–71. It was not a particularly distinguished architectural composition. The tower rose slightly awkwardly from a gateway whose flanking pediments failed to give it adequate visual support. These paired pediments were probably suggested by a plate in Francini's *Livre d'Architecture* of 1621, but there they answered one another without any tower in the middle. As for the architectural decoration, it was neither classically correct nor effectively deviant in the mannerist or baroque manner. The façade was handsome enough in its parts, but it lacked the assurance of a coherent architectural composition.

Of the rear elevation to Threadneedle Street only two representations appear to exist. One is an aquatint in Thomas Malton's *Picturesque Tour through*

FIG. 35. Giovanni David, *Royal Exchange, London* (rear elevation). Taken from his *Sketch Book, 1785–86*, vol. 1.
The Royal Collection, © 1993: Her Majesty The Queen

the Cities of London and Westminster (1792–1801) which incidentally shows a small portion of the arcade on the ground floor. The other is a wash sketch in the Royal Library at Windsor by Giovanni David (1743–90), dating from 1786. The sketch bears no inscription to identify its subject, but the building depicted agrees exactly with the plan of the Royal Exchange in the second volume of Campbell's *Vitruvius Britannicus* (1717). It shows most of the central portion of the north front, with one of the attics of the Mansion House in the right background. It reveals the north elevation as a rather more sophisticated composition than the south one. The centre is emphasised by a slightly projecting frontispiece which embraces the three entrances at ground-floor level. At the upper level a series of pilasters of the Corinthian order is crowned by a pediment. What gives the composition its distinction is the interpenetration of the spaces defined by the pilasters. Taken by itself the central feature reads as a large pedimented window flanked on either side by two smaller windows, one rectangular and one oval, one above the other. But these smaller windows also form part of a subordinate group with a large unpedimented window as its central feature. In other words, the two groups of windows have one bay in common, creating a

deliberate ambiguity of a kind that appealed to mannerist architects. A similar ambiguity in the grouping of the windows can be observed in several seventeenth-century English country houses with seven-bay fronts, for example, Lyndon Hall, Rutland, Longnor Hall, Shropshire (south front), Moresby Hall, Cumberland, and Uppark, Sussex (side elevation). But these are all astylar, that is, without pilasters to define the bays, and nowhere is this trick of composition so explicitly expressed as it is in the north front of the Royal Exchange.

For this interesting design as a whole no source suggests itself. But its basic unit — a large rectangular window flanked by two smaller ones, one oval, the other rectangular — was copied from the end bays of the front of Goldsmiths' Hall, as built in 1635–38 to the designs of Nicholas Stone. Goldsmiths' Hall was gutted in the Great Fire, but the main structure survived, to be restored in 1667–68 by none other than Edward Jerman (John Newman, 'Nicholas Stone's Goldsmiths' Hall', *Architectural History*, 14 (1971)). It is therefore to Jerman, rather than to Thomas Cartwright, who completed the Exchange after the former's death in 1668, that the north front should presumably be attributed.

CHAPTER XVI

'The Kingdom's Marble Chronicle': The Embellishment of the First and Second Buildings, 1600 to 1690

By KATHARINE GIBSON

As London was the glory of England, so was that Royal Exchange one of the greatest Glories and Ornaments of London. There were the statues of the Kings and Queens of England set up, as in the most conspicuous and honourable place (as well receiving lustre from the place where they stood, as giving lustre to it).[1]

AFTER THE REFORMATION and the havoc wreaked during the iconoclasm of Edward VI's reign, Elizabeth I attempted to lessen the Protestant rampage by forbidding further defacing of antiquities and monuments. She insisted that 'images of Kings, princes or noble estates of this realms' should be preserved.[2] Calvin and Erasmus had seen no reason why depictions of people, creatures and articles to be found in the actual world should not be permitted, and portraits of famous living people or great characters from the past could morally be defended as inspirational: powerful princes, courageous warriors, great thinkers, religious leaders, literary figures, etc., were worthy examples to ordinary people.

Sir Thomas Gresham must have seen the destruction of art and sculpture on a massive scale both in Britain and the Low Countries,[3] and in his resentment, perhaps, this innovative man promoted the remaining permitted arts with a patriotism that was no less than visionary. He moved internationally in exalted circles, and is credited with introducing the latest artistic developments from the Continent.[4] Having erected the Exchange, which quickly became the functional heart of his profession, he stipulated that the courtyard should be decorated with the larger-than-life statues of thirty British monarchs. The first series was destroyed in the Great Fire of 1666, but the Gresham Committee, faithful to the founder's memory, insisted on their replacement in the newly classical Exchange built in 1669–70. Many of these would in turn come to grief in the second fire of 1838. Throughout the seventeenth century the City was very closely embroiled in the history of the nation, and the tense relationship that existed between the City and the Crown was manifested in the changing attitudes towards the royal statues.

Such pantheons were not unprecedented. Since the Middle Ages, royal figures had been placed to intercede on behalf of the public with the holy offices of English cathedrals. The choir screens at Canterbury Cathedral and York Minster, dividing the choir from the nave, had life-size figures of the medieval kings of England, and the west doors of, for instance, Lincoln and Exeter, Wells, Lichfield and Rochester

I would like to pay tribute to the pioneering work of Katherine Esdaile, Margaret Toynbee, Margaret Whinney and Jean Imray. My thanks go to Ann Saunders, Ingrid Roscoe, John Watts, Curator for the Royal Exchange, Geoffrey Fisher and Philip Ward-Jackson of the Conway Library at the Courtauld Institute, and the staff of the Art Gallery, Library, Prints and Maps, and MSS departments of the Guildhall for their help.

Because this essay is to discuss not merely the 26 royal statues of the first Royal Exchange which were destroyed in the Great Fire in 1666, but also the 15 replacements in the second Exchange, plus additional kings and queens, rejected figures and other propositions for sculptures, a chart has been drawn up to show which figures from the line of kings stood in each incarnation of the building, giving any known details of sculptors and commissioning bodies. See pp. 171–73.

(All books published in London unless otherwise stated.)

[1] The Revd Samuel Rolle, *The Burning of London in the Year 1666* (1667), Part III, Meditation IX, p. 45.

[2] *Tudor Royal Proclamations, Vol. II The Later Tudors (1553–1587)*, ed. P. L. Hughes and J. F. Larkin (New Haven and Yale, 1969), proclamation no. 469, p. 147.

[3] Antwerp suffered a particularly awful onslaught in 1566 which was halted by the Duke of Alva the following year.

[4] E. Auerbach, *Tudor Artists* (1954), p. 74, mentions his friendship with Sir Philip Hoby, ambassador to the court of Charles V, who knew Titian, and his contact with the Fuggers, bankers of Augsburg, who 'rivalled the Medici as patrons of the arts'.

Cathedrals were flanked by standing or cross-legged monarchs who greeted the incoming congregation. By 1398 Richard II had decorated Westminster Hall, that cavernous secular edifice at the centre of power, with a dynastic series of thirteen kings placed round the walls at high level.[5] By the sixteenth century Westminster Hall was being used for sittings of the assize courts and trading-stalls were ranged round the remainder of the interior, and the Exchange statues were to preside over the transactions of the merchants conducting their business in the courtyard below, in a very similar manner.

By this means Gresham could invest his new building with an almost ecclesiastical dignity, dedicating its allegiance to God and the Crown and to the welfare of the nation. The mercantile purposes of the Exchange were thus given a strong moral justification, and the line of kings took on a particular meaning, expressing the interdependency between the City and the monarchy. The historical array also prompted national pride, and convinced foreign visitors that, although the country had changed religion, the English had sound stability through the continuity in their rulers stretching back in a glorious galaxy to Edward the Confessor, before the Norman Conquest. Edward III had earned the title of the 'Father of English Commerce', and Edward IV 'the Merchant King', and were particularly suitable representatives.[6]

Hogenberg's print (1568–69) of the quadrangle of the first Royal Exchange shows a full range of tiny sculptures (see Fig. 10, p. 43). There is no documentary proof, though, that they were installed by this early date, and the artist was probably illustrating Gresham's projected scheme.[7] The royal figures are not mentioned by the otherwise meticulous Stow either in 1598 or in 1603, and the first recorded reference to any statue dates from 10 May 1610,

when Nicholas Leate, later Master of the Ironmongers, suggested that a type of fine or penalty be imposed upon refractory guild-members who wished to avoid obligatory City responsibilities. The Court of Aldermen Repertory states:

Sir Thomas Gresham . . . whoe being cutt of by untymely death, left a p^te [of his project] unperformed, that is, xxx^ty pictures of Kings & Queenes of thys Land, and to that p^rpose the said Sir Thomas Gresham left 30 roomes to place them in.

The thirty 'roomes', or niches, were ranged 6:9:6:9 along the four internal faces of the quadrangle, at first-floor level. It was stipulated that the cost should be:

not exceeding 100 nobles, the pictures to be graven on wood, covered wth lead and then gilded and paynted in Oyle cullors, and for modelles or patternes, because the honorable Citty and wor^ll Company of Mercers doe receave good benefitte thereby, that they may make each of them one at their charges, wch will be a thing both memorable and honorable and noe man wronged.[8]

A singular and practically unheard-of technique for sculpture, the figures would be weather-proof, though not necessarily cheaper than stone.[9] With a vested interest in metalwork, Leate possibly hoped to benefit his own Company members. Wooden effigies were exhibited at the lying-in-state and carried on the catafalque at a royal funeral until the death of Henry, Prince of Wales in 1612.[10] But cladding a wood effigy in metal was unusual, to say the least.

Public sculpture was commonly brightly coloured and gilded at this date. Nonsuch Palace was painted in rainbow detail, and Bristol Cross and Gloucester Cross both had a series of polychrome stone royal figures.[11] Numerous royal statues did, thanks to Elizabeth I, escape destruction, and town gates,

---

[5] The 1995 exhibition at the British Museum 'Westminster Hall and the medieval Kings' featured the six surviving figures.

[6] J. E. Price, *A Descriptive Account of the Guildhall of the City of London* (1886), p. 33.

[7] Female figures can be seen to lounge in each bay under the arcades, along the back walls. Whether these were intended to be sculpted or painted, personifications of the virtues, or historical or mythological characters, is not known, and there is no written witness to them ever being installed.

[8] CLRO, Court of Aldermen, Repertory 29, f. 224 printed in *Extracts from the Records of the City of London . . . respecting the Royal Exchange 1564–1825*.

[9] I have consulted Adam White and Phillip Lindley, but have been unable to discover any surviving examples. The method probably related to such products as weathercocks and water-butts, etc. A thin lead layer might be hammered to take the shape of the wood-carving beneath, and soldered to prevent the rain entering. The painted effect could have been somewhat doll-like.

[10] Some of the wooden effigies are in Westminster Abbey Undercroft Museum.

[11] M. J. H. Liversidge, *The Bristol High Cross*, p. 1, unpublished typescript kept at Bristol Museum and Art Gallery.

bridges and city conduits were often decorated with colourful commemorative sculpture.[12] In London, Ludgate had a statue of Elizabeth, and Aldgate and Aldersgate both had gilded figures of James I. It was however, a question of topical debate in the first quarter of the seventeenth century whether new ideas about pure white marble sculpture and the classical ideal should be imported from the Continent.[13] The Gresham Committee stuck obstinately to polychromy, despite changing fashions. They were very hard to please, not only over colouring, but also over the questions of idealising features so much that they become unrecognisable, and dressing figures in the correct period costume. These were to become regular disputes. On top of this the pitfalls often associated with committee management would become painfully apparent.

The first figure, set up 'below in ye North end', in 1622, was that of Sir Thomas Gresham himself.[14] Contemporary sources record that this statue, by an anonymous sculptor, survived the Great Fire of 1666.[15] Evelyn reported it had 'fallen from its niche [but] remained entire'; like 'Noah was after the flood', wrote Rolle.[16] It was subsequently reinstated in its previous position, where it was illustrated by Sutton Nicholls in 1712 (Fig. 36).[17] George Vertue (1684–1756) engraved it for Ward's *Lives of the Professors of Gresham College*, and his charming preparatory drawing in pen and grey wash is in the Guardian

Royal Exchange collection (Fig. 37).[18] John Carter (1748–1817), the antiquary and recorder of vanishing splendours from the nation's past (whose pencil sketches of the second line of kings make such a valuable contribution and will be cited later), drew the same figure in *c.* 1790,[19] but it must have been destroyed in 1838.

A penalty of £200 was imposed in 1622 upon Richard Cheyney, Goldsmith, when he requested to be excused from aldermanic duties; this was later commuted in favour of his setting up 'one statute of some of the kings or queenes of this realme deceased'.[20] Nicholas Leate was held responsible for the project. Cheyney himself wished to provide the figure of 'that renowned King Edward the Sixt'.[21] Later the same year, he was instructed to set up 'another stature there att his own cost and charges'.[22]

From the Notebook of Nicholas Stone (1586–1647) we learn that this sculptor executed four carvings, of Edward V, Richard III, Henry VII and Elizabeth I.[23] The first three earned him £25 apiece, and were installed, only to be destroyed in the Great Fire of 1666. Raphe Stint paid for the figure of Richard III in 1626, thereby discharging himself from the duties 'of Shrievalty of the Citty of London and County of Middlesex'.[24] The Gresham Committee, however, did not approve of the figures of Elizabeth and James I, which had been 'made contrarye to the minde of this Court, and without their direccon'. They considered 'in what manner and hono^ble fashion

---

[12] Individual monarchs featured, for example, on the gateway leaving Salisbury Close, and on the Magazine Gate of the Great Bridge at Newcastle upon Tyne. In Oxford, Carfax Conduit supported an equestrian Queen Matilda.

[13] D. Howarth, 'Charles I, Sculpture and Sculptors', *The Late King's Goods*, ed. A. Macgregor (London and Oxford, 1989), p. 82; A. White, 'Nicholas Stone and Early Stuart Sculpture', *The Cambridge Guide to the Arts in Britain, Vol. IV The Seventeenth Century*, ed. B. Ford (CUP, 1989), p. 267.

[14] MC, GR 1 (1596–1625), f. 247, 18 April 1622; Gresham Accounts 1596–1625, f. 437 notes payment of the Mercers' moiety of £27 16s. 10d.

[15] E. Waterhouse, *A Short narration of the dreadful fire in London* (1667), p. 152; Rolle, op. cit., Part III, Meditation LI, p. 186; *The Diary of Samuel Pepys*, ed. R. C. Latham and W. Matthews (1970), Vol. VII, p. 276, 5 September 1666.

[16] *The Diary of John Evelyn*, ed. E. S. de Beer (Oxford, 1955), Vol. III, p. 460, 6 September 1666, and Rolle, op. cit., Part III, Meditation LI, p. 186.

[17] Nicholls pinpoints the exact situation with a letter 'A'. BM Prints and Drawings, Crace collection, 1880-11-13-3684.

[18] The drawing belonged at one time to Sir Mark Masterman Sykes, and was later in the Esdaile and Gardner collections. See also note 19. For the engraving, see Ward, *Lives*, Preface, p. xiii; and BM Prints and Drawings, Crace collection, 1880-11-13-3735.

[19] Carter's drawings, together with Vertue's drawing, were auctioned on day 12 of the Gardner collection sale, on 2 May 1924 (1863), and are also in the Guardian Royal Exchange Collection. For Carter's career see J. Mordaunt Crook, *John Carter and the Mind of the Gothic Revival* (1995), though the Exchange is not mentioned.

[20] CLRO, Court of Aldermen, Repertory 32, f. 146b, Repertory 36, ff. 125b–126.

[21] *Analytical index to the series of records known as the Remembrancia . . . A.D. 1579–1664* (1878), p. 212. He also wished his own name to appear beneath, as the donor.

[22] CLRO, Court of Aldermen, Repertory 37, f. 135b, 10 June 1622.

[23] W. L. Spiers, 'The Notebook & Account Book of Nicholas Stone', *Walpole Society*, Vol. VII (1918–19), pp. 57–58.

[24] CLRO, Court of Aldermen, Repertory 40, f. 208.

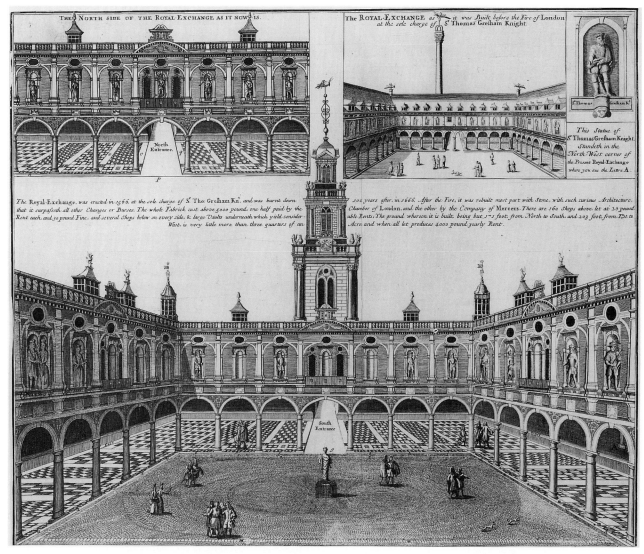

FIG. 36. Sutton Nicholls' engraving (1712) of the courtyard at the second Royal Exchange.
Guildhall Library, Corporation of London

they may be amended, and bewtified' and called for models of both, to be on the safe side.[25] No mention is made of the medium in which the statues should be fabricated, but the Committee insisted the Queen's figure should be dressed 'in the best and richest vestments and ornaments'.[26] Leate had to promise not to proceed in future without official instructions.

Stone would later be appointed Master Mason to Charles I. Possibly through his training in Amsterdam, or via his professional relationship with Inigo Jones, he knew of Michelangelo's Medici monuments in San Lorenzo in Florence, which bore no resemblance to the men commemorated, and instead personified their abstract virtues and strengths, as heroes of classical antiquity.[27] Wishing to symbolise the ethos of the Virgin Queen, he produced a female

[25] CLRO, Court of Aldermen, Repertory 37, ff. 176b, 208b, 219b.

[26] CLRO, Court of Aldermen, Repertory 39, f. 171, 22 April 1625.

[27] His admiration for the Medici tomb figures is most clearly expressed in the Holles monuments in Westminster Abbey.

FIG. 37. George Vertue's pen and grey wash drawing
(*c.* 1740) of the first statue of Sir Thomas Gresham by an
unknown sculptor (1622).
Guardian Royal Exchange collection

form reminiscent of the banned Virgin Mary. Elizabeth had strictly controlled her image during her lifetime, and was universally known as a stiff figure, bewigged and ruffed, and wearing stomacher and broad farthingale. The truthfulness of a likeness was important in Puritan ideology, and there could well have been an argument in committee over the rival merits of the real versus the ideal.[28]

A slender female draped *all'antica*, with long flowing tresses under a virgin's veil and a small crown, the

Virgin Queen can still be seen in the Guildhall Art Gallery (Fig. 38). The statue may have been avant-garde, but it was far too accomplished a piece to be discarded, so Nicholas Leate was directed to pay £40 for it to be 'taken downe undefaced' and resited on Guildhall Gate. Stone received £30.[29] Despite having a replacement right hand (which once held a sceptre), it is a very handsome work. It is clearly a portrait of the beak-nosed Queen, but the veil and classical drapery, which are so finely executed, rendered her unrecognisable at a distance. The figure was coated in grey stone-coloured paint, but this has recently been stripped to reveal 'repeated applications of tinted limewashes', proving her face was, at one time, painted a dull pink.[30]

Charles I in armour was duly added on his accession, though only after the original effigy by an unrecorded sculptor, too, had been rejected and sent to the Guildhall.[31] It is presumably the 6 ft. × 3 in. statue which is also still in the Guildhall Art Gallery (Fig. 39). The reasons for disapproval are nowhere spelled out. Perhaps the snake of Prudence slithering over the globe under his foot was too Platonic an allegory for the Aldermen. The execution is not of the same quality as Stone's Elizabeth. The detailing of fur, lace, armour, and jewels is painstaking, but the portrait is stereotyped and the head and crown curiously inept. This figure also bears vestigial traces of colour: an orange-red layer is visible on the underside of the left thigh.[32] Leate was instructed to pay £25 to 'one Andreas' (Andrew Kearne, Nicholas Stone's brother-in-law), for the replacement statue finally set up in April 1629, though there is no information as to how it differed from the reject.[33]

[28] The uncompromising portraits of Holbein and Durer were greatly prized. Oliver Cromwell would insist upon being depicted with all his 'ruffness. pimples warts & everything as you see me. otherwise I never will pay a farthing for it.' *Vertue Notebooks*, I, *Walpole Society*, Vol. XVIII (1929–30), p. 91.

[29] CLRO, Court of Aldermen, Repertory 37, f. 208b. Spiers, op. cit. Price, op. cit., p. 153 points out that the Guildhall Gate was better known as 'the Porch', and different from the Chapel, where this figure of Elizabeth is known to have stood.
[30] Helen Hughes, Historic Paint Research, Report commissioned by Nimbus Conservation, 1992, states that such limewashes use very common pigments which are difficult to date.
[31] CLRO, Court of Aldermen, Repertory 43, f. 152, 30 April 1629.
[32] Information from Helen Hughes. The figures of Elizabeth and Charles I, together with an earlier figure of Edward VI which was originally commissioned for the Chapel, are currently in storage until the Guildhall Art Gallery reopens.
[33] CLRO, Court of Aldermen, Repertory 43, f. 152. The German, Andreas/Andrew Kearne/Karne's dates are unknown.

FIG. 38.   Nicholas Stone's rejected figure of Queen
Elizabeth I from the first Royal Exchange.
Guildhall Art Gallery, Corporation of London

FIG. 39.   The rejected figure of Charles I from the first
Royal Exchange.
Guildhall Art Gallery, Corporation of London

The sovereigns from Henry II to Charles I stand in chronological order, running left to right, in the 1644 engraving entitled *Byrsa Londinensis* by Wenceslas Hollar (1607–77) (Fig. 17).[34] (The figures of Edward the Confessor to Stephen must therefore have stood underneath the Tower, which provided Hollar with an excellent perspective of the courtyard.) Many of the figures carry orbs and/or sceptres, and all wear crowns except for the youthful Edward V, whose crown is suspended above his head. Henry II, holding his Plantaganet shield with its heraldic lions, is the nearest statue on the left. Beneath the foot of the next king a lion slumbers, identifying Richard the Lionheart, and the sequence continues round to Henry VIII, followed by his heir, Edward VI, and his two daughters, Mary Tudor and Elizabeth, standing on the right.

By 1644, civil war had split the country and London was in ferment. Hollar was a devoted royalist who was forced into exile that very year.[35] Whether printed at home or abroad, the engraving conveyed a clear polemical message about the historical links between the monarchy and the economic heart of the nation. Trading continued willy-nilly, and Hollar included foreign merchants in their differing national costumes among the busy crowd. But public statues have always attracted unwelcome attention in times of unrest. Back in 1635 the citizens of Portsmouth were commanded to raise their hats to one bust of Charles I.[36] After his execution in 1649, reaction to such deferential attitudes set in. As Evelyn described it, 'Un-kingship was proclaimed'.[37] In a sweeping public act in December 1650, the Council of State ordered that the kings' statues (of James I and his son) at St Paul's, and of Charles I at the Exchange should be destroyed. Charles I was to have:

ye head . . . broaken off, and ye sceptre broaken out of his hand. And this inscription put upp by it Exit Tyrannus Regum Ultimus Anno Libtatis Angliae restitutae primo Anno Domini 1648 January 30.[38]

Any 'picture of ye late king' together with the royal arms, was to be removed from churches, 'Comon halls of Companies, & other publique places of meeting' in the City.[39] (The rejected figure of Charles I, by then standing on the Guildhall Chapel façade, was taken down, but was preserved intact, and replaced at the Restoration.[40])

The Gresham Committee were perturbed at the desecration of their property. The first entry in their Repertory is slashed through with a pen-stroke. Having obediently defaced the figure, the Committee decided it looked unsightly and they would remove 'what is remayning of ye statue'. Finally they required the Town Clerk to sign a certificate to the fact that they had been obeying an order of Parliament.[41] After the Great Fire, a Latin inscription expressing their regret was added under the replacement of Charles I, to the effect that the King had been twice martyred — 'Bis Martyris (in Corpore & Effigie)'.[42]

Disaffection was with Charles I only, and the other sovereigns were maintained throughout the Interregnum, being subjected to 'brushing washing and clensing' in 1657.[43] The whole history of the nation could not just be swept under the carpet. The first movement in 1656 towards persuading Cromwell to take the Crown, came from the City, from Sir Christopher Packe, and it is intriguing to discover that a portrait of Oliver Cromwell featured prominently. A poem was pinned up 'Under Gen. Cromwell's Picture, hung up in the Royal Exchange', which began 'Ascend ye Throne Greate Captaine . . .' and ended 'God save ye King!'[44] Another Latin couplet entitled *In Effigiem Oliveri Cromwell* is accredited to Andrew Marvell, the

[34] R. Pennington, *A descriptive catalogue of the etched work of Wenceslas Hollar 1607–1677* (Cambridge, 1982), p. 182, no. 1036i (1st state).

[35] He had been art-tutor to Charles I's second son, James, Duke of York, as a child; he is rumoured to have been at the Siege of Basing House with Inigo Jones, Robert Peake and William Faithorne; he took up residence in Antwerp from 1644–52 where he helped the royalist cause by issuing portraits of the exiled Charles II.

[36] *SPD*, 1635, p. 443: Viscount Wimbledon to the Mayor of Portsmouth, 22 October 1635.

[37] Evelyn's Diary, op. cit., Vol. II, p. 555, 30 May 1649.

[38] CLRO, Court of Aldermen, Repertory 60 (1949–50), f. 212.

[39] Ironmongers' Court Minutes, Guildhall MS 16,967/5, f. 101, 17 December 1650.

[40] Price, op. cit., p. 153.

[41] CLRO, Court of Aldermen, Repertory 60 (1949–50), ff. 219–220v.

[42] *A Compendious View of the late Tumults & Troubles in this Kingdom by way of Annals . . .*, by J. W. Esq. (1685) (occasionally referred to as *Wright's Public Transactions*), p. 169.

[43] MC, GR 1629–69, f. 170: payment to M. Derby.

[44] J. Friswell, 'Curious Epigrams on Oliver Cromwell', *Notes and Queries*, I, S.iii, no. 87, 28 June 1851, p. 516.

Protector's Poet Laureate. In translation it reads 'Before this shadow oft his en'mies fled: Beneath it lives secure the people led',[45] which suggests an inscription beneath something more solidly three-dimensional, but there is no documentation to suggest a statue of Cromwell was ever installed. Cromwell was, however, publicly mourned like a monarch when he died, with a crowned and purple-robed waxen effigy paraded upon his catafalque.

With the increasing certainty of the restitution of the monarchy early in 1660, there was a sudden revival in the importance attached to 'The Kingdom's Marble Chronicle', as the royal statues at the Exchange were called.[46] The City of London gave generously towards the subsidy sent to Breda for the purpose of bringing King Charles II home. Pepys wrote that the statues of the two kings, Charles I and II, were to be placed upon the Exchange, and the niche where the martyred King had stood was to have the anarchic inscription erased, and 'Vive le Roy' painted instead.[47] James Heath proclaimed the placing of these two 'Tutelar Angels' as

most pious, most due, and a most just veneration and reverence, (as it was the greatest glory among the Romans) which the City of London did to both Princes together.[48]

By 21 September 1660 both statues of father and son, 'most nobley cut in marble', had been installed.[49] Heath described the figure of Charles I with 'a Scepter in the King's right hand, a Church in his left Arme, a Globe at his left foot, and on his shield MAGNA CHARTA'.[50] The Guildhall's Charles I (Fig. 39) has many of the same attributes, so in the absence of the figure destroyed in 1649, the sculptor must have turned to the first statue that had been rejected in the 1620s.

Before Charles II had even set foot in England, Pepys noted that his statue was being made 'by the Mercers' Company (who are bound to do it) to set up in the Exchange'.[51] It was accompanied by a shield with the inscription, 'AMNESTIA: OBLIVION', expressing national agreement over the conciliatory conditions of the Restoration.[52] (When the image was replaced after the Great Fire, this inscription was dropped.) In 1668, Hollar reissued his, by then, invaluable documentary engraving, *Byrsa Londinensis*, adding Charles II in the vacant niche next to his father (Fig. 40).[53] The restored sovereign wore Garter robes with a high plumed hat, and held out a charter with a dangling seal. This statue stood in place for only six years.

Charles II had been in exile, apart from the brief Scottish interlude which ended at the Battle of Worcester in 1651, since 1646. He had left the country as a chubby-cheeked youth of 16, and returned a lean and world-weary cynic aged 30. The majority of the populace had no idea what he looked like, and I would suggest that the visit John Stone (1620–67) paid to Breda in early 1660, hitherto associated simply with his job-petition, may also have been an attempt to get a likeness for the Exchange commission.[54] Stone suffered a seizure while abroad,

---

[45] Andrew Marvell, *Complete Works*, ed. A. B. Grosart, Vol. 1 Verse (1872), p. 415. 'Haec est quae toties inimicos umbra fugavit,/ At sub qua cives otia lenta terunt'.

[46] 'The Conflagration of London Poetically Delineated' by Simon Ford, printed in *London in Flames London in Glory: Poems on the Fire and Rebuilding of London 1666–1709*, ed. R. A. Aubin (New Brunswick, 1943), p. 13, line 265.

[47] Pepys *Diary*, op. cit., Vol. 1, p. 89, 16 March 1660. See also 'The Loyal Subjects Teares for the Sufferings and Absence of their Soverign Charles II . . . with an Observation upon the Expunging of Exit Tyrannus . . . (etc.) by order of General Monk', BL Thomason Tracts, dated in MSS 21 March 1660.

[48] J. Heath, *The Glories and Magnificent Triumphs of the Blessed Restitution of His Sacred Majesty King Charles II* (1662), p. 165.

[49] Thomas Rugg, *Diurnal 1659–1661*, ed. Sasche (1961), p. 109. These were not minuted by the Gresham Committee, illustrating the turmoil of adjustment to the return of the monarchy.

[50] Heath, op. cit., p. 165, mentions shields for both Charles I and II which are not visible in Hollar's engraving. They may have been situated in the entablature of the arcade, under each royal figure.

[51] Pepys *Diary*, op. cit., Vol. 1, p. 113, 22 April 1660.

[52] Heath, p. 166. D. Lloyd, Bishop of Asaph, *Eikon Basilike or The True Pourtraiture of his Sacred Majesty Charls the II* (1660), p. 68 gives the full inscription: 'Monarchiarum Mag. Brit. tertius/ Franciae & Hiber. REX/ Aetatis Suae anno tricessimo, Regni/ duodecimo, Restaurationis primo/ Anno Dom. 1660.' Ford's poem, 'The Conflagration of London' (p. 13, line 280) commented that although the Royal Exchange statues had been destroyed, with 'Charles living, th'Amnesty'll ne're be forgot' (see note 46 above).

[53] Pennington, op. cit., p. 182, no. 1036iii (3rd state). Versions of both states i and iii are in the Guildhall Prints and Maps Department.

[54] Spiers, op. cit., p. 27. John Stone was Nicholas Stone's eldest son. His petition is *SPD*, 1660, SP29/3, f. 112, 11 June.

FIG. 40.   Hollar's *Byrsa Londinensis* reissued in 1668:
detail.
Guildhall Library, Corporation of London

and it has never been explained why a second competent sculptor, Caius Gabriel Cibber (1630–1700), the Dane who had recently been appointed Stone's foreman, was sent to bring him home, rather than a member of Stone's family.

When William Schellinks, the Dutch traveller, visited the country just after the Restoration, he listed all the monarchs at the Exchange, from Edward the Confessor on, together with the inscriptions which gave their dates of death, and the number of years, months and days that each had ruled.[55] Another visitor, Balthasar de Monconys, was not impressed with the old statues, however, describing them as 'de la hauteur du naturel, mais mal-faites'.[56]

One proposition, put forward in December 1660 by Hugh Morrell to Mr Secretary Nicholas, was that the English merchants of Rouen should establish a French Company in London. If this were to happen, 'the merchants should set up a brass statue of the King at the Exchange at their own cost like that of Henry IV at Paris'.[57] Henry's familiar armour-clad figure on horseback stood on the Pont Neuf. Although nothing more was heard of this suggestion, Ann Saunders' remark, about the replacement of the two royal statues in the line of kings, is equally relevant here:

It is worth noting that the chosen place of veneration was not a church or cathedral, or any place of political assembly, but the trading heart of London, the Royal Exchange.[58]

Then came the Great Fire. Vincent, in *God's Terrible Voice in the City*, described how 'By and By, the kings fell all down upon their faces'.[59] Evelyn lamented the loss of 'the sumptuous Exchange', and on 5 September 1666 Pepys recorded the holocaust's progress: 'The Exchange a sad sight, nothing standing there of all the statues or pillars but Sir Tho. Gresham's picture in the corner'. Although Samuel Rolle drew a moral about the 'craft and covetousness . . . overladen with pride and prodigality' which he saw in the mercantile transactions of the old Exchange,[60] I have found only expressions of regret at the loss of the royal sculptures. There is no contemporary comment to the effect that God had directed this particular blow at the line of kings as a condemnation of restored monarchy. Rather the reverse: Simon Ford in *London's Remains* wrote:

The dreadful Wrack now altogether flings
Crowns, Scepters, and the Trunks of Kings
And like your statues, kings, said she, you must
Once mingled be with common Dust . . .
. . .
And you, who dreamt o' th'Fall of Kings, at last
Grow wise, now Sixty-six is past.[61]

[55] *The Journal of William Schellinks' Travels in England 1661–1663*, trans. and ed. M. Exwood and H. L. Lehmann, Camden Fifth Series, vol. 1 (1993), p. 52.
[56] B. de Monconys, *Journal des Voyages de Monsieur de Monconys, Seconde partie: Voyage d'Angleterre . . . etc* (Lyon 1665), p. 11.
[57] *SPD*, 1660–61, p. 421.
[58] A. Saunders, *The Royal Exchange* (published for the opening by H.M. The Queen in 1991 of the restored and enlarged Royal Exchange), p. 17.
[59] Quoted by E. W. Brayley, *Londiniana or Reminiscences of the British Metropolis* (1829), Vol. III, p. 79.
[60] Rolle, op. cit., Part III, Meditation IX, p. 45.
[61] Printed in *London in Flames London in Glory*, op. cit., p. 100, lines 207–16.

After the rebuilding of 1669, two statues of the Founder presided over the Exchange. The old figure was reinstated, as recounted earlier, and John Bushnell (d. 1701) executed a second Gresham which was placed 'over the South Entrance' (Fig. 41).[62] It was heavily dependent upon the earlier statue, and could have been intended to replace it. Vertue stated that the original head by Bushnell was made of 'Clay. bak'd' and kept 'up Stairs' at the Exchange.[63] Bushnell may have enrolled the help of Edward Pearce Junior (d. 1695).[64] The full-length white purbeck stone statue (83 in. high) a bearded old fellow, survives, wearing slashed knickerbockers and flat cap, but the timeless 'toga', or stole, habitual in the seventeenth century, and hard-soled, high-tongued shoes, betray its date. In the 1820s it was moved to take pride of place, high up over the central archway of the Cornhill entrance.[65] It survived the fire of 1838, and today it is inaccessibly tucked away in the ante-chamber to the Central Criminal Court at the Old Bailey, together with Bushnell's melodramatic carvings of Charles I and Charles II (Figs. 42–45) which originally stood on the same façade overlooking Cornhill. The three figures represent Bushnell at his best. They are in excellent condition and it is a pity they cannot be viewed easily by the public.[66]

The magnificent new Cornhill frontispiece took the shape of a triumphal arch surmounted by a tower, and visitors were welcomed by the expansive gestures of the two royal statues, placed at first-floor level, either side of the main arched entrance. They can be

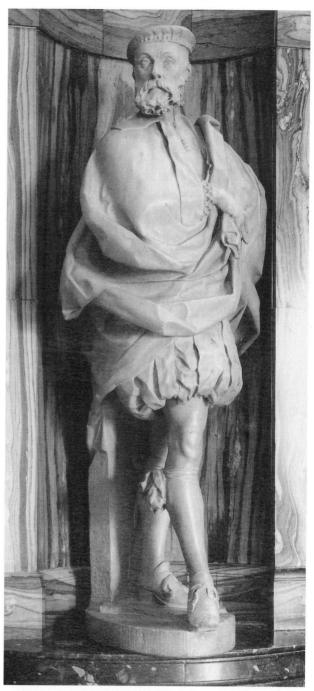

FIG. 41. John Bushnell's purbeck stone statue of Sir Thomas Gresham (1671) now in the Central Criminal Court, Old Bailey.
Corporation of London. Photo: Courtauld Institute

[62] MC, Gresham Account Books, 4 November 1671, Bushnell paid £75; Mercers' Rentwarden's Accounts 1658–75, f. 25 notes payment of their moiety of £37 10s.

[63] *Vertue Notebooks*, II, *Walpole Society*, Vol. XX (1931–32), p. 9.

[64] *Vertue Notebooks*, I, *Walpole Society*, Vol. XVIII (1929–30), p. 106 suggests Pierce 'cut' this figure, and M. Whinney, *Sculpture in Britain 1530–1830* (1988), p. 102 detected a second hand at work.

[65] K. Esdaile, 'John Bushnell Sculptor', *Walpole Society*, Vol. XV (1927), pp. 31–32, note 1. It can just be seen in the aquatint issued by Ackermann & Co. in 1836.

[66] Rescued undamaged in 1838, they were kept by the Gresham Committee, and housed at Gresham College until 1912 when that building was demolished. They then spent three years in the Guildhall Yard before being transferred to the Old Bailey where their unfortunate setting was remarked upon as long ago as 1927 when Esdaile wrote 'John Bushnell Sculptor', op. cit.

seen *in situ* in a detail of Robert White's inaugural engraving of 1671 (Figs 31, 46). Vertue gleaned the information from the sculptor's sons, in March 1726,

FIG. 42. John Bushnell's purbeck stone statue of
Charles I (1671) for the Cornhill façade of the second
Royal Exchange, now in the Central Criminal Court,
Old Bailey.

Corporation of London. Photo: Courtauld Institute

FIG. 43. Detail of head.
Corporation of London. Photo: Courtauld Institute

that their father was responsible for the figures,[67] but
it was Thomas Cartwright, who took over the supervision of the rebuilding project after Jerman's death,
who received £300 for setting up 'the statues of the
two kings; and all at his owne proper charge'.[68] He
must have sub-contracted Bushnell to make the royal
figures, just as he did John Bullimore for the six
dragons and four maidenheads which are also visible
round the tower in the detail of White's engraving.[69]

The kings were also carved in plain white purbeck
stone. Charles the Martyr (84 in. high) casts his eyes
to heaven, and touches his breast in exculpation. He

[67] *Vertue Notebooks*, II, *Walpole Society*, Vol. XX (1931–32), p. 9.
[68] MC, GR 1669–76, 25 January 1672/3.
[69] Bullimore's dates are unknown. He was paid £15 for this
work 'by appointment of Mr Cartwright', CLRO, Gresham
Accounts, Misc. MSS 150.5, sanctioned for payment 21 September 1677.

holds a tall staff reminiscent of a shepherd's stick,
alluding to his role as protector of his people, and to
the royal sacrifice. Bushnell's admiration for the work
of Bernini, with whom he had had some contact
during his recent visit to Italy, is visible in a number
of features. The head, particularly (Fig. 43), may have
been copied from Bernini's bust of Charles I, which
had been worked up from Van Dyck's famous triple
portrait of the ill-fated monarch, and which was,
until the fire of 1698, visible in Whitehall Palace.
Forceful diagonals and dramatic light and shade are
reminiscent of Italian baroque sculpture, but the rag-
like drapery is distracting. Both Cornhill figures were
intended to be viewed from a distance, like Bernini's
huge saints beneath the dome of St Peter's, and
Bushnell had studied the coarse finish which Bernini
used so cleverly to lend texture. The chisel marks and

FIG. 44 (*left*). John Bushnell's purbeck stone statue of
Charles II (1671) for the Cornhill façade of the second
Royal Exchange, now in the Central Criminal Court,
Old Bailey.
Corporation of London. Photo: Caurtauld Institute

FIG. 45 (*above*).   Detail of head.
Corporation of London. Photo: Courtauld Institute

clawing are obtrusive, however, when looked at close
to, as they can be, in their present unsatisfactory
situation.[70] Charles II ($83\frac{1}{2}$ in. high) is more substantial and stalwart than his father, and the likeness is
quite striking (Fig. 45), but Bushnell chose an awkward pose and the overall result is somewhat
ungainly.[71]

Bushnell's work attracted controversy not only for
artistic reasons. Offence was also caused because

both kings were dressed *all'antica*, in short tunics with
bare arms and legs, and cross-bound sandals. Plainly
Jerman and Cartwright thought these garments
would complement the handsome Corinthian façade.
But the classical dress of antiquity was by many
people irrationally associated with Roman Catholi-
cism.[72] Puritan notions had not necessarily vanished
with the return of the monarchy, and such a state of
'undress' probably seemed scandalous. It was also

[70] The polychrome marble of the niches at the Old Bailey
contributes further restlessness.
[71] Charles II was 6 ft 2 in. while his father was only 5 ft 8 in.

[72] A love of the past was often thought the equivalent to
recusancy. See J. Evans, *History of the Society of Antiquaries* (1956),
p. 19.

FIG. 46.   Robert White's engraving (1671) of the Cornhill façade of the second Royal Exchange: detail of frontispiece.
Guildhall Library, Corporation of London

important that the unities of time and place should be upheld: it was ridiculous to show an English king in the robes of a Roman *imperator*, wearing the medieval Garter round a bare leg, and a bouffant seventeenth-century wig upon his head. These anachronisms would have to go, and Gibbons' statue of Charles II, which later stood in the centre of the Exchange courtyard, would be one of the first to be archaeologically 'pure'.

On his return from Italy Bushnell had carved four royal statues for Temple Bar, the gateway between Westminster and the City (1669–70). James I was acceptable, but the Elizabeth was as willowy and

unrecognisable as Stone's rejected Queen, and the statues of Charles I and Charles II were the first full-length British kings to be dressed as ancient Romans. They sported beards and moustaches, and wore crowns over their long hair. The Cornhill façade statues followed closely upon Temple Bar, and almost immediately Bushnell began upon the line of kings for the courtyard. Vertue recounts how he

did those two statues at the Royal Exchange gate without. in Cornhill. & had agreed to make all the rest of the statues with in of the Kings. but some body haveing made interest to make some of them. contrary to agreement, which as soon as he understood. tho' he had begun seaven <six>

of them, he wou'd not proceed, & are unfinish'd to this day.[73]

Theophilus Philalethes in his encomium of 1672 upon the new Exchange, mentioned that six of the kings were in the building, ready to be installed:

> . . . on the North-side, here are to be seen
> Six of these Caesars there you may behold
> All in one shop, richly bedeckt with Gold.[74]

But Bushnell's statues for the courtyard were never put in place. Vertue discovered them in the sculptor's old studio after his death, in 1725:

> after long expectations I see the inside of John Bushnalls house . . . in which are several statues remaining in Marble . . . the other Statues where of several Kings & Queens, (none finish'd) beginning with Ed. sixt Qu. Ma. Que. Elisb. King James. I. K. Charles I & second. these two last most finisht Especially the heads.[75]

Caius Gabriel Cibber had a prior claim to do the work for the Exchange, and he came with infinitely more powerful recommendations. Cibber, as the inheritor of the Stone family workshop, had recently been appointed a member of the Royal Household and Sculptor in Ordinary to the King. As early as December 1667, the Lord Chamberlain had, with the King's approval, put his name forward for the job of replacing the line of kings.[76] The Mercer's Company received an approach they could hardly ignore:

> A Letter from the Right hon^ble the Earle of Manchester recommending one Cajus Gabriel Cibber to the makeing of the Statues for the Royall Exchange and the matter in regard he hath showed his Ma^ty some Modellos which have been well liked of; . . . The Committee . . . acquainted him that the buisinesse of making the statues is yett very remote from their thoughts haveing the wholle Exchange to build first . . .[77]

The Dane was encouraged to apply later, but in the meantime, he ran into debt and was thrown into prison.[78] During his incarceration he was allowed out daily to work on the Monument; this was probably permitted because of his status as a royal servant, but he had difficulty re-establishing himself afterwards.[79] Some of his models for the Exchange survive and will be discussed later.

There may have been some misunderstanding between Bushnell and the Gresham Committee, but they clearly rejected the six gilded 'Caesars'. The Committee very probably pointed him towards Cibber's models. Bushnell was a vain man, with modern ideas about the value of his own genius, and he would surely have flatly refused to copy another man's work. This, and Cibber's embarrassing absence, are possible explanations for the ensuing delay — an impasse which lasted for thirteen years. The records are silent on the subject.

Meanwhile the Gresham Committee had been approached with two proposals to place a statue of the reigning monarch in the centre of the courtyard. They politely turned down an offer made in March 1669 by Alderman Sir Robert Vyner of an ugly equestrian statue of Charles II,[80] on the grounds that it would 'take up too much of that roome which is too little already to contayne the concourse of Merchants', and they considered it important not to 'hinder the prospect through both the doores'.[81] They did not have the same reservations in 1682–83, when an offer was received from the Merchant Adventurers of Hamburg, of whom Sir Thomas Gresham had himself been a member. 'Out of Gratitude for some great Favour received from the King', they were

---

[73] Vertue Notebooks, I, Walpole Society, Vol. XVIII (1929–30), p. 86. John Gwynn, in London & Westminster Improved (1766), p. 29, described Bushnell as 'a humorist by disposition' and he seems to have lost his mind towards the end of his life.

[74] Lines 624–26 of 'Great Britain's Glory or a brief Description of the present State, Splendour and Magnificence of the Royal Exchange' printed in London in Flames London in Glory, op. cit., pp. 189 ff. This is obviously a pseudonym, but the writer has not been identified.

[75] Vertue Notebooks, II, Walpole Society, Vol. XX (1931–32), p. 8.

[76] Cibber's appointment is dated 20 June 1667 in PRO/LC3/25, p. 113 and confirmed LC3/26, p. 149.

[77] MC, GR 1629–69, f. 315.

[78] R. Gunnis, Dictionary of British Sculptors 1660–1851 (1951), p. 101.

[79] By 28 January 1680 he was able to sign a contract for seven garden statues for the Earl of Rutland at Belvoir Castle (see Lady Victoria Manners, 'Garden Sculpture by Caius Gabriel Cibber', Country Life, 27 September 1930, p. 382) but in November 1680 he was made to swear in front of the new Lord Chamberlain that he had been appointed in June 1667 (LC3/28, pp. 111, 169).

[80] Jasper Latham converted an Italian sculpture of Jan Sobieski of Poland defeating the Turk, into a portrait of Charles II trampling on the prone figure of Oliver Cromwell. It was later set up in Stocks Market, where it was greeted with derision.

[81] MC, GR 1626–69, f. 367.

Fig. 47.   Peter Vandrebanc's engraving of Grinling Gibbons' figure of Charles II which stood in the centre of the courtyard at the second Royal Exchange (1684).
Guardian Royal Exchange collection

Figs. 48–49.   Preparatory drawings for Roman statues attributed to Grinling Gibbons (*c.* 1683).
Trustees of the British Museum

(1648–1721), the King's Surveyor and Repairer of Carved Work at Windsor.[83] It marks the moment in the virtuoso wood-carver's career when he first personally undertook the execution of a stone figure in the round. His triumph in the harder medium was celebrated in poetry:

> Nor is the Conquest on the Marble less,
> The hardest Rocks thy softest Forms express.[84]

Gibbons' King Charles no longer exists, but its appearance is known from an engraving of imposing size (2 ft 2 in. × 1 ft 6½ in.) by Peter Vandrebanc, entitled 'Ex Marmorea Statua. G.Gibbons sculpta' (Fig. 47).[85] The medium was probably Portland stone, but it was variously described as grey stone, white stone or marble.[86] The statue faced south, and the Merchant Adventurers paid £500 for it and the 8 foot pedestal adorned with reliefs of cupids supporting the arms of France, Ireland and Scotland on the three lesser sides, while on the front were 'an Imperial Crown, Wings, Trumpets of Fame, Scepter and Sword, Palmbranches etc.'.[87]

The statue itself was in the idiom of several delicate preparatory drawings in the British Museum which are attributed to Gibbons, and of which the closest are illustrated (Figs. 48–49).[88] The result in stone must have looked very similar to the bronze Charles II by Gibbons which stands in Figure Court at the Royal Hospital, Chelsea, and which was fashioned

FIG. 50.   Grinling Gibbons' bronze statue of Charles II.
Figure Court, Royal Hospital, Chelsea. Photo: Courtauld Institute

willing to put up a full-length standing statue 'in the Garb and Habit of a Roman Caesar'.[82] This figure was designed and executed by Grinling Gibbons

[82] Aurelian Cook, *Titus Britannicus: An Essay of History Royal in the Life & Reign of his late Sacred Majesty Charles II. Of Ever Blessed and Immortal Memory* (1685), p. 464. See also *The Diaries and Papers of Sir Edward Dering, Second Baronet, 1644–1684*, ed. M. F. Bond (1976), p. 144. Between 1673–78, the King had also interceded in the repayment to the Merchant Adventurers of £35,000 'for the burning, takeing and destroying of certain Shipps by the Hollanders in the River of Elbe' on 24 August 1666 (CLRO, Misc. MSS 253.2–8 and GL MS 370).

[83] G. Beard, *The Works of Grinling Gibbons* (1989), p. 12. Gibbons did not receive the Master Carver's post until after the death of his predecessor, Henry Phillips, in 1693.

[84] Nahum Tate, 'To Mr. Gibbons on his Incomparable Carved Works' from *Poems Written on Several Occasions* (2nd edn, 1684) (BL 11626.d.59) printed in D. Green, *Grinling Gibbons, His Work as Carver and Statuary, 1648–1721* (1964).

[85] Windsor Castle, Royal Library, Engraved Royal Portraits Vol. VIII, p. 43. BM Prints and Drawings, Crace collection, 1880-11-13-3737.

[86] England has no natural deposits of fine white marble, and in the seventeenth century the word 'marble' was used to describe any stone used for statuary.

[87] E. Hatton, *New View of London or an Ample Account of that City* (1708), p. 616. *Wright's Public Transactions*, op. cit., p. 198.

[88] E. Croft Murray and P. Hulton, *Catalogue of British Drawings in the British Museum*, Vol. I (1960) i, pp. 333–36; ii, pls 135–36. These have been associated with the bronzes of Charles II at Chelsea, and James II, now in front of the National Gallery in Trafalgar Square.

soon after the prototype at the Exchange (Fig. 50).[89] The stone was 6 ft. 10 in., whereas the bronze is 7 ft. 4 in. in height. Vandrebanc shows the King with cropped hair, a laurel wreath, and wearing a Roman fish-scale cuirass, and lionshead lambrequins.[90] At Chelsea the right arm is thrust forward holding the baton of command, and the victor's cloak falls to the ground behind him. The figure is foursquare, lacking any *contrapposto*, and the head seems slightly too heavy for the body. But it is a powerful image, with a suppressed energy. The illusion of a real presence and Gibbons' 'matchless' and 'Majestic Figure' at the Exchange were euphorically praised in contemporary poetry and prose (Appendix I).[91]

It is evident that the King himself was responsible for this new style in royal statuary, purged of the anachronisms seen in Bushnell's controversial precursors at Temple Bar and on the Cornhill Front. Dr Martin Lister, FRS, writing in 1696, recalled being present when Charles had chosen such a design.

I remember I was at the Levee of King Charles the Second, when 3 Models were brought him, to choose one of, in order to make his statue for the Court at Windsor; he chose the Roman Emperours Dress, and caused it also to be executed in that other erected for him in the Old Exchange in London. The like is of King James in Whitehall, and at Chelsey Colledge, our Invalides. Now I appeal to all Mankind, whether in representing a living Prince now-a-days these Naked Arms and Legs are decent, and whether there is not a barbarity very displeasing in it.[92]

All British kingly allusions and all the familiar Garter references had been discarded in favour of uniformity of classical imperial detail in the bronze equestrian statue of Charles II at Windsor, which preceded the Exchange figure by Gibbons by four years.[93] This refinement in statuary was part of a Europe-wide artistic movement towards accuracy in the portrayal of the classical past. Some people may have been shocked and amazed by the equestrian image, but popular terminology frequently identified the British monarchy with the rulers of imperial Rome: Charles II's biographers entitled their books *Augustus Anglicus*, and *Titus Britannicus*, and the emulation of antiquity is often stressed in contemporary comment. Gibbons' statue 'does outdo old Memnon's Royal Shrine', and Gibbons himself is alternatively compared to Phidias, Deucalion and Pygmalion, and placed 'enthron'd at the head of all the Mechanical, and almost the Political Arts'.[94]

The literature which singles Gibbons out for praise, the engraving and other contemporary sources state he was the sculptor.[95] None the less Vertue, in the 1730s, alleged that this royal statue was 'actually the work of Quelline' and accused Gibbons of being 'neither well skilld or practized. in Marble or in Brass. for which works he imployed the best Artists he could procure'.[96] Recently discovered evidence shows that Gibbons and Arnold Quellin (1653–86) had indeed formed a 'Coepartnership' in 1681 which required the younger man to do 'all sort of Carvers worke in Stone, joyntly to be undertaken between them . . .'.[97] But Quellin had proved unreliable, and had been 'neglecting the p'formance & fineshing' of agreed work. There had been 'severall controversies and differences' and in May 1683 the partnership was dissolved.[98] In this light, the dates concerning

---

[89] Chelsea Hospital Audited Accounts for the years 1687–92 (PRO/AO1 1466/5) show that it stood in the refectory for some time before being moved into the centre of the Courtyard by 1690–91. The plinth is incised with Grinling Gibbons' name and has remained *in situ* since that date.

[90] The lion as a regal symbol is well-known; the fish-scale cuirass was also thought to be particularly royal. Lambrequins were the broad leather strips hanging from the breastplate at shoulder and hip.

[91] Apart from the anonymous poem in Appendix I, see also Tate's poem already quoted (note 84). Another, too long to print here, is Samuel Philipps' 'To the Learned and Worthy Artist Mr. Grinsted Gibbons' (prose) and 'On Mr. Gibbons his carving the Matchless Statue of the King Erected in the middle of the Royal Exchange' (poetry) (BL 806.k.16 [131]).

[92] M. Lister, *A Journey to Paris in the Year 1698* (1699), pp. 27–28. Lister wrote a parody of Horace's *Ars Poetica*, entitled *The Art of Cooking*. His remarks about nakedness may also have been tongue-in-cheek, poking fun at out-dated or provincial Puritan attitudes.

[93] The Windsor horseman, though cast by Josias Ibach, was also very probably designed by Gibbons.

[94] S. Philipps, op. cit., note 91 above.

[95] Apart from Cook and Wright, the following were written during Gibbons' lifetime: Edward Chamberlayne's *Angliae Notitiae* (1687), II, p. 301; Hatton, op. cit., p. 616; F. Colsoni, *Guide de Londres* (1710), p. 4.

[96] *Vertue Notebooks*, IV, *Walpole Society*, Vol. XXIV (1935–36), p. 35.

[97] Beard, op. cit., pp. 52–53.

[98] PRO, C9/415/250 (Plea to the Court of Chancery, 25 October 1683).

Gibbons' statue of Charles II need careful re-examination. Quellin would later execute the Garter figure of Charles II for the line of kings, which looked down upon Gibbons' Roman image in the centre of the courtyard, and the two strands of information became tangled very early on. (The confusion is exacerbated by the fact that Quellin was again sub-contracted by Gibbons during the last two years before his premature death.)

On 6 February 1683 the Gresham Committee gave permission for Mr Oliver to raise a scaffold, because he was 'preparing to set up a statue of his present Ma^ty'.[99] Anthony Wood, in Oxford, recounted that a statue of the King was actually erected at the Exchange on 25 May 1683.[100] But was it? Collaboration between Gibbons and Quellin came to an end at precisely this moment. It is quite possible that Quellin had failed to complete his commission on time, and the following facts prove that, after the parting of the ways, Gibbons himself shouldered the partnership's commitments, and began again.

On 11 July 1683 the King approved 'the model of it as it is prepared by Mr. Gibbon, a most famous artist in carving and eminent also for working in marble'.[101] The statue is mentioned in a letter of April 1684,[102] and it was unveiled on Wednesday, 14 May 1684. Next day the *London Gazette* published:

His Majesty being well satisfied with the performance of Mr. Grinling Gibbons in the making His Majesties Statue lately set up in the Royal Exchange, hath been pleased to forbid all Persons to Copy the same in Graving, Etching, or in Mezzo-tinto without the Approbation of the said Gibbons.

The announcement is a public assertion of Gibbons' authorship and leads to the suspicion that aspersions had been cast upon his abilities with 'marble', but his graduation to this most telling medium was celebrated not only in the written word, but in his portrait by his friend, Sir Godfrey Kneller, which shows him with a marble head, as England's answer to Bernini.[103] Gibbons, like Kneller, employed an engraver to bring him positive publicity, but this 'advertising' only partially paid off, and Vertue was left to query his responsibility many years later.

It is not disputed that Gibbons and his workshop were accountable for numerous other works in stone and marble, and his authorship of the two royal bronzes, of Charles II at Chelsea and of James II in Trafalgar Square, is not denied. Ironically, it was Vertue who provided proof that Gibbons carved the Exchange statue of the King when he repeated the sad story of Gibbons damaging a marble statue of the King in the royal presence:

upon a Certain Time King Charles ye 2d came to see a statue of marble that was done of himself. which Gibbons had got done. when the King was present Gibbons to shew his skill, found some small fault that wanted to be toucht, and to amuse the King took up a hammer and chisell and strikeing somewhat too hard, broke off a peice that should not have been at which the King laught at his pride & imprudent Vanity & sd could he not leave it when it was well.[104]

This can only refer to the statue for the Royal Exchange because no other work is known that could be described as a *marble* statue of the King by Gibbons. Vertue was unfair in accusing him of stealing the limelight. Gibbons was nothing if not an entrepreneur, with an overwhelming number of commissions from the Crown and the nobility. He could not spend nine to twelve months working solely on one figure. He designed it and saw it through to completion, carving certain features himself, as Vertue recounts. But the concept of a comprehensive sculptor's workshop, with numerous assistants to help prepare the blocks of stone and to carve the less important parts, and specialists to undertake different

---

[99] CLRO, Court of Aldermen, Repertory 88, f. 73b. Oliver was City Surveyor for the rebuilding of London.
[100] A. Wood, *Life and Times*, ed. Clark (1891), p. 56.
[101] Dering, op. cit., p. 144.
[102] John Verney to Sir R. Verney, 18 April 1684 (H.Ms.C. 7th Report, p. 481).
[103] The original is in the Hermitage; a copy in Beningborough Hall, North Yorkshire. J. D. Stewart in 'Sir Godfrey Kneller as Painter of "Histories" and Portraits Historiés', in *Art and Patronage in the Caroline Courts*, ed. D. Howarth (1993), p. 255, dates this painting to *c.* 1690. I would like to date it *c.* 1684 in view of the congratulatory poetry published that year.
[104] *Vertue Notebooks*, v, *Walpole Society*, Vol. XXVI (1937–39), pp. 58–59 (1742).

techniques, though well known in Italy and the Low Countries, was not yet accepted in England.[105]

A comparison with the full-length stone statue of Charles II known to have been carved by Quellin for the new Royal College of Physicians, shows a different style (Fig. 51).[106] The College's records prove it was made and paid for, together with a second figure of Sir John Cutler, in a suspiciously short time between July and December of 1683,[107] and the possibility arises that this is the statue begun for the Exchange under the terms of the 'coepartnership'. It could well have been rejected: the grimace, the flouncing contrapposto, the long wig, the medieval armour below and the Roman cuirasse above, all add up to decided lack of gravitas. If this was so, Quellin was lucky to find an alternative home for his statue.

Gibbons' progress was inextricably bound up with developments at the Exchange, but it is also attested in correspondence with the Dean of Christ Church, Oxford, over plans for 7 foot statues of Charles II and Henry VIII for Tom Tower. In September 1682, Wren is thought to have put forward the name of Cibber,[108] but by 14 June 1684 he had no hesitation in suggesting Gibbons for the task:

I found none more reasonable (of neer his ability) then Mr. Gibbons, and I am certain his hand in all Mens opinions will deserve this Mony, & though his Name is up yet he improves soe fast that he alwaies performes equall to the expectation of those that imploy him.[109]

The phrase 'his Name is up' may refer to the Merchant Adventurers' broken contract, but immediately after the unveiling of the Exchange statue of the reigning King, Gibbons was approached by the Haberdashers to make a Henry VIII, and by the Clothworkers for James I for the line of kings. A 'meeting of the giants' — Gibbons himself, with Samuel Pepys (by then Secretary to the Admiralty and a member of the Clothworkers' Company) and Sir Christopher Wren, Surveyor of the King's Works — was held on Boxing Day 1684, at which the full-size James I was inspected and officially approved.[110] Hotfoot upon this, Gibbons was commissioned to carve an Edward VI for the Drapers' Company, of which he was a Freeman and Court Member.[111] For the Mercers, he also executed the Mary Tudor, whose sceptre was knocked out of her hands at the time of the Glorious Revolution.[112]

Six days after the King died, the Gresham Committee set aside a yearly allowance for cleaning Gibbons' Roman statue of Charles II.[113] It was one of three sculptures of this most popular sovereign to reign over the second incarnation of the Royal Exchange for the next one hundred years. There is a sad irony, however, to Aglionby's praise, written the year after the King's death,

. . . we have him, as it were, yet living among us by that noble statue of his, made by the best of modern sculptors now living, I mean Mr. Grinlin Gibbons.[114]

Daniel Defoe in 1724 called the Exchange statue 'the best beyond comparison' among London statues,[115]

---

[105] The division of responsibility in the great workshops has only recently been examined: see K. Watson, *Pietro Tacca, Successor to Giovanni Bologna*, PhD thesis, 1973, University of Pennsylvania (New York, 1983), and J. Montagu, *17th Century Roman Sculpture, The Industry of Art* (1989).

[106] This statue is at present in store at the Guildhall. The College was rebuilt in Warwick Lane to designs by Robert Hooke, and the statue was placed over the main entrance against the façade. The statue measures approximately 7 feet, and the bulk of the body shows work had begun on shaping the back, which would not be necessary for a figure expected to stand high against a wall.

[107] Royal College of Physicians Cash Book, 1664–1726, ff. 86, 88, 90. Quellin was paid for the two figures together. He was given £20 'advance money' on 2 July, and £40 on 29 September; 16s. was paid to someone 'for Cutting the lettre under the statues' on 7 December, and a final payment of £20 was made to Quellin on 16 December.

[108] This is suggested in Wren Society, v, p. 22, Letter no. 7.

[109] Christchurch MSS no. 376, a letter to the Dean in Wren's legible hand which has been overlooked in the literature about both Wren and Gibbons.

[110] T. Girtin, *The Golden Ram: A Narrative History of the Clothworkers' Company 1528–1958* (published privately 1958), pp. 148–50.

[111] Gibbons was made free of the Drapers' Company by patrimony in 1672. The commission is recorded in the Drapers' Company Minutes (MB15), 19 December 1684 and 23 September 1685, and a note of his payment of £50 was recorded in the Warden's Accounts, 1685–86 (WA22), p. 39.

[112] Gibbons was paid £50 for the Mary Tudor: MC, 2nd and Renterwardens Accounts 1682–90, Extraordinary Payments 19 June 1685 and 31 July 1685. J. Ardagh, 'Notes on Statues at the Royal Exchange', *Notes and Queries*, 11 S.XI, 18 June 1915, p. 469.

[113] MC, GR 1678–1722, f. 130.

[114] W. Aglionby, *Painting Illustrated in Three Dialogues* (1685), Preface.

[115] D. Defoe, *A Tour Through England and Wales* (Everyman ed. 1948), p. 351.

FIG. 51 (*left*). Arnold Quellin's stone figure of Charles II, possibly rejected for the centre of the courtyard of the second Royal Exchange.
Guildhall Art Gallery, Corporation of London

FIG. 52 (*above*). John Spiller's marble figure of Charles II (1791), made to replace Gibbons' figure in the centre of the courtyard of the second Royal Exchange.
Guardian Royal Exchange collection. Photo: Courtauld Institute

but Gibbons' first essay in this supposedly most permanent of media proved less than satisfactory in the long term. He had carved the piece in a stone which weathered poorly, and by 1789 it was judged by the Gresham Committee to be 'very decay'd and Mutilated'. It was decided to have a replacement carved by a promising young sculptor, John Spiller (1762–94).[116] His idealised, unrecognisable Charles II, completed in 1791, still stands in the ambulatory of the third Royal Exchange (Fig. 52). It

[116] MC, GR 1774–1804, ff. 337, 373, 404, 406, 419. A student of John Bacon's, Spiller won the Silver Palette of the Society of Arts in 1778 and 1780.

was the crowning achievement of Spiller's career, for he died of consumption soon afterwards, having wasted all his energies on this royal figure.[117] The artist, R. B. Schnebbelie, gives a good idea of Spiller's sovereign presiding over the courtyard, in place of Gibbons' figure (Col. Pl. IVA), and Edward Hassell's beautiful subdued watercolour shows its surviving presence when all around it had been tumbled and blackened by the fire of 1838 (Col. Pl. VIIB).

The restoration of the monarchy had given Charles II a pivotal position in bringing order out of chaos and uniting the nation after civil war. His restoration carried implications of an optimistic renaissance, a reassertion of national pride, a pulling-together as one people in freedom again, after bitter divisions. The monarchy had been identified with the independence of the country since Henry VIII had broken away from Rome. With its restitution in 1660, promotion of the royal lineage became an important part of royalist propaganda. Such books as Ashmole's *Order of the Garter*, Baker's *Chronicle of Kings*, and Sandford's *Genealogy* were published and republished, and historical scholarship, particularly of the medieval period, was prolific.[118] The line of horsemen carrying the armour of each successive monarch at the Royal Armoury in the Tower of London was properly organised and opened to the public at this time.[119] A painting of the first Royal Exchange had featured on the second triumphal arch in the City's 'Entertainment' presented to Charles II on his Coronation in 1661, where it equalled the Tower of London in prestige.[120] The impasse over the replacement of the historical series of royal sculptures had to be broken.

The sovereign and the City were at legal loggerheads between 1682–88, however. In an episode which has become known as the *Quo Warranto* affair, Charles had withdrawn the Charter of the Corporation of London, as well as those of the leading Livery Companies. Claiming maladministration of the City's affairs, he was attempting to rid these bodies of his political opponents and pack them with Tories. The Mercers were foremost among the rebel Whigs, and the first to lose their Charter. The replacement of the royal statues appears to have been closely associated with the Livery Companies' attempts to recapture the King's favour.[121]

Early in 1684, Sir Thomas Beckford, with his Company, the Clothworkers, behind him, put before the Lord Mayor and the Court of Aldermen 'A Loyall proposall for setting up the Statues of the 24 Kings upon the Royall exchange . . .'. He recommended that 'the 24 superior Companys, by Subscriptions . . . [should] raise Money Each Company for the setting up of our Statues . . .'.[122] The Clothworkers hoped to break the deadlock and set 'a precedent and encouragement to other Companies of this City to set up the rest of the former Kings . . .'.[123] They themselves wished to replace the figure of Charles II, but were persuaded instead to reinstate James I, an action for which they sought, as a precaution, the King's approval.

To promote the City's renewed allegiance to the Crown, a Mayoral Precept was issued on 11 November 1684 which urged the Guilds each to

---

[117] 'Charles II. Statue in the Royal Exchange: John Spiller', Sequential articles in *Notes and Queries*, by R. Pierpont, II.S.II. 22 Oct. 1910, pp. 322–23; by J. T. Page, II.S.II., 5 Nov. 1910, pp. 371–72; by C. Clarke, II.S.II., 3 Dec. 1910, p. 454.

[118] Elias Ashmole, *The Order of the Garter* (1672); Sir Richard Baker, *A Chronicle of the Kings of England . . .* (1665) (5th edn 1684); F. Sandford, *Genealogical History of the Kings of England . . .* (1677). All were published under royal privilege.

[119] A. Borg, 'Two Studies in the History of the Tower Armouries: I. Heads and Horses from the Line of Kings', *Archaeologia*, Vol. CV (1976).

[120] Peter Mills' arch-designs are in the RIBA. They were engraved by David Loggan for John Ogilby's *The Entertainment of His Most Excellent Majestie Charles II in his passage through the City of London to his Coronation* (1662). The Exchange is mentioned on p. 66 as bearing a Virgilian motto: 'Generia Lapsi Sarcire Ruinas' about the industry of bees. The paintings on the actual arches were by Andrew Dacres and William Lightfoot. See also E. Halfpenny, 'The Citie's Loyalty Display'd', *Guildhall Miscellany*, X (1959), pp. 19–35, and R. Strong, 'A Note on Charles II's Coronation Entry', *Coat of Arms*, Vol. VI (1960–61), pp. 43–47.

[121] See particularly Guildhall MS 17,087.

[122] CLRO, Misc. MSS 152.6, n.d. My thanks to Ingrid Roscoe for this reference.

[123] Girtin, op. cit., p. 149.

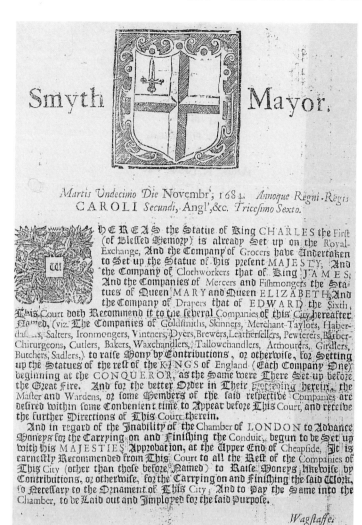

Smyth Mayor.

Martis Undecimo Die Novembr', 1684. Annoque Regni Regis
CAROLI *Secundi, Angl',&c. Tricesimo Sexto.*

ᵂHEREAS the Statue of King CHARLES the First (of Blessed Memory) is already Set up on the Royal-Exchange, And the Company of Grocers have Undertaken to Set up the Statue of this present MAJESTY, And the Company of Clothworkers that of King JAMES; And the Companies of Mercers and Fishmongers the Statues of Queen MARY and Queen ELIZABETH, And the Company of Drapers that of EDWARD the Sixth, This Court doth Recommend it to the several Companies of this City hereafter Named, (viz: The Companies of Goldsmiths, Skinners, Merchant-Taylors, Haberdashers, Salters, Ironmongers, Vintners, Dyers, Brewers, Leathersellers, Pewterers, Barber-Chirurgeons, Cutlers, Bakers, Waxchandlers, Tallowchandlers, Armourers, Girdlers, Butchers, Sadlers,) to raise Mony by Contributions, or otherwise, for Setting up the Statues of the rest of the KINGS of England (Each Company One) beginning at the CONQUEROR, as the Same were There Set up before the Great Fire. And for the better Order in Their proceeding herein, the Master and Wardens, or some Members of the said respective Companies are desired within some Convenient time to Appear before This Court, and receive the further Directions of This Court therein.

And in regard of the Inability of the Chamber of LONDON to Advance Moneys for the Carrying on and Finishing the Conduit, begun to be Set up with His MAJESTIES Approbation, at the Upper End of Cheapside, It is earnestly Recommended from This Court to all the Rest of the Companies of This City (other than those before Named) to Raise Moneys likewise by Contributions, or otherwise, for the Carrying on and Finishing the said Work, so Necessary to the Ornament of This City; And to Pay the Same into the Chamber, to be Laid out and Imployed for the said Purpose.

Wagstaffe

FIG. 53. Mayoral Precept of 1684.
Guildhall Manuscripts Department, Corporation of London

fund a single statue (Fig. 53).[124] All but the impoverished Salters from the top dozen Livery Companies complied. Some subsidised a statue of the first monarch to have granted them a charter; others chose a royal Company 'freeman' from the past. Some quarrelled over the monarchs they should represent. The Ironmongers won a contest with the Barber-Chirurgeons over which of them should sponsor Edward IV. The Mercers and the Fishmongers both wished to sponsor Elizabeth I, and settled their differences by agreeing to pay jointly for the two figures of Elizabeth and her less popular sister, Mary Tudor.

Several companies vied for the honour of putting up a statue to Charles II, and the Grocers' Company, who had elected Charles II a freeman at the Restoration, and 'bagged' him early on, nearly lost their prerogative.[125] The Gresham Committee had to persuade the Clothworkers to donate a figure of his

[124] Guildhall MS 17,087. CLRO, Court of Aldermen, Repertory 90, ff. 3–4, 2 November 1684, order that one hundred prints of the Precept be published and one delivered to each of the Livery Companies.

[125] Guildhall MS 11588, Vol. 5 of Grocers' Company Court Minutes, f. 86, 27 August 1669 talks of 'The Person that in in hand with the Kings Effigies for the Exchange'. This probably referred to Bushnell with whom they had been in contact over a statue of their current Master, Sir John Cutler. It is possible they would have been quite content with the statue of Charles II as 'Caesar' that Bushnell had completed by 1672, if the Gresham Committee had not disapproved.

grandfather.[126] The Founders' Company commissioned Jasper Latham (c. 1636–93) for a figure of Charles II, and he had actually begun work when the Grocers appealed that this was 'an affront and wrong to this Company', and he was forced to abandon his efforts.[127] Finally, on 22 May 1685, three months after the King's death, the Grocers made definite financial provision for the statue so that 'soe great a duty may no longer be neglected to the reproach of the company'.[128]

The reappearance of the royal martyr, Charles I, whose figure had already been replaced by November 1684, is unrecorded and remains a mystery. The lesser Companies' continued reluctance to vouch for any of the kings, together with the rapidly changing political fortunes following the death of Charles II in February 1685, and the flight of James II in 1688, meant that only 14 of the 24 niches (which ran 7:5:7:5 round the new quadrangle) had been filled by 1708.[129] They can best be seen in the fine pen and wash drawing on vellum, c. 1730, which hangs in the Guardian Royal Exchange collection (Fig. 33).

The repeated stipulations in the different Guilds' records make it clear that the royal replacements were to 'be made in proper habitts and as near as can be remembered to what they were in before the great fire', as stated in the Mayoral Precept.[130] For instance, Edward V was again portrayed with his crown suspended above his head. Gilding (which was now recognised as a particularly 'antique' feature, exemplified by the equestrian statue of Marcus Aurelius in Rome), was frequently specified, and an iron sword was provided for Henry VII. There are few references to painting in colour at this juncture, though one William Thompson, 'the Cities Painter', was paid

£11 'for painting and guilding the Kings and Queens Statues' in late 1695, and the figures were regilded and repainted in 1754.[131]

After all the criticism in the past, a careful effort was made by Edward Pearce to get a realistic likeness for the standing statue of Elizabeth I, which, it has been pointed out, was modelled closely upon her recumbent effigy by Maximilian Colt in Westminster Abbey.[132] Apart from memories of the lost figures, other royal tombs, portraits and statues could serve as examples. A drive to recapture historical authenticity was clearly attempted, but the Aldermen's praiseworthy ambition was very quickly forgotten, and certain eighteenth-century pundits would look down their noses at the old-fashioned figures. John Carter made his invaluable drawings of thirteen of the sovereigns in c. 1790, showing that period costume had been contrived reasonably successfully (Figs. 54–55). Carter's sketches are a major source of reference, because unfortunately only one of the large-scale figures that correspond to his drawings can be identified. Two 'medieval' torsos and some of the models have also come to light.

The names of the well-known sculptors of the period are interchanged with frequency in the many rebuilding projects after the Great Fire, and competitions for major sculpture commissions had become the norm by the end of Charles's reign in 1685. The Tallowchandlers considered 'Mr. Pearse at Arundell Ground', 'Mr. Bushnall at Hyde Park' and 'Mr. Sybbals' (Cibber), before deciding upon 'Mr. Arnold Qullin' to make their figure of Henry VII.[133] Together with Grinling Gibbons, and the obscure Joshua Fletcher (d. 1725), these men were responsible for the statues that were replaced after the 1684 Mayoral Precept.

Cibber's 'modellos' had been admired by the King back in 1667. The Gresham Committee may have insisted that Cibber's approved prototypes be referred to by the sculptors of the final statues. This deduction is reached because more than one name

[126] CLRO, Court of Aldermen, Repertory 88, f. 156 (28 June 1683) and Repertory 89, f. 111 (27 May 1684).
[127] Grocers' Company Minutes, Guildhall MS 11588, f. 673 (6 June 1684).
[128] Ibid., f. 691.
[129] They are listed by Hatton, op. cit., p. 615. Strype's 1720 edition of Stow's *Survey of London*, Book II, p. 137, and J. Halliday, *A Brief Account of the Kings and Queens whose statues (Now repaired and decorated in a most Splendid Manner) Are placed in the Royal Exchange of London* (1754) attempt to give more specific reasons why certain unpopular kings were not replaced.
[130] This phrase occurs in CLRO, Court of Aldermen Repertory 90, f. 15b. in relation to the Armourers' figure of Henry VI, but it is reiterated almost verbatim throughout.

[131] CLRO, Cities Cash Account 1695–96, f. 51v. See also Halliday, op. cit.
[132] J. Seymour, 'Edward Pearce, Baroque Sculptor', *Guildhall Miscellany*, January 1952, pp. 14–15.
[133] Guildhall MS 6153, Tallowchandlers' Court Minute Book 6, ff. 12–26.

can be associated with certain figures, and the Skinners' Company provides an example. They still possess a charming polychromed terracotta statuette, 14 inches high, of Edward III (Col. Pl. IVв).[134] In December 1684 they were recommended 'one Gabriel Sibart a Stone Cutter in St. James's for the setting the statue of Edward III on the Exchange'.[135] The following year

the Stonecutter appeared and demanded £70 for the Statue of King Edward the 3d . . . according to the Modell w.ch the Committee sawe at his howse . . . and £60 being proposed by ye Committee he accepted thereof and is to bring the Moddell to the hall . . .

The instructions continue:

. . . if the Company will guild it the paynter is to use the scaffold for that purpose when the Statue is sett up in its proper place. And the Clerke is to enquire . . . whether a Dossall or imperiall Crowne is to be putt by on it . . .[136]

In the event, however, it was 'Mr. Peirse' who set up the full-scale statue; he was paid £60 in October 1685, and a Mr Dyer was ordered to do the gilding 'in the best manner he can'.[137] Pearce had an independent practice by this juncture, but he had collaborated with Cibber on the Monument, and Cibber may have passed on the assignment.

Judging by the similar treatment of detail and the relaxed yet majestic pose, a second maquette may also be Cibber's original work, though once again another sculptor, in this case the mason, Thomas Cartwright, who subcontracted the actual work to Quellin, was paid for the large-scale carving.[138] The $12\frac{1}{2}$ inch statuette of Edward IV, still in the Ironmongers' Hall, is brilliantly coloured in scarlet with gold

armour (Col. Pl. IVc).[139] Edward IV had granted the Ironmongers their first Charter. It is unfortunately not possible to identify his statue in the vellum drawing of c. 1730, because it is in a far corner, but the model's sturdy proportions and style tally well with the other figures shown there.

A comparison of the 2 ft. $2\frac{1}{2}$ in. pale terracotta statuette of Charles II in the Sir John Soane Museum (Fig. 56) with the two foregoing models, suggests a different hand. 'Arnold Quelling' was paid £60 for carving the large-scale work,[140] and because the terracotta was acquired by Soane before the Exchange was demolished for the second time,[141] and could therefore be identified with the bigger work still *in situ*, this very fine figure has always been attributed to Quellin.[142] But, as we have seen, this assumption cannot be relied upon. Quellin was by 1685 working again for Gibbons, but it is difficult to think the woodcarver was responsible for this remarkably fine figure. Pin-point tracery is visible in the lace of the cravat, and *Honi Soit* . . . legible round the Garter. As a portrait it is one of the best to remain of the King's last years, and the tall proportions reflect the King's natural height. Carter's drawing of the completed large-scale work by Quellin shows a stockier figure altogether (Fig. 55h). Quellin was certainly working under pressure in the last years of his life and he died in September 1686, having produced six full-scale figures for the line at the Exchange in the last two years. (Over and above these, between 23 December 1685 and 1 June 1686 he fashioned four life-size lead statues of Stuart kings for Glamis Castle, which are different in composition from the figures recorded by Carter at the Exchange.[143])

There is a fourth model, of lesser quality, which can with more certainty be attributed to Quellin. A small hollow lead figure of Henry VIII (21 in. high) stands in the Library at Christ Church, Oxford

---

[134] In 1738 it was provided with a gilt and glass wall-bracket and set up over the Master's chair at the upper end of Skinners' Hall. In 1989, the figure and its frame were conserved by Malcolm Greene, but no opinion was sought as to the age of the polychroming which in the case of Edward III would appear to be original.

[135] Skinners' Company Court Minutes, f. 397, 3 December 1684.

[136] Ibid., f. 401. A dossal is an ornamental hanging, usually placed behind an altar.

[137] Ibid., ff. 414, 422, 424.

[138] Ironmongers' Court Minutes, Guildhall MS 16,967/6, 5 December 1684 and 13 January 1685; MS 16,967/7, ff. 3–4, 7 (April 1685); MS 16,988, Ironmongers' Accounts 1671–87, f. 403 (May 1685). The sources do not stipulate whether it was Cartwright father or son.

[139] It appears to be made of white clay or plaster, and the polychroming seems much fresher than on the Edward III.

[140] Grocers' Company, Accounts 1685–86.

[141] Sir John Summerson noted it was acquired at the sale of Richard Cosway's possessions held 22 May 1821 (Lot 30).

[142] The Victoria and Albert Museum possesses a bust-length copy of the Soane Museum statuette which has likewise been attributed to Quellin (Mus. Inv. no. A7-1945).

[143] M. R. Apted, 'Arnold Quellin's Statues at Glamis Castle', *Antiquaries Journal*, Vol. LXIV, pt. 1 (1984), pp. 53–61.

a.

b.

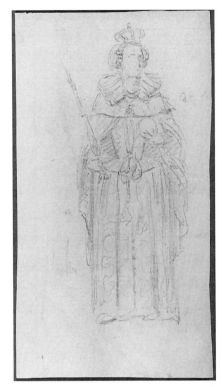

c.

d.

54a, Henry VII; b, Henry VIII;
c, Mary Tudor; d, Elizabeth I;
e, Elizabeth I, detail of head.
Guardian Royal Exchange collection

e.

f.

g.

h.

i.

FIGS. 54–55. John Carter's pencil drawings (*c.* 1790) of eight of the sovereigns from the line of kings at the second Royal Exchange.

55f, James I; g, Charles I; h, Charles II; i, James II.

Guardian Royal Exchange collection

FIG. 56.   Model of Charles II attributed to Arnold
Quellin.

By courtesy of the Trustees of Sir John Soane's Museum

FIG. 57.   Model of Henry VIII attributed to Arnold
Quellin (1685)

Christ Church, Oxford. Photo: Courtauld Institute

(Fig. 57).[144] The sculptor was no doubt directed to the Holbein mural in Whitehall Palace for a true likeness. As we have seen, in June 1684, Wren proposed that Gibbons make statues of Charles II and Henry VIII for Tom Tower.[145] At much the same time, the Haberdashers' Company sponsored the statue of Henry VIII for the Exchange. Their Minute Book for July 1685 records:

some Members of this Court . . . having seen the module of the statua of the King Henry the Eigth of one Mr. Gibbons Mr. Colynes . . . It is ordered that the standing committee . . . agree with Mr. Colyne for making the said statua with such Guilding for Ornament as they shall think fit.[146]

Although statues of Henry VIII and Charles II were never placed upon Tom Tower, the Christ Church statuette coincides closely with Carter's drawing of Henry VIII on the Exchange (Fig. 54). This one model was possibly made to do double duty therefore.

Few of the large-scale kings and queens appear to have been of outstanding quality and were probably no more than stock likenesses. This was certainly the way they were subsequently treated. St Bartholomew's Hospital Gateway followed with a very similar Henry VIII; Christ's Hospital and St Thomas's Hospital both possess figures of the boy king Edward VI wearing a crown somewhat curiously over a brimmed hat, as at the Guildhall and visible in engravings of the Exchange. Conversely, Carter's drawing of Mary Tudor reveals that Gibbons must have turned to the figure of Elizabeth I from Ludgate, which now stands on St Dunstans-in-the-East in Fleet Street, for her style of dress.

On his accession, James II's statue by Gibbons joined the line. The Merchant Taylors, with unexpected speed, decided upon the commission within days of Charles II's death in 1685.[147] It had a suitably 'Roman' character for this avowed Catholic. One of Carter's drawings illustrates the same stance adopted by Gibbons' bronze of James II now standing outside the National Gallery (Fig. 58).[148] For Tobias Rustat, Yeoman of the Robes to Charles II, Gibbons had duplicated the Merchant Adventurers' stone statue of Charles at the Exchange, in the bronze which stands at Chelsea. Gibbons may similarly have directed a duplicate be made of the stone figure of James II at the Exchange, when Rustat asked for a bronze of James II to stand in Pebble Court, Whitehall; it was installed in January 1687.[149] Strongly resembling the bronze (if of a very different standard of artistry), a full-length stone statue, covered in lichen, and almost forgotten in a garden in Dorset, may be the lost James II (Fig. 59).[150] Two bronze maquettes thought to be of James II exist, but neither duplicates this pose.[151]

A second great fire laid waste to the Exchange on the night of 10 January 1838. Many sculptural relics survived to be sold by auction later in the year, and at the sale 'The statues of the Kings and Queens . . . seemed to excite considerable interest, though sadly broken and mutilated'.[152] A quick glance again at Hassell's watercolour confirms that few could have remained undamaged, but the survivors from the line of kings were identified and listed in the sale catalogues issued by Joseph Pullen & Son (see Appendix II). The Ironmongers requested 'their' statue of Edward IV be returned to them, but it no longer exists, and it is a sad truth that, after the sale

---

[144] Kate Eustace kindly inspected this lead maquette, which has been filled with plaster, and stands on a $3\frac{1}{2}$ in. high by $10\frac{1}{4}$ in. wide marble block. She confirmed it could be late seventeenth century, though the legs and feet might have been restored since.

[145] See notes 108 and 109 above.

[146] Guildhall MS 15,842/3, Haberdashers' Court of Assistants Minute Books, 11 July 1685.

[147] CLRO, Court of Aldermen, Repertory 90, f. 47. Guildhall MSS Dept. Microfilm 331, Minutes of Merchant Tailors' Company, ff. 345–46, 1 and 12 March 1686; Microfilm 306, Accounts, 18 October 1686, 'Mr. Gibbons the Stone Cutter' paid £60.

[148] All the Carter drawings had been mounted on separate pieces of paper and given titles in a different handwriting. Ingrid Roscoe and I have reordered them as they are reproduced here (Figs. 54–55).

[149] Beard, op. cit., p. 61. John Lord discovered that Francis Bird made wooden models before he was given the commission for the skyline apostles at St Paul's. As Bird emerged from Gibbons' workshop, it may be that models were carved in wood as a matter of course before any large-scale work was undertaken. Such a model would have guided the stone-carver, and could equally provide moulds for the bronze-founder.

[150] RCHM Dorset, Vol. II, South-East, Part 2 (1970), p. 271; and plate 62 in Part 1. It stands at Creech Grange, Steeple, near Dorchester, is made of 'berestone', and is plainly a workshop production.

[151] Victoria and Albert Museum, Inv. no. A20–1948. Another was sold at Sotheby's, 8 December 1967 (33).

[152] *Gentleman's Magazine*, October 1838.

FIG. 58.   Gibbons' bronze statue of James II, now outside
National Gallery, Trafalgar Square.
Photo: Courtauld Institute

FIG. 59.   Stone statue of James II from the Gibbons
workshop, Creech Grange, Steeple, Dorset.
Photo: Royal Commission on Historical Monuments

in August 1838, most of the figures from the line of
kings have entirely vanished.[153] The broken heads of
Charles I and Edward VI, thought to have been
salvaged from the Exchange, were, until recently, in
the Museum of London.[154]

The builder John Mowlem acquired a certain
amount of the Exchange's architectural residue for
his home town of Swanage, which was expanding in
the late 1830s. Two torsos, whose provenance was
more or less certainly from the Exchange, have ended
up in the garden of Purbeck House Hotel in Swanage
(Figs. 60–61).[155] Little detailing survives which can
help identify them, but judging from the remaining
models, drawings and engravings, and by a process of
elimination, one can be said to be James I (Fig. 60),
and the other could represent either Edward I,

[153] A recent appeal via *Country Life*, and *Circumspice*, the newsletter
for the Public Monuments and Sculpture Association, brought
no new information.
[154] Museum of London, Acc. no. 7199 soft limestone head of
Charles I, 13 in. × 11 in.; and Acc. no. 7195 stone head of
Edward VI, 9 in. × 8½ in. × 8 in. They were said to be in store,
but could not be found on a recent search. My thanks to Hazel
Forsyth for this information. See *Notes and Queries*, 11 S.XI, 19 June
1915, pp. 468–69, when the heads were in the Guildhall Museum.

[155] RCHM, *South-East Dorset*, Vol. 11, pp. 295–96.

FIGS. 60–61.   Torsos of two medieval kings from the
second Royal Exchange (Purbeck House Hotel, Swanage).
Photos: Royal Commission on Historical Monuments

Henry V, or Henry VI.[156] At the same site, an
elaborate carved stone door pediment with a crown
in the centre might have come from a 'royal' building,
and two of the Mercers' symbolic 'maidenheads'
(possibly the 'Busts of Queen Elizabeth' listed in the
first day of Pullens' sale) can be identified high up in
the walls of the Town Hall overlooking Town Hall
Lane in Swanage.[157] These adorned the Cornhill
façade and were visible, it will be remembered, in
White's engraving of 1671 (Fig. 46). As they are of

different styles, one of them might be attributable to
the little-known John Bullimore.[158]

Bullimore was also responsible for the six dragons
poised round the second Exchange Clock Tower, and
clearly retained for the redesigned tower of *c.* 1822.
The arms of the City, the St George cross with an
upraised sword in the first quarter, were supported
by a heraldic dragon (also known as wyverns or
griffins), with its tongue breathing fire, and its bat-like
wings expanded. Although the St George cross had
been used for centuries as a City symbol, the dragons,
as an emblem of the City, do not appear before the

---

[156] The figure of James is intimated to be entire in the Pullens
sale catalogue. M. R. Apted, op. cit., Plate XIa illustrates
Quellin's Glamis Castle figure of James I wearing very similar
trunk hose, which would be anachronistic for any other king.
[157] For illustrations, see D. Lewer and J. B. Calkin, *Curiosities of
Swanage or Old London by the Sea* (revised edn 1986), nos. 32 and 40.

[158] See note 69.

1630s.[159] Their employment at the Royal Exchange in such numbers, as well as on the Monument and at St Mary le Bow, must have raised their popularity sharply in the last quarter of the century.[160] Like Bushnell's three figures which stood beneath the tower, they survived the fire of 1838, and are visible, intact, in Hassell's watercolour of the devastated building. Pullens sold four 'griffins' in 1838 which can no longer be traced. Similar dragons in cast-iron have recently become familiar boundary marks round the City.[161]

[159] J. Dallas, 'The City of London and its Dragons', *British Archaeological Association Journal*, 2nd series, Vol. 19 (1913), pp. 88–102. My thanks to Jeremy Smith, Keeper of Prints at the Guildhall Library for this reference.

[160] Robert Hooke's drawings of dragons in different poses round the base of the Monument column are in BL Add. MSS 5238.

[161] It is significant that they were adopted as a decorative feature for the Coal Exchange of 1847–49 (demolished in 1959) two of which now mark the City boundaries. The rest are modern copies made to half-scale in the 1960s.

The recommendation of a foreigner visiting London in 1693 was: 'La Premiere Chose a Voir A votre arrivee, visitez la Bourse Royalle.'[162] Joseph Addison charmingly sums up the national importance of the Royal Exchange at the start of the eighteenth century:

It gives me a secret satisfaction, and in some measure gratifies my vanity, as I am an Englishman, to see so rich an assembly of countrymen and foreigners . . . making this metropolis a kind of emporium for the whole earth . . . I have often fancied one of our old kings standing in person, where he is represented in effigy, and looking down upon the wealthy concourse of people.[163]

He obviously regarded the building with pride, and the kings with affection.

[162] Colsoni, op. cit. (1693 edn), p. 1.

[163] Quoted in Burgon, Vol. II, p. 512.

APPENDIX I

BL 11641.h.10(3)

A POEM UPON THE NEW MARBLE STATUE OF HIS PRESENT MAJESTY ERECTED IN THE ROYAL EXCHANGE BY THE SOCIETY OF MERCHANT ADVENTURERS OF ENGLAND TOGETHER WITH A COPY OF THE INSCRIPTION UPON THE PEDESTAL 1684

Hail Noble Founders of this vast Design!
Hail Thou the Artist who with Skill Divine,
Couldst shapeless Rock to this Perfection bring
Worthy such gen'rous Subjects, such a King.
See brave Adventurers with Triumph view
What Miracles united Zeal can do.
What wonders loyal Gratitude can raise,
That thus makes lifeless Stone speak *Caesar's* Praise!
Where with the[A] Emblems of his Pow'r, are seen,
His God-like Features and majestick Meen.
Nor do's this Piece that single Glory Claim,
It speaks with *Caesar's*, Your's and *Britains* Fame;
That now can of a nobler Statue boast,
Than[B] *Italy* preserv'd or *Greece* e're Lost.

Methinks I see Posterity Survey
(For sure such Sacred work can ne're decay)
This Marble-*Caesar*, with such God-like Grace;
As both Adorns and Consecrates the Place.
I hear them descant on his Awful Brow,
And Features that majestick Terrour throw,
Yet with such condescending Goodness join'd,
Displaying all the Mercies of his Mind,
That those Records they'll hold as false and vain
That register'd the Troubles of his Reign.

There was a Day (let Time for ever mourn
In Night, ere such another Day return)
That on our Monarchs sacred Form employ'd
A Rage more dire than what his Life destroy'd:
The first assay'd a Monarch's Blood to spill,
The Second, Monarchy it self to kill!
But late repenting years his[C] Image rais'd
More for the Zeal than Workman's Labour prais'd;

Yet by divine Instinct the Piece seems fram'd,
And for th'Event for ever shall be Fam'd,
Directly pointing with the Scepter'd Hand,
Where present *Caesar* do's in Triumph stand,
While the transported Figure seems to say,
Look Britains, *our Establisht Heir Survey;*
See how th'Assaults of Faction are in vain;
My Race, Heav'n's Choice, o'er Albion *still must Reign;*
If from no other Source your Love will spring,
Let Int'rest reconcile you to your King.
Since, in all frantick Changes you have past,
Heav'n first dislik'd, and you your selves at last,
From thence at least let now your Duty spring,
Know your own Int'rest and Obey your King.

Once more, ye brave Adventurers all Hail!
So may th'Example you have set, prevail;
Till each Society like yours shall join
(While yet we have an Artist so Divine)
To re-install each[D] Monarch in his Shrine.
While we the rising Figures shall admire,
(As from the Worlds last Flame) more glorious for the Fire!
Till of *Rome's* Capital th'Exchange has odds,
Our *British* Kings out-shine the *Roman* Gods.

All must confess who this warm Piece behold
That Marble now more precious is than Gold;
As if the Carver, with[E] Pygmalion's Art
Did, while he fram'd the Limbs, the Soul impart.
He grew ennamour'd on his own Design,
But, modest GIBBONS, all the World on Thine.

This Honour with just Gratitude is paid
By the first Masters of the Oceans Trade.
No less the Figure with the Place agrees,
Where else should stand the Monarch of the Seas?
Then let the World's united Treasure meet
T'enrich Their Bank, with each returning Fleet,
Who lay their Hearts and Wealth at *Caesar's* Feet.

[A] The Arms of the three Kingdoms carved upon the sides of the *Pedestal*.

[B] The Esteem that the Ancients had for Pictures and Statues of great Masters is incredible: of which we have this famous Instance. When *Demetrius* had laid close siege to the chief town in the Isle of *Rhodes*; he first prepared to set Fire to some Buildings without the Walls; which were slenderly defended; whereupon the People within the Town sent to him to make an Assault upon the City with all his Force, which if he could take by Storm the Buildings without would be his own; but if he proceeded to set Fire to them, he would destroy that famous Piece, fram'd by *Protogenes*, erected there. Which when it was once lost, their Town was not worth his taking. Upon this information, in reverence to that work, he withdrew his Forces and spared the Town.

[C] The Statue of His late Majesty erected (instead of that which was demolished) by remarkable Accident, pointing to the Center of the *Exchange*, where the new Figure of present Majesty is placed.

[D] The Statues of *English* Kings destroy'd in the general Conflagration.

[E] Reported by the Poets to have fram'd a Marble Nymph with which he fell in Love and laying it to his Breast the Statue took Life.

APPENDIX II

EXCERPTS FROM SALE CATALOGUES OF JOSEPH PULLEN & SON, 1838
(Guildhall Library, Pamphlet 1620)

THE VALUABLE MATERIALS OF THE ROYAL EXCHANGE

TUESDAY APRIL 3rd, 1838

MSS note of prices fetched	Lot no.	Description
£30.00.00.	51	*The two carved* GRIFFINS, *holding Shields of the City Arms*, next Cornhill
£35.00.00.	52	THE TWO DITTO, facing the Quadrangle
£18.00.00	53	*The two Busts of Queen Elizabeth*, on North and South Side
£10.15.00.	54	The TWO DITTO, on East and West Sides
Not Sold	55	THE COPPER GRASSHOPPER VANE, with the iron upright
£21.00.00.	56	THE ALTO-RELEIVO, in artificial stone, representing QUEEN ELIZABETH PROCLAIMING THE ROYAL EXCHANGE
£36.00.00.	57	*The corresponding* ALTO-RELEIVO, representing BRITANNIA SEATED AMIDST THE EMBLEMS OF COMMERCE, ACCOMPANIED BY SCIENCE, AGRICULTURE, MANUFACTURES, &c.
£110.00.00	58	THE VALUABLE CARVED EMBLEMATICAL FIGURE OF EUROPE
	59	DITTO, – ASIA
	60	DITTO, – AFRICA
	61	DITTO, – AMERICA

WEDNESDAY, AUGUST 29th, 1838

Statues and Figures, Grotesque Heads, &c.

	Lot no.	Description
*	26	*The finely sculptured* FIGURES OF WILLIAM AND MARY
	27	*Ditto of* QUEEN ANNE
	28	*Ditto* GEORGE III.
	29	*Ditto* GEORGE IV.
	30	*Ditto* GEORGE I. in Roman Costume
	31	*Ditto* GEORGE II.
	32	*The finely sculptured* FIGURE OF QUEEN ELIZABETH
	33	*Ditto* MARY
	34	*Ditto* EDWARD VI.
	35	*Ditto* CHARLES I.
	36	DITTO CHARLES II
	37	DITTO EDWARD III.
	38	DITTO JAMES I.
	39	DITTO HENRY VII.
	40	DITTO HENRY VIII.
	41	DITTO JAMES II.
	42	The sculptured head of one of the kings
	43	1 ditto
	44	Portions of statues
	45	Ditto
	46	3 stone crowns, and 2 figure heads
	47	A crown, a curious bull's head, and sundry pieces of carved stone and ornaments
	49	The highly enriched stone corbel at North Entrance, representing the head of an animal
	50	2 fine ditto, lions' heads
	51	*The lofty stone* PEDESTAL, *cased with* MARBLE, *on which* THE STATUE OF CHARLES II. *stood,* IN THE CENTRE OF THE AREA, and the wrought iron railing round ditto

* No MSS notes added for the second day of sale. The *Gentleman's Magazine* for October 1838 included: '29 August 1838 . . . Queen Anne fetched £10.5s., George II £9.5s., George III and Elizabeth £11.15s. each, Charles II £9, and the others, 16 in number, similar sums.'

TABLE 1

THE LINE OF KINGS AND QUEENS IN THE FIRST ROYAL EXCHANGE

[as listed by William Schellinks, 1661–1663. All destroyed 1666]

Kings and Queens	Sculptor/s	Payment by:	Date	Cost	Surviving Remains: full-size figures	(Engraved by:)
EDWARD THE CONFESSOR						
HAROLD						
WILLIAM THE CONQUEROR						
WILLIAM RUFUS						
HENRY I						
STEPHEN						
HENRY II						(Hollar 1644–LHS)
RICHARD I						(Hollar 1644–LHS)
JOHN						(Hollar 1644–LHS)
HENRY III						(Hollar 1644–LHS)
EDWARD I						(Hollar 1644–LHS)
EDWARD II						(Hollar 1644–LHS)
EDWARD III						(Hollar 1644–LHS)
RICHARD II						(Hollar 1644–LHS)
HENRY IV						(Hollar 1644–LHS)
HENRY V						(Hollar 1644–Far end)
HENRY VI						(Hollar 1644–Far end)
EDWARD IV						(Hollar 1644–Far end)
EDWARD V	N. Stone the Elder		c. 1625	£25		(Hollar 1644–Far end)
RICHARD III	N. Stone the Elder	Raphe Stint	c. 1626	£25		(Hollar 1644–Far end)
HENRY VII	N. Stone the Elder		c. 1625	£25		(Hollar 1644–Far end)
HENRY VIII						(Hollar 1644–RHS)
EDWARD VI		Richard Cheney	c. 1623			(Hollar 1644–RHS)
MARY TUDOR						(Hollar 1644–RHS)
ELIZABETH I	1. N. Stone the Elder rej., 2. Anon acc.		c. 1622 c. 1623		**Guildhall Art Gall.**	(Hollar 1644–RHS)
JAMES I			c. 1622–23			(Hollar 1644–RHS)
CHARLES I	1. rej., 2. A. Kearne acc.		pre-1629 1628–29	£25	**Guildhall Art Gall.**	(Hollar 1644–RHS)
CHARLES I Restoration replacement	?Cibber	Mercers Co.	1660			(Hollar 1644–RHS)
CHARLES II	?Cibber	Mercers Co.	1660			(Hollar 1668–RHS)

TABLE II
THE LINE OF KINGS AND QUEENS IN THE SECOND ROYAL EXCHANGE

Kings and Queens	Sculptor/s	Payment by:	Date	Cost	Models	Surviving remains: Full-size figures (Recorded by:)
EDWARD I	Joshua Fletcher the Elder	Vintners' Co.	1688–89	£50		**Swanage torso?** (*Hatton*)
EDWARD III	?Cibber (Model) Pearce (Full-size)	Skinners' Co.	1667? 1684	£60	**Skinners Hall**	(*Hatton*) (*s. Pullens Lot 37*)
HENRY V	Pearce	Goldsmiths' Co.	1686	£60		**Swanage torso?** (*Hatton*)
HENRY VI	Quellin	Armourers' Co.	1686	£50		**Swanage torso?** (*Hatton*)
EDWARD IV	?Cibber (Model) Full-size sub-contr. by T. Cartwright to Quellin	Ironmongers' Co.	1667? 1685	£50	**Ironmongers Hall**	(*Hatton*)
EDWARD V	Quellin	Leathersellers' Co.	1685–86	£38		(*Hatton*)
HENRY VII	Quellin	Tallowchandlers' Co.	1685	£57.3s		(*Hatton, Carter*) (*s. Pullens Lot 39*)
HENRY VIII	?Quellin (Model) Full-size Quellin	Haberdashers' Co.	1685	£49.12s.6d.	**Christ Church?**	(*Hatton, Carter*) (*s. Pullens Lot 40*)
EDWARD VI	1. Bushnell rej. 2. Gibbons	Drapers' Co.	1672 1684–85	£50		(*Hatton*)
MARY TUDOR	1. Bushnell rej. 2. Gibbons acc.	} Fishmongers' & Mercers' Cos.	1672 1685	£50		(*Hatton, Carter*) (*s. Pullens Lot 33*)
ELIZABETH I	1. Bushnell rej. 2. Pearce acc.		1672 1685?	£50		(*Hatton, Carter (2)*) (*s. Pullens Lot 32*)
JAMES I	1. Bushnell rej. 2. Gibbons acc. (exec. Quellin?)	Clothworkers' Co.	1672 1684	£50		**Swanage torso** (*Hatton, Carter*) (*s. Pullens Lot 38*)
CHARLES I	1. Bushnell rej. 2. Anon acc.		1672 1683			(*Hatton, Carter*)
CHARLES II	?Quellin (Models) 1. Bushnell [Full size] rej. 2. Quellin (Full-size) acc.	Grocers' Co.	1685 1686	£60	1. **Soane Mus.** 2. **V&A (bust)**	(*Hatton, Carter*) (*s. Pullens Lot 36*)
JAMES II	Gibbons	Merchant-Tailors' Co.	1686	£60		**Creech Grange?** (*Hatton, Carter*) (*s. Pullens Lot 41*)
WILLIAM III	John Nost I	Common Council	1695		**V&A?**	(*Hatton, Carter*)
& MARY II	John Nost I		1695		**V&A?**	(*Hatton, Carter*)

TABLE II (*continued*)

THE LINE OF KINGS AND QUEENS IN THE SECOND ROYAL EXCHANGE

Kings and Queens	Sculptor/s	Payment by:	Date	Cost	Models	Surviving remains: Full-size figures (Recorded by:)
ANNE	John Nost I?	Common Council	post 1702			(*Hatton, Carter*) (*s. Pullens Lot 27*)
GEORGE I	John Nost II?	Common Council	1716–18	£60		(*Carter*) (*s. Pullens Lot 30*)
GEORGE II	M. Rysbrack	Common Council	1727–28	£80		(*Carter*) (*s. Pullens Lot 31*)
GEORGE III	1. J. Wilton 2. J. G. Bubb	J.G.G. Committee	1761–64 1828–30	£300 £315		(*s. Pullens Lot 28*)
GEORGE IV	S. Gahagan	J.G.G. Committee	1830–31	£350		(*s. Pullens Lot 29*)

The CLRO Repertories of the Court of Aldermen, nos. 88–91 bear witness to the Corporation's control of the 1684 programme. The Court Minutes and Accounts of the Armourers, the Fishmongers, the Grocers, the Haberdashers, the Ironmongers, the Merchant Tailors and the Tallowchandlers are in the Guildhall Library MSS Department. The Clothworkers, the Drapers, the Goldsmiths, the Leathersellers, the Mercers, the Salters, the Skinners, and the Vintners still hold their own papers.

CHAPTER XVII

'The Statues of the Sovereigns of England': Sculpture for the Second Building, 1695–1831

By INGRID ROSCOE

THE RICHLY PAINTED SERIES of royal statues in the quadrangle of the first Exchange and their replacements commissioned in the 1680s 'in free stone and gilt in a gingerbread like manner'[1] can be read as testaments of romantic loyalty to the British monarchy. After the Glorious Revolution of 1688 a more discriminating attitude came to govern this form of commemoration, for new statues would only join the historic cavalcade after rulers earned the City of London's approval. William of Orange had been monarch for more than six years before his statue was raised on the east side in a double niche next to his more popular wife, and it was Mary's death that precipitated the decision to commemorate both. George I had to wait four years. The critical stance of the City Fathers was still more marked in the nineteenth century: George IV's effigy was erected posthumously and there was no move to immortalise his successor William IV.

There was also a change in patronage. The statues raised before 1688 were gifts of individual livery companies who must have striven to outshine one another, but William and Mary's, and those that followed, came instead from the City, sponsored first by the Common Council and later the Gresham Committee. Neutralisation of the competitive element might have led to economies and a diminution in technical quality, but a conscious effort was clearly made to employ the best available craftsmen. Until the 1760s, when English sculptors finally came into their own, commissions were going almost exclusively to prestigious foreign settlers, John Nost the Elder (fl. 1677–1710), and perhaps his cousin John (fl. 1710–29) who continued the business, Michael Rysbrack (1694–1770) and Peter Scheemakers (1691–1781).

Though immigrants were preferred over home-bred rivals, the statues were on the whole disappointingly conservative compared with Grinling Gibbons' figures of Charles II and his brother James, two of the first fully evolved Roman-style statues (with cropped hair) in an English public space. William and George I were presented in garter robes and both Mary and Anne wore coronation regalia. And despite the calibre of the sculptors, the general quality was apparently dubious: in 1734 James Ralph, the Opposition journalist and most perceptive critic of his day, admired John Bushnell's 'beautiful and admirable' figures on the outer entrance but condemned all those in the quadrangle:

I could wish tho' that either the statues were executed in a better manner, or that the city would condescend to excuse the setting up any more: for nothing can be more ridiculous than to hurt the eye with a fault, in the affectation of a beauty.[2]

Early relationships between *William and Mary* and the City augured a harmonious partnership. In November 1689, a year after their accession, they dined with the Lord Mayor at the Guildhall and in return restored the citizens' rights and privileges, eroded during the two previous reigns. The City on its part supported the new King with exemplary

I am grateful to Terry Friedman and Katherine Gibson for reading this essay and offering several excellent suggestions. Thanks are also due to Jean Imray, former archivist at Mercers' Hall, whose research material provided an excellent start to my own work on the royal statues, and Elizabeth Scudder of the Corporation of London Records Office, who meticulously checked my footnote references. Acknowledgements of generous help are also due to Ursula Carlyle, Matthew Craske, G. C. F. Forster, John Watts and Robin Harcourt Williams.

[1] *Royal Magazine*, vol. 10 (1764), p. 210.

[2] *A Critical Review of the Public Buildings, Statues and Ornaments In, and about London and Westminster* (1734), pp. 10–11.

loyalty during the succeeding war years, crippling themselves at a difficult time with loans totalling £500,000.³ Small wonder that projects for Exchange statues were put in abeyance.

Then, on 28 December 1694, Queen Mary, 'that excellent and incomparable Princess', died and the City delivered a melancholy address to the widower that owed quite as much to sympathy as convention. Three days later, the Common Council of the City resolved that statues of both monarchs should 'be sett up at the Royall Exchange at the charge of this Citty'.⁴

The official State portraits of William and Mary, painted in 1690 by Sir Godfrey Kneller, gave a pattern for the Exchange statues, though, ironically, William's pose was based on Martin Dejardins' colossal gilt-bronze statue of his enemy, Louis XIV, set up in 1685 in the Place des Victoires, Paris.⁵ The elder Nost, who was just beginning to emerge as 'a Master of reputation',⁶ received the order to carve both in Portland stone. His preliminary drawings have disappeared, but two terracotta maquettes have been linked to the commission (Figs. 62 and 63). A comparison of these models with an engraving of the Exchange quadrangle (Fig. 64), however, reveals significant differences, indicating that modifications were demanded by the supervisory committee, or conceivably, that the maquettes in fact relate to another commission.⁷ In the engraving William is crowned, the scroll in his right hand has been replaced by an upturned sword and there is an orb in the left, while Mary's image is divested of the emblems of monarchy (perhaps because she was by then dead)

and her torso twisted inwards to suggest amity and dependence on her husband. William's maquette, a superbly modelled figure with a *contrapposto* stance and rich surface textures, was at one time completely gilded, an indication that it came to be admired as an independent work of art. The model for Mary is slightly larger and looks less sophisticated because it is coated in polychrome paints, very likely original. The opulent colours, ranging from dark blues and reds to flesh-tones and gilding, are consonant with other Exchange statues in State robes.

The inscription *'Gulielmus III, Rex, & Maria II, Regina, A.D. MDCLXXXVIII S.P.Q. Londin, Optim, Principibus, P.C. 1695'* was inscribed on the plinths, and by the end of May 1695, both statues were ready for installation. The twelve man sub-committee, with Robert Hooke and John Oliver, two of the Exchange surveyors and the mason, Jasper Latham, then gathered in the quadrangle to choose an appropriate site. A first idea that the statues might be placed within an existing balcony on the east side was rejected 'by reason t'will firstly destroy the uniformity of the Exchange, and afterwards the building in that place', and it was instead decided 'that it will be best and most ornamentall to place the said Two Statues in the Two nisshes next to King James the Second', on the left corner of the east side.⁸ The City's Cash Accounts for Michaelmas 1696 record payments to the sculptor, mason, surveyor and painter:

Workmens Wages
To John Nost for two statues of King William and Queen Mary as per Order of Common Councill and Note from the Lord Mayor sett up at the Exchange.   120:00:00
To Robert Latham Mason for takeing downe of Nech in the Royall Exchange and Making a Double Nech for the King and Queen's Statues.   40:00:00.
To Robert Hook Gentleman Surveyor five Guineas for his care and diretton about the said Statues wch at XXXs charge is   7:10:00.
To William Thompson the Cities painter for painting and guilding the Kings and Queens Statues on the Exchange
        11:00:00
Being in all one hundred Seaventy Eight Pounds and Ten Shillings   178:10:00

A number of repairs were made in the mid-eighteenth century. In 1747 William Robinson, the Committee's

³ Among other problems there were several bad harvests, which made the price of corn rocket, and vast losses were suffered by the Turkey Company at French hands: W. Maitland, *The History of London*, vol. 2 (1766), pp. 492–98.
⁴ CLRO, *Journal of Common Council*, vol. 52, p. 36r (31 December 1694).
⁵ F. Souchal, *French Sculptors of the Seventeenth and Eighteenth Centuries*, vol. 1 (1977), pp. 251–52, figs. 41a–c.
⁶ *Vertue Notebooks*, IV, *Walpole Society*, 24 (1935–36), p. 35.
⁷ Though no other contemporary public statues of the two monarchs are known, there was a large private market for statues of William, particularly among members of the Whig party. An auction at Kistell's Coffee-House near Westminster Hall on 20 October 1690 included 'Queen Mary model'd in Clay' (lot 230), and on 11 November 1690, at the King's Arms Tavern, near St Clements in the Strand, lot 43 was 'K. Will. in Clay, in a fine Frame. Q.M. ditto' (BL Art Sale Catalogues, 1689–92).

⁸ MC, GR, 1678–1722, pp. 299, 300 (29 May 1695).

FIG. 62.   Terracotta model for King William III, perhaps
for the Royal Exchange, 53.5 × 18 cm.
Victoria and Albert Museum, London

FIG. 63.   Painted terracotta model for Queen Mary II,
perhaps for the Royal Exchange, H. 60 cm.
Victoria and Albert Museum, London

surveyor, recommended that 'new Iron Cramps &
run with Lead' should be placed behind the statues,[9]
and they were then repainted, an exercise that seems
to have been necessary every couple of decades.

The contract had a major impact on Nost's career.
In its immediate aftermath he received several orders
for monuments to members of the aristocracy including the 2nd Earl and Countess of Strafford, whose

memorial in York Minster, *c.* 1695,[10] was intended to
recall the Exchange statues. The Straffords are
presented in a double round-headed niche; he wears
garter robes like his King and the poses of both echo
the London statues. The sculptor also established a
profitable private market for statues of William,
having in hand at the time of his death one each of

[9] MC, GR, 1741–52, p. 158 (23 December 1747).

[10] G. E. Aylmer, 'Funeral Monuments and other Post-medieval
Sculpture' in G. E. Aylmer and R. Cant, *A History of York Minster*
(1977), pp. 447–48, pl. 147.

FIG. 64. Detail, east and south interior elevations of the Royal Exchange, engraved by Sutton Nicholls, 1712. William and Mary's statues and also Anne's, are clearly visible. The first three Georges were positioned in the three empty niches to the right and George IV occupied the first round the corner, here seen with Edward I's statue.

Guildhall Library, Corporation of London

William and Mary and three equestrian portraits of the King.[11]

No visual information is forthcoming on *Queen Anne*'s statue other than a rough sketch (Fig. 65) attributed to the antiquarian John Carter (1748–1817) *c*. 1790, who also made pencil drawings of William and Mary and the first two Hanoverians. Anne's figure was commissioned less than five months after her accession on 8 March 1702, a decision that reads as an endorsement of hereditary monarchy and the Anglican Church rather than as a specific reward for her contribution to the realm. It was probably the first of more than a dozen effigies, all perhaps after John Closterman's stocky portrait commissioned for Guildhall in 1702, raised in the metropolis and provincial cities in a decade when national feeling was running high, either as a result of Marlborough's victories or to celebrate the Union with Scotland in

1707.[12] The Queen's image was being promoted as an emblem of British patriotism in a manner rivalled only by Charles II and Queen Elizabeth.

In July 1702 a resolution to set up the Queen's statue in the niche next to her sister was passed by the Court of Aldermen, who appointed a committee of six to look into precedents and particularly to discover who had financed the earlier figures. They reported that 'the Statues of the Kings & Queens were Sett up by the several Companys of this Cittie. only the Statues of the said late King William and Queen Mary were sett up by Order of Common Councill at the charge of this Cittie'. The Council undertook to

---

[11] *Mr Van Nost's Collection of Marble and Leaden Figures*, 17 April 1712, lots 50, 51, 103, 104, 106.

[12] The best documented of these provincial statues, by Nost's former assistant, Andrew Carpenter (1670s–1737) for the Moot Hall in Leeds is finely analysed by Terry Friedman, 'A Noble Magnificent Statue', *Leeds Arts Calendar*, 72 (1973), pp. 5–13. See also T. F. Friedman, 'Foggini's statue of Queen Anne' in K. Lankheit (ed.), *Kunst des Barock in der Toskana Studien zur Kunst unter den letzen Medici* (1976), pp. 39–56, including note 64, which lists various Anne statues.

a.

b.

c.

FIG. 65a–e. John Carter,
pencil sketches of royal
statues, *c.* 1790. a, Mary;
b, William III; c, Anne;
d, George I; e, George II.
Guardian Royal Exchange collection

d.

e.

pay for the statue and overtures were made to the Queen that she might 'be graciously pleased to sitt for her Picture. This wee concieve will be a guide for the Statuary'.[13] The Lord Mayor was then made responsible for employing 'such Person, & give[ing] such direction for doing thereof as his Lordship shall thinke fitt'. There appears to be no further evidence either of the sculptor involved or of the commission's completion, though in 1708 a guide book recorded the figure in position and inscribed *Anna Regina Dei Gratia Mag. Britan. Franciae & Hiberniae, MDCCT*.[14]

George Ludwig, the fifty-three-year-old Elector of Hanover, became *George I* on 1 August 1714. He received an unexpectedly warm welcome in London and in November attended the Lord Mayor's celebrations, after which he created half a dozen new knights and gave a bounty of £1,000 to discharge poor debtors. These placatory gestures had little lasting effect on a discordant populace, uncertain about England's politico-religious future. In September the Old Pretender's standard was raised in distant Braemar, bringing fresh uncertainty, reflected in brawls in the metropolis, but by April 1716 the crisis was over. The sense of relief felt in London can be gauged by the Lord Mayor's address of 12 May, when he embraced 'the very first Opportunity of our being Assembled, to declare our Joy and Satisfaction that Your Majesty has suppressed the late and unnatural rebellion'.[15]

At this happy juncture the Common Council resolved to have a portrait for the Guildhall and a statue for the Exchange. A committee of fourteen, led by Sir Richard Hoare and Sir Robert Child, was instructed 'to imploy fit persons and give proper Orders and Directions for the making the Statue and drawing the Picture'.[16] The choice of Kneller, Principal Portrait Painter to the King, was a foregone conclusion and the canvas was again to provide a pattern for the statue. There was an unaccountable delay but on 27 September 1718 the *Weekly Journal or British Gazette* announced the statue 'quite finish'd' but not to 'be expos'd to publick view till the 20th of next month, being the most happy and glorious Anniversary of His Majesty's Coronation'. The citizens must have been impatient, for it was unveiled a full week early on 13 October, when it was tactfully 'judg'd by the most eminent Masters of that Art to be an Excellent and Accomplished Piece of Work'.[17] Posterity was less generous: the King's face must have been flamboyantly coloured, for a mid-eighteenth-century critic described an 'expression in the Harlequin or Quixot taste'[18] and Carter's drawing suggests that the torso was clumsily poised and the face lacked authority (Fig. 65d). When the statue was finally auctioned in 1838, it was mistakenly described as 'George I in Roman Costume'.[19] The sketch clearly shows the crown, orb, sceptre and trappings of State dress, and this uniform is indicated in several eighteenth-century engravings of the quadrangle.

The Cash Accounts record a payment of £60 made on 19 December 1718 to Edward Stanton, 'in full for making his Majesty's Statue set upp in the Royal Exchange'. It was his function as City Mason to disburse payments to the sculptor. The work has been misattributed to Rysbrack,[20] who was not in England until 1720, and a more plausible candidate is John Nost the Younger, whose family had already been involved with other sculpture for the Exchange. He was responsible for several contemporary statues of the King, notably 'a magnificent Statue in Metal at full proportion' for the Market Hall at Gosport, 1718.[21]

George II's statue is, however, Rysbrack's work. This time the resolution to erect the royal effigy, tabled on 5 October 1727, came only five months after the accession, a mark of confidence in the new reign.[22] Again the Guildhall canvas and Exchange

[13] CLRO, Repertory of Aldermen, 106, p. 226 (19 March 1701/2) and Repertory 106, pp. 236–37 (24 March 1701–02).
[14] *A New View of London*, vol. II (1708), p. 616. The only sum in the City's Cash Accounts that this author feels likely to include a payment for the statue details 'To Herbert Bourne the Cities Mason [as contractor] Two hundred pounds . . . dated the Xth day of April 1707 for work by him done'.
[15] *London Gazette*, 5433, 12–15 May 1716, p. 1.
[16] Journal of Common Council, 56, f. 217v (11 May 1716).
[17] *Weekly Journal or British Gazette*, 18 October 1718, p. 1178. Kneller's Guildhall portrait was unveiled on the anniversary of the coronation.
[18] *Royal Magazine*, vol. 10 (1764).
[19] *A Catalogue of the Valuable Materials of the Royal Exchange*, 29 August 1838, lot 30.
[20] M. I. Webb, *Michael Rysbrack* (1954), p. 216.
[21] *The Weekly Journal or British Gazette*, Saturday 1 November 1718, p. 1192.
[22] Journal of Common Council, 57, ff. 162r–v (5 October 1727).

figure were authorised in tandem, both at the instiga-tion of John Barber, an influential Alderman and future Lord Mayor. Charles Jervas, Kneller's suc-cessor as Principal Painter, depicted the King in traditional State robes, but Rysbrack, who had by then gained a position of primacy with his portrait busts and memorials for Westminster Abbey, was given free reign to create an independent three-dimensional image.

In 1728 Vertue noted that the sculptor 'has finished a Model of the Kings face in Wax',[23] an alternative to the customary terracotta head. Whether this was a mask or a profile portrait is not clear, but the advantages of using beeswax are obvious: it hardens naturally without shrinkage and is cleaner to use, though it is much more expensive than clay and convenient only for small-scale work.[24] Having pre-pared a wax mask 'thought very like' after two sittings,[25] Rysbrack made a clay model of the whole figure for inspection by the clients and this maquette remained in the sculptor's possession until his retire-ment sale of January 1766.[26]

The Cash Accounts for Michaelmas 1729 show a payment of £80 made through Edward Stanton 'in full for the Statue of His Majesty carved by Rys-brak'.[27] Joseph Thompson, the City's painter, was directed to coat the statue, not in the customary polychrome tints but in paint 'of a stone colour & writing inscription in gold',[28] which was considered more appropriate for a figure garbed all'antica.

In March 1746 a group of merchants met at the Crown Tavern behind the Exchange and came to a virtually unprecedented decision, to raise an Exchange statue to a commoner, Sir John Barnard and, moreover, in costly statuary marble.[29] They resolved to apply for funds to the Gresham Committee, the building's controlling body, comprised equally of members of the Mercers' Company and the Corpora-tion of the City of London. The proposal was well received and the choice of sculptor put to competi-tion, with models of Barnard 'in his magisterial Robes' assembled 'for that Purpose from several Statuaries in order to fix upon the best'.[30]

John Barnard (1685–1754), the Quaker merchant, financier, politician and Lord Mayor in 1737 and 1740, had a reputation for independence and integ-rity, and was particularly admired as 'one of those whom Walpole could neither buy nor corrupt'.[31] He rallied loyal elements in London during the '45 rebellion, designing proposals that stabilised sterling during the economic crisis of 1745–46, and it was in gratitude for this achievement that his supporters resolved to commemorate him, not among the mon-archs but 'under the Piazza' in the south-west corner, where there were twenty-eight niches, all vacant except one containing a statue of Gresham.

Peter Scheemakers won the contest. At this period he was at the peak of his career following the success of his memorial to Shakespeare in Westminster Abbey, 1741, and a succession of Abbey monuments to heroes of the French Wars. None the less the sculptor must have felt anxious about securing the contract, for he had been thwarted very recently in his sole attempt to obtain work in the City, the tympanum sculpture for the Mansion House pedi-ment, a prestigious commission which had also gone to competition and had been awarded to an English-born sculptor, Robert Taylor.

Though no records of payment have survived, the statue was evidently completed with the sculptor's characteristic punctuality, for on 6 May 1747 the gates of the Exchange were ordered to be closed to enable workmen to erect it without interference.[32] It later became a focus for adverse political comment-ary, for Barnard was no trimmer and he had many enemies.[33] An undated engraving (Fig. 66) super-scribed 'The LIVING STATUED PATRIOT, lately so justly celebrated, but now generally censured & exploded' was published with 'humorous lines . . . last Week

[23] Vertue III, p. 35.
[24] N. Penny, The Materials of Sculpture (1993), pp. 215–18. In 1738 the King would again sit twice for Rysbrack, but this time clay was used for the model: Vertue III, p. 84.
[25] Vertue III, pp. 35, 36.
[26] A Catalogue of the Collection of Models and Marbles of Michael Rysbrack, 24–25 January 1766, day 2, lot 52, 'A ditto [figure] of King George the Second, at the Royal Exchange'.
[27] 2/35, f. 63b.
[28] Ibid.
[29] London Magazine, vol. 15, 20 March 1746, p. 153. The only non-royal statues at this time were of Gresham.

[30] Westminster Journal, 29 March 1746.
[31] City Biography, vol. 84 (1800), pp. 170–75.
[32] MC, GR, 1739–53, 6 May 1747, pp. 142–43.
[33] R. Sedgwick (ed.), The History of Parliament: The House of Commons, 1715–1754, vol. 1 (1970), pp. 435–37.

The LIVING STATUED PATRIOT, lately so justly celebrated, but now generally censured & exploded.

Sic transit gloria Mundi.

The following humorous lines were last week Stuck up under ye Statue of S.J.B—d at ye Royal Exchange —

Art a Sleep old Friend Jack?   He did when Lord Mayor,
What more dost thou lack?   To Commons declare
What thoughts does thy Bosom now Harbour,   Bob Walpoles most wicked intention;
Do'st not see Rogues abrewing   If that M—r is a log,
Thy dear Countrys Ruin;   Prithee give him a jog,
Then why dost not act like John Barber?   Before too late for Prevention.

FIG. 66.   Engraving of Sir John Barnard presented in an illusionistic niche.

By kind permission of the Horace Walpole Library, Farmington

Stuck up under ye Statue', suggesting that he had lapsed from his customary vigilance. The great man must have had a sensitive core for he never returned to the Exchange again.[34]

George III, who succeeded on 25 October 1760, came in on a high tide shortly after the Year of Victories, which had given an unprecedented boost to national confidence. Enthusiasm for a King whose 'heart is truly English' was clearly uppermost when a motion was carried to commission his statue and a portrait for Guildhall on 18 November 1761, the day

after the Lord Mayor's annual party.[35] Five days later the Entertainments Committee received the royal assent to both projects. (Allan Ramsay, Painter-in-Ordinary, supplied canvases of the King and Queen in coronation robes.) On 28 November the sculptor Joseph Wilton (1722–1803), Coach-carver to the King, wrote the committee an obsequious letter from Great Portland Street, Cavendish Square, saying he had heard of a resolution to carve the statue in marble, a curious anomaly since the niched statues of monarchs were customarily of Portland stone. Wilton applauded 'a Proposal so truly noble and becoming the splendour of this great Metropolis' and he offered himself for the commission since it afforded 'such a favourable Opportunity for a Sculptor to acquire a Reputation'.[36] His euphuistic appeal had perhaps not yet won favour in January 1762 when William Tyler, 'Son & Grandson of a citizen & many years student under the late Mr Roubiliac', also offered his services.[37] There is no evidence of a competition and the contract probably went to Wilton soon after.

There was now an unexplained wait. Wilton may have been dilatory, or perhaps the cause lay with the King's foolish support for the Scottish Earl of Bute, whose peace policy antagonised the City and reflected badly on the monarch himself. George III intervened early in 1764 insisting that there should be no further delay in raising the statue[38] and on 14 February Wilton was summoned before the committee for instructions on the wording of the inscription. He was supplied with a variant of the conventional formula 'Georgius III D.G. Mag./ Brit. Fra. Et. Hib. Rex./ Anno Dom. 1760 S.P.Q.L.'.[39]

Following their monthly meeting on 15 March 1764 the committee went to Wilton's premises to inspect his work. They were apparently satisfied, for on 9 April the Press announced 'On Saturday the new statue of the King at the Royal Exchange was

[34] *City Biography* (1800), p. 175.

[35] Journal of Common Council, vol. 62, ff. 303r–v (18 November 1761).
[36] CLRO, MSS 5.18.
[37] George III, Committee Papers, 1761–64, CLRO, MSS 5.18 (28 January 1762). Louis-François Roubiliac had died on 11 January 1761.
[38] Undated news cutting, Guildhall Library, box file A512/12, p. 1821v.
[39] George III, Committee Papers, 1761–64, CLRO, MSS 5.18 (14 February 1764).

exposed to public view: it consists of the finest white marble, with a truncheon in his hand, and a laurel wreath around his head'.[40]

The marble may have been fine but there was apparently little else to recommend the work and the Mob's scorn, a perennial threat to public statues, must have made the committee wish they had supervised the work more thoroughly. A satirist signing himself 'the Lamplighter of Coleman-street' described a Hogarthian rout inside the Exchange, venting a range of criticisms: the effigy was poorly posed, the Roman draperies looked uncomfortably like the Highland dress associated with Lord Bute, the inscription was unintelligible and a marble statue was thought more appropriate for Westminster Abbey (see Appendix I).[41]

Wilton, who must have been anxious about his payment, countered by sending an elegantly written but querulous letter, reminding his patrons that they had approved the pose, that the height from which the statue would be viewed necessitated distortions and that there were distinguished precedents for Roman dress. As to verisimilitude, he had not been given the privilege of a royal sitting for the model, and marble could not be expected to look like flesh (see Appendix II).[42] He received his payment soon after. The white marble figure inevitably looked incongruous lined up with a series of polychrome effigies and in 1772 the Gresham Committee ordered that all the statues and 'the inside Fronts of the Area within the Exchange' should be painted in a stone colour.[43]

That was not the end of the matter. Repairs had to be made to the fabric in 1827 and George III's statue was taken down to be cleaned and mended. It was not put back and at a meeting of the Gresham Committee on 26 February 1828, enquiries were made about its state and current whereabouts. The Exchange surveyor, George Smith, returned a doleful tale: the figure was 'so dilapidated and defective' that repairs were not possible and it was currently in the workshop of the sculptor James George Bubb, by

Tottenham Court Road.[44] It seems possible that Bubb (1782–1853), who had an unsavoury reputation for opportunism, condemned the statue, realising that he was in a good position to provide a replacement. On 17 September a resolution was passed that yet another sub-committee should meet to consider a new statue and 'to confer with Artists thereupon: [to] inform themselves generally upon the Subject'.[45] There is no evidence that they looked any further than Bubb, whose letter, sent with a drawing to the Gresham Committee, reveals that the job was his:

Grafton Street East October 29th, 1828
I have made a sketch in Clay of a Statue of his late Majesty proposed to be erected in the Royal Exchange. I have represented him in his Robes of State (in preference to any foreign costume), which from their Grandeur will allow the Artist an opportunity of producing a Work which will be grateful to his own Feelings for taste and pleasing and honourable to his Employers.
In regard to your mention Mr Chantrey's Statue in the Council Chamber of Guildhall I beg respectfully to say that it would not be right for the Artist to copy the work of another, and in Addition to this that Statue is appropriate in the Situation it fills as his Majesty is represented receiving the City Address. The one for the Royal Exchange should, I conceive, be a Representation of the King in his Robes with his Sceptre.
My Estimate for executing this Work in my best style will be, if in Artificial Stone 200 Guineas, — Portland Stone 300 gns — Marble 1000 Guineas.[46]

The cheapest proposal immediately recommended itself and it was decided to settle for a statue in terracotta [artificial stone] 'representing his majesty at the Age at which he had arrived when he received the volunteers of the metropolis, in the Year 1803'. An optimum of £220 was considered quite sufficient to cover both the statue and its erection. But then there was anxiety about the use of artificial stone and D. A. Olivieri of Lambeth Walk, who would have cast the statue, was asked his opinion.[47] Olivieri's letter must have failed to reassure, for the committee now returned to Bubb, asking confirmation of his price for a Portland statue. He sent back a new design 'with the Crown placed upon a Pedastal by the side

[40] Undated news cutting, Guildhall Library, box file A512/12, p. 1085v.
[41] Royal Magazine, vol. 10, April 1764, pp. 209–10.
[42] CLRO, MSS 5.18 (12 April 1764).
[43] MC, GR, 1767–73, p. 108.

[44] MC, GR, 1824–29 (1 April 1828). The subsequent fate of Wilton's statue is not known.
[45] MC, GR, 1824–29 (17 September 1828).
[46] MC, GR, 1824–29 (29 October 1828).
[47] MC, GR, 1824–29 (12 November 1828).

of the Figure', together with an estimate 'for executing it in my best manner in portland stone . . . Three Hundred Guineas, and I will undertake that the Expences of Carriage, Scaffolding, and fixing complete, shall not exceed fifteen Guineas'.[48] The work now went ahead and on 20 September 1830 an invoice for £330 15s. (£315 for the statue and 15 guineas for its assembly on site) was approved by the Gresham Committee, with a moiety each to be paid by the City of London and the Mercers' Company.

The repairs to George III's statue were part of a much larger renovation programme in which Bubb was also involved. The Cornhill entrance front to the Exchange had long been one of London's landmarks with its elaborate frontispiece containing niches for John Bushnell's statues of Charles I and II and above that a wooden tower, soaring up 178 feet and topped with a grasshopper weathervane. By the early nineteenth century the tower was rotten and in 1821 it was replaced with a new one in stone designed by George Smith. This gave the opportunity for fresh sculptural embellishments. The *European Magazine* illustrated the elegant new entrance (Fig. 67) and described the proposed ornaments, then in the course of construction:

This tower consists of a square story, in the centre of which is a niche intended to be occupied by a full-length figure of Sir Thomas Gresham. On the top of the blocking-course, at each angle, is a colossal griffin, the fore paw sustaining, as one of the supporters, the Arms of the City of London; and in the centre on each side are intended to be placed four busts of the Virgin Queen, forming the Arms of the Mercers' Company . . . On either side the square story are facade walls, in each of which will be a panel containing a bas-relief: that on the west side representing the present state of the empire, as relating to its high attainments in the different branches of art, of science, and of government. — Britannia seated in the midst of Emblems of Commerce, Naval Power, Jurisprudence, and Mercy, accompanied with the Polite Arts on one side, and on the other Science resting on Manufacture and supported by Agriculture: that on the east is proposed to celebrate the present era, by depicting the great ascendancy of this Country among nations, the splendour of whose Naval and Military Triumphs may be considered as a principal cause of the security of Europe, Asia, Africa and America; and in the centre the Royal Arms of England.[49]

[48] MC, GR, 1824–29 (23 December 1828).
[49] The *European Magazine and London Review*, vol. 79, Jan–June 1821.

FIG. 67. The New Tower of the Royal Exchange, engraving c. 1812, frontispiece for the *European Magazine*, vol. 79, January–June 1821.

Some of the earlier sculpture was incorporated in the new front, notably Bushnell's royal statues and perhaps the Gresham, until now housed in the colonnade of the piazza. Bubb's new additions included the four personifications of Continents flanking his low-relief panels and four colossal busts of Queen Elizabeth in 'terracotta' (Fig. 68).

One relief tallies with the 1821 description, for it represents *Britannia seated amidst emblems of Commerce*

Fig. 68 (*above*).   J. G. Bubb, artificial
stone bust of Queen Elizabeth,
H. 4 ft.
Hatfield House

Fig. 69 (*above, right*).   J. G. Bubb,
artificial stone relief of *Britannia seated
amidst emblems of Commerce accompanied
by Science, Agriculture, Manufacture etc.*,
1823, 5 ft × 12 ft.
Hatfield House

Fig. 70 (*right*).   J. G. Bubb, artificial
stone relief of *Queen Elizabeth
proclaiming the Royal Exchange*, 1823,
5 ft × 12 ft.
Hatfield House

accompanied by Science, Agriculture, Manufacture etc
(Fig. 69). The second (Fig. 70) is not an allegory of
Empire building but the depiction of a specific and
pertinent historical moment, *Queen Elizabeth proclaiming the Royal Exchange*. The courtiers surrounding
the Queen include Gresham, the Lord Mayor, the
Bishop of London and Robert Cecil, Earl of Salisbury. The artificial stone panels are now sited at eye-
level in garden pavilions at Hatfield House: the
Britannia relief, inscribed 'J. G. BUBB/ SCULP Ft. 1823'
was cast in five vertical sections and the unsigned
companion panel, which shows evidence of fire
damage, in seven.

George IV succeeded on 29 January 1820 after eight
years as Regent, during which time he made scant
effort to charm the financial capital. As King he
delivered an unprecedented insult by refusing an

invitation to dine on Lord Mayor's Day of 1821; he
also declined to accept the Freedom of the City and
avoided hearing addresses and petitions from the
Livery.[50] It is not surprising therefore that no suggestion for a statue was made before October 1830, four
months after his death, and it was in the following
spring that the Gresham Committee finally resolved
to add one. The work was again put to competition
with an announcement advising entrants that they
should prepare tenders and models for submission in
person. There was an unusual rider: 'the sub-committee will not be bound to accept the lowest Tender,
nor will they pay any charge for forming Models, or
any charge relative thereto'.[51]

[50] Minutes and Reports of Common Council (11 September
and 18 October 1821).
[51] MC, GR, 1830–36 (31 March 1831).

PLATE V

A.   Interior of the second Royal Exchange; circle of Antonio Joli, oil on canvas.
By courtesy of the Mercers' Company

B.   Cornhill, with the Royal Exchange, 1778. John Chapman, oil on canvas.
By courtesy of the Mercers' Company

PLATE VI

A. Threadneedle Street and Cornhill in 1790 with the Bank of England,
St Bartholomew by the Exchange, the State Lottery office, the Royal Exchange and,
on the extreme right, the cupola of St Benet Fink and the tower of
St Michael Cornhill, by J. Paul.

Guardian Royal Exchange collection

B. Lloyd's Subscription Room, 1810, by Thomas Rowlandson and
Charles Augustus Pugin, for *Ackermann's Microcosm of London*.

Guardian Royal Exchange collection

PLATE VII

A.   The fire that destroyed the second Royal Exchange in the night of 10 February 1838 was the most spectacular London fire between the destruction of the Houses of Parliament, 1834, and the Tooley Street fire of 1861.

Guardian Royal Exchange collection

B.   Hassell's watercolour of the Royal Exchange after the fire shows the survival of Smith's tower (rebuilding of 1819–26) and Spiller's statue of Charles II.

By courtesy of the Trustees of the British Museum

PLATE VIII

A.   The façade of the second Royal Exchange was rebuilt entirely in stone by the Mercers' Company surveyor,
George Smith, between 1819 and 1826. John Hassell, watercolour, 1822.

By courtesy of the Mercers' Company

B.   W. Granville's 1839 competition design is representative of the unplaced entries: in the
'Cubic' style of Sir Robert Smirke, one of the referees. Competitors were allowed to submit only
two perspectives.

By courtesy of the Mercers' Company

Seven sculptors responded and their models (with estimates) were laid out together for consideration. The list[52] runs

Sebastian Gahagan	£420	
J. Manning	£288.15-	
B. Pistrucci	£525	
William Croggan	£210	to be executed by Mr. Kendrick
R. W. Sievier	£350	
J. G. Bubb	£330.15	
Rich'd Westmacott Jun'	£200	No Model submitted

With the King dead there was no reason to be niggardly over expenditure on what was now seen as a noble project and Gahagan's costly proposal was chosen as 'much superior to any of the others', though it was felt that adaptations would be necessary for 'the intended Situation'. The sculptor, however, had trials ahead: he was to make a fresh model incorporating suggestions from the committee, who expected a statue 6 feet 6 inches high and the budget was to be only £350.

The traditional English mistrust of Irishmen may account for a financial obstruction which now troubled Gahagan (fl. 1800–35), a little-known Dubliner, but a brother of Lawrence Gahagan, who had built up a successful London workshop at the turn of the century. It was common practice in England (though not apparently at the Exchange) to pay sculptors in parts, one before work began and one or two during and after completion. This enabled craftsmen to buy stone, always the most expensive item, and to pay assistants their customary weekly wage. On 3 June, when Sebastian Gahagan attended the sub-committee with his new model and a drawing, these were accepted, but he was told 'that it was not the practice of the Committee in cases of this kind, to pay any part of the charge until the whole of the work was completed'. As security for a payment essential for work to commence, he was obliged to nominate a guarantor, and the reputation of Mr Robert Ennever, Dairyman of King Street, Portman Square, was considered satisfactory. Thereupon £115 was released to the sculptor, with a similar sum paid when the statue was half finished, and the balance of £120 on completion.[53] It was ready for viewing in

December 1830 when Gahagan raised an important issue: there were no empty niches on the east side of the piazza where the statues from William and Mary onwards were housed, and a chronologically sensible site needed to be found for the new figure. The solution was to move the four later seventeenth-century statues on the South Walk (Edward I, Edward III, Henry V and Henry VI) 'and two of those on the West' (Yorkists and Tudors) into empty niches further along the line, so releasing space for George IV and any later successors considered worthy of commemoration. Messrs John Mallcot and Son, Statuaries and Masons, estimated the cost of taking down and refixing the six statues, effacing the letters cut below them, recutting and gilding the same, 'with an additional Expense of about £4 if a Pedestal is required for the statue of Edward 6th' at £37 15s. Their bill for £43 7s., submitted on 25 May 1832, exceeded the estimate because several new Portland bases were needed and there was also the cost of scaffolding.[54]

There would, however, be no more statues for the second Exchange. Soon after ten o'clock on the night of Wednesday, 10 January 1838, a fire broke out in Lloyd's Coffee-Rooms to the north-east of the quadrangle. It raged through the night, fanned by a wind that grew increasingly tempestuous and by the next afternoon many local dwellings as well as the Exchange itself were 'one body of flame'. The melodramatic crescendo came soon after four in the afternoon when 'The walls in the interior . . . fell with a tremendous crash, carrying with them the numerous statues of the Kings and Queens who have reigned from the time of William the Conqueror. At five o'clock, the fire was still raging; but all apprehension of danger to the surrounding buildings was at an end'.[55]

The auctioneers Joseph Pullen & Son of Cripplegate auctioned all the saleable building materials and ornaments at two separate sessions. On 3 April 1838 the tower on the Cornhill front and its surviving sculpture were sold, the Queen Elizabeth relief fetched £21 and its companion £36, and the

---

[52] MC, GR, 1830–36 (10 May 1831).
[53] MC, GR, 1830–36 (15 June 1831).

[54] MC, GR, 1832–36 (3, 15, 24 June and 20 September 1831, 24 February and 25 May 1832).
[55] *The Mirror of Literature, Amusement, and Instruction*, no. 875, Saturday 20 January 1838.

personification of the four Continents £110.[56] These latter have disappeared. At the second auction on 29–30 August all the other statues discussed in this

paper, with the exception of Sir John Barnard, whose effigy must have been reduced to an unrecognisable remnant, found buyers. It makes a frustrating end to a tale of corporate patronage that reveals much about relations between City and Monarch to record that neither the names of the purchasers nor information on the current whereabouts of those quaint and largely unremarkable royal statues have survived.

[56] The reliefs and two heads of Elizabeth were bought in by the Mercers' Company and eventually sold to the Marquess of Salisbury. Fifteen fragments of the Exchange were listed in the 1868 Hatfield Inventory.

APPENDIX I
RESPONSES TO WILTON'S STATUE OF GEORGE III, *ROYAL MAGAZINE*, APRIL 1764

The scaffold which has been erected for fixing the King's Statue in the Royal Exchange being struck, I had the curiosity to go and view it; and a great number of people I found assembled there on the same occasion, whose opinions concerning it were as various as their physiognomies . . . some of [the opinions] were so peculiar, that I cannot forebear mentioning them. Some condemned it totally, others partially. The first would assign no reason, or give a why or wherefore, other than they did not like it: some began their criticism at the head, foot, or other part, and proceeded to every member. 'The King, quoth one, is an upright man, and should not have round shoulders, or stoop like the statue; Poh! you fool, says another, don't you see the *architect's* intent by that attitude? He looks towards the north, with open arms, bestowing favours on the gentry in the Scotch walk; says a third, would you have him turn his posteriors on his ancestors, and pay his respects to his neighbour Log on his left hand. I think he should have been *gilt*, says a fat fish-woman, who stood not far from me; God forbid, says an old gentleman of 70, near to her. He has a lady's arm, says a country-farmer, with a wooden trundle in his left hand, such as we stir hasty-pudding with in the country. How comes it, says his companion, that he is dressed in the Scotch taste, without breeches, short-stockings, and plaid hanging loose over his shoulders, with a *broad* sword hanging loose at his side: it is plain to me he will become a rank Jacobite in time, Lord have mercy on us poor Protestants! . . . But what was most astonishing was, the construction of the initial letters of the inscription, or rather superscription underneath the Statue, viz S.P.Q.L. not one out of 300 present could decypher it (if I may be

allowed the expression). At legth a person in black attempted it thus, *Populus Scotorum Queritur Londino*; that is, says he, *the Scotch shall reign in London* . . . I drew him by the sleeve, and pointed to the same superscription under several other statues in the 'Change, to convince him that he was wrong in his application . . . that those letters were an imitation of the Roman S.P.Q.R. or *Senatus Populusque Romanus*, and that S.P.Q.L. intimated that the statue was erected *by the Legislature and Citizens of London* . . . I thought it would have been better if it had been done similar to the rest, in free-stone, and gilt in a gingerbread like manner; and if the expression had been in the Harlequin or Quixot taste, of James or George the First, it would have been more suitable to the place and intent. — That the present statue was more fit for a monument in Westminster-Abbey, being aptly and highly finished. That his being in a *Roman military habit*, and having a truncheon in his hand, was not intended to note its original as a warrior, or the position of the right-hand to express any partiality . . . But, on the contrary, indicates that he, as the fountain or source of peace or war, is ready to scourge his enemies by his soldiers and sailors, whenever there is occasion; but that his *greatest bliss* is the happiness of his people, which is well adapted and expressed by the fatherly and lowly attitude and expression of a reclined head, and a circling arm to all his subjects in general, instead of standing on tip-toe with a stiff-neck, insolent and haughty air of a tyrant. This is my confirmed opinion of the statuary's intent; if I am mistaken, the good-natured and sensible, I hope, will excuse me.

I am, Yours &c
The Lamplighter of Coleman-street.

APPENDIX II
'MR. WILTON'S LETTER TO THE COMMITTEE APPOINTED TO ERECT THE KING'S STATUE, 12 APRIL 1764'

Gentlemen,
    In the discourse concerning his Majesties statue, when I attended on Tuesday last at Guildhall and a Committee could not be made up, some Gentlemen were very earnest that I should publish a defence against the criticisms, which

have been wantonly made upon it. On mature deliberation, such appeal to the public, seems to me, neither reasonable nor necessary; as altercations, with thousands of people who understand nothing of the matter, might not only endanger my reputation, but would naturally give occassion to careless and malicious pens to work my ruin, by construing away the best meaning by the usual arts of equivocation. Give me leave Gentlemen to humbly represent to you, that the Intent & Position of the Figure, were clearly explain'd, and approv'd of by the Committee, anterior to their order for the execution of it, since which time no alteration has been made, from the original intention. When the Committee in a body examin'd the Statue, prior to its being erected, the faults now observ'd were not then found with it: then, was the time to have made the objection, when the defects / if there were any might probably have been removed.

The principal objections I have heard of, are, that the Statue is too reclining, that the truncheon is in the left hand, and the face is not like the King.

To the first, I answer, that no human figure could possibly with natural ease to himself look upon the height of 35 feet, on a multitude below him, and extend his arm at the same time, to enforce his Speech without such a reclination.

To the second, I refer the Connoisseurs to several beautiful and esteem'd antique statues, of Emperors &c: which have the truncheon, naked sword, or other emblems, in their left hand; I suppose the Artist, found it more convenient for the proper exposition of his Figure. See De Royse antique statues, and the Museum Capitolinum.

As to the likeness, exclusive of the impossibility of making white marble, without complexion, striking: I have perhaps done as much as any other might do, under the same disadvantage of not modelling it from the life.

I have the honour to be, very respectfully
   Gent
      Your most obedient
         most humble servant
           Joseph Wilton

CHAPTER XVIII

Exchanging Information: Print and Business at the Royal Exchange in the Late Seventeenth Century

By MICHAEL HARRIS

INFORMATION, NEWS, PRINT and business were locked together within the dynamic environment of the Royal Exchange. The structure hummed with activity organised through overlapping networks of formal and informal contact. The aim of this essay is to tease out some of the elements of this intricate system, as established at the end of the seventeenth and beginning of the eighteenth century, and to locate the Exchange, both as a place and an institution, within a general process of information transfer.

Information itself as a general category is rather enigmatic. Its flow through society, changing in form, direction and character over time, is hard to put into a shape that conforms to some sense of specific reality. The detail can be sharp enough, the outline is usually hazy and speculative. In focusing on the Royal Exchange in the late seventeenth century and tracking elements of the information system operating within and around it, the work of Jurgen Habermas, his successors and commentators, becomes of particular interest by suggesting a context for a study of this sort.[1] Bringing together approaches from several disciplines, Habermas identifies change in Western society in terms of the emergence and disintegration of what he calls 'a bourgeois public sphere'. In his account, the late seventeenth century figures as a pivotal point in the formation of bourgeois culture through which a new configuration of private and public interest was constructed. Lines of serial print identified closely with newspapers provided, in this analysis, a crucial mechanism for cultural formation and in this respect relates directly to the material which follows.

Physically located at the heart of the City of London and surrounded by some of its busiest and most commercially active thoroughfares, the Exchange also stood at the intersection of public authority and private interest. From its original construction the Exchange had provided a setting for forms of public display which in themselves carried messages concerned with the exercise of power. Within the rituals of authority it remained, with Temple Bar, Charing Cross and Tyburn, a primary location on the east/west axis of the metropolis for the publicity of the state.[2] Punishment under the law was represented at the Exchange by the pillory in which a string of individuals, usually with commercial associations, suffered serious consequences. Standing for specified periods in front of the Exchange at midday, the time of highest commercial activity, the victims of the law received the close attention of the public. In 1688 John Dykes, convicted of supplying labour to the colonies by kidnapping, stood in the pillory for an hour and was then whipped to Tower Hill.[3] Benjamin Harris, bookseller under the piazzas, was another who represented the force of the state in its response to print, receiving, it was claimed, an uncomfortable mauling from the public as he stood between noon and one o'clock in front of the Exchange.[4]

The elements of punishment and information organised by the state at this focal point of the life of the City were expressed in other ways. Announcements of all kinds resonated through the building in a

---

[1] Jurgen Habermas, *The Structural Transformation of the Public Sphere*, trans. Thomas Burger (Cambridge: Polity Press, 1989).

[2] For the printed representation of the legal process in serial form see Michael Harris, 'Trials and Criminal Biographies', in *The Sale and Distribution of Books from 1700*, ed. Robin Myers and Michael Harris (Oxford: Oxford Polytechnic Press, 1982), pp. 1–36.

[3] *London Gazette*, 2360, Monday 2 July 1688, conviction and sentence.

[4] *Mercurius Anglicus*, 25, Saturday 14 February 1680, 26, Wednesday 18 February 1680.

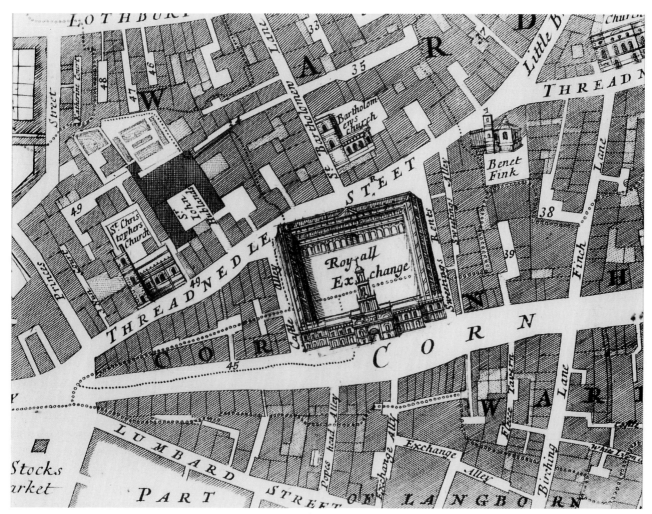

FIG. 71.   The section of the ward map that shows the Exchange with such prominence is: Richard Blome, 'Broad Street ward with its division into Parishes, taken from the last Survey, with Corrections and Additions / Cornhill Ward with its Division into Parishes taken from the last Survey, &c.' From John Stow, *A Survey of the Cities of London and Westminster*, ed. John Strype, for A. Churchill, J. Knapton, R. Knaplock, J. Walthoe, E. Horne, B. Tooke, D. Midwinter (1720). Although not published until 1720, the map was almost certainly engraved some twenty years earlier. Blome died in 1705 and his name was removed prior to publication.

combination of verbal and printed forms. The death and accession of monarchs, details of aggravated bankruptcy, books condemned and sometimes burned, were all manifested at a building which was plastered with notices including those which carried the imprimatur of government. The association of the structure with this form of publicity appeared most clearly in relation to the generalised commercial process. Ned Ward in the *London Spy* (1699–1700) remarked that at the Exchange 'Advertisements hang as thick round the Pillars of each Walk, as Bells about

the Legs of a *Morrice-Dancer*'.[5] The continuing use of this form of public display appeared in 1730 when the early issues of the successful newspaper, the *Daily Advertiser*, were published with a masthead printed on both sides of a single sheet specifically to facilitate posting at the Exchange and other centres of public

[5] Ned Ward, *The London Spy Compleat*, intro. by Ralph Straus (London: Casanova Society, 1924), p. 68.

activity.[6] In this setting, official and commercial information ran together, providing a clear sense of the interaction of public and private interest.

As an area of public space regularly used by national and City government, a centre of international commerce and a valuable store of commodities, the Royal Exchange was the subject of various kinds of official supervision. Its semi-official status was suggested in the news coverage of the rebuilding. In the government-sponsored *London Gazette*, advertisements for tenders from tradesmen appeared as early as March 1667 and each stage of the building leading up to the reopening was reported in some detail.[7] The subsequent concern of the authorities with the security of the new building appeared in 1682 when the presence of a routine guard by the City Trained Bands became a subject of public comment. The news serials reported a row which had developed between a captain of the militia and a local constable who, with the members of his watch, was refused access to his usual place 'in the Porch on the North-side' of the Exchange. The constable produced an order from the Corporation to which the captain was said to have replied, 'A fart for the Aldermen, and the Common Council'.[8] A fracas and legal proceedings followed, but clearly the physical security of the Exchange was seen to be a matter of more than local significance.

The public status of the building was directly related to the commercial activities that it contained. All of these, involving merchants, brokers, retailers and speculators of other intermediate sorts, were vital to the financial well-being of the City and were in turn crucially dependent on forms of recurrent information. Any engagement with long-distance commerce and with national and international markets required a flow of information regularly updated. From the sixteenth century merchants on the Exchange had established intricate lines of communication which were constructed and maintained through manuscript correspondence. Private links of this sort continued to be an essential element in the conduct of trade. But in and around the Royal Exchange the benefits of serial print containing a generally available, and therefore to some extent checkable, line of public information took an early shape.

Two lines of material began to roll forward from the early seventeenth century, each linked to the commercial system centred on the Royal Exchange. The first sequence consisted of what might be called hard-core material.[9] From 1608 a weekly price list of commodities was produced, apparently moving from duplicated manuscript into the more business-like form of print. By the 1630s the 'commodity price currents' were published by a broker with access to the Exchange, exercising a monopoly privilege granted by the Crown and supervised by the Corporation of the City of London. This basic but necessary information, policed by authority but run as a commercial speculation, conformed to other packages of privileged material published in London, including the *Bills of Mortality*.[10] Control passed through the hands of a string of City brokers who, from the 1670s when the licensing arrangements for the control of print began to disintegrate, found themselves faced with serious competition. Rival speculators, themselves based in or around the Exchange, began to publish price lists supplemented by a widening range of commercial information. James Whiston, printer and broker, John Castaing, broker, and John Houghton, broker and Member of the Royal Society, speculated in the publication of serials containing a mass of material in tabular form. Houghton even moved into the publication of serial essays which became a long-running feature of his

---

[6] Michael Harris, *London Newspapers in the Age of Walpole* (London/Toronto: Associated University Presses, 1987), pp. 50–51.
[7] *London Gazette*, 138, Thursday 14 March 1667, 205, Monday 4 November 1667, *passim*.
[8] *True Protestant Mercury*, 108, Wednesday 18 January 1682, 109, Saturday 21 January 1682.

[9] J. J. McCusker and C. Gravesteijn, *The Beginnings of Commercial and Financial Journalism* (Amsterdam: NEHA, 1991). This work contains a full account and bibliography of the serials carrying commercial information published in Europe and America before 1775.
[10] *The Bills of Mortality* authorised by the Corporation of London were published by the Company of Parish Clerks at varying frequency from the early seventeenth century.

monthly and weekly collections.[11] The practice of brokerage was not a respectable one and was usually combined with a variety of other forms of buying and selling. Consequently those concerned, unwelcome on the Exchange until well into the eighteenth century, were squeezed into the public houses concentrated around the building. These became in themselves satellite centres of business activity and it was out of this environment that Edward Lloyd produced the first marine list published from his coffee house in Lombard Street. As a result of the general expansion of output, it has been calculated that by 1716 a London merchant 'could have subscribed to seven different weekly or semi-weekly business newspapers' costing £6 a year.[12]

In tandem with the sequence based on commercial information, a second line of serial output began to take shape. Here again a shift in the balance of manuscript and print was involved, although in this case 'news' sustained a presence in its handwritten form over a long period. The printed news serial, initially imported from Holland, originated in close proximity to the Exchange. By 1620 the London book trades had already established a secondary centre of activity in and around the building, moving away from the officially dominated location at St Paul's Churchyard. The Exchange booksellers were mainly drawn from the lower levels of the trade and it was their speculative interest in ephemeral print which led into the line of public information generally classified as 'news'.

Among the principals within this highly competitive sector from the 1620s was Nicholas Bourne, whose imprints indicate that he ran a shop at the south (Cornhill) entrance to the Exchange. He may also have had storage space in the old building.[13] Bourne's involvement with news was extended in the 1640s when he became concerned in the publication

of a French-language serial. This venture embodied some of the links between booksellers and merchants in the supply of printed news and information. A flyer of 1644 announced:

These are to signifie, that all merchants and others that are desirous weekly to impart beyond seas the certain conditions of affairs here and of the proceedings of the war, they shall have it weekly published in print and in the French tongue. And every Thursday at nine of the clocke in the morning the Reader may have them (if he please) at Master Bourne's shop at the Old Exchange — the title of the thing is *Le Mercure Anglois* . . .[14]

This excursion into specialist publication was only to be continued if it received adequate public support. In the event the *Mercure* proved a durable product and remained in circulation for over four years. The use of French in a publication of this sort as well as in the price currents underlines the international character of the market for news and for a level of continental demand which underpinned the French language edition of the *London Gazette*.[15] Such lines of public communication locked the Exchange into a pan-European system of information transfer.

During the seventeenth century the two main sequences of serial print began to converge as the form of content of each was modified in line with changes in the framework of control and the nature of reader demand. The information serials began to adopt elements of news, while the news serials introduced an increasing amount of commercial information. Both circled around the Royal Exchange, from which they drew a substantial element of their content and within which a useful proportion of their readers were probably located. The nature of the commercial process made the Exchange one of the primary points for news gathering. Unlike Westminster Hall and the Sessions House in the Old Bailey where politics and the law were represented in a dramatic but formal process of public ritual, the Exchange was integrated with a

[11] Houghton published the monthly *Collection of Letters for the Improvement of Trade* between 1681 and 1684, and the weekly *Collection for the Improvement of Husbandry* between 1692 and 1703. Essays from the weekly collection were republished in four volumes in 1728.
[12] McCusker and Gravesteijn, *Financial Journalism*, p. 291.
[13] I am grateful to Ann Saunders for supplying me with references to Bourne which appear in MC, GR, vol. 2, ff. 63, 123, 143. Other entries identify a number of booksellers and stationers using the old Exchange building.

[14] Handbill cited in J. B. Williams, *A History of English Journalism to the Foundation of the Gazette* (London, 1908) [hereafter Williams, *Journalism*].
[15] The *Gazette de Londres* ran from 1666 to at least 1696; Carolyn Nelson and Matthew Seccombe, *British Newspapers and Periodicals 1641–1700* (New York: Modern Language Association of America, 1987).

wider and in many respects less structured community. Through the regular and far-flung correspondence of merchants and traders, a framework of potential news supply was established on a scale only equalled by the networks of government. At the same time, the Exchange was a magnet for individuals constantly on the move in and out of London in a kaleidoscope of unrecorded activity. Traders of all kinds, ships' captains and travellers arriving and departing, formed part of a procession offering eye-witness information relating to places near and far.

The pervasive presence of news from the Exchange in the content of the printed news serials filled with unattributed reports can only be stated fairly bluntly here. The general coverage of the movement of shipping was to some extent geared to a formal process of recording visible at the Exchange. In the early 1680s boards were hung up in the building to 'give notice where ships are going out'[16] and it seems likely that this sort of public information supply was extended to arrivals. Only occasionally was the shipping news in the printed serials identified under a Royal Exchange dateline. In the outcrop of news serials which followed the lapse of the licence in 1679, the Exchange had a higher profile. Such preliminaries as 'There is Advice on the Exchange . . .', 'Advice is brought upon the Exchange . . .' or 'There were Letters yesterday on the Exchange . . .' became a more regular element in the formulas of news, suggesting clearly the way in which the interests of merchants, publishers and readers interlocked. This was a continuing relationship. Fifty years later, in 1740, when a revamped but still generalised news section was included in the monthly *Political State of Great Britain*, it was entitled 'The Royal Exchange Intelligencer'. The universal and sometimes unwelcome emphasis on foreign news in the London newspapers of the eighteenth century (usually explained in political terms) was probably more an indication of the historically constructed response to the interests of merchants and traders preoccupied with events abroad. In the coffee houses round the

Exchange the supply of newspapers from the Continent was sometimes made a primary selling point in their printed advertisements.[17]

If the news gatherers made extensive and sometimes regular use of the private lines of communication running through the Exchange, the traders themselves used the printed serials to promote their miscellaneous interests. The physical structure of the Royal Exchange, imitated or reflected in the other 'Exchanges' strung out along London's east/west axis, contained a considerable diversity of commercial activity.[18] As well as the merchants organised around the central area, the 190 shop spaces 'above Stairs' as well as those located along the sides of the building represented a highly visible concentration of business.[19] The institution located at the heart of the City was clearly identified within the public sphere and to some extent projected its own message to the shoppers, dealers and visitors who poured through its much vaunted 'stately and Magnificent' spaces. A plan of the layout of the central area became a routine feature in the guide books to London.[20]

Even so, individuals within the Exchange found it useful or necessary to back up the generalised access with the forms of promotion and information which could be directed through the established lines of serial print. From the 1620s the London newsbooks had carried commercial advertising which was yoked with news under the licensing system as a monopoly interest. From the 1650s advertisements provided

[16] *Loyal Protestant*, 173, Tuesday 27 June 1682.

[17] The supply of City coffee houses with continental newspapers formed an important part of the business run by Charles Delafaye from the Secretary of State's office; Michael Harris, 'Newspaper Distribution in the Reign of Queen Anne', *Studies in the Book Trade* (Oxford: Oxford Bibliographical Society, 1975). An advertisement for Sam Wood's new coffee house in Exchange Alley emphasising this material appears in the *Daily Advertiser*, 5318, Thursday 28 January 1748.
[18] The three Exchanges in the Strand were the Exeter Exchange, the New Exchange and the Middle or Salisbury Exchange. A clear account of their activity and relative success appears in Katherine Swift, '"The French-Booksellers in the Strand": Huguenots in the London Book Trade, 1685–1750', *Proceedings of the Huguenot Society*, vol. 25 (1990), pp. 335–36.
[19] The number of upper-level shop spaces appears in Thomas De Laune, *The Present State of London* (London, 1681), p. 159.
[20] For example, *A Complete Guide to all Persons Who Have any Trade or Concern with the City of London . . .* (London, 1763), frontis. 'Plan of the Royal Exchange Shewing the Several Walks for Merchants, Traders, &c.'.

access to the government-sponsored serials including the *London Gazette*, and also appeared in the separately published advertising sheets noted below. From the late 1670s, as the system of state licensing tottered towards its close, the range and quantity of advertising material was extended and within it business at the Exchange came to form a recognisable element.

The merchants and brokers based in and around the Exchange, whose professional activities were mediated through the lines of printed news and information, also made use of the London serials to publicise specific and local interests. Their notices were constructed within the timetable of 'exchange time', the hours between noon and two o'clock, and the contacts were proposed on the Exchange itself or in one or other of the public houses located in the immediate vicinity. In March 1681 William Chambers, master of the ship *St Christopher* bound for Carolina, advertised that anyone wishing to transport themselves, their servants or their goods to the colony *'may speak to the said Master before and after Change-time, at the* Jamaica Coffee-House *in* Miles *Ally, and on the Exchange all Exchange time'*.[21] This sort of transaction appeared alongside the advertisements which laid out the public activities of such trading organisations as the Pennsylvania Free Society of Traders who offered subscription at Bridges' Coffee House in Pope's-Head Alley near the Exchange.[22]

Less usually, printed notices were applied by merchants to counter the flow of more insidious lines of information. Under the lash of rumours relating to the collapse of his finances, John Langley, a London merchant, used a news serial in an effort to prevent further damage. He combined his public defence with a spirited line of commercial promotion. Announcing his recent purchase of the Islington Wells and a rhinoceros, he went on to state that anyone claiming a just debt against him would be paid on the spot — 'And that he is dayly to be spoke with upon the Royal Exchange in the Barbadoes Walk, or at his Lodging at the three Bells in Lambard-street . . .'.[23] Merchants sometimes used the serials in property transactions and Captain South advertised

a 'Sugar House . . . ready fitted' to let on Bankside in Southwark. Interested parties could apply to him 'at Exchange-time, on the Barbadoes-Walk'.[24] In the mid-1680s 'A Broker, a considerable Dealer' advertised a willingness to 'Lett her House, and sell her Goods to one of the same Trade'.[25] Such interventions were spaced out through the London serials, while the intersection of print and business at the Exchange was primarily related to those involved in the conventional forms of buying and selling by retail.

In the advertisements published by retailers through the London serials, the use of Royal Exchange as a marker has an enigmatic quality. Such references as 'near the Royal Exchange' at least have the virtue of separating the location from the building. More often the identification of one or other of the adjacent streets with a reference to some part of the building, the corners or 'the backside of the Exchange', simply blur the distinction between the activities inside and outside the structure itself. The information was adequate to get a contemporary customer into the right neighbourhood but is hardly enough to satisfy a modern interest in accurate description. As a result the small-scale retailers stacked up in and around the Exchange are not easily distinguished within the advertising carried by the printed serials.

The businesses that could be carried on within the cramped spaces at the Exchange had a variable relationship to the information system centred on print. The dominant retailing presence at the Exchange was formed by the milliners' shops crammed into the building mainly at first-floor level. These gave the institution its most lively and raffish character and, at least from the mid-seventeenth century, figured prominently in the printed representations of the Exchange.[26] In his serialised perambulation, Ned Ward described how he mounted the stairs to the upper level:

---

[21] *Smith's Protestant Intelligence*, 11, Monday 14 March 1681.
[22] For example, notice by the society in *Loyal Protestant*, 148, Saturday 29 April 1682.
[23] *London Gazette*, 2072, Monday 28 September 1685.

[24] *London Gazette*, 2521, Thursday 9 January 1690.
[25] *From the Mercury Office at Charing Cross . . .*, 46 (1685?).
[26] For a discussion of the millinery business in relation to the New Exchange see James Grantham Turner, ' "News from the New Exchange". Commodity, erotic fantasy and the female entrepreneur', in *The Consumption of Culture 1600–1800: Image, Object, Text*, ed. Ann Bermingham and John Brewer (London/New York: Routledge, 1995), pp. 419–37.

where Women sat in their *Pinfolds*, begging of Custom, with such *Amorous Looks*, and after so *Affable* a manner, that I could not but fancy they had as much mind to dispose of themselves, as the Commodities they dealt in: My Ears on both sides were so Bruted with *Fine Linens, Sir, Gloves and Ribbons, Sir,* that I had a *Milliner's* and a *Sempstress's* Shop in my Head for a Week together.[27]

A similar, though more genteel, version of a visit to the Exchange, 'the Centre of the City, and Centre of the World of trade . . .', was offered in the daily *Spectator* in August 1712.

It was not the least of the satisfactions in my Survey, to go up Stairs, and pass the Shops of agreeable Females; to observe so many pretty Hands busy in the folding of Ribbands, and the utmost Eagerness of agreeable Faces in the Sale of Patches, Pins and Wires, on each Side the Counters, was an Amusement, in which I should longer have indulged myself, had not the dear Creatures called to me to ask what I wanted, when I could not answer, only *To look at you*. I went to one of the Windows which opened to the Area below, where all the several Voices lost their Distinction and rose up in a confused Humming . . .[28]

The milliners, like the other small-scale dealers in such commodities as tea, spectacles and haberdashery, seldom engaged directly with serial print through advertising. Word of mouth or occasional handbills could resonate through an area honeycombed with public houses and in which the commercial presence of the Exchange projected its own inescapable appeal. Most often the printed advertisements appearing in the serials announced reorganisation, or the start-up or closure of a business. In 1688 a characteristic advertisement stated that 'Mrs. Proctor's Shop at the Flower-de-luce on the Royal Exchange, being a large corner Shop at the North-East side, is to be Lett, and several sort of Points and Laces to be sold at reasonable Rates, she designing to give over her Trade before Midsummer next'.[29]

Such occasional visibility within the system of print was in stark contrast to the active engagement of the dealers in patent medicines with the advertising process. The presence of this small but noisy group

within the Exchange was signalled by a localised deployment of publicity material.

The Wainscote was adorn'd with *Quack Bills* instead of Pictures; never an Empirick in the Town, but had his Name in a Lacquer'd Frame, containing a fair Invitation for a *Fool* and his Money to be soon parted; thus he that wants *Physick* for a *Clap*, or a *Wet-Nurse* for a Child may be furnish'd here at a Minutes warning.[30]

At the same time, the medical retailers, whose trade crossed over with that of the printers and booksellers, many of whom also dealt in medicines, were amongst the most prolific users of newspaper and related advertising.[31] In the strings of locations at which such items as the Anodyne Necklace were offered for sale, an outlet at the Exchange was invariably included. One of the most visible of these was situated at the South entrance facing Cornhill. Identified as a fruit shop, it was included in 1695 in the advertisements for Boyl's Lozenges (with a printed book of instructions) and the ominously named Worm Cakes.[32] Run during the 1690s by Mr Levingston, Henry Garraway (fruiterer) and Mrs Garraway, the shop continued through the eighteenth century as a high profile centre of medical distribution.[33] Also in the building and identified through the overlapping and often abusive lines of newspaper advertising, were other dealers in patent medicines. Richard Stoughton advertised his retailing and wholesaling business at premises '3 or 4 Doors from the North-Gate of the Royal Exchange', while another of Mrs Garraway's competitors and detractors, Mr Payne, moved his medical business from Pope's Head Alley to the passage leading 'out of the middle of *Castle Alley* into the (West) Side Walk of the Royal

[27] Ward, *London Spy*, p. 68.
[28] *Spectator*, 454, Monday 11 August 1712, in *Spectator*, ed. Donald F. Bond (Oxford: Clarendon Press, 5 vols., reissue 1987), vol. 4, p. 102.
[29] *London Gazette*, 2344, Monday 7 May 1688.

[30] Ward, *London Spy*, p. 68.
[31] A remarkable though deeply confusing account of the promotion of the Anodyne Necklace and related materials appears in Francis Doherty, *A Study in Eighteenth-Century Advertising Methods* (Lewiston/Queenston/Lampeter: Edwin Mellon Press, 1992) [hereafter Doherty, *Advertising*].
[32] *London Mercury*, no number, Monday 30 December 1695.
[33] Advertisements with reference to these individuals in *City Mercury*, Monday 30 December 1695, Monday 21 June 1697. Doherty separates the Garraways at the fruit shop from the Garraways who kept the nearby entrepreneurial coffee house, *Advertising*, pp. 51–52. Mrs Garraway at the shop continued to be the focus of some vigorous skirmishing in print well into the eighteenth century.

Exchange'.[34] The active use of serial print to identify areas of commercial activity, particularly through medical advertising, represented only one level of engagement with the information system at the Exchange. More elaborate lines of communication developed within the framework of public advertising.

As might be expected, the mixed use of serial print to project information about businesses at the Exchange was focused within the book trades. Some of the serials, such as Benjamin Harris's *Domestic Intelligence*, were compiled and published, if not printed, at the Exchange itself. Shops run by booksellers and mercuries (pamphlet sellers) lined the adjacent streets and added a particular flavour of specialised trade which characterised the area through the seventeenth century. The presence of a concentration of dealers in print was reflected in the localised activity of a mob of hawkers more or less casually engaged in a local street trade. In 1679 when the Corporation took action against the 'loose and idle Persons, called Hawkers' engaged in selling seditious books and papers, they specifically targeted *'the Street of* Cornhill *and Passages to the Royal Exchange'*.[35]

The booksellers who ran shops in and around the Exchange during the late seventeenth century continued, as they began, to represent an active but low level sector of the trade. Those located in the Exchange building itself seem generally to have been lined up under the piazzas fronting Cornhill. As well as the usual forms of commercial activity laid out in the previous essay (pp. 85–98), the role of the booksellers also involved the collection and transmission of information from this site. Bookshops here as elsewhere provided meeting points for self-selecting groups of individuals and became in this way clearing houses for information passed about in the course of informal discussion. Equally, the booksellers were, perhaps in a more comprehensive way than other tradesmen, particularly through the supply of serial print, in recurrent communication with customers scattered across the London region and beyond. Through a combination of these characteristics the booksellers at the Exchange became intermediaries

in a flow of information channelled through their shops into the public sphere of print. The way this worked in practice can be suggested through the advertisements of Robert Horne. His connection with the Exchange was of long standing. He served an apprenticeship with Nicholas Bourne, was freed in 1657 and by the 1680s can be identified at a location which corresponded to that of Bourne's former premises in the old building. From his shop *'on the left-hand entry to the* Royal Exchange, Cornhill-*side* . . .'[36] Horne marketed the conventional products of the print trade. However, he also circulated information on behalf of individuals who identified his shop as a potential agency for such transactions. During the early 1680s he advertised, among other things, a bag of money lost in hackney coach number 50, a black boy born in Maryland and run away from Captain Richard Perry, and a large mansion house to be let near the church in Old Windsor.[37] His neighbour, Benjamin Harris at the Stationer's Arms, under the piazzas and near the entrance to the Exchange, was himself continuously represented in notices of this kind published in his *Domestic Intelligence.*

This agency role of the booksellers at the Royal Exchange leads towards a more highly developed point of intersection between information, print and this specific location. The presence within the building of a string of what were usually described as 'offices of intelligence' underpins the idea of the institution as a cog in the machine by which both economic and cultural formation were driven. The origins of this form of commercial speculation lay in monopoly grants made early in the century for the collection and supply of information about commodities and services.[38] Small-scale organisations of this kind were also established in France in the mid-seventeenth century by the founder of the official news serial *La Gazette* under the title of the Bureau

[34] Advertisements cited in Doherty, *Advertising*, p. 50.
[35] *London Gazette*, 1432, Monday 11 August 1679.
[36] *Loyal Protestant*, 245, Thursday 15 March 1683, advertisement for the Elixir Salutis.
[37] *Domestick Intelligence*, 25, Tuesday 30 September 1679; *London Gazette*, 1721, Thursday 18 May 1682, 2038, Monday 1 June 1685.
[38] For an account of the origins of the offices and of their ebb and flow to 1659 see Williams, *Journalism*, pp. 158–71.

d'Addresse et de Rencontre.[39] Both were geared up to exploit a form of public demand which required effective access to a line of public communication, and both relied on specially produced serials consisting entirely of advertisements.

In England these advertising sheets fell within the orbit of the state licence of print and after 1663 they were authorised as monopoly publications by Roger L'Estrange. In each case they were linked to an agency business conducted at one or other of the focal points of public commerce within the built-up area. The activity was modest in character and the serials through which it was promoted were both pragmatic and disposable. None the less, enough material survives to indicate the links to the Exchange from the 1670s. In January 1672 the *London Gazette* carried a notice announcing a grant under Letters Patent for an office dedicated to the supply of servants. Locations in Whitehall and Southwark were identified as contact points, but the business was centred 'against the *Assurance office* within the Royal Exchange'.[40] This attempt at specialist provision may not have been sustainable and in 1675 a new enterprise surfaced as it moved from St Michael's Alley, Cornhill, to the north-west corner of the Exchange. The business was linked to a serial advertising sheet initially entitled the *City Mercury* but later the *Mercury; or, Advertisements Concerning Trade*. This publication may have taken on a semi-independent existence as, at the end of the decade, an advertisement suggested that it was run from an office of its own at the Exchange.[41] The intelligence business itself was highly miscellaneous. The first surviving issue of the *City Mercury* contained notices from tradesmen, including a marble shaper at Vauxhall and a coffin maker, advertisements for public transport by land and water, for property to let and a lost and found section. It was also announced that 'At this Office does attend every day at Exchange time an able Accomptant and Book-keeper to receive the desires of all Persons of this Nature . . .'.[42] In later

advertisements servants wanted or looking for positions were given some emphasis. By 1680 competition from the unlicensed news sheets had undermined demand for the more prosaic *Mercury*. Consequently, the managers of what had become known as the Mercury Office formed consecutive alliances with established and apparently successful news serials. The publishers of *Mercurius Civicus* (1680) and subsequently of the *Impartial Protestant Mercury* (1681) made space available for the regular publication of advertisements from the intelligence office at the Exchange.[43] With the general suppression of printed news sheets in 1683 the enterprise sank from view, though its functions may have continued.

With the termination in state licensing in 1695 the lines of communication offered by serial print were again opened. By December a single sheet weekly composed entirely of advertisements was in publication under the title the *London Mercury: Published for Promoting Trade*. The earliest issue seen contained the announcement:

> The *Mercury* Office, Formerly Kept at *Trinity House* in *Finch-Lane*; is Remov'd to the Shop under the Stairs going up to the *Outropers Office* [see below], or *Million Bank*, at the West side of the *Royal Exchange*, and is called now, the *Mercury Office* or Office of Intelligence; where Blank and Benefit Tickets are bought and sold as formerly at the *Trinity House*: And also helps Masters and Mistresses: Commanders of Ships may be help'd to Surgeons, Stewards, other Officers and Apprentices; and also buys and sells Estates, helps to Mortgages, and Mortgage to Money.[44]

Advertisements for publication could be collected at a string of locations through the built-up area, and one of the first printed in this issue stated that at the Mercury Office 'is plac'd by a Gentleman, for the conveniency of Merchants and others (who come to Change) a *Cordial Water* called *Nectar* and Ambrosia . . .'. The entries in the short-title catalogue compiled by Caroline Nelson and Matthew Seccombe indicate that this serial continued in publication into 1697 and it is possible that a French language sheet under a similar title was linked to it in some way. However, without pursuing these ephemeral publications any further, it is possible to suggest the recurrent presence

---

[39] The originator of these offices in France was Theophraste Renaudot (1586–1653) who founded the newspaper *La Gazette*. The printed serials composed of advertisements and associated with these enterprises were later known as *Les Petites Affiches*.

[40] *London Gazette*, 646, Thursday 25 January 1672.

[41] *Domestick Intelligence*, 27, Tuesday 7 October 1679, advertisement for Major Choke's Anodyne Necklace.

[42] *City Mercury*, 1, Thursday 4 November 1675.

[43] Notices in *Mercurius Civicus*, 4, Thursday 1 April 1680; *Impartial London Intelligence*, 36, Friday 26 August 1681.

[44] *London Mercury* [no number], Monday 30 December 1695.

of an information-based business within the mixed economy of the Royal Exchange.[45]

The final element in this jigsaw again concerns the semi-official status of the Exchange as an institution and its relation to the City of London. The struggle of the Corporation to keep some sort of a handle on the activities within the building, suggested by the long-term effort to secure the licensing of brokers, appeared in 1688 in another form.[46] At this time of heightened political and economic confusion, an attempt was made to construct a new commercial monopoly based at the Exchange and promoted through print. Sales of all kinds by public auction had proliferated across London by the 1680s and were advertised through the serials at a wide variety of locations, including coffee houses, the Exchanges and specialist premises. In November 1688 a notice in the *London Gazette* announced that the Lord Mayor and Court of Aldermen had granted Thomas Puckle, Citizen and Ironmonger, the sole right to license individuals concerned in '*Publick Sales of their Goods, by Outcry, Auction, Candle or otherwise . . .*'.[47] This, it was claimed, was not an innovation but a reconstitution of the ancient office of 'Outroper', a term that had previously been applied to the City Cryer, and that the action was taken on behalf of the Court of

Orphans. Puckle was to be located at an office in 'the West-Pawn of the Royal Exchange' which had been specially prepared for the purpose. It was evidently up one flight of stairs in the gallery running round the central area. From the outset the attempt at this level of commercial intervention seems to have been hopeless. Early in 1689 Puckle was advertising his own auctions from the premises at the Exchange, becoming simply a component of the general system of public sales.[48] Auctions at the Exchange continued through the eighteenth century in parts of the building identified in the printed advertisements.

The Royal Exchange was an important conduit for the general flow of information. Through this channel material was directed into and out of London as well as through the intricately organised networks of public and private space within the metropolis itself. This flow assumed a public status through the various forms of serial print which were developed during the seventeenth century and which assumed an almost institutional force during the eighteenth. Some of the elements of the interaction between the Exchange and the medium of print have been sketched here, and through these, perhaps, a hint given at the way the spheres of commercial and cultural interest of bourgeois society were constructed and held together. During the late seventeenth century the Exchange acted as a sounding board, vibrating with commercial messages and giving off a most melodious twang to the entrepreneurial capitalists and their families who were consolidating their grip on sectors of English life.

[45] Ned Ward, in 1699, referred to an Office of Intelligence at the Royal Exchange 'pretending to help Servants to Places, and Masters to Servants; who have a knack of Bullying silly Wenches out of their Money . . .'; Ward, *London Spy*, p. 73.

[46] For an outline account of the documents relating to the licensing of brokers see Vivienne Aldous, *Brokers' Archives* (CLRO, 1995).

[47] *London Gazette*, 2404, Monday 26 November 1688.

[48] For example, advertisements in *London Gazette*, 2436, Monday 18 March 1689, 2533, Thursday 20 February 1690.

CHAPTER XIX

Merchants at the Royal Exchange, 1660–1720

By NATASHA GLAISYER

LEWES ROBERTS, in the second edition of his substantial volume, *The Merchants Map of Commerce* (1671), wrote 'that in all Cities and Towns of Traffique, there are always found five particular places, that only have a being and dependency upon the Trade thereof'. In four of these places customs are paid and collected, goods are stored and measured, and porters or carmen are employed. The first place on his list, however, is 'where Merchants and Tradesmen do assemble and meet at certain hours, and limited times of the day, to confer and treat together, concerning Merchandizing, Shipping, Buying or Selling, and the like; as is seen to be the Royal Exchange of London'.[1]

In the late seventeenth and early eighteenth centuries the Royal Exchange was *the* place in London where merchants, and other members of the London business community, gathered in substantial numbers. The Exchange was often full, and space in the area where the merchants met was at a premium. Robert Vyner, in 1669, had proposed placing a statue of Charles II on horseback, but was told by the Gresham Committee, 'Itt will take up too much of that roome, which is too little already to conteyne the Concourse of M[er]chants'.[2] Although it is difficult to estimate the numbers of merchants who filled the quadrangle, which was 40 by 50 yards in the post-Great Fire Exchange, it was probably in the high hundreds.[3]

As Roberts wrote, merchants assembled at the Exchange at certain times. These times were known as Exchanges and were regulated by the City authorities. In 1670 the noon Exchange was ordered to be between eleven and twelve o'clock, and the evening Exchange between five and six o'clock in the winter, and an hour later in the summer.[4] By the beginning of the eighteenth century both Exchange times had been extended to two hours with the noon Exchange beginning at noon.[5] According to these regulations merchants were to be fined if they stayed on the Exchange beyond the appointed times. In practice, however, there was sometimes confusion as to when Exchange time was. In 1684, for example, it seems that the noon Exchange was supposed to end at one o'clock, but the bell that rung at the end of Exchange time was interpreted as a signal to come on to the Exchange.[6]

The Exchange was closed on Sundays and fast days.[7] That an Exchange Keeper was reprimanded in the 1690s for allowing the gates to be shut on holidays suggests that the Exchange was usually open to merchants on all other days, including holidays.[8] As Thomas Watts wrote in a pamphlet concerning the business education of young men, 'Children may play by the Almanack, but he that is taking on him the Countenance of a Man, and intends for Business, should rather let the Exchange be his Oracle for Vacations'.[9]

I wish to thank Mark Goldie for his helpful comments. All dates are old style except that the year is taken to begin 1 January. All works were published in London unless otherwise stated.

[1] Lewes Roberts, *The Merchants Map of Commerce* (2nd edn, 1671), p. 12. First published in 1638, this volume was reprinted three times in the late seventeenth century.

[2] MC, GR, 1626–69, p. 367 (29 March 1669).

[3] For the dimensions of the Exchange see 'Plan of the Royal Exchange London', in Colen Campbell, *Vitruvius Britanicus, or The British Architect*, 3 vols. (1715–25), II (1717), plate 23.

[4] CLRO, Rep. 76 1670–71, ff. 4v–5r (10 November 1670).

[5] Comune Concil' tent' in Camera Guihald' Civitat' London [An order appointing hours for meeting in the Royal Exchange] (1703).

[6] MC, GR, 1678–1722, p. 118 (12 December 1684).

[7] CLRO, Rep. 111 1706–07, p. 88 (8 March 1707).

[8] MC, GR, 1678–1722, p. 309 (5 June 1696).

[9] Thomas Watts, *An Essay On The Proper Method For Forming the Man of Business* (1716; repr. Soldiers Field, Boston: Harvard University Graduate School of Business and Economics, 1946), p. 28.

The merchants met in the enclosed quadrangle, which was divided into areas called walks, each associated with a commodity or a trading region.[10] This made it easier for merchants to meet other merchants. There are numerous references to particular walks in contemporary sources. For example, Sir John Fagge and others were to meet one Saturday morning in 1661 on the French walk 'in order to the furnishing themselves with apparell suitable' for the King's Coronation.[11] Charles II was entertained in a shed on the Scottish walk in 1667 on the occasion of his laying foundation stones for the north entrance to the second Exchange.[12]

Many of the shops on the ground floor of the Exchange around the quadrangle provided services for the business community. In addition to the insurance office, which unlike the other shops could be accessed directly from the quadrangle, there were many notaries and scriveners doing business.[13] Stationers, engravers, perriwig makers, watchmakers, tobacconists, picture sellers and cabinet sellers, also had shops outside on the ground floor.[14] On the upper floor, in the rows of shops known as pawns, fancy goods such as lace, linen, silk, hosiery, buttons and baubles were for sale.[15] During this period, however, the Exchange's popularity as a centre for luxury shopping declined and parts of the upper floor were increasingly used for more commercial projects. As early as 1687 the Gresham Sub-Committee were considering letting the west outward pawn as warehouses.[16] In 1707 the Committee relaxed their prohibition of cranes at the Exchange in the hope that this would encourage prospective tenants to lease the recently converted warehouses on the north side of

the Exchange and ease the Committee's strained financial situation.[17] At the end of this period the Royal Exchange Assurance rented rooms in a section of the first floor.[18]

Fragmentary details in contemporary sources provide glimpses of the experience of merchants visiting the Exchange. Throughout the period the Cornhill Wardmote book contains complaints against the City and the Company of Mercers for a defective channel in front of the Exchange on Cornhill. In 1678 the problem lay in that 'before the Enterance into the Exchange there often happeneth a Stopage of great quantity of fowle water, mudd and other filth, into which some persons have fallen, and bin much damaged, and is very noysome'.[19] The other hazards to visitors of the Exchange in this period were the hackney coaches. The presentments to the Cornhill Wardmote for most years in this period contain mention of the great numbers of coaches and the resulting difficulties. In 1695 it was recorded:

That the Hackney Coachmen with their Coaches are very disorderly in their standing in the High street of Cornhill especially neer the Exchange where by pressing togeather and standing on each side the way they make frequent Stopps att Exchange time and great Soyle in feeding their horses in the streets with their Hay Which togeather w[i]th their abusive language profane Swearing and rudeness does disturb the Inhabitants of this Ward as well as Indanger the lives and Limbs of Gentlemen frequenting the Exchange and is contrary to all Civility [and] good Ord[er].[20]

Access to the Exchange was also hindered by 'multitudes of Vagabond beggars and other Vagrant persons . . . and more especially about the Exchange, whereby the Gentry cannot usually with freedome and quiett goe in, or come out to their Coaches, nor the Shopkeepers nor their Customers or others come to or goe out of their Shops, nor Merchants, to or from the Exchange'.[21] At the North and South entrances to the Exchange fruiterers displayed baskets of fruit which frequently led to complaints to

[10] For a depiction of merchants standing in groups on the walks see 'The Inside View of the Royal Exchange at London', BM Map and Print Collection, Crace collection, portfolio 22, items 66, 67 (1725, 1727).
[11] Letter from the Mayor and Jurats of Rye to Sir John Fagge, 10 April 1661, HMC, *The Manuscripts of Rye and Hereford Corporations* (HMSO, 1892), pp. 239–40.
[12] MC, GR, 1626–69, p. 308 (November 1667).
[13] MC, GR, 1669–76, p. 67 (7 April 1671). There may have been access from another shop, leased by Cowper, to the quadrangle.
[14] *Passim*, MC, GR, covering the period 1660–1720.
[15] Ehver Kynd (Henry Duke?), *Londons-Nonsuch; Or The Glory Of The Royal Exchange* (1668), sigs C2r–D1r.
[16] MC, GR, 1678–1722, p. 166 (7 April 1687).
[17] Ibid., p. 424 (15 August 1707).
[18] Ibid., p. 552 (15 July 1720).
[19] Corporation of London, Guildhall Library, Cornhill Wardmote and Wardmote Inquest Minute and Account Book 1652–1733, MS 4069/2, f. 334r (1678).
[20] Ibid., f. 400r (1695).
[21] Ibid., f. 325v (1675/6).

the Gresham Committee that the passage to and from the Exchange was hindered.[22] The constable and keepers of the Exchange were employed to keep 'mad people', footboys, beggars, shoe-cleaners, and other idle people out of the Exchange.[23]

Some merchants were such regular visitors to the Exchange that they used it as their address. In the 1677 directory of London merchants, a handful are listed as being available at the Exchange rather than at a street address. Thomas Gurden, for example, was listed in the directory as being available on the Turkey walk.[24] A declaration amongst the state papers is signed by a group of merchants, who could, they wrote, all be found on the New England walk.[25] Surviving business letters written by members of the mercantile community in this period contain occasional mentions of visits to the Exchange. Implicit in much of this evidence is the fact that many London merchants were very frequently at the Exchange. James Claypoole, for example, a London factor with correspondents in Europe and the West Indies, includes in letters written in the early 1680s, remarks about who went to the Exchange and who did not.[26]

Merchants went to the Exchange to do business, like Ward's 'Covetous Citizen' who 'There barters, buys and sells, receives and pays'.[27] It was a place where trade could be solicited. Nathaniel Harley, writing from Aleppo in 1696, reproached his brother Edward: 'How many jaunts do you take to the Exchange . . . to find me principals?'[28] Clearly, the merchants at the Exchange had dealings with the

notaries and scriveners whose shops were on the ground floor around the outside of the building, and probably they also shopped at the other booths there. Merchants could receive letters at the Exchange.[29] Generally, the nature of merchant political activity at the Exchange is difficult to uncover but, as Alison Olson has shown, Virginia merchants were 'politicised' there. 'A merchant who might have thought political lobbying a waste of time, if not, indeed, quite improper, might be persuaded to sign a petition circulated by a respected fellow merchant.'[30]

A lack of evidence does not allow a very precise picture of merchants' routine usage of the Exchange to be established. A merchant's diary from the early eighteenth century, however, is suggestive of one pattern of visits. Peter Briggins was a Quaker hop and honey merchant, who occasionally traded in other commodities, and invested in bonds. One volume of his diary survives, in which he records visiting the Exchange as many as six times a week. Over the two and a half year period covered by the diary, he usually went one to three times each week. Although he did go to the Exchange on Mondays and Saturdays, he was most likely to go on the other weekdays. In some periods he hardly attended the Exchange, and at other times he went very frequently. He did, like other merchants, go to the Exchange to meet other members of the business community. On various occasions he went to meet a Captain Bowrey, someone about wax, as well at other times to visit the insurance office, and specifically to strike a bargain over some tobacco.[31] However, although he records numerous visits to the Exchange where he does not mention his purpose, it seems from his brief diary entries that he met the majority of his business contacts, and did most of his dealing in hops and honey, in inns and at private houses, rather than at the Exchange. Briggins is representative of a merchant on the periphery of the commercial community at the Exchange. He did not attend the Exchange on

[22] MC, GR, 1669–76, p. 77 (23 September 1671), p. 99 (6 July 1672), p. 203 (28 July 1677).
[23] CLRO, Rep. 108 1703–04, p. 81 (14 December 1703); MC, GR, 1678–1722, p. 295 (19 December 1694), p. 530 (27 November 1719).
[24] A Collection of the Names of the Merchants Living in and about the City of London (1677), sig. D6r.
[25] 'Questions to be asked the New England men', 18 April 1676, Calendar of State Papers, Colonial Series, American and West Indies, 1675–1676, ed. W. Noel Sainsbury (HMSO, 1893), p. 377.
[26] See, for example, letter to Francis and George Rogers, London, 27 May 1682; letter to John Hodgson, London, 14 January 1682, James Claypoole's Letter Book: London and Philadelphia, 1681–1684, ed. Marion Balderston (San Marino: The Huntingdon Library, 1967), pp. 87, 116–17.
[27] [Edward Ward], The Character of a Covetous Citizen (1702), p. 12.
[28] Letter from Nathaniel Harley to Edward Harley, 3 April 1696, HMC, The Manuscripts of His Grace the Duke of Portland, 10 vols (HMSO, 1891–1931), II (1893), p. 246.

[29] Letter to Thomas Clutterbuck, 17 August 1681, James Claypoole, p. 51.
[30] Alison G. Olson, 'The Virginia Merchants of London: A Study in Eighteenth-Century Interest-Group Politics', William and Mary Quarterly, 40 (1983), pp. 363–88 (p. 367).
[31] GLRO, Peter Briggins, Diary 1706–08, ACC 1017/2, f. 36r (1 November 1707); f. 61r (28 September 1708), f. 40r (22 December 1707); f. 45r (4 February 1708).

an everyday basis, nor did he depend on the Exchange as a place in which to trade. It is reasonable to conjecture that Briggins went to the Exchange largely to keep abreast of the course of trade generally, and very occasionally to take advantage of the opportunity to engage in foreign trade, and speculation.

The Royal Exchange was indeed one of the central points in an early modern national knowledge network, as other contributors to this volume show. News was gathered and disseminated at the Exchange, declarations were made, and advertisements were displayed. Much of this information was directly related to the business conducted at the Exchange, or had a commercial bearing, as Michael Harris, in particular, shows in his essay on serial print in the publicity process. The oral aspect of this network is difficult for the historian to penetrate. However, by focusing on one important topic of conversation, that of merchant reputation, it is possible to begin to understand the spoken culture at the Exchange.

A good reputation was crucial to success in business. Being well esteemed on the Exchange was one sign of a good reputation, and probably the most important for those in the London business community. In January 1667 the King wrote to the Council of Barbados concerning the replacement of Lord Willoughby, who had been the island's governor. He was to be replaced by his brother, 'whose fair reputation and general esteem is such, that with one voice on the Exchange he was wished for his brother's successor, by the joint petition of the planters, merchants, and masters of ships, trading to the Caribbees'.[32] Being well esteemed on the Exchange signified a person was approved of by the business community.

Business manual writers in this period recommended that their readers visited the Exchange to determine the reputations of those with whom they were to do business. In a section on insuring ships, merchandise, and housing, in the fourth edition of the pocket-sized business manual, *Comes Commercii*

(1723), Edward Hatton explains the insurance procedure. After visiting an insurance office, like the one at the Royal Exchange, the 'next thing is to satisfy yourself of the Solvency of those who are to insure; and in order to that, you may desire the Office-keeper to give you the Names of 6 or 8 of their best Men; which done, you may enquire after their Credit on the Exchange'.[33]

What was thought on the Exchange was crucial to an individual's wider reputation, as Thomas Ludwell's attempt to clear his name, suspecting he had been slandered, demonstrates. He wrote to Secretary of State Williamson in November 1676, before departing for Virginia, concerned 'lest his maliciously unjust enemeies may have been as industrious to wound him by their whippers on the Exchange as he fears they have endeavoured to do at Court'.[34] Other members of the business community were undoubtedly slandered on the Exchange. Surviving depositions from a defamation case at the London Consistory Court provide insight into how a reputation could be damaged, and attempts that could be made to recover it. On 8 October 1667 Mr Wych, part-owner of a ship, met the master of the ship, Mr Wyld, on the Exchange. One of the deponents testified that Mr Wych said that he would do Mr Wyld 'all the mischeife that he could, and bid this dep[onen]t bid Mr Wyld to goe and look after his whore, or whores, or Bastard or Bastards in Jamaica'. The same words were later repeated at Change time. This deponent was concerned about what was said and the effect it would have on Mr Wyld's wife. The alleged defamation of Mr Wyld at the Royal Exchange did not focus on his business practices but his relations with women. All three deponents defended Mr Wyld's reputation. The third, for example, ended his deposition by saying that Mr Wyld 'hath the reputation of a very honest man'.[35] So members of the business community were abused on the Exchange and were prepared to take action in court to clear their names.

[33] Edward Hatton, *Comes Commercii* (4th edn, 1723), p. 291.
[34] Letter from Thomas Ludwell to Secretary Williamson?, 9 November 1676, *Calendar of State Papers, Colonial Series ... 1675–1676*, p. 487.
[35] GLRO, Consistory Court of London Deposition Book, June 1679–June 1681, DL/C/239, ff. 310r, 311v (21 November 1679). My thanks to Jennifer Melville for telling me about this case.

[32] Letter from the King to the Council of Barbados, January 1667, *Calendar of State Papers, Colonial Series, American and West Indies, 1661–1668*, ed. W. Noel Sainsbury (Longman, 1880), p. 438.

The Exchange was also a place where reputations could be saved. John Vernon, the author of *The Compleat Comptinghouse* (1678), an advice manual for apprentice merchants, noted that the reputation of a good substantial merchant could be ruined by failing to pay a bill. He gives instructions on the action to be taken when bills were not paid:

> you must go to the Exchange, when you see the Man will not pay it that it is Drawn upon, and there you may enquire if any Person will pay such a Bill for the honour of the Drawer, or of any of the Endorsers: and there you will find some body undoubtedly that will, and he must pay you the Principal and the Charges of the Protest, and Interest, if any due.

Saving another merchant's reputation by agreeing to pay his bill at the Exchange was a profitable activity. The merchant on whose behalf the bill was paid 'is bound by the Laws of Merchants' to pay the bill plus charges and give 'thanks for stepping in, and so upholding his Credit'.[36]

[36] John Vernon, *The Compleat Comptinghouse* (1678), pp. 103, 104, 105.

The first Royal Exchange had been built as a place for merchants to meet. In the late seventeenth century they continued to gather there regularly, and in substantial numbers. Although many of the shops selling luxury goods closed at the end of the century, and were converted to other uses, there is no evidence to suggest that the size of the Exchange's merchant community had declined by the beginning of the eighteenth century. Despite the 'hazards' of entering the quadrangle, the Exchange continued to attract merchants because it was one large place, located in the centre of the City, open most days at set times, with business services on hand, and walks that made meeting easier. Merchants were concerned there, however, with more than 'Merchandizing, Shipping, Buying or Selling'.[37] The Exchange was also a centre for commercial information, and the principal site in London where reputations of members of the business community were established, observed, determined, ruined, or saved.

[37] Roberts, p. 12.

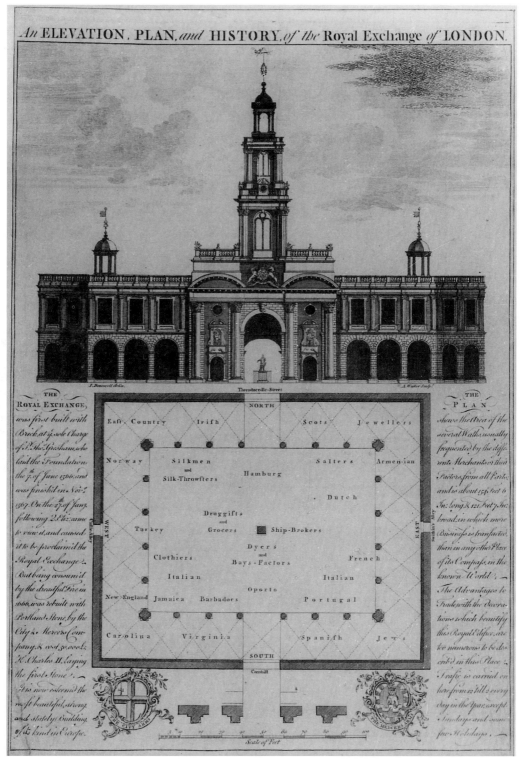

FIG. 72. Elevation and floor plan of the Exchange, indicating the particular positions of each nationality or trading group, drawn by I. Donowell and engraved by A. Walker.

Guardian Royal Exchange collection

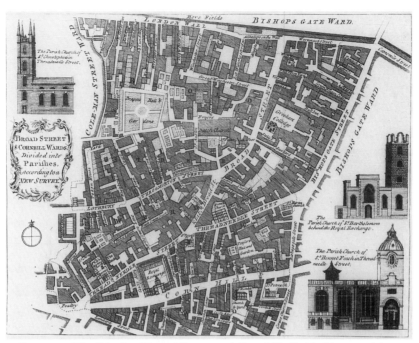

FIG. 73.   The Wards of Broad Street and Cornhill, divided into parishes,
1755. Four Wren churches — St Christopher's, St Benet's, St Martin's
Outwich, and St Peter le Poer — were all to disappear in redevelopment,
and Gresham College, Sir Thomas's own house, was soon to be
demolished to make way for the Excise Office. The Royal Exchange
stands out boldly, its southern entrance dominating Cornhill.

Guardian Royal Exchange collection

FIG. 74.   Interior of the Exchange, 1788. Building drawn by John
Chapman, figures by Philip de Loutherburg, engraved by Bartolozzi.
Notice the robed and turbanned Asiatic figure on the bench to the right;
beyond him, in the arcade, is a Jewish merchant. In the centre, his back
turned to us, is another turbanned figure, possibly a Hungarian, with a
Pole just beyond him, and a Dutchman with padded breeches towards the
left. The dog in the centre is muzzled.

Guildhall Library, Corporation of London

FIG. 75.   Arcade of the North front of the Royal Exchange by Thomas Malton, 1797.
Guildhall Library, Corporation of London

CHAPTER XX

THE SPECTATOR

No. 69   *Saturday, May* 19, 1711

THERE IS NO PLACE in the town which I so much love to frequent as the *Royal-Exchange*. It gives me a secret Satisfaction, and, in some measure, gratifies my Vanity, as I am an *Englisheman*, to see so rich an Assembly of Country-men an Foreigners consulting together upon the private Business of Mankind, and making this Metropolis a kind of *Emporium* for the whole Earth. I must confess I look upon High-Change to be a great Council, in which all considerable Nations have their Representatives. Factors in the Trading World are what Ambassadors are in the Politick World; they negotiate Affairs, conclude Treaties, and maintain a good Correspondence between those wealthy Societies of Men that are divided from one another by Seas and Oceans, or live on the different Extremities of a Continent. I have often been pleased to hear Disputes adjusted between an Inhabitant of *Japan* and an Alderman of *London*, or to see a Subject to the *Great Mogul* entering into a League with one of the *Czar* of *Muscovy*. I am infinitely delighted in mixing with these several Ministers of Commerce, as they are distinguished by their different Walks and different Languages: Sometimes I am justled among a Body of *Armenians*: Sometimes I am lost in a Crowd of *Jews*, and sometimes make one in a Groupe of *Dutch-men*. I am a *Dane*, *Swede*, or *French-Man* at different times, or rather fancy my self like the old Philosopher, who upon being asked what Countryman he was, replied, That he was a Citizen of the World.

Though I very frequently visit this busie Multitude of People, I am known to no Body there but my Friend, Sir ANDREW, who often smiles upon me as he sees me bustling in the Croud, but at the same time connives at my Presence without taking any further notice of me. There is indeed a Merchant of *Egypt*, who just knows me by sight, having formerly remitted me some Mony to *Grand Cairo*; but as I am not versed in the Modern *Coptick*, our Conferences go no further than a Bow and a Grimace.

This grand Scene of Business gives me an infinite Variety of solid and substantial Entertainments. As I am a great Lover of Mankind, my Heart naturally overflows with Pleasure at the sight of a prosperous and happy Multitude, insomuch that at many publick Solemnities I cannot forbear expressing my Joy with Tears that have stolen down my Cheeks. For this reason I am wonderfully delighted to see such a Body of Men thriving in their own private Fortunes, and at the same time promoting the Publick Stock; or in other Words, raising Estates for their own Families, by bringing into their Country whatever is wanting, and carrying out of it whatever is superfluous.

Nature seems to have taken a particular Care to disseminate her Blessings among the different Regions of the World, with an Eye to this mutual Intercourse and Traffick among Mankind, that the Natives of the several Parts of the Globe might have a kind of Dependance upon one another, and be united together by their common Interest. Almost every *Degree* produces something peculiar to it. The Food often grows in one Country, and the Sauce in another. The Fruits of *Portugal* are corrected by the Products of *Barbadoes*: The Infusion of a *China* Plant sweetned with the Pith of an *Indian* Cane: The *Philippick* Islands give a Flavour to our *European* Bowls. The single Dress of a Woman of Quality is often the Product of an hundred Climates. The Muff and the Fan come together from the different Ends of the Earth. The Scarf is sent from the Torrid Zone, and the Tippet from beneath the Pole. The Brocade Petticoat rises out of the Mines of *Peru*, and the Diamond Necklace out of the Bowels of *Indostan*.

If we consider our own Country in its natural Prospect, without any of the Benefits and Advantages of Commerce, what a barren uncomfortable Spot of

Earth falls to our Share! Natural Historians tell us, that no Fruit grows originally among us, besides Hips and Haws, Acorns and Pig-Nutts, with other Delicacies of the like Nature; That our Climate of its self, and without the Assistance of Art, can make no further Advances towards a Plumb than to a Sloe, and carries an Apple to no greater a Perfection than a Crab: That our Melons, our Peaches, our Figs, our Apricots, and Cherries, are Strangers among us, imported in different Ages, and naturalized in our *English* Gardens; and that they would all degenerate and fall away into the Trash of our own Country, if they were wholly neglected by the Planter, and left to the Mercy of our Sun and Soil. Nor has Traffick more enriched our Vegetable World, that it has improved the whole Face of Nature among us. Our Ships are laden with the Harvest of every Climate: Our Tables are stored with Spices, and Oils, and Wines: Our Rooms are filled with Pyramids of *China*, and adorned with the Workmanship of *Japan*: Our Morning's-Draught comes to us from the remotest Corners of the Earth: We repair our Bodies by the Drugs of *America*, and repose our selves under *Indian* Canopies. My Friend Sir ANDREW calls the Vineyards of *France* our Gardens; the Spice-Islands our Hot-Beds; the *Persians* our Silk-Weavers, and the *Chinese* our Potters. Nature indeed furnishes us with the bare Necessaries of Life, but Traffick gives us a great Variety of what is Useful, and at the same time supplies us with every thing that is Convenient and Ornamental. Nor is it the least part of this our Happiness, that whilst we enjoy the remotest Products of the North and South, we are free from those Extremeties of Weather which give them Birth; That our Eyes are refreshed with the green Fields of *Britain*, at the same time that our Palates are feasted with Fruits that rise between the Tropicks.

For these Reasons there are not more useful Members in a Commonwealth than Merchants. They knit Mankind together in a mutual Intercourse of good Offices, distribute the Gifts of Nature, find Work for the Poor, add Wealth to the Rich, and Magnificence to the Great. Our *English* Merchant converts the Tin of his own Country into Gold, and exchanges his Wooll for Rubies. The *Mahometans* are cloathed in our *British* Manufacture, and the Inhabitants of the Frozen Zone warmed with the Fleeces of our Sheep.

When I have been upon the *'Change*, I have often fancied one of our old Kings standing in Person, where he is represented in Effigy, and looking down upon the wealthy Concourse of People with which that Place is every Day filled. In this Case, how would he be surprized to hear all the Languages of *Europe* spoken in this little Spot of his former Dominions, and to see so many private Men, who in his Time would have been the Vassals of some powerful Baron, Negotiating like Princes for greater Sums of Mony than were formerly to be met with in the Royal Treasury! Trade, without enlarging the *British* Territories, has given us a kind of additional Empire: It has multiplied the Number of the Rich, made our Landed Estates infinitely more Valuable than they were formerly, and added to them an Accession of other Estates as Valuable at the Lands themselves.

JOSEPH ADDISON

No. 454   *Monday, August* 11, 1712

This Satisfaction encreased as I moved towards the City; and gay Signs, well disposed Streets, magnificent publick Structures, and wealthy Shops, adorn'd with contented Faces, made the Joy still rising till we came into the Centre of the City, and Centre of the World of Trade, the *Exchange of London*. As other Men in the Crowds about me were pleased with their Hopes and Bargains, I found my Account in observing them, in Attention to their several Interests. I, indeed, look'd upon my self as the richest Man that walk'd the *Exchange* that Day; for my Benevolence made me share the Gains of every Bargain that was made. It was not the least of the Satisfactions in my Survey, to go up Stairs, and pass the Shops of agreeable Females; to observe so many pretty Hands busy in the Foldings of Ribbands, and the utmost Eagerness of agreeable Faces in the Sale of Patches, Pins, and Wires, on each Side the Counters, was an Amusement, in which I should longer have indulged my self, had not the dear Creatures called to me to ask what I wanted, when I could not answer, only *To look at you*. I went to one of the Windows which opened to the Area below, where all the several Voices lost their Distinction, and rose up in a confused Humming; which created in me a Reflection that could not come into the Mind of any but of one a little too studious; for I said to my self, with a kind of Pun in Thought, *What Nonsense is all the Hurry of this World to those who are above it?* In these, or not much wiser Thoughts, I had like to have lost my Place at the Chop-House; where every Man, according to the natural Bashfulness or Sullenness of our Nation, eats in a publick Room a Mess of Broth, or Chop of Meat, in dumb Silence, as if they had no Pretence to speak to each other on the Foot of being Men, except they were of each other's Acquaintance. . .

RICHARD STEELE

No. 509   *Tuesday, October* 14, 1712

. . . there is at this Time, throughout the City of *London*, a lamentable Change from that Simplicity of Manners, which is the true Source of Wealth and Prosperity. I just now said the Man of Thrift shews Regularity in every thing; but you may, perhaps, laugh that I take Notice of such a Particular as I am going to do, for an Instance, that this City is declining, if their ancient Oeconomy is not restored. The Thing which gives me this Prospect, and so much Offence, is the Neglect of the *Royal Exchange*, I mean the Edifice so called, and the Walks appertaining thereunto. The *Royal Exchange* is a Fabrick that well deserves to be so called, as well to express that our Monarchs highest Glory and Advantage consists in being the Patrons of Trade, as that it is commodious for Business, and an Instance of the Grandeur both of Prince and People. But, alas! at present it hardly seems to be set apart for any such Use or Purpose. Instead of the Assembly of honourable Merchants, substantial Tradesmen, and knowing Masters of Ships, the Mumpers, the Halt, the Blind, and the Lame, your Venders of Trash, Apples, Plumbs, your Raggamuffins, Rakeshames, and Wenches, have justled the greater Number of the former out of that Place. Thus it is, especially on the Evening-Change; so that what with the Din of Squalings, Oaths, and Cries of Beggars, Men of greatest Consequence in our City absent themselves from the Place. This Particular, by the way, is of evil Consequence; for if the *Change* be no Place for Men of the highest Credit to frequent, it will not be a Disgrace to those of less Abilities to absent. I remember the Time when Rascally Company were kept out, and the unlucky Boyes with Toys and Balls were whipped away by a Beadle. I have seen this done indeed of late, but then it has been only to chase the Lads from Chuck, that the Beadle might seize their Copper.

I must repeat the Abomination, that the Walnut Trade is carry'd on by old Women within the Walks, which makes the Place impassible by reason of Shells and Trash. The Benches around are so filthy, that no one can sit down, yet the Beadles and Officers have the Impudence at *Christmas* to ask for their Box, tho' they deserve the Strapado. I do not think it impertinent to have mentioned this, because it speaks a Neglect in the Domestick Care of the City, and the Domestick is the truest Picture of a Man every where else. . .

RICHARD STEELE

CHAPTER XXI

The Book Trade at the Royal Exchange

By LAURENCE WORMS

THE IMPORTANCE OF the Royal Exchange in the history of commerce and finance has never been in doubt. The building itself and the tangle of streets, lanes and alleys that lie in its shadow, formed the hub of a trading empire that extended far beyond the confines of the British Isles for upwards of three hundred years. Rather less well known is that this same area was once also one of the major centres of the London book trade. Although the Exchange has never received the attention that historians of publishing have accorded St Paul's Churchyard, Paternoster Row, Fleet Street or the Charing Cross Road, it was for a very long period of time a centre of comparable importance. That this has not always been recognised is perhaps partly to do with the nature of the site: evidence for the history of the book trade to a large extent derives from surviving books and their imprints, and with addresses as diverse as Royal Exchange, Cornhill, Poultry, Lombard Street, Threadneedle Street, Pope's Head Alley, Castle Alley or Sweeting's Rents, it is not immediately obvious that these places formed in effect a single site, a small and contiguous cluster of streets and passages dominated by the Exchange at its centre. It is only when viewed on the ground or on a detailed map that their overall coherence becomes clear.

Some idea of how thick the concentration of bookshops in the area once was is given by a map published in the *London Magazine* in March 1748/49 (Fig. 76). The map was produced after a major fire in Cornhill and gives an unusually detailed view of the pattern of occupancy of the local shops. Running along Cornhill can be seen a dense little grouping of booksellers — Thomas Astley;[1] John Walthoe next door;[2] the stationer Warner;[3] next door again, this the sign of the Golden Ball, a long-established bookshop tracing its origins to the seventeenth century, is George Strahan;[4] beyond him a group of three more booksellers in John Brotherton;[5] William Meadows, at the sign of the Angel;[6] and, sharing

---

[1] For references to booksellers generally throughout the text the primary source remains the series of dictionaries published 1907–32 by The Bibliographical Society and amalgamated as H. R. Plomer & others, *Dictionaries of the printers and booksellers who were at work in England, Scotland and Ireland 1557–1775* (London, 1977). This is now supplemented by Ian Maxted, *The London book trades 1775–1800* (Folkestone, 1977) and by D. F. McKenzie's series, *Stationers' Company apprentices...* (Charlottesville/Oxford, 1961–78). Astley (fl. 1726–59) was a partner in the *London Magazine* and the publisher of the sumptuous four-volume *A new general collection of voyages and travels...* (1743–47), generally known simply as 'Astley's Voyages'. He is more usually recorded at addresses in St Paul's Churchyard: the Cornhill premises may have represented an additional retail outlet, or, just possibly, his private residence. A contemporary catalogue of his books is bound with the British Library copy of Isaac Watts, *Horae lyricae* (6th edn, 1748) [BL 11641.aa.48]. For his legal and medical problems at this time see D. F. McKenzie & J. C. Ross, *A ledger of Charles Ackers, printer of The London Magazine* (Oxford, 1968).

[2] Walthoe (fl. 1720–51) was a member of a distinguished bookselling family. His father, also John Walthoe, was Master of the Stationers' Company, the governing body of the book trade, in 1725–26. The British Library has a contemporary catalogue of the younger Walthoe's books [BL 1608/336].

[3] Most probably Matthew Warner, recorded at a new address in nearby Walbrook the following year.

[4] Strahan (fl. 1699–1748) was the son of a doctor of divinity, apprenticed to Joseph Hindmarsh, a previous occupant of the premises, in 1692. Dunton describes him as 'Honest Strahan... always for doing the fair thing'. His publications were mainly theological, although he also put out a number of medical books (see below).

[5] Brotherton (fl. 1700–53), whose shop sign was the Bible, was originally a bookbinder, having been apprenticed to Josiah Mitchell of Threadneedle Street in 1685. He was succeeded by his son James and the Cornhill premises subsequently passed to John Sewell, founder of the *European Magazine* (Fig. 79).

[6] Like Brotherton, Meadows (fl. 1719–53) had originally trained as a bookbinder, having been apprenticed to Ralph Simpson of St Paul's Churchyard in 1701.

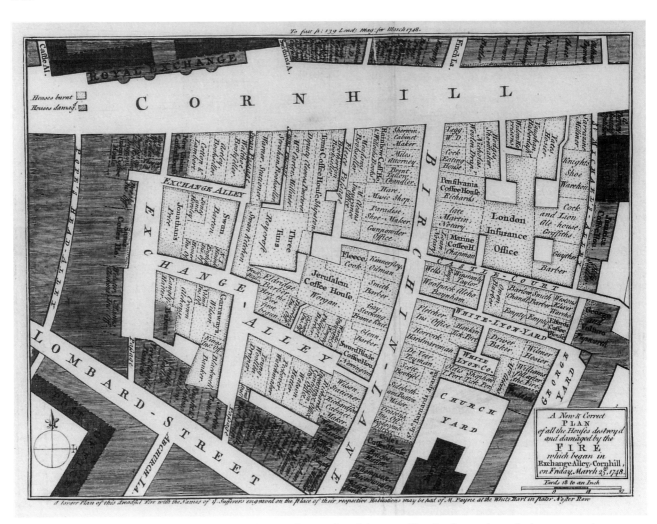

FIG. 76.   'A new & correct plan of all the houses destroyd and damaged by the fire . . .', 1748. An engraved map
published with the *London Magazine* for March 1748/49 showing the extent of a serious fire just to the south of the
Exchange — the worst fire in the City since the Great Fire itself. The map gives unusually good detail in showing the
names and trades of the occupants of many of the buildings destroyed. A thick concentration of booksellers can be seen
facing the Exchange along Cornhill.

Courtesy of Ash Rare Books

premises with the Rainbow Coffee House, the Scotsman Robert Willock.[7] In the heavily shaded area on
the Exchange side of Cornhill is another bookshop as

well as the print and mapseller Thomas Bakewell.[8]
To these could be added many similar shops in the
Exchange itself, and many more jostling for position
around the other three sides of the building. The

---

[7] Willock (fl. 1734–55) was another with long experience of the
area, having been apprenticed to his neighbour Strahan in 1719.
He was the son of a mariner from Montrose.

[8] Bakewell (fl. 1729–49) sold 'all sorts of mapps and fine French
Dutch and Italian prints'. He was a relative newcomer to
Cornhill, having spent most of his career 'next the Horn Tavern
in Fleet street'. He died in 1749 and is buried in St Michael
Cornhill, a church with records particularly rich in details of the
local bookselling community. His wife Eliza continued the
business, later taking into partnership Henry Parker, from whom
the still-surviving *Parker Gallery* traces its descent.

premises on the map are retail bookshops, but also in the area were printers, mapsellers, printsellers, music-sellers, newsmen, stationers, paper-merchants, a number of bookbinders (particularly in Thread-needle Street, on the less fashionable north side of the Exchange), and also the workshops of engravers — not just engravers of book-illustrations, but also of maps, commercial stationery, trade-cards, banknotes and the like.

There had been a book trade at the Exchange since its inception, building on a bookselling tradition in the area that goes back further still.[9] As early as 1571 a bookseller named Henry Saunderson was installed 'in the Burse at the Three Crowns Imperial'. He published an almanack from the Exchange in that year,[10] having moved there from the more established bookselling area in St Paul's Churchyard. Like a number of other books mentioned in the course of the text, it survives only in a single copy — much of the material published in and around the Exchange was of a particularly ephemeral nature. A vast quantity survives, but there is a strong inference that there must have been a great deal more.

The first book of major consequence to be published from the Exchange was not long in following. William Bourne's *A regiment for the sea . . .* (1574) was the first original work in English on the art of navigation and a book of paramount importance in its field. It contained the first printed description of the log and line in any language and was to become the vade-mecum of the great seamen of the days of Elizabeth I.[11] Intended for active use, its combination of theory and practical utility made it precisely the kind of publication that Gresham himself might have approved, for the founding of Gresham College, the precursor of all scientific institutions in England, had exactly that same aim of bringing scholarship and academic discipline to bear on practical problems. Bourne's book was brought out by the bookseller Thomas Hacket, and sold at his shop 'in the Royall Exchaunge, at the Signe of the Greene Dragon'.[12] Hacket had also moved across from St Paul's, although he had earlier been in Lombard Street, just south of the Exchange. He is the most substantial of the earliest generation of Exchange booksellers, in the sense that more is known of his life and career. Almost certainly the son of a French bookbinder,[13] he had already roused the imagination of a generation of Elizabethan explorers and colonists with the publication of his own translations of several import-ant early works: Jean Ribaut, *The whole and true discouerye of Terra Florida . . . (*1563); Nicolas le Chal-leux, *A true and perfect description, of the last voyage attempted by Capitaine John Rybaut, into Terra Florida* (1566); and André Thevet, *The new found worlde, or Antarctike . . . (*1568). These were some of the very earliest books in English on the Americas, and books that opened up entirely new horizons.[14]

FAMOUS BOOKS

It would be possible to make a case for the importance of the Exchange as a centre of the book trade simply in these kind of terms — first books, great books and

---

[9] There were 'bokeprynters' and booksellers in the area contemporary with Caxton himself, including Henry Frankenbergh, whose publication in the 1480s of [John Wotton], *Incipit liber qui vocatur speculum xristiani* (printed for him by William de Machlinia) appears to have been the first printed book published from the City of London. The famous old 'Long Shop' at the Exchange end of the Poultry was a bookshop from 1523 onwards, originally in the possession of Richard Bankes (fl. 1523–47), who published not only the first English herbal (*Here begynnyth a newe mater, the whiche is called an herball* (1525), STC 13175.1), but also the earliest extant printed sailing directions (Robert Copland's edition of Pierre Garcie, *The rutter of ye see* (1528), STC 11550.6). For some of the bookselling history of the Poultry in general see F. J. Froom, *A site in Poultry* (Idle, 1950).

[10] Philip Moore, *An almanack and prognostication for .xxxvij, yeres* (STC 485) printed for Saunderson by Henry Bynneman in 1571. A unique copy survives in the library of Corpus Christi, Oxford.

[11] For the significance of Bourne's work see D. W. Waters, *The art of navigation in England in Elizabethan and early Stuart times* (London, 1958), p. 132 *et seq.*

[12] Hacket (fl. 1557–90) produced a large number of titles throughout a long career. When he later moved from the Exchange, it was across the road to Pope's Head Alley, the short passageway off Cornhill facing the main façade of the original Exchange. He thus became the first of the Pope's Head Alley booksellers, an enclave of bookshops clustered opposite the Exchange entrance that came to exert an influence on the history of publishing out of all proportion to the size of the site.

[13] The Norman French bookbinder Thomas Hacket or Haquet (fl. 1534–82), who settled in London in the 1530s, married an Englishwoman, and became a denizen in 1544.

[14] The earliest account in English of the voyages of Columbus and Magellan, Richard Eden's translation of Sebastian Munster, *A treatyse of the newe India . . .* had appeared only in 1553, published in Lombard Street by Edward Sutton.

famous booksellers. *Loves' labours lost* — the first play to carry Shakespeare's name on the title-page — was published from the Exchange in 1598.[15] The first edition of Milton's *Paradise lost* (1667) bears the imprint of three booksellers, the first two of whom, Peter Parker and Robert Boulter, had premises on Cornhill.[16] Boulter also later published Andrew Marvell's *Miscellaneous poems* in 1681, in which many of the finest poems of the period made their first published appearance.[17] The first edition of Bunyan's *The pilgrims progress* was published by Nathaniel Ponder at 'the Peacock in the Poultrey near Cornhil', in 1678.[18] Boswell's *The life of Samuel Johnson, Ll.D*, still the most admired of all biographies, was published by Charles Dilly of the Poultry in 1791.[19] Tennyson's *Poems, chiefly lyrical*, his first regularly published work and one that took him immediately to the forefront of English poets, was first published from the Exchange in 1830, as was Robert Browning's *Paracelsus* in 1835 — 'the most miraculous and inexplicable of all the exhibitions of Browning's genius'.[20] The first edition of Charlotte Brontë's *Jane Eyre* was published in 1847 by 'Smith, Elder, & Co.' of Cornhill,[21] a firm that also published almost every other major writer of the period. Other literary associations abound, with Daniel Defoe, author of *Robinson Crusoe*, and *Moll Flanders*,[22] at one time in business as a hose-factor at premises in Freeman's Court, off Cornhill. He was stood in the Cornhill pillory for his *The shortest-way with dissenters . . .* in 1702, his route garlanded with flowers by his neighbours. Just across the street the poet Thomas Gray was born in 1716. Thomas Hood, known above all for his 'I remember, I remember, the house where I was born', was in fact born in the Poultry in 1799, where his father, also Thomas Hood,

[15] *A pleasant conceited comedie, called loues labors lost*, published by Cuthbert Burby (fl. 1592–1607; d. 1607). Burby also published an edition of *The most excellent and lamentable tragedie, of Romeo and Juliet* in 1599, as well as many other famous titles in Elizabethan literature, including Francis Meres' famous 'wits treasury', the *Palladis Tamia* 1598, Nash's *The vnfortunate traueller . . .* (1594), Greene's *The historie of Orlando Furioso . . .* (1594), and *A pleasant conceityed comedie of George a Greene, the pinner of Wakefield* (1599), the first edition of 'The Pindar of Wakefield'. Burby was at the Exchange between 1594 and 1602, and retained the lease on his premises even after his move to St Paul's Churchyard in the latter year. Another early play sometimes attributed to Shakespeare (even in his lifetime) was published from the Exchange by Sampson Clarke in 1591 as *The troublesome raigne of John King of England, also the death of King John* (STC 14644).

[16] Neither was actually in Cornhill at the time of publication — both having been burnt out in the Great Fire. Parker (fl. 1665–1703; d. 1712?) was working from temporary premises in Aldgate and Boulter (fl. 1666–83; d. 1683/4) in Bishopsgate. Both soon returned to Cornhill, Parker to the 'Leg & Star' and Boulter to the 'The Turk's Head', a sign also associated with the coffee house round the corner in Exchange Alley, where Pepys had his first ever cup of tea in 1660. Parker is probably to be identified with the Peter Parker, late deputy of Cornhill Ward, who was buried 'under the alderman's pew' at St Michael Cornhill in December 1712.

[17] Few of Marvell's poems were published in his lifetime and most appeared for the first time in Boulter's collection. Even though Marvell had died three years earlier, Boulter was still wary of publishing some of the material (see next note). Just two surviving copies of the book contain the suppressed poems in praise of Oliver Cromwell, but not a single known copy of the book appears to be absolutely complete — the missing text was either destroyed or never printed.

[18] Ponder (fl. 1664–96) came from Rothwell in Northamptonshire, only a matter of miles from Bunyan's Bedford, and shared not only his author's non-conformist background but also his experience of prison, having been jailed for publishing an edition of Marvell's *The rehearsal transpros'd*. He also published Bunyan's *A book for boys and girls . . .* (1686) and was again imprisoned, this time for debt, in 1688.

[19] Dilly and his brother Edward were famous literary hosts: even with dinner guests in the Poultry of the conversational prowess of Dr Johnson, Edward Dilly was said literally to have talked himself to death. It was in the Dillys' 'dusky, comfortable, pine-panelled drawing-room up the wide, shallow staircase, on the first floor overlooking the street' that Johnson met Wilkes on a famous occasion engineered by a Boswell stratagem of which Burke declared, 'there was nothing to equal it in the whole of the *Corps Diplomatique*'.

[20] Both were published by Effingham Wilson, see below.

[21] George Smith was just twenty-three when he received the manuscript from 'Currer Bell'. 'After breakfast on Sunday morning I took the manuscript of *Jane Eyre* to the library and began to read it. The story quickly took me captive. At twelve o'clock my horse came to the door, but I could not put the book down. I scribbled two or three lines to my friend, saying I was very sorry circumstances had occurred to prevent my meeting him, sent the note off by my groom, and went on reading the manuscript. Presently the servant came to tell me that lunch was waiting; I asked him to bring me a sandwich and a glass of wine and still went on with *Jane Eyre*. Dinner came; for me the meal was a very hasty one, and before I went to bed that night I had finished the manuscript'. Just six weeks later Smith had the book in print. After author and publisher had met, Charlotte Brontë became much attached to Smith and he is almost certainly the model for 'Doctor John Bretton' in her later and largely autobiographical novel *Villette*. For references see note 31 below.

[22] Originally published as *The life and strange surprizing adventures of Robinson Crusoe, of York, mariner . . .* (1719), and *The fortunes and misfortunes of the famous Moll Flanders . . .* (1721/2).

was the surviving partner in the publishing house of 'Vernor & Hood'.[23]

FAMOUS BOOKSELLERS

Among the booksellers and publishers that occupied premises in and around the Exchange, many were considerable figures in their own right. The scholarly Andrew Maunsell, at one time at the Exchange and later in nearby Lothbury, compiled and published the first ever catalogue of English printed books, the foundation of modern bibliography, in 1595.[24] The notorious John Wolfe, veteran of an assault against monopolies for which he suffered imprisonment, published John Stow's *A suruay of London* (1598), the foremost of all London books — 'the discovery of London, my native soil and country' — from Pope's Head Alley in 1598.[25] Nathaniel Crouch, a bookseller

in Exchange Alley and later in the Poultry, is remembered as both author and publisher of some of the first books specifically published for children.[26] The contumacious John Dunton of the Poultry, 'crack-brained scribbling bookseller', published an autobiography in 1705 that has the reputation of 'the maddest of all mad books': to connoisseurs of the eccentric, it still makes delightful reading, not least for its crackling pen portraits of his bookselling neighbours.[27] Thomas Guy, who built and endowed the celebrated London hospital that still bears his name,[28] was a bookseller at the top of Cornhill. The Scottish proof-reader ('corrector') Alexander Cruden compiled his famous biblical concordance while the

[23] The house in question was no. 31, once the site of the famous Rose Tavern. It ended its days as a Lyons Teashop before being demolished to make way for the Lutyens Midland Bank building. For an account of the career of the elder Hood see Peter Thorogood, 'Thomas Hood: a nineteenth century author and his relations with the book trade to 1835' in R. Myers & M. Harris, *Development of the English book trade, 1700–1899* (Oxford, 1981), pp. 106–72.

[24] *The first part of the catalogue of English printed books . . . (the seconde parte . . .)* (1595), STC 17669. Maunsell (fl. 1576–1604) had premises at the Exchange in 1592 (publishing in that year an edition of Thomas à Kempis, *Soliloquium animæ. The sole-talk of the soule . . .*). His main business was perhaps as a dealer in second-hand or antiquarian books. He compiled his catalogue because 'if learned men studie and spend their bodies and goods to further the knowledge of their countrymen for the good of the common weale, me thinketh it were pittie studies and the benefit of them should lie hidden . . .'. He hoped his work would be 'delightsome to all English men that be learned, or desirous of learning'. His fellow booksellers presented him a benevolence of 'money & bookes' in recognition of his 'paines and charges'.

[25] Wolfe's time in Italy, his epic clashes with the Stationers' Company over monopolies when he 'incensed the whole Citie', his illicit presses in secret vaults, appearances before Star Chamber, imprisonment in the 'Clinck', the production of so many books with fake imprints and other 'machiauellian deuices', have tended to obscure his other achievements. Wolfe (fl. 1579–1601; d. 1601) was one of the most important printers in London and had an extensive international trade. He was involved with Burghley in various covert propaganda exercises at the time of the Armada and fed by his contacts abroad and his friends in government he later began to produce news-books in large numbers. He is, so far as London is concerned, 'the father of news publishing' (Handover). He eventually became Printer to the City of London and the latter part of his career was spent at premises opposite the Exchange in Pope's Head Alley, from where many of his most important books were published. For Wolfe's wider career see D. B. Woodfield, *Surreptitious printing in*

England 1550–1640 (New York, 1973); H. R. Hoppe, 'John Wolfe, printer and publisher, 1579–1601' in *The Library*, new ser. 14.3 (December 1933); C. C. Huffman, *Elizabethan impressions; John Wolfe and his press* (New York, 1988); P. M. Handover, *Printing in London from 1476 to modern times* (London, 1960), pp. 103–09; and D. C. Collins, *A handlist of news pamphlets 1590–1610* (London, 1943).

[26] Crouch (fl. 1669–1708) wrote under the guise of 'R.B.', short for Richard (or sometimes Robert) Burton. His books were derivative and poorly produced, but they were cheap, pocket-sized, and highly popular. He was perhaps the first London publisher to bring out books that children actually enjoyed and his *Winter-evenings entertainments* (1687) is regarded as 'the nearest early approach to the modern children's book' (Froom). Dr Johnson was something of an admirer, finding the books 'very proper to allure backward readers'. In old age he wrote to his bookseller Charles Dilly asking him to find some of these mementoes of his youth.

[27] Dunton (1659–1733) was the uncle of John Wesley, and perhaps the brother-in-law of Daniel Defoe. In a typical aside, he notes of his neighbour John Salusbury, of the Rising Sun in Cornhill, 'he is a desperate hypergorgonic Welshman . . . a silly, empty, morose fellow. He had as much conceit, and as little reason for it, as any man I ever knew'. He also describes his own publisher, Sarah Malthus: 'a book-seller's daughter . . . free from all that pride and arrogance that is found in the carriage of some publishers'. By the following year they had quarrelled. He accused her of slander. She attached his goods for debt.

[28] It was the first purpose-built London hospital and cost some £250,000 even in the early eighteenth century. Although a figure of some substance in the book trade, Guy (1644–1724) was generally regarded as a miser from the parsimony of his private life. He made his fortune from financial speculation (this was the era of the South Sea Bubble) rather than bookselling.

tenant of a bookshop at the Exchange.[29] Effingham Wilson, who was at the Exchange for upwards of fifty years, became the determined champion of a free press — 'It is like the air we breathe, if we have it not, we die'. He published, among an array of other material that more timid publishers would not touch, John Wade's bible of nineteenth-century reform, *The extraordinary black book . . .*, that with its page-by-page listing of the entire workings of a corrupt system of government helped to bring about the passing of the Great Reform Bill of 1832 (Fig. 80).[30] George Smith, born over the shop at 65 Cornhill, was in sole charge of the publishing side of the family business, 'Smith, Elder & Co.' at the age of twenty-two. A recent biography is simply titled *The prince of publishers*[31] —

and so he was. With the sole exception of Dickens, he published all the great names of mid-Victorian England — Charlotte Brontë (not just *Jane Eyre*, but all her major works); Ruskin's *Modern painters*, *Pre-Raphaelitism*, and *The stones of Venice*; novels by George Eliot, Thackeray, Trollope, Meredith, Wilkie Collins and Thomas Hardy — the cornerstones of nineteenth-century literature. Later on, in an extraordinary feat of publishing for a single commercial concern, he organised and published the whole of the original edition of *The dictionary of national biography*.

BOOKS FOR THE CITY

Famous and enduring books are of course always exceptional. They are not typical of the general run of publishing and can never comprise more than a tiny proportion of the total number of books published in any given period. The fact that so many appeared in the vicinity of the Exchange presupposes a very large quantity of other, more humdrum, publishing. The key to the origins and distinctive features of most of this publishing lay in the nature of the area. For most of the period under review the Exchange was the leading financial and trading centre of the Western world. That in itself gave rise to an enormous weight of material published purely to serve the ends of that vast commerce. There is almost a sense in which we see printed information becoming a means of exchange, a type of currency, that the Exchange bookshops existed to supply. This is perhaps most clearly seen in the emergence and development in the area of the earliest newsbooks and newspapers, a topic that receives full attention elsewhere in this volume, but there are other indicators, too, of the way in which the Exchange created, fed, and fed upon, the bookshops that hemmed about it. Predictable staples were books, pamphlets and other items produced directly for use in the course of

[29] *A complete concordance to the holy scriptures of the old and new testament* (1738). A few months later Cruden (1699–1770) was forcibly restrained in a madhouse. Although the remainder of his life was clouded by recurring bouts of mental instability, as he launched various outlandish campaigns as 'The Corrector' of public morals, it none the less remained true for some two hundred years that 'his biblical labours have justly made his name a household word among the English-speaking peoples . . .' (*DNB*). See E. Oliver, *The eccentric life of Alexander Cruden* (London, 1934).

[30] Wilson (1785–1868) was given a public testimonial for his services to the passing of the Reform Bill. He also published Bentham's 'unpublishable' *The elements of the art of packing* (1821), T. Perronet Thompson's assaults on the corn laws, the 'revolting heresies' of William Godwin, the social visions of Robert Owen and the polemics of the Italian nationalist hero Giuseppe Mazzini. His obituary in the *City Press* (18 July 1868) remembered 'the longest career, and, we believe, the most independent, public-spirited, and fearless career of any publisher of his time . . . the producer of works for which it was difficult to find a publisher, containing as they did daring onslaughts on the established wrongs of the day'. He also published Burgon's life of Gresham, as well as an earlier history of the Exchange, *Wilson's description of the new Royal Exchange, including an historical notice . . .* (1844), which he appears to have written, or at least edited, himself. See L. Worms, 'Effingham Wilson' in C. S. Nicholls (ed.), *The dictionary of national biography; missing persons* (Oxford, 1993), pp. 720–21; E. W. Nye, 'Effingham Wilson: the radical publisher of the Royal Exchange' in *Publishing History*, vol. XXXVI (Cambridge 1994), pp. 87–102.

[31] J. Glyn, *The prince of publishers* (London, 1986). See also L. Huxley, *The house of Smith, Elder* (London, 1923), and, for a view of some of the more workaday publishing that underpinned the firm's success, B. Bell, 'The secret history of Smith & Elder . . .' in R. Myers, & M. Harris (eds.), *A genius for letters; booksellers and bookselling from the 16th to the 20th century* (Winchester, 1995). A genial and engaging figure, Smith (1824–1901) was in many ways the epitome of the Victorian entrepreneur. He recorded a revealing story of an encounter with Trollope —

Trollope came to see me . . . to arrange for a new serial. I told him my terms, but he demurred to my offer of £2,000, and said he had hoped for £3,000. I shook my head. 'Well', he replied, 'let us toss for that other

£1,000'. I asked him if he wished to ruin me . . . if my banker heard of my tossing authors for their copyrights he would certainly close my account; and what about my clerks . . . if they suspected me of tossing with an author for his manuscript! We ultimately came to an agreement on terms . . . but I felt uncomfortable — I felt mean — I had refused a challenge. To relieve my mind I said, 'Now that is settled, if you will come over the way to my club, where we can have a little room to ourselves for five minutes, I will toss you for £1,000 with pleasure'. Mr Trollope did not accept the offer. (*DNB*).

Smith died a millionaire with a mansion in Park Lane.

commercial transactions.[32] There were an inordinate variety of these, business aids of one kind or another, ranging from sophisticated text-books of economic theory down to the humblest of business necessities — where bookselling shades down into jobbing printing and stationery supply — pre-printed bills of lading, indentures, trade-cards, handbills, apprenticeship indentures and the like.[33] There was a solid and dependable trade in manuals of book-keeping and accounts, writing-books, copy-books,[34] ready-reckoners, tables of interest, tables of rates of duty, tables of exchange rates, tables of annuities, commercial dictionaries, street directories,[35]

diaries,[36] and books with names like *Debtor and creditor made easie . . .*, *The compleat comptinghouse*,[37] *The universal cambist*, *The London commercial dictionary*, *Drabwell's coal tables*, and *Corn, currency & consols*.[38] William Meadows, whose burnt-out premises are shown on the fire map (Fig. 76), was a typical case: he published Richard Hayes, *The broker's breviat* (1734) (a little pocket reckoner of early actuarial tables), the same author's *Interest at one view, calculated to the farthing . . .*, as well as *The merchant's magazine; or factor's guide . . .* (1743) and *The intelligencer or, merchant's assistant . . .* (an early street directory) in 1738. Also on Meadows' list was a pamphlet by the pseudonymous 'Philo-Britannicus', whose *The impartial accountant . . .* (1739) claimed to hold the secret of 'how to pay the National Debts'.

Alongside the publication of such practical aids, the Exchange booksellers would also on occasion make forays into larger economic theory. Nicholas

---

[32] This was a type of trade that had begun to emerge in the City even before the Exchange was built: Richard Kele of the 'Long Shop' in the Poultry was producing *The rates of the custome house bothe inwarde and outwarde . . .* (STC 7687), a handy pocket-book of customs duties, as early as 1545. Further editions were produced well on into the Exchange period by Kele's successors, John and Margaret Allde. The text of John Allde's edition of 1582 is reproduced in T. S. Willan (ed.), *A Tudor book of rates* (Manchester, 1962).

[33] The Exchange printseller, Thomas Jenner (fl. 1622–72; d. 1672/3) included among his stock 'blank bonds, blank bills peniall, plain bills, 2 bills of lading, indentures for Barbado's, indentures for London . . .', etc. (From a catalogue bound with Jenner's *A book of the names of all parishes . . .* (1662)). Jenner also had ideas of his own on the economic situation and his *London's blame if not its shame* (1651) attacks a supine policy towards the fishing industry 'which affordeth to our neighbor nations yeerly the revenue of many millions which they take up at our doors'. Jenner dedicated the book 'to the Corporation of the Poor in the City of London, being a member thereof'. For further material on an interesting and complex character see S. Tyacke, *London map-sellers 1660–1720* (Tring, 1978), and L. Rostenberg, *English publishers in the graphic arts 1599–1700 . . .* (New York, 1963).

[34] The ability to write in an attractive and legible hand was a much esteemed accomplishment, as well as a marketable secretarial and commercial skill. The best writing-masters enjoyed considerable celebrity and would give their name to copy-books of the sort exemplified by Richard Gethinge, *Calligraphotechnica or the art of faire writing . . .*, published by George Humble from Pope's Head Alley in 1619, with pages of specimen alphabets and examples of various standard commercial documents, or Thomas Watson, *A copy book. Enriched with a great variety of the most useful and modish hands . . .*, published by Nathaniel Ponder in 1680. See A. Heal, *The English writing-masters and their copy-books 1570–1800 . . .* (Cambridge, 1931).

[35] I believe all the earliest London directories appeared in the vicinity of the Exchange, commencing with Samuel Lee's *A collection of the names of the merchants . . .* published from Lombard Street in 1677. The originality and usefulness of such a business tool did not necessarily impress contemporaries. Dunton dismissed Lee as 'Such a pirate, such a cormorant was never before. Copies, books, men, shops, all was one, he held no propriety, right or wrong, good or bad, till at last he began to be known, and

the booksellers not enduring so ill a man among them to disgrace them, spewed him out, and off he marched for Ireland, where he acted as "felonious-Lee" as he did in London'. The earliest regular annual series of directories, long pre-dating the Post Office guides of the nineteenth century, was that inaugurated by Henry Kent of Finch Lane, just by the Exchange, in 1732. See P. J. Atkins, *The directories of London, 1677–1977* (London, 1990).

[36] The still well known brand of *Letts' Diaries* preserves the family name of John and Charles Letts, both booksellers at the Exchange in the nineteenth century. See *The romance of the business of a diary publisher* (Charles Letts & Co., London, 1949).

[37] See K. M. Bolton (ed.), *Historical accounting literature . . .* (London, 1975). The examples cited are by Stephen Monteage (1675) and John Vernon (1678) respectively, both published by Benjamin Billingsley (fl. 1669–1706) at the sign of the Printing Press in Cornhill (under the Piazza of the Exchange). The title of the second work continues in the 'swelling' fashion of the period, 'or, the young lad taken from the writing-school, and fully instructed, by way of dialogue, in all the mysteries of a merchant, from his first understanding of plain arithmetic, to the highest pitch of trade: whereby the master is saved much labour, and the lad is led by the hand to all his work and business; which to youth is accounted troublesome, but will here seem pleasant . . .'. Even Billingsley's *Advice to the women and maidens of London*, also 1678, offers the precept that they should 'apply themselves to the right understanding and practice of the method of keeping books of account: whereby, either single or married, they may know their estates, carry on their trades, and avoid the danger of a helpless and forlorn condition . . .'. Billingsley was a Londoner who had served his apprenticeship with Ralph Smith, another Exchange bookseller, between 1656 and 1664. According to Dunton he suffered a long period of mental illness during which his wife and son took charge of the business.

[38] The last four titles are taken from Effingham Wilson catalogues of the 1830s and 1840s.

Bourne of the Exchange[39] published, with what must have been considerable tact, the diametrically opposed theories of two leading seventeenth-century economists. If their argument was essentially an academic one, it was none the less conducted in the traditions of the spirited pamphlet duels of the period. The free-trader Edward Misselden, in *The circle of commerce . . .* (1623), attacked Gerard Malynes, whose arguments, he claimed, were 'as threadbare as his coat'.[40] Malynes coolly retorted in *The center of the circle of commerce*, also 1623, that Misselden's 'circle' represented not so much the flow of international trade as the gaping hole in his argument.

THE SHORTHAND BOOK

Some idea of the full extent of the market for these books produced for the local commercial community can be gauged by looking in more depth at one specific type of book at one particular period. It would be possible to do this with any of the various sub-species of business book, but the fact that Samuel Pepys formed a contemporary collection of books on shorthand writing that survives intact[41] allows an unusually direct and vivid glimpse of how rich and varied a field this may have been. The ability to write in shorthand was a much prized commercial skill. To cater for its would-be practitioners there were, *inter alia*, published or sold from the immediate vicinity of the Exchange in the seventeenth century (with many of the titles reprinted over and over again): John Willis, *The art of stenographie . . .* (1602), published by Cuthbert Burby — the same man that published

Shakespeare; Edmond Willis, *An abbreviation of writing by character . . .* (1627), stocked by Nicholas Bourne; across the street John Hancock 'at the first shop in Popes-Head Alley, next to Cornhill' published numerous editions of Theophilus Metcalfe, *Short writing the most easie exact lineall and speedy method that hath ever yet been obtained or taught . . .* from 1645 onwards,[42] as well as the same author's *School-master to radio stenography*. The writing-master Thomas Shelton, 'authour and professour' of various shorthand systems, retailed his own books, *Tachygraphy . . .* (1645) and *Zeiglographia . . .* (1650) from 'the Professours house in the Poultry near the Church'. Peter Cole, 'at the sign of the Printing presse in Cornhil neer the Royal Exchange'[43] published the original edition of Jeremiah Rich, *Charactery or, a most easie and exact method of short and swift writing . . .* in 1646, while in 1654 his neighbour 'Major' Nathaniel Brooke of the Angel in Cornhill[44] published Rich's *Semigraphy: or, arts rarity.*[45] Rich himself was selling copies of his broadside *The penns dexterity . . .* from his house 'at the Golden ball in Swithins-lane' in 1659. John Farthing sold his own *Short-writing shortned: or, the art of short-writing . . .* (1654)

[39] Bourne (fl. 1608–60; d. 1660) was an apprentice of Cuthbert Burby. One of the leading figures in the development of early newspapers, he became Master of the Stationers' Company in 1643 and 1651. At least five of his own apprentices went on to have their own businesses in the vicinity of the Exchange. See F. Dahl, *A bibliography of English corantos and periodical newsbooks 1620–1842* (London, 1952); also L. Rostenberg, *Literary, political, scientific, religious & legal publishing, printing & bookselling in England, 1551–1700: twelve studies* (New York, 1965), in particular the chapter on 'The debut of English journalism: Nathaniel Butter & Nicholas Bourne, first "masters of the staple"'.

[40] Malynes had been near ruined by the failure of his new farthing coins.

[41] Pepys wrote his diary in code and was evidently fascinated with writing systems. For a full catalogue see W. J. Carlton, *A descriptive catalogue of the library of Samuel Pepys. Part iv. Shorthand books* (London, 1940).

[42] A '55th' edition of this title was being sold at the Bible and Crown in Lombard Street by Edmund Parker as late as 1721.

[43] Cole (fl. 1637–65; d. 1665) was an apprentice of John Bellamy (see below). He was a printer as well as bookseller and at one time had his presses confiscated, presumably for printing unauthorised material. Amongst his other publications were *King Charls his speech from the scaffold* (1649) and *A true copy of Sir Henry Hide's speech on the scaffold, immediately before his execution before the Exchange, on the 4th of March, 1650.* Late in the plague year of 1665 Cole 'hanged himselfe in his warehouse in Leadenhall; reported to be distracted'.

[44] The rank presumably denotes a Civil War commission. A number of the local booksellers were actively involved on one side or another. The mapseller William Webb of Cornhill was a colonel, as was his neighbour, the puritan John Bellamy (see below). Among a wide variety of publications Brooke(s) (fl. 1652–77) also published John Tradescant, *Musæum Tradescantianum: or, a collection of rarities preserved at South-Lambeth . . .* (1656). He was later commissioned by the authorities to publish an important map of the City engraved by Hollar in the aftermath of the Great Fire. He ought not be confused with the Nathan Brooks tried and convicted at the Old Bailey in 1664 of publishing seditious works.

[45] Rich taught a deft and comprehensible shorthand method that was still in use as late as the nineteenth century. He offered 'the easiest, exactest, and briefest method of short and swift writing as ever yet was known; so that by the help of this book, and halfe an houres practise with the authour, an ordinary capacity may attain full knowledge therof'.

from his premises 'in the house that was Alderman Freemans in Cornhill, near the Royall Exchange'. Lodowick Lloyd, 'at his Shop, next the Castle-Tavern in Cornhil',[46] was the publisher of Job Everardt, *An epitome of stenographie . . .* in 1658. Peter Parker, who published Milton, stocked Samuel Shelton, *Brachygraphy, or the art of short writing* in 1672, as well as Elisha Coles, *The newest, plainest, and the shortest short-hand . . .* and a new edition of Thomas Shelton, *Tachygraphy . . .*, both 1674. William Mason, *A pen pluck'd from an eagles wing, or, the most swift, compendious, and speedy method of short-writing that ever was yet composed . . .* could be had from Brabazon Aylmer at the Three Pigeons in Cornhill in 1672. The writing-master Mason also stocked his own books and broadsides at the sign of the 'Hand & Pen', which hung at various addresses in the vicinity (in Lothbury, Bell Yard off Cornhill, in Scalding Alley, and in the Poultry) between 1682 and 1707. Benjamin Harris at the Stationers' Arms by the Exchange[47] co-published (with Richard Northcott of Cornhill) Nathaniel Stringer, *Rich redivivus or Mr Jeremiah Richs short-hand improved in a more breife & easy method . . .* in 1677. The Quaker Benjamin Clark,[48] in George Court off Lombard Street, offered Laurence Steel, *Short writing, begun by nature; compleated by art . . .* in 1678. Samuel Lee 'at ye Feathers in Lumbart Street near ye Post Office' published an edition of William Hopkins, *The flying pen-man, or the art of short writing . . .* in 1680. William Mason, *Arts advancement or the most exact, lineal, swift, short, and easy method of short-hand-writing hitherto extent . . .* could be had from Benjamin Harris above, or from his neighbour

Benjamin Alsop at the Angel & Bible in the Poultry, in 1682. Samuel Crouch at the 'Flower de luce' in Cornhil[49] was stocking William Addy, *Stenographia or the art of short-writing . . .* in 1684, as was Dorman Newman at the King's Arms in the Poultry.[50] The book was later advertised by John Laurence at the Angel in the Poultry in the 1690s. Dorman Newman also published late editions of Thomas Shelton, *Tachygraphy . . .* and *Zeiglographia . . .* from 1685 onwards. Both titles were later taken over by Thomas Speed of the Crown in the Poultry, and later of the Three Crowns in Cornhill. Also towards the close of the seventeenth century, John Man and his successors at the Heart and Bible in Cornhill were publishing repeated editions of Samuel Botley, *Maximum in minimo or Mr Jeremiah Richs pens dexterity compleated . . . .*[51] John Garrett 'At the South-side of the Royal-Exchange'[52] was one of the retailers of Abraham Nicholas, *Tho-ographia, or, a new art of short-hand . . .* in 1692, as was Samuel Manship at the Black Bull opposite the Exchange. Manship's successor at the Black Bull, William Davis, published a later edition in 1699. As one final example, George Ridpath, *Short-hand yet shorter: or, the art of short-writing . . .* could be

[46] Lloyd (fl. 1652–74) also published the works of Jacob Boehme. Catalogues of his books are found bound with John Norton, *Abel being dead yet speaketh* (1658) and Samuel Pordage, *Mundorum explicatio* (1661). He was perhaps a son of Llodowicke Lloyd, the poet.
[47] His shop was in Sweeting's Rents. Harris (fl. 1673–1708), who had 'a deal of mercury in his natural temper' (Dunton), had various brushes with the authorities. His *A protestant petition* (1681) earned him a £500 fine and the pillory. He later went to New England for several years, remarking that 'Old England is now so uneasie a place for honest men'. There he ran a book, coffee, tea and chocolate shop in Boston, and published (without permission) the first American newspaper. This was also suppressed.
[48] Dunton refers to him as 'Thee and Thou' Clark. George Yard was the particular home of a number of Quaker booksellers and printers.
[49] An apprentice and most likely a nephew of Nathaniel Crouch above.
[50] Newman (fl. 1662–94) also published Bunyan's *The holy war . . .* (with Benjamin Alsop) in 1682. His other output is fairly typical of a bookseller located near the Exchange, with books on economics and travel like *The trade of England revived: and the abuses thereof rectified . . .* (1681) or *The present state of New England . . .* (1675). His edition of Samuel Collins, *The present state of Russia . . .* (1671), contains a catalogue of his publications, and a further catalogue of about 1673 is to be found in the British Library (BL 1507/1255). He was, according to Dunton, who knew him well, a man of 'excellent parts'. Several of Newman's apprentices later had bookshops of their own in the vicinity. He apparently retired from bookselling after some misfortune and became a preacher.
[51] Carlton, op. cit., reports a copy with the contemporary inscription — 'To learn this book through your heed ought to be as large as St. Paul's doom by God!'
[52] A notable printseller who took over the premises of Thomas Jenner. Dunton refers to him as 'Indenture' Garrett, presumably from the amount of commercial stationery he stocked: a surviving broadside catalogue concludes with the offhand line, 'With many other things too many, here to be inserted'. The catalogue is reproduced in R. A. Skelton, *County atlases of the British Isles . . .* (London, 1970). Its main offerings are 'several maps and pictures, being very pleasant and delightful ornaments for houses studies, or closets, the which are printed and sold by John Garrett at his shop, as you go up the stairs of the Royal-Exchange in Cornhil'.

had both from Crouch and from the Scotsman Andrew Bell at the Cross Keys in the Poultry in 1696.[53]

TRAVEL BOOKS

Such an array of titles offered on a single and somewhat narrow subject over a limited period of time gives a reasonable indication of what the overall scale of bookselling at the Exchange may have been. It is possible to see a whole body of publishing feeding just on the demand created by the specific business environment of the area. But if some books may be characterised as following the demands of the City, there was another type of book, long specialised in by the Exchange booksellers, that can be seen as attempting to lead rather than to follow. Some of Thomas Hacket's travel books from the sixteenth century, some of the earliest books on the Americas, have already been mentioned. They were to set something of a pattern. Many similar books appeared down the years, including the first account of the rounding of Cape Horn[54] and the first reports of the *Mayflower*, the Pilgrim Fathers and the earliest permanent English settlements in America.[55] These travel books were often of a particular kind — not simply tales of adventure or reminiscence of life abroad, but books with a more specific agenda. This was often quite explicit. John Wolfe, whose career has already been touched upon, published a number of travel books in the late sixteenth century, including *John Huighen van Linschoten, his discours of voyages into ye Easte & West Indies* (1598), the book that really opened up the oriental trade to ships from northern Europe and one that was kept in service as a pilot guide for English ships voyaging to the Indies for almost a century. Wolfe also produced Duarte Lopes, *A report of the kingdome of Congo* (1597); Cornelius Gerritszoon, *An addition to the sea journal . . .* (1598); and Bernardt Langenes, *The description of a voyage made by certain ships of Holland* (1598). His intention, clearly stated in the introduction to *Linschoten*, a book he edited himself, was to foster an increase in international trade by inspiring more voyages to 'forraine partes . . . for the further benefitte and commodity of this land — by exportation of such thinges wherein we doe abound, and importation of those necessities whereof we stand in neede . . .'. The appeal of the travel book to the merchants that daily thronged the Exchange was rooted in a firmly practical interest in the existence of new and untapped markets. It is no surprise to find the Exchange booksellers alive to this type of publishing. The Exchange was the most obvious place for news of landfalls and fresh discoveries to surface. It was also the most obvious place for funds to be raised for a speculative trading venture. It was the place where such ventures were discussed and planned. It was, and remained, the obvious outlet for books of this type and similar books were to be published there for the next three hundred years. A typical early example is Richard Jobson, *The golden trade . . .*, published by Nicholas Bourne in 1623. Jobson had penetrated almost a thousand miles up the Gambia into the heart of Africa, and came back brimming with the possibilities and looking for backers for a full-scale trading venture. Bourne also published Philip Nichols, *Sir Francis Drake revived . . .* (1626), which called upon 'this dull or effeminate age, to

---

[53] Bell (fl. 1694–1720), like many booksellers of the period, also sold patent medicines. In 1712 he was advertising

Famous drops for hypocondriack melancholy: which effectively cure on the spot, by rectifying the stomach and blood, cleansing them from all impurities, and giving a new turn to their ferment, attenuating all viscous and tenacious humours (which make the head heavy, clog the spirits, confuse the mind, and cause the deepest melancholly, with direful views and black reflections), comforting the brain and nerves, composing the hurried thoughts, and introducing bright lively ideas and pleasant briskness, instead of dismal apprehension and dark incumbrance of the soul, setting the intellectuals at liberty to act with courage, serenity and steady cheerfulness, and causing a visible diffusive joy to reign in the room of weary doubts, fears, etc., for which it may be truly esteem'd infallible. Price 3s 6d a bottle, with instructions. Sold only at Mr. Bell's, book-seller at the Cross Keys and Bible in Cornhill, near the Royal Exchange.

[54] *The relation of a wonderfull voiage made by William Cornelison Schovten of Horne*, published by Nathaniel Newbery of Cornhill in 1619. Newbery (fl. 1614–36; d. 1636) was another of the local booksellers involved in early news-publishing.

[55] *A relation or iournall of the beginning and proceedings of the English plantation settled at Plimouth in New England . . .* (1622); *An historicall discoverie and relation of the English plantations, in New England* (1627); William Wood, *New Englands prospect. A true, lively, and experimentall description of that part of America* (1634), all published by John Bellamy of the Two Greyhounds in Cornhill. Bellamy (1596?–1653/4) was a co-religionist of the Pilgrims and published other important early works relating to the American colony. He

took an active part in the political and religious struggles of the day and at the outbreak of the Civil War he took up literary arms for Parliament, being given the rank of colonel. See L. Rostenberg, *Literary, political* (op. cit.), especially the chapter 'The new world: John Bellamy, "pilgrim" publisher of London'.

folowe his noble steps for golde & silver'. In like vein were Peter Cole's edition of John Underhill, *Newes from America; or, a new discoverie of New England* . . . (1638); Benjamin Billingsley's edition of Giacomo Baratti, *The late travels of S. Giacomo Baratti into the remote countries of the Abissins* . . . (1670); Robert Boulter's edition of Frans Caron, *A true description of the mighty kingdoms of Japan and Siam* . . . (1671); Richard Blome, *A description of the island of Jamaica* . . . (1678), published by Dorman Newman; Nathaniel Crouch's *A view of the English acquisitions in Guinea* (1686) and Sir Thomas Dalby, *An historical account of the rise and growth of the West-India collonies, and of the great advantages they are to England, in respect to trade* (1690), published by Joseph Hindmarsh of Cornhill.[56] As late as the nineteenth century, travel books of one kind or another still at times accounted for as much as a third of the annual output of the 'Smith, Elder' firm.[57] Henry S. King, who later took over the Smith, Elder premises in Cornhill,[58] continued the tradition. The frontiers of known and exploited markets had by now changed and King offered books on Alaska or Venezuela[59] rather than on long-settled and established trading routes, but the underlying principle remained the same.

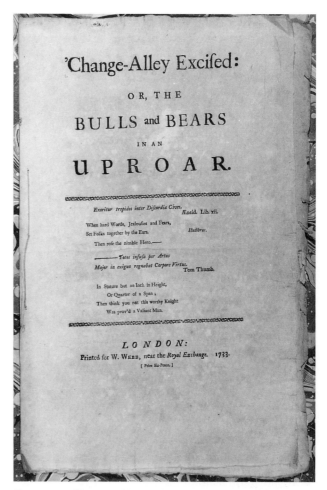

FIG. 77.   'Change-alley excised: or, the bulls and bears in an uproar', 1733. A rare political squib ostensibly published by 'W. Webb near the Royal Exchange'. The imprint is almost certainly a false one. The Royal Exchange was such a plausible address for a bookseller at this period that a vague form like 'near the Royal Exchange' was often used in conjunction with a stock name like 'Smith', or in this case 'Webb', to disguise the real origins of controversial or scurrilous material.

Courtesy of Ash Rare Books

[56] Hindmarsh (fl. 1678–96) had been bookseller to Charles II. To judge from some of his publications he was a staunch Jacobite: John Wilson, *A discourse of monarchy* (1684); Sir George Mackenzie, *The antiquity of the royal line* (1686); David Jenner, *The prerogative of primogeniture* (1685), and even the anonymous *A true account of the royal bagnio, with a discourse of its virtues* (1680). His geography was as perhaps as conservative as his politics, with Peter Blackborrow's *Navigation rectified* . . . (1684) claiming not only to prove Mercator 'notoriously false' but also to show 'the globe of the earth to be the centre of the heavens'.

[57] See B. Bell, 'Secret history . . .', op. cit., 'The majority . . . are travel guides, gazetteers and travel accounts . . . Even a cursory glance at the individual titles listed in the *English Catalogue* and *Publisher's Circular* for the 1830s and 1840s indicates attention to a clearly focused niche market. *Facts to illustrate the character of Indian natives* (1832), *China opened* (1838), *Van Diemen's Land as a place of emigration* (1840), are all typical . . .'.

[58] King had an impressive list, publishing works by De Tocqueville, T. H. Huxley, Thomas Hardy, George Macdonald and Walter Bagehot, whose masterly *Lombard Street, a description of the money market* King published in 1873. The firm was succeeded by the well known Kegan Paul & Co.

[59] Alexander Grant Dallas, *San Juan, Alaska and the north-west boundary* (1873); Charles Daniel Dance, *Recollections of four years in Venezuela* . . . (1876).

MAPS AND ATLASES

Closely related to the production of travel books was the production of maps, atlases and charts. From the earliest times this was another speciality of the Exchange shops. John Wolfe's travel books contained some of the very earliest maps engraved by London engravers, and he was the first London publisher regularly to use maps for book illustration.[60] It was possibly from Wolfe's old premises in Pope's Head Alley that John Speed's famous *The theatre of the empire of Great Britaine* . . ., the earliest published atlas of the British Isles and the first comprehensive collection of British town plans, was published by the uncle and nephew partnership of John Sudbury and George Humble[61] in 1611–12. The partners were early specialists in the sale of maps and prints[62] and George Humble went on to publish Speed's *A prospect of the most famous parts of the world* in 1627, the first general world atlas produced in this country. Less well known, and surviving only in isolated examples, are the separately printed news-maps of places of topical interest put out at this period by some of the Exchange booksellers involved in publishing the earliest newspapers.[63] Wenceslaus Hollar's famous

'Quarter-Master's Map'[64] was published from the Exchange at the time of the Civil War by the print and mapseller Thomas Jenner. The Yorkshireman Joseph Moxon, mapseller, globemaker, instrument-maker, printer, typefounder, author and translator, spent most of the early part of his career at the sign of the Atlas on Cornhill.[65] *A book of sea-plats* . . ., the atlas of sea-charts that he published from there in 1657, was the first maritime atlas produced by the London trade and marked an entry into an area previously wholly dominated by the Dutch publishers.[66] The sea-chart trade was further developed by Moxon's contemporary, John Seller, also both mapseller and instrument-maker, and himself a writer on mathematics, gunnery and navigation. Although he lived by the river at Wapping, Seller maintained retail premises in or near the Exchange for all of the most active part of his career, advertising his publications at various times from Exchange Alley, Pope's Head Alley, and in the Exchange itself.[67] He published

---

[60] Maps had regularly appeared in bibles since the mid-sixteenth century (see C. Delano-Smith & E. M. Ingram, *Maps in bibles 1500–1600* (Geneva, 1991)), but were otherwise seldom used as book-illustrations. Wolfe's *Linschoten*, with its fine series of folio maps of Africa and the Far East, preceded the first English general world atlas by almost thirty years. For the Exchange as a centre of the map trade see L. Worms, 'Mapsellers at the Royal Exchange' in *The Map Collector* (Tring, 1986), No. 34, pp. 2–7; No. 35, pp. 16–20.

[61] John Sudbury (fl. 1599–1618; d. 1621) came originally from Mapleback in Nottinghamshire and was apprenticed to Robert Hackforth, a London stationer, in 1568. The next thirty years of his life are obscure. His earliest surviving imprint dates from 1599, although he was probably in Pope's Head Alley somewhat earlier — his daughter Mary was christened at nearby St Michael Cornhill in January 1595/6. George Humble (fl. 1603–40; d. 1640) was the son of a local bookbinder, Thomas Humble, who was buried (as Umble) at St Michael Cornhill, 26 October 1588. See R. A. Skelton, *County atlases* . . . (1970), op. cit.

[62] See Rostenberg, *English publishers* . . . *(1963)*, op. cit.

[63] Two surviving examples of these news-maps, which were perhaps intended for public display, are *A thirde and last mape, both of the sedg of Breda by Spinola* . . . (STC 3597.5), and *A compendious card or map of the two armies lying by the R(hine)* . . . (STC 4606.5). Both are engraved maps with explanatory letterpress published by Thomas Archer in about 1624. Archer (fl. 1603–31; d. 1633) was a former apprentice of Cuthbert Burby who had premises in or near the Exchange throughout his career. He was the first London publisher of a regular series of corantos — in effect, the first London newspapers. He was 'laid by the heels [imprisoned] for making, or adding to, his corrantoes' in 1621. See J. B. Williams, 'The earliest English corantos' in *The Library*, 3rd series, Vol. 4, p. 437. Archer's neighbours Thomas Jenner and Nathaniel Newbery both produced similar maps.

[64] *The kingdome of England & principality of Wales exactly described* . . . (1644). A map 'intended to be vseful for all commanders for quarteringe of souldiers & all sorts of persons, that would be informed, where the armies be'.

[65] A man of remarkable talents, Moxon (1627–91) later became both Hydrographer to the King and a Fellow of the Royal Society. His *Mechanick exercises, or the doctrin of handy-works* . . . (1677–84) contains the earliest manual of printing in existence, and he also wrote on subjects as varied as astronomy, architecture and perspective. For biographical detail see the introduction to J. Moxon, *Mechanick exercises on the whole art of printing* . . ., ed. H. Davis & H. Carter (London, 1958).

[66] The only earlier maritime atlas published in England was an edition of Lucas Waghenaer's sea-charts, published as *The mariners mirrour* in 1588, a quasi-official project that owed its origins directly to the sponsorship of the Privy Council.

[67] Numerous map advertisements of the period are tabulated in S. Tyacke, *London map-sellers*, op. cit. Maps could be had from: George Baker's shop . . . North East Corner of the Royal Exchange; Billingsley . . . at the Royal Exchange; Christopher Browne . . . at the North Gate; John Cade at the Royal Exchange; S. Crouch by the Royal Exchange; Richard Davis at the 3 Ink-Bottles . . . Royal Exchange; Mr. Garret . . . under the Exchange; Robert Harford . . . near the Royal Exchange; J. Hide . . . behind the Royal Exchange; John Hills in Exchange Alley; J. Hindmarsh at the Golden Ball against the Royal Exchange; Robert Horne at the Royal Exchange; Mr. Mercer under the Exchange; Mr. Morgan . . . at Jo's Coffee-house . . . near the Royal Exchange; Mr. Ogilby . . . [who] has lately erected his standing-Lottery . . . near the Royal Exchange; R. Parker at the Royal Exchange; J. Pask . . . under the Royal Exchange; Robert Pask . . . under the North-side; S. Paske on the North side; Charles Price at the Lisbon Coffee-House behind the Royal Exchange; Godfrey Richards . . . over against the Exchange; R. Smith under the

maritime atlases of far more ambition than Moxon's early essay and, despite at one time having being found guilty of high treason,[68] was granted a monopoly of their manufacture and sale in an attempt to foster domestic production. Robert Morden, who took over Moxon's sign of the 'Atlas' in Cornhill and was perhaps his apprentice, was an innovative mapmaker, mapseller and globemaker of great distinction — and the first mapmaker regularly to lay his maps from the Greenwich meridian.[69] John Senex FRS began a distinguished career at a shop on Cornhill and, as well as producing maps, atlases and globes of great repute, also published important works in other fields.[70] John Bowles of Cornhill was the great 'pictureman' of the eighteenth century,[71] a dominant figure in the trade, retailing and wholesaling a wide range of maps, atlases and prints. His business was taken over by Robert Wilkinson, equally well-known as a publisher of prints, maps and atlases, who remained in Cornhill until 1816.[72] The first charts of Australia, brought back by Captain Cook, were engraved for publication by William Whitchurch in Bartholomew Lane, just behind the Exchange.[73] Another map-engraver, John Luffman, who for a time had premises in Sweeting's Alley,[74] not only engraved and published maps and atlases, but also wrote about his own travels to the West Indies.[75] As with bookselling, the mapselling tradition at the Exchange continued on well into the nineteenth century: the map-publisher James Wyld, who later built the extraordinary monster-globe in Leicester Square at the time of the Great Exhibition, had City premises at the Exchange. The instrument-maker Robert Brettell Bate, of the Poultry and later at the Exchange,[76] was granted the sole agency for Admiralty charts in 1829. The Letts family of diary fame also produced and sold maps. Effingham Wilson, too, published maps — but maps of a particular kind —

Piazza; Mr. Southby by the Royal-Exchange; Ed. Symon in Cornhill, against the Royal Exchange; and Anne Underwood on the Northside of the Royal Exchange going up the stairs.

The Mr Ogilby of the standing-lottery was of course John Ogilby, the mercurial Scot who began as a dancing master and only came to mapmaking at the age of sixty-six after losing everything in the Great Fire. He was a pioneer of this novel way of retailing by lottery. Another new method of bookselling coming into vogue at this time was the book auction, and some of the earliest recorded in England took place in the vicinity of the Exchange, most notably the first major sale of medieval manuscripts, which was held at Jonathan's Coffee-House in Exchange Alley in December 1682, organised by William Cooper, who had staged the first ever English book auction in 1676. See J. Lawler, *Book auctions in England in the seventeenth century*... (London, 1898).

[68] Seller and five others were tried at the Old Bailey in 1662 and found guilty. Four were hanged. Seller (1632–97) eventually received a pardon. It seems reasonably clear that he 'was not actually involved in the plot, although he was a friend of the conspirators'. See C. Verner, 'John Seller and the chart trade in seventeenth-century England' in N. J. W. Thrower (ed.), *The compleat plattmaker*... (Berkeley, 1978), pp. 127–57.

[69] Morden (fl. 1669–1703; d. 1703) is best known for his *Geography rectified; or a description of the world*... (1680), the county maps he prepared for *Camden's Britannia, newly translated*... (1695), and his *The new description and state of England, containing the mapps of the counties*... (1701). He also produced a great variety of other work and sold 'all sorts of globes, spheres, maps large and small, sea-platts, and other mathematical instruments'. He was churchwarden of St Christopher-le-Stocks in 1679–80 and was buried there, 'in ye North Ile', in August 1703. His career did not perhaps prosper as it might have done and he spoke somewhat bitterly towards the end of his life of having 'lain latent under the horizon of unknown obscurity, and irresistible poverty'. He looked for 'better rewards' in the next world.

[70] Senex (1678–1740) became Geographer to the Queen and a Fellow of the Royal Society. Among his apprentices was the first English encyclopaedist, Ephraim Chambers. When Senex died in 1740 he was remembered in a contemporary obituary as 'a sincere, worthy, honest man, and greatly valued by men of learning'.

[71] Bowles (1701?–79) began his career at the sign of the Screen opposite the Stocks Market and ended at the Black Horse (No. 13) on Cornhill. He was a member of an extensive family of map- and print-sellers. A cogent unravelling of the different members is given in D. Hodson, *County atlases of the British Isles published after 1703*, vol. 1 (Welwyn, 1984), p. 186 *et seq.*

[72] Wilkinson (fl. 1779–1825) was the publisher of *Wilkinson's general atlas of the world* (1794) and much else in similar vein.

[73] Whitchurch (fl. 1769–77) also engraved maps for Johann Georg Adam Forster, *A voyage round the world* (1777). He was born at Holborn in 1748.

[74] It was from Sweeting's Alley that Luffman (fl. 1776–1821) published his *Select plans of the principal cities, harbours, forts &c. in the world* (1799–1800).

[75] Luffman visited Antigua 1786–88, and published *A brief account of the island of Antigua*... in 1789. He also found time to produce *The charters of London complete* (1793), a work in which he asserts of his fellow Londoners, 'The Citizens of London have ever been looked up to by the nation at large, as the assertors of true liberty ... industrious, persevering, honest, generous and brave; the first of traders and the richest of all people depending on commerce in the world ...'. This was a commonly held view and indicative of the kind of confidence that people had in the mercantile system and the vast proportion of the world's trade that was funnelled through the Exchange.

[76] For an account of Bate's career see A. McConnell, *R. B. Bate of the Poultry 1782–1847: the life and times of a scientific instrument maker* (London, 1993).

FIG. 78a–d.   The imprints of four seventeenth-century Royal Exchange mapsellers. John Sudbury and George Humble (note 61) were the publishers of John Speed's famous maps of the counties of England and Wales. John Garrett's imprint is taken from a late edition of Wenceslaus Hollar's 'Quarter-Master's Map' (note 64). John Seller (note 68) published some of the earliest English maritime atlases, while Robert Morden (note 69) was one of the first truly innovative English mapmakers.

Courtesy of Ash Rare Books

statistical maps and commercial maps[77] — the first generation of maps developed, appropriately enough for the Exchange, as a new kind of business aid.

[77] See, for example, Sir John Stoddart's 'statistical, administrative, and commercial' charts of the British Isles, France, etc., published by Wilson in the 1830s.

BOOKS FOR THE CITIZENS

When George Smith left Cornhill in 1869–70, some three hundred years of major bookselling and publishing activity in the area was reaching an end. The book trade did not disappear at that point, for Smith's old premises continued under Henry S. King, and Effingham Wilson's firm continued trading on into

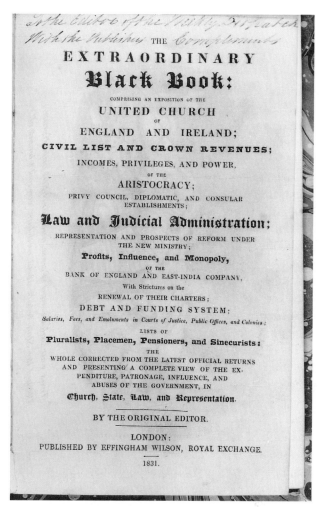

FIG. 79. 'The Bible, Crown and Constitution No. 32 Cornhill'. An early nineteenth-century engraving by Samuel Rawle of James Asperne's handsome bookshop on Cornhill. Asperne had taken over both the premises and the publication of the *European Magazine* from the previous occupant, John Sewell, who founded the magazine in 1782. Sewell, who was something of an authority on naval architecture, once proposed the construction of a reservoir under Cornhill. He was himself the successor of the bookselling Brothertons, who had rebuilt the premises after the Cornhill fire.

Courtesy of Ash Rare Books

FIG. 80. John Wade, *The extraordinary black book . . .* (1831). The bible of nineteenth-century reform, this edition published by Effingham Wilson from the Exchange in 1831. Booksellers in country towns were prosecuted for selling it, but the commotion that it helped to raise led inexorably to the passing of the Great Reform Bill in 1832. This particular copy was that sent to the editor of the *Weekly Dispatch* with Wilson's compliments.

Courtesy of Ash Rare Books

the twentieth century,[78] but the dynamics of the area had changed. The Exchange itself began to decline in

---

[78] The firm was eventually taken over by Sir Isaac Pitman & Sons in 1932.

importance and was no longer the great focal point of trade that it had been. The introduction of the London telephone system in 1881 in particular led to a different pattern of daily life in the City. All the vast business of the financial and trading centre of the nineteenth-century world became less and less a matter of daily attendance 'on 'Change'. The book trade, too, was coming to terms with new technology, mass production and more frenetic ways of doing business. Publishing and retail bookselling had gradually become quite separate activities. The older practice of combining the two perhaps lingered on longer in the City than elsewhere, but was by now a historical curiosity. But whatever external pressures may have been at work, and although the parallel should not perhaps be over-stressed, there is a reasonably clear correlation between the rise and fall of the Exchange as the focal point of the City's financial and mercantile activity, and the rise and fall of the book trade in the area. Given the nature of many of the books that have been discussed, that is natural enough, but this is not to suggest that bookselling in the area was wholly a matter of providing books for the local business community. For much of the period under review, the heart of the City was still a place where people lived and took their leisure, and many very different kinds of books were produced there.

There were large numbers of books on medicine, like those published by George Strahan, whose premises are shown on the fire map — William Beckett, *New discoveries relating to the cure of cancers* (1711), George Cheyne, *The English malady . . .* (1734), and Robert James's translation of Prosper Alpinus, *The presages of life and death in diseases . . .* (1746).[79] There were cookery books, including a famous title by Hannah Glasse, *The art of cookery made plain and easy* — the 'first catch your hare' book — that went on sale in 1747 at Mrs Wharton's toy-shop, 'The Blue-Boy', near the Exchange.[80] There were books

on sport, including the most famous of early cricket books, John Nyren's *The young cricketer's tutor . . .*, first published from the Exchange by Effingham Wilson in 1833.[81] There were important scientific treatises, like Edmond Halley's *A synopsis of the astronomy of comets*[82] or Isaac Newton's *A treatise of the system of the world*, the first generally accessible account of his analysis of the fundamental laws of physics, published by Francis Fayram at the Exchange in 1728.[83] Fayram also published Abraham de Moivre's *Annuities upon lives* in 1725 — a mathematical masterpiece that lays the foundation of modern actuarial calculation of life expectancy, probability, and insurance premiums.[84] There were books on religion, on education and on child-rearing.[85] There were books on architecture, like Moxon's translation of *Vignola: or the compleat*

[79] A few further examples from a particularly rich field are Nathaniel Brooke's *The compleat midwifes practice . . .* (1656); John Brown, *A compleat treatise of the muscles . . .* (1683), published by Dorman Newman; John Woodall, *The surgeons mate or military & domestique surgery . . .* (1639) and *The cure of the plague by an antidote called aurum vitæ* (1640). These two last were both published by Nicholas Bourne, who also sold the pills 'truly prepared of gold' that were advertised in the second work.

[80] A surprising number of cookery books were published from the vicinity of the Exchange. To cite just a few early examples — *The queen's closet open'd . . .* by 'W. M.' (perhaps William Meed), published by Nathaniel Brooke in 1655; *The perfect cook . . .* (1656), also published by Brooke; Hannah Wolley, *The accomplish'd ladies delight in preserving, physick, beautifying, and cookery*, published by Benjamin Harris in 1683, which combines advice on cooking 'both in the English and French mode' with tips on preserving food, remedies for illness, hints on beauty preparations and thoughts on catching fish; and the handsomely illustrated Charles Carter, *The complete practical cook*, published by William Meadows in 1730.

[81] 'The first cricket classic . . . constantly reprinted, discussed and quoted, these studies have proved wonderfully enduring, as stimulating now as when they were first written' (John Arlott).

[82] This was the work in which Halley first developed his theory of the periodicity of comets. He made a prediction of one great comet in particular that, 'I dare venture to foretell, that it will return again in the year 1758'. It duly reappeared on Christmas Day 1758 and has been known as Halley's Comet ever since. The English version of Halley's original Latin was first published by John Senex in 1705.

[83] Newton (1642–1727) deliberately chose to avoid public controversy, and although he wrote this popular account of his discoveries he declined to have it published in his lifetime. Fayram (fl. 1719–32) also published Newton's *Optical lectures . . .* (1728). In so far as scientific books are concerned there was obviously a certain amount of cross-fertilisation between the Exchange booksellers and the professors of Gresham College (who were paid from the rents of the Exchange shops).

[84] Fayram is the first-named of the three publishers that shared the publication. The son of a Tottenham blacksmith, apprenticed to the trade as early as 1687, most of his publishing consisted of similarly shared ventures. He was involved in the publication of works on mathematics, surveying, navigation, book-keeping, and medicine, as well as dictionaries, several works on Virginia, and John Woodward's pioneering *An attempt towards a natural history of the fossils of England . . .* (1728–29). One of the few books Fayram published on his account was an early edition in English of *The morals of Confucius a Chinese philosopher . . .* (1724). An advertisement for some his books is contained in Edward Strother, *The family companion for health . . .* (1729).

[85] A particular favourite in this last category is William Averell, *A dyall for dainty darlings . . .* (1584), published by Thomas Hacket. 'Drawe neere you dallying daddes, that marre the minds of your children, by excessive and overmuch cockering; beholde the iudgements of God, that punisheth you in those things that you cheefely love, because you make them your Gods, who ought to be theyr guides . . . you give them all things, and deny them nothing, and yet you complaine that your children are gracelesse, when you yourselves are not therein blamelesse . . .'.

Guardian Royal Exchange collection

architect ... (1655). Of even greater consequence for the development of English architecture was the first translation of the writings of Andrea Palladio, published by the cultured Godfrey Richards of Cornhill in 1663.[86] Richards also sold prints, as did numerous

others both before and after his time, from Sudbury and Humble whose shop in Pope's Head Alley was perhaps the first specialist print-shop to appear in London, on through Thomas Jenner, who numbered Pepys amongst his customers,[87] John Bowles in the eighteenth century,[88] and so on down to the colourful Victorian sporting prints published by Alfred Head

[86] *The first book of architecture by Andrea Palladio .... *Richards (fl. 1655–83) translated the work himself and was comfortable enough with his subject to add some ideas on house-frames of his own. He had noted 'The scarcity of books of architecture in English, and the zeal which I find our ingenious artists have to entertaine anything of that subject, incouraged me to this essay; wherein, I hope, I have rendered the authors sence, without disadvantage ...'. From his premises at the Peacock in Cornhill, and later at the Golden Ball opposite the Exchange, Richards provided an important conduit for ideas from abroad into seventeenth-century London. He also imported maps and prints, publishing, for example, the etched portraits of Guercino. We catch glimpses of him in the diaries of the scientist Robert Hooke, lending a book by Galileo or discussing Vitruvius. There is an account of him in L. Rostenberg, *English publishers*, op. cit., but his is a career that deserves further study. One would also wish to know more of the curious incident recorded in the parish register of St Michael Cornhill in which his servant, Robert Butler, was 'casually shot with a pistoll' in March 1660/1.

[87] Jenner was recommended to Pepys by John Evelyn. See S. Tyacke, 'Samuel Pepys as map collector' in R. Myers & M. Harris (eds.), *Maps and prints: aspects of the English booktrade* (Oxford, 1984), pp. 1–29.
[88] Two of the finest engravers of the eighteenth century also worked in the vicinity of the Exchange. The extravagantly gifted William Wynne Ryland (1732–83) — who introduced chalk-manner engraving to London, became engraver to the King and was later hanged for forgery — had premises facing the Exchange on Cornhill for a number of years. William Sharp (1749–1824), equally an engraver of international reputation, and honoured by the academies of Munich and Vienna, began his career as a writing engraver in Bartholomew Lane, just behind the Exchange. A radical and a friend of Tom Paine, Sharp was a follower in turn of Mesmer, Swedenborg and the lunatic Richard Brothers. He was later the chief supporter of Joanna Southcott.

Baily of Cornhill. One of the supreme achievements of nineteenth-century art publishing was the publication between 1842 and 1849 of the large folios of David Roberts' Middle Eastern landscapes by (Sir) Francis Graham Moon of Threadneedle Street.[89]

The book trade in and around the Royal Exchange was an extensive and varied one — a dense population of bookshops, a good many important books, and a number of distinct strands of publishing, very much inaugurated and sustained in the area. It was also large enough to encompass the publication of many books outside narrowly defined fields of special interest. For upwards of three hundred years it was an immediately noticeable feature of life at the very centre of the City. Much work remains to be done on tabulating the output of the Exchange booksellers and more still on uncovering the details of their lives, their relationships with one another and the patterns of trade both amongst themselves and with the wider bookselling and publishing community. But it is already amply clear that they offered much to London and its history, and to the life of the nation at large. They disappeared in the wake of changing circumstance, yet the shadows that they cast are not lightly to be erased.

[89] *The Holy Land, Syria, Idumea, Arabia, Egypt & Nubia. From drawings made on the spot* . . . (1842–49). 'One of the most important and elaborate ventures in nineteenth-century publishing . . . the apotheosis of the tinted lithograph'. The work required the use of several hundred printing stones, weighing in the order of 60 lb. each. See J. R. Abbey, *Travel in aquatint and lithography 1770–1860* . . . (London, 1957), pp. 334–41. Moon was later to become Lord Mayor of London.

FIG. 81.   The Royal Exchange from Threadneedle Street, by Thomas Malton, 1792.
By courtesy of the Trustees of the British Museum

FIG. 82.   The Courtyard of the Royal Exchange. Anonymous, undated engraving with an elaborate border.
Guildhall Library, Corporation of London

FIG. 83. Samuel Knights' shop, demolished to make way for the third Exchange. He was paid £1,500 in compensation for his book shop.

Guildhall Library, Corporation of London

FIG. 84. The Shops round the 'Change. Undated verses. Gace collection, XXII, 100.

By courtesy of the Trustees of the British Museum

FIG. 85.   The Royal Exchange from Cornhill, looking towards St Paul's, issued by
Ackermann & Co., 1836. Note the reconstructed tower over the entrance.
Guildhall Library, Corporation of London

FIG. 86.   The Royal Exchange, 1788. Building drawn by John Chapman, figures by Philip
de Loutherburg, engraved by Bartolozzi. Issued as a pair with Figure 74.
Guildhall Library, Corporation of London

CHAPTER XXII

Instrument-Making Around the Exchange

By GLORIA CLIFTON

THE MAKING OF mathematical instruments was just becoming established in London at the time when the first Royal Exchange was built. During the sixteenth century there had developed a growing interest in the practical applications of mathematics, in such areas as gunnery, navigation, surveying, mapping, and commerce, and in ways of making mathematical methods accessible to those who had enjoyed only a basic formal education. The beginnings of European settlement in the Americas, the opening up of oceanic trade routes, and the consequent intensification of rivalry between the major powers, placed a premium on effective military engineering, and on position-finding on land and at sea.[1] One way of both simplifying calculation and improving accuracy was to develop instruments with precise scales, such as the rules for gunners and carpenters devised by Thomas Bedwell.[2] Once out of sight of land, position-finding at sea depended on being able to measure the altitude of heavenly bodies, which required appropriate instruments. All these kinds of devices were provided by the mathematical instrument-makers.

The making of mathematical instruments, together with the publication of textbooks explaining their use, had been pioneered during the fifteenth and early sixteenth centuries in several regions of mainland Europe, including northern Italy, the Iberian Peninsula, the Low Countries and parts of southern Germany, and the emergence of the necessary skills

in the British Isles depended principally on Dutch, Flemish and German immigrants, encouraged by royal patronage. One of the first identifiable mathematical instrument-makers in London was Thomas Lambrit (*c.* 1510–62), an immigrant from the area around Liège, who used the name Thomas Gemini. He was a skilled engraver, who received an annuity of ten pounds from Henry VIII, and made a living as a printer, engraver of maps and illustrations, and mathematical instrument-maker, at his shop in Black-friars.[3] The scales of mathematical instruments were engraved by hand, and several of the earliest known makers were originally engravers, who applied their skills to the specific task of instrument-making.

During the seventeenth century a new type of instrument-maker emerged, the specialist in optical instruments. Both the telescope and the microscope were invented in the first decade of the seventeenth century in the Netherlands, and their manufacture quickly spread across Europe. The telescope, in particular, produced new discoveries in the realm of astronomy, and was one of the factors which helped to stimulate interest in natural philosophy, or science, as it would now be called. In 1660 the Royal Society was founded, receiving its charter from Charles II in 1662, and declared its purpose to be 'To improve the knowledge of naturall things, and all useful Arts, Manufactures, Mechanick practices, Engynes and Inventions by Experiments . . .'.[4] By the late seventeenth century there was also a growing interest in the problems of improving navigation, as Britain's overseas empire and international trade continued to expand. All these factors combined to produce a section of London society which was interested in

---

[1] E. G. R. Taylor, *The mathematical practitioners of Tudor and Stuart England* (Cambridge, 1954), pp. 3–48; D. W. Waters, *The art of navigation in England in Elizabethan and early Stuart times* (London, 1958); G. L'E. Turner, 'Mathematical instrument-making in London in the sixteenth century' in S. Tyacke (ed.), *English map-making 1500–1650* (London, 1983), pp. 93–106; S. Johnston, 'Mathematical practitioners and instruments in Elizabethan England' in *Annals of science*, vol. 48 (1991), pp. 319–44; G. Clifton, *Directory of British scientific instrument makers 1550–1851* (London, 1995), pp. xi–xv.

[2] Johnston, op. cit., p. 323.

[3] Taylor, op. cit., pp. 165–66; Turner, op. cit., pp. 96–97.

[4] R. Hooke, quoted in G. L'E. Turner, 'A very scientific century' in E. Lefebvre and De Bruijn (eds.), *Martinus Van Marum: life and work*, vol. 4, G. L'E. Turner and T. H. Levere, *Van Marum's scientific instruments in Teyler's Museum* (Leiden, 1973), p. 4.

discovering more about the workings of the natural world and set the scene for the emergence of the public demonstration lecture.[5] The first series was given by James Hodgson, Fellow of the Royal Society, in London in 1705, and was soon followed by others. Although there had been public lectures before, the use of apparatus to demonstrate the phenomena and experiments which were being discussed was novel, and stimulated further interest.[6] Such lectures helped to create a growing market for a third type of instrument, the philosophical instrument, designed to demonstrate or explore natural phenomena. This category included air pumps, to show the existence of a vacuum, electrical machines, and working models of the solar system, which were often called orreries, after the famous example built by the London instrument-maker John Rowley in about 1712 for Charles Boyle, 4th Earl of Orrery.[7] Such instruments were not only the province of lecturers and teachers, but were also acquired by prosperous individuals who were interested in pursuing their own studies in natural philosophy, and demonstrating their knowledge to family and friends. One early and particularly well known example was Samuel Pepys, whose diary during the 1660s records his growing interest in mathematics and in the workings of the natural world, with details of the instruments he acquired.[8] The rise of public demonstration lectures aroused the curiosity of other Londoners with some wealth and leisure to pursue their interests, such as the merchants and entrepreneurs who frequented the coffee houses. For those who traded overseas, astronomy and magnetism had a particular attraction because of their close links with navigation, and especially because they might offer a reliable method of finding longitude at sea, which remained the most intractable problem for mariners.

Although there were always some instrument-makers who specialised in only one of the three main types, by the mid-eighteenth century the leading shops sold all the principal kinds of mathematical, optical and philosophical instruments. By the middle of the eighteenth century the term 'optician' was sometimes used to denote an optical instrument-maker. There were also navigation warehouses, which combined the sale of nautical instruments with the supply of maps, charts, drawing instruments, globes and books. Rules and drawing instruments were sold by a number of other retailers, including stationers, ironmongers and cane sellers.[9] London remained the principal centre of mathematical, optical and philosophical instrument-making in the British Isles, from the origins of the trade in the sixteenth and seventeenth centuries through to the nineteenth century. By the late seventeenth century there were small numbers of makers in other major cities and ports, such as Bristol, Edinburgh and Oxford. But although provincial instrument-making expanded rapidly in the second half of the eighteenth century, even in the first half of the nineteenth century the Census reports show that about half the instrument-making workforce was in London.[10] By the second half of the eighteenth century London had become the most important centre in Europe for the production of precision instruments, especially those used in astronomy and navigation.

Within London, the areas where instrument-making was concentrated changed over time. The majority of the earliest makers, in the later sixteenth and early seventeenth centuries, set up in business close to the river, along the Strand and Fleet Street, at Blackfriars, by the Tower, and at Wapping and Ratcliff. Others were found near St Paul's, and around the edges of the City, in districts such as

[5] L. Stewart, *The rise of public science. Rhetoric, technology, and natural philosophy in Newtonian Britain, 1660–1750* (Cambridge, 1992), pp. 183–87, 257–60.

[6] A. Q. Morton and J. Wess, *Public and private science. The King George III collection* (Oxford, 1993), pp. 39–65.

[7] H. King with J. R. Millburn, *Geared to the stars. The evolution of planetariums, orreries, and astronomical clocks* (Bristol, 1978), pp. 154–55. See also below, p. 235.

[8] R. Latham (ed.), *The illustrated Pepys. Extracts from the diary* (London, 1978), pp. 119–20; M. H. Nicolson, *Pepys' Diary and the New Science* (Charlottesville, Virginia, 1965), pp. 18–27.

[9] For example, in the late seventeenth century searches by the Clockmakers' Company, which claimed jurisdiction over mathematical instrument-makers, included the shops of cane-sellers and ironmongers who sold rules: GL, Clockmakers' Company, Court Minutes, Search 21 February 1671 (OS), MS 2710/1, pp. 243–45.

[10] *Census of Great Britain*, 1831, 1841, 1851, tables of occupations. Clifton, op. cit., pp. xii–xiii, xv, 76, 151, 225.

Smithfield.[11] But by the middle of the seventeenth century the area surrounding the Royal Exchange was also beginning to emerge as a major centre for the sale of instruments, and it retained a significant number of the leading businesses through to the mid-nineteenth century. From the seventeenth century onwards most of the other important makers had their shops along the east–west route from Cheapside and St Paul's, via Ludgate Hill, Fleet Street and the Strand to Charing Cross, extending to Piccadilly by the late eighteenth century. The earliest reference traced to an instrument-maker having a shop near the Exchange occurs in a textbook for surveyors written by Edward Worsop and published in 1582: *Scales, compasses and sundry sorts of Geometricall instruments in metall, are to be had in the house of Humfrey Cole, neere unto the North dore of Paules, and at the house of John Bull at the Exchange gate.*[12] By the middle of the seventeenth century, instruments could be obtained at two shops in the vicinity of the Royal Exchange. Walter Hayes, who specialised in making mathematical instruments, initially worked in Birchin Lane, off Cornhill, although by 1652 he had moved to the Cross Daggers in Moorfields.[13] The other shop, to be found in 1653 at the sign of Atlas on Parnassus Hill, near St Michael's Church in Cornhill, was run by John Sugar and Joseph Moxon, who sold instruments alongside maps and globes. The business was apparently continued by Moxon alone for some years.[14] By the 1670s Robert Morden, also trading at the sign of the Atlas in Cornhill, likewise sold instruments as well as maps and globes.[15] A similar combination of goods

was offered by John Seller, who had a shop in Pope's Head Alley off Cornhill between 1678 and 1681, and at the West side of the Royal Exchange from 1682 to 1686. However, Seller had begun his career in Wapping as a compass maker and then added the sale of maps and charts to his business, before acquiring an additional outlet in the City, while retaining his original shop.[16]

The practice of combining the sale of maps and instruments remained a feature of several shops near the Exchange, no doubt prompted by the marketing opportunities offered by proximity to the principal meeting place for merchants and traders. Philip Lea, first at the sign of the Atlas and Hercules in the Poultry, and by 1685 at the same sign in Cheapside, advertised 'all Sorts of Globes Spheres Maps Sea:plats Mathematical Books and Instruments'.[17] Between 1703 and 1706 John Senex produced maps and globes from his premises 'next Door to the Fleece-Tavern in Cornhill', and also supplied books and mathematical instruments. In addition, he was one of the booksellers advertised as taking in subscriptions for James Hodgson's series of lectures and experiments in 1705.[18] From 1712 to 1716 Philip Lea's widow and successor, Anne, in partnership with her son-in-law, Richard Glynne, continued to advertise globes and maps, while Glynne, who had been apprenticed in the Clockmakers' Company to the mathematical instrument-maker, Henry Wynne, presumably produced instruments, as a number have survived bearing his signature.[19] In the early nineteenth century the practice of selling both charts and instruments in the neighbourhood of the Exchange was continued by several makers. Penelope Steel had a Navigation Warehouse at 70 Cornhill by 1803, which was continued by J. Steel from 1806, and had

[11] This conclusion was reached by analysing the addresses of all the makers at work before 1650, listed in Clifton, op. cit. The leading sixteenth-century maker after Gemini was Humfrey Cole, who was trading near St Paul's in 1582, and in 1590 the mathematical instrument-makers John Reade and Christopher Paine were both described as 'dwelling in Hosier Lane neere unto West Smithfield'; see D. J. Bryden, 'Evidence from advertising for mathematical instrument making in London, 1556–1714' in *Annals of science*, vol. 49 (1992), pp. 304–05.

[12] Quoted in ibid., p. 304.

[13] W. Oughtred, *Dialling performed instrumentally* (London, 1652), p. 34 (I am grateful to Dr D. J. Bryden for this reference); Taylor op. cit., p. 239.

[14] J. Booker, *Coelestiall Observations* (London, 1653), sig. C4, f. 5v; King with Milburn, op. cit., p. 95.

[15] S. Tyacke, *London map-sellers 1660–1720* (Tring, Herts., 1978), p. 123.

[16] Ibid., p. 139.

[17] Ibid., pp. 119, 121.

[18] A catalogue of Jeremiah Seller, Charles Price and John Senex's stock, BL 1509/1520, reproduced in Tyacke, op. cit., pl. 15, p. 137; Morton & Wess, op. cit., p. 42.

[19] *An inventory of the navigation and astronomy collections in the National Maritime Museum Greenwich* (London, 1971), section 23, p. 3; M. Holbrook with R. G. W. Anderson and D. J. Bryden, *Science preserved: a directory of scientific instruments in collections in the United Kingdom and Eire* (London, 1992), pp. 110, 113; Tyacke, op. cit., pp. 116–17.

become Steel & Co. by 1811.[20] Robert Brettell Bate opened his shop selling mathematical, optical and philosophical instruments at 17 Poultry in 1807, moving to 20 and 21 Poultry in 1824 (Fig. 87). Then, in 1829, he became principal Admiralty chart agent. In fact, the initiative came from the Hydrographer to the Navy, W. E. Parry, who wanted to simplify the supply of charts. Previously there had been numerous port agents for Admiralty charts, and Parry decided that it would be far more efficient if he dealt with a single agent, who would appoint his own sub-agents in the various ports. Bate was invited to apply for the post of principal chart agent, and was appointed in September 1829. Eventually Bate decided that the volume of chart business could be better accommodated in separate premises, and in 1844 he took a shop at No. 33 in the rebuilt Royal Exchange. After placing an advertisement in *The Times*, Bate appointed a Captain Pritchard as manager of his shop at the Exchange.[21] There was some dispute with the Gresham Committee over the size of board which would be allowed for displaying charts, but as the matter never appeared in the Committee's Minutes, it was presumably settled informally.[22] After Bate's death in 1847 his widow continued the business for a short time, but when she gave up in 1850 John Dennett Potter, who had previously been Bate's shopman, took over the chart agency and acquired premises at 31 Poultry. Like his former employer, Potter also sold all kinds of mathematical, nautical, optical and philosophical instruments, and after his death in 1882 the business was continued by his son, Septimus Charles Potter, at the same address.[23]

Besides those who sold instruments alongside charts, maps and globes, there were also a number of leading specialist instrument-makers in the neighbourhood of the Royal Exchange from the seventeenth to the nineteenth centuries. One of them, Walter Hayes, has already been noted, but he was only the first of a succession of leading makers who traded for at least a part of their career from that vicinity. By 1658 Henry Sutton had established a mathematical instrument shop behind the Royal Exchange in Threadneedle Street, supplying both wooden and the more expensive brass instruments, including astrolabes, quadrants, slide rules and sundials. He died in about 1665, probably from the plague,[24] but before the end of the seventeenth century there were two well known mathematical instrument-makers who had shops by the Exchange, Thomas Tuttell and Thomas Cooke. Tuttell was apprenticed to Henry Wynne in the Clockmaker's Company, freed in 1695 and quickly made a name for himself. His principal shop was at Charing Cross, but he also had premises 'against ye Royal Exchange in Cornhill'.[25] The title of one of his publications provides a useful summary of the market at which he and other instrument-makers around the Exchange were aiming: *The Description and Uses of a new contriv'd Elliptical double Dial: as also of the Universal Aequinoctial Dial: which serve to find the Latitude, Hour of the Day, the true Meridian, the Altitude, Azimuth and Declination of the Sun . . . very useful for all Seamen and Travellers and our curious Gentry . . .*. His pre-eminence was recognised in 1700, when he was appointed mathematical instrument-maker to William III, but, tragically, he died only two years later, drowned while undertaking a marine survey.[26] Thomas Cooke started in business at the back of the Royal Exchange in Threadneedle Street, from which address he issued an advertisement in 1695, but during 1704 he moved to Old Jewry. He was best known for his gauging instruments, which he supplied to the Excise Office. Later in the eighteenth century two other mathematical instrument-makers trading near the Exchange were especially well known for their marine compasses. John Fowler was at the Globe, Sweetings (Swithins) Alley by the Royal Exchange in the 1730s, while John

[20] *Holden's Triennial Directory* (London, 1802 and 1805); *Holden's Supplement of Names* (London, 1803); *Holden's Annual London and Country Directory* (London, 1811); *The Post-Office Annual Directory* (London, 1802–06).

[21] A. McConnell, *R. B. Bate of the Poultry 1782–1847. The life and times of a scientific instrument maker* (London, 1993), pp. 6, 41–46.

[22] Hydrographic Office, Taunton, Letters-in B.948, Bate to Beaufort, 18 December 1844, quoted in ibid., pp. 44–45.

[23] Ibid., pp. 53–54; *Post Office London Directory* (1851–85); Somerset House, indexes to wills, 1882 (I am grateful to Mr J. R. Millburn for drawing my attention to this reference).

[24] J. Collins, *The sector on a quadrant* (London, 1658), plates; Taylor, op. cit., pp. 105, 364.

[25] M. Crawforth, 'Evidence from trade cards for the scientific instrument industry', in *Annals of Science*, vol. 42 (1985), p. 535.

[26] J. Brown, 'Guild organisation and the instrument-making trade, 1550–1830: the Grocers and Clockmakers' Companies', in *Annals of Science*, vol. 36 (1979), pp. 33–34; Taylor, op. cit., p. 412.

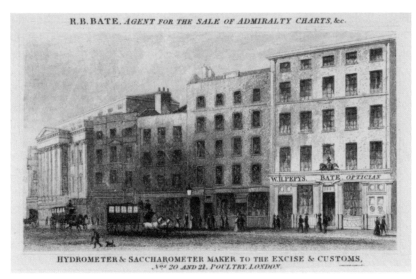

FIG. 87.   R. B. Bate's shop at 20/21 Poultry from John Tallis's *London Street Views 1838–40* (1969), part 38, p. 112.

FIG. 88.   The trade-card of J. D. Potter of 31 Poultry, about 1855.
Reproduced courtesy of the Trustees of the National Maritime Museum, Greenwich

Morgan was in Finch Lane, Cornhill in the 1750s. Morgan is remembered as the master who taught James Watt the trade of instrument-making, the basis for the latter's subsequent pre-eminence as an engineer, and was reckoned as one of the half-dozen most skilled scale dividers in London.[27]

Another kind of specialist found near the Royal Exchange was the optical instrument-maker or optician. Initially they confined themselves to optical goods, but during the eighteenth century there was a tendency for them to offer an increasingly wide range, including mathematical instruments, barometers and thermometers. One well known optical instrument-maker of the second half of the seventeenth century with a shop by the Exchange was Joseph Howe, a member of two London guilds, the Spectaclemakers' and the Broderers' Companies.[28] In the records of the Spectaclemakers' Company his address is given

[27] *London Gazette*, 2 September 1695; *Post Man*, 21 September 1704; C. Leadbetter, *The Royal Gauger* (London, 1739, and 3rd edn, 1750), p. xviii; G. L'E. Turner, *Antique Scientific Instruments* (Poole, Dorset, 1980), p. 38; J. P. Muirhead, *The Life of James Watt* (London, 1858), pp. 38–39.

[28] J. Brown, *Mathematical instrument makers in the Grocers' Company 1668–1800* (London, 1979), p. 5.

several times, with slight variations, which make it a little difficult to know whether he moved a short distance, or whether there were merely a number of different ways of describing the same shop. At a search for faulty goods in 1671, Howe's address was given simply as 'Exchang' [*sic*], at another search in 1676 it was 'Back side Exchang', in 1693 'Behinde Exchange', and in 1695 'Threadneedle street'. However, an advertisement in the *London Gazette* in 1691, asking for information about a gentleman's stolen horse, asked respondents to contact either the owner or 'Mr. Joseph Howe, Spectaclemaker in Threadneedle-street behind the Royal Exchange', a version which suggests that all the references in the Spectaclemakers' Company's records may refer to the same premises.[29] Joseph Howe was succeeded by his son John, and he also trained at least thirteen apprentices, some of whom were later in business on their own account in the vicinity of the Exchange.[30] His best known apprentice was John Rowley, and when the latter was made a Freeman in the Broderers' Company in February 1690 (OS), his address was given as being behind the Exchange, Threadneedle Street, so he was probably still working for Howe. References which are clearly to Rowley as an independent master in his own right give his address as being 'under St Dunstan's Church, near Temple Bar'. Rowley also appears to have offered a much wider range of goods for sale than his master. Whereas Howe was generally referred to as a spectaclemaker, and only made optical instruments, Rowley, while advertising himself as a mathematical instrument-maker, also supplied globes, orreries and telescopes.[31]

Joseph Howe had registered his earliest apprentices with the Spectaclemakers' Company, the first being William Longland in 1667. Apart from Rowley, those who went on to have their own shops traded as optical instrument-makers. Longland is recorded in searches by the Company in the 1690s in Cornhill, and a number of telescopes survive bearing the stamp 'Made by Will Longland at the ship in Cornhill London'.[32] Another apprentice, Thomas Gay, took premises even closer to his former master's, apparently in competition with Joseph Howe's son, John. Gay had been made a Freeman of the Spectaclemakers' Company in 1689 (OS), and in 1714 an advertisement gave his address as being 'at the Archimedes and Spectacles, near the Sun Tavern, behind the Royal Exchange London'. Besides spectacles, his stock included microscopes, telescopes, burning glasses and prisms.[33] Longland and Gay both trained several apprentices, and in each case one of them eventually had his own shop near the Exchange. Gay's apprentice, Matthew Loft, evidently succeeded to his master's business in about 1723, since the trade label pasted in the boxes of instruments he sold gave his address as 'the Golden Spectacles the Backside of the Royal Exchange' (Fig. 89).[34] Longland's apprentice, Thomas Brown(e), took a shop in the Exchange itself, advertising himself in the *Weekly Journal* of 1 July 1721 as a 'spectacle maker, at the Archimedes, west passage Royal Exchange'.[35]

The school of optical instrument-makers in and around the Royal Exchange, which could be traced back to Joseph Howe in the 1670s, continued by master-apprentice links throughout the eighteenth and into the nineteenth century. One of Matthew

[29] GL, Spectaclemakers' Company, Court Minutes, vol. 1, MS 5213/1, 3 August 1671, 28 July 1676, 4 October 1693, 27 June 1695; *London Gazette*, 30 July 1691 (I am grateful to the late Mr M. Crawforth for this reference).

[30] GL, Spectaclemakers' Company, Court Minutes vol. 1, MS 5213/1, generally; vol. 2, MS 5213/2, p. 5; Register of apprentice bindings, vol. 1, MS 6031/1; Broderers' Company, Court Minutes, vol. 1, MS 14657/1, 3 February 1681 (OS), 23 November 1682. (I am grateful to the late Mr M. Crawforth for this and subsequent references to the Broderers' Company.) See also Clifton, op. cit., p. 142.

[31] GL, Broderers' Company, Court Minutes, vol. 1, MS 14657/1, 26 February 1690 (OS); J. A. Bennett, *The Whipple Museum of the History of Science, catalogue 3, Astronomy & Navigation* (Cambridge, 1983), no. 20; Bryden, op. cit., pp. 319–21.

[32] GL, Spectaclemakers' Company, Court Minutes, vol. 1, MS 5213/1, 27 June 1667; *An inventory of the navigation and astronomy collections in the National Maritime Museum Greenwich* (London, 1971), section 32, p. 5. There is another telescope by Longland at the Museum of the History of Science, Oxford.

[33] GL, Spectaclemakers' Company, Court Minutes, vol. 1, MS 5213/1, 4 October 1682, 9 January 1689 (OS); F. Moore, *Vox Stellarum, Being an Almanack for ... 1714* (London, 1714), sig. C8v (I am grateful to D. J. Bryden for this reference).

[34] GL, Spectaclemakers' Company, Court Minutes, vol. 2, MS 5213/2, pp. 145–46; W. I. Cumiford, 'The Henze Collection of European Scientific Instruments', in *Bulletin of the Scientific Instrument Society*, No. 28 (March 1991), p. 17.

[35] Quoted in F. Buckley, 'Old English Glass. Optical Glasses', *Glass*, vol. 12 (1935), p. 428.

FIG. 89.   The label used by Matthew Loft (*c.* 1697–1747), optical instrument-maker, in the boxes of instruments he supplied.

Reproduced courtesy of the Trustees of the National Maritime Museum, Greenwich

Loft's apprentices was Edward Nairne, who succeeded to his master's business and became a leading maker of the second half of the eighteenth century, supplying mathematical and philosophical as well as optical instruments. He made a level for the Royal Observatory at Greenwich in 1772, several instruments for James Cook's second voyage of 1772–75, and supplied globes to Christ's Hospital School in 1774.[36] He had at least eleven apprentices between 1749 and 1788, three of whom went on to establish businesses in or near the Royal Exchange. James Long was apprenticed to Nairne in 1769, and by 1781 was trading as an optician at the Royal Exchange, where he remained until his death in 1811, when his address was 4 North Side.[37] Another of Nairne's apprentices was John Field, who was in business in the 1790s as an optician, mathematical and philosophical instrument-maker, at 74 Cornhill. But probably the best known instrument-maker trained by Nairne was Thomas Blunt, who was in partnership with his master between 1774 and 1793. Although primarily instrument-makers, Nairne and

Blunt also advertised that they supplied maps, charts and navigation books, suggesting that, like some of the booksellers around the Exchange, they found it worth while to offer the full range of aids likely to be required by master mariners. In 1785 both partners received a royal appointment from George III.[38] When the partnership ended in 1793 both men continued in business in Cornhill, Nairne at No. 20, and Blunt at No. 22. By 1795 Nairne and his apprentices made up four of the five optical, mathematical and philosophical instrument-makers trading around the Exchange. The fifth was Thomas Ribright, an optician at 40 Poultry, who, like Nairne and his apprentices, was a Freeman of the Spectaclemakers' Company.[39] Thomas Blunt and his sons, Thomas and Edward, carried on the business at 22 Cornhill until the 1820s. The death of Edward in 1826 marked the end of the chain of masters and apprentices going back to the seventeenth century, but there continued to be instrument-makers' shops in the area around the Exchange throughout the nineteenth century. The Bate and Potter businesses have already been noted, and William Harris took over at 22 Cornhill in the 1830s. Joseph Smith traded as an optician at the North Gate of the Royal Exchange from about 1811 to the mid-1820s, probably as successor to James Long. Stephen Bithray, optician and mathematical instrument-maker, was at 4 North Piazza in the Exchange from 1826 to 1838, moving to Finch Lane during the rebuilding, returning to 29 Royal Exchange from 1844 to about 1860. One of the leading firms of opticians, R. & J. Beck, noted particularly for their microscopes, were at 31 and then 68 Cornhill from the 1870s until the end of the century.[40]

The area around the Exchange attracted others who were not instrument-makers in the strict sense,

[36] GL, Spectaclemakers' Company, Court Minutes, vol. 3, MS 5213/3, p. 123; Christ's Hospital, ledger, vol. 6, MS 12823/6, p. 330; *General Advertiser*, 10 February 1752; J. R. Millburn, 'The Office of Ordnance and the Instrument-Making Trade in the Mid-Eighteenth Century', in *Annals of Science*, vol. 45 (1988), p. 276; E. G. R. Taylor, *The Mathematical Practitioners of Hanoverian England 1714–1840* (Cambridge, 1966), p. 214.

[37] GL, Spectaclemakers' Company, Registers of Apprentice Bindings, MS 6031/1, MS 6032; Court Minutes, vol. 3, MS 5213/3, 3 October 1781; vol. 4, MS 5213/4, 26 December 1811; *Holden's Annual London and Country Directory* (London, 1811).

[38] GL, Spectaclemakers' Company, Court Minutes, MS 5213/2, 27 June 1771. Millburn, op. cit. (note 30), p. 276; G. L'E. Turner, 'The number code on reflecting telescopes by Nairne and Blunt', *Journal for the History of Astronomy*, vol. 10 (1979), p. 180. Photocopy at National Maritime Museum of a Nairne & Blunt Catalogue in a private collection. Lord Chancellor's records of Royal Appointments at PRO, LC3/67, p. 178.

[39] Guildhall Library, London: Spectaclemakers' Company, Court Minutes, MS 5213/3, 5 October 1775; W. Lowndes, *The London directory* (London, 1794 and 1796 editions).

[40] *Post Office London Directories.*

FIG. 90. Trade-card of Henry Neale,
scale-maker, dating from about 1700.
*Reproduced courtesy of the Trustees of the National
Maritime Museum, Greenwich*

FIG. 91. Trade-card of Charles
Sommers, scale-maker, dating from
between 1765 and 1777.
*Reproduced courtesy of the Trustees of the National
Maritime Museum, Greenwich*

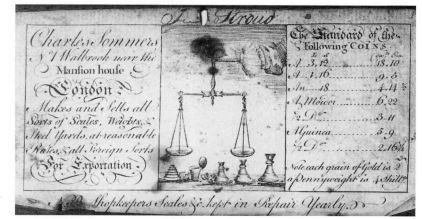

but who made closely related products. These included scale-makers, whose best balances were precision measuring devices, and chronometer-makers, whose products became part of the standard navigational equipment of ocean-going ships during the nineteenth century. Scale-making in the area around the Exchange can be traced back to the late seventeenth century, when Henry Neale was at the 'Corner of St Bartholomew Lane near the Royall Exchange' (Fig. 90). Thereafter there was a series of scale-makers' shops in Bartholomew Lane, including Timothy Roberts' and his son Richard's, from the beginning until the middle of the eighteenth century. Walter Phillips, who was active in the 1710s, had his shop at the Angel and Scales in Bartholomew Lane, and was succeeded in the 1720s by Thomas Overing. All these scale-makers were Freemen of the Black-smiths' Company. Another family of scale-makers, Joseph Sommers and his son Charles, were Freemen of the Skinners' Company and had their shop at the

'Corner of Bucklersbury against ye West side of ye Mansion House' in 1758.[41] By 1765 the street had been numbered and they were at 1 Walbrook. The firm advertised scales and weights, specifically including 'all Foreign Sorts For Exportation' (Fig. 91).

After John Harrison had invented an effective marine time-keeper, or chronometer, which was successfully tested in 1764, it was left to other watch-makers to develop commercially viable production. Among the most important pioneers were John Arnold, and his son John Roger, whose shop was in Cornhill. J. R. Arnold had moved to the Strand by 1815, but two other clock-making families continued to make chronometers in the vicinity of the Royal Exchange. Paul Philip Barraud and his sons and successors traded at various addresses in Cornhill until the 1890s, while William James Frodsham and

[41] GL, Blacksmiths' Company, Court Minutes, MS 2881/8–2881/11; Skinners' Hall, London: registers of apprentices and freemen; Clifton, op. cit., pp. 197, 234, 259.

his son Charles were in Change Alley in the 1830s. There were obvious commercial advantages in shops supplying chronometers being close to those of the chart sellers and nautical instrument-makers.

The Royal Exchange, by providing a meeting place for merchants, also attracted other dealers and craftsmen who supplied goods likely to be needed by those engaged in overseas trade. Although the area around the Exchange was never the most important district for instrument-making, it nevertheless attracted a number of the leading makers. However, there was a tendency for makers to move westward towards the Court, and the more fashionable residential districts, as they became more successful, particularly from the eighteenth century onwards. John Senex, the map- and globe-maker, moved to Fleet Street in 1710. Philip Lea, who began with a shop in Poultry, moved only a short distance to Cheapside, but his widow and successor transferred the business to Fleet Street by 1720, with her partner, Richard Glynne. The optician Thomas Ribright had premises in Poultry in the 1790s, but by 1802 he was at 20 Gloucester Street, Queen's Square, on the borders of Holborn and Bloomsbury. John Roger Arnold's move to the Strand has already been noted. In the mid-1820s, the optician Joseph Smith moved from the Exchange to Tottenham Court Road, and then to the New Road, now Euston Road.[42] In many ways instrument-making around the Exchange was a microcosm of the wider London trade. The tendency from around 1700 for successful retailers to stock a full range of mathematical, optical and philosophical instruments, whatever their own particular skill, was repeated elsewhere in the capital. Similar examples from other districts could be quoted of the importance of schools of instrument-makers created by the passing on of skills from master to apprentice. However, the combining of instrument-selling with the production of maps, globes and charts, does seem to have been a particular feature of the area around the Exchange. It is a good example of the way in which the character of a particular locality influenced the priorities of other local traders, just as the presence of the Royal Society's Rooms in Crane Court, Fleet Street, from 1710, encouraged instrument-makers to move to that area, and to concentrate on the astronomical, mathematical and philosophical pieces likely to appeal to Fellows and their associates.

[42] Tyacke, op. cit., pp. 120–22, 142; *Kent's Directories. Post Office London Directories.*

CHAPTER XXIII

Tokens of the Royal Exchange

By ROBERT H. THOMPSON

THIS CHAPTER IS CONCERNED with certain tokens of the mid-seventeenth, late eighteenth, and early nineteenth century on which appear representations of one of the buildings of the Exchange. Not all of them have been recognised hitherto as representing the Exchange, and some even have not been recognised as buildings. Their number and distribution is some sort of testimony to the symbolic importance of the Royal Exchange in the commercial life not only of London but of England and beyond.

As a preliminary, however, some pieces which might be expected amongst the tokens of the Royal Exchange need to be mentioned. Cast lead discs found on the site of the Exchange, bearing the Tudor royal arms and the legends ANGLIAE REGINA VBIQVE HONORATA or HONI SOEIT(!) QVI MAL Y PENSE, were published by Roach Smith as tokens or merchants' tickets commemorating the visit of Elizabeth I to Gresham's new building.[1] These are now seen, however, to be a class of German(?) merchants' seals intended for English cloths.[2] As such they have no essential connection with the Exchange, neither are they tokens. Omitted also is a mid nineteenth-century public house token-cum-medalet, which will be found in the chapter on medals (see Chapter XXX).

A. TOKENS OF 1651–69[3]

Arrangement is by places of issue, in order of their distance from the Exchange. Appropriately, the most dramatic representation occurs on the other side of Cornhill from the Exchange itself, in the alley which led towards it. Whereas an engraved source can be found for most of the representations on tokens, for example, the anonymous *Inside of the Royal Exchange as before the Fire* (Thompson, Fig. 1), for the view on A1 no drawing has been traced.

---

[1] Charles Roach Smith, *Catalogue of the Museum of London Antiquities* (London, 1854), p. 159, no. 777; Edward Hawkins, *Medallic Illustrations of the History of Great Britain and Ireland to the Death of George II*, 2 vols. (London, 1885), I, pp. 115–16; British Museum, Department of Coins and Medals, *Medallic Illustrations of the History of Great Britain and Ireland* (London, 1904–11), pl. vii, fig. 17.

[2] Geoff Egan, *Lead Cloth Seals and related items in the British Museum* (London, 1994), pp. 121–22 and fig. 46.

[3] References cited frequently in this section are as follows: John Yonge Akerman, *Tradesmen's Tokens current in London and its Vicinity between the years 1648 and 1672 . . .* (London, 1849); Jacob Henry Burn, *A Descriptive Catalogue of the London Traders, Tavern, and Coffee-house Tokens current in the Seventeenth Century . . .*, 2nd edn (London, 1855); William Boyne, *Tokens issued in the Seventeenth Century in England, Wales and Ireland . . .* (London, 1858); George C. Williamson, *Trade Tokens issued in the Seventeenth Century in England, Wales and Ireland . . .*, 2 vols. (London, 1889–91); R. H. Thompson, 'The Royal Exchange on seventeenth-century tokens', *Spink Numismatic Circular*, 101 (1993), pp. 78–80.

A1.   Change Alley: Stanley, Arthur: 1666 ½d.

Obverse: ·AVRTHOR·STANLEY·· around HIS|HALFE|PENNY ···

Reverse: ·IN·EXCHAINGE·ALLEY· 1666 around a view through two arches, bell-tower at left of facing range.

Literature: Akerman 639 (but reading AVTHOR, EXCHANGE, 1667); Burn 440 (but reading AVRTHVR); Boyne, London 772 and pl. 19, fig. 5; Williamson, London 962 (but reading PENY); Berry,[4] p. 62; Thompson, fig. 8.

Neither Arthur Stanley's trade nor his house is named, but there was a New Exchange tavern 'over against the Change' which Pepys visited on 17 November 1663, 'and I find my old playfellow Ben Stanly master of it'.[5]

The other tokens which are located by their legends in relation to the Exchange, or to Change Alley, may be listed briefly, with 'London' omitted from the Williamson references. All are undated. Several bear the device of a triangle of initials, in which the initial of the issuer's surname normally stood above those of his forename and his wife's, an example below being the Ship Tavern behind the Exchange, on which Y above C W can be expanded as Young, Charles and Winifred.[6] Thomas Corden's sign of the Grasshopper was a 'descendant' of those on the Exchange.[7]

Back side of the Royal Exchange

Globe Coffee House: [s.n.] (Williamson 969; Robinson,[8] p. 231).

Behind the Exchange [*i.e.* Threadneedle Street]

Antwerp Tavern: T[aylor], P[eter], T|PA (Williamson 963; Rogers, p. 74).

Globe Tavern: E., W. (Gilbert 127; Dickinson 960A);[9]

—W[illson?], S., W|SM (Dickinson 963A, cf. Rogers, p. 75).

Half Moon: H., T., H|TI (Williamson 961; Berry, p. 60).

[King's Head]: Browning, Tho., B|TS (Williamson 958, citing *The Newes*, 8 Dec. 1664, p. 786).

Ship Tavern: Y[oung], C[harles], Y|CW (Williamson 964 and note; Rogers, p. 75; Berry, p. 111).

Sun Tavern: C[olborne], N[icholas], C|NA (Williamson 959; Rogers, p. 74; Berry, p. 62).

Behind the Royal Exchange [therefore post-Restoration][10]

Towers, Sam: 2*d.* token, leather (Williamson, appendix A.14).

Grasshopper: Corden, Thomas, C|TA (Williamson 960).

Change Alley

Morat Coffee House: [s.n.] (Boyne 774–77 and pl. 19, figs. 6–7; Williamson 965–68; Robinson, p. 232 and fig. 2; Berry, p. 121).

---

[4] George Berry, *Taverns and Tokens of Pepys' London* (London, 1978).

[5] Samuel Pepys, *Diary*, ed. Robert Latham and William Matthews, 11 vols. (London, 1970–83), IV, p. 384.

[6] K. Rogers, 'On some issuers of seventeenth-century London tokens whose names were not known to Boyne and Williamson', *Numismatic Chronicle*, 5th ser., 8 (1928), pp. 61–97; addenda, p. 338. It has been suggested that with a triangle of initials the wife, too, accepted some responsibility for exchanging quantities of their small change; but there are too many cases in which three initials are accompanied by the legend HIS half-penny.

[7] Jacob Larwood and John Camden Hotten, *English Inn Signs* (London, 1951), p. 83.

[8] Edward Forbes Robinson, *The Early History of Coffee Houses in England* (London, 1893).

[9] W. Gilbert, 'Unpublished seventeenth-century tokens in the collection of William Gilbert', *Numismatic Chronicle*, 5th ser., 7 (1927), pp. 121–55, 342–69, pls. 6–7, 15; Michael Dickinson, *Seventeenth-century Tokens of the British Isles and their Values* (London, 1986).

[10] During the Interregnum the building was called the *Great Exchange*. Ian Doolittle, *The Mercers' Company 1579–1959* (London, 1994), p. 71.

A2.   Poultry, Exchange Tavern: K[ing], W[illiam]: 1651 [¼*d.*]

Obverse: THE·EXCHANGE·TAVERN around an interior view, bell-tower at centre of facing range.

Reverse: ·IN·THE·POVLTREY·1651 around W·K

Literature: Akerman 1534 (but reading W·V); Burn 915 (but reading POVLTRY·1671, and describing the view as the second building); Boyne, London 1832; Williamson, London 2277 (but restoring Burn's note which is irrelevant to a token dated 1651); Thompson, fig. 4.

In this view of three sides of the quadrangle there is an attempt to indicate the dormer windows in the roof, and the balconies on the bell-tower, but not the grasshoppers. The courtyard, which was paved with 'Turkey stones' and not cobbled, must be filled with the heads of a throng of merchants, as in Hollar's 1644 engraving. The issuer, identified on the token only by initials, was mentioned in F[rancis] K[irkman], *The Counterfeit Lady unveiled* (1673, 1679),

in connection with the arrival in 1663 of Mary Moders, alias Stedman, as the German princess, at 'the Exchange tavern, right against the Stocks, betwixt the Poultry and Cornhill, at five in the morning; Mr King being up, and standing at the bar telling of brass farthings'. This is one of the few contemporary references, outside corporation records, to individual tokens.

A3. Poultry, Exchange Tavern: [King, William?]: 1668 ½d.
Obverse: THE·EXCHANGE·TAVERN around an interior view, bell-tower at centre of facing range.
Reverse: ·IN·THE·POVLTREY·1668 around HIS|HALF|PENY
Literature: Akerman 1535 (but identifying the view as the façade of the second building), and fig. 48; Boyne, London 1831; Williamson, London 2276; Thompson, fig. 3.

This more elaborate version of A2 adds four grasshoppers above the roof and one of the two balconied galleries on the bell-tower (though not the clock), but the grasshopper at its summit has mistakenly become a cock. The issuer is unnamed, but Mr King returned after the Great Fire, for John Oliver 'sett out one

Foundac'on Feb: 28th 1667 for Mr Will: Kinge which was the Exchange in the Poultrey'. Oliver's plan adds Exchange 'Taverne'.[11]

[11] Peter Mills and John Oliver, *The Survey of Building Sites in the City of London after the Great Fire of 1666*, 5 vols. (London, 1962–67), IV, f. 16v.

A4. Fenchurch Street, Exchange: Morris, John: undated ½d.
Obverse: ·IOHN·MORRIS·AT·EXCHENG around an interior view, bell-tower at centre of facing range.
Reverse: ·IN·FANCHVRCH·STREET around HIS|HALF|PENY
Literature: Akerman 654; Boyne, London 794; Williamson, London 991; Thompson, fig. 2.

The bell-tower emerges from behind the roof-line, so this is not an exterior view of the whole building, as the straight sides might have suggested. Visible are

dormer windows in the roof, a grasshopper at either end, and the grasshopper at the top of the tower.

A5. Thames Street: Blake, Edward: undated [¼d.]
Obverse: ·EDWARD·BLAKE·IN· around an interior view, bell-tower at centre of facing range.
Reverse: ·THAMES·STREETE· around ·B·|E·H|·
Literature: Williamson, London 3083 (but describing the view as 'Fortress or ship with men'); Thompson, fig. 5.

This view is somewhat crude, but still clearly shows three sides of the building around a courtyard filled with heads. In the upper storey there is an attempt to show the round-headed niches in which were set royal statues, although they more closely resemble portholes, whence Williamson's description of the device as a ship.

A6.   Bury St Edmunds: Stanard, George: undated [$\frac{1}{4}d$.]
Obverse: ·GEORGE·STANARD·IN· around an arcaded building, above the centre of the roof a tower which perhaps incorporates a clock-face, initial mark a cinquefoil.
Reverse: ·s^T EDMONDS·BVRY· around ···|G·s|···, initial mark a cinquefoil.
Literature: Boyne, Suffolk 63 and pl. 28, fig. 8; Golding 72 and pl. 3, fig. 8; Williamson, Suffolk 77 (all give the reading ST); Sylloge 46, no. 4291.[12]

[12] Charles Golding, *The Coinage of Suffolk . . .* (London, 1868); R. H. Thompson and M. J. Dickinson, *Sylloge of Coins of the British Isles, 46: the Norweb Collection, Cleveland, Ohio, U.S.A.: Tokens of the British Isles, 1575–1750, Part V: Staffordshire to Westmorland* (London, 1996).

Boyne, Golding, and Williamson describe the obverse field as 'A view of a market-house'; see A8 below.

A7.   similar to A6, but initial mark on both sides a mullet
Literature: Fitch,[13] pl. xvi, fig. 7; Golding 73; Williamson, Suffolk 78; Sylloge 46, no. 4292.

[13] W. S. Fitch, *One Hundred and Seventy Suffolk Tradesmen's Tokens* (Lowestoft, [186–?]).

A8.   Bury St Edmunds: Stanard, George: 1667 [$\frac{1}{4}d$.]
Obverse: ·GEORGE·STANARD·1667 around a building.
Reverse: ·IN·s^T EDMONDS·BVREY around G·S
Literature: Golding 74; Williamson, Suffolk 79 (both give the reading ST).

Golding (copied by Williamson) described the building as the Market-House: 'This Token gives a correct view of the old Market Cross, as it then existed. A fine view of it is engraved on a scarce plan of the Town, by Alexander Downing, 1740, and published 1761'.[14]

The Market Cross, however, was a timber building of three storeys with a gabled roof and a portico at ground-floor level only. It was built soon after a fire in Bury St Edmunds in 1608; cased in stone from 1774, when it became the New Theatre (and subsequently the Concert Room), the main beams of the timber building were believed to have been found in the early 1970s when the building was altered to become the Art Gallery.[15]

No other similar building with a tower existed in Bury St Edmunds by 1667 (for the undated tokens can be taken to have preceded the dated). Comparison with A4 in particular (AT EXCHENG) leads to the conclusion that George Stanard's tokens are attempting to portray the Royal Exchange in London. The ground-floor and first-floor columns have been merged, but his tokens have the central bell-tower, straight roof-line, and even a hint of grasshoppers at either end.

The will of George Stannard of Bury St Edmunds, 'millener', was proved in 1670 in the Prerogative

[14] Golding (above, note 12), pp. 38–39. There is a framed copy of Downing's plan on the stairs of Moyse's Hall Museum in Bury St Edmunds, and the view of the building is reproduced in Margaret Statham, *The Book of Bury St Edmunds* (Buckingham, 1988), p. 92.

[15] Statham (above, note 14), pp. 89, 92, 94, 128.

Court of Canterbury.[16] In the Hearth Tax return for 1670 Jo. Stannard and Phill. Stannard appear, bracketed together with a total of no fewer than nineteen hearths.[17]

[16] Prerogative Court of Canterbury, *Wills, Sentences and Probate Acts, 1661–1670 (inclusive)*; arranged ... by J. H. Morrison (London, 1935), p. 231.

[17] S. H. A. H[ervey], *Suffolk in 1674, being the Hearth Tax Returns* (Woodbridge, 1905), p. 56.

A9. West Cowes, Royal Exchange: Warlaw's, John: 1668 $\frac{1}{2}$d.

Obverse: ·IOHN·WARLAWS·AT:ROYAL around an interior view, bell-tower at centre of facing range.

Reverse: ·EXCHANG·IN·WEST·COWES around HIS|HALF|PENY| 1668

Literature: Wetton, *IoW*, p. [7] and pl. [1], 'Warlaws'; Wetton, *Hants*, Cowes 6 and pl. 6, fig. D (but reverse inverted);[18] Dickinson, Hampshire 59A.

Wetton commented in 1962, 'There is apparently no present knowledge of the whereabouts of the Royal Exchange at Cowes'. One suspects that an actual exchange had been sought. Subsequently he added, 'It may have been an inn or a coffee house',[19] although this overlooks the extent to which signs were used by tradesmen other than innkeepers. From A8 and A10 appears the possibility of a milliner's warehouse but, whatever the issuer's occupation, his token gives a recognisable representation of the arcades of the Royal Exchange, thronging heads before, niches above, and only the roof wrong, with dormers and bell-tower but no roof-line. His surname is perhaps a form of Wardlaw with apostrophe 's'; the only similar name in the Hearth Tax return for West Cowes is 'Mr Warley' with six hearths in 1673, but this may not be the right man since he appears as 'Mr Worsley' in 1674.[20]

[18] J. L. Wetton, *The Isle of Wight Seventeenth-century Traders' Tokens* (Lymington, [1962]); J. L. Wetton, *The Hampshire Seventeenth-century Traders' Tokens* (Lymington, 1964).

[19] Wetton (above, note 18), *Isle of Wight*, p. [7], n. 3; *Hampshire*, p. 14.

[20] P. D. D. Russell, *Hearth Tax Returns for the Isle of Wight, 1664 to 1674* ([Newport, IoW], 1981), pp. 157, 178.

A10. Great Yarmouth: Crafford, Richard: [16]59 [$\frac{1}{4}$d.]

Obverse: ·RICHARD·CRAFFORD around an interior view, remnant of bell-tower at centre of facing range.

Reverse: ·IN·YEARMOVTH·59 around ·C·|R·D

Literature: Ewing, p. 194; Boyne, Norfolk 237 and pl. 23, fig. 11 (but reading CRATFORD); Tillett, p. 39, no. 287; Williamson, Norfolk 312; Thompson, fig. 6; Sylloge 44, no. 3325.[21]

Ewing described the device as 'A Garden', Boyne as 'Yarmouth Market-place', and Tillett, whom Williamson would copy, as 'A teasel':

The device upon this token has been supposed by some to represent Yarmouth Market-place, and by others a dock for the repair of ships. On close examination it will be seen to be a flower, as the stalk clearly appears. The teasel or fullers' thistle is a plant the heads or burs of which are employed in dressing woollen cloth.

This 'flower' is on its 'stalk' only if the obverse is placed with the start of the legend at about the seven o'clock position, a most unusual occurrence. Nevertheless, Richard Crafford has masqueraded ever since under the sign of the Teasel.

In fact the two dies which struck this token were sunk not only from individual letter punches, as were all other tokens described here, but also from a separate pictorial punch for the main obverse device. This was actually the same punch as for A2 (THE

[21] [William Creasy Ewing], *Norfolk Lists from the Reformation to the Present Time ...* (Norwich, 1837); Edward A. Tillett, *The Tokens of Norfolk ...* (Norwich, 1882); R. H. Thompson and M. J. Dickinson, *Sylloge of Coins of the British Isles, 44: the Norweb Collection, Cleveland, Ohio, U.S.A.: Tokens of the British Isles, 1575–1750, Part IV: Norfolk to Somerset* (London, 1993).

EXCHANGE TAVERN, 1651). Survival of such a punch for eight years is not unprecedented, even for more heavily used punches. The only difference from A2 is in the bell-tower, which has been reduced to a stump; although the lack of use of the punch otherwise, and the extent to which such a projection would have been vulnerable to damage, suggest that the bell-tower may not have formed part of the punch, but that it was engraved on the die of A2.

The name Crafford is from Crayford (Kent), and the distribution of the surnames Crayford, Crayfourd, Crafford and Craford does indeed centre on the Medway area, with a scatter in East Anglia.[22] Richard

Craford was admitted a freeman of Great Yarmouth in 1661 by purchase, and his son Michael in 1678 by apprenticeship to his father.[23] No trade is there mentioned, but Richard Craford of Great Yarmouth described himself as 'Milliner' in his will dated 23 April 1675 and proved 12 March 1676[-7].[24] He named as executrix his wife Dorothy, whence the D on the token.

[22] G. W. Lasker and C. G. N. Mascie-Taylor, *Atlas of British Surnames . . .* (Detroit, 1990), fig. 32.

[23] Norfolk and Norwich Archaeological Society, *A Calendar of the Freemen of Great Yarmouth, 1429–1800* (Norwich, 1910), pp. 93, 113.
[24] Norfolk Record Office, Archdeaconry of Norwich wills and administrations, 1676–77, ff. 226–28 (MF 306). I am grateful to Miss Jean Kennedy, Norfolk County Archivist, for finding this mention of his trade.

A11. Ludlow: Haughton, George: 1666 $\frac{1}{2}d$.

Obverse: ·GEORGE·HAVGHTON around a view through arches of a facing range, tower above.

Reverse: ·IN·LVDLOW·1666·· around HIS|HALF|PENY|···

Literature: Keary,[25] 369; Williamson, Shropshire 31; Thompson, fig. 9; Sylloge 44, no. 3895.

Keary described the obverse as 'Ludlow Castle', Williamson simply as 'A castle'; perhaps his subeditor, James W. Lloyd of Kington, had failed to identify the device with any view of Ludlow Castle. Indeed, it is difficult to identify any castle in the device. The 'windows' are too wide to be properly defensive; the structure is so open that arches opposite are directly visible; and the roof-line is odd, with

[25] C. F. Keary and Warwick Wroth, 'Seventeenth-century tokens in the British Museum not described in Boyne's work', *Numismatic Chronicle*, 3rd ser., 4 (1884), pp. 281–342.

bird-like shapes on top of the central tower and the four 'turrets'. The issuer is the same as for A12, and the device may be expected to be the same also, at least in name. The devices can indeed be reconciled if the 'birds' are grasshoppers, and the 'turrets' dormer windows. The tower will be the bell-tower of the Exchange. The view through arches, and the shape of the arches, are not unlike those on A1. The separate elements of the Royal Exchange do seem to be present, although the perspective is quite incompetent, with the roof opposite appearing above instead of through the arches in the foreground.

A12. Ludlow: Haughton, George, mercer: 1669 $\frac{1}{2}d$.

Obverse: ·GEORGE·HAVGHTON·MERCER around HIS|HALFE|PENY

Reverse: ·IN·LVDLOV·1669 around an interior view, bell-tower at left of facing range.

Literature: Boyne, Shropshire 23 (but reading LVDLOW) and pl. 26, fig. 10; Williamson, Shropshire 32; Lloyd 55;[26] Thompson, fig. 7; Sylloge 44, no. 3896.

Boyne and Williamson were defeated by this reverse device, describing it merely as 'An uncertain object'. Subsequent cataloguers attempted identifications ranging from 'possibly a fire-grate', through a 'water-gate?', to 'the object is a castle', this last doubtless influenced by the description of A11.[27] Clear on the specimen illustrated, however, is a gabled tower with

[26] J. W. Lloyd, 'Tokens', in *Catalogue of the Loan Exhibition of Shropshire Antiquities, Music Hall Buildings, Shrewsbury, May 10–21 1898*, Shropshire Archaeological Society, compiled and arranged by H. R. H. Southam (Shrewsbury, 1898), pp. 98–100.
[27] Glendining & Co., *Catalogue ... 16th ... 17th November 1977 ...* (London, 1977), lot 536; Norweb envelope; Spink Coin Auctions, *Sale no. 7 ... 5 December 1979* (London, 1979), lot 111.

a circular dial and a bird(!) above. Given the columns, and the angled structure enclosing what could be heads, the device can be taken for a view of the Royal Exchange, though wildly out of perspective. The Royal Exchange provides a common identity for the device on the two types of token of George Haughton in Ludlow, whose sign both are likely to have represented. In his will proved in 1694, as on his 1669 token, George Houghton of Ludlow was described as a mercer, a trade closely connected with the Exchange.[28]

[28] Prerogative Court of Canterbury, *Index to Wills ... Vol. 12: 1694–1700*, ed. Marc Fitch (London, 1960), p. 209.

A13. Waterford: Exton, Thomas, vintner: undated 1d.
Obverse: ·THO·EXTON·IN around an interior view, remnant of bell-tower at centre of facing range.
Reverse: ·WATERFORD·VINTNER around ·I·ᴰbetween T·E.
Literature: Green; Smith 525; Boyne, Ireland 572; Williamson, Ireland 731; Macalister 487.[29]

In the *Gentleman's Magazine* of 1786 'M. Green' (John Nichols) simply illustrated this as 'an uncommon trader's token'; Aquilla Smith omitted devices where there was a legend to transcribe; Boyne and Williamson described the device as 'A market-place'; while Macalister expanded it to 'a colonnaded market square'. Comparison with A2 and A10 in particular reveals its true identity as a representation of the Royal Exchange.

B. TOKENS OF 1796

A second wave of tokens began in 1787 in the industrial areas of the country. The various issuers naturally employed a variety of types, which created such interest that by 1795 there was a 'universal rage of collecting Coins'.[30] One consequence was the creation of types specifically intended for collectors, among them several series of architectural types published by the Birmingham medallist Peter Kempson. One of his series illustrated London buildings, paired either with a reverse die reading LONDON PENNY TOKEN, or with an otherwise similar die reading LONDON PROMISSORY PENNY TOKEN. A contemporary observer commented:[31]

[29] M. Green (i.e. John Nichols), 'Another uncommon trader's token', *Gentleman's Magazine*, 56 (1786), 825 and pl. 2, fig. 10; Aquilla Smith, 'Catalogue of the tradesmen's tokens current in Ireland between the years 1637 and 1679', *Proceedings of the Royal Irish Academy*, 4 (1847/50), p. 345 and Appendix No. 4, pp. xxvii–xlix; R. A. S. Macalister, 'A catalogue of the Irish traders' tokens in the collection of the Royal Irish Academy', ibid., Section C, 40 no. 2 (1931), pp. 19–185.
[30] T. Spence, *The Coin Collector's Companion ...*, 1st issue (London, 1795), p. [52], 'To the public'.
[31] Civis (i.e. James Wright), 'Observations on the genuine and forged Provincial Coins', *Gentleman's Magazine*, 67 part 1 (1797), pp. 31–34; letter dated 22 October 1796.

As to the undue expence of collecting such pieces as have got exclusively into the hands of the dealers, this must be chiefly confined to the purchase of such pieces as have been merely struck, for a limited sale to collectors, as medals or jettons, and never intended for circulation, or the use of tradesmen; such as . . . the London penny token, lately issued, bearing buildings, &c.

Only the Royal Exchange obverse, described below, occurs with both reverses, so tying together the two groups of dies, and making it likely that they were all produced at about the same time. Of all these linked dies only an obverse of the Guildhall bears what must be the date of issue, MDCCXCVI.

Another consequence of the rage for collecting was the publication of catalogues, both typographic and copperplate, while the tokens were still being produced. It is a copperplate dated 13 October 1796 which provides the first published record of the obverse illustrating the Royal Exchange. So it is that this undated token can be assigned to 1796.

B1. [Birmingham]:   [Kempson, Peter]:   [1796] London 1*d*.
Obverse: ROYAL EXCHANGE ERECT ^D 1669 around exterior view, bell-tower to right.
Reverse: LONDON PENNY TOKEN ·:· around the arms of the City of London within palm branches.
Literature: Denton, p. 132, 13 October 1796; Conder, Middlesex 37; Samuel, eighteenth century 779; Atkins, Middlesex 56; Dalton and Hamer, Middlesex 65; Bell, K 92.[32]

The dies were by Thomas and Peter Wyon of Birmingham.[33] The same obverse combined with the reverse reading LONDON PROMISSORY PENNY TOKEN was apparently first published by Sharp,[34] while the standard reference is Dalton and Hamer, Middlesex 45. Davisson[35] has added, as Middlesex 45*Bis*, an impression of the obverse on white metal muled with a reverse reading S^T BARTHOLOMEWS|HOSPITAL around a Gothick-style building, in the exergue REBUILT|1789. This building is in Gloucester (now a shopping centre), and the reverse properly pairs with a die bearing the arms of the city of Gloucester, signed P. KEMPSON FECIT.

C.   TOKENS OF 1811–13[36]

A renewed shortage of coin in the second decade of the nineteenth century stimulated a further wave of tokens, in silver in addition to copper. Only copper tokens, however, bear representations of the Royal Exchange, all of them issued in Staffordshire. The leading issuers were evidently Messrs Rushbury & Woolley of Bilston, with the only such token larger than a penny, and the greatest number of dies, which indicates the largest production. It may be supposed that it was the success of their tokens which led other issuers in the county to copy their device of the Royal Exchange, for it does not appear that the issuers were agents for the Royal Exchange Fire & Life Insurance

---

[32] M. Denton [and T. Prattent], *The Virtuoso's Companion and Coin Collector's Guide*, 8 vols. (London, 1795[–97]); James Conder, *An Arrangement of Provincial Coins . . .* (Ipswich, 1798); Richard Thomas Samuel, *British Tokens: Articles and Notes from 'The Bazaar, Exchange and Mart, and Journal of the Household'*, December 29, 1880 through August 28, 1889 . . . (Cold Spring MN, 1994); James Atkins, *The Tradesmen's Tokens of the Eighteenth Century* (London, 1892); R. Dalton and S. H. Hamer, *The Provincial Token-coinage of the 18th Century illustrated*, 14 parts ([Bristol], 1910–18); R. C. Bell, *The Building Medalets of Kempson and Skidmore, 1796–1797* (Newcastle upon Tyne, 1978).

[33] Thomas Sharp, *A Catalogue of Provincial Copper Coins . . . described from the originals in the collection of Sir George Chetwynd . . .* (London, 1834), p. v; L. Forrer, *Biographical Dictionary of Medallists . . .* , 8 vols. (London, 1904–30), VI, p. 637.

[34] Sharp (above, note 33), p. 16, no. 45.

[35] Allan Davisson, Prefatory update, in *The Provincial Token-coinage of the 18th Century illustrated* (above, note 32), 1st edn reprinted (Cold Spring MN, 1990), pp. [1], i–xxix.

[36] References cited in this section are as follows: Sharp (above, note 33); Josef Neumann, *Beschreibung der bekanntesten Kupfermünzen*, 6 vols. (Prague, 1858–72), IV, pp. 107–17; Samuel (above, note 32); W. J. Davis, *The Nineteenth-century Token Coinage of Great Britain, Ireland, the Channel Islands and the Isle of Man . . .* (London, 1904); E. A. Watkin, 'Staffordshire tokens and their place in the coinage of England', *North Staffordshire Journal of Field Studies*, 1 (1961), pp. 1–25, 2 pls.; R. C. Bell, *Copper Commercial Coins, 1811–1819* (Newcastle upon Tyne, 1964).

Office.[37] The other buildings differ only in detail, and since the same *imago* lies behind all the representations, there is little point here in illustrating more than the main issues of pennies, and the three denominations (twopence, penny, and halfpenny), particularly since work currently in progress will illustrate for the first time the die varieties of the nineteenth-century copper tokens.

[37] This seems unlikely: the fire offices listed for Bilston did not include the Royal Exchange in 1818, nor four years later; by that time Burton upon Trent had acquired a Royal Exchange agent, but his name was Henry Hodson; Wednesbury at that date appears to have had no insurance agents. James Pigot, *The Commercial Directory for 1818–19–20* (Manchester, 1818); Pigot & Co., *London & provincial new commercial directory for 1822–3 ...* (Manchester, s.d.).

C1. Bilston: Rushbury & Woolley: 1811 2*d*.
Obverse: ONE POUND NOTE FOR 120 TOKENS|bust [George III] to right|1811.
Reverse: PAYABLE BY RUSHBURY & WOOLLEY|a building|BILSTON .
Literature: Sharp, p. 191, Staffordshire 1; Neumann 23828; Samuel, nineteenth century 88; Davis, Staffordshire 30–31; Watkin, N.19; Bell, Staffordshire 8.

The dies were by Thomas Halliday of Birmingham. Messrs Rushbury and Woolley were engaged in making a variety of metal and wooden objects, including ornaments for military uniforms, and chafes. In addition to copper tokens for 2*d*. and 1*d*. they issued silver tokens in 1811 for 1*s*. and for 6*d*. After complaints about tokens by Wolverhampton tradesmen a meeting of Bilston tradesmen resolved

That the town and neighbourhood, having derived great advantage from the silver and copper coins issued by ... Messrs Rushbury and Woolley, any attempt to impede the circulation thereof will be impolitic and materially prejudicial to commercial intercourse in the town and neighbourhood.

In 1815 George Rushbury with his son, George junior, went on to issue banknotes for £1 and 10*s*.,

and Corksheets Colliery near Bilston issued a cheque-type note on them.[38] However, they were unable to redeem all their notes, and in November 1815 they were declared bankrupt. The other token issuer, Edward Woolley, was listed in contemporary directories as a locksmith and wood screw maker, and on 18 November 1818 he patented an improvement for making screws. There is a portrait of Woolley in Stafford Central Library.[39]

[38] G. L. Grant, *The Standard Catalogue of Provincial Banks and Banknotes* (London, 1977), pp. 10–11, 124, pl. 4.
[39] Davis (above, note 36), p. 118; James O'Donald Mays, *Tokens of those Trying Times: a Social History of Britain's 19th-century Silver Tokens* (Ringwood, 1991), pp. 121–22.

C2. Bilston: Rushbury & Woolley: 1811 1*d*., obverse only dated
Obverse: ONE POUND NOTE FOR 240 TOKENS|bust [George III] to right|1811.
Reverse: PAYABLE BY RUSHBURY & WOOLLEY|a building|BILSTON
Literature: Sharp, p. 198, Staffordshire 13; Samuel, nineteenth century 96; Davis, Staffordshire 51–55; Watkin, N.26; Bell, Staffordshire 9.

Dies by Halliday. There is also a variety (Davis, Staffordshire 56–57) with a dated reverse similar to the next.

C3.   Bilston: Rushbury & Woolley: 1811 1*d*., reverse only dated
Obverse: ONE POUND NOTE FOR 240 TOKENS|bust [George III] to right.
Reverse: PAYABLE·BY··RUSHBURY··&·WOOLLEY|a building|1811|BILSTON
Literature: Samuel, nineteenth century 97; Davis, Staffordshire 58; Watkin, N.28.

Dies by Halliday. There are also anonymous Bilston pennies which name the ROYAL EXCHANGE, executed by William Turnpenny of Birmingham (Davis, Staffordshire 59), and by Halliday (Davis, Staffordshire 60–71).

C4.   Burton upon Trent: [s.n.]:   undated 1*d*.
Obverse: STAFFORDSHIRE|laureate bust [George III] to right|PENNY TOKEN.
Reverse: PAYABLE AT THE EXCHANGE|a building|BURTON.
Literature: Neumann 23848; Davis, Staffordshire 25; Watkin, N.38.

The dies were by Benjamin Patrick of Birmingham. There are also anonymous Burton mules of dies by Wyon and Turnpenny, and by Halliday and Turnpenny (Davis, Staffordshire 78–80).

C5.   [Wednesbury]:   [Round, Abel]:   1812 1*d*.
Obverse: ONE PENNY TOKEN|bust [George III] to right|1812.
Reverse: FOR PUBLIC ACCOMMODATION|a building|ROYAL EXCHANGE.
Literature: Sharp, p. 200, Staffordshire 43; Neumann 23898; Samuel, nineteenth century 122; Davis, Staffordshire 116; Watkin, N.56; Bell, Staffordshire 25.

Issued anonymously, but according to Thomas Sharp (1770–1841), 'This Token was executed for Abel Round, of Wednesbury, and a very large quantity was issued'. Samuel adds that Abel Round was a maltster and victualler. The dies were by Turnpenny, according to Sharp; Davis attributes them to Halliday.

C6. [Wednesbury]: [Round, Abel]: 1812 ½d.
Obverse: HALF PENNY TOKEN|bust [George III] to right|1812.
Reverse: FOR PUBLIC ACCOMMODATION|a building|ROYAL EXCHANGE.
Literature: Sharp, p. 210, Staffordshire 5; Neumann 23899; Davis, Staffordshire 117 and
pl. D, no. 8; Watkin, N.57; Bell, Staffordshire 26.

Dies by Turnpenny, according to Sharp; Davis attributes them to Halliday.

D. CONCLUSION

Thus the Royal Exchange provided an icon for seventeenth-century token-issuers, not only in London, but also in Suffolk (Bury St Edmunds), the Isle of Wight (West Cowes), Norfolk (Great Yarmouth), Shropshire (Ludlow), and Ireland (Waterford). The significance of this distribution is brought out by Fuller's explanation for the absence of any Lord Mayor of Devonshire birth, that Devonians had made little use of the Exchange in London on account of their distance from London.[40] In the nineteenth century the Second Exchange was an icon for token-issuers in Staffordshire, particularly in Bilston, and thence Burton and Wednesbury.

If the seventeenth-century issues are placed in chronological order, London appears from 1651, Great Yarmouth in 1659, Bury St Edmunds by 1667, Ludlow in 1666 and 1669, and West Cowes in 1668. Waterford must date from the 1650s, for it bears the mullet initial mark and other characteristics of David Ramage, moneyer in the Tower of London, who changed his initial mark in 1660.[41]

In London with the Exchange Tavern and so on, in Waterford where Thomas Exton described himself as a vintner, and in nineteenth-century Wednesbury where Abel Round was a maltster and victualler, the Exchange presumably would have been seen as a

suitable sign to attract a mercantile clientele. There are also indications that by the third quarter of the seventeenth century the Exchange might be adopted as an emblem for trades related to its commercial operations. George Haughton in Ludlow was a mercer, and the Exchange of course was partly owned by the Mercers' Company. George Stanard in Bury St Edmunds, and Richard Crafford in Great Yarmouth, were both milliners, a trade not unrelated to that of mercer;[42] and there were milliners in the Exchange.

Sources of illustrations
(Figs. i–x are at 2:1, the remainder 1:1)
- i   Norweb Collection, W. London 962, 39137 ex Nott.
- ii   British Museum, W. London 2277, 1847 3-4-467 ex Pulham.
- iii   Norweb Collection, W. London 2276, ex Baldwin.
- iv   British Museum, W. London 991, T.2671.
- v   Norweb Collection, W. London 3083, 43503 ex Nott.
- vi   British Museum, W. Suffolk 78 [*recte* 77], T.5104.
- vii   R. H. Thompson, W. Norfolk 312, ex Norweb 3325.
- viii   R. H. Thompson, W. Shropshire 31, ex Norweb 3895.
- ix   British Museum, W. Shropshire 32, 1994 5-16-212 ex Norweb 3896.
- x   British Museum, W. Ireland 731, 1933 4-13-1018 ex Fletcher.
- xi   British Museum, D. & H. Middlesex 45 [*recte* 65], SSB 189.121 ex Sarah Sophia Banks.
- xii   British Museum, D. Staffs. 30, 1870 5-7-1542 ex Freudenthal.
- xiii   British Museum, D. Staffs. 53, 1855 10-4-114 ex Cureton.
- xiv   British Museum, D. Staffs. 58, 1855 10-4-115 ex Cureton.
- xv   British Museum, D. Staffs. 25, 1870 5-7-1553 ex Freudenthal.
- xvi   British Museum, D. Staffs. 116, 1870 5-7-1587 ex Freudenthal.
- xvii   British Museum, D. Staffs. 117, 1870 5-7-1588 ex Freudenthal.

---

[40] 'And because they had a Little London (Exeter) wherein wealth is gained near at hand'. Thomas Fuller, *The History of the Worthies of England, first printed in 1662*, new edn, 2 vols. (London, 1811), I, p. 292.

[41] R. H. Thompson, *Sylloge of Coins of the British Isles, 38: the Norweb Collection, Cleveland, Ohio, U.S.A.: Tokens of the British Isles, 1575–1750, Part II: Dorset ... [to] Gloucestershire* (London, 1988), p. xix.

[42] For example, John Barrett in Oxford, 'milliner' in 1665, had been apprenticed to a mercer; H. E. Salter, *Surveys and Tokens ...* (Oxford, 1923), p. 381.

PART THREE
THE THIRD EXCHANGE

1841 –

SCENE SHIFTING

THE THIRD EXCHANGE

CHAPTER XXIV

The Setting of the Royal Exchange: Continuity and Change in the Financial District of the City of London, 1300–1871[1]

By DEREK KEENE

There never was so much borrowed money collected in the world as is now collected in London.

I venture to call this Essay 'Lombard Street' and not the 'Money Market' or any such phrase, because I wish to deal, and to show that I mean to deal, in concrete realities . . . the Money Market is as concrete and real as anything else.

In this constant and chronic borrowing Lombard Street is the great go-between . . . Why particular trades settled in particular places it is often difficult to say; but one thing is certain, that when a trade *has* settled in any one spot it is very difficult to oust it.[2]

BY 1870, WHEN WALTER BAGEHOT began to write his classic analysis of the London money market, there had emerged at the heart of the City that distinctive neighbourhood later to be labelled, in the ungainly language of urban studies, as the Central Financial District, a subdivision of the Central Business District.[3] London's financial district in 1870 was a compact area, nowhere more than 350 yards across, and taking less than ten minutes to traverse on foot. It extended, more or less as it still did in 1980, from just beyond the Bank of England on the west to Gracechurch Street on the east (Figs. 93 and 94). At its heart was the Royal Exchange, which in key respects had served as the kernel around which the neighbourhood had formed. Here the city's traditional intermixture of dwelling houses, shops, warehouses, and counting houses had given way to a landscape dominated by the office in its many different forms. Work rather than domestic residence now supplied the underlying social framework for the area. There was a vast daily influx of workers in banking, insurance and other financial services, as well as of brokers, jobbers and other dealers. The Bank of England alone employed more than 800 clerks,[4] and in 1871 some 500 stockbrokers had offices in the area.[5] The loss of the residential population was all too obvious. By night, in 1871, the total resident population within the line of the ancient city walls was only 44 per cent of what it had been in 1801, and 40 per cent of the total in 1695, when the number of inhabitants within the walls was not far short of the total on the eve of the Great Fire of 1666,

[1] Another version of this essay has been published as 'The financial district of the City of London: continuity and change, 1300–1871' in *Cities of Finance*, ed. H. A. Diederiks and D. Reeder (Amsterdam, 1996), pp. 279–302. In part the paper arises from the research project 'From Counting House to Office', funded by the Economic and Social Research Council (grant no. R000231022) and based at the Centre for Metropolitan History. Using rating lists, street- and business-directories, and census returns, the project traced in detail the pattern of change within the study area shown on Fig. 94, mainly from 1800 onwards. I am grateful to Jon Lawrence, researcher on the project, and to Martin Daunton, my co-supervisor of it, for supplying information and ideas, especially concerning the nineteenth century. Parts of this paper are derived from one drafted by Jon Lawrence, and destined for separate publication.

[2] W. Bagehot, *Lombard Street, a Description of the Money Market* (new edition, 1912), pp. 1, 11, 17.

[3] Cf. R. E. Murphy, *The Central Business District* (Chicago and New York, 1972); M. J. Bowden, 'The growth of Central Business Districts in large cities', in *The New Urban History: Quantitative Explorations by American Historians*, ed. L. F. Schnore (Princeton, 1975), pp. 75–109, covers financial districts, but its account of London is misleading and anachronistic.

[4] D. Morier Evans, *City Men and City Manners. The City; or, the Physiology of London Business; with Sketches on 'Change, and at the Coffee Houses* (1852), p. 7.

[5] W. H. and L. Collingridge, *The City of London Directory for 1871*.

the maximum ever achieved.[6] The loss was even more marked in the parishes of the financial district, where the total of residents in 1871 represented 34 per cent of that in 1801 and 27 per cent of the 7,500 or so persons who had lived there in 1695.[7] By contrast, the 170,000 persons who in 1866 were 'residing, occupied or employed' during working hours in the City each day were more than twice as numerous as the dwindling total of night-time residents. The streets were fuller than ever before, so that in 1822 it was claimed that 200,000 people a day passed the corner of the Royal Exchange, while in 1866 549,613 people were counted as entering the city over a twelve-hour day.[8]

What the financial district had lost in domesticity it gained in a new monumental aspect. 'The Roman Corso, The Neapolitan Toledo or even the glories of the Rue de Rivoli . . .', wrote an enthusiastic critic in 1866, 'will be overtopped and out-vied by the continuous line of merchant palaces in Cornhill, and Lombard-street, and Bishopsgate-street, and Cheapside', streets which would be even more monumental and picturesque than the 'once matchless streets of the grandest old German towns or even the glorious canal-ways of Venice herself'.[9]

The financial district was but one of several central neighbourhoods of the city to have been transformed in this way, although the architectural expression of that change was less grandiose elsewhere. To the south and east, centring on Mincing Lane, was a specialised district associated with the market in 'colonial goods'; to the west, around Wood Street, was an area dominated by the warehouses and offices of textile dealers and manufacturers; and to the north-east, in Old Broad Street, there was a lesser concentration of the establishments of 'general merchants'. All those areas were characterised by new, large-scale buildings, often in a plain but inventive style, and by a loss of the resident population.[10] The financial district lay at the centre of a network of specialisation, both physically and in terms of the services it provided to other districts and to the world at large. These specialised districts grew naturally out of patterns of residence and trading which had existed in the city for many centuries. They arose from the growth of London's business as the dominant national market place, as an international centre for maritime trade and commodity markets, as the focus of government finance, as a machine for recycling savings and rural rent, and as a general provider of banking, insurance, and other services. The process of transformation and localised specialisation was not fundamentally different from that which had characterised earlier phases in the City's growth. It was distinguished, rather, by the great scale and rate of physical and social change, which was notable from the late seventeenth century onwards and became dramatically frenetic during the two decades before 1870. The pace of change directly reflected underlying trends in business, and some legislative innovations which facilitated new types of activity in the City.

Above all, the Napoleonic Wars mark the period in which London rose to undisputed prominence as an international as well as a national centre of business and finance. From then on, despite the slumps which followed the booms, the market carved out for itself an exclusive space at the heart of the City, at a pace which matched increases in the quantity and rate of circulation of money and in the overall level of trade. For the purposes of this paper the root causes of change at each historical stage should be taken as

[6] Census totals for 1801 and 1871: see W. Page (ed.), *The Victoria History of the Country of Middlesex*, II, Appendix IV, 'Table of Population, 1801–1901' (1911). For 1695, see P. Jones and A. V. Judges, 'London population in the late seventeenth century', *Economic History Review*, 6 (1935–36), pp. 45–63. For issues concerning the population trend in the seventeenth century, see V. Harding, 'The population of London, 1550–1700: a review of the published evidence', *The London Journal*, 15 (1990), pp. 111–28. For the general picture in the nineteenth century, see K. G. Grytzell, *County of London Population Changes, 1801–1901* (Lund, 1969).

[7] For sources, see previous note. The parish units for which figures are available do not correspond exactly with the study area defined in Fig. 93. The parishes used for the comparison are: All Hallows Lombard Street, St Bartholomew by the Exchange, St Benet Fink, St Benet Gracechurch, St Christopher le Stocks, St Edmund the King and Martyr, St Margaret Lothbury, St Martin Outwich, St Mary Woolnoth, St Michael Cornhill, and St Peter Cornhill.

[8] Local Government and Taxation Committee of the City of London, *Report on the City Day-Census 1881* (1881), p. 8; S. Leigh, *Leigh's New Picture of London* (1822), p. 240.

[9] D. J. Olsen, *The City as a Work of Art: London, Paris, Vienna* (1986), p. 27, quoting *The Builder*, 24 (1866), p. 810.

[10] E. I'Anson, 'Some notice of office buildings in the City of London', *Papers Read at the Royal Institute of British Architects, Session 1864–65* (1864–65).

given.[11] Instead, the focus is on the complex and highly concentrated physical environment within which business was done, that concrete reality which Bagehot identified as an essential feature of the market in money and which was the setting of the Royal Exchange.

Neither Lombard Street nor the Royal Exchange served as the City's original focal point for commerce and finance. That lay in the wide market street of Cheapside which extended east from St Paul's Cathedral towards Lombard Street and Cornhill (Fig. 92).[12] The money and bullion market seems originally to have been located among the goldsmiths at the western end of Cheapside near St Paul's, and the likely site of the pre-Conquest royal palace in the City, a situation at the focal point of power very similar to that of the money market in early medieval Winchester. By 1300 the London money market had moved, as is indicated by the local place-name 'Old Change'.[13] The new focus was just to the east of Cheapside in the vicinity of Bucklersbury (Fig. 92), a

district notable at that time for its group of large houses and business establishments known as 'wardrobes'. In the late thirteenth century landed magnates used the wardrobes as city bases for managing both their financial affairs and the supplies of luxury goods which they purchased in London.[14] Some of the wardrobes had once belonged to wealthy Jewish families before their expulsion in 1290.[15] Others had belonged to Italian ('Lombard') or Provençal merchants, came subsequently into Lombard hands, or were managed on behalf of their owners by Italians, who towards the end of the thirteenth century became prominent as traders in London, providing both magnates and the King with banking and commercial services as well as luxury goods.[16] One of the largest of those establishments belonged to the society of the Bardi of Florence. For a while in the mid-fourteenth century it was used by the King as his Great Wardrobe in London; the site was later occupied by the Pope's Head Tavern which lay in the heart of the Lombard Street banking district.[17] The Italians were drawn to this neighbourhood in the later thirteenth century, perhaps by a money market associated with the Jews, but more certainly by business connected with the wardrobes and by their interest in the trade in imported spices and luxury textiles, which had probably been established in the vicinity since the twelfth century, when there may even have been a

[11] For guidance as to these underlying trends, see M. Buchinsky and B. Polak, 'The emergence of a national capital market in England, 1710–1880', *The Journal of Economic History*, 53 (1993), pp. 1–24; M. Daunton, 'London and the World' in *London — World City, 1800–1840*, ed. C. Fox (1992), pp. 21–33; F. G. Dawson, *The First Latin American Debt Crisis: the City of London and the 1822–25 Loan Bubble* (New Haven, 1990); P. G. M. Dickinson, *The Financial Revolution: a Study in the Development of Public Credit, 1688–1756* (1967); P. Earle, *The Making of the English Middle Class* (1989); E. Kerridge, *Trade and Banking in Early Modern England* (Manchester, 1988); D. Kynaston, *The City of London, volume 1, A World of Its Own, 1815–1890* (1994); F. T. Melton, *Sir Robert Clayton and the Origins of English Deposit Banking, 1658–1685* (Cambridge, 1986); *idem*, 'Deposit banking in London, 1700–90', in *Business in the Age of Reason*, ed. R. P. T. Davenport-Hines and J. Liebenau (1987); L. Neal, *The Rise of Financial Capitalism: International Capital Markets in the Age of Reason* (Cambridge, 1990); L. S. Pressnell, *Country Banking in the Industrial Revolution* (Oxford, 1956); R. D. Richards, *The Early History of Banking in England* (1929); J. C. Riley, *International Government Finance and the Amsterdam Capital Market, 1740–1815* (Cambridge, 1980); B. E. Supple, *The Royal Exchange Insurance: a History of British Insurance, 1720–1970* (Cambridge, 1970); C. Trebilcock, *Phoenix Assurance and the Development of British Insurance* I *1782–1870* (Cambridge, 1985).
[12] D. Keene, *Cheapside before the Great Fire* (1985).
[13] C. E. Challis (ed.), *New History of the Royal Mint* (Cambridge, 1992), pp. 95, 114; E. Ekwall, *Street-Names of the City of London* (corr. ed., Oxford, 1965), pp. 197–98. For the Winchester money market, see M. Biddle (ed.), *Winchester in the Early Middle Ages: an edition and discussion of the Winton Domesday* (Oxford, 1976), pp. 396–422.

[14] D. Keene and V. Harding, *Historical Gazetteer of London before the Great Fire*, 1, *Cheapside* (Cambridge, 1987), nos. 95/8–12; D. Keene, 'Medieval London and its region', *The London Journal*, 14 (1989), pp. 99–111; D. Keene, 'The Walbrook study: a summary report' (typescript in library of Institute of Historical Research, London, 1987), no. 156/12.
[15] For the localities associated with the Jewish community, see J. Hillaby, 'London: the thirteenth-century Jewry revisited', *Jewish Historical Studies*, 32 (1990–92), pp. 89–155.
[16] E. B. Fryde, 'The deposits of Hugh Despenser the younger with Italian bankers', *Economic History Review*, 2nd ser., 3 (1951), pp. 344–62; R. W. Kaeuper, *Bankers to the Crown: the Riccardi of Lucca and Edward I* (Princeton, 1973), pp. 17, 31.
[17] C. L. Kingsford, 'Historical notes on London houses', *London Topographical Record*, 11 (1917), pp. 70–73; T. F. Tout, *Chapters in the Administrative History of Mediaeval England*, IV (Manchester, 1928), pp. 395, 401–05.

market in gold nearby.[18] Thus by the early fourteenth century the name Lombard Street, the original form of which had no connotation of an Italian presence, had acquired much of its modern meaning,[19] and several of the key functions later associated with the financial district around the Royal Exchange had come to be established in that part of the City.

By the 1340s the King's exchange, where bullion and foreign coin were changed for coins of the realm, was being held in Bucklersbury. By 1378, however, it had been moved to Lombard Street, perhaps on account of the Bardi who had been involved from time to time in running it.[20] In the fifteenth century the exchange was unified with the mint at the Tower of London, but the earlier developments appear to have been sufficient for Lombard Street to emerge as the nucleus of the City's money market, and for goldsmiths to be attracted there from elsewhere. Certainly, there appear to have been no goldsmiths in the street before the Italians and the exchange came to it.[21] It was in Lombard Street that rates of exchange with foreign currencies were publicly known, where bills of exchange facilitating the City's overseas trade (especially with the international markets in the Low Countries) could be encashed, and where merchants engaged in that trade could exchange news and be confident of finding others whose business was relevant to them. The street served as a more or less direct link to the Place de la Bourse in Bruges, and thence to the money markets of the Mediterranean. In the sixteenth century, if not before, Lombard Street was also the site for ship broking, where merchants could find ships to carry their wares to the ports they wished.[22] A distinctive space had been established in which finance, overseas commodity trade, and commercial and maritime information flowed together, and which was to play a crucial role in the City's future development as an international centre.

The meetings of merchants and brokers in Lombard Street, which acquired the character of regular and predictable assemblies, were open to the weather and took place in a narrow street where there was a steady flow of traffic. By the 1530s the disadvantages of this arrangement were apparent, especially by comparison with the elegant, protected environment provided, from 1531, by the new bourse at Antwerp, now London's principal, and indeed dominant, trading partner. A proposal to establish a London bourse at Leadenhall came to nothing. Leadenhall was a magnificent and very suitable fifteenth-century market building with a courtyard plan, just five minutes away from Lombard Street, and already had some connection with the money market. The episode provides a striking demonstration of Bagehot's principle concerning the strong physical association between specialised markets and particular places. A more realistic scheme to establish a bourse in Lombard Street, on a site where some of the fabric of the former Great Wardrobe probably still stood, also failed. The eventual outcome was Thomas Gresham's Exchange, erected in the angle between Cornhill and Threadneedle Street, and opened by 1570. In design, function and facilities the Royal Exchange was closely modelled on the Antwerp bourse. It incorporated skills and materials brought directly from Antwerp and was a striking, and perhaps inappropriately optimistic, affirmation of what one would now

[18] Keene, *Cheapside*; P. Nightingale, 'The London pepperers' guild and some twelfth century English trading links with Spain', *Bulletin of the Institute of Historical Research*, 58 (1985), pp. 123–32; eadem, 'Some London moneyers and reflections on the organisation of English mints in the eleventh and twelfth centuries', *Numismatic Chronicle*, 142 (1982), pp. 34–50; eadem, *A Mercantile Community: the Grocers' Company and the Politics and Trade of London, 1000–1485* (1995), pp. 35–42; S. Dempsey, 'The Italian community in London during the reign of Edward II', *The London Journal*, 18 (1993), pp. 14–22.

[19] Ekwall, *Street-names*, pp. 83, 98–99.

[20] T. F. Reddaway, 'The king's mint and exchange in London, 1343–1543', *English Historical Review*, 82 (1967), pp. 1–23 (1967).

[21] This is contrary to the view expressed in Reddaway, 'The king's mint'. For the concentration of the City's goldsmiths at the western end of Cheapside, and their absence from the Lombard Street area in 1319, see E. Ekwall, *Two Early London Subsidy Rolls* (Lund, 1951).

[22] Burgon, *Gresham*, p. 261; A. Hanham, *The Celys and their World: an English Merchant Family of the Fifteenth Century* (Cambridge, 1985), pp. 352, 401, 405; S. Jenks, 'Kredit im Londoner Aussenhandel um die Mitte des 15 Jahrhunderts' in *Kredit im spätmittelalterlichen und frühneuzeitlichen Europa*, ed. M. North (Cologne and Vienna, 1991), pp. 71–102 ; R. de Roover, *Money, Banking, and Credit in Mediaeval Bruges* (The Mediaeval Academy of America, Cambridge, Mass., 1948), p. 17; *Statute 32 Henry VIII c. 14,*, 'The mayntenaunce of the navye', section 8.

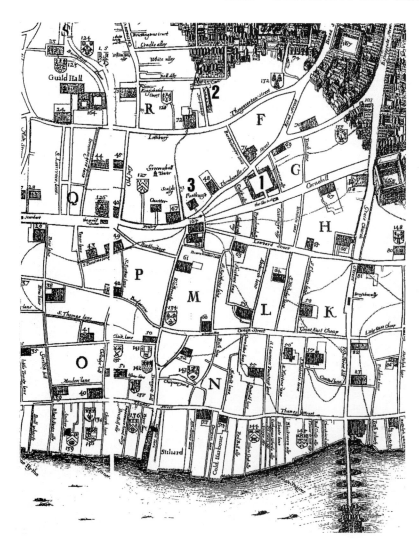

FIG. 92.   The river, London Bridge, and
the Royal Exchange after the Great Fire of
1666. From the 'Exact surveigh of the
streets, lanes and churches contained
within the ruins of the city of London'
made by John Leake *et al.* and engraved by
Wenceslas Hollar, 1667. **1** denotes the site
of the first Royal Exchange, **2** that of Inigo
Jones's office for the issue of tokens, and
3 that of the Post Office established in 1660.

describe as the 'modernity' of London as a commercial centre.[23]

The Royal Exchange retained very much its original form through successive rebuildings after the Great Fire of 1666 and another fire in 1838. Both the first construction and its successor impressed visitors with their scale, elegance and opulence. The vaults came to be used for the goods of the East India Company. In the eighteenth century the shops above gave way to office uses, although there continued to be a brisk trade in expensive consumer goods in the shops surrounding the Exchange. In the courtyard

and galleries, which remained open to the sky until they were roofed over in the 1880s, merchants, factors, and brokers assembled to do business twice a day, in the late morning and early evening, a practice already established by 1578. By that same date it was customary for merchants to group themselves within the Exchange according to their nationalities.[24] By the early eighteenth century, when the City's overseas trade was well advanced in its expansion and a market in government and other stocks had been established, the merchants had recognised places or 'walks' where they gathered according to the commodities or countries with which they dealt. Thus it

[23] See C. E. Challis, *The Tudor Coinage* (Manchester, 1978), pp. 60–61; for the fifteenth-century buildings at Leadenhall, see M. Samuel, 'The fifteenth-century garner at Leadenhall', *The Antiquaries' Journal*, 69 (1989), pp. 119–82.

[24] L. Grenade, 'Les Singularitéz de Londres' (Rome, Vatican Library, Reg. Lat. 672), ff. 52–53.

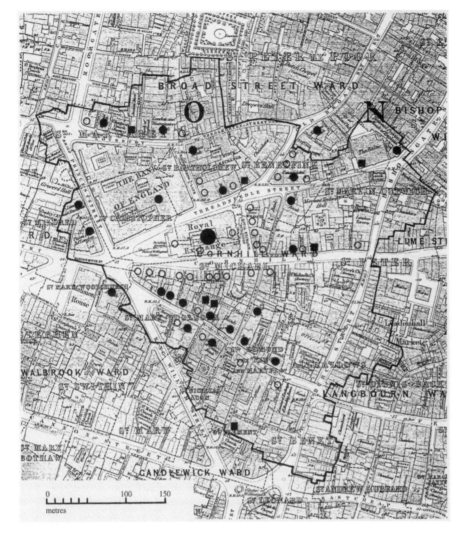

FIG. 93.   The financial district
of the City of London in 1873.
The study area, defined in terms of
administrative units, is shown in
heavy outline on the Ordnance
Survey map of 1873.
It corresponds closely to the
financial district at that date.

● the Royal Exchange as
rebuilt after 1838.

◗ clearing banks (both joint-
stock and private): all the
clearing banks are shown.

■ finance and discount
companies: all those
recorded in contemporary
directories.

○ insurance company offices:
only those within the study
area.

was possible readily to do business with the Hamburg
or the Jamaica merchants, with the clothiers, with the
brokers of stocks, or with the small number of Jews,
who like other brokers were licensed by the City
authorities.[25] Ship-broking and other maritime business rapidly became established at the Exchange, and
the shops round about sold the books, maps, and
scientific instruments essential to those concerned
with seafaring. These trading practices continued
well into the nineteenth century, despite the proliferation of other, more specialised places for doing

business.[26] Even in the 1850s, when the Exchange
had 'no longer the prominence as a place for the
meeting of merchants it once had',[27] the Rothschilds
used to appear there daily to deal in bills of exchange,
while a few minutes away at their offices in St
Swithin's Lane a band of clerks handled the essential

[25] E. V. Morgan and W. A. Thomas, *The Stock Exchange: its History and Functions* (1962), p. 65.

[26] Earle, *Middle Class*, pp. 40–41; W. Maitland, *The History of London from its Foundation to the Present Time* (1756), pp. 898–902; W. H. Quarrell and M. More (eds.), *London in 1710: from the travels of Zacharias Conrad von Uffenbach* (1934), pp. 15, 124; *The Royal Exchange: Extracts from the Records of the City of London . . . respecting the Royal Exchange and the Gresham Trusts, 1564–1825* (c. 1825), p. 46 (for regulations concerning the hours of assembly); see also *supra*, Chapter XI.

[27] *A New Survey of London*, 1 (1853), p. 377.

but more routine record-keeping aspects of the business.[28]

The foundation of the Royal Exchange reinforced the existing trend towards the concentration of financial and mercantile business away from Cheapside, but even in the later sixteenth century the Cheapside goldsmiths were more numerous and on the whole more prosperous than their fellows in Lombard Street. The importance of Lombard Street as a centre for the bullion market, however, is clear from the residence there of the very wealthy goldsmith Martin Bowes (d. 1566–67), who for twenty-five years controlled the operation of the Mint at the Tower.[29] In the seventeenth century this position was reversed. Goldsmiths evolved into 'goldsmith-bankers', and moved away from Cheapside into Lombard Street. They began to give interest on deposits and to provide facilities for credit transfers between London and the provinces. The London goldsmiths who issued notes were said to keep 'running cashes', and according to a list of them published in 1677 twenty-eight had addresses in or close to Lombard Street, while only three had addresses in Cheapside. City goldsmith bankers might expect, for example, to provide facilities for the merchants who assembled at the Royal Exchange.[30]

The 1677 list reveals a second notable feature of London's financial geography. Eleven of the goldsmiths who kept running cashes had addresses in Fleet Street or The Strand, close to the legal quarter and to the fashionable and expanding residential districts to the west of the City later to be known as the West End. Ready access to legal services and to a market in mortgaged properties, either for investment or as security for loans, could be important for a banker's business. Moreover, the scriveners, who seem to have been the immediate predecessors of the goldsmiths in London banking, were a part of the legal world, drawing up documents, negotiating

loans, and managing property.[31] The bankers also provided credit services for the landowners who periodically resided in the West End for the 'Season' or parliamentary sessions, thus providing a crucial link between landed income and commercial investment.[32] This pattern persisted, so that in the 1820s, and even in the 1870s, London bankers were distributed in a very similar way between Lombard Street and the West End. The effect of these two distinct types of demand, the fashionable or landowning on the one hand and the mercantile on the other, is also evident in the London addresses of the insurance companies which proliferated during the eighteenth and nineteenth centuries. Since their business concerned buildings and lives, as well as commercial goods and shipping, the insurance offices were more evenly distributed between the two localities, and often a single firm had offices in both.[33] It was the great concentration of banking, finance, and commodity markets, and the circulation of money arising from that association, which distinguished the business life of the City from that of the West End.

At the end of the seventeenth century, when London was poised to assume a leading role as a world centre of commerce, the district surrounding the Royal Exchange is clearly recognisable as the centre of the City's financial and commercial life. To an extent, with the notable exception of the goldsmiths in Lombard Street, it retained some of its earlier diversity. Cornhill was still dominated by linen drapers, as it had been in the past, but was in addition noted for luxury trades, which by 1750 were coming more to the fore. Further north, but certainly related to the needs of the financial and commercial district, was a zone where scriveners and attorneys were

---

[28] Morier Evans, *City Men*, pp. 99; R. W. Davis, *The English Rothschilds* (1983), pp. 35, 47–48, 135.
[29] T. F. Reddaway, 'Elizabethan London — Goldsmiths' Row in Cheapside, 1558–1645', *Guildhall Miscellany*, 2, no. 5 (1963), pp. 181–206; Challis, *Tudor Coinage*, p. 31.
[30] Kerridge, *Trade and Banking*, pp. 70–71, 76–78; Earle, *Middle Class*, pp. 48–49; *A Collection of the Names of the Merchants Living in and about the City of London* (1677).

[31] Earle, *Middle Class*, pp. 48–49; Richards, *Early History of Banking*, p. 15.
[32] M. G. Davies, 'Country gentry and payments to London, 1650–1714', *Economic History Review*, 2nd ser., 24 (1967), pp. 15–36.
[33] This pattern is clearly apparent from: Critchett and Woods, *The Post Office Annual Directory for 1815*; Pigot & Co., *Pigot and Co's Metropolitan New Alphabetical Directory* (1827); Collingridge, *Directory 1871*.

especially numerous.[34] A distinctive feature of the district was its numerous places of entertainment, serving those who had business at the Royal Exchange and elsewhere. The taverns, relatively spacious establishments, and often containing stylish and imposing rooms where public meetings, auctions, and concerts were held, had performed this role since the Middle Ages and continued to do so into the nineteenth century. Pontack's Tavern in Abchurch Lane, for example, was known in 1756 for its 'elegance in entertainments' and was used both 'by rich merchants and by persons of quality from the Court End of town'. From the 1650s onwards the taverns were joined by the newly fashionable coffee houses, which, unlike the taverns, were distinctively concentrated near the Royal Exchange, notably in Exchange Alley, Pope's Head Alley (the site of the former headquarters of the Bardi), and other lanes off Lombard Street and Cornhill. Here brokers, merchants, monied men, ship owners, and agents assembled and 'could be spoken to' outside the hours of 'Change. The widely perceived importance of this dense network of places for the exchange and authentication of information is apparent from the way in which the coffee houses served also as places for promoting philosophical and mechanical demonstrations. There was no attempt to restrict business to the Exchange, and so taverns and coffee houses were widely advertised as places where stocks were available. They came to be centres for speculation, and traders set up deals there before going on 'Change. Just as the 'walks', associated with specialised trade, evolved in the Exchange itself, so individual coffee houses came to be associated with particular groups of dealers — Lloyd's with marine insurance, Jonathan's with stockbrokers, and so on. As the eighteenth century progressed, so too did the mercantile specialisation of the coffee houses, and names such as 'The

Virginia and Baltic' or 'The Jamaica' proclaimed the interests of their users.[35]

The high demand for this type of informal trading space promoted intensive use of the buildings in the immediate vicinity of the Exchange. That is apparent in the distinct shift in the concentration of high land values within the City from Cheapside to this neighbourhood which took place between the 1630s and the 1690s.[36] The dense network of alleys itself reflected the need for ease of communication among the participants in this 'grand market for buying and selling stocks, lottery tickets, etc.', as Exchange Alley was described in 1756. As an observer unsympathetic to speculation had remarked earlier in the century, 'the center of the Jobbing is in the kingdom of Exchange Alley and its adjacencies: the limits are easily surrounded in about a minute and a half'.[37] Face-to-face contact, the facility to identify people who specialised in particular types of business and to establish their credibility, and above all speed of communication, emerge as essential to the operation of a complex system, which even today in its preoccupations and language remains mystifying and impenetrable to outsiders.[38]

The provision and circulation of news was one of the key services in the district. In 1576 'the Dowche poste' occupied a house in Lombard Street.[39] When the General Post Office was set up in 1660, it occupied

---

[34] Characterisation based on J. Alexander, 'The economic and social structure of London , *c.* 1700' (unpublished University of London PhD thesis, 1989); *idem*, 'The economic structure of the city of London at the end of the seventeenth century', *Urban History Yearbook 1989*, pp. 47–62; *idem*, 'The City revealed', in *Surveying the People*, ed. K. Schurer and T. Arkell (Oxford, 1992), pp. 181–200; see also Maitland, *History of London*, p. 897.

[35] B. Lillywhite, *The London Coffee Houses: a Reference Book of the Coffee Houses of the Seventeenth, Eighteenth, and Nineteenth Centuries* (1963), pp. 23, 282–86, 305–09, 330–35, 626–27; Morgan and Thomas, *Stock Exchange*, pp. 20–21, 35–36; Maitland, *History of London*, pp. 898, 996. L. Stewart, *The Rise of Public Science: Rhetoric, Technology, and Natural Philosophy in Newtonian Britain, 1660–1750* (Cambridge, 1992) is the most vivid demonstration of the vitality and significance of the network.

[36] Most readily apparent in the comparison of property values per acre in 1638, derived from T. C. Dale, *The Inhabitants of London in 1638* (1931) with those in the 1690s: Alexander, 'Economic and social structure'; C. Spence, *A Social Atlas of London in the 1690s* (forthcoming, 1997). See also E. Jones, 'London in the early seventeenth century: an ecological approach', *The London Journal*, 6 (1980), pp. 123–33, for the 1638 material.

[37] Maitland, *History of London*, p. 898; Morgan and Thomas, *Stock Exchange*, p. 37.

[38] B. Attard, 'The jobbers of the London Stock Exchange, an oral history', *Oral History*, 22 (1994), pp. 43–48.

[39] Also apparently known as 'the post master's house': Bethlem Royal Hospital Archives and Museum, MS Minutes of the the Court of Governors of Bridewell and Bethlem III, ff. 13v, 28 (I owe these these references to Laura Wright).

a house in Threadneedle Street, and after the Great
Fire, when it developed an important role as a source
of commercial information, maintaining packet boats
to Spain, the West Indies and elsewhere, it moved to
a site in Lombard Street, directly opposite Pope's
Head Alley. By the 1680s the Office had made
arrangements with coffee houses nearby for the
deposit and collection of letters, and it was almost
certainly the value of easy access to shipping information, available via the Post Office, which in 1691
caused Edward Lloyd to move his coffee house to
Lombard Street from a site near the Custom House
on the river, where the City's commerce was most
tangibly manifest.[40] Coffee houses also attracted
customers by providing information in the form of
specialised journals and newspapers from overseas.[41]
That practice continued into the 1850s, although by
then other types of reading room and information
services had begun to be provided. The decision of
Julius Reuter, that great entrepreneur of marketable
news, to set up his 'Submarine Telegraph' office in
Royal Exchange Buildings in 1851, a month before
the opening of the Channel cable, thus was entirely
consistent with established practice and also presaged
radical changes in the methods and speed of communication. In 1848 a capacious and imposing
'Central Telegraph Station', connected to the new
railway termini, had been erected immediately
behind the Bank of England, and in 1859 the English
and Irish Magnetic Telegraph opened equally grand
offices in Threadneedle Street.[42] Throughout the
period, proximity to the key central sites for business
and information was regarded as essential to the
success of an enterprise. As with Amsterdam in an
earlier period, the single most important function of
the district was probably as an information
exchange.[43] Even government institutions were

affected. It was, for example, conscious policy until
1848 to maintain the Excise Office, which administered the duties on inland trade, close to the heart of
the City, both for the convenience of the merchants
who congregated there and for ready access to
warehouses and the Custom House.[44] Sale notices for
properties suitable for domestic or commercial occupation by merchants, brokers or lawyers stressed the
value of their location for those who 'require immediate intercourse with the Royal Exchange, Bank, Stock
Exchange, Post Office, India House or other places
of commercial resort', as an advertisement of 1806
put it.[45]

Indeed, in attempting to understand the development of this area it may be best to characterise it as a
market place, accommodated within a complex
framework inherited from the medieval City, where
trading in paper interests, information and services
steadily drove out first the direct trade in material
goods, and then the residential population. In the
1690s we find that merchants engaged in overseas
trade, who would have attended the Royal Exchange
and the coffee houses, resided not within the area
itself but just beyond its limits, where there was space
for their dwellings to include warehousing, a pattern
evident in earlier centuries in relation to other market
centres in the City.[46] In the seventeenth and eighteenth centuries the headquarters of new trading
associations, such as the East India Company and the
South Sea Company, occupied similar positions on
the margins of the district dominated by the Royal
Exchange. Those headquarters were notable for their
size, and incorporated extensive provision for the
storage of goods and for sale rooms, as well as
administrative offices.[47]

The distinctive geography of the financial district
and the institutions associated with it was already

[40] D. Defoe, *A Tour through the whole of Britain*, 1 (Everyman edition, 1962), p. 341; Maitland, *History of London*, pp. 997–98; Lillywhite, *Coffee Houses*, pp. 18–20; D. W. Gibb, *Lloyd's of London* (1957), pp. 6–7.
[41] *New Survey of London*, 1 (1853), p. 378.
[42] D. Read, *The Power of News: the History of Reuters, 1849–1989* (Oxford, 1992), pp. 7, 13–16 and pl. 6; *The Illustrated London News*, 22 January 1848, pp. 34–36.
[43] W. D. Smith, 'The function of commercial centres in the modernization of European capitalism: Amsterdam as an information exchange in the seventeenth century', *Journal of Economic History*, 44 (1984), pp. 985–1005.

[44] J. Imray, *The Mercers' Hall* (1991), pp. 257–71; *The Royal Exchange: Extracts from the Records of the City of London*, pp. 55–56.
[45] Oxford, Bodleian Library, Gough Additional Folios A261, no. 160.
[46] Alexander, 'Economic and social structure' and 'Economic structure'; D. Keene, 'Well Court documentary evidence' and 'The character and development of the Cheapside area; an overview' in *Transactions of the London and Middlesex Archaeological Society*, 41 (1993 for 1990), pp. 89–113, 178–94.
[47] Defoe, *Tour*, 1, pp. 339–40; Maitland, *History of London*, pp. 848–53, 997, 1003.

apparent to contemporaries by 1666, for Christopher Wren's proposal for replanning London after the Great Fire included the provision in that neighbourhood of a central piazza which was to contain the Royal Exchange, with the Excise Office, the Post Office, the Mint, and the shops of the goldsmiths fronting on to it.[48] But this was not to be, and, with the exception of the Royal Exchange itself, the development of the area after the Fire was characterised by the adaptation of existing, essentially domestic, buildings for use by commercial and other institutions. Thus the Post Office in 1678 came to occupy the large private house of Robert Vyner, a goldsmith banker, and was to remain there until the 1820s, when it was finally decided that such a setting was no longer 'worthy of its role and of British opulence'.[49] The East India Company occupied a warren of former private houses, and the South Sea Company had similar accommodation, while the Excise Office occupied the former dwelling of Sir John Frederick. Shortly after its foundation in 1694, the Bank of England moved into the hall of the Grocers' Company, which in fact provided the Bank with spacious, efficient and central accommodation for its business.[50] All these establishments, like the great merchant houses of the past, were set back from the street frontage, where they made no distinctive architectural statement. This landscape reflects the *ad hoc* development of institutions, the relative shortage of resources for building after the Great Fire, and perhaps the discretion of the post-Restoration monarchy.

Apart from the Royal Exchange, the first specialised business building in the area to make a coherent architectural statement was Inigo Jones's little known, but striking and probably influential, office for the issue of tokens, erected in Lothbury at the end of the

1630s.[51] It is possible that the Token House, used as offices for only a brief period, contributed in the long term to the slow but steadily increasing trend towards monumentality which can be detected in the financial district from the time of the Great Fire onwards. The new Royal Exchange, for example, was significantly more obvious to passers-by than its predecessor.[52] The next specialised business buildings were associated with the trading companies. In the 1720s the South Sea Company and the East India Company each erected large-scale headquarters buildings with imposing, if clumsy, façades to the street. Far more truly Palladian and impressive were the Bank of England's new headquarters erected in 1732–34. They were soon joined by the Mansion House, the Lord Mayor's official residence, built nearby between 1739 and 1752 on the site of the Stocks provision market, and the new Excise Office, erected in Broad Street between 1769 and 1775, both of which made a distinctive contribution to the dignity of the area. These palatial buildings were in striking contrast to the small-scale domestic structures which adjoined them. The Bank's new building, however, was distinctly traditional in scale and layout. It did not require the storage and trading space of East India House, and so could be accommodated within the relatively narrow limits of the site of a former merchant's house. In functional terms its plan, with a hall set back from the street, and offices behind, closely resembled that of the premises at Grocers' Hall.[53]

[51] For Jones's designs, previously considered not to have been built, see J. Harris and G. Higgott, *Inigo Jones: Complete Architectural Drawings* (1990), pp. 256–57. The site came to be known as Tokenhouse Yard, and it is clear that at least the long range of offices or warehouses was built and survived the Great Fire: R. Ruding, *Annals of the Coinage of Great Britain*, 1 (3rd edn, 1840), pp. 389, 398–400; J. Leake, *An Exact Surveigh of the Streets, Lanes, and Churches contained within the Ruins of the City of London* (1667), relevant portion reproduced as Fig. 92; Maitland, *History of London*, p. 840.

[52] Cf. *supra*, Chapter XIV; V. Harding and P. Metcalf, *Lloyd's at Home* (1986), pp. 82–83.

[53] H. M. Colvin, *A Biographical Dictionary of British Architects, 1600–1840* (3rd edn, 1995), pp. 288–89, 419, 832, 841, 1276; Harding and Metcalf, *Lloyd's*, pp. 94–95, 123–26; S. Jeffery, *The Mansion House* (Chichester, 1993); W. Marston Acres, *The Bank of England from within, 1694–1900*, 1 (1931), p. 47 and pl. XVII; Maitland, *History of London*, pp. 846, 848, 1003; T. Shepherd, *London in the Nineteenth Century* (1829), pp. 62–63, 72.

[48] T. F. Reddaway, *The Rebuilding of London after the Great Fire* (1940), pp. 51–67; see *supra*, pp. 122–23; C. Wren, *Parentalia* (1750), pp. 269–71.

[49] H. A. Harben, *A Dictionary of London* (1918), p. 483; *Leigh's New Picture*, p. 248.

[50] Defoe, *Tour*, 1, pp. 336, 339–40; Imray, *Mercers' Hall*, pp. 262–71.

While regretting its confined situation in Thread-needle Street, contemporaries recognised the quality of the Bank's new building, and its drawing power as a centre of business close to the Royal Exchange. Over the following century the needs of the Bank constituted the main force in the physical transformation of the district. Three principal requirements can be identified: the need to accommodate the expanding business of the Bank, which was largely associated with government finance, and to provide more light and air for its clerks; the need to protect the Bank from fire and disorder in the taverns, alleys, and streets which adjoined it; and the need for a more dignified and spacious approach for pedestrians and carriages. From 1764 onwards this led to the steady enlargement of the area occupied by the Bank; to the creation of Bank Buildings (1766–67), a group of private houses and offices to the west of the Royal Exchange and on either side of a new approach to the Bank; and to the laying out of Prince's Street (1808), flanked by Soane's curtain wall.[54] The culmination of this process came with the rebuilding of the Royal Exchange after the fire of 1838: the new structure was given a grand portico facing on to the new open space in front of the Bank where Bank Buildings had stood, in a conscious expression of the acknowledged role of finance and commerce in city life. A more general programme of street improvements enhanced the centrality of that space, eased movement within the district, and improved communications with residential areas which now lay at some distance from the City. In the eighteenth century three parish churches had made a distinctive visual contribution to the immediate neighbourhood of the Bank and the Exchange, demonstrating its historic residential character.[55] By the mid-1840s they had gone, and the architectural landscape was dominated by the palatial monuments of finance (Fig. 94).

Meanwhile, other businesses, principally the insurance companies, private bankers, brokers, merchants, and lawyers continued to occupy private houses more or less modified for business purposes. The insurance company buildings were the most purely commercial in function. In the eighteenth century many of them acquired elaborate façades, a process facilitated by rebuilding after two fires in Cornhill, where the companies congregated. One insurance company leased more specialised premises in the Royal Exchange from the 1720s onwards, and the Sun Fire Office (along with at least one banking business) moved to Bank Buildings soon after their completion.[56]

Contemporaries also noted the high quality of the houses occupied by bankers in Lombard Street. One of them, Charles Asgill, in about 1756 employed the rising architect, Robert Taylor, later to become his friend and Surveyor to the Bank of England, to design him a 'banking house' there (later occupied by an insurance company), along with a country villa at Richmond, fourteen miles from the City.[57] Asgill was following the practice, common for centuries among leading City men, of maintaining several places of residence, of which one was at his place of business and another was a 'retiring house' an hour or more out of town. From about this time on, however, it became increasingly common for City merchants to travel daily to their work from a house in one of the newly expanding suburbs or from a semi-rural location such as Hackney. Even so, many banking houses in the City retained a domestic character up to the mid-nineteenth century, with well-appointed living rooms upstairs and the 'shop', as it continued to be called, on the ground floor where bank business was done. Often it fell to the younger partners to reside in the City. Thus, on Census night in 1851 the banking house of Barnard, Barnard and Dimsdale in Cornhill was inhabited by the junior partner, his wife, his three young children, and six domestic servants, along with two clerks and a bank messenger who were in their

[54] Marston Acres, *Bank of England*, I, pp. 190–91, 194, 197–98, 397, 402–03; Colvin, *Dictionary* (1978), p. 964.
[55] The churches of St Bartholomew by the Exchange, St Benet Fink, and St Christopher le Stocks, removed in 1840–41, 1781, and 1842–44, respectively: Harben, *Dictionary*, s.n. For the contribution of the churches to the landscape, cf. Harding and Metcalf, *Lloyds*, pp. 82–83; Marston Acres, *Bank of England*, pls. XXVIII, LIII; Shepherd, *London in the Nineteenth Century*, pp. 132–33.
[56] Supple, *Royal Exchange Insurance*, pp. 19, 34; D. Hughson, *London; being an Accurate History and Description of the British Metropolis and its Neighbourhood* (1805), I, p. 412, and II, pp. 115, 119, 123, 140–41; Marston Acres, *Bank of England*, pp. 197–98.
[57] Colvin, *Dictionary*, pp. 962–63; Hughson, *London*, II, pp. 534–38; Maitland, *History of London*, p. 996.

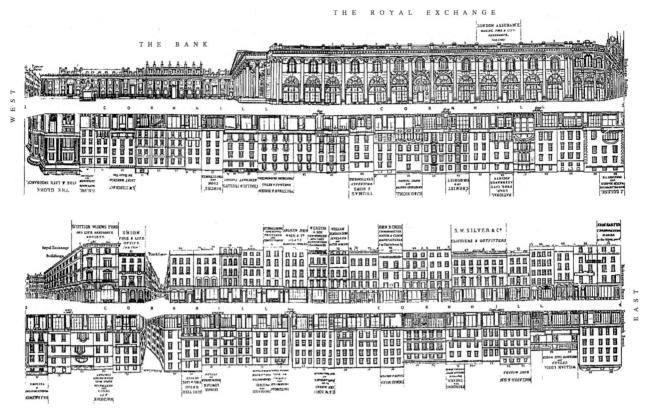

FIG. 94. From *Tallis's Street Views and Pictorial Directory* (London, 1847). The palatial character of the Bank of England, the Royal Exchange, and some of the insurance company headquarters contrasts with the domestic scale of most of the other buildings, many of which still included the shops of retailers or small manufacturers. Tallis's views have been arranged so as to produce a panorama extending along Cornhill from the Bank on the west to Gracechurch Street and Bishopsgate Street on the east (cf. Fig. 93).

early twenties. At Martin, Stone and Martin's bank in Lombard Street, James Martin, an unmarried partner who also had lodgings at Camden outside the City, was dwelling with his clerks and servants, while his elder brother, the senior partner, and his younger brother both lived with their families in fashionable new houses in the West End.[58] By the 1850s it was more common for the domestic rooms at banking houses to be occupied by senior clerks and their families, or by groups of unmarried clerks under the eye of a housekeeper. Even the managers of the banks tended to live outside the City.

Up to the early decades of the nineteenth century the insurance and private banking premises were relatively small in scale and were generally contained within a pattern of house and plot boundaries inherited from the medieval City. A growing business was often accommodated by extending the building over the yard at the rear. That created the gloomy, cramped environment typical of much of the nineteenth- and twentieth-century City, where architects had to exercise great ingenuity in providing light wells and ventilation shafts.[59] Even so, up to about 1820 most of the houses in the financial district were valued equally as residences and as commercial premises. Sale notices continued to stress the comfort and splendour of the domestic accommodation, and even after Princes Street had been laid out (1808) family houses for professional men were being built

---

[58] Census enumerators' returns for Nos. 49–50 Cornhill and 68 Lombard Street; *Post Office London Street Directory 1851*; J. B. Martin, '*The Grasshopper' in Lombard Street* (1892), pp. 102, 226–28, 275; cf. D. Kynaston, *City of London*, p. 61.

[59] I'Anson, 'Some notice of office buildings'; Martin, *Grasshopper*, pp. 226–28.

across the street from the Bank of England.[60] A 'mercantile residence' in Warnford Court, 'within three minutes walk of the Royall Exchange' was in 1805 described in terms of its domestic accommodation, but with the suggestion that the 'handsome dining and drawing rooms' might be converted to counting houses. In the more crowded conditions of Pope's Head Alley, a house offered for sale in 1806 was subject to slightly different expectations: potential occupiers identified included not only the merchant or broker (apparently as residents), but also the 'office keeper', presumably one who made his living by renting out office space.[61] Evidently it was already an established practice to let out rooms in houses as offices, and even to split entire houses into office units, for the use of those who, unlike banks and insurance companies, needed only a room or two as a working base. As business demand grew, the attractions of letting out rooms for offices became correspondingly great, and so professional families sought houses elsewhere. The construction of Finsbury Square in 1777 and Finsbury Circus, just beyond the line of the former City wall, in 1815, demonstrates the demand for grand houses within a few minutes walk of the Bank, and it was among the prosperous medical men of Finsbury Square that Julius Reuter and his family found lodging when they arrived in London in 1851.[62] Improvements in transport, however, meant that those working in the City could more readily live elsewhere. Thus the opening of Blackfriars Bridge in 1768, and more especially of Southwark Bridge in 1819 and of Broad Street railway station in 1861, brought new residential territories within reach and changed perceptions of the City and its surroundings. As a commentator on the City's depopulation put it in 1872:

the citizen may now live in a suburban villa or even in a Belgravian or Tyburnian mansion, upon the rent he obtains for the drawing-room floor of the house wherein his ancestors lived for generations.[63]

From 1820 onwards, but especially from 1840, 'stacks of offices', purpose-built structures occupying narrow house sites, became more and more common.[64] Their origin, and the early stages in the spread of small-scale office buildings, are far from clear. An important stage in the development may have been in the later eighteenth century, when buildings described as 'chambers' began to appear in the area.[65] They may have been modelled on the lawyers' chambers at the Inns of Court, and were perhaps originally intended as residential accommodation for bachelor merchants, whose requirements had certainly made a distinctive impact on the housing stock of the Cheapside area in the seventeenth century. Such rooms soon came to be used for business. Dickens, in *A Christmas Carol* (1843), tells us that Scrooge 'lived in chambers . . . a gloomy suite of rooms, in a towering pile of building up a yard . . . nobody lived in it now but Scrooge, the other rooms being all let out as offices'. By that date, substantial, purpose-built blocks of offices were being built. Among the most obvious of them was Royal Exchange Buildings (1842), on a new street opened as part of the replanning of the area which followed the fire at the Exchange.[66]

As the eighteenth century progressed and business grew, the informal dealing and associations in the coffee houses led to the emergence of new institutional forms. That was accompanied by a growing perception among specialised groups of traders that they should control the space in which they made their markets. The common trading space, such as that at the Royal Exchange, or the informal, multi-purpose environment provided by the coffee house, had no long-term future. Even within the coffee house it became the practice to restrict use of parts of the establishment to specialised groups of subscribers. In the 1760s the 150 or so brokers who dealt in government stocks and company shares at Jonathan's coffee house formed an association and rented a room there, where they ran their market for three hours a day. In 1773 they acquired independent premises at the corner of Sweetings Alley, and in

[60] Marston Acres, *Bank of England*, II, pp. 402–03.
[61] Bodleian Library, Gough Additional Folios A261, no. 160, and A262, no. 223.
[62] Colvin, *Dictionary*, pp. 289, 670; Read, *Power of News*, p. 15.
[63] E. I'Anson, 'On the valuation of house property in London', *Papers Read at the Royal Institute of British Architects, Session 1872–73* (1872–73), p. 40.

[64] I'Anson, 'Some notice of office buildings'.
[65] Harben, *Dictionary*, pp. 181, 430.
[66] Harben, *Dictionary*, p. 513; I'Anson, 'Some notice of office buildings', pp. 25, 29.

1801 moved to more spacious purpose-built premises at Capel Court, the direct ancestor of the present London International Stock Exchange.[67] In the 1770s the 71 merchants, brokers and marine insurance underwriters meeting at Lloyd's coffee house likewise formed a society with the intent of building their own premises, for which Robert Adam prepared magnificent designs. In the event, they leased rooms at the Royal Exchange, and after the fire of 1838 the provision of rooms for Lloyd's was a major element in the design for the new Exchange.[68] A similar initiative, by surveyors and auctioneers, led to the building, in 1808–09, of the Auction Mart, an impressive structure described as a 'national edifice' close to the Stock Exchange, which, by contrast, was plainer and more concealed from view. The Auction Mart accommodated sales of landed estates and works of art, and a reading room where the prospectuses of canal and railway companies were to be found. It did not develop the institutionalised, regulatory role of the Stock Exchange or Lloyd's and so ultimately faded away.[69]

The provision of exchanges for particular markets had been anticipated in the commodity trading areas outside the financial district by the Corn Exchange and the Coal Exchange, first built in 1747 and 1769, respectively, and both of some architectural pretension. The Commercial Hall, erected by subscription in Mincing Lane in 1811, provided spacious and elegant accommodation for the sale of colonial goods.[70] The process continued. In 1858, for example, South Sea House was converted to accommodate the Baltic Exchange, run by an association of traders in Baltic and Russian goods who had previously met at the Virginia and Baltic coffee house and had traded in the Royal Exchange.[71] The most ambitious of the exchanges in the financial district was the private enterprise by a biscuit baker (one of the distinctive service trades of the area), Edward Moxhay. His 'Hall of Commerce' of the early 1840s was intended to capture trade displaced from the destroyed Royal Exchange, and probably also to provide a market for industrial goods. Industrial marketing, however, developed in a different way, and the Hall of Commerce was ultimately a failure. It became reading rooms, and provided accommodation for those 'who had no office of their own', before being taken over in about 1855 as the headquarters of a bank.[72]

The exchanges were competing enterprises, offering space for fluid and highly volatile markets. From its construction in 1765–70 the Rotunda in the Bank of England housed a lively market in government stocks, which persisted into the 1830s, despite growing competition from the Stock Exchange.[73] During the railway boom of 1845, trading in railway shares was conducted in the Stock Exchange, at the Royal Exchange, in the Auction Mart, at the Hall of Commerce, and in coffee houses and the street; but that hectic business, much of it conducted by disreputable 'stags' and 'alley men', quickly faded away.[74] Such rapid flows of dealing beyond the conventional spatial limits, followed by equally rapid ebbs, have continued to be characteristic of City business, even in the more regulated and constrained environment of the twentieth century.

The new exchanges were few in number, but during the 1830s and 1840s there was a more widespread rebuilding of the headquarters of banks and insurance offices. This reflected both a sharp increase in insurance business and the legislative

[67] Colvin, *Dictionary*, p. 744; S. R. Cope, 'The Stock-Brokers find a home: how the Exchange came to be established in Sweetings Alley in 1773', *Guildhall Studies in London History*, 2 (1975–77), pp. 213–19; Morgan and Thomas, *Stock Exchange*, p. 71.
[68] Harding and Metcalf, *Lloyds*, pp. 85–94, 99–103.
[69] Auction Mart, *A Detailed Prospectus of the Auction Mart, Instituted 1808* (1809); Colvin, *Dictionary*, p. 1020; *Leigh's New Picture*, p. 241; *New Survey of London*, I, p. 378. For views of the Auction Mart, see D. Kynaston, *Cazenove and Co.: a History* (1991), following p. 96, and of the Stock Exchange, Shepherd, *London in the Nineteenth Century*, pp. 129–30.
[70] *London and its Environs Described* (1761), s.n. 'Corn Exchange'; J. Britten (ed.), *The Original Picture of London* (1826), p. 144; Colvin, *Dictionary*, pp. 288, 1078; *Leigh's New Picture*, p. 251; Shepherd, *London in the Nineteenth Century*, p. 80; R. Smith, *Sea Coal for London, History of the Coal Factors in the London Market* (1961), pp. 84–87.
[71] H. Barty-King, *The Baltic Exchange: the History of a Unique Market* (1977), pp. 35–61, 89–128.
[72] Barty-King, *Baltic Exchange*, pp. 90–91; Lillywhite (1963), pp. 257–58; *New Survey of London*, I, p. 378; *The Illustrated London News*, 30 July 1842, p. 180; 17 December 1842, p. 500; 29 December 1855, p. 700.
[73] *Leigh's New Picture*, p. 236; Marston Acres, *Bank of England*, I, pp. 216–17; Morgan and Thomas, *Stock Exchange*, pp. 52–54.
[74] Morgan and Thomas, *Stock Exchange*, pp. 108–09; *New Survey of London*, I, p. 378.

changes of 1826 and 1833 which enabled joint-stock banks to come into being and to establish themselves in the City.[75] The new insurance buildings, larger and architecturally more ambitious than their predecessors, were especially prominent, and spread beyond the limits of Cornhill and its environs, into Cheapside and beyond.[76] On the other hand, the leading banks had developed a clearing system, requiring a daily interchange of papers at the Clearing House in Lombard Street,[77] and that restricted them almost entirely to the central district (Fig. 93). In the same period the West End witnessed an extensive rebuilding both of the insurance company headquarters located there and of the offices of the non-clearing banks.[78]

A forerunner of future developments in the central district was provided by the headquarters of the newly formed joint-stock bank, the London and Westminster Bank, erected in Lothbury, behind the Bank of England, between 1837 and 1839. This capital-rich institution, intent on establishing its reputation, acquired a block of several private properties on which was erected a large-scale building designed by the leading architects of the day. Its imposing façade stood in sharp contrast to the smaller-scale and traditional buildings of the private bankers, Jones Loyd and Company, which stood next door and had been rebuilt as recently as 1808, incorporating residential accommodation for a partner.[79] During the 1850s and 1860s there was a sharp rise in the demand for new, large-scale sites on prime frontages to be occupied by the headquarters buildings of banks (especially the growing number of joint-stock banks), insurance companies, and the finance and discount companies which proliferated after the Companies Act of 1856 (cf. Fig. 95). Cheap money facilitated rapid change. Investment in building now underpinned as well as accommodated a business. As *The*

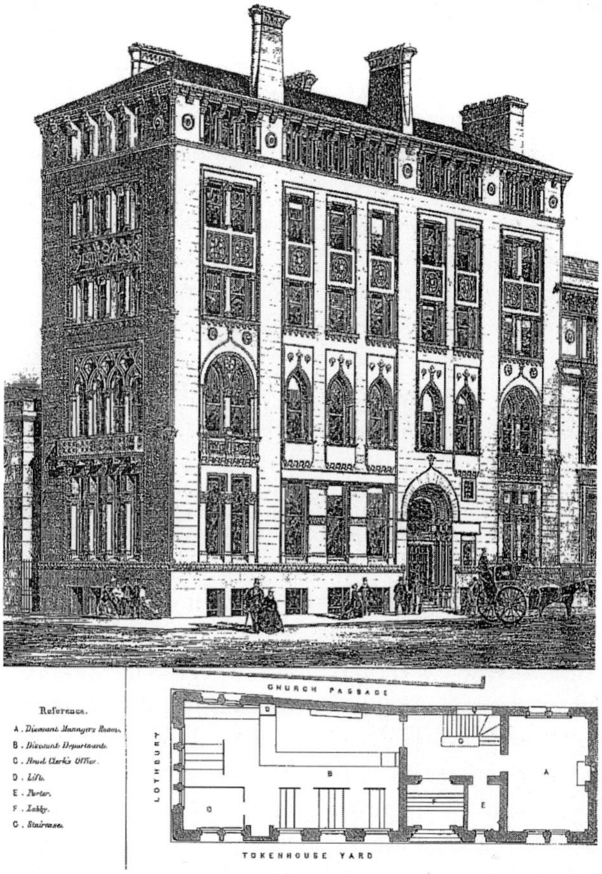

FIG. 95. The Lothbury offices of the General Credit and Discount Company, 1868. From a sale notice. A striking example, in the Venetian style, of the imposing office buildings erected during the building boom of the 1860s.

Builder wrote of the new National Provincial Bank building of 1865, adjoining the Baltic Exchange, 'architectural effect . . . in the case of a bank can . . . help the impression of stability of the concern'.[80]

Many of the new headquarters buildings, like some of their public counterparts, included lettable office space on upper floors — a source of income which would help finance the development, and a reserve of space to accommodate future growth in the organisation. Yet equally typical of the last decades of the period, and a measure of increasing demand, was the large-scale speculative office block. Significantly, some of the key developers of such premises began

[75] Pressnell, *Country Banking*, pp. 507–10; Richards, *Early History of Banking*, pp. 196–99; Supple, *Royal Exchange Insurance*, p. 112.
[76] J. Summerson, 'The Victorian rebuilding of the City of London', *The London Journal*, 3 (1977), pp. 163–85.
[77] C. Knight, *Knight's Cyclopaedia of London* (1851), pp. 639–40.
[78] Colvin, *Dictionary*, pp. 116, 259, 514, 735, 863, 1013.
[79] T. E. Gregory, *The Westminster Bank through a Century* (Oxford, 1936), pp. 100, 165; I. S. Black, 'Symbolic capital: the London and Westminster Bank headquarters, 1836–38', *Landscape Research*, 21.1 (1996), pp. 55–72.

[80] Olsen, *The City as a Work of Art*, pp. 27, 29.

their careers in the conversion of domestic buildings to multiple office use.[81]

These dramatic changes were obvious to observers at the time. Historians of the eighteenth- and nineteenth-century City have the opportunity of measuring their impact more precisely in terms of the numbers and values of properties assessed for local taxation, of the businesses carried on there, and of the resident population (Table 1). A study of the central financial district[82] reveals that change was decidedly uneven across the area, although by 1870 it had been transformed entirely. Over the eighteenth century (between 1693 and 1817) the rate of change was greatest in the immediate neighbourhood of the Bank of England, even if we discount that part of the area which came to be occupied by the Bank itself. Here houses, banks, and other business buildings (including the Auction Mart and the Stock Exchange) were altered or rebuilt on a larger scale than elsewhere, as revealed by the reduction in the number of separately assessed properties and the increase in their mean rental value. The increase in the total rental value of the neighbourhood was not so great as that of the area immediately to the east (containing South Sea House), because several properties close to the Bank had been removed in the course of street improvements. By contrast, some parts of the district, most notably at the eastern end of Lombard Street towards the commodity trading area, hardly changed at all. In two parishes, again in the south-eastern quarter of the district, populations actually increased between 1695 and 1801.[83] That perhaps was caused by a displacement of poorer residents from the more central areas, combined with a rise in the demand for their services as porters and servants. By 1811, however, the populations of even those parishes had begun to fall.

Between 1817 and 1851 all parts of the district experienced a reduction in the number of properties

TABLE 1

NUMBERS OF PROPERTIES AND TOTAL RENTAL VALUES FOR SELECTED PARTS OF LONDON'S FINANCIAL DISTRICT
(INDEX VALUES 1693–1871)

Date	Bank*	Area Cornhill†	Lombard Street: west	east
1693:				
properties	100	100	100	100
value	100	100	100	100
1817:				
properties	67	82	79	105
value	158	138	128	119
1851:				
properties	45	63	44	89
value	368	273	185	184
1871:				
properties	30	46	34	60
values	965	760	593	570

SOURCES. For 1693: CLRO, Four Shillings in the Pound Tax (totals supplied by J. Alexander); J. Ogilby and W. Morgan, *A Large and Accurate Map of the City of London* (1676). For other years: Guildhall Library, MSS 2137–38 (Sewer and Consolidated Rate valuations).

NOTES TO TABLE
* Excluding site of Bank and Royal Exchange.
† Excluding site of Royal Exchange.

and an increase in property values. The increase in mean, as well as total, values was most marked near the Bank of England, with Cornhill in second place, and seems clearly to reflect the demand for new bank and insurance premises, and the changes associated with the rebuilding of the Royal Exchange. Once again the south-eastern quarter, represented by the eastern part of Lombard Street, experienced the lowest rate of change.

By 1851 few financiers or merchants remained resident in the area, which was by now the most depopulated part of the City. On the other hand, large numbers of the resident population were still, as in the eighteenth century, employed in retailing and small-scale production, mostly at their places of residence (31 per cent of resident adults with a given occupation). It seems that many of the shopkeeping families of this type, including bakers, tailors, watchmakers, printers, bookbinders, and bootmakers, were able to continue living in the area, despite increasing rents and land values, because they could sub-let

[81] For these general developments, see J. Summerson, *The London Building World of the Eighteen-Sixties* (1973).

[82] See above, note 1.

[83] The index value for the entire district in 1801, taking the 1695 population total as 100, was 79; the index values for All Hallows Lombard Street and St Benet Gracechurch were 106 and 108, respectively.

rooms in their houses for use as offices. Characteristically, the small businesses carried on in such offices were those of agencies associated with the stock market, shipping, insurance, and merchandising, the trades whose growth was transforming the City. The second largest occupational group among the residents serviced the office sector as office keepers, housekeepers, messengers or porters. They represented 18 per cent of the resident working population overall, rising to 31 per cent in the neighbourhood of the Bank of England, where change was most advanced. The employed company messenger, carrying letters and bills from office to office within the area, was an important development of the period, replacing the casual 'ticket porters' of earlier times.[84] Resident messengers were often married to female 'housekeepers' (although housekeepers could also be men), and it was the couple's job to look after the office building in the garret of which they lived.

The rate of change reached a new peak in the 1850s and 1860s. In all parts of the area property values rose more quickly than before. The rate of increase was now greatest in the south-eastern quarter, which came finally to be transformed by the construction of banks and office blocks. In that area, the relatively poor working-class families who in 1851 had lived in acutely overcrowded houses in a maze of courts and alleys just a few paces from Lombard Street, were displaced. So, too, were the resident retailers and small-scale producers, who were unable to resist the pressures and lures of the property market. In 1871 resident heads of household in that category represented no more than 9 per cent of the total. The housekeepers and messengers, however, had risen to 35 per cent of the resident population, and despite a 40 per cent decline in the total population of the area between 1851 and 1871,[85] the number of housekeepers and office keepers actually rose from 216 to 261.

Despite the huge capital assets and public visibility of the banks, insurance companies, and finance houses, the business life of the district was dominated by the numerous small-scale concerns within the world of broking and merchanting. In 1871 the area contained 2,128 businesses with office addresses, an increase of 18 per cent since 1851, and of 70 per cent since 1817.[86] By far the greatest part of the increase was accounted for by the small businesses, and in 1871 the banks and other large concerns represented only about 3 per cent of the total. There were distinct geographical patterns in the distribution of the smaller businesses. The stockbrokers, for example, were by far the largest single group, and 63 per cent of them had offices in buildings almost immediately adjacent to the Stock Exchange. Insurance brokers were to be found along Cornhill, and shipping agents, general merchants and company agents in the new stacks of offices along Gracechurch Street and Bishopsgate on the eastern edge of the area. They were the sort of people who might once have used a coffee house as an address but whose scale of business now demanded an office, and ledgers as well as a pocket book.

To a large extent the patterns in the distribution of businesses reflected the need for access to particular markets, or to more than one market, as in the case of the merchants in Gracechurch Street who might require banking, insurance and shipping services, as well as access to the 'colonial goods' area to the east. It seems likely, however, that close analysis of spatial patterns will reveal more complex relationships within the highly concentrated nexus of businesses which made up the financial district. Those relationships probably arose from the interdependence of numerous separate, small-scale specialised enterprises which provided services to each other and to outsiders on a flexible basis. Combinations of different types of enterprise — accountants, civil engineers, and company agents, provide one example — within the highly localised environment of the alley or office block, are likely to have been just as significant in the working life of the district as an exclusive concentration like that of the stockbrokers. Such forms of personal and business association, reinforced by membership of clubs, livery companies, and vestries, were an essential attribute of patterns of work and enterprise in the City.

---

[84] W. M. Stern, *The Porters of London* (1960), pp. 178–85; Morier Evans, *City Men*, pp. 167–68.
[85] The index value for the population of the whole area in 1871 was 27.

[86] Statistics and distributions based on: *Johnstone's London Commercial Guide and Street Directory* (1817–18); *Post Office Directory 1851*; Collingridge, *City of London Directory 1871*.

The distinctive feature of London's financial district surrounding the Royal Exchange was the combination of services it provided: in commodity, share and stock markets; in finance; in insurance; in shipping, and in information. Crown or government interests were also present, both in the continual need for loans and in the form of institutions such as the Exchange and Wardrobe in the Middle Ages and the Post Office and Excise Office in later times. That conjunction of markets, facilities, and power, which in many significant respects resembled that present in Wall Street during the nineteenth century,[87] made the area central to the economic life of the City, and for a while to that of a world financial system. Bagehot's implicit question as to why the money market came to be established where it did is to be answered in terms of an accumulation of causes which explain why it settled *neither* in the original main market place of the City *nor* in the riverside district which was the focus of its overseas trade. In that respect, the market was less concrete than Bagehot's terminology implies: fundamentally, it was an occasion or performance, involving sets of ideas and assumptions common to the actors involved, which on account of its complexity and very intangibility could only function within a universally recognised and well-defined space where many networks intersected. With hindsight, it is possible to see how the interests of high finance, luxury consumption, the recycling of rent, and long-distance trade converged in an area which hitherto had been peripheral to the City's main centres of business. The gradual establishment of public institutions and buildings — above all the Royal Exchange and later the Bank of England — consolidated the area's role and identity, but informal habits of association among merchants and others were also a powerful force for continuity. By 1666 the monumental potential of the financial district was recognised by some, but adaptation within existing structures and topographical frameworks was to remain the predominant means by which the area accommodated its growing and increasingly specialised business.

Up to the nineteenth century the Bank and the Exchange were the only major structures which expressed the financial character of the district, although overall the density and scale of building was increasing. New exchanges and the headquarters of insurance companies and banks followed; there was also a steady increase in the demand for office space by brokers, agents and other small businessmen, and a corresponding decrease in the use of the facilities provided by coffee houses and taverns. Those stages paralleled and expressed ones in the organisation of business. The destruction of the Royal Exchange in 1838 provided an opportunity for localised redevelopment, but overall the amalgamation of sites and the physical transformation of the area proceeded fairly slowly until the 1850s and 1860s. Even in the mid-nineteenth century, when the availability of capital and the head of demand for large prime sites and lettable office space had built up to unprecedented heights, rebuilding on a large scale could be a protracted business. A powerful force inhibiting change was the extreme fragmentation and heterogeneity in the ownership and tenure of both land and buildings, which had characterised the City for many centuries. In the 1860s, for example, the City Offices Company undertook a large-scale office development in the south-eastern quarter of the district and had to acquire twenty-three separate properties, freehold and leasehold, at a cost of £70,000 down and £653,000 over 99 years, before spending £70,000 on building.[88] Even then the company could not buy out all the existing interests, and was forced to adjust the plan of its new buildings accordingly. Only after 1830 or so was it possible for private or joint-stock, rather than civic or semi-public, enterprises to undertake such comprehensive transformations of the fabric in this central district.

Study of the physical evolution of the financial district aids interpretation of London's commercial fortunes over the long term and of its image in the wider world. The Royal Exchange was the focal point

---

87 W. Werner and S. T. Smith, *Wall Street* (New York, 1991).

88 City Offices Company, *Third Annual Report, 22 March 1866* (among the records of the City Offices Company, held by Greycoat Group plc, London); *The Building News and Engineering Journal*, 26 January 1866. The number of properties to be acquired is indicated by the rate lists of 1851: Guildhall Library, MSS 2137–8. These processes and problems are well-described in City of London Real Property Company, *The City of London Real Property Company Limited, 1864–1964* (published by the company, 1964).

of that district and a powerful element in that image, yet in the latter part of the period the increase in its physical prominence was matched by a decline in its functional significance, except simply as an office building. Likewise, geographical analysis of the activities in the district provides indications of the ways in which the internal business life of the City was organised, information which is all the more valuable since few detailed records of the small-scale enterprises which dominated that life have survived. That complex business network underpinned, though it eventually undermined, the life of the Exchange, supplying the people and the ideas which for three centuries came together twice a day in a spectacular, theatrical and productive expression of London's commercial life.

CHAPTER XXV

The Excavation for the Third Royal Exchange

By PETER MARSDEN

THE EXCAVATION OF THE SITE of the Royal Exchange, prior to the erection of the third building, provided the climax to a prolonged struggle between Richard Lambert Jones, Chairman of the Royal Exchange Development Committee, and Charles Roach Smith, a chemist by profession but an antiquary and a scholar by instinct. Jones has been in control of the Committee for the Rebuilding of London Bridge and for Improving and Making Suitable Approaches Thereto; although he had been instrumental in the setting up of the Guildhall Library in 1824 with a museum as an adjunct two years later, and although he served them as chairman thereafter, he was not a man to let the past stand in the way of the splendid modern future he foresaw for London. To this end, he had organised the sacrifice of Wren's unusual church, St Michael's, Crooked Lane, in the cause of road-widening and was very ready to let the trenches for the capital's new sewerage system rip through previously undisturbed layers of Roman London with no real attempt to preserve the treasures revealed. Roach Smith viewed all this with horror, saved what he could, and organised a team of juvenile watchers to report on excavations and to offer money on the spot for significant finds. An armed truce existed between the two men which broke into open warfare over the Royal Exchange site, the road-rationalisation for the new building having required the demolition of Roach Smith's shop in Lothbury. He sued the Corporation over the destruction but without success.

Before the redevelopment, the Corporation of London and the Mercers' Company, who comprised the Joint Gresham Committee responsible for the rebuilding, had decided that this time the City should be seen to be concerned about antiquities discovered on this supremely historic site. The contractor agreed to hand in all discoveries; the workmen were to be 'liberally compensated' for their finds, but punished if found selling antiquities; and a large room in a house in Freeman's Court nearby was to be set aside temporarily for the 'reception, arrangement, and custody of all antiquities so discovered'.

The hope that there would be important discoveries was realised during 1841 when a Roman gravel pit full of exceptionally well preserved antiquities was found at the west end of the site.[1] The objects were placed in the London Institution where in due course they were catalogued, drawn, and eventually published in a special report by Tite which was given to every member of the Court of Common Council. But in spite of this the Redevelopment Committee, under the chairmanship of Lambert Jones, refused to hand the antiquities over to the City Library and museum. However, this did not stop the Corporation from considering that, having examined the Royal Exchange site, it had shown that it was indeed caring for the history and antiquities of the City of London, and that Roach Smith's accusations were untrue.

In 1845, even though the excavations had long been completed, the Gresham Committee had still made no decision about where the antiquities would be preserved. They could have formed the basis for a new city museum, but the Guildhall Library, itself badly stored in cramped conditions, had totally inadequate storage facilities; and Lambert Jones, the one man on the Library Committee who could still have done something helpful, did nothing. In fact at one stage it looked as if the City might give the Royal Exchange antiquities to the London Institution where the space had been found.

At the end of January 1845 Thomas Lott, a Deputy of the Corporation and a good friend of Roach Smith, raised the museum question before the Court of Common Council, by requesting them to ask the

---

[1] See *supra*, Chapter I.

Library Committee to reconsider setting up a museum. Lott was to be disappointed, however, as the meeting was adjourned due to insufficient members of the Court being present.

Censure of the Corporation quickly followed from the Press: 'the apathy', said one magazine, 'is really disgraceful to the City of London, and cannot be sufficiently reprobated. There are few towns in England in which some public repository of local antiquities cannot be found; yet in London . . . where curious remnants of the past are turned up every day, there is nobody appointed for their preservation, there is not even a place at which they may be gathered together: they are at once sold to individuals, and so dispersed . . . and in too many instances, are unnoticed and destroyed.'

In October *The Builder* launched an attack on the City for deciding to demolish the Church of St Benet Fink as part of the 'improvements' in the Royal Exchange area. This was an unusual and historical Wren church, and the magazine was 'forced to cry, shame on those who may be concerned in the wanton destruction of this valuable example of our great countryman's skill'. Lambert Jones was chairman of the committee responsible.

This criticism was the limit as far as the Corporation was concerned. On the evening of Monday 17 November, William Tite gave a speech at an ordinary meeting of the Royal Institute of British Architects, of which he was the vice-president, in which he publicly attacked Charles Roach Smith. He accused him of distorting the truth, and claimed that private collectors, particularly Roach Smith himself, who had been buying antiquities from workmen, had actually stopped the City from acquiring a collection, and had therefore delayed the setting up of a museum. Tite also accused Roach Smith of stealing antiquities from the Royal Exchange site, and of threatening to shoot the Clerk of Works. Tite said that he had suffered much trouble from collectors 'amongst the most active was Mr. Roach Smith who secured many [antiquities]'.

This was the last straw as far as Roach Smith was concerned. He was furious that Tite had tried to discredit him with falsehoods, and that 'he had the affrontery . . . to make me appear as the great

impediment to the Corporation's preservation of City antiquities. This was not to be endured'. Since Tite had publicly accused Roach Smith, the latter 'challenged Mr. Tite to a public discussion'.

Tite did not attend the public debate, but he was not so easily able to ignore Roach Smith's reply to its original accusations in *The Builder*. Roach Smith wrote that he found it 'rather remarkable that Mr. Tite should have allowed so many years to elapse before he had venture to rebut my assertions and to counter charges'. He said that he had never purchased objects from the workmen on site, since the Gresham Committee was collecting them, and although he had encouraged the workmen to hand in objects, 'I much doubt if the chief mass of antiquities collected, ever reached the London Institution'. Indeed, many people visited the site and took antiquities, even from the room in which they were supposed to have been preserved.

Tite's accusation that Roach Smith had stolen antiquities and had threatened to shoot the Clerk of Works on the Royal Exchange site was based on two curious incidents that are also fully documented. The first was when Roach Smith was accused of being responsible for the loss of a broken sculpture of Charles II brought to him by workmen from the Royal Exchange. He ordered them to return it and 'I paid them to do so, and moreover paid for a barrow to convey it in. I perfectly well remember telling them that a museum was being formed for such things and that they must take it there'. The other incident occurred when Roach Smith was ordered off the site and was threatened with physical violence. He returned to the site on the following day and later recalled his conversation with the Clerk of Works. 'I then said that if his [Tite's] order could not protect me from personal violence, if I came again, I should feel it necessary, in self defence, to come armed. When if the Gresham agent should think it fit to put his threats into execution and lay hands or feet on my person, he might run the risk of being shot.'

On safety grounds, Roach Smith gave up visiting the site.

In the published correspondence in *The Builder*, Roach Smith attacked the Corporation for its apathy, and, in addition to refuting the accusation by Tite that he had taken antiquities from the Royal

Exchange site, he added his own sharp words privately directed at Lambert Jones, the chairman of the committee.

Had I been a servant of the Corporation, and seized some thirty or forty gold nobles, on behalf of the city,[2] and had never rendered to science or to the City Exchequer a proper account of the *treasure trove*, then Mr. Tite might . . . have worthily stood forward as a public accuser. But, I trust, I have said enough to show that the accusations brought against me are frivolous, vexatious, and false; that they have all the appearance of being an *afterthought*, and are calculated to mislead the public, and to injure private character . . . they are unworthy of the office Mr. Tite holds, through which office he has thought proper to disseminate them.

Before the rebuilding of the Royal Exchange, Roach Smith had been given by the owner of a site an object that subsequently proved to be a sixteenth-century inscription cut in lead referring to the opening of the first Royal Exchange by Queen Elizabeth I. Tite accused him of illegally receiving this important object and asked him to return it. To Roach Smith there were more important principles at stake here; he stated that he had been given the object by the owner so thus it was legally his, and publicly invited the Corporation of London and the Gresham Committee 'to institute an action in law for its recovery'. Of course, nothing was done.

In spite of Tite's attempts to discredit the chemist, Roach Smith added: 'I hope before long to render such a complete account of our stewardship, as will not be discreditable to our exertions to preserve the City antiquities from the *vandalism* of committees, and from the whole tribe of "City authorities", and from general profound ignorance and indifference.' This was to be a book about the discoveries in Roman London, a publication that is, after more than a century, still fundamental to the study of Londinium and an enduring credit to its author.

This was the final confrontation between Charles Roach Smith on his own and the City, for hereafter he would have friends — many friends to help establish the cause of London's heritage. The issues had been clear, and Roach Smith had made the

destruction of London's historic buildings, monuments and antiquities a matter of public concern. The issues had become widely accepted, and the pressure on the Corporation of London to adopt a more positive attitude to its past was increasing all the time. But while Richard Lambert Jones was in power there was resistance, and the Corporation refused to discuss the matter. The public row about the Royal Exchange antiquities solved one problem, however, for in 1846 the Gresham Committee gave all the discoveries to the Guildhall Library.

Lambert Jones was at the height of his power in 1845 when the Royal Exchange row became public. He was on ten committees of the Corporation, and was chairman of three. But just as his ascent to power had been rapid after 1819, so his decline was equally quick. By 1848 his drive was spent and, perhaps due to his age — he was sixty-five — or due to ill health, he retired from most of his City activities. In that year he was only on three committees, and in the year following just one. Although Lambert Jones finally retired from public life in 1851, the Corporation of London had recognised his achievements in 1846, by collecting about £1,000 towards a permanent memorial to him. They commissioned a marble bust of him to be placed in the Common Council Chamber of Guildhall, and they struck a special gold medallion bearing his portrait. A Lambert Jones Scholarship at the City of London School was established with the remainder of the fund, to perpetuate the memory of this man who had undertaken some of the greatest public 'improvements' in the City. The 'City Dictator' was no more, and with him was removed the greatest impediment to the study and preservation of the history of London. The way was clear for the creation of a city museum by the Corporation of London.

For fourteen years Charles Roach Smith lived at No. 5 Liverpool Street, by day following his profession as a chemist, but in the evening entertaining scholars who had come to visit his remarkable 'Museum of London Antiquities' housed in a room above his shop. When failing health forced him to retire in 1855, he offered his collection to the Corporation of London to form the basis for their embryonic museum then housed in the small room by the Guildhall Library. Unfortunately the policy of

[2] A reference to the taking of gold coins by R. L. Jones from the London Bridge rebuilding excavations.

Richard Lambert Jones still prevailed and the Library Committee bluntly refused both his collection, and the gift of another private collection of antiquities. Roach Smith sold his to the British Museum for £2,000, far less than it had cost him to acquire, but he accepted the loss that his collection might remain available to scholars. In 1854 he published a catalogue of his museum which contained over 1,000 objects, and in 1859, after he had retired to Strood in Kent, he published his great work, *Illustrations of Roman London*.

In 1869 the Corporation of London decided to build the long-awaited library and museum on a site in Basinghall Street, adjacent to the medieval Guildhall. At last the battle for a City museum had been won, and one of its delighted visitors was the ageing Roach Smith himself, who knew that his endeavours had not been in vain.

Roach Smith was a man of vision who in 1845 wrote of the Corporation of London that: 'had they ever possessed a feeling for the works of art which illustrate the history of old London, they would have possessed a mansion solely devoted to them, an entire building for such a museum as might have been formed, and such as the valuable monuments demanded.' That mansion became a reality 131 years later when on 2 December 1976, Queen Victoria's great, great grand-daughter, Queen Elizabeth II, opened the Museum of London. Standing there in the foyer during the opening ceremony I could not help wondering if the spirit of Charles Roach Smith was present, watching the conclusion of the work he had started so long ago. Perhaps he would forgive his old enemy, the Corporation of London, if he knew that it was a partner in the enterprise. He would certainly remember that it was the Royal Exchange excavation that provided the starting point for the whole undertaking.

BIBLIOGRAPHY

THE BUILDER (1845), pp. 55, 181–82, 497, 558, 569–70, 582–83, 585, 595–96, 612, 621.

JONES, R. L. *Reminiscences of the public life of Richard Lambert Jones Esq.* (London, 1863).

SMITH, CHARLES ROACH *Illustrations of Roman London* (London, 1859).

——*Journals*, vol. III, in the care of the Department of Medieval and Later Antiquities, British Museum.

—— Correspondence relating to the Royal Exchange in the libraries of the Museum of London and the Society of Antiquaries.

TITE, W. *A descriptive catalogue of the Antiquities found in the excavations at the New Royal Exchange, preserved in the Museum of the Corporation of London* (London, 1848).

THE WESTMINSTER REVIEW, Vol. XXXVI (July–October 1841), pp. 405–24.

FIG. 96 (above).   Guildhall, with the merchants
assembled there after the destruction of the Royal
Exchange. Watercolour by C. Matthews, 1838; later
issued as an engraving in which the anxious
merchants, clearly drawn from the life, have been
tidied up into top-hatted City gentlemen.

Guildhall Library, Corporation of London

FIG. 97 (below).   Nathan Rothschild, the
great financier, standing by his favourite pillar
in the south-east corner of the Royal
Exchange.

Guildhall Library, Corporation of London

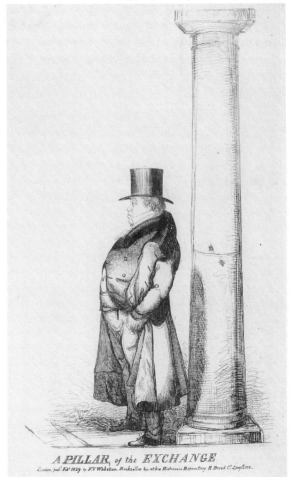

Following the fire, Lloyd's sought temporary refuge at the Guildhall
and the temporary Exchange subsequently erected in the quadrangle
of the Excise Office, Broad Street; this same quadrangle formed part
of Gresham's House, later the Gresham College, having served a
similar purpose as a temporary home for the Merchants following the
destruction of the first Royal Exchange in 1666. On 17 January 1838
Lloyd's took possession of South Sea Hall at the corner of Threadneedle Street and Bishopsgate.[1]

London Assurance moved to Birchin Lane[2] and The Royal
Exchange Assurance purchased on 12 January 1838 21 Lombard
Street, lately the Banking House of Messrs Esdaile & Co. with all
desks and fittings for £16,000.[3]

[1] See 'A History of Lloyd's' by Charles Wright and C. Ernest Fayle (1928),
pp. 334, 338.
[2] *Idem*, p. 335.
[3] REA Board Minutes.

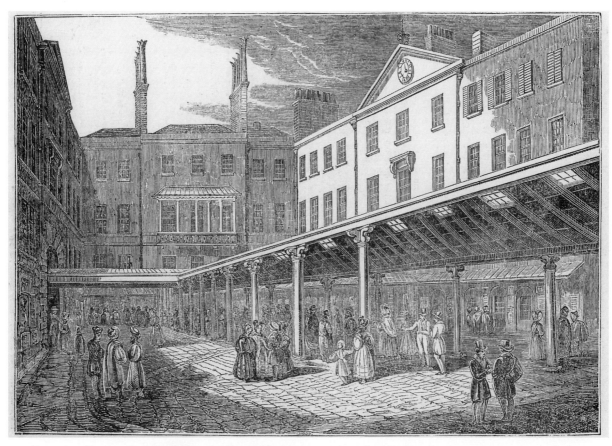

FIG. 98.   During the rebuilding, the Royal Exchange continued operations in temporary accommodation in the quadrangle of the Excise Office, Broad Street.

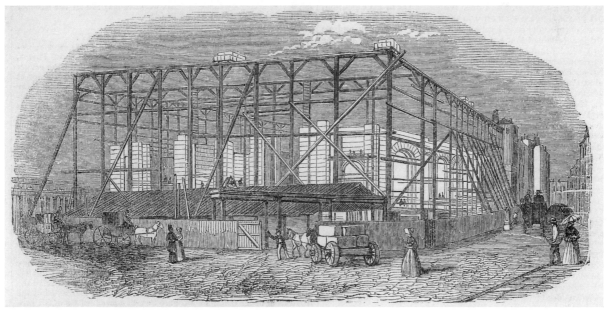

FIG. 99.   Scaffolding around the shell of the devastated Royal Exchange.

Guardian Royal Exchange collection

FIG. 100.   Opening the Royal
Exchange.
Guildhall Library, Corporation of London

FIG. 101.   Popular print celebrating
the Opening.
Guardian Royal Exchange collection

CHAPTER XXVI

Destruction, Competition and Rebuilding:
The Royal Exchange, 1838–1884

By M. H. PORT

THE SECOND ROYAL EXCHANGE was destroyed by fire on the night of 10 February 1838 (Col. Pl. VIIA). The fire started in the Captains' or Coffee Room of Lloyd's, in the north-west corner of the Exchange, where it was noticed by porters across the road in the Bank of England at about 10.50 p.m. A severe frost hindered the fire-fighters, who had to procure hot water 'before the engines could be got to work'. By 3.30 a.m. the flames had reached the east end, and at 9 o'clock, when the Mercers' surveyor, George Smith, arrived, 'no hopes could be entertained of checking the Element until the whole Building should be reduced to a heap of Ruins'.[1] The timber floors, galleries and panelling fuelled the flames, fanned by a strong north-east wind; while the space between the gallery skylights and the roof, uninterrupted by party walls, 'formed a complete channel for the flames into which no engine could be applied'.[2]

City opinion demanded that the Exchange be rebuilt as soon as possible. So serious was the situation regarded that special administrative machinery was immediately devised. The Grand or Joint Committee of the Corporation and the Mercers' Company for Gresham affairs was reinforced by a Special Committee appointed by Common Council (the City's legislature), composed of the Lord Mayor, two Aldermen, and one commoner for each ward, to confer with the Mercers' Company; the Mercers for their part appointing a corresponding Special Committee.[3] The Mercers were anxious to limit their financial liability, unless there were a reasonable prospect of an adequate return on any additional expenditure 'beyond what appertains to their proportion on re-instatement'.[4] But the role of London as the world's greatest city called for a worthy grandiloquence in the new building and its setting.[5]

While the Mercers appeared somewhat parochial in their outlook, the City side had a clear concept of the opportunity offered by the destruction of the old Exchange. The impetus came probably from Richard Lambert Jones (1783–1863), chairman since 1823 of the Bridge House Estates Committee, responsible for the rebuilding of London Bridge, and subsequently in charge of the extensive works of improving the bridge approaches.[6] He was therefore an expert on the City's traffic problems and contriving improved thoroughfares. A plumber by trade, he had become a builder, valuer and surveyor.[7] His enthusiasm overrode any

---

[1] MC, GR (unfoliated), 18 January 1838; J. G. White, *History of the Three Royal Exchanges* (1896), p. 30.

[2] MC, GR, 18 January 1838, report of special committee, from which a long quotation is given by D. Kynaston, *The City of London*, I (1994), p. 111.

[3] MC, GR, 24 January 1838.

[4] Ibid., 6 February 1838.

[5] There are four principal modern accounts of the rebuilding: K. Esdaile, 'Battles Royal: No. 1. The Royal Exchange' (several entries illustrated), *Architect and Building News* (hereafter *Archt & BN*), 9 January 1931, pp. 47–49; H.-R. Hitchcock, *Early Victorian Architecture in Britain*, I (London and New Haven, 1954), pp. 305–06; D. Watkin, *The Life and Work of C. R. Cockerell* (1974), pp. 207–10, pls. 119–25; and J. Bassin, *Architectural Competitions in Nineteenth-Century England* (Ann Arbour, 1984), pp. 42–47 (also usefully illustrated, pls. 4–10). All these are based, more or less, on White, *Three Royal Exchanges*, and reproduce his inaccuracies.

[6] Elected Common Councilman for Cripplegate Without in 1819, he had also become chairman of the corporation's Public Improvements Committee, which handled the very extensive work of improving the approaches to London Bridge. See R. L. Jones, *Reminiscences of the Public Life of Richard Lambert Jones Esq.* (priv. printed, 1863).

[7] F. Shepherd, *The Treasury of London's Past* (1991), p. 7.

doubts about the necessity for an enlarged replacement building, though these later came to be aired in the public prints.[8]

The City Special Committee proposed rebuilding on an enlarged scale 'to afford increased accommodation to the Mercantile Interests; to improve the contiguous approaches; and to render the Building in all respects worthy of this great Metropolis', for which purposes it would be necessary to demolish the adjacent Bank Buildings to the west, and houses between Cornhill and Threadneedle Street at the east of the old Exchange. Such an enlarged building might be erected for £150,000, the City committee had already determined; the City and the Mercers should contribute equal shares, to be reimbursed out of the (non-existent) surplus of the Gresham Estates.[9] So much of the old site would be given up as was required for widening the street, and in lieu the additional site would be vested in the Gresham Trust. But the Corporation was also keen to seize the disastrous opportunity in order to improve adjacent thoroughfares, break traffic jams in the neighbourhood, and create an island site for the new Exchange — improvements costing probably a further £200,000.[10] As all expenditure beyond £150,000 would be for the benefit of the public, the government should be asked for the additional funds. Four members from each side were nominated to form a deputation to the Chancellor of the Exchequer.[11]

The Mercers' surveyor, George Smith (1782–1869), at first regarded the tower (rebuilt by him in 1819–26, see Col. Pl. VIIIA) as safe, and the Gresham Committee hoped that it would be possible to incorporate some portion of the ruin in a new building (Col. Pl. VIIB); but the exceptionally severe weather soon ensured that it was 'neither prudential or economical' to retain any part.[12] The City Corporation and the Mercers' Company as joint trustees of the Gresham Estates[13] then agreed to raise £150,000 for rebuilding[14] 'on a very splendid scale', adequate for 'an extended commerce of the country' and the influx of provincial merchants expected once the new railways were operating.

When the City deputation waited on the Chancellor of the Exchequer to seek additional funds, Mr Spring Rice referred the matter to a select committee already sitting on the question of metropolitan improvements,[15] which interrogated Richard Lambert Jones. He explained that the trustees were, from their own funds, 'quite willing to re-build the Royal Exchange on a very splendid scale, suitable to the mercantile demands and the commercial interest' (although there was, he claimed, no legal obligation to do so),[16] at a cost of £150,000; it was very unlikely, he thought, that more than a few thousands could be raised from City men in aid of the enterprise, a view shared by other City witnesses before the committee.[17] Jones urged the need for street improvements around the Exchange that would permit its enlargement from about 35,000 square feet to nearly 40,000.[18] All the witnesses agreed that the existing site was 'far the most convenient place for the transaction of business generally in the city of London', but that the old Exchange (203 ft east–west by 171 ft north–south) was not large enough:[19] 'persons have said "You ought not to build an

---

[8] Thus, *The Sunday Times*, leader, 17 November 1839: 'It is notorious to all persons, that the real business of the city is not done at the Royal Exchange at all'; Nathan Rothschild was 'almost the last man of commercial consequence who personally went upon 'Change', and that was because it fed his vanity as well as his purse. See D. Kynaston, *The City of London*, 1 (1994), p. 54.

[9] In evidence before the select committee, Jones declared that the Gresham Trust was in debt to the City 'upwards of £100,000', but that they would sacrifice that. *Parliamentary Papers* (hereafter *PP*) 1837–38 (661) XVI, S.C. on Metropolitan Improvements, 2nd report, q. 210.

[10] *PP* 1837–38 (661) XVI, 2nd report of S.C. on Metropolitan Improvements, statements of R. Lambert Jones, qq. 210, 227, 307–08, 310 (26 February 1838).

[11] MC, GR, 6 February 1838.

[12] MC, GR, 16 and 20 February 1838.

[13] Hitchcock, *Early Victorian Architecture*, 1, p. 305, fails to understand that the Corporation and the Mercers composed the Gresham Trustees. It is true that there were differing views within the two component bodies.

[14] *PP* 1837–38 (418) XVI, 1st report of S.C. on Metropolitan Improvements. This sum included the insurance of £45,000 on the burned building.

[15] Ibid.

[16] But counsel's opinion was that, though there was no express trust, the Mercers were so obliged, MC, GR, 19 April 1839.

[17] *PP* 1837–38 (661) XVI, 2nd report of S.C. on Met. Improvements, qq. 210, 219, 263–64, 272, 297, 615–16, 711, 714, 898–99.

[18] Ibid., q. 357.

[19] Ibid., qq. 369, 500 (Jones), 529 (G. R. Jones, chairman of Lloyd's), 602–04 (Samuel Gurney), 635 (Sir J. Reid, Bt, Deputy-Governor of the Bank of England).

Exchange for our present wants, but you are to look forward to an extended commerce of the country, and what accommodation may be required when railways come into operation"', or as one M.P. put it, 'It must be a species of emporium for the commerce of the whole world'.[20]

Although Lambert Jones as yet had no plan, he had definite views about the future Exchange: the front 'ought to be a western front', rather than the old front looking south. If Parliament would grant £200,000 for street improvements — desperately needed because Threadneedle and the adjoining streets were always greatly impeded by stage coaches and omnibuses, so that a wagon would take three hours to travel from Aldgate to Charing Cross[21] — it would be possible to improve the site of the Exchange: an oblong building, somewhat narrower — about 150 feet, against 171 feet, allowing for widening the street opposite the Bank — but some 60 feet longer east to west could be constructed, contrived by the demolition of Sweetings Alley and Rents to the east. In front (to the west) an open space would be obtained by demolishing Bank Buildings. There would be a large upstairs room, 'on a different class . . . to what was there before'; although previously the upstairs had not been open to the public but was, Jones admitted, 'a subscription room', yet he planned 'entirely new' accommodation for merchants and trade in general, for the meeting of merchants and public companies, 'such as they now have at Lloyds'. It would, he added when pressed, be largely for brokers and such parties, and the Royal Exchange Assurance Company and Lloyd's.[22]

In view of the plan ultimately adopted, it is comment-worthy that at this stage Lambert Jones declared that the Trustees would not seek to maximise income by laying out shops — the Mercers, he remarked, were anxious that no part should be let for shops, and 'I think it more difficult to produce an architectural view with shops'. They wanted to serve the mercantile interests rather than the retail; they had applications that the whole of the ground floor, apart from the open area, should be coffee shops of different natures, for refreshments and meetings: the Baltic coffee house, the North American, and so forth, 'so constructed, that when a merchant goes upon 'Change, he can obtain any information, east, west, north or south'.[23] Part would be open in the traditional way, part covered. The roof would be of iron, to obviate any risk of fire, and the open court itself might be covered by a dome, but 'we must look to the hot weather'.[24]

The committee enquired into the rental of the old Exchange (£5,150 for shops and offices in 1837), whether anyone was under an obligation to rebuild it, and whether City men would subscribe for that purpose. Satisfied that street improvement in that quarter was necessary and that the Trustees would rebuild the Exchange at their own expense (despite the indebtedness of the Gresham Estate), they nevertheless declined to embellish the capital at the cost of taxpayers in general. 'Notwithstanding the very extensive interests connected with the transactions which are conducted at the Royal Exchange, the burden of effecting any improvements incidental to the rebuilding of the edifice, ought not to be cast upon the resources of the Nation at large'.

Fortunately a proposal by Lambert Jones offered 'an easy and practicable mode of raising the necessary funds . . . without any material pressure upon the inhabitants of London and its vicinity': the Coal and Wine Duties had been ever since the rebuilding after the Great Fire the accepted means of financing metropolitan improvements. Currently levied under an Act of 1831 for discharging the cost of making new approaches to the rebuilt London Bridge, their yield of £84,515 in 1834 had risen to £100,585 in 1838. The new approaches' debt would be paid off by 1852 rather than 1858, as had been envisaged. Thus the duties for 1853–58 would be available. The committee therefore recommended that from this source £150,000 — enough for 'all those changes absolutely required, if it be . . . economically administered' — be provided for enlarging the site and improving the

---

[20] Ibid., qq. 307–08, 310.

[21] Ibid., qq. 470–71, 637–41, 736–38, 751.

[22] Ibid., qq. 278–84, 407, 411, 466, 499. The Lloyd's underwriters wanted a merchants' room added to their establishment to provide a sort of commercial club-room for businessmen visiting London (E. Wilson, *Wilson's Description of the New Royal Exchange* (1844), pp. 64, 97).

[23] *PP* 1837–38 (661) XVI, qq. 288–90, 386, 400.

[24] Ibid., qq. 360, 388.

streets.[25] That this sum was precisely that which the Gresham Trustees undertook to spend on the rebuilding was to provide a fertile source for misunderstandings among the public — and historians.[26]

The Royal Exchange Bill of 1838 to effect this subsidy proved a contentious measure. Radicals found it unpalatable that building improvements should be financed by a tax on one of the necessaries of life. Rich merchants should follow Liverpool's example and raise the money themselves. But the bill's advocates pointed out that the purpose was not to erect an Exchange but to make new streets; 'it was notorious to everyone who passed through the city that there was no greater thoroughfare and no greater embarrassment than that between the Bank and the old Exchange'. The measure was carried by 102 to 38, with government and opposition members voting indiscriminately on either side.[27]

An unfortunate dispute then developed between the Treasury and the Corporation, which rejected the Chancellor's demand to approve any design for the new Exchange. The City men were very suspicious of having some expensive design foisted on them by the Treasury: a not unreasonable fear given the recent history of government building.[28] Lambert Jones insisted that the Trustees would 'not be parties to the Government having any control in the building of the

Exchange'.[29] 'Without the control of the Lords of the Treasury, the public will have no assurance', countered the Chancellor, 'that a building adequate to the purposes of trade and worthy of the present time will be erected'. The Metropolitan Improvements Committee's recommendation that the advance of £150,000 to the Corporation should be 'subject to the sanction and direction of the Lords Commissioners of the Treasury, without whose approbation of the plans and estimates no portion of the works ought to be proceeded on', could be interpreted to support the view of either party.[30] Lambert Jones pointed out that the Trustees had not asked any parliamentary aid for the Exchange itself; that a direction in the Bill (as drafted by the City Remembrancer) that 'all plans and estimates of the said improvements shall be submitted' to the Treasury had been struck out on his instructions; and that, by the Act, the Treasury's only control was over the site.[31] Deputations to the Chancellor and even to the First Lord, Lord Melbourne, brought no resolution.[32] Ministers referred the issue to the select committee, reappointed in 1839, where Jones was grilled but stood defiant: 'this is a control which ought not to be asked . . . because they [the Gresham Trustees] are about to expend their own money.'[33]

By the New Year, there was widespread criticism of the delay. *The Times* reported a joke at the Stock Exchange: a drawing of the ruins exhibited with a board inscribed, 'This ground to be let for 99 years, on a building lease, after which it will be wanted for a Royal Exchange' (Fig. 102).[34] City passions mounted,

---

[25] *PP* 1837–38 (418) XVI, 1st report of S.C. on Met. Improvements, p. 5. The Coal and Wine Duties Act of 1831 (1 & 2 Wm IV, c.76) provided an 8*d.* tax on coals imported into London until 1858 to pay off City borrowings of £1,250,000 for improving the approaches to the new London Bridge (ibid., Appendix). Hitchcock, *Early Victorian Architecture*, I, p. 305, assumes that the parliamentary £150,000 was for rebuilding the Exchange — pardonable as members of the 1839 Metropolitan Improvements committee were similarly confused, see below; Watkin, *C. R. Cockerell*, p. 207, likewise mistakenly states that 'The Treasury was to provide the money though its attempts to control the whole project were successfully[!] resisted by the Trustees'.

[26] See third reading debate on Royal Exchange Bill, 16 July 1838, 3rd ser., *Parliamentary Debates* (hereafter 3 *Parl. Deb.*) XLIV, col. 223 ff.

[27] 3 *Parl. Deb.* XLIV, cols 223–28.

[28] See J. M. Crook and M. H. Port, *Hist. of the King's Works*, VI (1973), *passim*.

[29] *PP* 1839 (136) XIII, 1st report of S.C. on Met. Improvements, q. 11 (26 February 1839). Jones was so instructed by J. Horsley Palmer (Governor of the Bank of England, 1830–33). Cp. Common Council's resolution, 17 January 1839, '. . . the Lords of the Treasury are not entitled, under the terms of the Act of Parliament, to require the Corporation of London to submit for their approval the plan of the intended new building for the Royal Exchange', J. G. White, *Three Royal Exchanges*, p. 35.

[30] *The Times*, 2 February 1839, p. 6 f.; *PP* 1837–38 (418) XVI, q. 5, and 1839 (136) XIII, q. 459.

[31] *PP*, 1839 (136) XIII, qq. 14, 17.

[32] White, *Three Royal Exchanges*, pp. 32–36.

[33] *PP*, 1839 (136) XIII, qq. 80–81.

[34] *The Times*, 4 February 1839, p. 5. Sir P. Laurie reported this to Common Council as a bill placed in the ruins, inscribed 'To let for 99 years, and after that probably an Exchange may be built', *Spectator*, 30 November 1839, p. 1174.

and one member of the Gresham Committee published a personal attack on Spring Rice, the Chancellor, echoing criticisms already made by the *Spectator*, which had accused him of lying about the views of members of the Commons' committee, and declared: 'the petty insolence of an ill-bred banker's clerk, anxious to show his consequence by making you wait, would seem habitual to this man'.[35] A report that a Mr Baily [*sic*] had been given the commission was claimed to have emanated from the Treasury.[36] The *Civil Engineer and Architect's Journal*, the only professional periodical of that day, complained in March of the 'disgraceful delay', but put the blame on the City.[37]

Faced with the City's intransigence — and threats even of resorting to the law courts[38] — the Chancellor devised an assurance that the Treasury would not cause any excess of expenditure above the agreed £150,000, or impose any plan that the Trustees had not themselves previously approved.[39] The committee then agreed that 'the plans and estimates of the said Building and of the approaches thereto, as proposed by the Trustees and the Corporation, ought to be submitted to and approved by the Lords of the Treasury before any of the said works shall be undertaken'.[40] The City had given way, but only after securing its main objectives.

Meanwhile, the Gresham Joint Committee of the Corporation and the Mercers' Company that had been entrusted with the rebuilding, chaired by Richard Lambert Jones, resolved on 4 January 1839 that 'plans and designs for the intended Royal Exchange

should be procured by open competition'.[41] By the 1830s, competition was a rule of life among businessmen. The trading monopoly of the East India Company had been abolished with effect from 1813; joint-stock banks had been allowed to set up in London from 1826, breaking the Bank of England's monopoly; insurance companies were competing for business. In the architectural world, new churches and commercial buildings alike were the object of competitive designs. Lambert Jones himself as chairman of the Bridge House Estates had presided over a competition for designs for rebuilding London Bridge in 1823. Government building had been thrown to the market when the old Office of Works with its 'Attached Architects' was smothered in 1832. When the Houses of Parliament were burned down in 1834, pressure from the Press demanded open competition in choosing an architect for the new buildings; public attention focused on an architectural competition for the greatest building of the age, no fewer than 217 entries contesting for the prize,[42] although the competition arrangements were widely criticised. Consequently in 1839 the Institute of British Architects drew up a code for competitions.[43]

It was therefore unsurprising that the Joint Committee should decide on a competition for designs for the new Exchange. But the drawbacks evidenced by the Houses of Parliament open competition persuaded some members of the committee that it should be limited to a chosen list of architects. This idea, however, was rejected in favour of open competition by eleven votes to six.[44] Details of the competition were promulgated on 26 March: on payment of £1, competitors could obtain a set of instructions,

[35] Richard Taylor's letter to Sir Harry Inglis reported *Spectator*, 21 March 1839; ibid., 26 January 1839, p. 85.
[36] *The Sunday Times*, 10 March, citing *Morning Advertiser*; *The Times*, 13 March; *Spectator*, 16 March, p. 250, reporting Common Council meeting of 14 March 1839. 'Mr Baily' was perhaps the surveyor James Bailey (*c.* 1771–1850) — or there may have been confusion with the Nelson Memorial competition (see below) and E. H. Baily.
[37] *Civil Engineer and Architect's Journal* (hereafter *Civ. Eng. & Archt's Jnl*), II (1839), p. 114.
[38] White, *Three Royal Exchanges*, pp. 34–36.
[39] *PP* 1839 (136) XIII, after q. 93.
[40] Ibid., p. iv.

[41] *Royal Exchange. Report to Court of Common Council from the Royal Exchange and Gresham Trusts Committee, with Extracts from Proceedings of the Joint Gresham Committee on procuring plans for the new Royal Exchange from 14th March 1839 to 14th May 1840* (1840) — hereafter *Proceedings*.
[42] See M. H. Port (ed.), *The Houses of Parliament* (1976), ch. III.
[43] See J. Bassin, *Architectural Competitions*, p. 41.
[44] MC, GR, 4 January 1839. *The Times*' correspondent subsequently remarked (5 October 1839, p. 3f.) that 'It seems that the well-known first-rate architects of the metropolis, such as Sir Robert Smirke, Cockerell, Decimus Burton, Wilkins, Barry, Joseph Gwilt, Hardwick, &c, would not enter into a general competition', — a belief which had long been a ground of objection to open competition.

FIG. 102.   Drawing exhibited at the Stock Exchange early in 1839, satirising the delay in erecting a new
Royal Exchange, showing the still-uncleared site, with the Bank of England in the background, right.

together with a site plan. These instructions[45] were strongly influenced by those for the Houses of Parliament competition.

Entries were to be submitted by 1 August, which was by contemporary standards a reasonably generous preparation time (though the IBA requested a longer period).[46] Three premiums were offered, of £300, £200, and £100, for the 'designs adjudged by the committee to be the best'. This compared

favourably with the £500 awarded to each of the four winners in the Westminster battle, as the total expense for the new Exchange was not to exceed £150,000, whereas the Houses of Parliament were costed at about £750,000. Experience in a hundred competitions for new churches, as well as for some public buildings (notably the General Post Office in St Martin's le Grand, and — even more pertinently — Lambert Jones's own London Bridge Competition of 1823), had taught the wisdom of safeguarding a building committee from having to employ the winner of a competition, and the Exchange committee stipulated that he should not necessarily have a claim to be entrusted with the work; but were his designs to be executed by another, he was to receive a further £500, the committee retaining all premiated drawings — a necessary clarification when there was

---

[45] *Proceedings*, pp. 20–23. Both Hitchcock and Watkin state that neither the Trustees' own retained architect (George Smith) nor any of his pupils should compete; this latter rule, however, does not appear in the 'Resolutions and Instructions to Architects' (which would have excluded Grellier and David Brandon as pupils of Smith), which merely note that 'The Architect of the Gresham Trust and his Partner do not intend sending in any design'.

[46] MC, GR, 24 April 1839.

no legal certainty about the ownership of competition drawings.

As in the Westminster competition, the style of the new building was stipulated, but this time Gothic was excluded, the specification calling for 'the Grecian, Roman, or Italian style of architecture, having each front of stone of a hard and durable quality' (a current concern in the parliamentary building). The scale required for the drawings was ten feet to one inch and a half (80:1), half the size of the parliamentary designs, not imposing too great a labour on contestants, but adequate for judging. Elevations of each front were to be supplied, with plans of each storey, and longitudinal and transverse sections, together with an interior elevation. As at Westminster, drawings were to be tinted in brown Indian ink only. Another Westminster rule was observed, that no perspective drawings were to be admitted save two from specified viewpoints. This, like the ruling against coloured drawings, was to prevent the judges being deluded by mere artistic display, a very genuine risk as many competitions have proved. Models, similarly (though less wisely), were excluded.

Some of the other rules for the Exchange competition also arose from that for the Houses of Parliament, but out of the competition experience and criticisms made of the Westminster pattern, rather than the actual instructions. Thus the Exchange committee demanded a specification and an estimate of the cost, which had been omitted at Westminster, whereby the judges had been persuaded, in the opinion of some critics, to choose an excessively expensive design. As further security against running into excessive expenditure, the committee was empowered to withhold the premium and reject the design if there was doubt about the feasibility of carrying it out within the estimate and the architect was unable to prove the accuracy of his calculations. Whereas the anonymous Parliamentary entries were to be distinguished by a motto or device, those for the Exchange were to bear no identificatory mark of any kind; instead, the receiving officer would attach a number to each entry as it was delivered, giving a counterfoil to the depositor. This was because some Westminster competitors had used flagrantly obvious devices, such as J. C. Buckler's buckle surrounding an R. For further security, a sealed letter containing the name

and address of the competitor was to accompany each entry, and would be returned unopened to the unsuccessful.

Further instructions related to what was required within the building, of which the trapezoid site was carefully demarcated: the basement to be appropriated to vaults, cellars and strong-rooms; the ground floor to shops and offices. Each part of the building intended to be held as a distinct tenement was to be separated by brickwork or equally fireproof materials on every side, above and below, from adjoining parts — the fear of fire, naturally, in the forefront of committee-men's minds. The space allocated for the meeting of merchants and others was specified at about 20,000 square feet, of which 7,000 were to be open — a somewhat puzzling requirement, as in the previous October, when thirty merchants had been asked their opinion on the point, nine (including Nathan Rothschild) had favoured a covered space, compared with only four for an open space.[47] The answer may lie in Lambert Jones's view that 'we must look to the hot weather'.[48] Forty-one rooms of specified sizes were to be provided, as well as kitchens, waiting-rooms, water-closets and washing-rooms. Despite the degree of detail supplied, the Architectural Society (a rather select rival to the IBA) vainly asked for more.[49]

Carefully elaborated as the instructions were, the competition yet met with criticism from both the profession and the public prints. 'An Architect' complained in the *Civil Engineer and Architect's Journal* that there was no guarantee of fairness given. He wanted to know who the judges were to be, whether strict adherence to the instructions was necessary to secure an inspection of one's plan, whether a public exhibition would precede the judging, and — crucially — whether the prize-winner would execute the work (his standing and experience being adequate). Until these questions were satisfactorily answered, he called for a

---

[47] Ibid., 12, 19 October 1838. A fifth voter classed as 'open' had observed that a covering was inconvenient unless properly ventilated — whereas Rothschild had put it the other way round asking for a 'lofty covering with means for Ventilating'. But according to Wilson, the leading merchants had by a 'very large majority' favoured an open area; E. Wilson, *Wilson's Description of the New Royal Exchange* (1844), p. 103.

[48] *PP* 1837–38 (661) XVI, q. 360.

[49] MC, GR, 24 April 1839.

unanimous boycott of the competition. The journal's
editor attacked the 'paltry meanness' of the Gresham
Committee's charging £1 for the ground plan and
instructions, which he condemned as being 'as
remarkable for their incompleteness as they are for
their worthless character'. In protest against the
imposition, he reprinted the instructions and offered
a free tracing of the plan.[50] Similar criticisms were
voiced in the following issue by E. B. Lamb (c.
1805–69) in the light of his experience with the nearly
simultaneous Liverpool (St George's Hall) competition. He also wanted a report by disinterested professional judges to be printed so as to allow reply by
competitors.[51] Thomas Hopper (1776–1856), a fashionable country-house architect and inveterate (but
disappointed) competitor, called for an elaborate
scheme for choosing an impartial judge whose
decision would be final.[52]

The 38 entries received — the modest number for
so valuable a commission perhaps reflecting these
objections — were arranged at Mercers' Hall for the
committee to inspect. Some provincial architects had
probably argued that they would stand no chance for
a City job,[53] and, since there was to be no exhibition
of the rejected designs (a valuable means of advertisement), even London architects may have felt that
without City connections they were unlikely to reap
any benefit for the months of labour required. But
there were also two rival important competitions, for
a Nelson Memorial in Trafalgar Square (April 1838-
January 1839, producing 124 entries); and for concert
halls (St George's Hall) for the rich city of Liverpool
(March-July 1839, with 75 entries).[54]

Unlike the parliamentary connoisseurs of 1835, the
City men realised that they needed professional
assistance in choosing the best entries: they sought
three eminent London architects who had in no way
been concerned in the competition to advise them.
This was replicating the practice of Lambert Jones's
committee in the London Bridge competition of
1823, when the Crown architects (Robert Smirke,
Soane and Nash) had acted. The committee now by
ballot chose Sir Robert Smirke, Philip Hardwick and
Charles Barry to select six of the designs for the
committee's decision.[55] Barry refused, so placing the
other two, in the view of *The Times*, 'in an awkward
predicament, as their immediate relations are understood to be competitors'.[56]

Nevertheless, Smirke and Hardwick agreed to act,
and Joseph Gwilt was elected to join them.[57] Smirke,
as the last surviving Crown architect, stood at the
head of his profession; he had for some years been
closely engaged with Lambert Jones in designing
street façades for the new London Bridge approaches.
Hardwick (1790–1870) had designed the St Katharine's Dock warehouses, the new Goldsmiths' Hall,
and additions to St Bartholomew's Hospital, so that
he too was well known in the City. Joseph Gwilt
(1784–1863), a prolific architectural writer, born and
bred a Londoner, was surveyor to City companies,
brother of George who in 1835 was Master of the
Masons' Company — again, no stranger in the City.

The survival of Gwilt's papers[58] enables us to
penetrate to an unusual degree the arcana of the
judging process. He started by sorting the sheep from
the goats, paying considerable attention to the plan
(11 September). Thus he rejected twenty. He then
attempted to arrange the remaining eighteen in order
of merit, a listing he reconsidered extensively, still
'*non sine dubio*', the next day. No. 50 (Donaldson's, see

[50] *Civ. Eng. & Archt's Jnl*, II (1839), pp. 171–72, 173.
[51] Ibid., pp. 211–13.
[52] Ibid., p. 218. Hopper then incorporated his criticisms in a pamphlet, *A Letter to Lord Melbourne on the rebuilding of the Royal Exchange* (1839).
[53] But the Manchester Architectural Society complained at the brushing off of the London societies' requests, MC, GR, 12 August 1839.
[54] See R. P. Jones, 'Life and Work of Harvey Lonsdale Elmes', *Architectural Review*, xv (1904), pp. 231ff. H. L. Elmes, who won this competition, was nephew and sometime pupil of Henry John Elmes, a member of the Joint Committee who helped to draw up the Exchange instructions (MC, GR, 14 March 1839). It seems that at least one entrant submitted much the same design for both competitions, viz., George Gilbert Scott's then partner, W. B. Moffatt (K. Esdaile, 'Battles Royal: No. 1', *Archt & BN*, xxx (1931), pp. 48–49.

[55] MC, GR, 27 August 1839; the votes cast were Barry 11, Blore none, Cockerell 2, J. Gwilt 6, P. Hardwick 12, Sir R. Smirke 9, Tite 2.
[56] *The Times*, 2 September 1839, 4e — i.e., R. Smirke's younger brother, Sydney.
[57] MC, GR, 6 September 1839. Gwilt was chosen by 8 votes against 5 for Cockerell and 2 for Tite. James Savage and Decimus Burton were included in this ballot but received no votes. Smirke pointed out that his brother was a competitor, but the committee had no doubt of his integrity.
[58] Guildhall Library, MS 4952, on which this and subsequent paragraphs are based.

Fig. 103), of which he had originally noted 'Expense against it' and 'Exhibits talent', he moved up from fifth place to second, then adding 'Quare if not first', thereby demoting no. 46, sent in under the name of Henry Richardson — 'A very extraordinary and fine composition and drawing' — from the place it had held for two days. No. 36 (Grellier's) — originally marked 'Must certainly be further considered', he promoted from sixth to third. Of no. 51 (Penne-thorne's, ranked 7th and then 8th) he noted 'perhaps much higher rank'. Nos. 37 (Sydney Smirke: 'Yes! single order', and then 'deserve higher rank'), and 27 (Mocatta: 'Very considerable merit — feeling of old Exch. about interior') seemed also in the running. By 14 September, Gwilt had demoted 'Richardson's' to eighth, promoting Grellier's to second, and retaining no. 43 (Chateauneuf and Mee's — 'A very clever design of the Renaissance') in fourth place, with Pennethorne fifth, Sydney Smirke sixth and Mocatta tenth. Third was no. 22, J. B. Bunning's ('Florid Roman Circular Court'), a design he later demoted and ultimately was unranked (Figs. 104–05). Four days later, he commented of 'Richardson's', 'Not consistent with Plan and could not be done for the money'; Donaldson's, too, 'Could not be done for the money'. Nevertheless, by 23 September, Gwilt had decided that Donaldson's was the best, and Richard-son's second.

Although at this stage and for some months longer the entries were still anonymous, we may now ask who these commended competitors were. Thomas Leverton Donaldson (1795–1885) came of a family of architects, and was 'virtual founder' (Colvin) and secretary of the Institute of British Architects in 1834; in 1841 he was appointed professor of architecture at University College London. Henry B. Richardson was a pupil of Charles Robert Cockerell, RA (1788–1863), architect to the Bank of England, who was the effective author of the design, as Richardson revealed in November: the entry submitted under his name was 'framed by the co-operation of Mr Cock-erell'. 'Cockerell's position was a very curious one', remarks his biographer.[59] Cockerell distrusted com-petitions, as *The Times'* correspondent had accurately observed, but Richardson had asked him to help with his own Palladian entry. Cockerell insisted that his part in the design be concealed unless it were chosen.

William Grellier (1807–52) — youngest of those in the final selection — as we have observed, a pupil of George Smith (the Mercers' Company's and Gresham Trustees' surveyor), had won the Royal Academy Schools' gold medal in 1829, and the second premium (£30) in a competition for a town hall and market place for the capital of Newfoundland in 1838. Arthur Mee (1802–68), a pupil of Sir John Soane, had in 1837 exhibited designs for a villa near Hamburg, where he presumably met Alexis de Chat-eauneuf (1799–1853), an inhabitant of that city, evidently responsible for the chief features of their design. Sydney Smirke (1797–1877) was the younger brother and pupil of Sir Robert, whom he had been assisting on the Oxford & Cambridge University Clubhouse in Pall Mall.[60] These men were the sort of architect, with a few works already to their credit but no well established practice, who were most likely to be caught by the lure of the architectural competition, men who had not yet matured the judgement or skill that would have put the prize firmly within their grasp.

Gwilt met his fellow judges at Mercers' Hall on 28 September, when he noted of 'Richardson's' design that 'Not more than $\frac{2}{3}$ of Court could be treated with Sun's Ray'. His continuing indecision is revealed by his comments on Grellier's: 'false bearing in upper story. Still upon the whole looking to Estimate Etc — This is perhaps the best — All his flues are brought up'.

At this point we need to interrupt our history of the proceedings to give some idea of the leading features of the principal designs under discussion. The two of the highest quality in today's eyes were those submit-ted by Richardson and Donaldson. Donaldson's was a superb exercise in neo-Grec, influenced by recent French interpretation of that style (Fig. 103). His noble giant octostyle Corinthian portico, surmounted by a strong pediment, its tympanum writhing with classical marine symbols, was flanked by short wings with a round-headed arch in each; behind, the

[59] D. Watkin, *C. R. Cockerell*, p. 208.

[60] See, *sub* respective names, H. M. Colvin, *Biographical Diction-ary of British Architects* (3rd edn, 1995).

MR DONALDSON'S DESIGN FOR THE ROYAL EXCHANGE, 1839.
Nº 50 THE FIRST OF THE BEST CLASS.

FIG. 103.   T. L. Donaldson's magnificent neo-Grec competition design (no. 50) was widely admired,
but adjudged too expensive.

Guildhall Library, Corporation of London

windowless wall of rusticated stonework was broken by a wide (three intercolumniation) set of Grecian-style doors and crowned (under the portico) by a frieze of marine symbols. The keynote was one of restrained grandeur appropriate to the world's commercial metropolis. A contemporary found it 'a magnificent design . . . as far superior to all the rest as Mr Barry's design for the Parliament Houses was to its competitors'. Admitting some resemblance to the Paris Bourse, he declared that it was no imitation, but a finer building.[61]

The Richardson-Cockerell entry is well known from the frequently reproduced magnificent lithographs (Fig. 106). The predominant feature was, as Cockerell explained to the Gresham Committee,

'the Triumphal arch expanded [from four to six columns] and . . . rendered habitable by floors', achieving an effect rather similar to Salvi's Trevi Fountain in Rome (1732–62), but derived from Palladio's Loggia del Capitaniato in Vicenza and antique sources. An entablature broken forward over each of the columns of the giant Corinthian order carried statuary; continued round the whole building, in three-quarter columns on the south front and pilasters on the north, the order supported an unbroken cornice of 161 feet on either side, which Cockerell thought would please 'the fashionable amateurs of the day . . . who consider the unbroken line . . . to be the grand nostrum of architectural beauty'. An early sketch shows a vast tower reminiscent in outline of Hawksmoor's Christ Church

61 *Spectator*, 26 October 1839, p. 1022.

Spitalfields, a further repetition of the triumphal arch theme;[62] Cockerell argued that a tower was necessary, particularly in view of the demolition of the neighbouring towers of St Benet Fink and St Bartholomew by the Exchange, but finally settled for small towers at the corners. Interweaved throughout was a subordinate Doric order, employed also for the interior, above which, 54 feet from the ground, a range of 28 windows admitted the sun's rays. Crowning these, at 80 feet, a cove partly covered the open area. At the wider east end, a transverse arcade, as well as the east front itself, allowed for wide openings for shops which in Cockerell's view 'the dignity of the edifice' did not permit in the three principal fronts.[63] But Cockerell was designing, not for 'the architectural amateurs of the day', but for hard-fisted commercial men. And even the *Spectator* found his design 'too showy for its purpose, and overstepping the bounds of pure taste'; it has, indeed, a baroque quality foreign to the commercial metropolis.

Grellier's exquisitely drawn design, like Donaldson's, owed something to modern French neo-classicism. His six-column Corinthian portico substituted an attic storey for a pediment; the ground floor stonework was channelled; an eastern tower recalls another Hawksmoor church, St Mary Woolnoth. The *Spectator* characterised it rather harshly as 'bold, but commonplace, and somewhat vulgar'.[64] Chateauneuf and Mee's design is known in a revised form 'showing an Alteration to the West Front . . . as suggested by Members of the Committee' and lithographed for circulation in a puffing exercise (Fig. 107). 'A species of Loggia dei Lanzi [from Florence] has been added to a massive block of building suggesting the [Roman] Capitol'; Mrs Esdaile in 1931 was 'tempted to wish' that it had been carried out, apart from its 'dreadful little towers'. Contemporaries were quick to spot its German character, and it was chiefly the work of Chateauneuf from Hamburg, a pupil of Schinkel. The competition version, however, had 'three tiers of arcades' at the west front, which the *Civil Engineer* preferred to a large portico of a single order as less

overpowering of the nearby centre of the Bank of England's façade. The *Spectator*, however, thought the style out of sympathy with the surrounding buildings.[65] Sydney Smirke's (no. 37) was yet another with a Corinthian portico, this time spread across the whole front, but appearing divided because the four central columns (or, presumably, intercolumniations) opened into the area of the Exchange; monotonous rows of three-quarter columns, north and south, were compared with the Royal Institution in Albemarle Street.[66] The only other design calling for comment was that of Nash's heir, James Pennethorne, a powerful 'essay in the style of the early Roman Empire', its 'deep Corinthian [octostyle] portico surmounted by a low pediment' with sculpture in the tympanum; at the east end rose a dominant, massive bell-tower, having a colonnaded top storey.[67]

Despite his doubts, Gwilt stuck to his decision of 23 September that Donaldson and 'Richardson' headed the list. In this view, he found that his fellow-referees coincided, as in putting no. 27 third (Mocatta: 'Wish Pediments were away, but plan good', Gwilt had noted; 'bizarre' in the *Spectator*'s opinion). But whereas Gwilt now put Grellier fourth and Chateauneuf fifth, Smirke put his own brother fourth with Chateauneuf again fifth; whilst Hardwick preferred Pennethorne as fourth (placed thirteenth by Smirke) to Sydney Smirke at fifth; both placing Grellier seventh.

The umpires then had a prolonged discussion, deciding to jettison Donaldson on grounds of expense, and 'Richardson' on grounds of both expense and impracticability ('as represented in the Drawings impracticable in Construction . . . Sculpture [an important element of cost] here is not foreign to the design for if omitted half of the value of the Design would be gone').[68] That left five 'upon which all agree': Pennethorne, Sydney Smirke, Wyatt and Brandon (no. 33), Grellier, and Chateauneuf and Mee. But Wyatt and Brandon's 'could not be

[62] See D. Watkin, *C. R. Cockerell*, pp. 210–11, pls. 119–22.

[63] Cockerell's own report to the Gresham Committee on his design is extensively quoted in *Westminster Review*, xxxv (1841), pp. 71 ff.

[64] *Spectator*, 26 October 1839, p. 1022.

[65] *Archt & BN*, 9 January 1931, p. 48; *Civ. Eng. & Archt's Jnl*, ii, pp. 440–41; *Spectator*, 26 October 1839, p. 1022.

[66] *Spectator*, 26 October 1839, p. 1022.

[67] G. Tyack, *Sir James Pennethorne and the making of Victorian London* (Cambridge, 1992), p. 40 and pl. 19.

[68] Cockerell was strongly conscious of the traditional extensive adornment of the Exchange with sculpture.

FIGS. 104 and 105.   J. B. Bunning, later the
City Corporation's Architect, submitted a
grandiose Roman design that had many
admirers but failed to secure a ranking in the
competition.

104 (left).   View of the interior looking east.

105 (opposite).   View of the western front,
behind which lay a circular court.

Guildhall Library, Corporation of London

executed as shewn from False bearings', Smirke's had
only one entrance, and Grellier's was impracticable.

In this puzzling situation, and finding that no
design was strictly fireproof, the umpires decided
that they could recommend none of the designs to be
carried into execution; but to satisfy, in some
measure, the unhappy competitors, they made a
two-fold award. Three designs, though 'possessing
for magnificence and beauty, great claims as works
of art', were, they declared, too expensive: those of
Donaldson (no. 50), 'Richardson' (no. 46), and
Mocatta (no. 27). As the building committee had

requested, they named five that fell within the cost
limits: nos. 36 (Grellier), 43 (Chateauneuf and Mee),
37 (S. Smirke), 33 (Wyatt and Brandon), and 51
(Pennethorne).

Their judgement shows a weakness that became
evident in even the most judiciously conducted
competitions: by sifting the entries in the light of their
strict adherence to the instructions, judges all too
often were left with only mediocre designs: they
sought to select a design, where they ought to have
looked for a designer. As the candid critic W. H.
Leeds remarked in the *Westminster Review*:

They could not more completely have frustrated the objects of the committee in consulting them, nor have more effectually damaged the system of competition, to which individually they are known to be opposed . . . They exhaust their critical power on 'what are called false bearings,' . . . and such like technical and minute particulars, and say nothing whatever of the various systems or principles of design and arrangement of which the site is susceptible, and every class of which had been worked out in a variety of ways, and with the utmost ichnographical skill, by many competitors of great ability.

He added that Donaldson had in his 'Statement of Facts' concerning his own design, pointed out 'what is perfectly notorious, especially in the recent practice of architecture', that false bearings were unavoidable in large public buildings where large rooms and innumerable small ones had to be combined, and that it was no longer important because the introduction of iron framing had revolutionised the art of planning.[69]

As the anonymous entries were returned to their authors, the great majority of designs have been lost from view.[70] One surviving set was identified by Mrs Esdaile as W. B. Moffatt's ('The use of round-headed windows and the admirably planned arcades are most satisfactory'), and she thought that 'it is at least significant of the high level of designs submitted that they are not even mentioned by the assessors'.[71] *The Times* shared her view, regretting (before the referees reported), that 'very splendid and admirably executed drawings' differed so much from the printed instructions as to be placed 'out of the pale of competition',

[69] *Westminster Review*, xxxv (1841), p. 58.

[70] We have the names for 14 entries: the 8 selected, viz. Cockerell and Richardson, Donaldson, Mocatta, Grellier, Chateauneuf and Mee, S. Smirke, T. H. Wyatt and D. Brandon, and Pennethorne; and 6 others: J. B. Bunning (GR, 29 November 1839), H. Baddock (ibid., 3 December 1839), W. Granville (perspective at Mercers' Hall), G. Pownall and F. Wigg (*Globe*, 9 June 1840), W. B. Moffatt (*Archt & BN*, 9 January 1931; entry in RIBA Dwgs Coll.), and John D. Paine who sent in his R.A. Schools gold medal design of 1833.

[71] *Archt & BN*, xxx (1931), pp. 48–49.

FIG. 106.   C. R. Cockerell was drawn into the competition by his pupil H. R. Richardson.
His superb design, interweaving the Corinthian and Doric orders, would have given the City a
world-class structure rivalling Soane's Bank of England (visible on the left).
Guildhall Library, Corporation of London

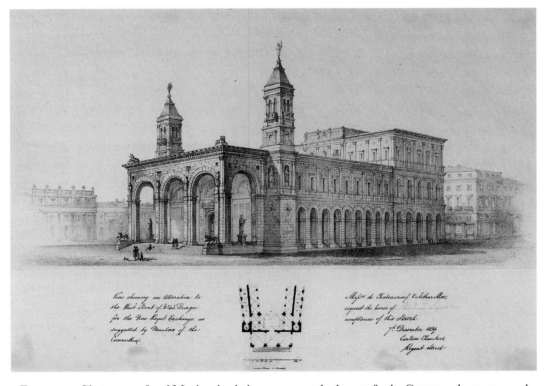

FIG. 107.   Chateauneuf and Mee's submission was remarked upon for its German character, and
this revised version reflects the strong enthusiasm for the Florentine Renaissance in
Germany at that time.
Guardian Royal Exchange collection

especially as those instructions appeared 'to be as clear and explicit as any ever issued for any public work' — though it acknowledged that 'it must be extremely difficult to avoid such departure', and hoped that 'there will be found amongst the 38 designs some splendid specimens of taste and genius for a building worthy of this most noble metropolis' (see Col. Pl. VIIIB).[72]

These favourable views were not held universally, however. After the Gresham Committee had viewed the designs set out in Mercers' Hall, the keenly interested public was admitted by ticket for seven days; but there was, complained the professional journal, no catalogue, no list, no order in the arrangement — and no note-taking allowed. 'Upon the whole, we were disappointed; few of the designs came up to what we expected to find . . . there were many designs so greatly inferior . . . as almost to stagger us'. The judges' universal condemnation of the entries looked 'very much as if the competition has been no more than a stratagem, to enable the Committee to obtain ideas for the guidance and assistance of those whom they now, it seems, have determined to employ' — the referees themselves.[73] The *Spectator* made the same point more crudely: 'the 38 sets of drawings that line the Mercer's Hall are merely a screen to the proceedings of a trio of deep dogs whose business it is to pick the brains of their less profound brethren'.[74] The *Civil Engineer*'s editor made in his December issue the interesting comment that some competitors were so buried in their books 'as to be utterly ignorant of all that has been doing in architecture in this and other countries during the last ten or fifteen years'.[75]

The Sunday Times was even more condemnatory, declaring that 'surely, such a heap of rubbish was never collected . . . such a melange of higgledy-piggledy abortions as would have disgraced the shop windows of a pastrycook on Twelfth-day, and with which no *traiteur* would degrade the decorations of a goose-pie'.[76] The *Spectator* was little more restrained:

'the great mass of victims [of the competition system] manifest a prodigious quantity of misapplied labour and perverted ingenuity . . . an assemblage of structures of all sorts of styles, known and unknown; domed and steepled, porticoed and colonnaded — some plain to Quakerism, others too tawdry for a gin-shop', the majority appearing to be 'anything, in short, but an exchange for mercantile purposes'.[77]

In this difficult situation, the Joint Committee sought to throw back responsibility upon the referees, whom they naïvely asked on 18 October 1839 to consider the first three recommended permissible plans, nos. 31 (Grellier), 43 (Chateauneuf and Mee) and 37 (S. Smirke) — to which they now awarded the premiums — and 'prepare a plan and specification for a new Exchange, such as in their judgement should be carried into execution, having reference to the printed instructions', so justifying the Press attacks.[78] Smirke, who had been criticised previously for carrying out a similar exercise in respect of a competition for a new General Post Office,[79] refused because he thought that three architects could not agree in a joint design; the two others accepted.[80] But by 5 November protests were pouring in from the competitors, demanding to show that their plans could be carried out, and that within the sum allotted; *The Sunday Times* had just published a letter from 'A Merchant' asking if the 'architectural triumvirate' were about to enter 'the arena over which they formerly presided', — as the *Spectator* and the *Civil Engineer* had already suggested — and pointing out that, of the five permissible designs, the first and fifth were the work of clerks of the Mercers' own architect (Smith), and the third (S. Smirke), brother and partner of one of the judges.[81] In Common Council itself, criticism was voiced, supported even by Lord Mayor Wilson: 'It appeared to him that the whole of the proceedings of the Committee with respect to the plans for the new Royal Exchange were conducted with too much privacy and secrecy. In fact, he had

[72] *The Times*, 5 October 1839, p. 3 f. *Atlas* also admired the exhibition, 16 November 1839.

[73] *Civ. Eng. & Archt's Jnl*, II (November 1839), pp. 440–41.

[74] *Spectator*, 26 October 1839, p. 1022.

[75] *Civ. Eng. & Archt's Jnl*, II (December 1839), p. 473.

[76] *The Sunday Times*, leader, denouncing the system of public works, 17 November 1839.

[77] *Spectator*, 26 October 1839, p. 1022.

[78] *Proceedings*; *John Bull*, 27 October 1839, however, had high expectations of such a 'combination of ability'.

[79] *King's Works*, VI, p. 147.

[80] MC, GR, 5 November 1839.

[81] *The Sunday Times*, 3 November 1839.

been refused admittance himself to view the designs.'[82]

Thus when the committee met on 5 November, the request to the referees to prepare a plan was promptly abandoned. Gwilt and Hardwick were instead asked to communicate with the architects of all eight recommended designs, and 'to report any two or more which they thought, with specified alterations, could be most beneficially adopted with reference to expense of construction and rental', an embarrassing commission that Hardwick sensibly declined, followed by Gwilt.

Unwilling wholly to abandon their competition, the Gresham Committee, on 19 November 1839, resolving that the eight selected plans were those 'possessing the most architectural merit', decided that these designs be referred to 'one or more competent architects and surveyors, to report as to the relative expense and rental [capability] of such buildings, with such alterations as may be deemed requisite (after communication with the architects by whom they were designed) for making them durable edifices'. Having failed to persuade the original referees, the committee nominated George Smith (1782–1869) and William Tite (1798–1873) — a name suddenly plucked from the blue as it seemed (though now President of the small Architectural Society) — with instructions to report on 'the superior eligibility of two or more' of the designs, 'after such alterations as they might suggest, and with reference to the printed instructions to the architects'.[83] At the same time they ordered payment of their three premiums to the men who headed the referees' list of five permissible entries: William Grellier, no. 36; Messrs Alexis de Chateauneuf and Arthur Mee, no. 43; and Sydney Smirke, no. 37; an award sufficiently correct in law, but hardly one that satisfied either contestants or critics.[84]

The award of the premiums, however, did not commit the City powers to adopt any of those designs

for the new Exchange.[85] *The Sunday Times* reported that 'a system of "canvassing" for the job is going on'.[86] Clearly, the more meritorious proposals were those on the referees' other list, excluded on grounds of non-conformity with the instructions, primarily excessive cost. Conscious of the popular demand for a building that would do credit to London's world standing, the committee sought some way of satisfying such expectations without abandoning their competition altogether. The reference to Smith and Tite was one way forward: but Tite wisely declined to interfere.

Smith, however, as the Gresham Committee's surveyor, felt it his duty to accept. 'A careful and meticulous man',[87] who as district surveyor of the southern division of the City, surveyor since 1814 to the Mercers' Company, and sometime Master of the Coopers' Company, was at the heart of the City establishment, Smith had himself undertaken major repairs of the late Exchange in 1820–26, rebuilding the entrance front and tower. Contemporaries noted that he had also trained Grellier and David Brandon, T. H. Wyatt's partner in the fifth place. It was doubtful whether he could be considered an impartial referee: he had expected himself to receive the commission for rebuilding, and according to W. H. Leeds 'felt aggrieved in not being employed as architect, nor allowed to take part in the competition . . . though he had twice petitioned the Court, after the first competition, to be allowed to do so'.[88]

But who was William Tite? In 1838 he had been elected President of the Architectural Society, as noted above, a small if rather select body of architects soon to merge with the more widely supported Institute of British Architects, which gave him professional credibility.[89] More significantly, he too was a City man. He inherited a fortune from his father, a

[82] *Spectator*, 2 November 1839, p. 1031; *The Times*, 1 November 1839, has a fuller report.
[83] *Proceedings*, p. 24; MC, GR, 5 November 1839.
[84] *Proceedings*.

[85] Hitchcock, *Early Victorian Architecture*, I, p. 306, argues that the commission 'should have gone either to Grellier [as first prize winner] or Donaldson [as head of the list of aesthetic winners], provided one or the other so reduced his scheme that it could be built with the sum fixed by the Treasury'. Clause 10 of the instructions, however, distinctly repudiates any right of the winner to be entrusted with the work. Moreover, the referees were merely called in to advise the committee, and their award was so qualified that Hitchcock's argument is unsustainable.
[86] 17 November 1839.
[87] Colvin, *loc. cit.*
[88] *Westminster Review*, XXXV (1841), p. 61.
[89] Colvin, *Dictionary*; *DNB*.

Russia merchant, and married City money. He sat from 1832–36 as a Common Councilman for Aldgate Ward. His numerous City connections included Richard Lambert Jones, the Joint Committee's chairman: as 'A Constant Reader' of the *Globe* pointed out maliciously, Lambert Jones was valuer of the Eastern Railway's property, and Tite surveyor to that railway; and the same paper in a leading article alleged that the two men divided £3,000 per annum as joint surveyors to the Blackwall Railway.[90] In 1837 he had been appointed jointly with his rival C. R. Cockerell as architect for the new Westminster Bank building in Lothbury, after a deadlock in the building committee.[91]

The in-fighting on the committee was fierce: but it is difficult to discern a pattern from the brief reports of voting. A motion to refer Grellier's entry (no. 36) also to two surveyors was replaced by an amendment carried by nine to four that nos. 50, 46 and 27 were the best and most splendid designs, and that one of them was to be selected if it was found to be practicable and to cost less than £150,000. A further amendment that six principal architects be invited to a limited competition was defeated likewise nine to four, and the three 'best designs' were referred to Smith. When the three protested against the ruling that their designs would cost more than the permitted £150,000, the committee allowed them to employ their own estimators in collaboration with George Smith.

It looked as if Cockerell's design might be successful, and decision was deferred over Christmas. However, the canvassing that *The Sunday Times* had warned against was continuing: Grellier and Wyatt and Brandon had petitioned Common Council, and on 31 December a motion to refer Grellier's design also to Smith was carried in committee only by Lambert Jones' casting vote[92] after a tie, eight each way. This may be read as an anti-Cockerell move. The other four selected designs were then added to the reference.[93] Compounding his error of passing his work under Richardson's name, Cockerell now asked William Tite's opinion as to the cost of his design. 'Richardson was uneasy at this', recorded Cockerell's long-serving assistant Goodchild,[94] and office opinion thought that Tite was out to secure a role for himself, as in the London and Westminster Bank affair in 1837.[95]

Smith stated in his report, dated 30 January 1840, to the Joint Committee, that he had interviewed the various competitors, pointing out difficulties of construction and arrangement that he had observed, 'suggesting remedies or receiving explanations, and, in some instances, proposing alterations'.[96] The architects of the three architecturally outstanding designs — Donaldson (no. 50), Richardson/Cockerell (46) and Mocatta (27) — supplied him with their detailed estimates; Grellier and Sydney Smirke gave 'only a general calculation'; while the remaining three firms (Chateauneuf and Mee, Wyatt and Brandon, and James Pennethorne) 'deemed it unnecessary to go further into the estimates', presumably realising theirs were but forlorn hopes. Smith did his best with the available material, 'but, in the absence of working drawings, and of any common principle with respect to the nature and depth of the foundations and the style and extent of the finishings', expected a considerable difference of opinion. Nevertheless, he thought that all had seriously underestimated the cost of their designs. According to Dr Watkin, Smith found — 'as a result of Tite's help', he comments cynically — that of the three designs, only Cockerell's fell within the prescribed limits.[97] This is not borne out, however, by Smith's report, pricing Cockerell's at £174,648, Donaldson's at £159,337, and Mocatta's at

[90] *Globe*, 15 and 17 June 1840. According to Leeds, Lambert Jones's crucial opposition (as chairman of the relevant committee) to extending the Blackwall Railway to Shoreditch had been bought off by this joint appointment, *Westminster Review*, XXXV (1841), p. 85n.

[91] I. S. Black, 'Symbolic Capital: the London and Westminster Bank headquarters, 1836–38', *Landscape Research*, XXI (1996), pp. 55–71.

[92] Are we to conclude that Lambert Jones was in the minority voting against the reference of only the 'three best designs'? Did he bring about the reversal of that vote on 3 February 1840?

[93] MC, GR, 29 November and 31 December 1839.

[94] MS scrapbook compiled by J. E. Goodchild, 1889, entitled 'Reminiscences of my Twenty-six years Association with Professor C. R. Cockerell, Esqr.', cited by Watkin, p. 209. The RIBA's charges have prevented my consulting this source personally.

[95] Watkin, pp. 221–22. See I. S. Black, cit. n. 91.

[96] *Proceedings*, p. 25.

[97] Watkin, p. 209. Smith does not mention this in his report in *Proceedings*.

FIG. 108.   John Davis Paine's design for a Royal Exchange, in the French Beaux Arts manner, had won the Royal
Academy Schools Gold Medal in 1833.

£150,285, with potential rentals of £6,060, £4,000 and £6,360 respectively.[98]

Smith admitted that much larger rentals could be expected from nos. 46 and 27, as well as Grellier's, than from the others. But there were two fundamental requirements, however, that he distinguished: a satisfactory arrangement of the specified offices and rooms, with sufficient light and convenient access; and the complete fireproofing of each distinct set of rooms. All the designs, Smith concluded, were 'essentially deficient in some one or more' of the required particulars:

It is comparatively easy to design a splendid architectural portico and façades, or to ornament a building with elaborate and tasteful decorations in turrets and towers; but much difficulty is often found in duly sustaining such superstructures consistently with the necessity for large and airy apartments below, or to reconcile deep recesses of porticos with the light so much required in this metropolis and for the wants of this building.

⁹⁸ MC, GR, 31 January 1840, printed in *Proceedings*, pp. 24–26.

From the shape of the site, any towers or turrets placed at right angles to the north and south fronts would not be parallel with the principal or west front. It is possible to avoid the manifestation of these or other objections in drawings (submitted to non-professional inspection), though it is of great importance that perspective views should accurately represent the actual effect of the building when completed.[99]

Having considered Smith's report, the committee decided unsurprisingly at a crucial meeting on 3 February 1840 when Smith gave more detailed verbal information, to reject the five 'permissible' designs (nos. 36, 43, 37, 33 and 51). The fate of the architecturally 'best' designs was then similarly resolved: Donaldson was refused a hearing by 11 votes to 5, and finally rejected by 12 to 2; Mocatta and Cockerell refused a hearing by 12 to 4, and further consideration of the former rejected by 12 to 1, despite endorsement of Mocatta's low estimate by

⁹⁹ Ibid. The last point strikes at Cockerell's design, as well as others.

the great contractors Grissell and Peto.[100] The struggle over no. 46 then reached a climax: a move to reject Cockerell's design was defeated by 12 to 3 — but a follow-up motion to employ Cockerell subject to his remodelling the interior with Smith's help was amended 'to ballot for five eminent architects, to each of whom, together with the architect of No. 46 (*Mr C. R. Cockerell*), it should be referred to send in a ... design ... at a cost not exceeding £150,000'; provided two or three accepted, no others were to be substituted. This was then carried by 10 votes to 6, thereby reversing the defeat (9:4) of a similar proposal on 29 November previous. A ballot nominated Tite (8 votes), Barry (7), and the original referees, Sir Robert Smirke (9), Hardwick (12) and Gwilt (9).[101] Meanwhile all the remaining plans (including no. 46) were to be returned to their authors.

All the invitees declined the Gresham Committee's invitation save Tite, although Hardwick and Gwilt expressed their willingness to have taken part in a limited competition in the first instance — while Cockerell offered his old design with modifications. A motion to allow Donaldson, Mocatta and Cockerell to give personal explanations was negatived.[102] Tite suggested to Cockerell that they should again collaborate. When the latter reminded him that he was already bound to a collaborator, the manipulative Tite remarked that Richardson might be persuaded to stand aside 'for a consideration'.[103]

The committee then determined on a competition between Tite and Cockerell, their designs to be submitted within two months; alterations in the instructions were referred to Lambert Jones and Smith, the assurance companies and Lloyd's furnishing the rivals with necessary information.[104] The digging of five dry wells to determine the nature of the foundation was authorised on 20 March, the two

competitors reported progress, and the committee 'neither sanction nor object to Mr Tite' showing his plans. The contending plans were received on 28 April, and the accompanying reports ordered to be printed and circulated to committee members; Tite was instructed to furnish a detailed statement of the area in each of his storeys provided for letting, with a block plan on a fly-sheet — to be printed and circulated.[105] On 4 May Tite and Cockerell were allowed two hours each to explain their designs before the committee, and the latter's detailed statement as read ordered to be printed and circulated.[106] But it availed him nothing. Nor did his request to exhibit an elaborate model which — rather than his drawings — embodied his revisions: Tite, model-less, secured its rejection on grounds of unfairness, and non-compliance with the rules of the original competition.[107] The committee resolved, after a 'protracted discussion' on 7 May, in favour of Tite by thirteen votes to seven.[108]

Hitchcock suggests that the constructional problem posed by Cockerell's proposed roof, with its 'tremendous round [*sic*] opening' (Fig. 109), may have been 'sufficient to discourage the committee' from selecting his project. But the 'bold Late-Imperial air' of his grandiloquent main front probably struck in the minds of contemporaries a note of continental baroque despotism or Romanism that was still more discouraging than technical problems they are unlikely to have comprehended. Still more fatal was the disposition of shops in an arcade at the east; the former tenants feared the loss of their conspicuous frontages, and opened up the 'batteries of shopocracy' against it. Cockerell vainly referred to his illustrious sources and explained that he drew inspiration from Nerva's Forum in Rome, which he thought appropriate as he saw the space in front of the Exchange as

[100] W. H. Leeds reported that the respected measurers Meredith and W. H. Hunt (the latter employed by Barry) had guaranteed the architects' prices, and that Hicks & Sons, well-known contractors, had tendered at Cockerell's figure, *Westminster Review*, XXXV (1841), p. 61.
[101] The unsuccessful were Bunning (5), Papworth (4), Donaldson (3), Mocatta (1), Decimus Burton (1) and Hoskins (1), MC, GR, 3 February 1840.
[102] Ibid., 11, 19 February 1840.
[103] Watkin, p. 209, citing Goodchild.
[104] MC, GR, 11, 19 February 1840.

[105] Ibid., 28 April 1840.
[106] Cockerell had drastically remodelled the original design, discarding the huge entrance front tower that would have been an extremely expensive feature: cp. Watkin, pls. 120 and 123.
[107] Lambert Jones told Common Council that 'he found all the best authorities opposed to models'; and that a City builder, a friend on whose judgment he relied, had seen the model and assured him 'it was a complete deception', *Westminster Review*, XXXV (1841), p. 67.
[108] MC, GR, 7 May 1840; *The Times*, 8 May 1840.

the 'Forum Londinium'[109] — but of course that was an overstretch of imagination.

Tite's octostyle pedimented Corinthian portico (Fig. 110), on the other hand, was a big example of a familiar type, even if 'banal' and borrowed from Donaldson's (which had, of course, in its original form been on public exhibition in Mercers' Hall for a week),[110] likely enough to appeal to businessmen unlearned in the finer points of architectural discrimination.[111] Effective drawing may well have helped Tite win — use of false shadow in his perspective made the portico appear deeper than it would be. The shape of the site, a trapezoid or irregular oblong, meant that all the drawings gave a somewhat inaccurate representation, and presented Tite with a discord between the plane of the flanks of his portico and those of the north and south sides that he failed to resolve. But to Hitchcock, Tite's design 'perhaps suffers no more than Cockerell's . . . from the disparity in treatment between the main front and the other three sides'. While the portico 'is both conventional and overpowering', the long north and south sides (Fig. 111), in his sympathetic view, offer more 'real novelty' than did Cockerell's: they contain features 'in the continental Baroque tradition, although not without parallels in late Stuart work by Wren and Archer', with an 'elaboration of relief in the handling of wall planes' which are not found in Victorian architecture before the mid-fifties[112] — and, one may add, are much less distinct than the Baroque element of Cockerell's magnificent façade or even the subtle interplay of his two orders. The contemporary critic W. H. Leeds complained of the flatness of Tite's long north and south fronts, pilasters on isolated pedestals separating niches for flat shop-fronts, a concept Tite justified by reference to the much shorter flat façade of Barry's Reform Club. Cockerell's apologist Watkin

condemns Tite's 'complex but flaccid articulation'. Cockerell in contrast, he believes, had integrated 'structure, function and adornment into one triumphal whole'. His design was 'one of the great triumphs of his career and hence of the whole of nineteenth-century architecture', superb in its 'panache and vigour'.[113] To Leeds, it was 'the best Palladian design we have seen since Sir William Chambers'.[114]

Cockerell's design commanded widespread admiration, and much Press comment took the common modern view that the Gresham Committee was perpetrating an architectural injustice. A correspondent in the *Globe* evening newspaper urged reconsideration; a 'constant reader' of *The Times* found 'very little novelty' in Tite's design, commenting unfavourably on his departure from Vitruvius' rules about the space between columns of a portico, and the inadequate depth of his 'preposterous' portico, a feature the beauty of which depended not merely on its frontage (Tite's at 90 feet the widest in London), but on its projection, depth of shadow and general effect.[115] *The Times* and the *Globe* gave the widest coverage to the issue, the latter particularly pluming itself on sustaining discussion, though its editorial attitude was essentially hostile to Tite's appointment: 'there are not, amongst competent judges, two opinions on the conduct of the City Committee of Taste. The thing passes for what it ought to pass — a gross blunder, or a still grosser job.'[116] Tite's supporter, the *Chronicle*, was disparaged as the 'newspaper organ of a railway company', and the man himself as 'a clever coadjutor in City transactions, an able Railway suveyor and valuer'.[117]

Indeed, Cockerell still had something to fight for, since both the general court of the Mercers' Company and the City Corporation itself had yet to endorse the committee's recommendation. But it was hardly surprising that the City's merchants were complaining about the delay in starting work on a new

[109] A. E. Richardson, *Monumental Classical Architecture in Great Britain and Ireland* (1914), p. 79, cited Watkin, p. 211. See above, p. 288.

[110] Along with the rest of Donaldson's main features, 'except just in those points which form its [Donaldson's] principal merit' (*Westminster Review*, XXXV, p. 69).

[111] It also won the approval of the critic of the *Surveyor, Engineer and Architect*, I (1840).

[112] Hitchcock, p. 308. There is a detailed analysis of the defects of Tite's design in the *Globe*, 8 June 1840, and a more favourable description in *The Times*, 21 May 1840, p. 4.

[113] Watkin, p. 210.

[114] *Westminster Review*, XXXV, p. 70.

[115] *The Times*, 9 June 1840, p. 4d. Leeds also condemned Tite's anti-Vitruvian internal composition of two almost equal storeys, Doric and Ionic.

[116] *Globe*, leader, 3 June 1840; see also 8, 9, and 17 June.

[117] Ibid., 8 and 6 June 1840.

FIG. 109.   The courtyard of C. R. Cockerell's design, showing the remarkable coving and
the balustrading to his elliptical opening, and the statues of
English sovereigns above his Doric arcade.

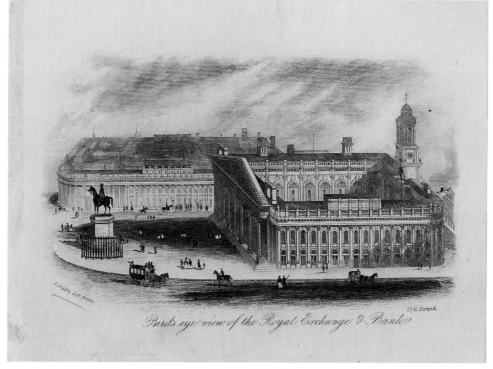

FIG. 110.   William Tite's approved design had a very shallow western portico,
a defect vigorously attacked in the Press.

FIG. 111. The sides of Tite's design display a rich ornamentation and variation in the wall plane anticipating High Victorian elaboration.

FIG. 112. The interior of Tite's design, unadorned with statuary, looked respectable but inexpensive.

building. The Inquest of Cornhill Ward made a presentment to the Court of Aldermen regarding the suffering from the commercial interest's being diverted into other channels, the failure of charitable contributions and the increase in rates resulting from the loss of the Exchange; and the ghost of Sir Thomas Gresham was visualised on the ruins of the Exchange, demanding where the spirit of London's merchantmen was sleeping and whether Enterprise had fled.[118] 'Mercator' — an old merchant of London with 'too much business of his own to undertake the office of common-councilman' — declared roundly in *The Times* that 'The question in the city is not "Who is to be the architect?" but "Are we to have an Exchange?".' The two and a half years' delay since the destruction of the old Exchange, 'a great commercial city in itself', had caused 'excessive inconvenience'; 'whatever solicitude may have been felt as to the architectural embellishment of the city, the great interests at stake have made that rather secondary to the restoration of those facilities to trade and commerce which the new building is expected to afford'. In any case, Tite's design was 'far superior in elevation and general effect to its neighbour, the Bank, and it immeasurably surpasses any other specimen of civil or commercial architecture in London'.[119]

Nevertheless, the minority vote coming from the Mercers' side of the Joint Committee, Cockerell attempted to exploit this division by appealing to the Mercers' committee.[120] A statement that Tite's portico columns were 42 feet 6 inches high, but the depth from inside the columns to the pilasters of the wall was only 8 feet 4 inches was considered at two meetings of the Mercers' side of the Gresham Committee, but the Joint Committee then recommended the Mercers' court to adopt Tite's plan 'with the clear understanding that any Alteration which can be made to improve the Structure or increase the Rental will be attended to' — and indeed the criticism was soon to bear fruit. The court then resolved 'by a very large majority' to adopt Tite's plan, but with the

significant addition of a rider to the committee's recommendation, 'and that due attention will be paid . . . to the Rental thereof'.[121] The City Corporation followed suit. The final step was to obtain the sanction of the Treasury, which Cockerell in a last despairing throw had now memorialised. Approval was ultimately secured on 27 September 1840.[122] Thus one of England's finest architects was outplayed by a City slicker only too familiar with the terrain.

The design approved, the committee had to organise the building. Tite had already on 3 July, as soon as the Mercers had approved his plan, recommended excavating the foundations and laying concrete.[123] It was decided to obtain lump-sum contracts, then becoming general for extensive new works, and particularly popular with businessmen,[124] but to divide the contracts between foundations (with all the necessary excavation work) and superstructure. On 6 October 1840 the first contract, that for foundations, was let to Messrs Robert and George Webb at £7,638, exclusive of excavating the central open area (subsequently included for an additional £486).[125]

During the summer, criticism of Tite's showy but shallow portico had been making its impact, and he was instructed to consider alterations; the model and drawings that he produced on 12 February 1841 doubled the depth of the portico by inserting a

[118] *The Times*, 15 January 1840, p. 3e; 10 March 1840, p. 7c.
[119] Ibid., 6 June 1840, p. 5d.
[120] *Globe*, 5 June 1840; MC, GR, 19 May 1840; Cockerell's letter, 'entering very fully into grounds for such objection' to the appointment of Tite, has not survived.
[121] Ibid., 5, 10, and 16 June, 3 July 1840; see also *The Times*, 19 May, 10, 16 June, 3 July 1840.
[122] MC, GR, 27 July, 30 September 1840. Interviewed on Cockerell's memorial by the First Commissioner of Works, Lambert Jones had satisfied him 'and particularly as to the Committee not having visited in their official capacity the Model prepared by Mr Cockerell' (ibid., 27 July). An objection by the Bank of England that Tite's building came too close was also removed by widening the juxtaposition from 40 ft to 43 ft, ibid.
[123] Ibid., 3 July 1840.
[124] See Port, 'The Office of Works and building contracts in early nineteenth-century England', *Econ. Hist. Rev.*, n.s., xx (1967), pp. 94–110.
[125] MC, GR, 6 October 1840. Tite's estimate had been £10,829. The other tenders were, to the nearest pound: Jos. Bennett £11,181, N. Winsland £11,302, G. and G. W. Baker £10,932, Jas. & Jos. Lee £10,837, G. and J. W. Bridger £10,627, Grissell and Peto £10,165, T. and T. Piper £9,980, H. Ward £9,587, J. and J. Little £9,432, Wm Cubitt £8,985, S. Grimsdale £8,738.

column at each side. He also showed his arrangement of office space.[126]

For the major work of the superstructure, competitive tenders were invited in May 1841 from fourteen leading builders, who returned bids for a building of Portland stone ranging from Herbert Ward's £135,500 down to Thomas Jackson's successful £115,900; the building was to be completed by 20 June 1844, with a penalty of £20 a day for late delivery.[127] The first stone was laid by Prince Albert on 17 January 1842 (Fig. 113).[128]

As the building rose, the committee considered some additional embellishments. Tite was authorised to prepare a contract for architectural carving with C. H. Smith (sculptor of the capitals of the National Gallery portico) at £6,500 (see Fig. 111).[129] He then pointed out that the tympanum of the west front pediment was 'highly favourable to the display of the art of the sculptor' (Cockerell's having been criticised for its excessive sculpture); 'the uninterrupted view of this part of the building, the height, and the aspect offer advantages which do not often present themselves', he urged. To strengthen his case, he resorted to Richard Westmacott, ARA (1799–1872), learned son of a more famous father, who prepared a sketch. Tite estimated that 'such a mass of sculpture could be executed in the best style of art for £3,000 or three thousand guineas'.[130] The committee approved this

proposal, directed Tite to obtain designs and estimates from Westmacott and his rivals, E. H. Baily, RA (1788–1867), sculptor of Nelson's statue in Trafalgar Square, and M. L. Watson (1804–47), who had just carved the frieze on the façade of Moxey's 'Hall of Commerce' in Threadneedle Street (itself intended as rival or substitute for the destroyed Exchange). Baily declining, Samuel Joseph (1791–1850) — whose memorial statue of Wilberforce had been erected in Westminster Abbey in 1838 — was substituted.[131] The committee heard the sculptors in explanation of their designs, and selected that by Westmacott, as recounted in fuller detail by Mr Leith below (pp. 336–43). A model was inspected on 31 March 1843, and approved with some alterations.[132]

Other embellishments included a chiming clock by Dent (which the Astronomer Royal had no doubt was 'the best public clock in the world');[133] a peal of bells by Mears of Whitechapel which was to cause inordinate trouble;[134] and free-standing statuary, including a statue of Queen Victoria (by T. G. Lough) for the centre of the merchants' arena, and the restored Charles II that had stood in the centre of the old Exchange.[135] Others by Watson, Behnes, J. E. Carew, and Joseph[136] are discussed below.

The ferment of ideas about decorative painting unbottled by the Royal Fine Arts Commission relating to the New Palace of Westminster also sprayed the Exchange: Tite reported that encaustic painting of the ambulatory ceiling with heraldic devices could be done for £1,740, and recommended Frederick Sang of Munich (Fig. 114).[137] This proved little more satisfactory than Henry Pether's tessellated pavement

---

[126] Ibid., 6 October 1840. The committee also ordered payment of 50 guineas to Robert Smirke, Hardwick and Gwilt for their report on the competition, as well as 100 guineas to Mocatta, Donaldson and Cockerell for their expenses in supplying detailed estimates; Cockerell returned his fee, suggesting it be 'applied to some really charitable purpose' (Watkin, quoting, *Cockerell*, p. 210).

[127] MC, GR, 25 May and 1 September 1841. Tenders were required for both Portland stone and the slightly more expensive Magnesian limestone 'of equal quality to that used for building the new Houses of Parliament'. The Portland stone bids were: H. Ward £135,500, N. Winsland £134,219, Wm Cubitt £134,200, G. and J. W. Bridger £131,519, Jos. Bennett £131,500, R. and G. Webb £130,150, J. and J. Little £129,800, J. Jay £129,609, T. and T. Piper £128,700, Grissell and Peto £127,400, S. Grimsdale £126,762, H. and J. Lee £126,390, G. and G. W. Baker £122,765, and Jackson £115,900. *Proceedings*, p. 28.

[128] The elaborate ceremonial on the laying of the stone, as well as for the Queen's opening of the Royal Exchange, is set out in R. L. Jones, *Reminiscences*, and in White's *Three Royal Exchanges*.

[129] MC, GR, 20 April 1842.

[130] *Proceedings*, p. 38, 28 October 1842.

[131] Ibid., p. 40. For the sculptors, see R. Gunnis, *Dictionary of British Sculptors* (rev. edn, n.d.).

[132] MC, GR, 28 October, 25 November 1842; 31 March 1843.

[133] White, *Three Royal Exchanges*, p. 44.

[134] Summarised in White, and to be followed in detail in MC, GR from 28 February 1844 to 5 October 1855, when one bell was still out of tune. They played the Old Hundredth, God Save the Queen, Auld Lang Syne and The Roast Beef of Old England until 1894, when they 'came entirely to grief' and were reconstructed (White, pp. 46–47).

[135] A work of John Spiller in 1789–92, MC, GR, 19 May 1789, 24 July 1792.

[136] MC, GR, 31 May 1844, printed in *Proceedings*, p. 40.

[137] *Proceedings*, p. 40. The painting is described in *Illustrated London News*, 9 November 1844, p. 291.

FIG. 113.   Prince Albert laid the foundation stone in a splendid civic ceremony on 17 January 1842.

for the open area (Col. Pl. IXB) — executed by A. Singer at the Vauxhall Pottery — judged a failure and ordered to be removed in November 1844, to be replaced by asphalt of Seyssel, until in September 1845 Tite was instructed to prepare a specimen of the pavement he had originally proposed, using in part the Turkey stones of Gresham's original Exchange, stored since the fire at Mercers' Hall.[138] Sang's ceilings were in need of restoration by 1853, but not until 1859 was a small part cleaned, after which an advertisement was issued for designs for fresco painting in the ambulatory. Eventually Sang's estimate of £1,830 was accepted for this work, but his claim to

be reimbursed for a loss of £825 in executing it was declined.[139]

However, the formal completion of the new building was signified by its opening by Queen Victoria on 28 October 1844 (four months late), though it was not opened to the public until 1 January 1845, and the accounts were not completed until 1852, when the total cost of rebuilding, including the cost of the associated ceremonies and the architect's commission of £3,350, was stated at £168,534 6s.[140] But already in May 1852 the committee was having to contemplate the cost of securing the imperfect cornices of the new building.[141]

---

[138] MC, GR, 20 September and 8 November 1844, 26 September 1845. Seventy cartloads of the Turkey stones from the old Exchange had been removed to Mercers' Hall early in 1840, *The Times*, 3 February 1840.

[139] MC, GR, 22 April 1853; 8 April, 17 June, 13 July, 1 November, and 2 December 1859.
[140] White, *Three Royal Exchanges*, p. 46. The cost of the site extension and surrounding avenues was given as £233,700 7s. 4½d.
[141] MC, GR, 7 May, 9 July 1852.

FIG. 114.   Frederick Sang's encaustic painting in the arcades was inspired by the Royal Fine Arts Commission's recommendations for the new Houses of Parliament.
Guardian Royal Exchange collection

Consumer reaction to Tite's work was not wholly favourable. The Royal Exchange Assurance Company required additional windows for its offices, and the tenants of the shops wanted, contrary to Tite's opinion, to move their shopfronts forward. Ironically, this proposal was referred to Cockerell, who reported, but begged to be relieved from giving further advice. The shopfronts on either side of the north gateway were brought out, against further protests by Tite, at a cost of £1,194.[142]

More important was a request from a deputation of merchants in 1860 for the open central area to be roofed: it had proved to be the cold and wet, rather than hot weather, that needed to be considered. The committee advertised for designs, and received 33 proposals, from which a sub-committee selected three, requesting their estimates. But a week later they asked to be relieved from recommending a plan: it sounds like a repetition of the original competition of 1839. The complaining merchants were then told that the area could be enclosed if a suitable design and the means were provided, and the Exchange's tenants agreed to the plan. The Lord Mayor and the Master of the Mercers were asked to consider the

relative merits of designs, and on their report a premium was awarded. A light rough structure springing from the lower entablature was then put up at the east end in March 1861, but met with no approval: the merchants protested against half-measures, while the public — and Tite (now Sir William) — disliked it. Tite produced his own model, but the Mercers at first declined to finance it. After a viewing of Tite's model at Lloyd's, it was declared inexpedient to proceed further, and the temporary half-roof was removed in March 1862.[143]

Nearly twenty years later, a memorial from foreign bankers, merchants and brokers re-started the discussion; a design by Handyside & Co. was approved by merchants and brokers; but Lloyd's and Royal Exchange Assurance objected to a covering from the top, as this would have diminished the light in their rooms. The 1861 design was brought out again, the adoption of Handyside's design rescinded, and a limited competition for a £10,000 project initiated. Eight designs were received, and that of Charles Barry, junior, accepted. Barry himself proposed a modification whereby semicircular openings in a solid

[142] Ibid.,   11 December   1851,   21 January,   6 February, 15 September, and 22 October 1852.

[143] Ibid., 26 July, 27 September, 5 and 13 December 1860; 3, 10, 22, and 31 January, 22 February, 5 March, 23 April, 27 June, 9 and 17 July 1861, 17 March 1862.

FIG. 115.   After prolonged complaints, a roof, designed
by Charles Barry, junior, was erected over the courtyard
in 1884.

cover were to be glazed (Fig. 115). The work, carried
out at a cost of £20,000 by Whitford & Co. in 1884,
was 'much admired for its elegance and lightness'.[144]

144 Ibid., 18 February, 12 October, 20 December 1881; 10 and
17 March, 24 April, 16 and 23 June, 21 July, 6 November,
15 December 1882; 17 January, 2 February, 25 May 1883;
25 January, 18 July, 12 December 1884; White, *Three Royal
Exchanges*, p. 46.

CHAPTER XXVII

Opening of the Royal Exchange
by Queen Victoria

COPY OF A LETTER deposited in the Guildhall Library by an anonymous donor, inscribed:

Written by my grandmother (Mrs. Thomas Wilkinson, late of 5 Portland Place, Clapton) to her sister, Maria Brookes (daughter of Dr. William Brookes, of Much Wenlock, Shropshire)

November 10th 1844

My dear Maria,

Let me have the pleasure of conducting your attention to the great National Event of 28th October. We were in the interior of the Royal Exchange the day it was opened by Her Majesty. The order was for all gentlemen invited to the Déjeuner in the Queen's apartments to be attired in Court dress and ladies in full evening dress (not full court dress which would have required us to wear trains, lappets and feathers).

I will therefore give you an account of Thomas's dress which is the principal feature on that subject; mine being a more *general* style of costume. A rich, dark claret was the colour of his coat and knee breeches made in the *older* style which I must leave you to imagine and which in many old paintings you may have seen portrayed. The coat was lined throughout with a rich white silk and ornamented with 24 steel buttons of the value of 5/– each; the nether garment required 8 of these costly courtly buttons of a smaller size value 2/6 each which Thomas did me the honour to permit me to select, and superb they were. The waistcoat was white silk embroidered with a very exquisite wreath of lilac coloured flowers intermingled with green leaves, the centre was covered with pretty little corresponding sprigs; *that* was my superior taste also! But I love to go a-shopping and to see what I can see as you very well know. A pretty little bag, covered with black satin loops was attached to the collar of the coat behind; formerly the repository for the tail of the wig which

was then worn and which still bears the denomination of a *bag wig*. A cocked hat of black silk looped together with a 5/– button, the same as those on the coat. Shoes ornamented with large silver buckles which we preferred to steel, with smaller ones to match for the knees — value 3 guineas. A glittering sword in readiness to defend Her Majesty. Silk stockings, fine as gossamer to adorn and set off his legs (and a very handsome leg it is!) and white rich silk gloves — Andrew's wedding gift, and you may reflect upon the portrait I have given you of your courtly brother. His shirt was trimmed in the front with three rows of the richest point lace about 3½ inches wide, very full, and coffee coloured, which looked so much the handsomer as it is the *fashionable* tint, ruffles of narrower point lace to match.

I will now say all that is to be said of my dress. The pink satin was of course the very thing and suited me in every way, the only addition made to it being a very beautiful white rose, which considerably improved the body by being placed in the centre of the blonde bertha in front. A very beautiful spray of white flowers we purchased (22/– the cost) at Foster's to adorn my head with — part of which extended quite over the *upper* part of my plaited hair behind and then fell down in two very négligée sprays at the side of the head. A hair dresser from London was in requisition to set my hair off to the best advantage, and very beautifully he did it certainly. He made several trellis work kind of plaits behind (twisting my hair up with a comb first) and looped them in a very pretty elegant way. Curls in front, without the aid of curling irons, for I had taken special care to curl it carefully in paper the night previously, and he finally placed the flower I mentioned as the last touch. My snowy kid gloves just from Paris were elegantly trimmed with a gimp composed of a silver cord with white silk tassels — white satin shoes from Regent

Street, all my jewellery and best pocket handkerchief and I was equipped for the grand Déjeuner.

On the Sunday previously Mr. Freeze and his son Henry together with Mrs. Wilkinson and Mary dined with us and after showing them our various trappings for the use of the following day which they were very anxious to see, they very thoughtfully wished us Good Evening at 9 o'clock, enabling us thereby to retire to rest at an early hour, for at 4 o'clock in the morning of Monday we had to quit our warm beds, for the following reasons. On the Saturday previous Thomas wishing to give his servants and children a treat, he and I together sought and procured places for them in Cornhill just opposite to the site of the great western door where Her Majesty and all the Nobility (ourselves of course among the number) were to enter, a most admirable situation. Mrs. Wilkinson and Mary wished for seats also, for which they paid a guinea each and half price was given for each child. They of course kindly took care of the children and were all together in one room — about the third story, above which was erected by the occupants of the house for the purpose of forming other seats, five of which we engaged for the domestics, three for our three and two for Mrs. Wilkinson's servants who treated hers likewise, these seats were half a guinea each, but commanded an equally good view of the whole procession, as those in the rooms below and they were all much enchanted and have not ceased to talk about the fairy-like scene. I provided them with wine, apples, biscuits and plenty of sandwiches, so that they were not uncomfortable upon that point and had no occasion to leave their seats the whole time. The children were similarly provided with the exception of *wine* (which was substituted by toast and water) and apples.

It was observed in the papers as one of the regulations that no carriages would be permitted to pass the *barriers* after 7 a.m. excepting those containing the visitors to the Royal Exchange. This regulation was afterwards, unknown to us, altered till 9 a.m. they were permitted to pass. At 4 a.m. therefore all our household began to be on the alert in order to have a comfortable breakfast and dress in readiness for the coach which conveyed them all away at *6 a.m.* calling for the inmates of Grove Place on the way. A very large roomy vehicle it was and

conveyed them all most comfortably — by 8 o'clock it was at the door of 5 Portland Place in readiness for the second party, namely Thomas and myself, and Thomas's tailor (Mr. James of Alfred Street) who came down to us by 6 o'clock to bring Thomas's coat etc. and assist him in dressing. Thomas's study was converted into my dressing room, and at 6.30 my hair dresser arrived. The baby, of course, was left at home, having provided a very nice steady girl to take care of her, and the house, who came in the evening before.

Henry Freeze came to look at us at 8 in the morning, just before we departed. We then drove off to the West End where a party was awaiting to accompany us — the principal person being a young lady, a niece to the gentleman, Mr. Newnham of Cornwall Terrace, Regents Park, who gave us the tickets and was placed under Thomas's care to chaperone. Her dress was white tarlatan (alias white book muslin) over white satin being pretty and elegant, a pink rose in front of a wreath of pink flowers in her hair, similar in size to mine and placed in the same position.

Thomas and this young lady of eighteen (I think I ought to be jealous!), a young gentleman (her cousin) and my beau for the day — and myself now occupied more fully our carriage and without delay we proceeded to the Royal Exchange, having to pass the barrier in Cheapside before 10 o'clock. We entered at the great western door, and paused a few minutes ere we passed onwards to wave our handkerchiefs to our little ones and all *our* party of spectators who were anxiously watching for us and speedily recognised our group. Mary Anne's little voice I distinctly heard calling 'Mamma, Mamma' — we then passed into the Quadrangle and walked around it for the purpose of inspecting the paintings which adorn its walls and ceiling, and then ascended the staircase where we first of all looked at our ticketed places, and then walked about as we liked.

The Duke of Wellington arrived shortly after and you may fancy how my heart glowed when the band proclaimed the arrival of this illustrious hero with 'See the Conquering Hero comes'. Most gloriously was he cheered and he appeared much pleased with the enthusiasm of his admirers, as he walked with somewhat tottering steps through both the rooms. I

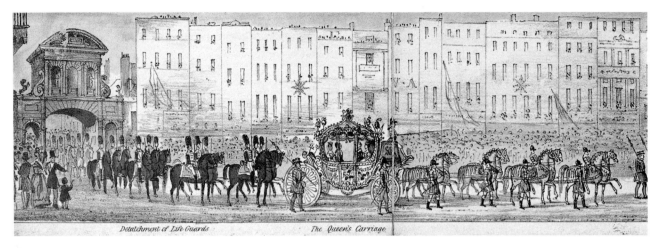

Detatchment of Life Guards   *The Queen's Carriage*

FIGS. 116, 117.   Panorama of the Royal Procession on the opening of the third Exchange, 28 October, 1844. The complete engraving is nearly twelve feet long. These details show Queen Victoria's coach entering the City at Temple Bar, and the head of the procession reaching the Exchange.

Private Collection

had an excellent view of him for I stood within a yard of him as he entered the commercial room of Lloyds in which I had a seat, the next one (the Subscribers' room) was Thomas's apartment, and the one in which the Queen and Royal Family lunched; the Queen's table being at the top of the room, and Thomas's seat at only twenty-one of the central tables from Her Majesty — a most delightful situation. Sir Robert Peel soon afterwards was warmly greeted with music and voices, the Duke of Cambridge and many other nobles of the land.

At last as the hour of one drew nigh all were commanded to take their places and shortly afterwards to rise up in readiness for Her Majesty, and 'God save the Queen' was struck up immediately upon her arrival. She walked first I believe around and then through the centre of the Quadrangle and ascended the staircase as we had previously done, leaning on the arm of her interesting husband Prince Albert, who wore the scarlet uniform, as Colonel of the City Artillery Company, preceded by the Lord Mayor and followed by her Maids of Honour, — one of them very lovely. She walked through our room and from thence into the State room and subsequently into the Throne Room, situated on the left hand side of the State room. There Her Majesty held a Court and received the City Address which was delivered by the Recorder surrounded by the Aldermen and City Functionaries to which she replied in a

distinct and silvery voice, a queenly voice indeed, — she read the reply to the address presented to her. Thomas entered the Throne Room and had the satisfaction of listening to her and was much gratified. Afterwards she retired for a few minutes into her withdrawing room and then appeared at the table appointed for the Royal party. The Bishop of London advanced from his seat to the Queen's table and said Grace, he then retired and the déjeuner was at once cordially commenced.

I really felt exceedingly and provokingly hungry and very gladly performed operations on a chicken's wing and a slice of tongue — every thing was excellent, and of the very best description and in abundance; likewise the grapes were like plums in size, pineapples very fine, various ices and choice wines, — champagne alone I patronized. The band played at intervals, and previous to each toast being given, heralds stationed at either end of the room proclaimed silence with trumpets which had a grand and thrilling effect, a flourish of trumpets concluded the toasts. The Lord Mayor first proposed at Her Majesty's Command the health of Her Majesty, shortly afterwards silence was proclaimed again and by the Queen's Command was proposed the health of Prince Albert, then the Prince of Wales and the rest of the Royal Family, lastly — prosperity to the City of London.

Presently the feast was at an end and at 3 o'clock Her Majesty departed in the same ceremonious order

Life Guards   *Police Officers*

as she entered, proceeding down the grand staircase into the Quadrangle.

I have not yet described her dress, which was a rich figured white satin brocaded in front with silver tissue, a tiara of diamonds in her hair — crowning her forehead and a very small crown of diamonds placed at the back of her head just in the centre of the plait. In stature she is short, shorter than Mary Wilkinson and inclined to be stout. She looked *well* but *serious*, — and many thought melancholy, her countenance is open and the features large (the eyes) but wanting animation, — decidedly only *good looking* but no approach to beauty, in fact she was precisely what I had previously conceived from various representations of her — except that I had fancied a more smiling and less stern countenance.

The Prince her husband, I much admired, for he is certainly handsome, but looking very ill and it is said he is in a decline, — surely if so, his Queen may well look sad. Whilst walking through the rooms the Queen and Prince both continued bending their heads increasingly [*sic*] by way of acknowledging the warm salutations of Her affectionate subjects. The Maids of Honour were dressed in white satin with trains which they held very gracefully on their arms.

After Her Majesty's departure the company began to disperse; we left at about half past four and once more we had the opportunity of waving handkerchiefs to the group who knew us even in the midst of such a throng. We called for Mrs. Wilkinson, Mary and the children whom we took with us to the West End, and after taking a cup of tea, we very gladly hastened

homewards and as we came through the City for the purpose of showing the children the illuminations they were entertained to the very last.

I did not tell you that opposite to Thomas sat the very ugly Lord John Russell and the handsome Lord Ernest Bruce, with the latter Thomas took wine at his Lordship's request. Sir Robert and Lady Peel, the renowned, sat also very near Thomas. I exceedingly admired the fine open countenance of Sir Robert Peel. Sir Henry Pothinger sat also very near Thomas, another very interesting character, but nearer still and almost opposite to him sat Lady Seymour — the 'Queen of Beauty' at the Eglinton Tournament, Lady Dufferin, her sister — (two of the beautiful Misses Sheridan upon whom he principally feasted his eyes) also the Hon. Mrs. Norton the celebrated authoress being the other, who is also very beautiful. Also Lady Lincoln and the Earl of Westmorland.

Nay, one thing more I must tell you, namely that during the déjeuner we were each presented with a silver medal which I shall one day have the pleasure of showing you. Her Majesty in remembrance of the event, expressed her wish to retain her table napkin, which was exceedingly exquisite, being embroidered with point lace, worth I should think about £20. She was presented with a gold medal I believe.

Do you not think we spent a delightful day? a very *golden* day, — a sunbeam in one's life, a thing to be remembered to amuse our rising generation, a nursery story to entertain our little grandchildren with. Furthermore let me tell you that we shall one day be in all probability introduced at Court, and very useful it would be in the event of travelling abroad where it would be a sufficient 'card' of recommendation to other Courts.

. . . To return to the Royal Exchange, Prince Albert informed the Lord Mayor, Mr. William Magnay, that Her Majesty had directed Letters Patent to pass the great seal, creating him a baronet upon which he was presented by Lord Chamberlain, and kissed hands and in turn presented, as was previously arranged, the Master of the Mercer's Company, Mr. Tite the architect, the chairman of the Gresham Committee and Thomas . . .

Transcribed by ANN SAUNDERS
Noble Collection, A512/12. Guildhall Library, Corporation of London. The text breaks off abruptly.

CHAPTER XXVIII

The Mural Decoration at The Royal Exchange

By CLARE A. P. WILLSDON

WHILST STATUES HAD BEEN a distinctive feature of the first and second Royal Exchange buildings, it was not until the completion of the third and present Royal Exchange that consideration was given to mural painting. Having been consulted by the Gresham Committee on 'the subject of additional Sculptural Decorations at the New Royal Exchange', its architect Sir William Tite responded with a radical proposal:

The liberal vote of money for sculpture decoration at the new Royal Exchange has induced me to turn my attention to other modes of decoration adapted to the purposes and circumstances of the Edifice in order that the Committee might have a choice of subjects on which to exercise their judgement and taste. At your last meeting you were good enough to entertain with some favour a suggestion for painting the ceilings of the Ambulatory of the Merchants area with Wax color [*sic*] as lately introduced into Germany and France to direct me to report further upon it . . . This Ambulatory is ceiled with beams and pannels [*sic*] and is exceedingly well adapted for such a style of decoration . . .[1]

Tite submitted a 'sketch showing the general effect of two or three of the pannels' when so painted which he had asked the German decorative artist Frederick Sang to prepare, and then proceeded to a panegyric on the merits of 'Wax color' in which he cited its use in Antiquity — 'in the Roman baths in Rome though exposed to dampness and every vicissitude of the weather for 1800 or 2000 years the paintings in Wax will still preserve their freshness and vividness of

color' — and the recent successful revival of 'this long lost art' in Munich and in the 'Church of the Madeline [*sic*] and other buildings at Paris'.

He urged that such painting

could be introduced with great propriety and effect in the situation pointed out by me. It would tend greatly to increase the beauty of this most important part of the Exchange and if greater Decoration is wished for I know of no situation and no application of modern science which could be more gracefully and usefully introduced than this mode of Decoration.[2]

The Exchange was, after all, almost exactly contemporary with the new Houses of Parliament of Sir Charles Barry and was felt to represent the great 'nation of shopkeepers' almost as importantly as Westminster itself; by the end of the century it would be known, indeed, as 'the heart of Empire'.[3] In 1844, Sir William Tite was clearly looking to emulate the decorative splendours of Barry's great new building. At Westminster, as part of the Gothic Revival style, mural painting was being attempted under the direction of a specially established Royal Fine Arts Commission headed by Prince Albert. What more natural than that, for his design based on a classical temple, Tite should turn to the type of decoration used both in ancient Greece and Rome and in some of the most famous modern re-interpretations of the temple idiom, the Munich Glyptothek of King Ludwig, and the Madeleine Church in Paris? Following the Reformation, mural painting by British artists had suffered a severe decline, and strenuous efforts were being made at Westminster by Prince Albert to establish a modern British 'School of High [i.e.

The author wishes to acknowledge the assistance of a Research Grant from the British Academy and a Research Support Award from the Faculty of Arts of the University of Glasgow in the preparation of this chapter. All illustrations by courtesy of the Joint Grand Gresham Committee.

The following abbreviation is used: GCM — Gresham Committee Minutes, Archives of the Worshipful Company of Mercers, London.

[1] Report from Sir William Tite to 'the Sub-Committee appointed to consider the subject of additional Sculptural Decorations at the new Royal Exchange', GCM, 26 April 1844.

[2] Ibid.

[3] As, for example, in Niels M. Lund's painting *The Heart of Empire: View of London looking west from the top of the Royal Exchange* of 1901 (Guildhall Art Gallery); the image persisted as late as 1924 in the *Morning Post*'s account of the unveiling of the mural of *Women's Work in the Great War* of 30 April 1924 ('. . . there, in the heart of the Empire, the memorial picture would stand').

mural] Art' which could equal continental, and especially modern German, achievement. Whereas the medium of fresco, as used by the Italian Renaissance artists and revived by the German Nazarene painters, was being attempted at Westminster and in a number of private schemes, it was something of proven durability (as he believed), a wax-based paint (also known as encaustic)[4] that Tite significantly recommended at the Royal Exchange, and he clearly also wanted an experienced practitioner because he turned to Sang. Unfamiliar with mural techniques, British artists were having to learn them from German mentors, and the results were of highly variable quality.[5]

Emboldened by the Gresham Committee's interest in his proposal, Tite next, however, approached the enthusiastic British advocate of mural painting, B. R. Haydon, for an estimate for frescos — the Westminster form of mural art — to fill the 24 large panels, each 17 feet high by 11 feet wide, around the ambulatory of the Exchange. This would not be some modest encaustic ornament on beams and ceilings, but a full-blown scheme of grand pictorial compositions in the manner of the great Italian Renaissance decorative schemes. Fresco technique involved painting directly on to wet plaster and the work thus became integral with the very fabric of the building. Haydon, an entrant to the competitions for murals at Westminster, responded with aplomb:

Dear Sir,
    I was honoured by your question, and I am most happy to answer it, as you know I have always entertained a conviction that historical fresco decoration was essential to the completion of the new Royal Exchange.

There are twenty-four large spaces and eight small ones. The large ones might be filled with a series of beautiful fresco illustrations of our rise, from the earliest to the latest period of commercial greatness. The small might contain, in chiaroscuro, portraits of the greatest men who have contributed to that rise. The whole series might be, like the ceiling and the building, under the direction of one man and his assistants, as abroad: but if other artists have to share, they should be constrained in their respective sides to carry out their part only of one great consistent object . . .[6]

Not surprisingly, since it had only been quoted a sum of £1,740 for Sang's ceiling ornamentation,[7] the Gresham Committee balked at Haydon's offer to paint his proposed series of ambulatory frescos for a total sum of £3,500. They did agree, however, that 'Armorial bearings Shields and appropriate Designs in Encaustic Painting'[8] should be carried out by Sang on the ceiling of the ambulatory at a total cost of £2,240, and that further decoration should be placed in the panels around the ambulatory to 'harmonise' with this. The latter appears to have taken the form of 'Arms of Lord Mayors and the Masters of the Mercers Co who have held office during the erection of the building', along with those of the Chairman of the Gresham Committee (and the architect, too!), all within '16 small circular panels in the ambulatory'.[9] As yet, the opportunity to decorate the 24 large panels round the ambulatory which so excited Haydon seems to have remained unfulfilled.

Sang was also responsible for mural work at the Adelphi Theatre in the Strand (1848) and Bunning's Coal Exchange (1849), and although little is known of him, he clearly won a reputation in London in the 1840s as a practitioner of the art which Prince Albert, inspired by the traditions of his own nation, so dearly wished to revive in Britain. Although Sang's Exchange work has long since perished, the plans for it provoked the satire of *Punch*, which dubbed the building 'a sort of Valhalla of City Worthies' because it thought the scheme was to include portraits, and offered fanciful illustrations of what it anticipated the

[4] Encaustic technique was described by Dioscorides and Pliny, and colours used in the technique were discovered at Pompeii. A revival of encaustic had taken place in eighteenth-century France and Sir Humphry Davy was one of the early nineteenth-century investigators of the ingredients used in Antiquity for this painting method. Details of the process whereby wax was fused with colours for wall painting are given in F. Hamilton Jackson, *Mural Painting* (London, 1904), pp. 101 ff.
[5] See the Reports of the Royal Fine Arts Commissioners during the 1840s, T. S. R. Boase, 'The Decoration of the New Palace of Westminster 1841–1863', *Journal of the Warburg and Courtauld Institutes*, XVII (1954), and C. Willsdon, *Mural Painting in Britain 1840–1940* (forthcoming, Oxford University Press) for the experiments at the Palace of Westminster and elsewhere by British artists following German fresco techniques.

[6] B. R. Haydon, *Autobiography and Memoirs*, edited from Haydon's Journals by T. Taylor (London, 1926), p. 772 (Haydon's letter to Tite is dated 11 July 1844).
[7] GCM, 26 April 1844.
[8] GCM, 18 December 1844.
[9] Ibid.

murals would look like, such as 'Hope: a large proprietor of Pennsylvania Bonds, holding out a blank receipt'.[10]

That Sang's decoration in fact made extensive use of arabesques inspired by Italian Renaissance models (a favourite motif of early nineteenth-century German mural painters) is indicated by the *Art Journal*'s account in 1859 of the fate which had already by then befallen it:

When the Royal Exchange was decorated by Sang we foretold the total obfuscation of that thin and wiry ornament in a few years. This is now accomplished — Giulio Romano's naiads, with their vegetable continuations, are embalmed in city smoke.[11]

Sang was employed to restore his work[12] and the *Art Journal* reported later in the year:

. . . we took a walk round the interior . . . the other day, and found that Mr Sang and his large staff of assistants were progressing rapidly with the work of redecoration, on which they have been engaged for some weeks. The embellishments are in fresco, not simply painted as before; and so far as we could judge from the portion already finished, the arcade, or ambulatories, will have a splendid appearance. The ornamentation is remarkably rich in colour, and elegant in design.[13]

The use now of fresco as the medium — as had been employed at Westminster under Prince Albert — was presumably partly why the latter, on a visit to the Exchange in 1860,

proceeded to a very minute inspection of the decorations [with] the general appearance of which and of the harmony of the colouring . . . [he] expressed himself much pleased displaying at the same time a very accurate knowledge with this peculiar style of art.[14]

Some two-thirds of Sang's assistants were German, and B. R. Haydon indeed learnt that 'Prince Albert had *personally* . . . asked the [Gresham] Committee to employ Sang to decorate the Exchange'[15] back in 1845.

[10] *Punch* (1844), vol. 7, p. 192; I am grateful to Dr A. Saunders for drawing this reference to my attention.
[11] 'The Royal Exchange' in the *Art Journal*, vol. v, new series (1859), p. 31.
[12] See GCM, 1 and 8 April, 16 May and 17 June 1859 and 3 March 1860.
[13] *Art Journal* (1859), op. cit., p. 319.
[14] GCM, 3 March 1860.
[15] B. R. Haydon, *Diary*, ed. W. B. Pope (Harvard, 1963) (entry for 19 February 1845).

When Sang's second decorations also perished later in the century, however, the Gresham Committee turned down his request for 'leave to submit suggestions for the redecoration of the whole of the interior of the Royal Exchange'.[16] By this point, the Royal Exchange's central courtyard had during 1883–84 been roofed over and the Gresham Committee clearly felt that this improvement merited a fresh start. In contrast to the German style favoured earlier, there was now, in 1889–90, a specific move to create a distinctively British scheme of decoration, and more particularly one which emphasised the Exchange's place at the heart of the City of London. The London decorating firm of J. G. Crace having been called in to remove Sang's work, its advice on a more permanent type of decoration was sought, and when it recommended 'a good oil painting' in place of encaustic or fresco, and 'a scheme of pictorial illustration in the large wall panels',[17] the Gresham Committee seems to have turned to the plan which Haydon had put forward so many years before for historical subjects. The Committee approached the President of the Royal Academy, Lord Leighton, and its Council

with a view to filling in the panels of the Royal Exchange with scenes painted by the students of the Academy illustrating English history or the history of the City of London.[18]

Leighton and his fellow Academicians Sir E. J. Poynter and P. H. Calderon (Keeper of the Royal Academy) advised, however, that 'well-known artists of proven ability' should instead be employed for such a major building.[19]

Leighton clearly saw an opportunity further to promote the revival of mural painting which, following the decay of so many of the Westminster frescos, had received something of a check in Britain. Despite significant schemes in various British town halls such as Manchester and Rochdale during the 1870s and 1880s, and Leighton's own work at the South Kensington Museums, Britain still lagged far behind the

[16] GCM, 20 June 1890, p. 328.
[17] 'Report from Mr. J. D. Crace' in ibid.
[18] See letter from Eaton (Secretary of the Royal Academy) to J. Watney, 18 June 1890, pp. 28–29, GCM.
[19] Letter from Leighton to Gresham Committee, 13 July 1892 in MC, and GCM, 1 July 1892, pp. 26–29.

achievements of Paris, Munich, Berlin or Vienna, for
example, whose public buildings were lavishly decorated with murals. The recent historical and allegorical
murals in the Paris Hôtel de Ville and Panthéon, or
in many of the German town halls, were, moreover,
painted in oil on canvas and as such could be seen by
both British artists and businessmen visiting the
international exhibitions in Paris or Vienna where
they were shown before being installed as murals by
means of a special technique of 'marouflage' which
bound them to the walls. London City Councillors,
who, of course, with the Lord Mayor formed the 'City
side' of the Gresham Committee, had themselves had
plenty of opportunities in recent years to attend
functions in the newly ornamented civic 'palaces' of
Europe.[20] It is easy to see why the Gresham Committee responded enthusiastically to Leighton's recommendation of established artists rather than students
for the Royal Exchange work; political reasons,
however, can be identified as prompting the alacrity
with which a working committee on the Royal
Exchange decoration was appointed in 1891 (consisting of Leighton, Poynter, and Calderon from the
Royal Academy and the Mayor (David Evans),
Deputy Joseph Snowden, and the Master of the
Mercers' Company), and a list of subjects from
London history was drawn up already by 1892. This
was presented to the Royal Academy representatives
who selected twenty subjects from it which they
considered suitable for painting.

THE 1892 MURAL SCHEME: POLITICS AND
PICTURES

Ruskin, that great arbiter of artistic taste, had as long
ago as 1849 condemned heraldic decoration such as
Sang had painted as certain 'utterly to destroy both
the power and beauty of any building;[21] whilst
Leighton was a fervent admirer of modern French
monumental art. Yet in seeking to install a pictorial

scheme at the Exchange in the early 1890s, the
Gresham Committee was not simply trying to rival
foreign counterparts like the Paris Bourse in which
four huge murals illustrating trade with the different
Continents were completed during the late nineteenth century, or the slightly earlier historical murals
by Jan Swerts in the Antwerp Exchange.[22] A more
pressing motive can be recognised in the establishment in 1889 of the London County Council as a
means to reform London's government. Its elections
were fought on ambitious manifestos for municipalisation of the many areas which for centuries had
been controlled by the Livery Companies, the Corporation, and private enterprise, such as the dock-
yards, building, poor relief and education. As we shall
find out, all these areas of responsibility and the
Corporation of London's and its Mayors' and Livery
Companies' contributions to them are clearly commemorated in the historical subjects which were
selected for the Royal Exchange murals in 1892. By
then, significantly, the Lord Mayor and therefore
Chairman of the Gresham Decoration Committee,
was Sir Stuart Knill, who had recently donated mural
paintings to the Guildhall which symbolised allegoric-
ally the ancient rights and status of the Corporation
and included a frieze of figures representing the
different Livery Companies — the very City institutions which a Royal Commission on Livery Companies of 1884 had deemed to be corrupt and requiring
dissolution, recommending that their monies, lands
and charities should be taken under the control of a
central municipal authority. The symbolism of Knill's
Guildhall murals, carried out by Hardman's decorative company, would have been easily understood in
this context (the paintings are no longer extant). They
showed St George, Patron Saint of the City of
London, conquering the dragon, whilst 'the Citizens
with their Mayor, are anxiously awaiting the result of
the combat'; St Paul before old St Paul's Cathedral
offering his sword of Martyrdom in illustration of the
words, 'Put on the whole armour of God'; and a
maiden personification of the City, protected by
dragons, and 'holding and pointing to an ancient
Charter of the City'. A symbolic rose-tree bound

[20] References to these visits appear in the Minutes of Common
Council and the London County Council Reports for the late
nineteenth/early twentieth centuries. The Lord Mayor visited
the Paris International Exhibition of 1889 and in 1891 the
German Emperor Wilhelm II attended a reception at the
Guildhall (Guildhall Library, London).
[21] J. Ruskin, *The Seven Lamps of Architecture* (London, 1906),
p. 199 (first published 1849).

[22] These were in fact destroyed by fire in 1858.

together the arms of the twelve great Livery Companies above the motto, 'Now join your arms, and with your arms your hearts, that no dissention hinder government'.[23]

The mural scheme at the Royal Exchange can be seen as a still more ambitious use of art to present the City's 'propaganda', and the Gresham Committee's search for a durable painting method (Leighton recommended and introduced a special medium of spirit-fresco for this purpose) as simply part of the Corporation's and Companies' concern to assert their role and rights in London City. Writ seventeen feet high upon the ambulatory walls, their traditions and ideals would be visibly, and (it was hoped) permanently present, to protect, like St Paul with his sword on the Guildhall walls, the cause of the City in the face of invective such as Sidney Webb's Progressive pamphlets or J. B. Firth's *Reform of London Government and City Guilds*.[24] They would serve vividly to remind both the businessmen and the ordinary citizens of London who daily used the Exchange exactly where their electoral interests and their 'liberty'[25] and livelihood lay. Before we look in detail at the significance of the mural subjects, however, it is helpful to note the system which was evolved for realising this ambitious enterprise.

The first panel was painted and donated by Leighton himself, and showed the beginnings of commerce by *Phoenicians trading with the Early Britons on the Coast of Cornwall*; the second was also donated, by Deputy Snowden, and illustrated the *Opening of the Royal Exchange by Her Majesty Queen Victoria 28th October 1844* (Figs. 118 and 136) The artist was another Royal Academician, R. W. Macbeth. Both were unveiled in 1895 by the Lord Mayor, and invitations to choose a subject from the list determined under Knill's chairmanship were sent to the eleven other principal Livery Companies (the Mercers were already part of the Gresham Committee). Clearly the Gresham Committee was aiming at a representation

of City strength not simply in terms of iconography, but, even more literally, through the very mechanism of the murals' patronage. Whereas the Committee had itself funded the earlier decoration by Sang, the system now adopted of donation of individual panels was both a natural extension of the Companies' philanthropic and charitable traditions which were so much threatened by the growing powers of the new London County Council, and a manifesto for the role of private enterprise which the LCC was determined to curtail in so many areas of City life ranging from control of the docks (under four private companies) to responsibility for construction and building. A press release was widely circulated which, significantly, announced that 'amidst the turmoil of the election contests, Art, in the City of London is making satisfactory progress . . .',[26] and not only the Livery Companies but also prominent City businesses and individuals were wooed as mural donors. In turn, this system of funding the murals (each of which was to cost £500), enabled the employment of the 'well-known artists of proven ability' whom Leighton had recommended, and whose services would otherwise have lain beyond the means of the Gresham Committee alone. It was hoped that, following an initial cluster of donations, murals would be completed at a steady rate of one per year so that in course of time the entire ambulatory would be adorned, an aim which was in the event only achieved by 1924. Eight smaller portrait panels were then added which were completed by 1927.

The installation of each panel was marked by a special unveiling ceremony performed by a prominent City personality, or in a number of cases a member of the Royal Family, which thus maintained a level of public as much as artistic interest in the project; by 1921 the celebrations indeed ran to a lunch of 'Huîtres Naturels, Tortue Claire, Sole Colbert' and 'Mousse de Foie gras aux Truffes' amongst other delicacies, and press photographers were present, although an application from Fox News

[23] *Report of the City Lands Committee No. 29*, 16 June 1892: 'The Decoration of the Outer Lobby of the Council Chamber', CLRO.

[24] See especially S. Webb's *The London Programme* (London, 1891); Firth's *Reform . . .* was published in 1889.

[25] J. G. White, *History of the Royal Exchange* (London, 1896), p. 48 (description of the mural scheme).

[26] *Memorandum as to filling ambulatory of Royal Exchange with Pictures* (1892), MC. This appears to have been the basis for the various press reports of the project which were published in 1892.

for 'one of our kinematograph operators to take a picture' was declined for want of space.[27]

The relationship of the scheme to contemporary events was something with which Leighton must readily have sympathised. Although his own mural of *Phoenicians trading with the Early Britons on the Coast of Cornwall* was perhaps less a political than an artistic credo (he called the Phoenicians a race which contributed 'more than any other to the scattering of the seeds of Art'[28] through their trade, and they are shown giving pottery to the Britons in exchange for skins, and thereby introducing Classical art to British shores), he had told his students at the Royal Academy in 1883 that 'art has an organic connection with the temper of the times'[29] and had called in his first Presidential Address at the Royal Academy for the artist to have 'in modern society a lawful place, a meaning, a justification'.[30] In this first mural, Leighton symbolises the concept of 'exchange' in trade which was the *raison d'être* of the building itself. So enthusiastic was he about his own contribution to the scheme that, despite the demands of painting on such a scale (he was nearing the end of his life), he travelled to Cornwall to observe the cloud effects which form the backdrop to his composition, and claimed, 'I can work at that picture like an athlete, but when I lift a light hand to brush my hair in a hurry, I sometimes turn faint'.[31] He agreed to act as overall artistic co-ordinator of the scheme and was able to lay down guidelines for a common horizon level, colour scheme and figure height, before his illness resulted in the role of artistic adviser passing in 1897 to Alma Tadema. The artists of the murals, who were selected by the donors with the agreement of the Gresham Committee, were further required to submit a preliminary design for their work first to the Gresham

Decoration Committee and then to the Royal Academy Committee (originally Leighton, Poynter and Calderon) before proceeding with it.

Let us look now in more detail at the unfolding of the mural scheme, the meaning of its subjects, and the achievements of the various artists involved.

The scheme as a whole, arising as it did within the context of the 'struggle for the City' in 1890s London, is essentially an example, for a particular political purpose, of what the historian Cannadine has termed 'the invention of tradition'.[32] 1889, the year preceding the Gresham Committee's request for advice from Lord Leighton, had been not only the date of the LCC's foundation, but also the 700th anniversary of the Mayoralty. The celebrations for this included the revival of the originally water-based Lord Mayor's procession in a land version, an event which finds an echo in the mural by Solomon J. Solomon for Sir S. Montagu MP, of *Charles I demanding the Five Members at the Guildhall* with its prominent motifs of the Lord Mayor's coach and City topography (Fig. 134). Revivals of civic pageantry took place in many other towns at this period,[33] and in London the iconography of the Royal Exchange murals offers direct comparison with the historical floats of the Lord Mayor's revived processions, which were designed 'to show how, from time immemorial, the Corporation has been loyal to the crown and to the people'.[34] With their realistic re-creation of historical events, the Exchange murals have a particularly close affinity to such pageantry, and so mark a development beyond the convention of allegorical personification used in Knill's Guildhall murals to present anti-LCC sentiment. Something far more vivid also than the coats of arms and arabesques produced by Sang was now in process of creation.

The *Reconciliation of the Skinners and Merchant Taylors* mural, for example, which was presented by the two

[27] Details of the event (when Salisbury's *National Peace Thanksgiving Service on the Steps of St Paul's Cathedral July 6th 1919* was unveiled) from papers in 'Royal Exchange Box 3.9', MC.

[28] F. Leighton, *Addresses delivered to the Students of the Royal Academy by the late Lord Leighton* (London, 1897), p. 99 (Address of 1885).

[29] Ibid., p. 93 (Address of 1883).

[30] Ibid., p. 9 (Address of 1879).

[31] Quoted in W. Meynell, 'The Pictures in the Royal Exchange', *The Windsor Magazine* ((?) 1904) (copy kindly supplied by Miss A. Sutton, Archivist to the Mercers' Company).

[32] D. Cannadine, 'The Transformation of Civic Ritual in Modern Britain: the Colchester Oyster Feast', *Past and Present*, no. 94 (February 1982), p. 108; the idea is amplified in E. Hobsbawm and T. Ranger (eds.), *The Invention of Tradition* (Cambridge, 1983).

[33] As for example in Colchester where the 'Oyster Feast' was revived; see Cannadine, op. cit.

[34] Quoted in R. Withington, *English Pageantry A Historical Outline* (New York, 1963), p. 122.

Companies in 1904, portrays Lord Mayor Billesden's judgement in 1484 as to the Companies' order of precedence in Lord Mayors' processions, and was entrusted to an artist, E. A. Abbey, who was renowned for his 'Neo-Pre-Raphaelite' ability to fuse authentic costume and 'prop' details with decorative, even heraldic, design (Fig. 131). He was also a stage designer for Sir Henry Irving. Lord Mayor Billesden is seated high on a dais, the City arms emblazoned on a red banner behind him, and his chain and mace picked out in gold at the exact centre of the mural. Beneath him, and with their chains and ceremonial ermine-trimmed robes equally prominent, are the feuding masters of the two Companies, about to drink from a loving cup as a token of their reconciliation. This act was recognised when the mural was unveiled as 'perhaps the most remarkable piece of arbitration the City of London has ever experienced, inasmuch as the award has been faithfully fulfilled for a period of over four centuries'.[35] Even though the subject of his mural had originally been determined during the white heat of the LCC's first years, attacks on the Corporation continued well into the twentieth century as the LCC's powers increased, and the prominence Abbey gave to the symbols of the City's ancient power would have represented a robust riposte to challenges like that of the Demon Bumblebeadalus in Walter Crane's satirical *Masque of Beauty* of 1899, who asked, 'And what if a tub-thumping socialist boggles/ At your mace and your furs and your goggles?'.[36]

The continuing concern at the LCC's growth probably explains why the Gresham Committee was adamant right up to the First World War that no alterations should be made to Knill's 1892 historical programme. It took, indeed, the personal intervention of the King before a contemporary subject was then unveiled, whilst as late as 1912 an offer by the Australian government of a mural illustrating the opening of its Parliament by the King was turned down after John Horseley Palmer, a leading Mercer

and donor of another mural, objected to 'the insertion of a picture … of a modern subject, in no way directly connected with the City' as being 'both incongruous and inartistic'.[37] Already before this, in 1896, an offer of a portrait of Oliver Cromwell had even more tellingly been rejected by the Gresham Committee:[38] Cromwell, after all, had been adopted as a hero by the Liberals and Progessives.[39]

A clear indication of the philosophy which lay behind the mural iconography is afforded by an after-dinner speech given by Knill to the Society of Ye Sette of Ye Odde Volumes in 1895, which argued for the Livery Companies' contemporary relevance by reference to their past achievements in welfare, trade and construction.[40] The speech gave particular emphasis to a number of medieval episodes which are found at the Exchange. With regard to *King Alfred the Great repairing the Walls of London* (Col. Pl. XA) for example, Knill explained, 'It is in Alfred's time that we first hear of a municipal government … King Alfred, rebuilding London after its fourth destruction by fire, placed it in the keeping of Alderman Othelred [sic], and a frith guild or peace guild, was established …'.[41] Likewise, he cited *William the Conqueror granting a Charter to the Citizens of London* (Fig. 119), another mural subject, as the occasion on which the Conqueror addressed the Portreeve as the 'official to whom secular authority was given';[42] the Gresham Committee indeed insisted that the artist, Seymour Lucas, amend his original sketch in such a way 'that the Bishop standing in front of the Portreeve should be placed at the back of him so as to make his figure more important'.[43] Knill, along with the Chairman and Clerk of the Gresham Committee, was responsible for the choice of Lucas, and the panel was donated by the Corporation, although Sir Frank Salisbury, who painted *King Alfred* …, gave a more

---

[35] 'Royal Exchange Frescos a Notable Addition', *The City Press*, 21 December 1904 (press cutting in MC).

[36] *Beauty's Awakening A Masque of Winter and Spring* 'presented by members of the Art Workers' Guild', June 1899; text given in *The Studio*, Special Number (1899) (the quotation is from p. 28). This masque was performed by Crane, Lethaby, Henry Holiday and others — with remarkable effrontery — in no less a venue than the Guildhall itself.

[37] Letter from Palmer read at a meeting of the Joint Grand Gresham Committee on 12 January 1912, GCM for that date, p. 367.

[38] GCM for 15 May 1896 records the refusal of an offer from H. Hadwyn of a portrait of Cromwell to be funded by public subscription.

[39] Lord Rosebery, Leader of the LCC, presented a statue of Cromwell to Parliament in 1899–1900.

[40] S. Knill, *A Pot Pourri of London Antiquities* (London, 1890).

[41] Ibid., p. 18.

[42] Ibid., p. 28.

[43] GCM, 5 February 1897.

colourful account of having been told by Lucas that the donor was 'a Billingsgate fish merchant (who) asked . . . if he would take the payment out in fish'.[44]

Lucas, like Abbey, had designed for the theatre, and his mural sets the charter incident within a dramatically lit 'stage-set' of Norman architecture. This, however, in contrast to the strongly decorative character of Abbey's mural, Salisbury's *Alfred* or Brangwyn's *Modern Commerce*, creates more a 'window in the wall' than a painting which takes account of its purpose as surface ornament. Such discrepancies of style were particularly noticeable after Leighton's death, and of course they also reflect the inevitable changes in taste during the lengthy period over which the scheme was carried out. Despite the Gresham Committee's concern to create a tightly integrated thematic ensemble, from an artistic point of view the end product was so varied in character as to provoke Abbey already by 1906 to speak of the 'hideous result (which) the court of the Royal Exchange presents — which is a standing example of how *not* to do it';[45] a view which was widely shared and which echoed Haydon's earlier warnings about using more than one artist.[46]

Given the undeniably variable success with which the artists, who in most cases were attempting their first mural work, responded to the Gresham Committee's iconography, it is easy, perhaps, to dismiss the scheme as dusty history painting with no particular merit or significance. To do so is to overlook the potent symbolism which underpins its iconography and which we have begun to uncover through the clues like the detail of Abbey's picture and Knill's speech on the Livery Companies; the pride which artists and patrons alike took in what were regarded as highly prestigious commissions; the individual interests of the donors; and perhaps, above all, the distinctive character of the ensemble as an icon of a place and an epoch, rather than merely an aesthetic exercise. All these facets are subtly interwoven in the scheme and need to be appreciated in any thoughtful evaluation of it.

The range of subjects and the way they are illustrated are, for example, not only a reflection of the political 'temper of the times', but also of radical changes in the writing of history. The ready association which Knill and the Gresham Committee made between their forebears in the City and their modern contemporaries parallels the new approach of historians such as W. Stubbs, E. A. Freeman and J. R. Green, who, in contrast to Macaulay's view of the past as a roll-call of famous heroes, believed in what Freeman called 'the unity of history'.[47] Past and present were felt to be linked in a continuum and in that process, the ordinary people, their local traditions, and the endurance of their buildings through the centuries were the definitive factors. Whilst the historical subjects at the Royal Exchange were devised as a chronological sequence, they also function as a cycle, and the 'unity of history' is vividly sensed through the recurrence of specific themes throughout the ages. Leighton's *Ancient Commerce* (Fig. 118) is thus paired with Brangwyn's *Modern Commerce* (Fig. 137) so as to frame the main entrance to the central courtyard, at the west, and their common theme of sea/river trade, which of course lay close to the heart of the Exchange as the seat of international commerce and the home of Lloyd's the marine underwriters, was echoed in many of the other murals, setting up a Freeman-like vision of the continuum of history.

At the same time, the Royal Exchange scheme involves a selective representation of the past. The seventeenth century so favoured in the earlier murals at the Palace of Westminster (on which Macaulay advised) is largely disregarded for the medieval, Tudor and nineteenth-century periods preferred by the new generation of historians.[48] Given this selectivity, and the 'cyclic' character of the mural scheme, it is easier to understand its overall significance if we

---

[44] F. O. Salisbury, *Sarum Chase* (London, 1953), p. 19.

[45] Letter from E. A. Abbey to Lord Carlisle, 17 July 1908, Castle Howard Archives (quoted by kind permission of the Hon. Simon Howard).

[46] Haydon, op. cit. (1926); he predicted that unless either one artist or a strictly controlled team of artists was employed, 'confusion and failure will be the result' (p. 772).

[47] Quoted by J. W. Burrow, *A Liberal Descent Victorian Historians and The English Past* (Cambridge, 1981), p. 222.

[48] See for example Freeman's *History of the Norman Conquests of England* (Oxford, 1867–79); and the selective emphasis in Green's *History of the English People* (London, 1877–80) and Stubbs' *The Constitutional History of England in its Origin and Development* (Oxford, 1866).

consider the murals not in chronological order (their completion, indeed, depended upon the availability of donors rather than historical sequence), but instead according to themes.

THE THAMES, SHIPPING AND THE SEA

Modern Commerce was given in 1906 by Sir Thomas Lane Devitt, President of the Shipping Federation and a prominent Skinner. Its Thames-side dock subject would have had particular significance in the context of the reform of London's government, since Sidney Webb and his Progressive supporters made the municipalisation of the Port of London a key goal of the new LCC, claiming that 'The bulk of the shipping trade of the Capital of the Empire lies at the mercy of an unregulated crowd of private wharfingers and the boards of directors of four giant dock companies'.[49] In turn, Sir Frederick Green, the donor of *Philip the Good presenting the Charter to the Merchant Adventurers* (not actually unveiled until 1916), was Chairman of the Shipping Federation. Both Green and Devitt were also managers of the Orient Steam Navigation Company, whilst Green was Director of the Suez Canal Company. It is easy to see why, even though the immediate urgency of shipping matters *vis-à-vis* the LCC had by 1916 of course passed, Green was nevertheless attracted to a subject which commemorated the City origins of modern overseas trade (the Merchant Adventurers were originally based at Mercers' Hall). The thematic relationship of Green's *Charter . . .* to Brangwyn's *Modern Commerce* which Devitt had presented was indeed reinforced by Green's selection of Cox as his artist. Cox was a pupil of Brangwyn and closely emulated Brangwyn's style in his mural's high colour key and foreground motif of piled fruit.

The choice of Brangwyn himself as the artist of the one panel in the whole scheme which illustrates modern London — and, as the symbolic counterpart to Leighton's *Ancient Commerce*, therefore points to the essential message of correspondence and continuity between past and present which underpins the entire mural ensemble — was particularly felicitous. Brangwyn had offered to design and donate a panel

to the Exchange as early as 1894,[50] but Leighton refused his offer on the grounds of inexperience, even though Brangwyn, still a young artist, was being extravagantly praised in Paris, Germany and Belgium.[51] By 1900, however, when Devitt proposed him for his chosen *Modern Commerce* subject, the Gresham Committee agreed.[52] Devitt's commission, followed by his choice of Brangwyn again for important schemes at Skinners' Hall and Lloyd's Register of Shipping, substantially sealed Brangwyn's British reputation and he became the nation's foremost, and virtually sole, professional mural painter in the first half of the twentieth century.

Modern Commerce has the rolling cumulus clouds and common quayside labourers shifting exotic fruits and heavy crates in the play of sun and shadow caused by giant cranes and towering ships which would become the artist's hallmark. The mural also already reveals Brangwyn's characteristic sympathy with the old and the inexperienced (see the grey-bearded man sharing some word of confidence with the two young boys in the foreground), and those who toil. A group of thumbnail preparatory sketches for the mural show that he originally experimented both with the mural's key figure of a man shouldering a packing case (whom Goldsborough Anderson in turn echoed in *William II building the Tower of London*, Fig. 120) and with the dockside setting which at this stage included a view of the River Thames in the distance.[53] A more advanced study[54] dispensed entirely with the packing case carrier, and when he reappears in both the final sketch[55] and the mural he is, interestingly, given a similar prominence and pose to the man with a crate

[49] S. Webb, op. cit., p. 65.

[50] GCM, 8 June 1894.

[51] In Paris, Brangwyn's paintings were being exhibited to great acclaim at the Salon, and in 1895 he was commissioned by Samuel Bing to provide murals for his renowned Maison de l'Art Nouveau (murals now lost/detached); in 1892 he had been appointed a Corresponding Member of the Munich Secession; his work was also enthusiastically received in 1894 in the United States.

[52] GCM, 26 January 1900.

[53] These studies are in a private collection.

[54] Dundee Art Gallery (collection no. 4/65/196; red chalk and black/grey watercolour wash).

[55] Reproduced in *The Studio*, vol. XLV (1909) as 'First sketch in oils for panel of "Modern Commerce" at the Royal Exchange, London. By Frank Brangwyn, A.R.A.'; this appears to be the same sketch as was sold by the Fine Art Society, London as *Unloading Merchandise*, Fine Art Society, File 3528 no. 352686.

in a huge mural of *Les Halles* painted by Léon Lhermitte for the Paris Hôtel de Ville[56] which Brangwyn would have known from his years in Paris. Brangwyn was thus clearly attempting to emulate modern French mural art, just as Leighton before him had based his *Ancient Commerce* on a mural by Chassériau in the Paris Cour des Comptes. Brangwyn's emphasis on the common man can, indeed, be placed not only within the context of Freeman's, Stubbs' and Green's concern as historians with the shaping of the modern nation by the actions and traditions of its ordinary citizens, but also within that of the preoccupation with the anonymous 'man in the street' which characterised both Lhermitte's view of the Parisian markets and the work of other late nineteenth-century continental history painters such as the members of the Düsseldorf School. We find this emphasis repeated in the prominence given to the crowd of onlookers in the mural of *The Opening the First Royal Exchange by Queen Elizabeth* (Col. Pl. Xʙ), by Ernest Crofts, who had trained at Düsseldorf, as well as in the way that Nelson, leaving Portsmouth to join HMS *Victory* in A. C. Gow's panel for the Corporation of Lloyd's,[57] is presented not as the Christ-like hero enduring a noble death of Maclise's 1850s Westminster mural of *Nelson*, but rather as a little man, clearly lacking his arm lost in battle, who is rendered heroic by the adulating, flag-waving common crowd who see him off at the dockside.

Although Brangwyn's is the only panel to portray a generic, rather than specific incident, he clearly took a decision at a later stage in its evolution to render the wharfside setting as more explicitly contemporary. His detailed oil sketch includes a distant detail of smoke pouring from funnels, but chiefly illustrates old-fashioned rigged shipping.[58] The final mural, however, shows the soaring scaffolding of modern shipbuilding and the high jib and gantry of a crane alongside a steamship funnel. Whilst the dockers still toil manually, the advanced technology of a modern port is also visibly evident. Was this change urged by Devitt or the Gresham Committee, to show the Progressives that private dock enterprise was progressive, too? It certainly enabled Brangwyn to build a tautly decorative composition, whose play of rigid verticals against the sinewy labourers creates the arresting visual rhythm so essential to a successful large-scale mural, whilst it also echoes the distinctive preoccupation of modern French mural art with contemporary life as seen in Lhermitte's *Les Halles*.

Just as Brangwyn's panel stands as a focus for the theme of shipping and sea trade as associated with the City of London, so other groupings of murals, all with 'political' significance in the context of 1892 when the iconography was chosen, may be identified within the overall scheme at the Exchange. Building and rebuilding, the assignment of rights and powers to the City and its inhabitants via charters (which echo as a visual *Leitmotiv* through many of the panels), the connections of the City with Royalty, and its role in national as well as municipal government, and the City's traditions of charity and welfare provision, are key recurrent themes, as well, of course, as the endurance of civic ritual which we have already met in Abbey's *Reconciliation of Skinners and Merchant Taylors*. A number of murals involve several of these themes, like Cox's *Philip the Good presenting the Charter to the Merchant Adventurers* (Fig. 128) in which the incident is not just a reminder of the continuity of the City's (specifically the Mercers') involvement in maritime commerce, but also an echo of the 'charter' motif represented in Lucas' *William the Conqueror granting a Charter to the Citizens of London* (Fig. 119).

BUILDING, DESTRUCTION AND REBUILDING

One of the prime issues on which the first elections were fought for the new LCC was the need to provide housing for the poor and to initiate an integrated renewal and building plan for London's City.[59] The Corporation responded by drawing attention to its

---

[56] Léon Lhermitte, *Les Halles*, completed 1895; the mural was detached from the walls of the Hôtel de Ville in the early twentieth century but is preserved in the collections of the City of Paris (see T. Burollet *et al.*, *Le Triomphe des Mairies* (Paris, 1987), p. 336).

[57] Unveiled in 1903. The incident illustrated in the mural is based on Southey's biography of Nelson (1861), and 1903 was the centenary of Nelson's departure from Portsmouth.

[58] This is the sketch for which details are given in n. 55.

[59] See for example H. M. Hyndman, *A Commune for London* (London, 1887), and 'Questions to Candidates', *The Star*, 6 December 1888. Housing was a key issue in 1892, the year of the Exchange programme.

FIG. 118.   *Phoenicians trading with the Early Britons on the Coast of Cornwall.*

FIG. 119.   *William the Conqueror granting a Charter to the Citizens of London.*

FIG. 120.   *William II building the Tower of London.*

FIG. 121.   *Women's Work in the Great War, 1914–1918.*

FIG. 122. *King John sealing Magna Carta.*

FIG. 123. *Their Majesties King George V and Queen Mary visiting the Battle Districts in France, 1917.*

FIG. 124. *National Peace Thanksgiving Service on the steps of St Paul's Cathedral, 6 July 1919.*

FIG. 125. *Sir Henry Picard, Master of the Vintners' Company, entertaining the Kings of England, France, Scotland, Denmark and Cyprus.*

323

Fig. 126.   *The Destruction of the Second Royal Exchange in 1838.*

Fig. 127.   *Sir Richard Whittington dispensing his Charities.*

Fig. 128.   *Philip the Good presenting the Charter to the Merchant Adventurers.*

Fig. 129.   *Henry VI Battle of Barnet, 1471. The Trained Bands Marching to the Support of Edward IV.*

FIG. 130. *Blocking of Zeebrugge Waterway, St George's Day,*
23 April 1918.

FIG. 131. *The Reconciliation of the Skinners' and*
Merchant Taylors' Companies by Lord Mayor Billesden,
1484.

FIG. 132. *The Crown offered to Richard III at*
Baynard's Castle.

FIG. 133. *The Foundation of St Paul's School, 1509.*

FIG. 134. *Charles I demanding the Five Members at the Guildhall, 1641–42.*

FIG. 135. *Founding of the Bank of England, 27 July 1694.*

FIG. 136. *Opening of the Royal Exchange by Her Majesty Queen Victoria, 28 October 1844.*

FIG. 137. *Modern Commerce.*

substitution of wide and convenient thoroughfares for the narrow streets of fifty years ago, and commercial and other buildings, which may not unfitly be termed palatial, for old and inconvenient and often squalid houses,

its recent Aldgate 'Dwellings for the Working Class', and its Cannon Street, Holborne Valley and Ludgate Hill improvement projects.[60] Architectural palimpsest, meanwhile, was an image used by the historian Freeman to present his notion of the 'unity of history'. A number of the Royal Exchange murals both reinforce the Corporation's and Companies' concern to publicise their tradition of achievement in this area, and reflect the historians' new ways of looking at the past.

Panel two, for example, showing *King Alfred the Great repairing the Walls of the City of London* (Col. Pl. XA), deals with medieval reinforcement of the Roman wall. Knill referred to this in his speech about the ancient origins of the Corporation and Companies given to Ye Sette of Ye Odde Volumes, and Roman remains had also been recently excavated in the early 1890s around the sites of the Mercers' Hall, Guildhall and Royal Exchange. In panel four, *William II building the Tower of London* (Fig. 120), the Norman king is shown in consultation with Bishop Gundulph, his architect who holds the Tower plans just as those of the new London appear in *Alfred* and just as the City's charter is granted by William the Conqueror in panel three. Tower Bridge was, of course, in process of construction by the Corporation when the iconography was conceived (it was completed in 1894), and Goldsborough Anderson's mural of the building of the Tower clearly shows the river it would span. That Sir Frank Salisbury, who painted *King Alfred the Great repairing the Walls of London* was sensitive to the link between successive phases of Anglo-Saxon and Norman construction which is illustrated by this group of subjects, and their connection in turn with the Corporation's history, is suggested by the way he portrayed Alfred's architect. Standing beneath a primitive canopy slung over rough construction scaffolding, the latter points to the Royal Commission for the rebuilding of London which Ethelred, the new

deputy leader of London, has given him.[61] Even though the immediate motive of riposte to the LCC's designs on control of City building was naturally by 1911–12, when Salisbury's panel was painted, somewhat less pressing than in 1892, it is clear that the larger principle of the continuity of tradition in the construction of the City by its Corporation and citizens was still at work in the conception of the picture. It was presented by Alderman (later Lord Mayor and Viscount) Wakefield, just as Anderson's showing the Tower was given by the Mercer William Wallis Aston.

Although Wakefield, the manufacturer of 'Castrol' oil products, was a keen supporter of air travel already in 1910 and was later to back the flights of Sir A. Cobham and Amy Johnson, he was also an enthusiast for the history and traditions of London, and his choice of Salisbury was probably a reflection of this. Royal Academy trained, Salisbury was part of the 'Neo-Pre-Raphaelite'[62] group of artists led by E. A. Abbey, and in *Alfred* he shows the same antiquarianism (if not complete historical accuracy) allied to a highly decorative style of golds, rich reds and blacks within a shallow picture space as does Abbey in his *Skinners and Merchant Taylors*. Salisbury copied shields from Anglo-Saxon manuscripts,[63] and made preparatory studies of surviving fragments of the Roman wall. The mural illustrates a piece subsequently covered by the Post Office in Newgate Street behind the scaffolding where Alfred's architect stands with his commission, which is labelled 'Londinium'.[64] The scaffolding squares off the arched top of the mural panel and creates a taut geometric framework for Alfred's arrival on a powerful black and

[60] The Right Honourable Polydore de Keyser Lord Mayor, *Fifty Years' Progress in the City*, speech at a banquet at the Guildhall, 9 November 1887, CLRO, p. 9.

[61] For identification of the personnel portrayed in this and other murals, see C. Welch, *Illustrated Account of the Royal Exchange and the Pictures therein* (London, 1913).
[62] A nascent 'school' of 'Neo-Pre-Raphaelite' ('Neue Präraphaeliten') decorative artists was identified by the German critic Hermann Muthesius in 1902 and included Abbey and Salisbury ('Kunst und Leben in England', *Zeitschrift für bildende Kunst*, neue Folge XIII, No. 3 (1902).
[63] Miscellaneous preparatory studies for the mural from Anglo-Saxon manuscript illustrations of shields were sold at Christie's, 25 September 1985. (See the catalogue of this sale, p. 43 (No. 118) for a small colour study for the panel, and No. 34 in it for studies of Alfred's horse (wrongly identified)).
[64] See B. Barber, *The Art of Frank O. Salisbury* (Leigh-on-Sea, 1936), p. 24.

white horse in the lower part of the mural. Arm raised aloft, Alfred gives instructions to the architect and workmen above him; his bodyguards hold spears at the left and the Royal 'Raven Standard' at the right. Seen in profile, Alfred recalls a Roman Imperial equestrian monument and the addition of Latin inscriptions to the border of the mural which record his achievements — 'Londinium restituit. Imperium populi. Classem paravit . . .' ('He rebuilt London. He established the sovereignty of the people. He built a fleet . . .') — confirms his implied line of inheritance and succession from the Roman era. Freeman's view of history as a continuum, created by the successive accretions of the different ages, and the Corporation's comparison of its achievements in building with those of Ancient Rome,[65] could hardly be more graphically illustrated.

The *Great Fire of London 1666* (Col. Pl. XIA) and the *Destruction of the Second Royal Exchange in 1838* (Fig. 126) subjects are a reminder that the building and rebuilding of the Exchange itself and the contributions of its users shaped modern London as had Alfred and William II in earlier times. Stanhope Forbes' *Great Fire . . . 1666* took Pepys' descriptions of the event as inspiration[66] and, as was explained at the unveiling of the panel in 1899, its donor, the Sun Fire Insurance Company, 'had at one time been housed almost on the spot where the picture now was'.[67] Forbes introduced the subtle firelit effects he had already explored in a number of his Newlyn oil paintings,[68] and indeed painted the panel in his Cornwall studio at Trewarveneth, but he also made preliminary studies of period architecture and costume in the British Museum.[69] Like Leighton's, his mural is in fact a hidden allegory on the value of art as much as an illustration of the Gresham Committee's purposes. Showing the citizens' escape from their burning homes by the river, the mural gives prominence to a framed painting, held aloft by one of the escapees who hastily descend riverside steps to a boat. The low viewpoint and the foreground oarsmen looking up to the scene of the conflagration guide the viewer's eye, past a frightened girl and sleeping boy who are being helped down the steps, to the precious picture, which, as a portrait, cleverly reinforces the scheme's central message of the enduring links between successive generations of City life.

Forbes' *Destruction of the Second Royal Exchange in 1838*, given by the Royal Exchange Assurance Company (later Guardian Royal Exchange) actually represents one of the post-First World War amendments to the 1892 iconography,[70] but it may be considered here since it is consistent with the 'building/destruction' theme in the original programme. Although the donors, whose interests it obviously reflects, initially proposed a mural showing either the *Destruction* subject or the proclamation of peace on the Exchange steps, sketches prepared by Eric Kennington, who had been an Official War Artist, were rejected[71] and the Royal Academician Sir William Orpen recommended Forbes. Had Kennington contributed, his work would have introduced a more avant-garde element to the scheme, which, after its initial espousal of such 'progressive' trends in art as had been represented by Abbey's and Brangwyn's panels at the turn of the century, was now essentially conservative in the style of its commissions. Forbes' mural is, none the less, a highly accomplished re-interpretation of William Heath's period print of the 1838 fire,[72] with characteristic anecdotal detail amongst the crowd of onlookers and escaping citizenry. The box being carried to safety in the foreground recalls the story of the rescue of a safe filled with Lloyd's secretaries' books, and cheques and banknotes; when the safe was subsequently opened, 'the air rushing in upon the tender fragments, blew them about', but it was none the less possible for them to be 'collected carefully,

[65] De Keyser, op. cit., p. 9.
[66] See Mrs L. Birch, *Stanhope Forbes A.R.A. and Elizabeth Stanhope Forbes A.R.W.S.* (London, 1996), p. 98.
[67] 'A New Fresco at The Royal Exchange. "The Great Fire" ', *The Daily Graphic*, 17 February 1899. I am grateful to the Sun Alliance Insurance Group for bringing this article to my attention.
[68] E.g. *Forging the Anchor* (1891) and *The Smithy* (shown at the Royal Academy in 1895).
[69] L. Birch, op. cit., p. 99. Some of the other muralists were far less concerned with historical accuracy; Crofts' *First Royal Exchange* (Col. Pl. XB), for example, looks more Jacobean than Elizabethan.

[70] The mural was donated by the Royal Exchange Assurance Company in 1920 to commemorate the bicentenary of its tenancy of the Exchange.
[71] GCM, 26 September and 28 November 1919 and 12 March, 28 May and 9 July 1920.
[72] The print is reproduced in *Six Historic Fires* (London, 1951), published by the Fire Protection Association.

and the numbers and dates traced'.[73] Forbes' emphasis on such an incident can be compared with the interests of G. M. Trevelyan, later author of the *Illustrated English Social History*, who was beginning to establish his distinctive interpretation of history as something which must be rendered 'living, many-coloured and romantic' for the modern reader.[74] Having mirrored the stirrings of this new historical school in the writings of Freeman, Stubbs and Green, the Royal Exchange murals thus now began, in fact, to shape it, for already by 1920, when Forbes' panel was installed, they were in demand for reproduction as postcards, school posters and illustrations in children's history books.[75]

MONARCHY, MAYORS AND MUNIFICENCE

Murals already considered, such as *Alfred repairing the Walls of London* or *William II building the Tower of London*, involve, of course, a 'Royal' element, but several panels make a more specific association between the Corporation or Companies and King or Queen, which can be read as another aspect of the scheme's attempt to reinforce the authority of the City's historic mode of government and institutions. Likewise, others remind the viewer of the City's contribution to national, and not just civic, government.

Reference has already been made to the Lord Mayor's coach in *The Opening of the First Royal Exchange by Queen Elizabeth* (Col. Pl. XB), given by the Mercers in 1899. Less artistically accomplished is Deputy Joseph Snowden's donation (1895) of the *Opening of the Royal Exchange By Her Majesty Queen Victoria* (Fig. 136), painted by R. W. Macbeth. Set to the immediate left of Brangwyn's *Modern Commerce* subject by the west door, this makes a clear nineteenth-century partner not only to *Queen Elizabeth*, but also to *Alfred repairing the Walls of London*, which occupied the space to the right of the door, since Macbeth includes a sweeping vista down Cornhill, seen through the entrance to the Exchange, as the backdrop to the Queen's ceremony; the modern London, in fact, whose foundations were laid by Alfred. Associations with Queen Victoria were also implicit in the subject of *Sir Henry Picard, Master of the Vintners' Company, entertaining the Kings of England, Scotland, Denmark and Cyprus* (Fig. 125), which was given by William Vivian, JP, DL, in 1903, and painted by A. Chevallier Tayler, an artist who, like Forbes, was part of the 'Newlyn' group. At her recent Jubilee celebrations in the City, Queen Victoria had also entertained four kings. The incident, taken from the Elizabethan John Stow's famous *Annales of England*,[76] illustrates a feast given in 1363 by Picard, who had been Mayor in 1357, for Edward III and the Scottish and continental monarchs. Consistent with the interests of modern French and German history painters, like J. P. Laurens, under whom Tayler had studied in Paris, and also with the emphasis we have noted in Brangwyn's mural, Tayler relegates the feast to the background and places the servants filling goblets in the foreground, the common folk whose actions in the eyes of Freeman and his fellow historians, were the decisive factor in the shaping of modern Britain. With them is Edward's fourth son the Duke of York, and a Bishop who, along with another at the feast table, was modelled by 'Old McNab'. This 'crotchety ancient', a well-known character in London artists' studios, was also the model in several other murals,[77] and thus intriguingly encapsulates the artists' and historians' concerns with the contribution to history of the ordinary man in the street.

In Goetze's *The Crown offered to Richard III at Baynard's Castle* (Fig. 132; 1898), the Lord Mayor is again the real subject of the picture, as he intercedes for Richard, his mace to the fore, in the centre of the

[73] Quoted in ibid., p. 14.
[74] G. M. Trevelyan, *Clio a Muse and other Essays Literary and Pedestrian* (London, 1913), p. 39.
[75] As early as 1913 the Acts of Court of the Mercers' Company in the MC record a request from C. H. Letts of the Fine Art Publishing Company to reproduce one of the murals, and by c. 1922 *The Children's Encyclopaedia* had been granted permission to reproduce the *Foundation of St Paul's School* (see GCM). Prior to 1933 W. Hutchinson's *Story of the British Nation* included Royal Exchange murals as illustrations, whilst Cassell's *Stream of Time* history book of as late as 1952, and Jan Juta of South Africa's *Junior History Course* of c. 1955, were still reproducing them. The murals were printed as Christmas cards even in 1953, when a British Transport filmstrip on Cornwall also included Leighton's panel.

[76] The relevant passage in Stow's *Annales* . . . is quoted in an extract from A. Crawford, *A History of the Vintners' Company* (London, 1977) which was kindly supplied to me by the Vintners' Company.
[77] Information kindly supplied by Miss A. Sutton, Archivist to the Mercers' Company, from an unidentified printed source.

composition. The incident is taken from Shakespeare's *Richard III*, Act III, and the donor of the panel, Sir Carl Meyer, was in fact one of the supporters of the scheme for a Shakespeare National Memorial Theatre.[78]

Similar prominence is given to the Lord Mayor, resplendent in robes and chain of office in the very forefront of the composition, in J. H. Amschewitz's *Trained Bands marching to the Support of Edward IV* (Fig. 129; 1911). He leads the citizens who have assumed arms for their King in the Wars of the Roses; their wives wave farewell from half-timbered houses either side. An ecclesiastic holds up a cross behind the Mayor's head; a white rose of York flag flutters amongst the army led by the King on horseback. Amschewitz had recently won the 'Prize for the decoration of a portion of a public building' awarded by the Royal Academy[79] and had also been chosen to provide murals for Liverpool Town Hall; his Royal Exchange panel makes skilful use of the arched vertical format to suggest the congestion of the scene as it unfolds within the narrow City street, punctuated by the rhythmic diagonals of the band's weapons. With its black and rich reds, the panel stands alongside Abbey's *Skinners*, Goetze's *Richard III*, Salisbury's *Alfred* and Solomon's *Charles I* to form a distinctive stylistic grouping in the Exchange which compares closely with the manner adopted for the 1906 East Corridor mural scheme at the Palace of Westminster of which Abbey was co-ordinator and to which Solomon contributed. Amschewitz's panel was in fact given to the Exchange by the sons of Ellis Abraham Franklin in memory of their father, who had been a partner in the banking business Samuel Montagu and Co.; as Member of Parliament for Whitechapel, Montagu in turn gave the Exchange mural by Solomon of *Charles I demanding the Five Members at the Guildhall* (Fig. 134) and, after he became a baronet, the Westminster panel by Solomon.

The closeness of these connections between donors, artists and mural themes thus vividly illustrates the social-political significance of the Exchange commissions. The *Charles I* panel, with its prominent Lord Mayor's coach, commemorates the origins of the City MPs' privilege of sitting on the Treasury Bench on the opening day of Parliament,[80] a right which would have had particular significance for Montagu with his banking background, as well as being a clear demonstration of the historic involvement of the City in the government not just of London, but also of the nation. It stands beside the south entrance to the Exchange ambulatory, symbolically opposite *King John sealing Magna Carta*, which of course commemorates the origins of the British Parliamentary system.

Magna Carta, presented by the Kimberley merchant John Paddon in 1900, is an atmospheric scene which reveals its artist Ernest Normand's experience of painting in the French *plein air* artists' colony at Grez. Normand's wife, Henrietta Rae, was commissioned to paint the panel of *Sir Richard Whittington dispensing his Charities* (Fig. 127), which was donated also in 1900 by the South African financier and statesman Sir Abe Bailey, whose first wife was the daughter of John Paddon who gave Normand's mural. Again, therefore, we find a close interrelationship of patronage and choice of artist, and Bailey's wife indeed was Rae's model for Whittington's wife in her mural, making it an interesting 're-invention' of the medieval and Renaissance genre of 'donor' portraiture.

With *Whittington* we move from the Royal-Mayoral group of murals to a subject which draws attention to the Corporation's and Companies' traditions of charity and welfare; the areas in which the Progressives accused the Companies of incompetence. Whittington, of course, was not only Lord Mayor, but also a Mercer. Sir Abe Bailey, who was to become famed for the welcome which he extended at his own home to men of all opinions,[81] must have identified with Whittington, who in the mural holds a well-filled purse and supervises his servants as they offer loaves and garments at his door to the needy in the depths of winter. His wife Mistress Alice (Paddon's daughter), meanwhile provides alms. A poor woman warms herself at a brazier at the left and a child receives alms from Whittington's own, contrastingly well-clothed

---

[78] See Meyer's obituary in *The Times*, 19 December 1922, p. 10.
[79] Amschewitz won the RA Prize for the Decoration of a Portion of a Public Building in 1905; the competition had been instituted by Leighton in 1878. He was, at 27, the youngest Exchange artist.

[80] See Welch, op. cit., p. 87.
[81] See the *DNB* entry on Bailey.

child; once again the ordinary citizens of London are given primary emphasis. Rae's highly realistic vision of history here invites the modern viewer to identify with the past events; a device which, like the symbolic pairing of past and present which characterises the Exchange scheme as a whole, was a feature of much continental history painting in the late nineteenth century. *The Lady of the Castle distributing Bread*, for example, a Düsseldorf School mural of 1899 at Schloss Burg an der Wupper in Germany,[82] offers a direct comparison and reminds us that the Exchange decoration, for all its distinctive connections with the City of London, also forms the first substantial British contribution to the wider European revival of historical mural painting in the nineteenth and early twentieth centuries. As we shall see, the Exchange work in turn became a key stimulus for the installation of murals in many other public buildings in Britain.

The theme of charitable provision is continued in another mural with Mercers' connections, *The Foundation of St Paul's School, 1509* (Fig. 133), painted in 1905 by W. F. Yeames, again a Royal Academician. Opened in St Paul's churchyard by John Colet, the son of a Lord Mayor and Dean of St Paul's, the school was governed by the Mercers and the mural was fittingly given by the prominent Mercer John Horseley Palmer, thus again reinforcing the 'past into present' symbolism of the entire scheme. It portrays Henry VIII presenting the foundation charter, and so also recalls the City's 'Royal' connections.

FIRST WORLD WAR MEMORIALS AND THE SMALL PORTRAIT PANELS

Given the close and often subtle interface of historical iconography with modern concerns about the future of the Corporation and the varied interests of the donors and artists, it is not at all surprising that the Gresham Committee was at first loath to interrupt the programme of subjects it had devised in 1892 under Mayor Knill with the contemporary themes which were proposed by a number of donors to commemorate the First World War. By the war period, however, there was an increasing feeling that the variety of styles already present at the Exchange had in any case disrupted its unity, whilst the original

propaganda motive *vis-à-vis* the LCC which we can identify behind the 1892 choice of subjects was no longer relevant. So it came about that the subject of *Scene of a Folk-Mote in St Paul's Churchyard* (i.e. people's assembly or council), which had not been selected by any donor even though in 1892 it would obviously have provided a strong thematic counterpart, laden with anti-LCC symbolism, for *Magna Carta* and *Charles I demanding the Five Members*, was abandoned to make way for *Their Majesties King George V and Queen Mary visiting the Battle Districts in France, 1917* (Fig. 123). This was painted by Salisbury and presented in 1917 by Sir W. H. Dunn, the Lord Mayor. Salisbury later related how Dunn swept aside his concern that the Gresham Committee would not accept a modern subject:

The Lord Mayor said 'Nonsense! I will not have a word of objection. I am chairman ex-officio and I have a subject of worldwide interest and national importance, and furthermore, here is a letter from the king promising all the help necessary to the painter . . .[83]

If Salisbury's initial remonstration suggests he would have preferred another historical theme like *Alfred*, he thus found himself designated a Colonel, given a car 'without speed limit', and instructions to follow the route through France being taken by the King and Queen on their 1917 visit. It was planned that the panel would be completed within eight weeks so that Dunn could present it before leaving office,[84] and it was no doubt intended to boost morale in a City (and nation) overrun with Kitchener's 'Your Country Needs You' posters. Arms of Britain and her Allies (whom the King decorated on his visit) adorn the frame, where Latin inscriptions had decorated that of *Alfred*. The panel was given wide publicity and in the event exhibited at the Royal Academy and in Liverpool (where Salisbury was subsequently commissioned to paint murals in the Town Hall as the City's War Memorial) before being unveiled in the Exchange by the Duke of Connaught in the presence of Services representatives.

The documentary purpose of the painting perhaps explains its departure from the richly decorative treatment of colour and space which make *Alfred* so

---

[82] *Die Burgherrin verteilt Brot*, painted by Peter Janssen.

[83] F. Salisbury, op. cit., p. 38.
[84] Ibid.

effective, although Salisbury introduced an ingenious reminiscence of a Renaissance altarpiece predella panel in his treatment of Queen Mary's visit to a military hospital in France as a separate horizontal section in the lower part of the mural. This of course confers a quasi-religious overtone to the event and enables the King, in the upper section of the mural, to appear still further elevated as a commanding presence above the viewer. Standing on rising land, and dressed in the uniform of a Field Marshall, he holds field-glasses, whilst Field Marshall Sir Douglas Haig, map in hand, points to what, in keeping with the Censor's requirements, lies beyond the picture frame. This, of course, is the 'scene of desolation and despair'[85] as Salisbury later termed the region of the Somme he had visited in the footsteps of the Royal party. Salisbury indeed claimed to have been the first civilian to have travelled so far forward in the front, and he obtained sittings there from the commanding generals assembled behind the King and Haig, as well as from the Prince of Wales who stands in the left foreground. King George V gave him the honour of coming to his own studio for a sitting back in London.[86]

The novelist Arnold Bennett wrote, somewhat extravagantly, of the mural that, 'You have to pinch yourself in order to be sure that you have not fallen into a tranced vision',[87] and illusion, however 'staged' by the artist, was clearly the prime objective also in Salisbury's post-war, and last, Exchange panel, *National Peace Thanksgiving Service on the steps of St Paul's Cathedral, 6 July 1919* (Fig. 124). This features life-size portraits of Archbishop Davidson of Canterbury giving a blessing, and the Bishop of London, with the King and Queen slightly behind them at the top of the Cathedral steps. Salisbury described the incident he selected as

the end of the beautiful service, when the royal procession, the archbishops with the representatives of the Churches, and the Lord Mayor and Sheriffs, moved in stately dignity to the great west door . . .

and he 'took up a position at the foot of the steps, where I had a fine view of the impressive group, and

a vista through the open doors as far as the great dome', with 'a rich red and cream canopy' overhead; 'hurrying home, I quickly made my sketches and in a few days the Lord Mayor secured the King's approval . . .'.[88] The panel was donated by Sir Horace Marshall who had been Lord Mayor when peace was declared, and unveiled in 1919 by the Duke of York, the future King George VI. Although a trace of Salisbury's pre-war decorative flair survives in the heraldic banners and ecclesiastical robes, his style, for all its accuracy of portraiture (which was achieved in part by using photographs) is now curiously stilted as if the devastation he had witnessed had oppressed his abilities.

With Salisbury's two war panels, a decisive break had been made with the original conception of the scheme, although the Mayoral and City emphasis was of course still to the fore in the *Peace* mural. The way was now open for two further First World War commemorations to complete the main decoration, although these too remained essentially conservative in style.

The first was W. L. Wyllie's *Blocking of Zeebrugge Waterway*, for the small panel above the Keeper's Lodge. This also involves a strong element of careful 'reportage' but, with its dramatic lighting effects and conflict of struggling sailors and hostile seas, it is arguably far more moving a memorial than Salisbury's *Peace*, and of course complements the existing sea/naval element in the Exchange iconography.[89] The British Dominions Insurance Company which, after its amalgamation with the 'Eagle' and 'Star' companies, donated the panel, was originally a marine insurer.[90] Wyllie was a seaman himself and painted the picture from meticulous sketches 'of everything that had to do with the occasion' as well as from the accounts of eye-witnesses.[91] It shows the survivors from the block-ship 'Iphigenia' (seen at the far right) as they escape in a motor launch under the guidance of Lieutenant W. B. Leake; another escape boat is alongside and, as Wyllie explained, 'in the

[85] Ibid., p. 46.
[86] Ibid., p. 47.
[87] B. Barber, op. cit., p. 31.

[88] F. Salisbury, op. cit., p. 52.
[89] The GCM for 23 May 1919 indicates that the artist initially chosen was Norman Wilkinson (who was to become famous for his poster designs).
[90] Information kindly supplied by the Eagle Star Group.
[91] M. L. Wyllie, *We were One. A Life of W. L. Wyllie* (London, 1935), p. 228.

extreme foreground a part of the Carley craft is seen in which Lieut. Bonham-Carter escaped from the "Intrepid" with five others'.[92] The wrecks of the 'Thetis', 'Vindictive' and 'Daffodil' are illustrated in the background. The grossly overladen escape boats form a dark mass against the lurid brightness of the battle sky, upon which the motor launch's mast etches a faint but suggestive cross shape. Wyllie's wife wrote an entertaining account of the unveiling, which took place in the presence of Leake and other survivors:

... the Lord Mayor on one side, and two of the Sheriffs on the other, laid hold of the ropes, pulling gently at first. Nothing happened. They increased the pull, till they hung like sacks, with their robes spread on the ground around them. A tense moment ensued. Then a voice from the expectant crowd began singing: 'With a long pull, and strong pull', and suddenly the flag came down with a rush.[93]

The final panel, *Women's Work in the Great War* (Fig. 121), by Lucy Kemp-Welch, also continues the naval theme as it shows representatives of women's different contributions to the war set against a sunlit sea. Destroyers punctuate the distant horizon whilst planes fly far above the brightening sky. Soldiers glimpsed beneath the terrace attract the attention of a woman in khaki seen shifting boxes at the left, a nurse standing in the centre, and a Voluntary Aid Detachment member who is using a hand-drill, and is poised on a heap of chains, tools and industrial debris to form the picture's focal point. A widow with two children at the far left, however, poignantly averts her face. In the foreground a landworker selects a spade and a pickaxe from the pile of tools; another woman operates an industrial sewing machine and the remaining two study a book, with a stack of ledgers and invoices at their knees. The picture was presented by the Empress Club, of which the artist, a well-known woman painter who had recently won medals at the Paris Salon, was a member. The Club had been significantly involved in the war effort through its Emergency Voluntary Aid Committee. Princess Mary performed the installation ceremony in 1924, taking the opportunity to speak

personally to Kemp-Welch,[94] and expressing her delight in a note to Colonel Watney of the Gresham Committee at 'being able to unveil so interesting + striking a picture – + one (which) ... will become a very historical addition to those already in the building'.[95]

Meanwhile, a decision had been taken to complete the ambulatory decoration in the manner which Haydon had advised some seventy-five years before. Colonel Watney

In March 1921 ... suggested to the Gresham Committee that the 8 small panels should be filled with portraits of past eminent bankers and merchants of London, and it was left to me to suggest names and to carry the matter out.[96]

The work was completed in 1927 following the same method of donation as had secured the large panels, and with the advice of a number of experts including, for example, Sir Aston Webb the architect, who recommended Alfred Hayward of the Chelsea Arts Club as the painter of the Bank of England's gift of *Sir John Houblon* (first Governor of the Bank of England), and Sir William Orpen who supervised this picture. The Committee of Lloyd's gave a copy by Madame Ruelle of Sir Thomas Lawrence's portrait in the Louvre of John Julius Angerstein, the banker whose art collection formed the nucleus of the National Gallery, and who secured Lloyd's its Royal Exchange tenancy, whilst the other portraits, representing the founders of the banks and businesses of their donors, are *Abel Smith* and *Pascoe Grenfell* (both painted by Harcourt, who had done the *Bank of England* large mural); *Nathan Mayer Rothschild* (by Edward Horwitz); *Sir Francis Baring*, *Sir Richard Glyn*, and *Anthony Gibbs* (by E. B. Patry). Most of these were copies or adaptations of period portraits.[97] Even in this late

---

[92] Letter from Wyllie to the Gresham Committee, 31 October 1919, in GCM, 28 November 1919, p. 369.

[93] M. L. Wyllie, op. cit., p. 230.

[94] Information from press cuttings of 1924 in MC, Royal Exchange Box 3.6.

[95] Letter from Princess Mary's Lady in Waiting to Colonel Watney, 30 April 1924, in MC, Royal Exchange Box 3.6.

[96] Letter from Watney to Sir William Soulsby, 14 June 1927 in MC, Royal Exchange Box 4.1.

[97] *Pascoe Grenfell* was 'taken from various pictures of the time' but 'with the face a little older in the final work' (letter from E. C. Grenfell to Watney, 2 March 1923); *Baring* was based on Sir Thomas Lawrence's portrait at Stratton; and Glyn on Zoffany's painting at Bridewell Royal Hospital. See MC, Royal Exchange Box 4.1.

extension of the Exchange decoration, the Corporation/Livery Company element remained prominent, for Houblon had launched the business of the Bank of England in the Mercers' Chapel in 1694, whilst Sir Richard Glyn was not only the founder of Glyn Mills Currie and Company in the eighteenth century, but also (as Houblon too had been) an Alderman, Sheriff and Mayor of London.

A PIONEERING EXAMPLE: THE PLACE OF THE ROYAL EXCHANGE SCHEME IN BRITISH ART

Although Lionel de Rothschild regarded the panel showing his ancestor as 'the best of the portraits',[98] Roberson, the artists' supplier since Leighton's day, confided to Colonel Watney that its artist, Horwitz, was 'in our experience . . . one of those unable to come to a decision or make up his mind'![99] The task of the Exchange artists was, in fact, for many of them a novel, if not testing and troublesome experience, and there were numerous delays in the completion of large as well as small panels. The Exchange was, after all, the most ambitious programme of mural decoration attempted in a public building in Britain since the abortive Palace of Westminster scheme of the 1840s and '50s. What was a typical form of art in numerous continental buildings had largely to be pioneered at the Exchange.

The 'marouflage' process, for example, by which the paintings were permanently fixed to the walls, had to be demonstrated by French workmen brought over specially by Leighton.[100] Leighton in turn took the opportunity to promote the 'spirit-fresco' technique at the Exchange which he had learnt from its

British inventor Gambier Parry.[101] Most of the 1890s and early 1900s work was carried out in this medium, but later panels tended to be painted in oils, the continental norm which could just as successfully be marouflaged. Canvases of large enough dimensions had to be secured from the Low Countries, and the sheer size of the panels — 17 feet high by 11 feet wide — led Stanhope Forbes, Henrietta Rae, Ernest Normand and W. L. Wyllie to devise special pit and pulley arrangements in their studios to facilitate painting. Forbes wrote desperately in 1899 to his patron the Sun Fire office seeking a large enough studio in London.[102] Lucy Kemp-Welch fainted after working at her mural on scaffolding and 'the doctor sent her away to Devon for 3 or 4 months and forbade all work'.[103] In some cases it was difficult even to find a willing artist: the Mercers' Company attempted a competition, but had to resort to direct commission.[104] Unlike the well-established patronage methods in France, Germany and Austria, the system at the Exchange was essentially experimental, and it is hardly surprising that the work was criticised for

[101] The technique was invented by Thomas Gambier Parry and published by him in 1862; it was promoted by Parry at Highnam Church, Gloucestershire, and in Ely Cathedral, and enthusiastically taken up by Leighton at Lyndhurst Parish Church and the South Kensington (Victoria and Albert) Museum before he used it at the Exchange. It had also been demonstrated in the 1880s at Manchester Town Hall by Ford Madox Brown. For an account of the technique, see D. Farr (ed.), *Thomas Gambier Parry as artist and collector*, Courtauld Institute Galleries (London, 1993).

[102] See letter from Edward Banner (? of the Sun Fire Office) to Stanhope Forbes, 12 January 1899, in Secretary's Letter Book, Sun Fire Office Archives MS 18. 243/9, Guildhall Library, London.

[103] Letter from Williamson Milne to Watney, 16 February 1922 in MC, Royal Exchange Box 3.6.

[104] See the Acts of Court of the Mercers' Company, 21 June 1895–25 September 1896. The Company initially approached P. H. Calderon, and when not only he but subsequently Poynter also declined the commission (Calderon on grounds of ill health), a small competition between William Hole (artist of murals in the Scottish National Portrait Gallery) and Walter Horseley was mounted but failed to produce a sketch acceptable to the Company, whilst both E. A. Abbey and Ernest Crofts declined to compete. (Abbey explained, 'I do not consider that the best artistic results are obtained by competition . . . I have never entered into a competition with my brother artists . . .'.) Crofts was willing to submit a sketch once the competition had proved abortive. The whole situation represents an intriguing reaction by Abbey and Crofts to both the competition procedure used earlier at Westminster and the competitive systems much used in France and Germany (where Crofts had trained).

[98] Letter from J. A. Archer (of Messrs Rothschild) to Watney in ibid.

[99] Letter from Roberson to Watney, 29 January 1925, in ibid.

[100] See letter from John Watney to the Joint Grand Gresham Committee, 5 October 1894, in GCM for that date. Even the 'base' on to which the first two murals (Leighton's and Macbeth's) were marouflaged on the wall was created with foreign expertise: Roberson the artist's colour maker recorded that it was 'a Roman cement of extraordinary hardness: this work was done by an Italian, who unfortunately died, and the secret of his preparation died with him', so that subsequent panels had to be fixed with slate as their backing. The object of these backings, whether of cement or slate, was to protect the murals from moisture in the walls. See letter Roberson's to Watney, 28 October 1926, MC, Royal Exchange Box 3.7.

stylistic disunity. Yet, as we have seen, there was a very high degree of iconographical co-ordination, at least until the changes following the War. Though the original 'propaganda' purposes were naturally obscured by time, the richly interwoven strands of Corporation, Company and City history proved a remarkably evocative stimulus and synthesis for the artists' work. Christian allusions — from the cross carried to the Wars of the Roses by Amschewitz's Trained Bands to that created by the motorboat mast in Wyllie's *Zeebrugge* — and the increasing awareness of the Exchange as the 'heart of Empire' (from Cox's *Merchant Adventurers* to Salisbury's arms of the Allies) likewise integrate the scheme at further symbolic levels, just as the notion of history as a continuum which united the original programme indeed permitted, paradoxically, its 'interruption' with modern panels from 1917. The scheme is undoubtedly variable in its quality, but it afforded a highly important opportunity for a number of artists, like Brangwyn and Amschewitz, to win their spurs, and for particular trends in decorative art, such as the 'Neo-Pre-Raphaelite' style of Abbey, early Salisbury, Solomon, Amschewitz and Goetze, to be consolidated. It directly stimulated the resumption of mural painting at the Palace of Westminster from 1906,[105] and was emulated in civic schemes as far away as Glasgow. The murals also inspired banks, Lloyd's Register of Shipping, and most notably, Skinners' Hall where Brangwyn was employed, acting as a vital catalyst in Britain's contribution to the nineteenth- and twentieth-century European mural revival.[106] The murals deserve to be treasured and it is very much to be hoped that one day it will again be possible to view them as they were originally, without the visual interruption of the present interior layout at the Exchange.

[105] Here, a deliberate attempt was made to overcome the problem of stylistic disunity in evidence at the Exchange by appointing Abbey (who had done an Exchange panel) artistic co-ordinator of the East Corridor mural scheme (1906–10). Other Exchange artists who contributed were Salisbury and Solomon, and the scheme featured the 'Neo-Pre-Raphaelite' style they had demonstrated with Abbey at the Exchange.
[106] This is discussed in C. Willsdon (op. cit., forthcoming) and C. Willsdon, 'Mural Painting in Europe *c.* 1810–1930', *The Macmillan's Dictionary of Art* (London, 1996).

ROYAL EXCHANGE MURALS

The murals are displayed in the following sequence:

Fig. 118. *Phoenicians trading with the Early Britons on the Coast of Cornwall*, painted and presented by SIR FREDERICK LEIGHTON, Bart. PRA, 1895.

Col. Pl. XA *Alfred the Great repairing the Walls of the City of London*, by [SIR] FRANK O. SALISBURY. Presented by Sir Charles Wakefield (afterwards Viscount Wakefield), 1912.

Fig. 119. *William the Conqueror granting a Charter to the Citizens of London*, by JOHN SEYMOUR LUCAS, RA. Presented by the Corporation of London, 1898.

Fig. 120. *William II building the Tower of London*, by CHARLES GOLDSBOROUGH ANDERSON. Presented by William Wallis Aston, Mercer, 1911.

Fig. 121. *Women's Work in the Great War, 1914–1918*, by LUCY KEMP-WELCH. Presented by C. Williamson Milne on behalf of the Empress Club, 1922.

Fig. 122. *King John sealing Magna Carta*, by ERNEST NORMAND. Presented by John Paddon, 1900.

Fig. 123. *Their Majesties King George V and Queen Mary visiting the Battle Districts in France, 1917*, by [SIR] FRANK O. SALISBURY. Presented by Sir William H. Dunn, Bart., Lord Mayor, 1917.

Fig. 124. *National Peace Thanksgiving Service on the steps of St Paul's Cathedral, 6 July 1919*, by [SIR] FRANK O. SALISBURY. Presented by Sir Horace Marshall, Lord Mayor, 1919.

Fig. 125. *Sir Henry Picard, Master of the Vintners' Company, entertaining the Kings of England, France, Scotland, Denmark and Cyprus*, by ALBERT CHEVALLIER TAYLER. Presented by William Vivian, 1903.

Fig. 126. *The Destruction of the Second Royal Exchange in 1838*, by STANHOPE A. FORBES, RA. Presented by the Royal Exchange Assurance, 1920.

Fig. 127. *Sir Richard Whittington dispensing his Charities*, by HENRIETTA RAE. Presented by Sir Abe Bailey, KCMG, 1900.

Fig. 128. *Philip the Good presenting the Charter to the Merchant Adventurers*, by ELIJA A. COX, RBA. Presented by Sir Frederick Green, 1916.

Fig. 129. *Henry VI Battle of Barnet, 1471. The Trained Bands Marching to the Support of Edward IV*, by JOHN H. AMSCHEWITZ. Presented in memory of Ellis Abraham Franklin by his sons, 1911.

Fig. 130. *Blocking of Zeebrugge Waterway, St George's Day, 23 April 1918*, by WILLIAM L. WYLLIE, RA. Presented by the Eagle, Star & British Dominions Company Ltd, 1920.

Fig. 131. *The Reconciliation of the Skinners' and Merchant Taylors' Companies by Lord Mayor Billesden, 1484*, by EDWIN A. ABBEY, RA. Presented by the two Companies, 1904.

Fig. 132. *The Crown offered to Richard III at Baynard's Castle*, by SIGISMUND GOETZE. Presented by Carl Meyer, 1898.

Fig. 133. *The Foundation of St Paul's School, 1509*, by WILLIAM F. YEAMES, RA. Presented by John Horsley Palmer, Mercer, 1905.

Col. Pl. XB *The Opening of the First Royal Exchange by Queen Elizabeth, 23 January 1570–71*, by ERNEST CROFTS, RA. Presented by the Mercers' Company, 1899.

Fig. 134. *Charles I demanding the Five Members at the Guildhall, 1641–42*, by SOLOMON J. SOLOMON, ARA. Presented by Sir Samuel Montagu, Bart., MP, 1897.

Col. Pl. XIA *The Great Fire of London, 1666*, by STANHOPE A. FORBES, ARA. Presented by the Sun Fire Office, 1899.

Fig. 135. *Founding of the Bank of England, 27 July 1694*, by GEORGE HARCOURT. Presented by Members of the Stock Exchange, 1904.

Col. Pl. XIB *Nelson leaving Portsmouth, 18 May 1803 to join HMS Victory*, by ANDREW C. GOW, RA. Presented by the Corporation of Lloyd's, 1903.

Fig. 136. *Opening of the Royal Exchange by Her Majesty Queen Victoria, 28 October 1844*, by ROBERT W. MACBETH, ARA. Presented by Joseph Snowden, Deputy, 1895.

Fig. 137. *Modern Commerce*, by [SIR] FRANK BRANGWYN, ARA. Presented by Thomas Lane Devitt, Skinner, 1906.

All illustrations are reproduced by kind permission of the Joint Grand Gresham Committee.

CHAPTER XXIX

The Sculpture of the Third Exchange

By IAN LEITH

AFTER THE FIRE OF 1838, most of the sculpture within the central courtyard was either destroyed or dispersed in the sale later that year. Only two pieces were considered suitable for re-erection in the new Exchange: the statue of King Charles II by Spiller[1] and the partly damaged Lydekker monument.

It is significant that the chosen plan, whilst perpetuating the central open courtyard and the tradition of a free-standing figure of a monarch within it, did not continue the scheme of niches containing the monarchs and worthies which had been such a feature of the previous building. Given the accepted understanding of this tradition in English art, it is perhaps surprising that this key element was not considered essential by the City authorities who determined the architect's brief: the omission of royal figures in the new Exchange does not represent any lessening of loyalty on their part, but it does reflect the confident early Victorian taste for grand civic buildings which, instead of being decorated with a varied collection of inherited figures, were, if the opportunity existed for complete rebuilding, to be selectively embellished with contemporary sculpture. Certainly Queen Victoria, Prince Albert, Gresham and other appropriate persons were to be properly commemorated, so the decision to discontinue the tradition of a royal gallery was quite conscious.

Sir William Tite, the architect, has received a uniformly bad press. However, the Royal Exchange, his magnum opus, was planned and executed with great thoroughness according to the exacting supervision given by the Joint or Grand Gresham Committee (henceforth described as the Committee) and the structure was accepted as a success from both a functional and symbolic point of view. The Royal Exchange was endowed with the right image for a dynamic business city, and the use of architectural sculpture reflects how such elements were to be manipulated within such an undertaking.

The sculpture consisted of two distinct elements: the architectural sculpture and the quite separate commemorative free-standing figures provided by independent sculptors. The sheer scale and elaboration of the important pediment sculpture meant that this fell into the second category rather than the first, but it is worth noting that the first mention of Richard Westmacott, junior (1799–1872)[2] is in connection with supplying just such applied surface ornament[3] similar to the Royal Arms over the west entrance carved by J. E. Carew.[4]

As the form of the Exchange became distinct, so Tite began to implement the particular sculptural schemes which he considered desirable. These were authorised by the Committee and were subject to at least a nominal form of competition or tendering. It is difficult to interpret the extent of Tite's influence, but it is probable that his well known dominant personality controlled the decision. Apart from the records at Mercers' Hall, there is little original correspondence as opposed to quoted extracts from letters or reports. However, the Committee did at least once expressly refuse his recommendation for a

The author would like to acknowledge the help he has received from Ursula Carlyle of the Mercers Company, Ben Read of the University of Leeds, Philip Ward-Jackson of the Courtauld Institute and to all the helpful staff at the Guildhall Library, the City of London Record Office and the Greater London Record Office.

[1] See Chapter 16, Gibson, for the earlier sculpture; this figure was restored by M. L. Watson for the new Exchange. See below for Watson's statue of Elizabeth I.

[2] Throughout this paper he will be referred to as Richard Westmacott and should not be confused with his sculptor father Sir Richard Westmacott (1775–1856) who has no known connection with the Royal Exchange.

[3] MC, GR, 28 October 1842. Tite made a subsidiary contract with Westmacott for modelling, carving and sculpture for £2,700 consisting of shields of arms, swags, festoons, etc.

[4] MC, GR, 29 March 1844. Carew was paid £350. See below for his statue of Whittington.

FIG. 138.   Pediment sculpture by Richard Westmacott, junior, 1844.
Courtauld Institute of Art

pedestal modelled on that of King Charles at Charing Cross, when they upheld the height and proportion of the plinth of the equestrian Duke of Wellington.[5]

Tite knew that this latter piece was the fulcrum of the whole site: it acted as a 'prow' to the grand entrance front opposite the Mansion House. Tite was peculiarly unable to grasp the importance of scale in this vital context: a 'small' Wellington would have been lost against his imperial portico and could not have acted as a sufficiently focal counter-weight in the new triangular 'piazza' created at such a critical junction in the City. Indeed, it has to be remembered that we now take for granted that the portico and the space in front of it is *the* central focus of the entire City of London. Before 1838 other views of the centre of the City, such as St Paul's from Ludgate Hill or the vista down Cheapside towards St Mary le Bow, would have been considered the worthy candidates for popular or symbolic depictions of the centre of the metropolis.

Given the now increased elevation of all the other buildings at this junction, especially the Bank of England itself, it is fortunate that Chantrey's original

proportions were adhered to. It is even possible to speculate that the strength of this spatial relationship has helped to counteract any later tendency to isolate Wellington in the middle of a traffic island, a fate that has overtaken a number of other statues in central London. This official equestrian statue commemorating the role Wellington played in the city (not on the battlefield) is the centre of the web of geometric streets which were still evolving. This should be compared with the similar but enormous statue by M. C. Wyatt (1846) at Hyde Park Corner.[6]

London has few grand urban vistas — only a few other set pieces like the Mall and Trafalgar Square can be compared with the way the early Victorians managed to open up several axial views focusing on the new Exchange. Such is the formality that one is inevitably reminded of Wren's unexecuted masterplan after the Great Fire.

Tite first described his conception of his Exchange pediment in October 1842 when he stated that it 'would seem to demand that [it] should be filled but not crowded, that the masses should be simple, well

[5] MC, GR, 31 May 1844; see below for discussion of this piece.

[6] J. Physick, *Designs for English Sculpture 1680–1860* (1969), p. 183.

23

defined and boldly relieved'. He also alludes to the fact that he had 'recourse to some assistance [and] valuable cooperation of a gentleman very eminent in his profession'. While admitting to the Committee that this was in fact Westmacott, he was careful to qualify that they should not consider themselves committed to him.[7] They authorised £3,000 for the pediment and voted for the following artists: Richard Westmacott (unanimous), 'William Bailey' (11), W. L. Watson (7), Samuel Joseph (6), and Carew (5).[8] The first three were instructed to supply designs and estimates. Baily declined and thus Joseph was included in the short-list. The sealed designs were examined and the artists interviewed in alphabetical order. This was further reduced to Westmacott and Watson, and the former eventually won the ballot by fourteen votes to two.[9] The speed of assessing and making this major artistic decision provoked comment, and Watson created yet more controversy when he sent his refused drawings to the Royal Academy.[10]

The British trading empire was consciously represented by Westmacott within the pediment by a clear programme of Portland stone figures which were quite explicitly designed to illustrate the manifold extent and wealth 'in the very heart and centre of the great mart of the world'.[11] The realism is emphasised by the fact that with two exceptions all the figures are detached and not merely in relief. Either side of the central crowned figure of Commerce are groups depicting the range of actual people engaged in the different activities of such international business. Below the central figure is the inscription 'The Earth is the Lord's And the Fullness thereof' (Psalm 24.1). The fact that Commerce is the only allegorical figure should be compared with the closest contemporary exercise in recreating the classical tradition of providing pediment sculpture: the British Museum (1847).

Not only is it full of neo-classically correct draped figures which must have been thought appropriate in view of the Elgin marbles and the cultural aspirations of the users, but it was actually executed by the more prolific and better known father of Richard Westmacott, junior: Sir Richard Westmacott (1775–1856).

The fact that the subjects of the Exchange pediment executed by the younger Westmacott between 1842 and 1844 are consciously rooted in the commercial present evokes a much rarer Victorian concern to deliberately elevate 'trade' within an art world which was preoccupied with either a Gothic or a Greek past. This contrast in pedimental subject matter could also be a filial reaction against such ideal tastes. Richard Westmacott never again attempted such a massive commission and, indeed, produced very little other architectural sculpture and far less portrait sculpture than his father, yet he was committed to his art and later became Professor of Sculpture at the Royal Academy where he analysed and taught the very tradition of ancient Greek art so evident in his father's work.

By August 1844 Westmacott had completed the pediment and was paid £3,150. At least one commentator remarked that the central figure should have been different in order to complete the historical reality of the tableau: 'We should prefer Gresham in the flat bonnet and other costume of his time, to this allegorical creation, which reminds us too much of a fire insurance office.'[12] Such consistency is understandable, though the latter remark is somewhat puzzling given that the Exchange *was* actually the home of such an office. The elevation of Gresham to the status of a personification of trade was perhaps thought by the City authorities as being reminiscent of the worship of Mammon.

In his published lectures on sculpture, Richard Westmacott stated that Greek sculpture was not an art

---

[7] MC, GR, 28 October 1842.

[8] MC, GR, 28 October 1842. Presumably these refer to E. H. Baily, M. L. Watson, S. Joseph and J. Carew. Baily executed the Nelson statue in Trafalgar Square (1845).

[9] MC, GR, 25 November 1842.

[10] H. Lonsdale, *The Life and Works of Musgrave Lewthwaite Watson, Sculptor* (1866), p. 178.

[11] Royal Exchange, Report to The Court of Common Council from The Royal Exchange and Gresham Trusts Committee, 23 January 1845, p. 90.

sustained by the opulent few, who bought the services of the sculptor to execute works merely to gratify the patron's fancy. In Greece the artist, himself a Greek, and having a common feeling for the beautiful with his countrymen, *produced his works for the public* . . . No mere personal motives

[12] *Illustrated London News*, 17 February 1844.

FIG. 139.   Duke of Wellington, by Sir Francis Chantrey,
1844.
Courtauld Institute of Art

influenced his labours. These were the conditions which
carried the art to its highest perfection.[13]

The sculptural articulation of entrepreneurs and
workers was expressly intended to be read above the
main portico by a public whose daily sustenance was
dependent on the very transactions which took place
below and behind the main front of a building which
accurately reflects financial and commercial realities.
They also would have comprehended that the central
allegorical figure, like Britannia, specifically avoided
the placing of a temporal ruler or individual: the
substitution of Queen Victoria or even Thomas

Gresham would have implied a hubris incongruous
to the man in the street who knew a 'colossal
impersonation of Commerce'[14] when he saw it
precisely because of its similarity to the symbols to be
found on a common fire insurance office. Westmacott
wanted his pediment to be 'seconded by public
encouragement' if he was to achieve the excellence
required 'to carry art beyond mediocrity'.[15] This
huge panorama of figures dressed in everyday
working clothes should be appreciated after glancing
at another pediment (of 1744) by Sir Robert Taylor
virtually opposite the Royal Exchange: the Mansion
House. Though also intended to typify London's
commercial prosperity, it is 'trivial in conception and
undistinguished in execution'[16] because it cannot be
understood from the ground as being more than a
purely decorative embellishment whatever the allegorical programme proclaimed by the sculptor or
discerned by the cognoscenti. Westmacott's groups
are identifiable by dress, nationality (Russian, Indian,
Chinese, Greek, Armenian, Persian and the Levant),
by station in life and even by religion: the two
intermediate hatted 'Asiatic' figures on Commerce's
right-hand side are 'natives of our Indian possessions,
the one a Hindoo, the other a Mahomedan, each
readily distinguishable in person as well as costume'.[17]
Westmacott is being faithful to his interpretation of
Greek art and by implication criticises the forms
unrecognisable to the public which were used by his
father at the British Museum.

The 1844 Duke of Wellington equestrian statue by
Sir Francis Chantrey (1781–1841) provides , as noted
above, the introductory apex to the space in front of
the Exchange façade. Though sited close to a war
memorial, this piece does not commemorate the
general, but the politician. Wellington was instrumental in helping to get a bill for rebuilding London
Bridge through Parliament. What is puzzling is why
the statue cost so much: over £9,000 seems excessive,
especially in view of the fact that it was cast from
captured Waterloo cannon. Though Chantrey died

[13] Richard Westmacott, junior, *History of Sculpture*, p. 84; my
emphasis.

[14] *Illustrated London News*, 17 February 1844, p. 104.
[15] R. Westmacott, junior, *Handbook of Sculpture Ancient and Modern*
(1864), p. 86.
[16] H. Colvin, *A Biographical Dictionary of British Architects* (2nd
edn, 1978), p. 815.
[17] *Illustrated London News*, 17 February 1844, p. 104.

in 1841, substantial elements had been completed and the work was finished by Henry Weekes (1807–77).[18] The similarity of the horse to that of the same sculptor's George IV in Trafalgar Square suggests a certain economy in design.

Tite's initial proposals for the two niches high up on the North front involved statues of Queen Elizabeth and Queen Victoria,[19] and he also suggested 'four statues for the two central pedestals of the north and south fronts — these statues might appropriately represent the four quarters of the world'.[20] Neither of these schemes was executed. Even after the sculptors had been selected for the two niches on the Threadneedle Street front, the identities of the statues 'were not at present fully defined leaving the allegorical sculpture for the south and north fronts of the Exchange open for further consideration'.[21] Apart from the pediment, only the North and East fronts were to receive any sculptural attention.

The three standing figures in Portland stone to be put in the two niches on the northern side (Threadneedle Street) and in the single niche at the base of the eastern tower were assigned as follows:

Sir Richard Whittington by John Edward Carew (1785?–1868) on the North front (1844) for £430.

Sir Hugh Myddleton by Samuel Joseph (1791–1850) on the North front (1845) for £430.

Sir Thomas Gresham by William Behnes (1795–1864) on the East front (1845) for £550 who was further authorised to study a Holbein portrait of Gresham to ensure an accurate likeness.[22] Behnes was declared bankrupt in the same year.[23]

These three exterior statues were by artists who had all achieved sculptural distinction, but in this architectural context they are 'simply typical portrait figures stuck into niches'[24] and in addition they are all very difficult to see from the ground: in Gresham's

case 'nothing can be seen from the street except his knees'.[25] However, Tite thought that this twelve-foot figure would be more effective from a distance, that is, from the eastern fringes of the City where, until the later rebuilding of Royal Exchange Buildings, it would indeed have been prominent.[26] The previously noted interchangeability of the subjects for these niches proves 'that they could as well be separate monuments placed on pedestals in some open public place'.[27]

The three new interior statues were Elizabeth I by Musgrave Lewthwaite Watson (1804–47), and Queen Victoria and Prince Albert, both by John Graham Lough (1798–1876).

Watson had been runner-up for the pediment and he had a rather better claim to this commission than Westmacott if one takes into account his well received frieze for the façade of the Hall of Commerce on Threadneedle Street in 1842.[28] This substantial work (it was 73 feet long) also had a commercial theme and had cost only £500. His failure to secure the Exchange pediment was hardly offset by securing the Elizabeth statue which occasioned friction with the Committee who had specified a Portland stone statue for £400 to be completed in three months. Both Behnes and Joseph had been given six months, and when Watson asked for an extra three months his request was refused.[29] Nevertheless it was finished by August 1844, but was criticised as being unsightly and Tite was told to communicate the Committee's dissatisfaction with the execution.[30] In reply the sculptor declined to make any alterations and the Committee was reluctantly advised that the (unexplained) 'defect' could form no legal impediment.[31] Watson also repaired for £35 the damaged Charles II statue by Spiller.[32] Watson never again had the opportunity to prove his ability in architectural sculpture: he died in 1847 aged forty-three.

[18] The long inscription on the plinth also records that a stone from London Bridge has been set in the adjoining pavement to commemorate the bridge's re-erection in Lake Havasu City, Arizona, in 1971.
[19] MC, GR, 29 March 1844.
[20] MC, GR, 29 March 1844.
[21] MC, GR, 26 April 1844.
[22] MC, GR, 28 June 1844. The portrait was owned by John Thurston of Weston Hall near Botesdale, Suffolk, who later presented it to the Committee.
[23] MC, GR, 28 February 1845.
[24] B. Read, *Victorian Sculpture* (1982), p. 217.

[25] Lord Edward Gleichen, *London's Open-Air Statuary* (1928), p. 119.
[26] MC, GR, 29 March 1844.
[27] B. Read, *Victorian Sculpture* (1982), p. 217.
[28] The remains of this can now be seen at Napier Terrace, Islington, where they decorate the walls of a recreation area.
[29] MC, GR, 29 May 1844.
[30] MC, GR, 27 September 1845.
[31] MC, GR, 28 February 1845.
[32] MC, GR, 18 April 1845.

FIG. 140. Sir Richard Whittington, by John Carew,
1844.
Courtauld Institute of Art

FIG. 141. Sir Hugh Myddleton, by Samuel Joseph, 1845.
Courtauld Institute of Art

The other two statues inside were entrusted to Lough and are important since they are among the first examples of this type of commemoration of Queen Victoria and Prince Albert.

Lough was paid £1,050 for Queen Victoria, his marble centrepiece to the new courtyard. Quality was uppermost in the minds of both the sculptor and the Committee, but the fact that the marble was exposed to the elements was from the beginning seen as a problem and it is now very difficult to separate the physical degradation from the aesthetic response. The surprising absence of any photographic records

between 1845 and 1891 (when the statue was destroyed) suggests that depiction of this royal symbol was embarrassing, but when such images are discovered they will show not only the effects of weather and pollution but also the fact that the marble used was 'of the veined or piebald variety'.[33] The Committee minutes are peppered with references to cleaning, restoration and, as early as 1859, replacement.[34] The eight-foot figure with pedestal designed by Tite was

[33] J. Lough and E. Merson, *John Graham Lough* (1987), p. 69.
[34] MC, GR, 18 November 1859.

FIG. 142.   Sir Thomas Gresham, by William Behnes.
RCHME, © Crown copyright

statue 'very bad'[37] though there is another version of the Prince's reaction. The later destruction of this piece will be discussed with its replacement by Thornycroft in 1896.

In 1845 Lough was also commissioned by Lloyd's to erect a statue to Prince Albert to commemorate his laying of the foundation stone of the Royal Exchange in 1842. This was unveiled in Lloyd's rooms on 19 July 1847 and later transferred to the ambulatory of the Exchange in 1921–22.[38] It is currently in store, but must have some public future since it is probably the earliest known statue to the Prince: virtually all the other public memorials derive from the period after his death, despite his instructions that the Queen should not raise even a single marble image to his name.[39]

Other sculpture in Lloyd's rooms included a plain testimonial in tablet form to *The Times* by Thomas Piper, junior (fl. 1800–50), designed by Tite, which was placed in the vestibule close to Prince Albert's statue.[40] Another statue was also situated in Lloyd's: the solemn marble figure in a toga of William Huskisson by John Gibson (1790–1866) which had been considered by both Mrs Huskisson and Gibson as being not suitable for its intended Liverpool location.[41] It was unveiled in Lloyd's on 7 February 1848 and was later given to the LCC in 1915 and re-erected in Pimlico Gardens. The classical garb has occasioned scholarly and comic comment which should be examined in the context of the propriety of sculptural dress discussed later under the Peabody and Rowland Hill statues.[42]

It has been claimed that Gibson also refused the Queen Victoria commission because Lough was not known to have obtained a royal sitting.[43] However, the Queen *did* sit for Lough and in contradiction to the previously quoted negative remark by Gibson on Prince Albert's reaction to Lough's Victoria, the Committee minutes record the Prince's *satisfaction*

only completed in plaster for the official opening in October 1844. The vexed marble version was unveiled one year later (28 October 1845) when it was immediately suggested that a glass covering should be placed over it.[35] Only in 1884 was the courtyard roofed, but by then it was too late for the exclusion of the elements to have any effect. Prince Albert himself remarked to the sculptor John Gibson[36] that he thought Lough's

[35] E. Darby, 'Statues of Queen Victoria and of Prince Albert', PhD thesis (University of London, 1983), vol. 2, p. 160.
[36] See Huskisson statue discussed below.

[37] National Library of Wales, MSS 20, 566.7E, 1847. Quoted in E. Darby thesis.
[38] E. Darby, PhD thesis (1983), vol. 2, pp. 166–67.
[39] E. Darby, *The Cult of the Prince Consort* (1983), p. 6.
[40] *Illustrated London News*, 29 August 1846. R. Gunnis, p. 306.
[41] Lady Eastlake, *Life of John Gibson* (1870), p. 116.
[42] For reactions to Huskisson see J. Blackwood, *London's Immortals* (1989), p. 180.
[43] E. Darby, PhD thesis, vol. 1, pp. 112–13.

FIG. 143. Prince Albert, by John Graham Lough, 1847.
Courtauld Institute of Art

about Lough's visit and sketch.[44] Without further evidence the merits of this contentious statue will have to wait until the written documentation is augmented by original sketches or photographs. It has also been suggested that the haste of the Committee to complete all the sculptural works succeeded in losing the services of Gibson.[45]

Apart from Spiller's Charles II, the only other piece of sculpture which may have survived the fire was the marble wall monument to John Lydekker (1778–1832) by J. J. Sanders (fl. 1812–46)[46] which had been situated on the North staircase of the old Exchange and whose survival 'amidst the general wreck is very extraordinary'.[47] It is unclear whether any of the original was incorporated since both versions feature a pair of figures of wounded seamen

and the panel now contains a whaling scene which replaced a presumably damaged view of the stern of the Dreadnought hospital ship. Lydekker bequeathed enough money to the Seamen's Hospital Society to enable their Act of Incorporation.[48] The replacing of this memorial in Lloyd's rooms was endorsed by Tite.[49] It is now in store.[50]

To sum up the sculpture put up after the opening of the new Exchange, there seems to be a common feeling that the exterior figures on the East and North fronts were too high. This has to be balanced by the reminder that the height of most of the surrounding buildings allowed at least distant views. The inscriptions relating to these niche figures are in some cases now invisible and the man on the omnibus who can see them would be hard pressed to identify Whittington, Myddleton or Gresham. Regarding the interior, some form of public access would until quite recently have been possible at least for exhibitions or other functions, and judging by the availability of popular guide books there must have been some demand for information on the sculpture and murals even after the Second World War. Outside the Royal Exchange the evidence that today's sculptural display was assembling became evident in the 1860s. The initial spate of sculptural achievement between 1844 and 1848 was only relieved by a brief respite before new monuments began to appear in the surrounding area.

The Metropolitan Drinking Fountain and Cattle Trough Association (henceforth known as the Association) was founded in 1859 to provide pure water for needy people and animals. In the same year the first drinking fountain was erected outside St Sepulchre's church on Snow Hill. This does not now exist in its original form but the Association's second fountain put in 1861 outside the main front of the Royal Exchange still exists, though at a different location. A simple circular granite bowl is surmounted by a bronze female figure by W. and T. Wills (fl. 1856–84). She is probably the first symbolic representation of Temperance on a public drinking fountain and has also been described as The Woman

[44] MC, GR, 31 May 1844.
[45] H. Lonsdale, *The Life and Works of Musgrave Lewthwaite Watson, Sculptor* (1866), p. 179.
[46] R. Gunnis, p. 339.
[47] Guildhall Library A512/12: unidentified press cutting of 1838 which also refers to pieces of monarchical statues being purloined as mementoes by importunate parties.

[48] W. R. Dawson, *John Lydekker: The Memorial at Lloyd's* (1927), p. 5.
[49] MC, GR, 29 March 1844.
[50] Information from Lloyd's Information Centre, 1996.

FIG. 144.   George Peabody, by William Wetmore Story,
1869.
Courtauld Institute of Art

of Samaria.[51] Between 1861 and 1911 when it was relocated north-east of Blackfriars Bridge, this unassuming figure was calculated to have been used by no less than 5,603 individuals during one twenty-four-hour period.[52]

In 1869 the seated bronze statue of the philanthropist George Peabody was unveiled at the North end of Royal Exchange Avenue by the Prince of Wales on 23 July. That both the subject and the sculptor, William Wetmore Story (1819–95), were American is not coincidental: the public subscription committee presided over by the Lord Mayor in 1866

had been formed to discuss the gift by Mr George Peabody of £250,000 for the 'benefit of the industrious poor of London' and how best to express gratitude for this gift in some lasting form.[53] The Committee had invited Story, Foley, Marochetti, Theed, Durham, Woolner and Bacon to submit designs for a competition, but when four of these declined the committee 'proceeded with what had evidently been the original plan: to gain the services of the American sculptor . . . in deference to the nationality of George Peabody',[54] Story, who had spent a large part of his life in Rome (as had John Gibson) was selected in 1867 and was paid £2,300 in July 1869. It is signed 'w.w. STORY inv. et sculp/ROM 1868' as is the founder 'FERD. V. MILLER fudit/MUNCHEN 1869'. The result has been described as 'stark [and] all but devoid of artistic identity' and as being typical of the growing number of similarly undistinguished pieces in towns throughout England.[55] Contemporary observers rather bizarrely agreed that the character of modern dress was to blame for these deficiencies, but more acute sculptors like Boehm[56] and Onslow Ford (1852–1901) were to make costume a challenge and were 'to take a positive delight in its textures, fit and detail'.[57]

Just such a contrasting figure was erected in 1881[58] at the south end of Royal Exchange Buildings to commemorate Rowland Hill, the famous instigator of the Penny Post. This was Onslow Ford's first major public commission and his lively handling is acknowledged to have affected the 'by now established form and style of the standing bronze figure [which] is treated in a wholly different way'.[59] The statue was relocated to its present position outside the GPO on King William Street in 1911.

[51] P. Davies, *Troughs and Drinking Fountains* (1989), p. 49.
[52] GLRO, 3168/160/396. A large part of the Association's archive is deposited here, but individual fountains are not fully catalogued.

[53] Quoted in S. Beattie, *The New Sculpture* (1983), p. 201. Another version of Peabody is in Baltimore, USA.
[54] S. Beattie, *The New Sculpture* (1983), p. 202.
[55] Ibid., p. 203.
[56] Boehm was later invited to supply the replacement Victoria statue inside the Exchange, but died before commencing this commission. It was subsequently executed by Thornycroft (see below).
[57] S. Beattie, *The New Sculpture* (1983), p. 203.
[58] CLRO, Engineers Papers, Misc. 1/17 (1–10). Letters from Ford state that a full-sized model was finished in late 1881 and that plans for the pedestal were ready by April 1882.
[59] B. Read, *Victorian Sculpture* (1982), p. 292.

FIG. 145. *Motherhood*, by Jules Dalou, before 1911, and removal of canopy.
RCHME, © Crown copyright

A more sculpturally significant and still existing addition to Royal Exchange Buildings was erected at the northern end a few years before Rowland Hill: in 1878 the Broad Street Ward Fountain designed by J. S. Edmeston (d. 1887) and, more significantly, modelled by Jules Dalou (1838–1902). Dalou was an eminent French artist who lived in exile in England and through his teaching at South Kensington became a pivotal influence in English sculpture. He was the celebrated creator of *The Triumph of the Republic* in the Place de la Nation in Paris and was assisted by Alfred Drury who will be discussed in the context of his war memorial figures at the Exchange.

The canopied fountain shelters a bronze figure of a mother and child entitled 'Charity' (or 'Motherhood') which heralds the end of the old neo-classical stiffness of early Victorian sculpture. Again the Drinking Fountain Association supported the joint funding with City and Ward sources.[60] It is unclear when the canopy was removed. The original marble figure was replaced in bronze in 1897.

By 1889 the courtyard had been roofed over but the state of the Queen Victoria statue by Lough could be ignored no longer and the Committee asked the President of the Royal Academy, Sir Frederick Leighton, to assess its condition. He was

. . . sorry to find the light obscured beyond my expectation by the heavy glass roof of the Quadrangle. As far as I could make out the face of the Queen is almost wholly obliterated by the effect of exposure or at least entirely disfigured. The stone used must have been extremely perishable.

Meanwhile there is of course no remedy. Shall I be forgiven if I say that the Gresham Committee seems to me to be favoured by circumstances in being virtually forced to replace so poor a work altogether.[61]

This was enough to persuade the Committee to commission a new piece, and without any selection procedure Sir J. Edgar Boehm was asked to submit a design in marble similar to the one he had just finished for Sydney, Australia, for a sum not to exceed £2,000.[62] However, Boehm died in 1890 before he could execute any part of this work, and the Committee, perhaps feeling that there were no artists with such an obvious royal pedigree, went through a full process of requesting applications which were reduced to three: C. B. Birch, E. Brock (*sic*) and H. Thorneycroft (*sic*), and finally selected the latter at the same cost as Boehm.[63] William Hamo Thornycroft (1850–1925) was a deservedly popular sculptor whose works still attract attention, and unlike Lough he was given much more time to find the proper materials. The old statue was destroyed in 1891[64] and the new one unveiled on 20 June

[60] *The Builder*, 6 April 1878, p. 350.
[61] MC, GR, 7 February 1890, quoting his letter of 7 January.
[62] MC, GR, 23 July 1890.
[63] MC, GR, 30 January 1891. Presumably this refers to Sir Thomas Brock (1847–1922). The other unsuccessful candidates were: J. A. Acton, Alfred Gilbert, J. Milo Griffith, H. Morris, Walter Merritt, and F. J. Williamson.
[64] GR, 13 November 1891.

1896.[65] The new Victoria held the prime central position until 1953 when, after temporary removal to provide space for the Mermaid Theatre, she was not subsequently re-installed and remained in the north-west corner until being recently put into store with Prince Albert.

1911 was the Jubilee of the Drinking Fountain Association who were determined to replace the existing simple piece with a more elaborate one. George Frampton and the Doulton Company were linked to the first proposals in 1909, but the former was blocked by charity regulations and the latter was not thought suitable owing to the desirability of granite. The Jubilee fountain was designed and built by Joseph W. Whitehead (Whitehead & Sons fl. 1882–1920) for £1,094 and was erected on the site of the present war memorial and contained yet another bronze female figure under a canopy which was surmounted by a bronze Roman Standard carrying a lamp for electric light.[66] In 1959 it was described as not having been used since early in the last war and its water supply was cut off. The bronze figure of the Jubilee fountain was stolen on 11 February 1989 and replaced by a similar piece by Stephen Robert Melton on 9 November 1993. The 1861 fountain was removed to Blackfriars, where it remains today.

The increasing awareness of the sculptural import-ance of the Royal Exchange was perhaps acknow-ledged by the permanent loan offer in 1913 of seven statues from Westminster Hall. These 'modern' statues in a 'Renaissance' style were considered suit-able to stand between the main piers of the Quad-rangle, but the Committee rejected this proposal.[67] Further evidence that the Exchange was used as a temporary sculptural exhibition space is confirmed by a reference to the display in 1919 of yet another statue of Queen Victoria for British Columbia.[68]

Inevitably the space outside the Exchange was thought suitable for one of the main City war memorials, and in 1920 a series of monumental moves enabled the memorial by Aston Webb (1849–1930) and Alfred Drury (1856–1944) to be put in place on the site of the Jubilee drinking fountain, which was relocated to the Royal Exchange Buildings position of the Rowland Hill statue, which was itself moved to its current position on King William Street.[69]

The Portland stone war memorial consists of a square panelled pillar surmounted by a lion sup-porting armorial shields and is flanked on either side by statues of men of the London regiments, signed 'A Drury 20'. It was unveiled by the Duke of York on 12 November 1920. Webb had, earlier in 1919, proposed erecting two Venetian masts sheathed in copper, standing 75 feet high, which were to fly flags for ceremonial occasions.[70]

Inside the Exchange Lloyd's also erected a large war memorial by Sir Edwin Lutyens (1869–1944). Two tall pylons flanked by flags and inscribed with the names of Lloyd's men were placed on either side of a doorway over which was a cartouche and dedication. This was unveiled on 31 January 1922 by Field Marshal Earl Haig. It is currently in store.[71]

The exhibition of a limestone bust of Abraham Lincoln by Andrew O'Connor (1874–1941) inside the courtyard was granted by the Committee in 1928. This aroused admiration, and a presentation commit-tee chaired by the Marquess of Reading offered it as a permanent monument. This was accepted and the giant bust was unveiled by the Lord Mayor on 12 February 1930.[72] O'Connor, like W. W. Story, was an American sculptor who spent part of his life in Europe — in this case, Paris. He was influenced by Dalou and supplied a number of statues for the USA, including the figure of Lincoln for the President's birthplace in Springfield, Illinois. In his last years the sculptor spent his time in London and Dublin, leaving many pieces to the Dublin Municipal Gallery.[73]

[65] E. Manning, *Marble and Bronze: The Art and Life of Hamo Thornycroft* (1982), p. 211. A letter (p. 134) from the sculptor describes the fifteen-hour physical effort required to move the piece into position safely: 'Her Majesty was very obstinate in going on to her pedestal and we fought hard to save her sceptre'.
[66] See CLRO, P.D.60.12 for the Programme of Ceremonies on 3 May 1911 and a description of the fountain.
[67] MC, GR, 25 July 1913.
[68] MC, GR, 11 July and 26 September 1919.

[69] CLRO, Streets Committee Papers 1920/9A; GLRO, 3168/160/396.
[70] CLRO, Streets Committee Papers 1916–47; file 1920/9A: there are letters from Webb describing both versions.
[71] Lloyd's Information Centre, 1996.
[72] MC, GR, 23 May 1930.
[73] H. Potterton, *Andrew O'Connor 1874–1941* (1974), p. 60. This accompanied an exhibition at Trinity College, Dublin, in September 1974. There are several versions of this composition which was originally intended for Providence, Rhode Island.

FIG. 146.   War memorial after 1920, by Aston Webb and Alfred Drury, 1920.
RCHME, © Crown copyright

The most recent sculptural manifestations outside the Royal Exchange commenced with the appropriate bust of Paul Julius Reuter by Michael Black (1976) which is close to the original Reuters office on Royal Exchange Buildings. The striking grey granite herm, while incorporating a bust, proves its modernity by transforming the inscription into a monumental block of deep relief lettering which arrests the eye in contrast to the keenness of observation needed to identify the elevated figure of Gresham in his niche opposite. Black is also responsible for the replacement heads of Emperors around the Sheldonian Theatre, Oxford. For the 1993 Art in the City sculpture trail, two steel armatures by Marcel Baettig in the forms of a Bull and a Bear were temporarily sited on either side of the portico. The more permanent bronze memorial sited in the middle of Cornhill to the engineer James Henry Greathead by James Butler was commissioned by London Underground Ltd and only erected in 1995.

With the cessation of its trading functions in the late 1930s, the Royal Exchange took on an uneasy life as a semi-public space for exhibitions and City functions. This trading on symbolic and historical associations was temporarily interrupted by the advent of the London International Financial Futures Exchange in 1982 which led to the removal of Queen Victoria and Prince Albert from the courtyard: both of these have been restored by the Mercers' Company but remain in store until the future of the Exchange becomes clear. Elizabeth I, Charles II and Lincoln remain the last evidence of the interior sculpture accumulated since 1844: there is an echo here of the sculptural losses after the fire of 1838. By 1930 more

FIG. 147.   Paul Julius Reuter, by Michael Black, 1976.
RCHME, © Crown copyright

than fifteen pieces of executed sculpture meant that the Exchange and its surroundings now housed another sculptural generation which replaced the lost public art of the second Exchange. Within the Exchange the loss of *two* such collections, one by fire and one by default, begins to look like evidence for national carelessness. The existence of what is tantamount to a sculpture park (doubly so if one adds all the pieces remaining from the second Exchange) needs to be recognised and built into any future plans relating to the history of London and the history of English sculpture. Perhaps the central courtyard figure where Charles II and Victoria have stood should be graced with the first statue of Queen Elizabeth II.

CHAPTER XXX

Medals of the Royal Exchange

By CHRISTOPHER EIMER

BY THE MIDDLE OF THE nineteenth century medal making in Britain was reaching a zenith, with production occurring in the Mint at Tower Hill and at a large number of private die-sinking establishments in London and in Birmingham. Medals were an ideal medium on which to commemorate events of national or local interest, and those of the Royal Exchange, which were struck after the old building burned down in 1838, on the erection of Wellington's equestrian statue in front of the new building in June 1844, and on its opening by Queen Victoria four months later, represent the largest group to commemorate an event in the history of the City of London.

William Wyon, the celebrated Mint engraver, had only recently cut the definitive portrait of Queen Victoria for the first postage stamps, when he produced two medals with variations of this image (Nos. 8 and 32). Wyon's large-size medal of Thomas Gresham and the only one to carry his portrait is perhaps the finest of all the Royal Exchange medals,

with its intricately detailed exterior view of the building on the reverse (No. 15).

The medal for the laying of the foundation stone, by Alfred Joseph Stothard, the sculptor and designer, is described in a contemporary advertisement as having been executed from sittings kindly given by Prince Albert. The obverse legend is said to have been based on a medallet found on the site of the old Royal Exchange, its inscription — 'Angliae Regina Ubique Honorata' — recording Queen Elizabeth I's patronage of the original building (No. 7).

The large variety of white metal medals, principally the product of Birmingham medallists, constitute the largest group in the series. The majority were available for a matter of pence and some are frequently found pierced at the top, having been worn from a ribbon. The portrayal of the Duke of Wellington, for whom public sentiment was running high at this time, only added to the popularity of these medals.

1. Destruction of the old Royal Exchange, 1838.

Obverse: elevation to Cornhill of the ROYAL EXCHANGE. Ex. BUILT. BY. SR. THO. GRESHAM. 1566

Reverse: Queen Elizabeth standing, half-left, surrounded by courtiers. Ex. QUEEN. ELIZABETH.

DESTROYED. BY. THE. FIRE. OF. LONDON. REBUILT. 1669. AGAIN. BURNT JANRY. 10. 1838. *Signed*: I. BARBER. FECIT. PUB. BY. GRIFFIN & HYAMS. CORNHILL. in the exergue.

PROCLAIMING THE. BURSE. TO. BE. CALLED THE. ROYAL. EXCHANGE. FOR. EVER. 1570. 61 mm   a) copper;   b) copper-gilt;   c) white metal. *Literature*:   Brown 2071; Taylor 36a.

A white metal example is in a case, the outer-lid gilt-embossed with the Cornhill elevation (collection of the Guardian Royal Exchange).

---

2.   Sir William Tite, Architect of the new Royal Exchange, 1840.

Obverse: two-line inscription WILLIAM. TITE. ARCHI-TECT Around, NEW ROYAL EXCHANGE. MDCCCXL.

Reverse: three armorial shields upon a decorative square-shaped device.
Edge: SIR CHAPMAN MARSHALL KNT. ALDERMAN.
50 mm   ivory.
Literature: Unpublished.

An open competition was held in order to find the architect of the new Royal Exchange, but none of the entries were deemed satisfactory. Five eminent architects were then invited by the Rebuilding Committee to take part in a further competition, although submissions, received in April 1840, only came from Charles Robert Cockerell and William Tite, the eventual winner.

---

3.   Stone Laying for the new Royal Exchange, 1842.

Obverse: conjoined busts of Prince Albert and Queen Victoria, left. VICTORIA BRITAN: REGINA, ET ALBERT SAX COBURG GOTHA PRINCEPS.
Signed: HALLIDAY on the truncation.

Reverse: façade of the NEW ROYAL EXCHANGE Ex. THE FOUNDATION STONE LAID BY H.R.H. PRINCE ALBERT JANUARY 1842.
Signed: T.H. at the right-hand edge, and PUBLISHED BY HYAM HYAMS. CORNHILL. in the exergue.
61 mm   a) copper; b) copper-gilt; c) white metal.
Literature: Brown 2074; Eidlitz 99; Taylor 146b.

4.   Stone Laying for the new Royal Exchange, 1842.
Obverse: (as the reverse No. 3) façade of the NEW ROYAL EXCHANGE Ex. THE FOUNDATION STONE LAID BY H.R.H. PRINCE ALBERT JANUARY 1842.
Signed: T.H. at edge, and PUBLISHED BY HYAM HYAMS. CORNHILL.

Reverse: (as No. 1) Queen Elizabeth standing, half-left, surrounded by courtiers. Ex. QUEEN. ELIZABETH. PROCLAIMING. THE. BURSE. TO. BE. CALLED. THE. ROYAL. EXCHANGE. FOR. EVER. 1570
61 mm   a) white metal.
Literature: Brown 2075; Taylor 146c.
Not illustrated.

5.   Stone Laying for the new Royal Exchange, 1842.

Obverse: (as the reverse of No. 3) façade of the NEW ROYAL EXCHANGE Ex. THE FOUNDATION STONE LAID BY H.R.H. PRINCE ALBERT JANUARY 1842.
Signed: T.H. at the right-hand edge, and PUBLISHED BY HYAM HYAMS. CORNHILL. in the exergue.
Reverse: (similar to the obverse of No. 1) elevation to Cornhill of the ROYAL EXCHANGE. Ex. BUILT. BY. SR. THOS GRESHAM 1566 DESTROYED BY THE FIRE OF LONDON REBUILT 1669. AGAIN BURNT JANY 10. 1838
Signed: PUBLISHED BY HYAM HYAMS CORNHILL in the exergue.
61 mm   a) white metal.
Literature: Brown 2076; Taylor 146d.
Reverse only illustrated.

6.   Stone Laying for the new Royal Exchange, 1842.

Obverse: conjoined busts of Prince Albert and Queen Victoria, left. ALBERT BORN AUGT. 26TH. 1819. VICTORIA BORN MAY 24TH. 1819.

Reverse: view of the portico of the NEW ROYAL EXCHANGE LONDON Ex. FIRST STONE LAID BY H.R.H. PRINCE ALBERT IN THE 5TH YEAR OF THE REIGN OF H.M.G.M. VICTORIA JANY. 17. 1842 W. TITE ESQR. F.R.S. F.G.S. & C. ARCHITECT.
Signed: DAVIS BIRM in the exergue.
54 mm   a) copper; b) white metal.
Literature: Brown 2072; Taylor 146a.

7.   Stone Laying for the new Royal Exchange, 1842.

Obverse: head of Prince Albert, right, ALBERTVS VBIQVE HONORATVS.
Signed: A. L. STOTHARD. F.

Reverse: elevation of the portico to the Royal Exchange. SVB AVSPICIO PRINCIPIS. Ex. RESTAVRATIO IANVAR: XVII MDCCCXLII.
45 mm   a) silver; b) copper.
Literature: Brown 2077; Taylor 146e.

A pair of these medals in copper are in a fitted case, its lid gilt-embossed with the City of London arms (collection of Guardian Royal Exchange).

8.   Stone Laying for the new Royal Exchange, 1842.

Obverse: bust left, wearing a diadem. VICTORIA D: G: BRITANNIARUM REGINA F: D:
Signed: W. WYON on the truncation.

Reverse: ten-line inscription IN COMMEMORATION OF LAYING THE FIRST STONE OF THE NEW ROYAL EXCHANGE BY H: R: H: PRINCE ALBERT CONSORT OF H: M: QUEEN VICTORIA 17 JANUARY 1842 IN THE FIFTH YEAR OF HER REIGN
45 mm   a) silver; b) copper; c) copper-gilt.
Literature: Brown 2078.

9.   Stone Laying for the new Royal Exchange, 1842.

Obverse: view of the NEW ROYAL EXCHANGE Ex. THE FOUNDATION STONE LAID BY PRINCE ALBERT JAN. 17. 1842.

Reverse: a candlestick, knife and fork. Above, BEST SHEFFIELD PLATE Below, SILVER SPOONS KNIVES & FORKS GOLD GUARDS & C. SPLENDID AND APPROVED MEDALS OF THE THAMES TUNNEL.

31 mm   unsigned a) white metal.

Literature: Brown 2073.

The description of this medal is taken from Brown, who attributes its publication to William Griffin. An example has not been examined. Griffin describes himself on an advertising ticket as a silversmith, jeweller and medallist at 25 Change Alley, Cornhill, London (Hawkins, p. 812, No. 8).

———————————

10.   Stone Laying for the new Royal Exchange, 1842.

Obverse: view of the NEW ROYAL EXCHANGE Ex. THE FOUNDATION STONE LAID BY PRINCE ALBERT JAN. 11. 1842.

Signed: W. GRIFFIN LONDON at the bottom edge.

Reverse: eleven-line inscription GOOD CHEER THE FINEST WINES CAPITAL STABLING AND EVERY POSSIBLE COMFORT WILL BE FOUND AT THE OLD HAT INN EALING MIDDLESEX CHARGES VERY MODERATE.

30 mm   a) brass.

Literature: Hawkins, p. 811, No. 1.

The description of this medal is taken from Hawkins. An example has not been examined. It is unclear whether the date of 11 January — as opposed to 17 January on all other medals — is an incorrect transcription of the example cited by Hawkins, which is in a private collection.

———————————

11.   Equestrian Statue of Wellington, 1844.

Obverse: façade of the NEW ROYAL EXCHANGE Ex. THE FOUNDATION STONE LAID BY H.R.H. PRINCE ALBERT JANUARY 17. 1842.

Signed: T.H. at the edge, and PUBLISHED BY HYAM HYAMS. CORNHILL. in the exergue.

Reverse: equestrian statue, its base inscribed WELLINGTON / ERECTED JUNE 18 1844.

Signed: PUB. BY. H. HYAMS, and T.H.F. [= Thomas Halliday, fecit] at the edge.

62 mm   a) white metal.

Literature: Brown 2198; Eimer 120; Taylor 146v.

Francis Chantrey's statue was erected in front of the Royal Exchange on the anniversary of the battle of Waterloo. His designs are in the National Portrait Gallery (Archive Nos. 1331–37). Reporting on the ceremony and the statue itself the following week, the *Illustrated London News* remarked that the horse's chest and shoulders were disproportionately large, its head too sharp and its neck too short. The Duke's head was also thought to be ill-proportioned to the entire figure and the omission of stirrups 'a modern invention'.

---

12. Equestrian Statue of Wellington, 1844.

Obverse: bust left. ARTHUR DUKE OF WELLINGTON.
Signed: JOS. DAVIS BIRM at the edge.

Reverse: equestrian statue inscribed SERINGAPATAM ASSYE TALAVERA BADAJOZ SALAMANCA VITTORIA TOULOUSE WATERLOO on the pedestal. THE WELLINGTON STATUE IN FRONT OF THE ROYAL EXCHANGE LONDON ERECTED JUNE 18 1844 COST £9000 RAISED BY PUBLIC SUBSCRIPTION.
51 mm   a) copper; b) white metal.
Literature: Brown 2195; Eimer 121.

---

13. Equestrian Statue of Wellington, 1844.

Obverse: view of the Royal Exchange. On ribbons, above: ROYAL EXCHANGE LONDON; and below, OPENED BY H.M.G. MAJESTY VICTORIA OCT: 28: 1844. Ex. FOUNDED BY SIR THOMAS GRESHAM, A.D. 1566. PROCLAIMED ROYAL EXCHANGE 1570. DESTROYED IN THE GREAT FIRE 1666 RESTORED, 1667. AGAIN DESTROYED BY FIRE, 1838 FIRST STONE OF PRESENT

Reverse: (as No. 12) equestrian statue inscribed SERINGAPATAM ASSYE TALAVERA BADAJOZ SALAMANCA VITTORIA TOULOUSE WATERLOO on the pedestal. THE WELLINGTON STATUE IN FRONT OF THE ROYAL EXCHANGE LONDON ERECTED JUNE 18 1844 COST £9000 RAISED BY PUBLIC SUBSCRIPTION.
51 mm   a) white metal.

EDIFICE LAID BY H.R.H. PRINCE ALBERT JANUARY 17. 1842.

Signed: J. DAVIS MEDALLIST BY COMMAND TO H.R.H. PRINCE ALBERT on the exergual line.

Literature: Brown 2194; Eimer 122; Taylor 146t.

14. Equestrian Statue of Wellington, 1844.

Obverse: bust left. ARTHUR DUKE OF WELLINGTON.
Signed: ALLEN & MOORE BIRM: below the bust.

Reverse: equestrian statue. THE WELLINGTON STATUE LONDON ERECTED JUNE 18 1844. SIR F. CHANTRY. SC: Ex. COST £9000 RAISED BY PUBLIC SUBSCRIPTION. THE METAL WORTH £1500 GIVEN BY GOVERNMENT.
39 mm   a) copper; b) white metal.
Literature: Brown 2191; Eimer 125.

15. Opening of the new Royal Exchange, 1844.

Obverse: robed bust of Thomas Gresham, left. EMPO-RIVM REGIVM A. THOMA GRESHAM EQ. AVR. CIVE LONDINENSI CONDITVM A. S. MDLXXI.
Signed: W. WYON R.A. on the truncation.

Reverse: courtyard of the Royal Exchange, with a statue of Queen Victoria, its base inscribed A: S. MDCCCXLIV XXVIII OCT., in the foreground, REST. ET. APERT. AVSP. VICTORIA REG Ex. W. TITE F.R.S. ARCHT.
Signed: W. WYON R.A. FECIT in the exergue.
72 mm   a) silver; b) copper.

An example in copper is in a fitted case, its lid gilt-embossed with the City of London arms (collection of Guardian Royal Exchange). William Wyon's wax model of Gresham is in the Fitzwilliam Museum, Cambridge.

16.   Opening of the new Royal Exchange, 1844.

Obverse: view of the ROYAL EXCHANGE LONDON 1844 Ex. FOUNDED BY SIR THOMAS GRESHAM A.D. 1566, VISITED IN STATE BY QUEEN ELIZABETH AND PRO-CLAIMED 'ROYAL EXCHANGE' 1570. DESTROYED BY THE GREAT FIRE 1666. FIRST STONE OF SECOND BUILDING LAID BY KING CHARLES II, 1667, WHICH WAS ALSO DESTROYED BY FIRE JAN. 10. 1838.
Signed: J. DAVIS. MEDALLIST TO H.R.H. PRINCE ALBERT on the exergual line.

Reverse: another view of the building ROYAL EXCHANGE LONDON NORTH-EAST Ex. FIRST STONE OF THE PRESENT EDIFICE, LAID BY H.R.H. PRINCE ALBERT. JAN. 17. 1842. OPENED BY H.M.G. MAJESTY VICTORIA OCT. 28. 1844. W. TITE ESQR. ARCHT.
60 mm   a) copper; b) white metal.
Literature: Brown 2176; Eidlitz 996; Taylor 146u.

17.   Opening of the new Royal Exchange, 1844.

Obverse: (as No. 13) view of the Royal Exchange. On ribbons, above: ROYAL EXCHANGE LONDON; and below, OPENED BY H.M.G. MAJESTY VICTORIA OCT: 28: 1844. Ex. FOUNDED BY SIR THOMAS GRESHAM, A.D. 1566. PROCLAIMED ROYAL EXCHANGE 1570.

Reverse: Queen Victoria upon a dais, attended by Prince Albert, receiving an address from the Lord Mayor of London. Ex. PRESENTATION OF THE CITY ADDRESS.
51 mm   a) copper; b) white metal.

DESTROYED IN THE GREAT FIRE 1666 RESTORED, 1667. AGAIN DESTROYED BY FIRE, 1838 FIRST STONE OF PRESENT EDIFICE LAID BY H.R.H. PRINCE ALBERT JANUARY 17. 1842.
Signed: J. DAVIS MEDALLIST BY COMMAND TO H.R.H. PRINCE ALBERT on the exergual line.

Literature: Brown 2177; Eidlitz 990; Taylor 146s.

18. Opening of the new Royal Exchange, 1844.

Obverse: conjoined and draped busts of Prince Albert and Queen Victoria, left, she diademed. QUEEN VICTORIA & PR: ALBERT. Above, crown and crossed sceptres on cushion. Around, a broad raised border of oak, shamrock, rose and thistle.

Reverse: view of the ROYAL EXCHANGE LONDON Ex. FIRST STONE LAID JAN. 19 1842 BY H.R.H. PRINCE ALBERT OPENED BY H.M.G.M. VICTORIA OCTR 23 1844 On the exergual line W. TITE ESQ ARCH: Standing figures, left and right, on a broad raised border inscribed, on upper section FOUNDED BY SIR THOMAS GRESHAM KNT: 1566, OPENED IN STATE AND PRO-CLAIMED 'ROYAL EXCHANGE' BY Q: ELIZABETH 1570, DESTROYED BY THE GREAT FIRE 1666 and on lower section FIRST STONE OF THE SECOND BUILDING LAID BY KING CHARLES THE SECOND 1667 WHICH WAS ALSO DESTROYED BY FIRE JANY 10 1838.
Signed: ALLEN & MOORE BIRM. on the exergual line.
51 mm   a) copper; b) white metal.
Literature: Brown 2173; Taylor 146k.

19. Opening of the new Royal Exchange, 1844.

Obverse: view of the NEW ROYAL EXCHANGE LONDON Ex. FIRST STONE LAID JAN. 17. 1842 BY H.R.H. PRINCE ALBERT. OPENED BY H.M.G.M. VICTORIA OCT. 28. 1844.
Signed: DAVIS BIRM. in the exergue.

Reverse: (similar to No. 17) Queen Victoria upon a dais, attended by Prince Albert, receiving an address from the Lord Mayor of London. Ex. PRESENTATION OF THE ADDRESS.
44 mm   a) copper; b) white metal.
Literature: Brown 2179; Taylor 146r.

---

20.   Opening of the new Royal Exchange, 1844.

Obverse: conjoined busts, left. QUEEN VICTORIA & PRINCE ALBERT.
Signed: J. DAVIS BIRM below the busts.
Reverse: (as the obverse of No. 22) view of the NEW ROYAL EXCHANGE LONDON Ex. FIRST STONE LAID JAN. 19. 1842 BY H.R.H. PRINCE ALBERT. OPENED BY H.M.G.M. VICTORIA OCT. 28. 1844.
Signed: DAVIS BIRM at the edge.
43 mm   a) white metal.
Literature: Brown 2178; Taylor 146q.
Obverse only illustrated.

---

21.   Opening of the new Royal Exchange, 1844.

Obverse: (as No. 19) view of the NEW ROYAL EXCHANGE LONDON Ex. FIRST STONE LAID JAN. 17. 1842 BY H.R.H. PRINCE ALBERT. OPENED BY H.M.G.M. VICTORIA. OCT. 28. 1844.
Signed: DAVIS BIRM. in the exergue.

Reverse: equestrian statue inscribed SERINGAPATAM ASSYE TALAVERA BADAJOZ SALAMANCA VITTORIA TOULOUSE WATERLOO on the pedestal. THE WELLINGTON STATUE IN FRONT OF THE ROYAL EXCHANGE LONDON Ex. ERECTED JUNE 18. 1844.
43 mm   a) copper; b) white metal.
Literature: Eimer 123.

22. Opening of the new Royal Exchange, 1844.

Obverse: (as the reverse of No. 20) view of the NEW ROYAL EXCHANGE LONDON Ex. FIRST STONE LAID JAN. 19. 1842 BY H.R.H. PRINCE ALBERT. OPENED BY H.M.G.M. VICTORIA. 1844
Signed: DAVIS BIRM. in the exergue.

Reverse: (as No. 21) equestrian statue inscribed SERINGAPATAM ASSYE TALAVERA BADAJOZ SALAMANCA VITTORIA TOULOUSE WATERLOO on the pedestal. THE WELLINGTON STATUE IN FRONT OF THE ROYAL EXCHANGE LONDON Ex. ERECTED JUNE 18. 1844.
43 mm   a) copper; b) white metal.
Literature: Brown 2196; Eidlitz 992; Eimer 124; Taylor 146p.

---

23. Opening of the new Royal Exchange, 1844.

Obverse: conjoined and draped busts, left, she diademed. QUEEN VICTORIA AND PRINCE ALBERT.
Signed: ALLEN & MOORE BIRM. at the edge.

Reverse: view of the ROYAL EXCHANGE LONDON At the edge WM TITE ESQ ARC. Ex. FIRST STONE LAID JAN: 19 1842 BY H.R.H. PRINCE ALBERT OPENED BY H.M.G.M. VICTORIA 1844.
Signed: ALLEN & MOORE. BIRM. at the edge.
39 mm   a) copper; b) white metal.
Literature: Brown 2174; Taylor 146j.
Allen & Moore's signature is occasionally indistinct.

24.   Opening of the new Royal Exchange, 1844.

Obverse: (similar to the reverse of No. 23) view of the ROYAL EXCHANGE LONDON W TITE ESQ: ARCH: Ex. FIRST STONE LAID JAN: 19. 1842 BY H.R.H. PRINCE ALBERT. OPENED BY H.M.G.M. VICTORIA 1844.
Signed: ALLEN & MOORE. BIRM. at the edge.

Reverse: (as No. 14) equestrian statue. THE WELLINGTON STATUE LONDON ERECTED JUNE 18 1844. SIR F. CHANTRY. SC: Ex. COST £9000 RAISED BY PUBLIC SUBSCRIPTION. THE METAL WORTH £1500 GIVEN BY GOVERNMENT.
39 mm   a) copper; b) white metal.
Literature: Brown 2192; Eidlitz 991; Eimer 126; Taylor 146i.
Allen & Moore's signature is occasionally indistinct.

25.   Opening of the new Royal Exchange, 1844.

Obverse: view of the ROYAL EXCHANGE LONDON Ex. FIRST STONE LAID BY H.R.H. PRINCE ALBERT JAN. 17. 1842 OPENED BY THE QUEEN OCT. 28. 1844
Signed: J. TAYLOR BIRM at the edge.

Reverse: equestrian statue almost facing. THE WELLINGTON STATUE LONDON ERECTED JUNE 18. 1844.
39 mm   a) copper; b) white metal.
Literature: Brown 2199; Eidlitz 993; Eimer 127; Taylor 146w.

26.   Opening of the new Royal Exchange, 1844.
Obverse: view of the ROYAL EXCHANGE LONDON Ex. FIRST STONE LAID BY H.R.H. PRINCE ALBERT JAN. 17. 1842 OPENED BY THE QUEEN OCT. 28. 1844.

Reverse: view of THE NEW HOUSES OF PARLIAMENT Ex. C. BARRY ESQ: ARCHT:
39 mm   a) white metal.
Literature: Brown 2184.

The description for this medal has been taken from Brown, who attributes it to W. J. Taylor. An example has not been examined.

27.   Opening of the new Royal Exchange, 1844.
Obverse: view of the ROYAL EXCHANGE Ex. LONDON.

Reverse: three-line inscription WILLIAM TITE ARCHI-
TECT 1844.
32 mm   Unsigned. a) copper.
Literature: Brown 2187; Eidlitz 988; Taylor 146y.
Not illustrated.

---

28.   Opening of the new Royal Exchange, 1844.

Obverse: view of the NEW ROYAL EXCHANGE Ex. FIRST
STONE LAID JAN. 17. 1842 BY PRINCE ALBERT OPENED
BY THE QUEEN OCT. 28. 1844.
Reverse: equestrian statue. THE WELLINGTON STATUE
LONDON ERECTED JUNE 18. 1844 Ex. COST £9000.
31 mm   Unsigned. a) white metal.
Literature: Eimer 128.

---

29.   Opening of the new Royal Exchange, 1844.
Obverse: head of H.R.H. ALBERT PRINCE OF SAXE
COBURG AND GOTHA

Reverse: view of the NEW ROYAL EXCHANGE Ex. FIRST
STONE LAID JAN. 17. 1842 BY PRINCE ALBERT OPENED
BY THE QUEEN OCT. 28. 1844.
31 mm   Unsigned. a) white metal.
Literature: Brown 2188.

The description for this medal has been taken from Brown. An example has not been examined.

---

30.   Opening of the new Royal Exchange, 1844.

Obverse: conjoined busts, left. QUEEN VICTORIA &
PRINCE ALBERT.
Reverse: view of the NEW ROYAL EXCHANGE Ex. THE
FIRST STONE LAID BY H.R.H. PRINCE ALBERT 1842
COMPLETED 1844.
Signed: DAVIS BIRM. in the exergue.
30 mm   a) copper.
Literature: Brown 2180; Taylor 1460.

---

31.   Opening of the new Royal Exchange, 1844.
Obverse: Conjoined and draped busts, left. QUEEN
VICTORIA & PRINCE ALBERT OF SAXE COBURG &
GOTHA.

Reverse: (similar to No. 30) view of the NEW ROYAL
EXCHANGE Ex. THE FIRST STONE LAID BY H.R.H.
PRINCE ALBERT 1842 COMPLETED 1844.
Signed: DAVIS BIRM. in the exergue.
30 mm   a) white metal.
Literature: Brown 2181.

The description for this medal has been taken from Brown. An example has not been examined.

32.   Opening of the new Royal Exchange, 1844.

Obverse: bust of Queen Victoria, diademed, left. ROYAL EXCHANGE OPENED BY H:M: QUEEN VICTORIA OCT. 28 1844.
Signed: w. w. on the truncation.
Reverse: three shields upon a wreath, a grasshopper (Sir Thomas Gresham's personal badge) above. FIRST STONE LAID BY H.R.H. PRINCE ALBERT JANY. 17 1842.
28 mm   a) silver; b) copper.
Literature: Brown 2186.
Obverse only illustrated.

33.   Opening of the new Royal Exchange, 1844.

Obverse: (similar to No. 32) bust of Queen Victoria, diademed, left. ROYAL EXCHANGE OPENED BY H:M: QUEEN VICTORIA OCT. 28 1844.
Reverse: three shields upon a wreath, grasshopper above. FIRST STONE LAID BY H.R.H. PRINCE ALBERT JANY. 17 1842.
Signed: H. HYAMS LONDON below wreath.
28 mm   a) white metal.
Literature: Unpublished.
Reverse only illustrated.

34.   Opening of the new Royal Exchange, 1844.

Obverse: view of the ROYAL EXCHANGE LONDON Ex. FIRST STONE LAID JAN. 19. 1842 BY H.R.H. PRINCE ALBERT OPENED BY H.M.G.M. VICTORIA 1844.
Signed: ALLEN & MOORE BIRM. at the edge.
Reverse: equestrian statue. THE WELLINGTON STATUE LONDON ERECTED 1844. Ex. RAISED BY PUBLIC SUBSCRIPTION TOTAL VALUE L10500.
27 mm   a) white metal.
Literature: Brown 2193; Eimer 129; Taylor 146h.
Allen & Moore's signature is occasionally indistinct.

35.   Opening of the new Royal Exchange, 1844.

Obverse: view of the NEW ROYAL EXCHANGE Ex. LONDON.
Reverse: seven-line inscription THE FIRST STONE LAID BY PRINCE ALBERT JAN. 17. 1842 OPENED BY QUEEN VICTORIA OCT. 28. 1844.
25 mm   Unsigned. a) brass.
Literature: Brown 2189.

36. Opening of the new Royal Exchange, 1844.

Obverse: bust right. PRINCE ALBERT BORN AUGUST 26. 1819.

Reverse: view of the NEW ROYAL EXCHANGE Ex. THE FIRST STONE LAID BY H.R.H. PRINCE ALBERT 1842 COMPLETED 1844.

Signed: DAVIS on the groundline.

24 mm a) copper.

Literature: Brown 2182; Taylor 146m.

---

37. Opening of the new Royal Exchange, 1844.

Obverse: bust left. VICTORIA BORN MAY 24. 1819. CROW. JUNE 28. 1838. MARR. FEB 10. 1840.

Reverse: (as No. 36) view of the NEW ROYAL EXCHANGE Ex. THE FIRST STONE LAID BY H.R.H. PRINCE ALBERT 1842 COMPLETED 1844.

Signed: DAVIS on the groundline.

24 mm a) white metal.

Literature: Brown 2183; Taylor 146l.

---

38. Opening of the new Royal Exchange, 1844.

Obverse: (as the reverse of No. 36) view of the NEW ROYAL EXCHANGE Ex. THE FIRST STONE LAID BY H.R.H. PRINCE ALBERT 1842 COMPLETED 1844.

Signed: DAVIS on the groundline.

Reverse: equestrian statue. THE WELLINGTON STATUE LONDON. ERECTED JUNE 18. 1844 Ex. WATERLOO.

24 mm a) copper; b) white metal.

Literature: Brown 2197; Eimer 130; Taylor 146n.

---

39. Opening of the new Royal Exchange, 1844.

Obverse: conjoined and draped busts, left. QUEEN VICTORIA AND PRINCE ALBERT.

Signed: A & M on the truncation.

Reverse: view of the ROYAL EXCHANGE LONDON Ex. FIRST STONE LAID 1842 BY P: ALBERT OPENED BY QUEEN VICTORIA 1844.

22 mm a) copper; b) brass.

Literature: Brown 2175; Eidlitz 995; Taylor 146f.

40.   Opening of the new Royal Exchange, 1844.

Obverse: (similar to the reverse of No. 39) view of the ROYAL EXCHANGE LONDON Ex. FIRST STONE LAID 1842 BY P: ALBERT OPENED BY QUEEN VICTORIA 1844.

Reverse: equestrian statue. WELLINGTON STATUE LONDON ERECTED 1844 Ex. COST L9000 RAISED BY SUBSCRIPTION.

22 mm   Unsigned. a) copper; b) brass.

Literature: Brown 2200; Eimer 131; Taylor 146g.

---

41.   Opening of the new Royal Exchange, 1844.

Obverse: view of the NEW ROYAL EXCHANGE LONDON Ex. FIRST STONE LAID 1842 BY P: ALBERT OPENED BY QUEEN VICTORIA 1844.

Reverse: (as No. 40) equestrian statue. WELLINGTON STATUE LONDON ERECTED 1844 Ex. COST L9000 RAISED BY SUBSCRIPTION.

22 mm   Unsigned. a) copper.

Literature: Eimer 132.

---

42.   Opening of the new Royal Exchange, 1844.

Obverse: view of the ROYAL EXCHANGE LONDON Ex. FIRST STONE LAID JAN. 19 1842 OPENED OCT. 28. 1844.

Reverse: Imperial crown within closed wreath.

22 mm   Unsigned. a) brass.

Literature: Brown 2190.

The description for this medal has been taken from Brown. An example has not been examined.

---

43.   Royal Exchange, 1842 / Houses of Parliament, 1845.

Obverse: view of the Houses of Parliament. Ex. PARLIAMENT HOUSE DESTROYED BY FIRE OCT 16 1835 REBUILT 1844–5.

Signed: PUBLISHED BY HYAM HYAMS. CORNHILL. in the exergue.

Reverse: (as No. 3) façade of the NEW ROYAL EXCHANGE Ex. THE FOUNDATION STONE LAID BY H.R.H. PRINCE ALBERT JANUARY 1842.

Signed: T.H. at edge, and PUBLISHED BY HYAM HYAMS. CORNHILL. in the exergue.

61 mm   a) white metal.

Literature: Brown 2212; Taylor 179f.

Obverse only illustrated.

44. Equestrian Statue of Wellington, 1844 / Death of Wellington, 1852.

Obverse: bust right. FIELD MARSHAL ARTHUR DUKE OF WELLINGTON. K.G.

Reverse: equestrian statue upon a pedestal, inscribed BORN MAY I. 1769 DIED. SEP. 14. 1852 on its base. THE WELLINGTON STATUE IN FRONT OF THE ROYAL EXCHANGE LONDON ERECTED JUNE 18 1844.
41 mm   Unsigned. a) copper; b) white metal.
Literature: Brown 2493; Eimer 157.

ARTISTS, MEDALLISTS AND PUBLISHERS

John Allen and Joseph Moore, Birmingham: Nos. 14, 18, 23, 24, 34, 39.
J. Barber, London: No. 1.
Joseph Davis, Birmingham: Nos. 6, 12, 13, 15, 17, 19–22, 30, 31, 36–38.
William Griffin, London: Nos. 9, 10.
Thomas Halliday, Birmingham: Nos. 3–5, 11, 43.
Hyam Hyams, London: Nos. 1, 4, 5, 11, 32, 43.
Alfred Joseph Stothard, London: No. 7.
James Taylor, Birmingham: Nos. 25, 26.
William Wyon, London: Nos. 8, 15, 32.

ABBREVIATIONS

AE	COPPER/BRONZE
AR	SILVER
BM	BRITISH MUSEUM
Ex.	EXERGUE
NAM	NATIONAL ARMY MUSEUM
PC	PRIVATE COLLECTION
WM	WHITE METAL

PHOTOGRAPH CREDITS

1	BM (AE)		23	BM (WM)
2	Spink & Son Ltd		24	PC (AE)
3	BM (AE)		25	NAM (AE)
4	—		26	—
5	BM (WM)		27	—
6	BM (AE)		28	NAM (WM)
7	BM (AE)		29	—
8	PC (AR)		30	BM (AE)
9	—		31	—
10	—		32	BM (AR)
11	NAM (WM)		33	BM (WM)
12	NAM (WM)		34	PC (AE)
13	BM (WM)		35	PC (AE)
14	PC (WM)		36	BM (AE)
15	PC (AE)		37	BM (WM)
16	BM (WM)		38	PC (WM)
17	PC (AE)		39	PC (AE)
18	BM (WM)		40	NAM (AE)
19	BM (AE)		41	PC (AE)
20	BM (WM)		42	—
21	BM (AE)		43	BM (WM)
22	PC (WM)		44	PC (WM)

BIBLIOGRAPHY

BROWN, L.   *British Historical Medals*, Vol. 2, 1837–1901 (London, 1987).

EIDLITZ, R.   *Medals and Medallions relating to Architects* (New York, 1927).

EIMER, C.   *Medallic Portraits of the Duke of Wellington* (London, 1994).

HAWKINS, R.N.P.   *A Dictionary of Makers of British metallic tickets, checks, medalets, tallies, and counters 1788–1910* (London, 1989).

TAYLOR, J.   *The Architectural Medal: England in the Nineteenth Century* (London, 1978).

CHAPTER XXXI

Office Buildings in the City:
Royal Exchange Buildings (1841–45)

By PETER JEFFERSON SMITH

OFFICE BUILDINGS IN THE CITY

OFFICES, ESPECIALLY THOSE built for letting, are apt to have short lives and to be little regarded by historians. The first Royal Exchange Buildings, an office block just to the east of the Royal Exchange in the City of London, was no exception; built in 1845, it was demolished in 1907. It appears in the architectural histories as an example of the Italianate palazzo style, and as an illustration of the early work of its distinguished architect, Edward I'Anson, jun., and indeed the building that made his reputation. An adjoining block, 22 Finch Lane, was probably built as an associated development, almost certainly by I'Anson, and remarkably still stands. Little known, it is probably the oldest extant office block in London.

I first came across Royal Exchange Buildings when researching the history of the firm of Edward I'Anson and Son. There was a conflict in the literature over who I'Anson was building for,[1] and that led me to look for source material. The development (to use twentieth-century terminology) turned out to be exceptionally well documented, partly because the landowner was an Oxford college, and partly because negotiations and disputes between the developers, the City Corporation and adjoining owners or occupiers have left plenty of traces in the archives.

Edward I'Anson, jun., became one of the leading commercial architects of Victorian London. Born in

1811, the son of an architect and surveyor of the same name, when he died in 1888 he had recently completed a term as President of the Surveyors' Institution and was still in office as President of the RIBA — the only person ever to hold both posts. He was a distinguished and prolific designer of City offices, and a pioneer of one type, the lettable office.

In the nineteenth century, as now, there were two different types of office building, or more precisely, two types of client. One of these was the single large firm, building premises for its own occupation. In the City, this was often a bank or insurance company, but it could also be a large commercial business, combining sales or administration premises with a warehouse. Well before I'Anson started practising, banks and insurers had set the trend, at first in Westminster and Fleet Street, but then starting to build imposing new premises in the financial centre of the City in the late 1830s.

The other sort of building was the lettable office block — the 'spec' office, we would now call it. This is a type of building now familiar in all cities, designed for and built by a landlord or property developer without a specific occupier in mind, and intended for letting in anything from single rooms to whole floors or blocks. The lettable office first emerged in the early nineteenth century, and I'Anson did more than anyone else to take it forward.

In 1864, he read a paper to the RIBA entitled 'Some Notice of Office Buildings in the City of London'.[2] This readable account is still a major source for historians. In it, he described the growth of office buildings, and his own share in it:

There were in the City of London, in my recollection, some thirty years ago, certain houses let out in separate

This study is based mainly on archival material held by Magdalen College, Oxford and the Corporation of London. I am very grateful for the access and help I have had, from Dr J. B. Cottis, the former College Archivist, and from the staff of the Corporation of London Record Office and the Guildhall Library.

[1] Henry-Russell Hitchcock, *Early Victorian Architecture in Britain* (Yale, 1954), p. 381: the commission may have come from Magdalen College, Oxford. Edward I'Anson, jun., in *Transactions of the Royal Institute of British Architects (TRIBA)* (1864), pp. 25–26: for Sir Francis Moon.

[2] *TRIBA* (1864), pp. 25–36.

floors, and used as offices — but these were few — and it is quite within my recollection when merchants dwelt in the city over their counting-houses, and next to their warehouses, going to their country houses at Edmonton, Tottenham, and Hackney . . .

But in those days buildings erected expressly for offices were not known, and the first building which I remember to have been erected for that special purpose was a stack of office buildings in Clement's Lane, at the end nearest to Lombard Street. They were erected by the late Mr. Voysey, about the year 1823, and although he was a skilful and able man, there was not sufficient professional occupation for him here, and he finished his professional career and his life in Jamaica. [He was grandfather of the more famous architect of the same name.]

The first building in which I was myself engaged was an office building, forming one of a large block in Moorgate Street, built about the year 1837; but the adjoining buildings were built on the old plan of offices and dwelling-houses over, and although in the course of their erection another of the buildings was built principally for an office, yet, as originally designed, it was for a dwelling house. Shortly after this period, however, the building of offices increased largely. In 1842 I was engaged in building Royal Exchange Buildings, and some buildings adjoining, for Sir Francis Moon; and these latter buildings, more particularly, were built with special reference to being let as offices, and as a financial operation, it has, I believe, been eminently successful.[3]

The lettable office met a demand to accommodate more and more businesses in the confined space of the City, in the nineteenth century the world's leading financial and trading centre. At first the demand could be met, as I'Anson pointed out, by turning over existing houses to office use. Those of us who live in the suburbs tend to assume that the City residents moved out because they preferred our sort of living. But in an 1872 paper to RIBA 'On the Valuation of House Property in London'[4] I'Anson said:

The families which, in my youth, lived in its narrow lanes have utterly deserted it, not because the City is unhealthy or inconvenient, but because the rooms formerly used as living rooms are more valuable as offices, a citizen may now live in a suburban villa or even in a Belgravian or Tyburnian mansion, upon the rent he obtains for the drawing-room floor of the house wherein his ancestors lived for generations.[5]

Those who had left included the I'Ansons themselves; their practice was run from a house next to that where Edward and his brothers and sisters had been born and brought up; but by 1841, none of the family lived there. The residential population of the City as measured by the Census peaked in 1851 and then started to fall rapidly. But this peak resulted from still rapid growth in the parishes outside the ancient walls; within the walls, the population was already static or declining. In 1866, the City made its first estimate of the day-time population.[6] By that time, the day-time population exceeded the residents by 80,000. How many daily incomers there were in the early 1840s is not known; but it is fair to assume that the build-up had already started.

'Old London, the London as rebuilt after the great fire of 1666 (for there are but few and isolated houses of an earlier period) is fast wearing out', said I'Anson.[7] Although his own firm worked from post-fire houses for over a century, many businesses, typically the banks and insurance companies, found the old houses no longer adequate. Their new buildings produced as a by-product a further important source of lettable office accommodation. Summerson comments that the Victorian rebuilding had the objects of commodity, prestige and investment. The firms got the specialist accommodation they required, behind a rich façade which advertised their worth; and the remaining space in the building could be flexibly partitioned and let as offices.[8]

A third source of supply of offices was rebuilding linked to street improvements. These started about 1830, with the rebuilding of London Bridge, and were carried through by the City Corporation's London Bridge Approaches Committee. The driving force was its Chairman, Richard Lambert Jones (1783–1863). He began his career as a builder and was later described as a house agent. He had a plain-speaking manner, and ambitions as a City improver, impatient with those who made difficulties. 'Any success that I was entitled to obtain', he wrote in his

---

[3] Ibid., pp. 25–26.
[4] *TRIBA* (1872), pp. 39–54.
[5] Ibid., p. 40.

[6] Benjamin Scott, *A Statistical Vindication of the City of London* (London, 1867).
[7] *TRIBA* (1872), p. 42.
[8] 'The Victorian Rebuilding of the City of London, 1840–1870', in *The Unromantic Castle* (London, 1990), pp. 195–96.

Reminiscences,[9] 'must be ascribed to a certain firmness of character which I possessed, and to a resolute determination to discharge with fidelity every trust reposed in me.' He showed an extraordinary ability to push his schemes through City colleagues, Cabinet ministers and Church leaders, who he persuaded to demolish Wren churches. (But if we regret that, London historians should remember him with gratitude whenever they use his creation, the Guildhall Library.)

Under Jones, the Approaches Committee gradually took its remit far beyond what anyone could regard as the Bridge approaches. Its original task was to build good approaches, north and south, to the new Bridge; to do this, it had powers of compulsory purchase under private Acts of Parliament, backed by powers to borrow secured mainly on duties on coal and wine shipped into London. From 1831, the year the Bridge opened, it started to use the same procedures, backed by its considerable income, to promote legislation to take the improvements further, to east and west, but mainly to the north. A new street was pushed through, from the main Bridge approach, to the Mansion House and Bank; by the late 1830s, Princes Street had been improved and a new street cut to Moorgate. By the early 1840s, the Committee was prepared to handle improvements anywhere in the City, whether connected with the Bridge approaches or not.

The method followed in street improvements was to buy up the houses needed to provide a widened or new thoroughfare with adequate buildings flanking it. The resulting building sites were then let or sold off to developers, who could build as they wished, but subject to uniformity in outward appearance. Thus, on the streets from the new Bridge to Moorgate, all the façades had to conform to designs by Sir Robert Smirke. Behind the façades, the buildings could be designed traditionally, as houses over ground-floor offices or shops. But whatever the appearance, the rooms above the ground floor were more likely to be occupied as offices than lived in. The office building which I'Anson designed as part of the Moorgate Street improvement would have looked from the outside like a house.

There was profit to be made from City redevelopment — but the extent was critically affected by time and place, as I'Anson pointed out in his 1872 paper on valuation. He explained how the City is divided up into distinct markets. Round the Royal Exchange was the money market, with the Stock Exchange, the Bank of England and the offices of the great insurance companies and the merchant banks.

> This is the most valuable part of the City, as much as £40 per superficial foot having been given for land in this situation; £30 a foot is by no means an uncommon price for land in good positions, but precious as is the commodity the extreme value obtains over a very limited area, and a very short distance from this favoured locality the value of land falls to one half or even one third of the price realised in the best portions.[10]

So Royal Exchange Buildings was on one of the most valuable sites in the City.

At a discussion at the RIBA in 1864, which followed I'Anson's paper on office building, he said that 'the value of land had, in some parts, trebled within the last few years, until it had increased beyond all proportion to that of the buildings placed upon it'.[11] In his 1872 paper, he referred again to the trebling in value, and added:

> This increase in value, although subject to some fluctuations, dependent upon the prosperity or depression of commerce, has upon the whole, been constantly maintained, so that it has grown to be a proverb, that you must make a profit upon building in the City.[12]

These were the conditions which made the lettable office an attractive proposition. With hindsight, therefore, it is not surprising that Royal Exchange Buildings was intended as offices; a rebuilding following a street improvement was more likely to be that than anything else. But — with the possible exception of Voysey's building in Clement's Lane, which is known only because of what I'Anson said about it — it was the first office building to be designed as such, and to express its purpose, both internally and externally.

---

[9] *Reminiscences of the Public Life of Richard Lambert Jones Esq.,* privately printed (London, 1863) (copy in Guildhall Library (GL)).

[10] *TRIBA* (1872), pp. 39 and 40.
[11] *TRIBA* (1864), p. 34.
[12] *TRIBA* (1872), p. 40.

NAE LUCK ABOOT THE HOOSE

The opportunity for Royal Exchange Buildings came from the fire which on 10 January 1838 destroyed the Royal Exchange. The tune the chimes played as the tower fell was 'There's nae luck aboot the hoose' — 'which seemed', writes a recent historian, 'only too apt a comment'.[13]

After the fire, the City Corporation decided not only to rebuild, but to do so on a grander scale and to promote further street improvements. The destroyed Royal Exchange stood on its present site, but occupied only about two-thirds of it, at the western end, with its main façade facing south to Cornhill. As it was separated from the Mansion House/Bank crossroads by only a few houses, it was logical to link up with the main London Bridge Approaches improvements, and make the new building more visible. But the policy of taking available opportunities for improvements meant that the eastern end of the building could be tackled as well. In the summer of 1838, a private Act of Parliament was obtained, to allow the compulsory purchase of the houses at both ends of the site.[14] Those at the west end (around the present site of the Duke of Wellington's statue) were to be pulled down, to create the vista of the main portico. At the eastern end, the houses which stood round the small courts and alleys between Threadneedle Street and Cornhill were to be cleared, partly to allow for a larger site for the new Royal Exchange, and partly to allow a new roadway at its eastern end.

The land required for this roadway was the western side of a court leading off Cornhill. This was Freeman's Court, or Freman's Court, as it appears in the records of its owner, Magdalen College Oxford, which had been given the land in 1760 by Dr William Freman. This followed a fire, after which the College had built the houses then standing. John Buckler had surveyed them for the College in 1805, and his plan and elevations show a court lined by handsome houses of five storeys, with shops on the ground floor.[15] After two houses on each of the corners with Cornhill, there were six, nos. 1 and 2 on the east, nos.

5 and 6 on the west, and nos. 3 and 4 closing in the far end, and backing on to the churchyard of St Benet Fink, a Wren church on Threadneedle Street. No. 3 was the largest house, with six bays overlooking the churchyard.

At this period, the College depended for its income on property rentals, and its London portfolio was a main contributor.[16] It was actively managed, in order to make the most of its potential. In the early years of the century, the College started using the services of Edward I'Anson, sen., at that time partner of Daniel Alexander in a City-based firm of architects and surveyors. By the second decade of the century, I'Anson was being given a free hand by the College to value properties and settle rentals, as well as approving rebuilding plans.[17] Now in his sixties and nearing retirement, he had recently been joined in practice by his talented son, who, as we have seen, had been working since 1837 on City buildings.

The general policy of the College appears to have been to let for 21 years, though they would sometimes go up to 40. It would let a house as a whole; and in Freeman's Court for the most part the head lessees, even where they were occupiers, in turn sublet to a variety of small businesses. No. 3 was let to Messrs Pirie and Powles. Alderman John Pirie was a wealthy ship broker and ship owner, who became one of the original directors of P&O on its incorporation in 1840. No. 3 Freeman's Court was his business premises (he lived in Camberwell) and much of it was let out to other tenants. The house had a controversial place in the redevelopment, and the documents and plans usually refer to it as 'Alderman Pirie's'.

In 1837, the lease of Alderman Pirie's came up for renewal. Following a report from I'Anson, the College decided to offer another 21 years. They tried to get £320 a year, but after negotiation settled for £300, and early the following year Edward I'Anson, jun., drew up floor plans of the house for copying into a new lease — the plans are full of pin holes.[18] The lease was completed a few weeks after the Royal Exchange fire. It may have looked a good move at the time, but any advantage was very short term: a few months later, the Corporation's Act for

---

[13] Ann Saunders, *The Royal Exchange* (London, 1991).
[14] 1 & 2 Vic cap c. passed 10 August.
[15] Magdalen College Oxford (MCO), plan MP/1/29.

[16] Information from Dr J. B. Cottis, the College Archivist.
[17] MCO, College Order Books (typed transcript) CP/1/13.
[18] MCO, MP/1/30.

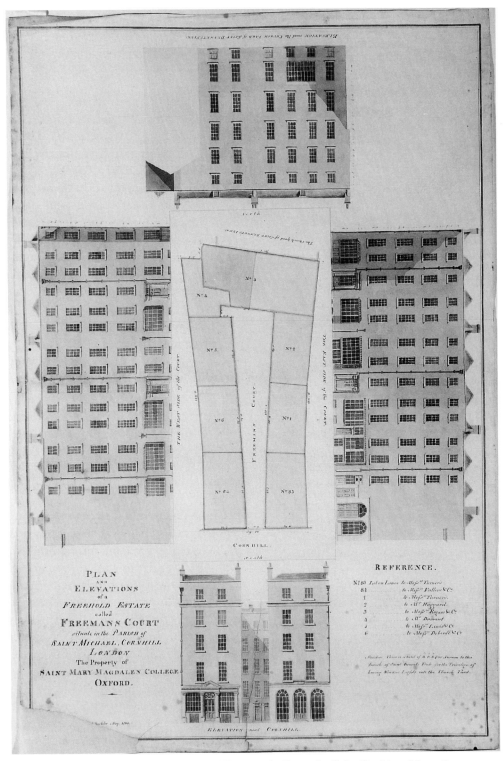

FIG. 148.   Plan and elevations of Freeman's Court, by John Buckler, May 1805.
The President and Fellows of Magdalen College, Oxford

rebuilding the Royal Exchange obliged the College to sell all the northern and western sides of Freeman's Court and 84 Cornhill, five houses in all, including Alderman Pirie's.

The College did not oppose the sale. The price, determined by a referee, was £26,071: this may seem a large sum; but at something over £5,000 a house, it was in line with what other owners in the same area received.[19] A valuer for the Corporation assessed the remainder of Pirie's lease at £875 (including compensation for loss and damage on removal of fittings); but it is not clear from the records whether this was paid.[20] Most of the house remained in being, and during 1841, the Corporation used it as the New Royal Exchange Architect's Office;[21] at the time of the Census, it was lived in by the Clerk of the Works, an architect, Henry Russell, with his wife and young family.[22] By the end of the year, the Corporation had demolished part of it, and cleared the rest of the site.

The process of improvement and redevelopment could have stopped there. There would have been (from south to north) one house at the corner with Cornhill, then two houses in the Court itself, then, projecting forwards, most of Alderman Pirie's house, presenting a flank wall to the new Exchange. But the Corporation had already decided to go further, and was able to do so, because it needed further powers. The main reasons were that the money authorised for purchase of property was not enough, and the time limit insufficient. R. L. Jones persuaded the Commons Select Committee on Metropolis Improvements that more money and time should be allowed,[23] and a Bill was prepared to do this.

Only one copy of the Bill has survived, as it happens in the archives of Magdalen College.[24] It

enabled the Corporation to raise more money and gave it longer to make the purchases authorised by the 1838 Act; and it authorised compulsory purchases for a miscellany of street improvements for various parts of the City. One of these was for the area to the east of the new Royal Exchange. A wide public way was to be achieved by the compulsory purchase and demolition of the east side of Freeman's Court and to its north the Church of St Benet Fink; from there eastwards, Threadneedle Street was to be widened by demolition of most of the south side.

In a Schedule, as was customary, the Bill listed all the freeholders, lessees and occupiers affected; and this brings into the story a wealthy and influential City figure who was to play a major part in the redevelopment, Francis Graham Moon. At that time a Common Councillor, he was soon to become a Sheriff of London and Middlesex, in 1844 an Alderman, and later still Lord Mayor and a baronet.[25] He had made his money as a successful book- and printseller, and invested in property. He was directly affected by the Bill, which would have taken his shop on the corner of Finch Lane and Threadneedle Street; and he was also acquiring other property in the area affected. The outcome for him was very successful, and in 1864, Edward I'Anson, jun., felt able to state that that he had built Royal Exchange Buildings for Moon, without even mentioning the College.

How far Moon planned or foresaw this outcome cannot be known. But by early 1841, he had obtained the leases of 1 and 2 Freeman's Court. The Schedule to the Bill shows him as sole lessee of No. 2, which he taken over from a firm of solicitors, Smith and Alliston. At No. 1, he had become co-lessee with the Eagle Insurance Company. The Eagle was also co-lessee of 83 Cornhill, the corner building, with Messrs Baily, a firm of stationers and booksellers.

The Corporation's Bill was promoted in Parliament in February 1841. This time, Magdalen College decided to oppose what they described in their College Orders as a bill 'by which it is intended to deprive the College of their property in Freman's Court'. They instructed Parliamentary agents, and on 4 May fixed the College seal to a petition against

[19] CLRO, Final Report to the Court of Common Council from the London Bridge Approaches Committee (LBAC), 27 January 1847, Appendix: Claims in respect of property.
[20] CLRO, Royal Exchange and Gresham Committee. Box of loose documents: award dated 4 December 1840.
[21] Kelly's *Directory* for 1842. (All references to Kelly's *Directory* taken from microfilm set in GL.)
[22] Census returns for Parish of St Michael Cornhill (Microfiche in GL). CLRO, Minutes of the Royal Exchange and Gresham Committee for 22 November 1841 describe Russell as 'late Clerk of the Works'.
[23] Second Report of the Select Committee on Metropolis Improvements 1840.
[24] MCO, EP/251/19.

[25] CLRO, Biographical notes folder.

the Bill.[26] A month later to the day, Lord Melbourne lost a 'no confidence' motion by one vote, and Parliament was dissolved for the General Election. So the Bill was for the time being lost. On 15 November 1841, however, the London Bridge Approaches Committee of the Corporation decided to renew its application to Parliament;[27] and some time around then, the moves started which led to the Freeman's Court site being developed under the ownership of the College.

A material factor was that the Corporation had decided on a less ambitious redevelopment. It dropped the scheme for widening Threadneedle Street, and decided not to extend the public highway to cover the entire site of Freeman's Court. It is probable that by the late autumn this was known to Moon, the I'Ansons and the College, and this made it possible for the College as freeholder, with a willing tenant, to prepare its own scheme.

The first evidence of this is two plans at Magdalen College, dated December 1841, prepared by Edward I'Anson and Son. One shows the whole area around the new Royal Exchange, and on it there are notes in the handwriting of Edward I'Anson, jun., of some of the present occupiers, notably banks and insurance companies, and in Princes Street the offices of the Great Western Railway: it shows very clearly the commercial importance of the Freeman's Court site, in the heart of the City's financial sector.[28]

The other plan, also with detail in Edward I'Anson, jun.'s handwriting, is titled 'Plan showing the proposed new frontage of the Freeman's Court Estate'. The frontage is drawn as a straight line, parallel to the eastern edge of the new Royal Exchange. Two options are shown for the width of the roadway, one of 40 feet, the other of 45 feet. The consequence of drawing the frontage parallel to the Royal Exchange was a wedge-shaped site; at the southern end it was 17 to 22 feet deep; further north, at Alderman Pirie's house, it had widened out to 45 to 50 feet. The line is drawn to run beyond that, taking in the churchyard of St Benet Fink: but someone recognised the difficulty of building over the churchyard; on the College copy of the 1841 Bill, there is pencilled sidelining

against the Clause which provided for the churchyard to remain open space.[29]

There followed discussions with the Corporation. Partial agreement was reached, and in February 1842 a formal proposal was made. Edward I'Anson, jun., wrote to the Royal Exchange and Gresham Committee (also chaired by R. L. Jones):

As the idea of appropriating the site of the remaining buildings in Freeman's Court for the enlargement of the Public way is now understood to be relinquished, the President and Fellows of Magdalen College presume you will no longer think it necessary to retain their property in that locality in the Schedule to the Bill which you are about to introduce in the present session of Parliament: when you are assured that they are ready to promote your views as to the general improvement of the property in the immediate neighbourhood of the Royal Exchange.

To further this object I am authorised to submit to you the accompanying plan whereby it is proposed to erect on the line A-B a façade to be approved by your Architect — the site of the House late Alderman Pirie's to be reconveyed to the College . . .

This, and two other houses, were proposed to be rebuilt forthwith: but a third house 'being in lease for an unexpired term of 15 years cannot be rebuilt until the expiration of that period'.[30] This was probably 83 Cornhill, leased by Messrs Baily.

When the plan came to the Committee, it noted that the width of the public way was to be 48, not 35 feet. The significance of these figures is that 35 feet was the distance from the Royal Exchange to the nearest existing building, 83 Cornhill, and 48 feet was the distance to the remaining flank wall of Alderman Pirie's. The implication is that in the informal discussions the College had tried for the narrower public way, to maximise the land on which to build, but without success. The wider public way was acceptable; but the Committee did object to the plan on the ground that the whole redevelopment should be carried out at once.[31] This was understandable, since I'Anson's proposal would have meant that the view of the east front of the new Exchange from

[26] MCO, CP/1/13.
[27] CLRO, Minutes of the LBAC, 1841–45.
[28] MCO, MP/1/32 and 33.

[29] MCO, EP/251/19.
[30] CLRO, Royal Exchange and Gresham Committee, box of loose documents.
[31] CLRO, Minutes of Royal Exchange and Gresham Committee, 21 February 1842.

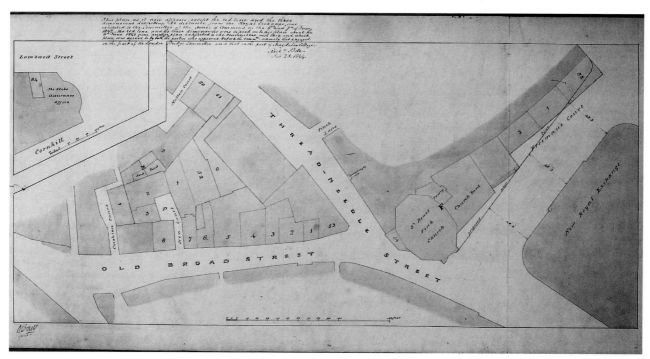

FIG. 149.   Plan exhibited to the Committee of the House of Commons on 6 and 7 June 1842, to which was
added the new line of Royal Exchange Buildings.
Corporation of London Record Office

Cornhill would have been partially obscured for the next fifteen years.

The College and the Corporation had still not reached agreement by the time the Bill came before Parliament. So once again, the College petitioned against it, and when the Bill went before a Commons Committee in June, the Committee heard from Counsel, both for the College and the Corporation. On 6 June, Richard Bell, the architect and surveyor acting for the Corporation, gave evidence. Then, as the Committee minutes record,

Mr Baines was heard on behalf of Maudlin College Oxford to propose Clauses in reference to some property belonging to them, the effect of which were to enable them to carry into effect the improvements contemplated upon that property.

Mr Gurney [Counsel for the promoters] was heard to object to a portion of the proposition of Mr Baines.

The parties were desired to confer together to endeavour to arrange the Clauses.[32]

[32] House of Lords Record Office. Evidence HC 1842, v7. London Bridge Approaches, pp. 17–18.

The record does not show how the parties differed; but they did confer, and did reach agreement. On the matter in issue in February, the College gave way: the site was to be redeveloped as a whole, with the College being given powers to purchase compulsorily existing leasehold and tenant interests. They would have six months from the Bill becoming law to declare whether they would take down and rebuild the east side of the Court. If they decided to do so, and rebuild according to the City's improvement plan, 'and according to an elevation to be prepared by the Architect of the said college within two calendar months from the passing of this Act' and approved by Common Council, they would then have $2\frac{1}{2}$ years from the passing of the Act to build and roof the buildings. Any College land not covered by the new buildings would become part of the public way.

The agreed outcome was copied on to the Corporation's plans, in the form of a red line showing the frontage of Royal Exchange Buildings and three indications of distance from the new Royal Exchange. From the central projecting portion of the Exchange, the distance was to be 46 feet 3 inches, and on either side of it 48 feet 3 inches. These were the exact distances from a frontage line drawn through the nearest undemolished corner of Alderman Pirie's house. Richard Bell wrote on one of the plans that the copying was done about 11 June and on the other, about 14 June; the inconsistency suggests that he made his notes two years later, when these distances had become an issue.[33] The Act passed on 16 July 1842.[34]

THE COLLEGE AND THE CORPORATION

The next steps, as the plans at Magdalen College show, were twofold: to sort out the property interests and to design the building. There was an unwelcome third matter, which was a dispute with the City over the distance between the proposed frontage for the new building and the Royal Exchange; but that came later. Both I'Ansons, father and son, were involved; to judge from surviving papers, Edward I'Anson, jun., designed the new building and supervised the building contract, while his father brought his experience and seniority to the negotiations and dispute with the City.

By the end 1842, it looked as if the essentials of the redevelopment had been settled. As well as the College itself, the leasehold interests to be accommodated in the new building were those of Francis Moon and Messrs Baily. The I'Ansons drew up a plan for a building that would be in a wedge shape, the frontage parallel to the new Royal Exchange, and tapering to a blunted point at the junction with Cornhill. The College was to get the premises nearest Cornhill; then there was a section for Bailys, and then for Moon (marked in both cases 'ground to be appropriated in exchange for their [or his] present site'). The final section, to the north and the widest part of the wedge, was for the College, but Moon was to 'have the first refusal if the College approve'.[35] This was mostly the site of Alderman Pirie's house. There was a formal agreement between the I'Ansons and Bailys in June[36] — perhaps also with Moon, though there is no evidence for it.

Both the rebuilding plans and the repurchase of Alderman Pirie's were approved by the College in July,[37] and the ground plan is marked by Edward I'Anson, sen., as having been 'arrang'd and agreed upon' with R. L. Jones. The next step was to obtain the formal approval of the Corporation, as the Act required, for the elevations for the new buildings. These were the work of Edward I'Anson, jun. He submitted two designs, the first in September 1842, the second, and agreed version, on 31 December.[38]

Both designs are for a four-storey building of thirteen bays. At ground level, there is what appears as a glazed-in arcade, though in fact it was intended for individual shops or merchants' premises. The two storeys above have large windows, and the top storey has square attic windows, under a bold Italianate cornice. One of the reasons why the building was significant was in giving emphasis to the upper storeys, as compared with a house, so that they became more attractive to commercial tenants. If the first elevation had been built, this would have been even clearer: the first floor windows had plain square-topped pediments, while the second floor windows had alternating angled and segmental pediments; so whilst the windows were the same size, the second floor was architecturally more significant. For whatever reason — perhaps it was too unlike a familiar City elevation — in the December plan the window surrounds were reversed, giving the more conventional prominence to the first floor. At the same time, the significance of the third floor windows was reduced by squashing them under the cornice.

This elevation got through: it is inscribed at the top, 'This elevation approved pursuant to the Provisions of the Act of Parliament for extending the Avenues to the Royal Exchange passed 16 July 1842'.

Opposite the site for Royal Exchange Buildings, the new Royal Exchange was going up. Prince Albert had laid the foundation stone in January 1842, with Lord Mayor Pirie in attendance. (By the summer he had become Sir John Pirie, Bt., in recognition of the fact that the Prince of Wales had been born on the first day of his Mayoralty.[39])

[33] CLRO, plans 27.J.4 and 27.J.7.
[34] 5 & 6 Vic cap ci.
[35] MCO, MP/1/31.
[36] MCO, EP/220/28.
[37] MCO, CP/1/13.
[38] MCO, F.1.3.1842; CLRO, plans 27.J.6 and 27.J.5.
[39] CLRO, Biographical notes folder.

In 1843, comparatively little appears in the records. It can be assumed that in the I'Ansons' office, detailed design work was going on, with the intention of drawing up bills of quantities as a basis for tendering. By July, sufficient had been done for the College to 'consent to the immediate commencement of the New Buildings' — as it turned out, a year before the event.[40] There was also the matter of transferring the ownership of Alderman Pirie's house. Around September, a valuer's award was made for the sale to the College for £7,500, and in November or December, the Corporation published the legally required notice of its intention to sell.[41]

This seems to have been retrospective, since the College had already taken possession. On 13 September, all the materials and internal fittings of the old buildings — 83 Cornhill and 1, 2 and 3 Freeman's Court — were sold by auction. Everything went — tiles, rafters, floorboards, windows, doors, shopfronts; stoves, fireplaces, gas fittings, cisterns, wcs; stone floors and copings, lead gutters and pipes; the bricks the houses were built of; and finally the stone paving of the Court itself.[42]

In November, the College decided on future lettings. Following a letter from I'Anson to Edward Blagrave, the Estates Steward of the College, they agreed that a large part of the buildings should be let to Moon for 30 years from Christmas 1844. There were conditions contained in the correspondence which has not survived; and Moon later said (at a meeting of the Approaches Committee) that he had 40 years.[43] Letting the corner house was 'left to Mr I'Anson', and the plan and cost of the new buildings delegated to the President and Bursars.[44]

But before building could begin, there was a major set-back, leading to a fierce dispute between the developers of the new building and the Corporation. As with many of the disputes in this story, reading these papers is like watching a television drama with the sound turned off: you can see the parties quarrelling and eventually agreeing, but you have to infer most of the arguments.

It started about the end of 1843 or the beginning of 1844. A wooden fence had been put across St Benet Fink churchyard, parallel to the Royal Exchange, and marking what the Corporation regarded as the eastern boundary of their new roadway. It was indeed the correct distance from the Exchange, in accordance with the 1842 Parliamentary Plan, but further east than it should have been. The disturbing conclusion was that the new Royal Exchange had been built further to the east than expected.

The developers had to work out the implications. They could establish where the frontage of the Royal Exchange ought to have been, because, under the terms of the 1838 Act, this had been approved by the Treasury and recorded on a plan, one copy of which was available for reference in the Town Clerk's office. But the question was whether the frontage of the new building should be measured from where the Exchange ought to have been, or where it actually was. If the latter was the case, the practical effect was that the whole building would be shallower than intended, and the land not used would be surrendered for the public roadway — and under the 1842 Act, the College would get no compensation; they simply lost what they did not need.

In January 1844, Edward I'Anson, jun., prepared a plan, to enable the College to take Counsel's opinion.[45] In February, Blagrave wrote to the Approaches Committee; his letter appears to have been a bid for the College to get the space it had expected, since the reply, to quote a note on the agenda paper, was in summary — 'Committee cannot alter the dimension of the roadway'.[46] This went down badly in Oxford; the College decided that 'agreeably to the opinion of Mr Tinney (the QC they had consulted) a bill for specific performance and injunction be filed without delay against the Corporation . . . to compel them to carry out the Award made by Mr Higgins on the resale to the College of a portion of the late Alderman Pirie's house . . .'.[47]

[40] MCO, CP/1/13.
[41] CLRO, Minutes of the LBAC, 11 September 1841, and Minutes of the Royal Exchange and Gresham Committee, 7 November and 18 December 1841.
[42] MCO, EP/220/5.
[43] CLRO, London Bridge Approaches Minute Papers and Letters 1841–43. Misc. MSS 69.12. Paper dated 22 April 1844.
[44] MCO, CP/1/13.

[45] MCO, MP/1/34.
[46] CLRO, Minutes of the LBAC and Misc. MSS 69.12.
[47] MCO, CP/1/13.

In late February, Lawrance and Plews, a firm of City solicitors acting for the College, started a correspondence with the Corporation. All this came before the Approaches Committee, with Tite and the Town Clerk in attendance. There was debate both on whether the Committee was in the wrong, and on what the remedies might be. One of the members of the Committee, Edward Harrison, had a stationer's business at 82 Cornhill, immediately adjoining the Royal Exchange Buildings site, and as will be seen later, an involvement with the developers. No doubt briefed by them, he 'considered that the College would meet the Committee on any equitable arrangement to give the whole space required'. This sounds like a renewed bid to allow the College to build to its intended frontage; but against this, R. L. Jones, the Chairman, 'stated the obligation of the Committee to abide by the Act of Parliament as to the Plan deposited in the Town Clerk's office'. Tite promised a report in writing; but without waiting for that, the Committee preferred to approach the College to try to agree compensation.[48]

The first attempt at a resolution for the Committee minutes was for a communication with the College 'to arrange what amount of compensation shall be paid or received by either party in consideration of property appropriated to the public way'. The agreed version was that the City Solicitor should communicate with the Solicitor of the College 'relative to any misunderstanding between themselves and the Corporation' — all without prejudice. The difference between the two motions may be partly an attempt to avoid any admission of error; but it may also be that the Committee wanted to shift the argument away from the loss of land by the College to the public way. Compensation for the loss of a strip of land, running the whole length of the new building, would be considerable; it would also be inconsistent with the provision of the 1842 Act for surrender of unused land. Instead, it would be better for the Corporation to focus on the point at which the College had an evident grievance, as Tinney's advice appeared to recognise, namely that they had bought more land from the site of Alderman Pirie's house than they would be allowed to use.

The wording of subsequent Committee minutes and papers suggests that this was the argument which Tite and the City Solicitor pursued with the College. During March, April and May negotiations took place. Tite went back to the Committee on 1 April; having met one of the I'Ansons, he thought an offer of 'a deduction' should be made at once. The Committee authorised £500, which was rejected. The developers stepped up the pressure, and now Francis Moon entered the fight himself; he wrote to Jones and Harrison, and also attended the 22 April meeting of the Committee.

At that meeting, Tite explained that £500 had been rejected, but £1,000 would be accepted. Moon 'proposed reference to Mr Barry or any other eminent and disinterested architect'. He added that he had an agreement for 40 years but would continue to pay the same rent, and made a comment about 'not so much as should be left of Sir J. Pirie's house', an indication of where the compensation argument was now focusing. This was confirmed by the Town Clerk, who 'stated extent of legal claim — no oblign on the City to pay any amot except for peace except as to the angle of Sir J. Pirie's house'. There was close debate on what more to offer: a proposal for £750 was lost 7:8, and then £1,000 carried 8:7. The payment was to be conditional on Tite certifying that the new buildings had been erected on the line in the Parliamentary plan.

Moon and the College accepted, a final round of solicitors' letters was exchanged, and the agreement was finally approved at the Approaches Committee on 13 May. On 22 May Richard Bell and Edward I'Anson, sen., agreed and signed a plan, which not only marked out the ground, with measurements from the plinth of the Royal Exchange, but also set out the land to be conveyed from the Corporation to the College.[49]

Taking account of all the changes to the site, the loss to the College, as compared with their plans when they started out, had been considerable. The outcome of the disagreement in early 1842 had been to set them back behind the building line they probably first tried for; and now they were set back further. Measuring from the extant maps is difficult;

[48] CLRO, Misc. MSS 69.12, 11 March 1844, and Minutes of LBAC, same date.

[49] CLRO, same vol. of Minutes and Misc. MSS and plan 27.J.3.

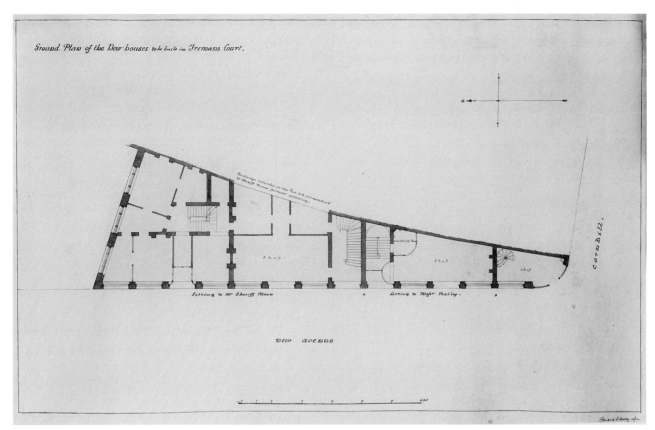

Ground Plan of the New-houses to be built on Iremans Court.

FIG. 150.   Edward I'Anson, jun.'s final ground plan for Royal Exchange Buildings, May 1844, showing the intended link
with Moon's premises in Finch Lane.
The President and Fellows of Magdalen College, Oxford

but it looks as if the worst loss was at the southern end, where the the building that I'Anson had planned to be some 20 feet deep was reduced to under 10 feet. At the northern end, it was not so bad; the lost section of Alderman Pirie's house was no more than two feet. But with built-up land changing hands at over £5 a square foot, as evidenced by the sales from and to the College, £1,000 was little enough compensation. The land lost from Alderman Pirie's house was only a few square feet; but compared with what had been agreed in June 1842, the total reduction in the size of the site for building was (very roughly) 300 square feet or more.

ROYAL EXCHANGE BUILDINGS, AND SOME BUILDINGS ADJOINING

This dispute held up work on the new buildings, which under the Act should have been built and roofed by January 1845. But now it was out of the way, building could proceed. In May 1844, Edward I'Anson, jun., settled the ground plan of the new buildings. Starting at the blunted point of the wedge (the southern end, on the right as you stood with your back to the Royal Exchange and looked at the site) there was: first, a shop with one bay and a curved corner entrance, with stairs at the back to the upper floors; that would be available to the College for letting. Next, four bays for letting to Messrs Baily, equivalent to their former premises; there was a ground-floor shop with a counting house in one corner, and one bay was filled by a staircase to the upper floors. Thirdly, the next three bays were those which had been allocated in 1842 to Moon as equivalent to his former premises; but in fact he got the whole of the remaining eight bays, divided into two sets of accommodation, with two staircases. This was both the widest and deepest part of the new building; and in the middle of it, at the back, there is a note in Edward I'Anson, jun.'s hand, 'Buildings intended at this point to be connected with Mr Sheriff Moon's premises adjoining' — these, in Finch Lane, will be described later.[50]

On 2 July a contract was signed by the College with Thos and Wm Piper, a large firm of London builders, for £12,466.[51] Before they could start, there was yet another skirmish with the Approaches Committee. This time, I think it was the I'Ansons who found themselves on the wrong foot, since they appeared to have taken for granted Corporation approval of the vaults they intended to build under the roadway. In July, the Approaches Committee instructed the Comptroller of the City to write to Lawrance and Plews to say that the College could not proceed with vaults until plans had been approved. Edward I'Anson, sen., pressed for a decision; he wanted nineteen vaults; the sub-committee to which the matter was referred recommended fourteen, and the main Committee approved ten.[52]

Pipers started on site in the late summer 1844, and got their first payment on account in October. By early in 1845, they were up to roof level — which gave rise to another dispute, between Moon and the owners of a neighbouring property.

At the back of Royal Exchange Buildings, there was an alley which ran from Finch Lane in an L-shape through to Threadneedle Street; then called Spread Eagle Court, what remained of it later got the grandiose name of Royal Exchange Avenue. Some houses there were owned by two people called LeMann; and they were aggrieved to find that their property was being overhung by a cornice of the new building, for which they held Moon responsible.

A draft deed settling the dispute was sent to Magdalen College in April 1845.[53] It explains that Moon is the lessee of certain premises adjoining those of the LeManns, held under Magdalen College, on which he 'is now erecting certain buildings and premises which front the East end of the Royal Exchange' and 'is possessed of certain premises adjoining thereto in Spread Eagle Court aforesaid

and which return on the North Side towards Spread Eagle Court aforesaid abutting on the premises' of the LeManns. Moon, it says, 'has carried the buildings he is now erecting higher than the adjoining Buildings [of the LeManns] and has placed and built a cornice at the North East corner of the said premises projecting onto and over the properties and premises' of the LeManns. The draft deed acknowledges that Moon had no right to do this; but 'the said F. G. Moon has conceived that it would add much to the architectural beauty and effect of his said premises if the said projection and cornice were suffered to remain for the present'. So the agreement was that he would remove it at one month's notice and meanwhile pay the LeManns a shilling a year 'if demanded'.

The deed is of interest in that it says that Moon was erecting what is evidently Royal Exchange Buildings, and it is the first document which suggests what is likely to have been the case, that he had a principal role and was more than just a prospective tenant. It also mentions premises adjoining in Spread Eagle Court: it is not clear which these were, but it could be a reference to the Finch Lane buildings flanked by the Court, which Moon was about to redevelop.

Royal Exchange Buildings was finished externally in the spring of 1845, and in May there was another, and probably final encounter with the Approaches Committee. Lawrance and Plews sent in a certificate from Tite that the buildings had been erected on the approved line, and applying for payment of the £1,000 compensation. The Committee decided to keep them waiting until the areas and gratings were completed and the scaffolding removed. But they did allow the College its legal costs of £350 10s. 10d.[54] Internal work went on for some time after that: there were further payments to Pipers running through to late November 1845, for the balance of the amount of the contract, and then what was really the final amount in February 1846.[55] The excess over contract was £2,600, and is explained by extra work which the College had approved, twice for Moon and once for Bailys. In each case, they agreed on condition that 6 per cent was added to the rent (this was the annual

---

[50] MCO, MP/1/37 and 38.
[51] In archives of MCO.
[52] CLRO, Minutes of the LBAC, 8, 18 and 31 July and 12 August 1844.
[53] MCO, EP/220/17.

[54] CLRO, Minutes of the LBAC, 19 May 1845.
[55] MCO, DBJ/117.

amount appropriate to 'twenty-five years' purchase' — that is, the amount which would repay the capital in twenty-five years, at an assumed interest rate of 4 per cent).[56]

The College granted three leases, the major one being to Moon at an annual rental of £1,176. He got the northern part of the building, which became Nos. 1 and 2 Royal Exchange Buildings. Then came Bailys at £370 a year for No. 3. The corner section, No. 4, was nearly let to a Mr Thomas for £300 a year (there was a stationer of that name round the corner in Finch Lane); but in July 1845, it was reported that it had just been let for 40 years at £320 a year to the Scottish Widows Fund Society.[57]

Scottish Widows were involved in what was to outward appearances an extension of Royal Exchange Buildings along Cornhill. We know about it because it greatly upset Bailys, who started legal action against the College and against the other party involved, Harrisons the stationers at 82 Cornhill. Their grievance is not known, but has to be inferred from an undated proposal by Scottish Widows for a settlement. Bailys were to have within four months their lease of No. 3 Royal Exchange Buildings, as had been agreed in 1842; Harrisons were 'to continue to carry their business upon the premises at the corner of the Royal Exchange Buildings and Cornhill for the space of three months from the present time'; and the lease to be granted to Scottish Widows was to contain covenants to prevent their premises being occupied by a 'bookseller, printseller, printer, [illegible] or stationer'.[58]

The most likely explanation of all this is that Harrisons had or were about to move into the corner building, to get a new shop on a prime site. Bailys could reasonably have been aggrieved, since before redevelopment they had been on the corner themselves. Whatever the explanation, Harrisons not only stayed at 82 Cornhill but had it rebuilt. Edward I'Anson, jun., was the architect: at the end of 1845 and early 1846, he was negotiating the Union Assurance Office, next door and at the corner with Finch

Lane, to rebuild the party wall between them.[59] The façade of the new 82 Cornhill was identical to Royal Exchange Buildings, so that it looked like a part of it.[60] In a sense it was, since Scottish Widows' offices extended into the upper floors.[61] It may be that this was what they planned when they took the lease of the small corner part of Royal Exchange Buildings. (They remained there until the late 1860s, until they moved to another building in Cornhill which Edward I'Anson, jun., designed for them, replaced in the 1930s by their present head office.)

I was engaged in building 'some buildings adjoining' Royal Exchange Buildings, for Francis Moon, said Edward I'Anson, jun., in 1864. This is almost certainly a block which still stands in Finch Lane, the next street to the east, with an entrance from Royal Exchange Avenue. It appears as 22 Finch Lane in the official list of Grade 2 buildings. The list picks up a reference by Hitchcock, who attributed the building to Thomas Hague (about whom little else is known) and dated it c. 1855. He did not cite his source.[62]

Hague was building in Finch Lane in 1855;[63] but it is much more likely that this block was built for Moon by I'Anson in 1846. A year or so previously, he had acquired 22–24 Finch Lane; the houses were gradually emptied, and the October 1846 Land Tax assessment register described them as 'pulled down and rebuilding'.[64] At the same time, they dropped out of Kelly's *Directories*, and remained out until the early 1850s, when a wine merchant was shown at No. 22. There was no other entry for what had previously been three houses; but what the *Directories* also show is that the number of tenants in Moon's part of Royal Exchange Buildings was disproportionately greater than the numbers in the other parts — indeed it would be hard to see how he got them all in. The plans which Edward I'Anson, jun., had prepared in

[56] MCO, CP/1/13, 11 December 1844, 2 April 1845 and 2 February 1846.
[57] MCO, Freman's Court Account Book CP/1/37 and College Orders CP/1/13 14 March and 25 July 1845.
[58] MCO, EP/220/28.

[59] GLRO, papers of the Metropolitan Buildings Office, Vol. 91 (case nos. 69, 72 and 73).
[60] John Tallis's *London Street Views, 1838–40 and 1847* (LTS, 1969).
[61] GL, MS 11316, vol. 432.
[62] Henry-Russell Hitchcock, *Architecture in the Nineteenth and Twentieth Centuries*, 3rd edn (Harmondsworth, 1968), pp. 237–38.
[63] *The Builder* (1855), p. 420. I am grateful to Simon Bradley for this reference.
[64] GL, MS 11316, vols. 428, 430, 432.

1844 for Royal Exchange Buildings showed provision for a link with Moon's adjoining premises; so a reasonable conclusion is that the Finch Lane building was treated as a back annex to Royal Exchange Buildings, and entered through it. There is confirmation in the Corporation's collection of Ward maps of 1858.[65] The sheet for Cornhill ward shows No. 1 Royal Exchange Buildings (the northernmost part) and No. 1 Royal Exchange Avenue as all the same building, with no dividing line at all. No. 2 Royal Exchange Buildings is separated from 22–24 Finch Lane by a thin line, whereas all the other properties are divided by bold lines.

This view of things also makes stylistic sense. The building is of red brick with thin piers of stone, now painted, and a strong cornice. It looks dignified, but the relative plainness of the stonework and the lack of any significant entrance suggests either a modest building in its own right, or an attachment to a building from which it was planned not to detract.[66]

In what is now Royal Exchange Avenue, there is also a rendered building, with the dates 1845 and 1854 on the pediment. This appears to be part of the same block, and a final addition to the complex. It may have been built on the site previously owned by the LeManns, overhung by Moon's offending but architecturally beautiful cornice. Its architect is unknown. But 22 Finch Lane was certainly earlier, certainly owned by Moon, and can reasonably be attributed to I'Anson.

Royal Exchange Buildings and 22 Finch Lane were gradually finished and occupied from late 1845 onwards (the Land Tax records for September 1845 show Royal Exchange Buildings as part occupied and part empty but do not make clear which part is which[67]). Occupiers of Moon's part of Royal Exchange Buildings appear in Kelly's for 1847, and for the two smaller parts (Bailys, and the Cornhill corner premises) in 1848. Occupiers of the shops included booksellers (Bailys), and a wine merchant and an outfitter in the corner premises. In Royal Exchange Buildings, there were other merchants who could have been retailers. Mostly, the occupiers were small businesses, stockbrokers, ship brokers, commodity and other merchants, and solicitors. The *Directories* for those early years[68] also show a number of companies. As might be expected at this time, there were several railway companies (The Great Luxembourgh Railway Co., the Boulogne and Amiens Railway Co., the Wexford and Valentia Railway, and the Reading, Guildford and Reigate Railway!); there were also insurers, shipping companies and two emigration businesses. There was the Daily News Office, and (briefly) the Electro Magnetic Telegraph. It all gives a good picture of the booming 1840s.

THIS HANDSOME PILE

Illustrations of the completed buildings are few, and include only one photograph. I'Anson exhibited his designs twice at the Royal Academy; the first time, in 1843, he showed 'The intended new frontage', whilst the second time, in 1845, he showed a model of the south-west corner.[69] Magdalen College also has a finely drawn elevation.[70] This has lost its date — the bottom right-hand corner is damaged — and it is titled 'proposed elevation', but I think it shows the building as it was completed. It is of the 'architect's impression' type, taken from a slight angle, with people in it. Compared with the approved 1842 elevations, it shows a greater elaboration, with swags between the windows immediately under the cornice, and some large shields over the second floor central windows.

The first illustration to be published is the best known, and has been reproduced in a number of later books.[71] It was published in the *Illustrated London News*

[65] CLRO, The City Secondary's ward maps.
[66] The full description from the statutory list is: '(?)1855 by Thomas Hague (Hitchcock, *Architecture in the Nineteenth and Twentieth Centuries*). Office building of painted stone and red brick. 5 bays. 4 storeys. Ground and 1st floors linked by thin stone piers rising to form tall openings with rounded angles between jambs and head; the slenderness of the piers is accentuated by a cavetto moulding continuous around the angles and across the heads. These tall openings contain recessed windows with moulded timber mullions and only a narrow transome between the 2 floors. The design is visually reminiscent of a framed structure of cast iron. Upper storeys with architraves to windows. Simple crowning cornice with egg and dart enrichment to bed mould. Return elevation to Royal Exchange Avenue of 3 bays similar to main front.'

[67] GL, MS 11316, vol. 430.
[68] Kelly's *Directories* for 1847–50.
[69] Royal Academy Exhibition catalogues, 1843 and 1845.
[70] MCO, E.1.8 (n.d.)
[71] For example in Hermione Hobhouse's *Lost London* at p. 174.

FIG. 151. Royal Exchange Buildings, undated elevation by Edward I'Anson, jun., but showing the final design of
the building.
The President and Fellows of Magdalen College, Oxford

for 4 October 1845.[72] It is a sketch taken from a
position in Cornhill, opposite the Royal Exchange;
compared with the I'Anson elevation at Magdalen
College, some of the shields do not appear; and the
latter also shows roundel windows in the roof, which
appear in neither of the published drawings, possibly
because they were difficult to see from the ground.
The next illustration appeared in the *Companion to the
British Almanack for 1846*,[73] and shows the two left-
hand bays; it looks precisely drawn, but omits the
glazing bars in all windows above ground level, and
the roof has the non-perspective appearance of
having been drawn by someone who could not see it.
The following year, a small drawing taken from
Cornhill appeared in the *Supplement* to Tallis's *Street
Views*; this is the evidence that 82 Cornhill was rebuilt
as a continuation.[74]

There is one photograph. When Ernest George
and Yeates built the replacement of I'Anson's building in 1907, they started with the northernmost
section, leaving the remains of the old building to the
south standing. Their building was illustrated in *The
Architect* in January 1908,[75] and three bays of the
I'Anson building are visible, including what appear
to be the roundel windows in the roof.

At the back, 22 Finch Lane is still there to be seen;
one bay of it appears in a drawing in the *Illustrated
London News* of the 1860s, showing the recently
completed next door bank.[76] The main subsequent
change has been that the ground and first floor
windows have been merged by weakening the appearance of the intermediate transom, giving a rather
more modern vertical emphasis to the ground and
first floor window openings.

[72] *Illustrated London News*, 4 October 1845, p. 216.
[73] *Companion to the British Almanack for 1846*, p. 235.
[74] John Tallis's *London Street Views, 1838–40 and 1847* (LTS, 1969).

[75] *The Architect*, 10 January 1908.
[76] Copy in GL, Noble Collection. I have not identified which edition it came from.

Nothing is known about the internal arrangements of Royal Exchange Buildings beyond what can be seen from the 1844 ground plan. But there were two external features which became common in mid-nineteenth-century offices, intended to ensure that the rooms received the greatest possible natural light. On all but the top floors, the windows were large; those in the Finch Lane addition are so large as to put one in mind of a criticism by a speaker at the RIBA in 1864 — had Mr I'Anson not found an objection to the introduction of large surfaces of plate glass, in what was familiarly known as 'the banker's draught?'[77] The other feature was the use of glazed white tiles for lining the walls of the light wells.

'This gives a very great advantage,' said I'Anson in 1864,

not only in reflecting light, but the appearance is very pleasing, and it is very easily cleansed; every shower, in fact, helps to do this. They were first used by me at the suggestion of Sir Francis Moon, at Royal Exchange Buildings, and this, so far as I know, is the first instance of their application on a scale of any magnitude in City buildings. It is obvious that they may be made hexagonal in form, or square or diamond shaped . . .[78]

On the side of the Finch Lane building, facing the back of Cornhill, hexagonal tiles are still to be seen.

The first commentary on the external appearance of Royal Exchange Buildings is the text accompanying the *Illustrated London News* drawing. It ran:

This handsome pile . . . has just been completed from the designs of Mr J. Anson, the architect, to whose taste it is highly creditable. It comprises four stories; about 60 feet in height, and 284 feet in length [an error: the length was just under 16oft]; the depth varies from 47 feet to 9 ft 2½ in . . . The lower floor will be first-rate shops, railway offices, &c; and the upper stories will form handsome suites of chambers. Altogether, this is a very striking and meritorious addition to the architectural character of this very important locality of civic improvement.

The commentary accompanying the elevation in the *Companion to the British Almanack for 1846* was more long-winded. Leaving out most of the verbosities, it ran:

Freeman's Place . . . distinguishes itself . . . by having more the air of a single large edifice, than of a mere piece of

street architecture. This range . . . is in a style of noble simplicity which says much for the good taste and judgment of its architects, Messrs I'Anson and Son . . . this façade is exceedingly well proportioned both as to the quantity of *window opening* as compared with the entire surface, and well-proportioned also in regard to mass (about 160 feet by 60 high), wherefore the eye takes in the whole of it a distinct architectural object . . . The character is Italian *astylar* . . . For simple grandeur of mass, and also for size, this range of building will bear comparison with the Excise Office in Broad Street; and while it is of sufficient extent for importance and dignity, it is not carried on to such length that continuity of design becomes monotony and wearisome repetition. One peculiarity . . . is that of colour, the whole of the front above the ground-floor being of *red brick*, with stone dressings . . . Instead of decreasing in ornaments upwards, as is usually done, the architect has given more than ordinary richness and importance to the upper part of the façade by the series of festoons between the attic or mezzanine-proportioned windows; which, together with the cornicione (whose blocks we may observe are somewhat too heavy, and should have partaken more of the cantilever form), give no small degree of character to the whole. Freeman's Place is certainly a great architectural acquisition to the city . . .[79]

This critique brings out the points which subsequent commentators have noted. The unbroken façade with the uniform, large windows above, gave the building an air of distinction and unity of purpose. Stylistically, there may have been echoes of Fowler in the arcade of shops (Nicholas Taylor, *Monuments of Commerce*[80]) or of New Oxford Street (Summerson[81]). Hitchcock noted the device of tying the top storey windows 'with a sort of frieze as Barry had already done in the second storey of the Reform Club'.[82] Elsewhere, he suggested that I'Anson had knowledge of, and respect for the work of contemporary or even earlier French architects[83] — which is very likely since he was partly educated in France, as well as spending time there and in Italy in 1835–36.

The use of red brick was the other architectural innovation. As Hitchcock pointed out, it broke the rule of stucco without resort to stone overall,[84] and its

77 *TRIBA* (1864), p. 35.
78 Ibid., p. 29.

79 *Companion to the British Almanack for 1846*, pp. 234–36.
80 Published London, 1968.
81 Summerson, op. cit., p. 208.
82 Henry-Russell Hitchcock, *Architecture in the Nineteenth and Twentieth Centuries*, 3rd edn (Harmondsworth, 1968), p. 235.
83 Henry-Russell Hitchcock, *Early Victorian Architecture in Britain* (Yale, 1954), p. 382.
84 Ibid., p. 381.

use could be explained by I'Anson's family link with Edward Walters, then establishing himself as an architect of offices and warehouses in Manchester. I'Anson certainly liked red brick, which he used to good effect elsewhere (for example, the façade of the Corn Exchange in Seething Lane). A good reason for using it here would have been to create a sympathetic link between Royal Exchange Buildings and the older post-fire houses which still filled most of the streets. But sympathy with surroundings was not a characteristic of the architects (including I'Anson) who rebuilt the City from then on.

But 'the air of a single large edifice' was deceptive, and with the Cornhill and Finch Lane additions would become even more so. Taking all these together, there were three freeholders, three lessees and, within a few years of completion, nearly 50 occupiers, spread over four or five units of greatly varying size. The largest of these was a block running from the Royal Exchange side through to Finch Lane; neither of its façades gave any clue that this was what lay behind them. This sort of irregularly shaped block, using an assemblage of sites, with façades on to more than one street, and with an internal warren of passages, stairs and light wells, was to become a common type of City office block, gradually giving way to the larger redevelopments of the late twentieth century.

In the end, however, a City office building is judged not by the beauty of its cornices, but whether and by how much it pays.

The outcome for Magdalen College can be worked out from their accounts; but only up to point, because of the way they were kept. The College bursars kept cash accounts in their Day Books and annual summaries, neat ledgers in English and Latin. The President also kept, in his own untidy handwriting, a book of New Building Accounts.[85] When capital was needed for building work, the College drew on its investments; and when the work was done, the first charge on the rents was a payment into the New Building Accounts. This was like a mortgage payment, part interest on the capital outstanding and part repayment. Because there were no capital accounts and no valuations, the system did not show

the return on capital; but it did lead the President to the important figure for him — the net amount available from any part of the estates for spending on the College.

For the Freman's Court Estate, there is also an account book which shows the rents received, related management expenses, and the net amounts transferred to College funds.[86] The book starts in 1822 and shows gross rents of £1,240 a year, rising to £1,520 a year in 1839, the last complete year of the old buildings. After deductions for expenses, debt interest and repayments, the balance for the College was £1,272.

The proceeds of the forced sale of about two-thirds of the estate to the City Corporation and some other surplus money was invested in Exchequer stock at 3 per cent interest. Some of this was cashed in, probably for the repurchase of Alderman Pirie's house. But over £20,000 remained in 3 per cent gilts, with the income being paid into the Freman's Court account, until 1862, when it was used to buy an estate in Sussex.[87]

The building cost of Royal Exchange Buildings was met in the way described above. Tranches of money were drawn from the New Building Fund between 1844 and 1846, totalling by that year £16,776 5s. From 1846, the Royal Exchange Buildings rents were charged with repayments of £800 a year; in the early years, this was to pay off old debt, but by 1850, it was all going to pay off the cost of Royal Exchange Buildings, the debt being finally extinguished in 1878.[88]

The expenses of building, and everything connected with it, like the legal fees for the College's dispute with the Corporation, have to be picked with difficulty out of the bursars' Day Books.[89]

Pipers the builders received a total of £15,066. The next largest payments were to the I'Ansons, of £1,954. There were offsets; the auction of the old buildings got in £910,[90] but there were other receipts from items sold separately and deleted from the catalogue. A later entry in the accounts is for a sum

[85] MCO, CP 2/53.

[86] MCO, CP 1/37.
[87] Ibid.
[88] Ibid.
[89] MCO, DBJ/116, 117 and 118.
[90] MCO, EP 220/5.

of £1,557;[91] this is either the total from the sale of the old buildings, or it could be the compensation plus legal fees and interest, which the Corporation paid to settle the 1844 dispute.[92]

There must be numerous other items I have not picked up. So it is best not to second guess, but accept as the total building cost the figure in the New Buildings Accounts of £16,776.

When the building was complete, the annual rental income was £1,866 a year; with the investment income from sale of the old buildings, that was £2,468, an improvement of nearly £1,000 on the old estate. There were various minor expenses, and property tax of £54 a year, and £800 a year was repayable to the New Building Fund; this left a net income of £1,614 a year — and of course the new building had a much greater potential for future rents than the old.[93]

This is the sort of calculation the College accounts point to, and on this test, their disposable income was up by nearly 30 per cent. They were well pleased: in 1847 the College Orders record the award to Blagrave of 150 guineas 'for the eminent services rendered to the Society in the settlement of their property at Freman's Court'.[94]

But others in the City appear to have done much better, especially Francis Moon. His rent, like Bailys, was on favourable terms, and some measure of this can be gained from a comparison with the rent paid by the only new lessee, Scottish Widows. It is difficult to be quite sure how much space each tenant occupied; plans prior to rebuilding cannot be a reliable guide, since the outcome of the dispute with the Corporation was to reduce the space available. But measurements can be taken from the City's 1858 ward plans,[95] which were an enlargement of the Ordnance Survey. These show that Scottish Widows leased a fifteenth part of Royal Exchange Buildings, but paid about a sixth of the total rents. Bailys paid only £50 a year more, but got for that three times as much space. And Francis Moon became the tenant of three-quarters of the buildings, but paid only two-thirds of the total rent. With a favourable rent and a 40-year lease for a top class new building, he had ample scope for high profits from letting at market rents to his own tenants. In his paper to the RIBA in 1864, I'Anson said, in a passage where he spoke of building for Moon, that 'as a financial operation, it has, I believe, been eminently successful'.

Lettable office buildings by their nature are apt to have short lives, and Royal Exchange Buildings was no exception. By the start of the present century, it probably looked rather shabby and was certainly unfashionable. Edward I'Anson, jun.'s son was still in practice (working at this time on major extensions to St Bartholemew's Hospital); but Magdalen College no longer used him. They turned to Ernest George and Yeates to provide the building that is now on the site. (It also took in 82 Cornhill, the Harrisons building; but not the offices linked to Royal Exchange Buildings which Moon's successors owned.) Tastes have changed again, and we would now be more likely to admire I'Anson's early Victorian classicism than the overblown Edwardian replacement.

As a Victorian building development, I cannot say whether Royal Exchange Buildings is in any way typical (that is, if any development in somewhere as complex as the City of London could be 'typical'). What it does, however, illustrate is the complexity of the process that starts with a site and ends, not just with one tenanted building, but an irregular block in mixed ownership. Summerson remarks that, 'As building became more an industry than a trade, so architecture became more a business than a profession';[96] but it was driven that way not just by the building firms but other factors like the need to negotiate with what we would now call the planning authorities and with adjoining property interests.

The story also shows some complex relationships between the parties to the development. To a twentieth-century mind, one would think the I'Ansons had difficulties in balancing their responsibilities to the College and to Moon. I started off this research to try to resolve which of the parties Edward I'Anson, jun., was really working for — Magdalen College as the legal owner which commissioned his firm, or

[91] MCO, College accounts, 1846.
[92] CLRO, Minutes of the LBAC, 19 May 1845.
[93] MCO, CP 1/37.
[94] MCO, CP 1/13, 2 February 1847.
[95] CLRO, The City Secondary's ward maps.
[96] Summerson, op. cit., p. 181.

Francis Moon, for whom he later said he was working? At the end of it, I am still unclear. It is likely that in financial terms Moon had the best of the outcome; and the I'Ansons may have found themselves leaning towards the influential City financier and politician rather than the more distant Oxford College. But the one certainty is that both parties did well out of it: as I'Anson himself said thirty years later,

It has grown to be a proverb, that you must make a profit upon building in the City.[97]

[97] *TRIBA* (1872), p. 40.

CHAPTER XXXII

Royal Exchange Restaurants

By PETER JACKSON

ON 14 MAY 1875 the Gresham Committee[1] resolved to lease the Royal Exchange vaults and eleven days later the following advertisement appeared in *The Times*: 'To be LET, on LEASE, the extensive VAULTS, under the Royal Exchange. The Gresham Committee are prepared to receive TENDERS for taking on LEASE, for 21 years, from Midsummer-day next, in two divisions, the valuable ARCHED VAULTS, under the ambulatory and other portions of the Royal Exchange, according to a plan deposited at the office of their surveyor, where also a form of lease may be seen.'[2] There was no rush of applicants; in fact, at a meeting on 16 July, it was revealed that there had been no tenders and the Committee decided that 'The question of letting the Vaults be postponed'.

In December a letter was received from a Mr Dyer who proposed to use the vaults for a skating rink and billiard saloon. Not surprisingly, the Committee turned him down. They looked more favourably on the application from Messrs Akhurst & Butterworth who wished to establish a 'high class restaurant and series of refreshment rooms of which accessory this City is lamentably dificient'. Their offer was, however, withdrawn without explanation and the advertising was resumed.

The Committee received a letter on 26 July 1876 from Edward Tyrell Smith offering to lease the vaults from Michaelmas next for 21 years at a rent of £1,000 a year and to 'expend £5,000 upon the premises for fitting them up as a first class refreshment establishment'. Smith was 'called in and heard'. He must have made a good impression as his offer was

accepted subject to some minor conditions. It was to prove a controversial choice.

E. T. Smith was an extraordinary character. George Augustus Sala, reminiscing in the *Daily Telegraph* said, 'Among the curious people I have known — I can scarcely remember one more eccentrically interesting than Mr Edward Tyrell Smith'.[3]

Born in 1804, the son of an Admiral, his mother rescued him from a life at sea by fetching him back the night before the ship on which he was to serve as a midshipman sailed away.[4] After a spell as a police constable, he became a sheriff's auctioneer, then a wine merchant, but soon realizing that this would not fulfil his avowed intention of getting rich quickly, he embarked upon his first piece of chicanery. Each morning he would set out with a £1,000 banknote in his pocket which he had hired from a money-lender named Sam Genese at the rate of £1 a day plus $36\frac{1}{2}$ per cent interest.[5] Knowing that with this note shopkeepers would find it impossible to give change, he was able to enjoy unlimited credit. And he was not above flourishing it to impress business contacts. With whatever capital he amassed he became, in the early 1850s, the landlord of a tavern in Red Lion Street, Holborn, where he first demonstrated his flare for publicity by dressing his barmaids in the newly introduced Bloomer costume.[6]

His career as a theatrical impresario began in a small way when he became the lessee of the humble Marylebone Theatre, Church Street, Edgware Road in 1851,[7] but in the following year he made the giant leap to Drury Lane and ran it successfully for ten

---

[1] Unless stated otherwise, the material for this article has been taken from the Minutes of the Gresham Committee in the Mercers' Company Archives. Reference to specific entries are prefixed by the initials GCM (Gresham Committee Minutes.) I am greatly indebted to the Mercers' Company Archivist, Anne Sutton, and her Assistant, Ursula Carlyle, for their help and advice.

[2] *The Times*, 25 May 1875.

[3] *Daily Telegraph*, 7 August 1894.

[4] Edward Leman Blanchard, *Life & Reminiscences*, II (1891), p. 472.

[5] J. H. Mapleson, *The Mapelson Memoirs*, I (1888), p. 29.

[6] Article by George Augustus Sala in *The Daily Telegraph*, 7 August 1894.

[7] Malcolm Morley, *The Old Marylebone Theatre*, St Marylebone Soc. Pubns 2 (1960).

THE ROYAL EXCHANGE CO-OPERATIVE RESTAURANT & WINE SUPPLY ASSOCIATION, LIMITED.

INTERIOR VIEW OF THE PREMISES OF THE ASSOCIATION. (FROM THE WEST ENTRANCES.)

FIG. 152. Anonymous, undated lithograph of a restaurant in the vaults of the Royal Exchange. It is not known whether this establishment ever really existed but the print shows clearly the vaulting, and a possible layout for the tables and service areas.

Private collection

years.[8] While at Drury Lane he took over the Panopticon of Science & Art in Leicester Square, turning the pseudo-scientific exhibition into a circus and later, by adding a stage and proscenium arch, into the Alhambra Palace Music Hall.[9] In 1860 he became lessee of Her Majesty's Theatre where he put on Italian opera.[10] He owned Cremorne Gardens from 1861 to 1869[11] and his management did little to improve its dubious reputation. During this time he was not only running the Lyceum Theatre but was lessee of Astley's, where he caused a sensation by producing Byron's *Mazeppa* starring the notorious Adah Isaacs Menken wearing nothing but a body-stocking and tied to the back of a real horse which galloped around the stage.[12]

He entered the restaurant business early in his career when he acquired Crockford's, the gambling club in St James's Street, at a very small cost as the lease had less than ten years to run. He turned it into a fashionable restaurant called The Wellington and opened it in 1857.[13]

Two years later he purchased the bank premises at the Holborn corner of Chancery Lane and fitted them up as a refectory which he called The Radnor, and in 1860 he opened the Cremorne Supper Rooms in Leicester Square on the corner of Wardour Street.[14]

It was probably Smith's experience as a caterer which prompted the Gresham Committee to accept his application to turn the vaults into a restaurant, to which, it subsequently appeared, was to be added a billiard room.

There was some opposition from the other tenants, Lloyd's, Royal Exchange Assurance and London Assurance expressing concern over the extensive work which had to be undertaken to provide additional light and ventilation. The ventilation necessary for the kitchens consisted of three galvanised iron shafts painted to imitate stonework which ran up by the side of each pilaster at the eastern end. The extra lighting was supplied by enlarging the gratings outside the north and south sides of the building. These alterations were approved by the Royal Exchange surveyor, George Barnes Williams.[15]

[8] *Survey of London*, XXXV (1970), p. 26.
[9] *Survey of London*, XXXIV (1966), p. 495.
[10] Frederic Boase, *Modern English Biography*, III (1901), p. 625.
[11] Warwick Wroth, *Cremorne & Later London Gardens* (1907), p. 12.
[12] Samuel Edwards, *Queen of the Plaza* (1969), Ch. 2.
[13] Boase, op. cit.

[14] *The Era*, 2 December 1877.
[15] GCM, 1 December 1876. It was not the first time in the history of the Royal Exchange that there had been trouble with an eating-place in the vaults; see p. 91.

The tenants' protests, however, were as nothing compared with the outcry which greeted the news that E. T. Smith was about 'to start a subterranean Cremorne in the City of London'.[16] On 26 February 1877 a deputation waited upon the Lord Mayor at the Mansion House headed by the Revd Harvey Brooks, rector of St Margaret's Lothbury, and presented him with a memorial signed by the whole of the committees of Lloyd's and the Stock Exchange, the Postmaster-General, twenty-five City bankers, the Young Men's Christian Association and 1,275 young men in wholesale houses and trades, begging him, as chairman of the Licensing Justices of the City, to reject Smith's application. They gave as their reason 'that there were too many opportunities for drinking and betting already in existence in the City without so vast an addition being provided'.

The Lord Mayor replied that, 'if the decision rested with him the petitioners need have no fear as to the result'.[17]

Smith even had the City Press against him. In a long editorial it wrote: 'There are now about 550 licensed houses in the City employing 2,000 barmen and barmaids, more than amply sufficient to provide for the present daily wants of the City in the matter of eating and drinking.'[18] In the same issue the *City Press* reprinted articles which had been published in the *Daily Telegraph* and the *Echo* protesting against the inclusion of a billiard saloon as part of the restaurant: '. . . billiard rooms are only the resort of "sharps" to prey upon the unwary', thundered the *Echo*, 'if the magistrates wish to have evidence of the danger they need only ask the governors of Newgate and Holloway as to the pernicious influence of billiard-rooms west of the City.'[19] Smith sensed the danger and withdrew his application for permission to include billiards in case it jeopardised his chances of getting his wine and spirit licence.

The Gresham Committee had already agreed to support him in this. But the final word rested with the City authorities, and on 21 March a full bench of City magistrates, sitting at Guildhall for licensing purposes, considered Smith's application.[20] Mr Poland, acting on behalf of the petitioners (whose numbers had now increased to '50 clergymen, 230 bankers and others numbering together 1,700 persons') pointed to the temptations offered to young men who 'instead of going home after the business of the day, would resort to Smith's billiard-rooms for the rest of the evening'. (It was not revealed until the end of the hearing that Smith had already abandoned the idea of introducing billiards.) But clearly Smith's slightly shady reputation went against him and the Bench arrived at the conclusion that the full licence, including wine, be refused.

Smith protested in a letter to *The Times* that the petition had been rigged. He claimed that petitions presented to various banks were 'sent round the desks stating the establishment was to be opened for gambling and the ruin of young men, with rooms for improper purposes'. Moreover, 'Clergymen were written to, their signatures cut off, and pasted on the petitions'. To refute the assertion that there were rooms for gambling and improper purposes, 'the whole area is open; one grand saloon for luncheons. Every part of the building can be seen from any spot within'.[21]

The failure to obtain a licence was a major setback but Smith, not a man to be easily defeated, found a solution. On a placard posted at the entrance of the Exchange vaults he put up a notice announcing that 'the magistrates, having refused to grant him a licence, he has let the premises to a "Free Vintner" who will, at once, open them for the sale of wines, etc.'.[22] A Free Vintner was, by ancient custom, not liable to the jurisdiction of licensing laws.

There was an immediate outcry in the Press from leader writers and correspondents protesting that Smith was putting himself above the law and abusing the Vintners' privilege: '. . . it is hardly to be supposed', wrote a correspondent to *The Times*, 'that the Lord Mayor and Aldermen will quietly submit to their authority being so completely set at defiance within a few yards of the Mansion House and in so public a manner.'[23]

[16] *The Times*, 22 March 1877.
[17] Ibid., 27 February 1877.
[18] *City Press*, 10 March 1877.
[19] Ibid.

[20] *The Times*, 22 March 1877.
[21] Ibid., 17 April 1877.
[22] *City Press*, 31 March 1877.
[23] *The Times*, 17 April 1877.

By now Smith was also in financial trouble. In May he was asking for a modification of his lease, abatements of his rent or whether 'the Committee will accept a surrender of the lease and pay the amount (£8,000) that has been expended in making the vaults fit to carry on a business of a first class restaurant'.[24] The Committee refused his application, but Smith went ahead anyway and in the first week in June 1877 his Royal Exchange Vaults Restaurant was opened 'for the sale of wines and refreshments'.[25]

His ruse of overriding the licensing laws by obtaining his wines through a Free Vintner clearly succeeded, and the Press continued their anti-Smith campaign. '. . . The system of licensing in the City may become a nullity', wrote the *City Press*. 'No doubt questions will be asked in the House of Commons on the subject.'[26]

Finance, however, was still Smith's major concern and on 6 July he was allowed to assign his lease by way of a mortgage to Susan Donnison of Oval House, Kennington, for £6,000 and unspecified further advances.

But he remained active in running the restaurant and, living up to his reputation for publicity, he engaged as a barmaid the beautiful Alice Rhodes who had recently been pardoned for a sensational murder in Penge.[27]

It was his last flourish of showmanship for on 26 November 1877 Edward Tyrell Smith died, 'the greatest impresario London has ever known'.[28] He died at Oval House, Kennington, the same address as the Susan Donnison to whom he had assigned his lease, though what their relationship was is not clear.[29]

She continued to run the restaurant after Smith's death, but on 12 July 1878 she was allowed to assign to the People's Cafe Company Ltd provided arrears of rent were paid and the ventilating shafts were completed or entirely removed.

On 8 April 1879 there was a further underletting to one Henry Clifford at a rent of £1,400, and on 26 September he, in turn, was allowed to assign to the Coffee Public-Houses National Society Ltd. This time there would be no controversy over wine and spirit licences; they were a temperance society which had already opened five coffee public houses in London and three in the country.[30] They sought permission to lease No. 4 Royal Exchange, then occupied by the Society for Promoting Christian Knowledge, to make an entrance through the shop to the vaults. They were granted permission at an annual rent of £180, and on 12 May 1880 they formally opened their restaurant in the presence of a large and influential company. *The Times* reported the opening:

The area set apart has been handsomely decorated and furnished with every convenience for serving breakfasts, luncheons and dinners to a large number of customers, while the counters are supplied with tea, coffee, milk, aerated and mineral waters, and other drinks. The arrangements are so made as to prevent overcrowding, and the new restaurant is well ventilated, lighted by electric lamps, and will be both cool in summer and pleasurably warm in winter. There are smoking and reading rooms, with telephonic and electric communication with the Stock Exchange, and other business centres. The great object sought has been to provide for the wants of the rapidly-increasing class of customers who, whether professed abstainers or not, yet desire to take a mid-day meal where no alcoholic liquors are supplied.[31]

It was not, however, a success. They must have seriously misjudged the number of teetotal City businessmen, for they could not pay the rent and, in just over a year, went bankrupt. In June 1881 the Gresham Committee were dealing with the Official Liquidator who undertook to see that nothing was removed from the vaults, and a firm of auctioneers was called in to sell 'all Trade Utencils and Furniture on the premises'.[32] Emergency action by the Clerk and Surveyor prevented the uprooting of the parquet flooring, so essential to the appearance of the vaults, by puchasing it for £150. It had originally cost ten times that amount. They also bought some gas piping and glass cups under the ventilators for £2.[33]

[24] GCM, May 1877.
[25] *City Press*, 9 June 1877.
[26] Ibid., 23 June 1877.
[27] Erroll Sherson, *London's Lost Theatres of the Nineteenth Century* (1925), p. 73.
[28] Ibid., p. 74.
[29] Boase, op. cit.

[30] *Illustrated London News*, 15 May 1880.
[31] *The Times*, 13 May 1880.
[32] GCM, 23 June 1881.
[33] Ibid., 12 October 1881.

On 12 October 1881 the Coffee Public-Houses National Society gave up the keys of No. 4 Royal Exchange and the vaults were once more vacant.

In February 1882 an application was received from Spiers & Pond to rent the vaults for 'City Clerks Commercial Dining Room'.[34] Spiers & Pond were the largest and most famous caterers of the time with restaurants all over London, including the Gaiety, and were catering contractors for the South Eastern Railway running station buffets and supplying take-away hampers for travellers. But the Gresham Committee had had enough of restaurants and declined their offer.

In the following month an application was made for the vaults to be used by a safe deposit company which was about to be formed. The offer was accepted but came to nothing, and in June permission to use the vaults for an exhibition of electric lights was turned down.[35]

In February 1883 a Mr Ross wrote a letter proposing to turn the vaults into a Turkish Bath. No doubt visualising the effect this would have on the troublesome ventilation system, the idea was totally ignored. On 26 October 1883 an outstanding debt of £1,000 arrears of rent on the vaults was written off as irrecoverable and the Committee decided to start advertising again. This time the advertisement specified that the Gresham Committee 'will not let the vaults for the purpose of a Restaurant or for any other occupation which will necessitate the cooking and sale of any fresh provisions'.[36]

This resolution was adhered to for twenty-three years until 1906 when a licence was granted to Mrs A. M. Sayer to use the basement under Nos. 16 and 17 as a tea-room,[37] and five years later she was allowed to erect a sign outside the entrance.[38]

'The Royal Exchange Tea Room' flourished under a succession of lessees, and in June 1914 the business was purchased for £300 by Miss Millicent Gibson[39] who continued to run it successfully throughout the Great War.

Towards the end of the war, however, the City authorities began to suspect that the entertainment she and her three waitresses, Hilda, Alice and Betty were offering the troops went a little beyond the provision of tea and biscuits.[40] The police put the place under surveillance and a detective named Johnson, posing as a customer, became a regular visitor for nine days in October and November 1918, during which time he became very friendly with the proprietress Miss Gibson, who preferred to be called Millie. As a result of his observations Millie was summoned before the Lord Mayor at the Mansion House for permitting disorderly conduct to take place on the premises. This, according to the detective's evidence, consisted of Alice putting her arm round the neck of an Army officer, Hilda rolling about on a settee with a sailor, and the girls flirting with two customers named 'Len' and 'Tea and a Bun'. Then there was the gambling. Detective Johnson had taken part in a game of Pontoon and also another game called 'Slippery Sam'. He lost all his money, about £1, and Millie lent him 10s. At the end of the game he had lost 25s. And he was presented with a bill for 3s. 6d. for a pot of tea with a biscuit.

Millie's defence council, Mr Huntley Jenkins, pointed out that at no time did any act of immorality take place and that 'what happened on the day after Armistice Day, when there was a sailor there, was merely harmless "larking", such as prevailed in the streets and everywhere at that time'. The Lord Mayor, however, took a different view. He imposed the full penalty of £5 and 3 guineas costs on each of the eight summonses — £65 4s. in all — and said that he considered it a very bad case.[41] The Tea Room closed, quietly.

---

34 Ibid., 7 February 1882.
35 Ibid., 10 March 1882 and 16 June 1882.
36 Ibid., 16 November 1883.
37 Ibid., 25 May 1906.
38 Ibid., 17 February 1911.

39 The Times, 16 January 1919.
40 The following account is given in The Times for 1 January 1919 under the headline, 'A City Tea Room. Alledged Disorderly Conduct'.
41 The Times, 16 January 1919.

FIG. 153.   Traffic outside the Royal Exchange, *c.* 1900.
Guildhall Library, Corporation of London

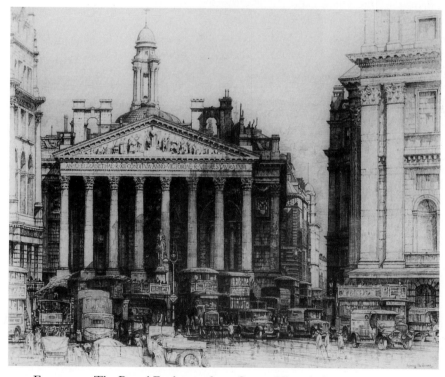

FIG. 154.   The Royal Exchange from Queen Victoria Street. Etching by
Sydney R. Jones, *c.* 1927.
Guildhall Library, Corporation of London

FIG. 155.   Armistice Day,
11 November 1931. Crowds attend the
Memorial Service outside the Royal
Exchange, marking the Exchange as
the true heart of the City.
Guardian Royal Exchange collection

FIG. 156.   The Acclamation of
Edward VIII, 29 May 1936, on the
steps of the Royal Exchange.
Guardian Royal Exchange collection

A.   The Bank of England and Tite's Royal Exchange, engraved by T. A. Prior from a drawing by
A. L. Thomas.

Guildhall Library, Corporation of London

B.   Henry Pether's tessellated pavement for the courtyard, executed by A. Singer at the Vauxhall Pottery,
proved a failure and was soon removed.

Guardian Royal Exchange collection

PLATE X

B. *The Opening of the First Royal Exchange by Queen Elizabeth, 23 January 1570–71*, by Ernest Crofts, R.A. Presented by the Mercers' Company, 1899.

A. *Alfred the Great repairing the Walls of the City of London*, by Frank O. Salisbury. Presented by Sir Charles Wakefield (afterwards Viscount Wakefield), 1912.

By courtesy of the Joint Grand Gresham Committee

PLATE XI

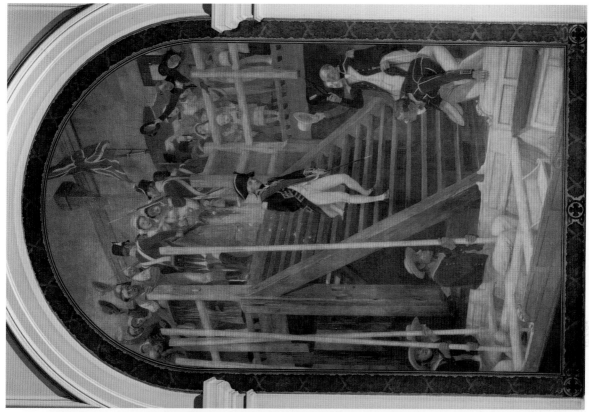

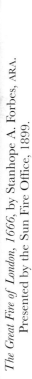

B. *Nelson leaving Portsmouth, 18 May 1803 to join HMS Victory,* by
Andrew C. Gow, R.A. Presented by the Corporation of Lloyd's, 1903.

A. *The Great Fire of London, 1666,* by Stanhope A. Forbes, A.R.A.
Presented by the Sun Fire Office, 1899.

By courtesy of the Joint Grand Gresham Committee

PLATE XII

A.   Edwin Hughes, circus manager, drawn by his elephants through the streets of the City in
1847, the year in which he appeared before Queen Victoria at Drury Lane Theatre.
The Royal Exchange fills the background.

Guildhall Library, Corporation of London

B.   *The Heart of the Empire*, by Niels Moeller Lund (1863–1916).

Guildhall Art Gallery, Corporation of London

PLATE XIII

A.   Royal Exchange from Queen Victoria Street, 1898, by A. F. Werner, oil on canvas.

By kind permission of the Mercers' Company

B.   London's largest bomb crater, painted by H. S. Merritt. The bomb fell in front of the Royal Exchange on the evening of Saturday 11 January 1941, with the loss of eighty lives.

Guardian Royal Exchange collection

PLATE XIV

A. The interior of the enlarged Royal Exchange, showing the additional upper storey,
where a skilful use of the Corinthian order has preserved the architectural harmony.

Guardian Royal Exchange collection

B. The Royal Exchange, 1991.

Guardian Royal Exchange collection

CHAPTER XXXIII

The Courtyard of the Royal Exchange

By JOHN WATTS

THE COURTYARD and its enveloping ambulatory was the centrepiece and, of course, the glory of Gresham's Royal Exchange and subsequently two replacement buildings. From the opening of the first in 1568 to the closure of the third in 1939, due to the outbreak of the Second World War, trading took place in a period of some 370 years apart from the time devoted to the construction of the second building, 1666–69, and the third, 1838–44. An additional period of trading took place between 1982 and 1991 when LIFFE (London International Financial Futures Exchange) was established in what can only be described as an enlarged prefabricated Portakabin sitting on and completely covering the original Turkey sets and extending to the surrounding ambulatory.

Whilst great use of the courtyard in the first two buildings was made by trading merchants, this was not the case with the third one. Initial enthusiasm gave way to a gradual decline in use and, less than 50 years after the glittering state opening in 1844 by Queen Victoria, an article in *The Graphic* dated 9 May 1891 painted a very different picture of the transacting of business in its precincts —

Much of the research material used in this chapter and indeed elsewhere in this book has come from the GRE Archives which have been built up over a period of many years. Nearly forty years ago I recall learning many things about the historical background of the Royal Exchange and the formation of the REA in 1720 from conversations with the then Company Secretary, David Baker, and his assistant, Dick Dunster. The subsequent appointments of company archivist Doug Thomson and later Audrey Button did much in bringing order to the documents library, and the establishment of an Archives Committee under the enthusiastic chairmanship of Reg Wells was a further milestone in building up the archives.

For the history of the Guildhall Museum in the Royal Exchange I am indebted to Francis Dimond for bringing to my attention the Library Committee Minutes and the Librarian's Reports in the City Corporation's Records Office.

All illustrations are from Guardian Royal Exchange collection.

That business, however, is a mere tithe of what at one time daily transacted within its walls. Within the memory of many living merchants to go 'on Change' was as much a part of daily routine as attending the office, or opening correspondence. Nearly all classes of business — apart from the Stock Exchange and Lloyd's, which early in their history sought separate headquarters — were represented on the flags, and had their separate corners and regular hours of meeting. The enormous growth of the City and of its business led gradually to the hiving off of separate interests. The corn merchants took to meeting in Mark Lane, the produce-brokers in Mincing Lane, other trades found accommodation at the 'Baltic', until practically only one regular assembly has been left faithful to its old associations. The dealers in foreign bills of exchange still meet in the Courtyard twice every week, on Tuesdays and Thursdays, and representatives of all the leading bankers doing a foreign business may here be seen, on those days from half-past one to half-past two o'clock. The assembly is not a large one, comprising usually about one hundred regular attendants, but it represents an enormous aggregate of capital and enterprise. The site of the meetings, where each man may usually be found in his accustomed position, is towards the eastern end of the building, and clusters are formed round the various pillars of the structure.

Transactions on 'Change are exclusively confined to foreign money. Bills drawn on and payable in London are handled by the various banks and discount houses, in their own offices, but when any of these institutions have foreign Bills to 'melt', as it is termed, the most ready means is to offer them through a broker on the Royal Exchange, where a market price can be obtained without going a round of the leading banks. Payment is made on the following day by the principals direct, so that as little risk is run as possible by the employment of intermediaries.

It seems somewhat a pity that the 'gentle and very fryndely gift' of the good knight, and the subsequent donations of the City authorities, are not now as widely useful to business interests as formerly, but the reason is obvious, and the remaining frequenters of 'Change still comprise most of the 'Pillars of London Finance.'

In the years immediately prior to the closure in 1939, trading had become even more sporadic and the lack of activity must have resulted in a rather

FIG. 157.   The Essex Art Club Exhibition, 1954.

FIG. 158.   The Mermaid at the Royal Exchange, by Michael Stringer, 1953.

FIG. 159.   Cover of booklet describing the beginnings of the Mermaid Theatre.

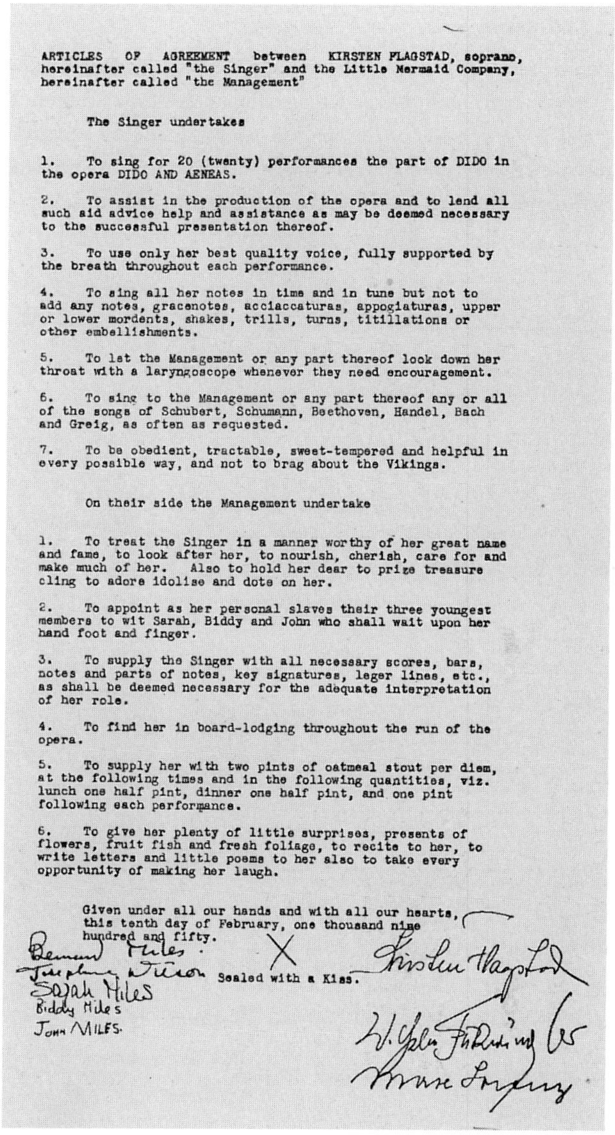

ARTICLES OF AGREEMENT between KIRSTEN FLAGSTAD, soprano, hereinafter called "the Singer" and the Little Mermaid Company, hereinafter called "the Management"

The Singer undertakes

1.   To sing for 20 (twenty) performances the part of DIDO in the opera DIDO AND AENEAS.

2.   To assist in the production of the opera and to lend all such aid advice help and assistance as may be deemed necessary to the successful presentation thereof.

3.   To use only her best quality voice, fully supported by the breath throughout each performance.

4.   To sing all her notes in time and in tune but not to add any notes, gracenotes, acciaccaturas, appogiaturas, upper or lower mordents, shakes, trills, turns, titillations or other embellishments.

5.   To let the Management or any part thereof look down her throat with a laryngoscope whenever they need encouragement.

6.   To sing to the Management or any part thereof any or all of the songs of Schubert, Schumann, Beethoven, Handel, Bach and Greig, as often as requested.

7.   To be obedient, tractable, sweet-tempered and helpful in every possible way, and not to brag about the Vikings.

On their side the Management undertake

1.   To treat the Singer in a manner worthy of her great name and fame, to look after her, to nourish, cherish, care for and make much of her.   Also to hold her dear to prize treasure cling to adore idolise and dote on her.

2.   To appoint as her personal slaves their three youngest members to wit Sarah, Biddy and John who shall wait upon her hand foot and finger.

3.   To supply the Singer with all necessary scores, bars, notes and parts of notes, key signatures, leger lines, etc., as shall be deemed necessary for the adequate interpretation of her role.

4.   To find her in board-lodging throughout the run of the opera.

5.   To supply her with two pints of oatmeal stout per diem, at the following times and in the following quantities, viz. lunch one half pint, dinner one half pint, and one pint following each performance.

6.   To give her plenty of little surprises, presents of flowers, fruit fish and fresh foliage, to recite to her, to write letters and little poems to her also to take every opportunity of making her laugh.

Given under all our hands and with all our hearts, this tenth day of February, one thousand nine hundred and fifty.

Sealed with a Kiss.

FIG. 160.   Contract between the soprano, Kirsten Flagstad, and the Little Mermaid Company, as appeared in the booklet of 1951.

depressing atmosphere. This contrasted greatly with the congestion at Lloyd's which occupied most of the first floor of the building. In the early 1920s the situation was then apparent as reported in *The Times* for 3 June 1921 (p. 14, col. d):

Congestion at Lloyd's

Frequenters of the Rooms on the first floor of the Royal Exchange know well the severe congestion of the market and the difficulty of conducting business comfortably under such conditions and it is recognized that if business continues to develop a solution will sooner or later have to be found.

Neglected Royal Exchange

In the meantime the poor use which is now being made of the main portion of the Royal Exchange is the subject of comment. Judged by the business which is now being conducted there, the title is hardly justified. Some three months ago the bill brokers intimated that they would not for the present desire to continue frequenting it for an hour on two days a week. A few dealers in oils and chemicals are to be discovered there for a short time in the afternoon: but even when these markets are in progress the great quadrangle has a deserted appearance. A few admirers of the pictures, and a few individuals resting on the benches and the beadles provide most of the signs of life. It is certainly an anomaly that in the very heart of the greatest business

University of Copenhagen
Students' Choir

Conducted by
J. HYE-KNUDSEN
Conductor of the Royal Opera. Copenhagen

Royal Exchange
City of London

Noon, Saturday, June 23rd, 1928

FIG. 161.   Cover of concert programme from 1928.

centre in the world with the surrounding buildings over-crowded there should be a quarter of an acre of closed in little-used space — a relic of the past.

In 1928 Lloyd's solved their problem by moving to a new specially designed building on the corner of Leadenhall Street and Lime Street. The Royal Exchange Assurance established under Royal Charter in 1720, then the only other tenant on the first floor, took over the former Lloyd's area and carried out the first major refurbishment of the building since it had been opened 84 years previously.

The outbreak of the war not only put paid to any trading activity in the courtyard but also resulted in the evacuation to the Home Counties of non-essential insurance staff from the upper floors.

The war years meant that the building was being safeguarded at night by a regular team of firewatchers who had to deal with numerous incendiary devices.

It was spared direct bombing, the nearest incident being the bomb which dropped at the Bank crossing on the evening of Saturday 11 January 1941 with the death of more than 80 people sheltering in the underground station. The cavity caused was 1,800 square feet in area, 150 feet long and 10–30 feet deep and was described at the time as London's largest crater. On 12 January, the Royal Engineers commenced clearing away the wreckage where the seven streets converging on this spot were blocked. They erected a trestle (Bailey) bridge measuring 164 feet from Queen Victoria Street and Poultry to Cornhill capable of carrying $12\frac{1}{4}$ ton London Passenger Transport buses and other traffic. The bridge was opened by the Lord Mayor, who was the first civilian to cross it, and was used for seven weeks during which time 39,520 buses and 158,000 other vehicles passed over the cavity. The fact that the bomb exploded below ground meant that the surrounding buildings such as the Royal Exchange, Mansion House and the Bank of England were spared serious damage, albeit at the great loss of life.

As business activity gradually returned to the City so did the increasing numbers of office workers look for something to raise their spirits. In the years 1942 and 1943 a series of lunch-time concerts organised in the courtyard by Hilda Bor featured many well-known artists. The 1942 season consisting of some 70 concerts mainly of chamber music and piano and song recitals were attended by 34,000 people, each paying one shilling (10p) plus a similar sum for refreshments from a specifically installed canteen. Two hundred volunteers acted as cashiers, ushers, programme sellers, and so on. In 1943 the number of concerts increased to 112 with a total attendance of 40,000 people. The seating capacity was 800–1,000 and the profit of £350 made over the two years was donated to the Duke of Gloucester's Red Cross and St John's Fund.

A typical series of concerts on 8, 9, 10, and 11 June 1943 included Maggie Teyte accompanied by Gerald Moore, pianists Nina Milkina and Denis Matthews, the Teyte recital on 9 June being broadcast by the BBC. The first concert on the 8 June comprised the London Philharmonic Orchestra conducted by Edric Cundell in a concert of Mozart and Bach which was reviewed in the following day's *Times*:

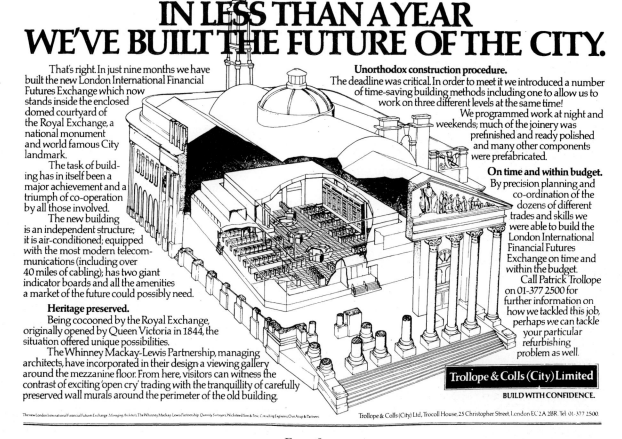

FIG. 162.

Yesterday's concert at the Royal Exchange was a gift from the Royal Exchange Assurance, and being thus a special occasion was distinguished by the presence of an orchestra. It is not often possible, nor indeed is it altogether desirable, to have orchestral music provided at cheap rates in a series devoted to chamber music. But the visit of the L.P.O. proved immensely popular, and filled the L-shaped concert hall that has been carved out of the great (and otherwise much too resonant) building. Acoustics, if a trifle sharp, are good for the ear; amenities in the shape of a sandwich bar feed the inner man and an exhibition to nourish his eye make the short lunch-time programme of music a time of refreshment for his spirit.

Yesterday's programme was appropriately enough directed by Mr. Edric Cundell, who as principal of the Guildhall School of Music is an officer of the City of London. He chose for programme a movement from Mozart's "Haffner" Serenade, Bach's third Brandenburg Concerto, and Mozart's little (i.e., three-movement) symphony in C that Sir Thomas Beecham used to play so often. His readings of Bach and Mozart were alike in being taut and virile. This sort of vigorous playing is common enough in Bach, but its application to Mozart proved to be unexpectedly successful. The familiar idiom was alive with new cogency, and the effect was stimulating.

Hilda Bor, writing in Hinrichsen's *Musical Year Book 1945–46* (pp. 305–06) says, 'Although the two seasons took place in the middle years of the war, and the Royal Exchange was situated in the heart of the devastation caused by enemy bombing, no air-raid noise ever occurred to disturb the concerts'. The 1944 season was abandoned after one week due to the start of the VI flying bomb attacks.

However, these were not the first concerts to take place in the courtyard. Annual Carol concerts by Lloyd's Choir and Orchestra took place each December in the 1920s, and on 23 June 1928 the University of Copenhagen's Students' Choir gave a concert. Armistice Day services, an annual feature since 1919, took place in the courtyard whenever bad weather prevented the usual ceremony taking place in front of the building.

After the war, trading was not resumed until the formation of LIFFE in 1982. The courtyard which was normally opened to members of the public was used for various exhibitions and charity events organised with the permission of the Gresham Committee. The annual Essex Art Club exhibition was held along with others by the Wapping Artists. Later the Red Cross Christmas Charity fairs were held together with sale of Charity Christmas Cards. The Festival of Britain in 1951 was celebrated with an Exhibition by the British Insurance Companies under the auspices of the British Insurance Association (now ABI).

An important event took place in 1953, the year of Queen Elizabeth II's coronation, and this was the construction in the courtyard of the Mermaid Theatre, the City's first for more than 200 years. This was to be a forerunner of the Mermaid Theatre reestablished later in Blackfriars under its enthusiastic director, Bernard Miles (appointed CBE in 1953, knighted in 1969 and created a Life Peer as Baron Miles in 1979). Built of stone and glass, the majestic quadrangle posed an acoustic problem of cathedral-like dimensions, which was only solved by hanging a false ceiling 32 feet above floor level, thus cutting the building horizontally into two halves. This ceiling, suspended from the barrel-vaulted roof by a network of some 6,000 feet of steel wires, was made of acoustic boards slotted into a light metal framework and weighing $4\frac{1}{2}$ tons, was completed in just over three weeks.

At ground level, the open stage with balcony above, bars, boxes, dressing rooms, cloakrooms and stairways, as well as 1,000 seats, all had to be fitted into the available space without in any way damaging or defacing the historic stone fabric, and all within six weeks. This seemingly impossible problem was solved by using 32,000 feet of tubular steel, 9,800 fittings and 10,000 feet of timber to mould the entire structural framework from which everything was either supported or hung, besides thousands of wooden wedges to cushion it from the walls. The architect was Ernst L. Freud, the son of Sigmund Freud.

On Mayday the whole company in their stage costumes went from Regent's Park to the Royal Exchange, headed by a mermaid represented by former Sadler's Wells Ballet dancer Penny Asserson. She was presented to the Lord Mayor, who then gave her this licence to perform in the City:

We, the Lord Mayor and Aldermen of the City of London, at the contemplation of the Letters of Bernard Miles and other poor players of London, and having regard to the Season and that Her Majesty sometimes takes delight in such pastimes, do welcome the said Bernard Miles and his Mermaid Theatre company to use the exercise of playing at the Royal Exchange and nowhere else within the City between the Feast of Easter and Lammas Day next coming, providing they play not upon the Sabbath Day, nor play any matter tending to the dishonour of Almighty God, nor to the quiet peace and government of the City.

Purcell's opera[1] featured the famous Norwegian soprano Kirsten Flagstad, long associated with Wagner's great music dramas, and in fact, Mme Flagstad gave her farewell stage performance to the world during the season on the night of 5 June. Kirsten Flagstad's original contract with Bernard Miles must be unique amongst any contract between management and a singer in that it contained a clause whereby the former undertook to supply the singer with two pints of oatmeal stout per diem, at the following times and in the following quantities, namely, lunch one half-pint, dinner one half-pint, and one pint following each performance.

On 22 April 1953, *The Times* published an article by Dr F. S. Boas pointing out that

in this year especially it should not be forgotten that the Royal Exchange and its association with the Sovereign and the City figure prominently in an almost contemporary play by another Elizabethan dramatist, Thomas Heywood. It is the second part of the play with the proverbial title *If You Know Not Me, You Know Nobody*, printed in 1606.

---

[1] The repertory for the three months' season was: Shakespeare's *As You Like It*, on 4–9, 11–16 May at 6.00 and 8.40 with matinées on 9 and 16 May at 2.50 p.m.; Kirsten Flagstad in Purcell's *Dido and Aeneas*, on 21–23, 25–30 May and 1–5 June at 6.00 and at 8.00, with one performance only on 2 June at 8.00 p.m.; Ben Jonson, Chapman & Marston's *Eastward Ho*, on 10–13, 15–20, 22–23 June at 6.00 and 8.40, with matinées on 13 and 20 June at 2.50 p.m.; Shakespeare's *Macbeth*, on 1, 5–6, 8, 10, 13, 15, 17, 20, 22, 24 July at 6.00; 2, 4, 7, 9, 11, 14, 16, 18, 21, 23, 25 July at 8.15 with matinées on 4, 11, 18, 25 July at 2.50 p.m.; twelve lunch-time recitals in association with the City Music Society at 1.05–1.45 p.m. on Fridays, 8, 15, 22, 29 May, 5, 12, 19, 26 June, 3, 10, 17, 24 July. The prices of the seats ranged between 2s. 6d. and 12s. 6d. ($12\frac{1}{2}$p–$62\frac{1}{2}$p).

The Central figure is Thomas Gresham, who had been the financial agent of the English Crown in the Netherlands. Ignoring this, Heywood introduces him in controversy with Sir Thomas Ramsey over the purchase of some land. Both, however, accept a decision by the Dean of St. Paul's as umpire, and are reconciled. Thereupon follows a violent storm which gives Gresham an inspiration:

> I do not like 't, nay and it angers me that such a famous City as this is,
> Wherein so many gallant merchants are,
> Have not a place to meet but in this,
> Where every shower of rain must trouble them.

He declares that he will have a roof built under which the merchants with their wives and friends will have shelter. His good resolution is confirmed by the display to him by the Dean of portraits of former citizens famous for their charitable deeds. He meets with a ready response from the civic authorities who buy and provide a site. As a Sheriff announces:

> We in name of the whole citizens
> Do come and give you full possession
> Of this our purchase, whereon to build a Burse,
> A place for merchants to assemble in,
> At your own charges.

It was a happy time when no further formalities were needed. Gresham at once buys the first brick of his 'new Burse,' and has 100 workmen ready to follow suit immediately. He announces the date as 'this seventh of June,' without adding the year, 1566. And to his admiring friends he shows 'plot', or model of the projected edifice, which was not completed till December 22, 1568. With the vague statement, 'It hath been long in labour', Heywood through Gresham's lips bridges over the three years' period between that date and the Queen's visit. The civic presentations made for it, and the stress on the details of the route taken by her, anticipate in their minor degree the processional arrangements of this year. The Lord Mayor orders that all things be ready to give her Majesty such entertainment as may grace London, and become the state her Highness brings along.

He asks, 'Where's the Queen now?' and is told:

> She comes along the Strand from Somerset House,
> Through Temple Bar, down Fleet Street, and the Cheap,
> The North Side of the Burse to Bishopsgate,
> And Dines at Master Gresham's, and appoints,
> To return on the South side through Cornhill.

Trumpets in the distance give note of her coming, and she enters attended by the Earls of Leicester and Sussex, and is met by Ambassadors with each of whom she speaks in his own language. Then calling for a herald and a trumpet she gives her orders:

> Proclaim through every high street of this city
> The place to be no longer call'd a Burse
> But since the building's stately, fair and strong
> Be it for ever call'd The Royal Exchange

Heywood then seriously violates chronology by making Elizabeth knight Gresham on the stage. He had attained that dignity for his services to the Government about 10 years previously. But it added to the theatrical effect and the queen particularizes the date of her visit:

> A thousand, five hundred and seventy one, Elizabeth
> Christens this famous work, Now to our Court
> Of Greenwich. Gresham, thanks for our good cheer.
> We to one people, they to us, are dear.

Could the effectionate bond today between Queen Elizabeth II and her loyal folk throughout the Commonwealth find fitter expression than in this last line spoken by Elizabeth I on a stage with a scenic presentation of the first Royal Exchange of which a later counterpart is to house a temporary Renaissance Theatre?

In April 1978 Bernard Miles endeavoured to secure the return of the Mermaid Theatre to the Royal Exchange for a period of eighteen months whilst his theatre at Blackfriars was being enlarged. The negotiations did not succeed due to likely problems concerning security, fire risk, disturbance of noise affecting the offices overlooking the courtyard, lack of heating and ventilation and the difficulties in providing lavatory accommodation. The general tone of the discussions was to discourage any attempt to rehouse the Mermaid Theatre.

Following the discovery of the Mithras Temple in the excavations at Walbrook, the sculptures raised considerable public interest and in 1953 a member of the City Corporation's Library Committee suggested that the courtyard might provide a permanent home for the Guildhall Museum, then occupying cramped temporary space in the Guildhall itself. The Gresham Committee agreed to allow the museum to use the courtyard for five years on condition that the main area continued to be available for the various temporary art exhibitions, and so forth.

This meant that the offices for the museum staff and the display cases had to be confined to the ambulatory. Featured items included specimens relating to all periods of the City's past, but special emphasis was given to the Mithras finds. The new museum was opened by the Lord Mayor on 29 June 1955 and by 1957 annual attendances had risen to over 122,000. By 1959 when four years of the initial five-year term had elapsed, a report to the Library Committee stated that 'the accommodation was by no means satisfactory'. There was no heating except in the offices, no water and no lavatories. The report further complained that at frequent intervals the work and displays of the museum were interrupted by 'totally irrelevant exhibitions' mounted in the centre of the courtyard. Negotiations for the amalgamation of the Guildhall Museum with the London Museum, which had started in 1959, had reached agreement by 1966 and the City Corporation decided to move the collection to further temporary accommodation on the newly built Bassishaw High Walk, not far from the brand new Museum of London being built in London Wall. This further temporary home was opened on 4 January 1968.

The removal from the Royal Exchange was really accelerated by press reports about the plight of the museum staff. The *Daily Mail* told its readers on 7 December 1966, 'people hurry from the Guildhall Museum in the City to the nearest Tube station, Bank. They aren't catching early trains home. They are all going to the lavatory'. A reporter from the *Daily Sketch* watched members of staff slip out of the Exchange 'clutching bits of paper and vanish into the Bank Underground station close by', where they presented their Corporation chitties to the attendant at the public 'wash-and-brush-up' (price 3*d*.) and were admitted free of charge.

By the end of 1967 the courtyard had reverted to its role as a haven for the public from inclement weather, courting couples and temporary exhibitions.

The Royal Exchange Assurance merger with Guardian Assurance in 1968 resulted in a new company called Guardian Royal Exchange plc (GRE) which continued to occupy the offices above, but

three major landmark events concerning the company took place in the courtyard, each being attended by 800/900 guests.

The first took place on 24 June to commemorate the 250th Anniversary of the formation under the Royal Charter on 22 June 1720 of the Royal Exchange Assurance; the second took place on 15 December 1971 to commemorate the 150th Anniversary of the foundation of the Guardian Assurance; and the final event was on 8 June 1978 to celebrate the retirement of Mr E. F. Bigland, the first Managing Director of GRE following the merger.

Early in 1980 deterioration of the cast iron dome (which had been erected in 1884 to a design by Charles Barry) caused by rain water penetration resulted in sections of the internal surrounding plaster cornice to fall, and this led to an immediate closure of the courtyard. As the Gresham Committee was unable or unwilling to authorise repairs, the closure continued until 1982 when a Government-supported scheme to establish a London International Financial Futures Exchange was agreed to be located there. This, like the Mermaid Theatre nearly thirty years before, was to be a prefabricated structure, but built on a concrete base covering the original Turkey sets. The building was not allowed to touch the stonework and was to be capable of easy removal at some later date. Trading commenced on 30 September 1982 and terminated on 13 December 1991 when LIFFE outgrew the premises and moved to a new market floor above Cannon Street station.

It is ironic that, for this period, Gresham's original trading concept was re-established, and although he may not at first have comprehended this form of 'open outcry' dealing one can be sure that, given his financial acumen, he would have soon grasped the rules and joined the ranks of the successful.

CHAPTER XXXIV

Decline and Redevelopment of the Third Royal Exchange

By COLIN CHRISTMAS

WHEN IN OCTOBER 1991, almost a hundred and fifty years after it was built, H.M. Queen Elizabeth II re-opened the Royal Exchange following a complex building programme to restore, extend and revitalise this Grade I listed building and former Ancient Monument, a royal association was maintained which had begun four centuries earlier, when on the same site Elizabeth I, accompanied by Sir Thomas Gresham, the founder, visited the original Exchange.

The ceremonial re-opening of the Royal Exchange marked the culmination of twelve years of intense activity and planning by Guardian Royal Exchange Assurance, the principal lessees of the building and their advisors, and drew to a conclusion over forty years of concern and debate by the freeholders, the Joint Grand Gresham Committee, for whom the ageing Exchange had become an anachronism, and with its decaying fabric and outmoded services, an increasing moral and financial burden.

In May 1979, Guardian Royal Exchange Assurance, a company formed some eleven years earlier by the merger of Royal Exchange Assurance with Guardian Assurance Company, advised the Joint Grand Gresham Committee that they not only wished to continue their occupation of the Royal Exchange but would be willing, if economic, to finance and undertake a scheme for the refurbishment and enlargement of the existing offices with a view to ensuring the suitability of the Royal Exchange as their International Headquarters office.

This far-reaching decision by GRE to consolidate their historic relationship with the Royal Exchange, first established in 1790 when Royal Exchange Assurance occupied part of the Second Exchange, signals a turning-point in the fortunes of a building which had been in decline since the beginning of the twentieth century and which had long since ceased to fulfil the function for which it was expressly built in 1844.

The present Royal Exchange was designed by the architect Sir William Tite in 1839 and is regarded as one of London's great civic monuments.

Tite's plan is a regular trapezium 90 metres long, reducing in width from 53 metres at the east end to 27 metres at the west, in the middle of which is a rectangular courtyard with direct access on its axes to the four surrounding streets and around which is arranged a deep arcade. At the eastern end of the building rises the campanile, surmounted by a gilded grasshopper, symbol of the Gresham family and possibly the only surviving relic of the First Exchange. In the organisation of the plan, with its courtyard open to the sky, shops around the perimeter and offices at first floor level, Tite remained faithful to the examples of the first and second Exchanges which themselves were based on the great sixteenth-century Bourse at Antwerp.

It was some forty years before Charles Barry, jun., won a limited competition to design a roof over the courtyard. Tite's parapet was demolished to allow Barry's barrel-vaulted and glazed roof to spring from a coving supported on the existing cornice, and a glazed dome over the centre three bays completed the composition. Ironically, the 'improvement' would, less than a hundred years later, be the cause of a great deal of anxiety, as the inappropriate and poorly fixed plaster embellishments rotted and began to fall away.

The usefulness of the Exchange, as a pre-eminent centre of commerce, was even more short-lived, and towards the end of the nineteenth century business began to drift away as the various trades and professions acquired their own Exchanges. Specialist

FIG. 163.   Proposal for the redevelopment of the Royal Exchange; drawing by Messrs Collins, Melville and Ward.
Guardian Royal Exchange collection

Coal, Corn and Hop Exchanges each contributed towards the inexorable decline of the Royal Exchange. Even more important was the trend towards transacting business in private offices. After the First World War, according to Kent's *Encyclopaedia of London*, merchants assembled for only an hour or so on Tuesdays and Thursdays to transact business, but by 1921, even this desultory activity had ceased.

Lloyd's departure in 1928, after an occupation on the site which had dated back to 1774, would seem to be the *coup de grâce* for the Exchange, and even as a symbol of a glorious past when the building was

FIG. 164.   Proposal for the redevelopment of the Royal Exchange; drawing by Messrs Collins, Melville and Ward.
Guardian Royal Exchange collection

synonymous in the public mind with 'commerce', the Exchange lost its relevance in the national conscience.

In the report of the Royal Commission on Historic Monuments of 1929, the Royal Exchange was not included among the buildings recommended as worthy of preservation, and a decade later, when the building was closed to the public at the request of the Police as a precaution against the danger of air raids, not one protest was heard.

The Exchange, however, was built to last, and in the course of the Second World War its substantial structure of load-bearing stonework survived,

FIG. 165. Silver gilt and enamel casket presented to Her Majesty Queen Elizabeth II by Guardian Royal Exchange on the occasion of the re-opening of the Royal Exchange on 23 October 1991.
Guardian Royal Exchange collection

virtually undamaged, the impact of high explosive bombs which fell close by in Cornhill and Threadneedle Street.

As the war drew to a close, the Joint Grand Gresham Committee confronted the fundamental question of what to do with the Exchange, and on 17 May 1944 their Surveyor summarised the conundrum which the freeholders, and their consultants and advisors, would address at regular intervals for the next forty years. The Surveyor reported that:

The Royal Exchange is more in the nature of an historic monument of the past rather than serving any real function in the commercial life of the city.

Most of its features indicate its character as a building designed for a special purpose rather than a commercial building in the accepted sense.

As a percentage of net income, the cost of upkeep is abnormally high for a building 100 years old and these costs will have a tendency to increase in the future.

Disregarding the historical and sentimental interest, the building as a commercial investment must already be regarded as obsolete.

The building occupies an area of approximately 1 acre in a position which is unique.

In addition to the Surveyor's report, and no doubt reflecting the climate of opinion at the time, Dr A. H.

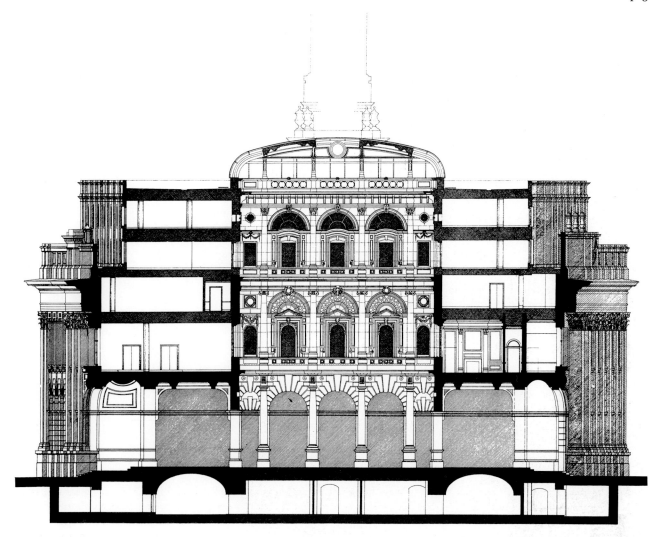

FIG. 166.   Cross-section showing new courtyard of the Royal Exchange, drawn by Alan Rafter-Phillips.
Private collection

Thomas, Deputy Keeper of the Records of the Royal Exchange, in his contemporary report to the Town Clerk on the propriety of disposing of the Exchange to the Bank of England, observes that 'people consider it a gloomy building, ill arranged and old fashioned, a heavy example of early Victorian taste'.

Six years later, with the tide of public and architectural opinion turning in favour of conservation, the freeholders' options were severely diminished by the Minister for Town and Country Planning, who gave notice that the Royal Exchange would be Listed Grade I as the 'symbolic centre of commercial life in the City as much as for its architectural quality'.

By 1950 the Exchange's architectural status was consolidated by its inclusion in the list of ancient monuments, as a building of such national interest that it should be preserved. Within, many offices continued to operate in near Dickensian conditions.

It seemed by now that the slowly decaying building could only be preserved as an historic relic, and when in 1963 exploratory discussions took place on proposals to demolish the Exchange, with the exception of the portico, and rebuild on the same site, the Minister of Public Buildings and Works responded that it was his duty to preserve such buildings, and added somewhat frostily that he would strongly resist

Fig. 167.   Perspective drawing showing the courtyard unencumbered, by Paul Freeman.
Private collection

any attempt to demolish or reconstruct the building, even if it became 'no more useful than a Medieval Castle'. During the course of the meeting, a proposal that the Royal Exchange could perhaps be used as a museum was roundly condemned by the Inspector of Ancient Monuments and Historic Buildings, on the grounds that it was too obsolete for this purpose!

For Royal Exchange Assurance, the principal lessees at that time, who had instructed Sir William Holford and Collins, Melville and Ward to prepare the exploratory studies, the verdict was conclusive, and it was accepted that no development could take place.

With the passing of another decade, the plight of the Royal Exchange was becoming more acute, and the Joint Grand Gresham Committee in collaboration with Guardian Royal Exchange decided to examine the possibility of remodelling and enlarging the existing building. From a shortlist of architects which included the President of the RIBA, Alexander Gordon, Sir Giles Gilbert Scott & Partner, and William Whitfield who, being pre-eminent in the field of modernisation of prominent buildings in the City, was chosen to explore the possibilities. By 1978, however, although the outline studies had been generally approved at planning officer level in 'design concept terms', the project was abandoned when the required level of support from Guardian Royal Exchange could not be guaranteed.

Meantime the Surveyor's Annual Structural Reports spoke prophetically, as it would turn out, for the need to carry out repairs to Barry's roof, which by now was exhibiting serious signs of rusting and general deterioration.

Such, then, was the backdrop to GRE's offer in 1979 to the Joint Grand Gresham Committee to undertake a scheme, at their own expense, to refurbish and enlarge the Royal Exchange.

A joint committee of the freeholders was immediately set up and within two months it was agreed that their policy

should be to encourage GRE to produce as commercial a scheme as was practicable, to refurbish and enlarge the existing office space and retail areas within the constraints imposed by the fabric of the building and its status as a Grade I Listed Building and Ancient Monument, consistent with the dignity of the Corporation and the Mercers' Company.

The freeholders' measured response provided the catalyst for GRE to appoint the Fitzroy Robinson Partnership as architects, to see what could be achieved to meet the aspirations of both GRE and the freeholders. Whilst the architects addressed the overall problems of the Exchange, in a separate exercise, Ian Kennard, Surveyor to the Joint Grand Gresham Committee, began negotiations with the London International Financial Futures Exchange (LIFFE) to explore the possibility of housing its operation in the Royal Exchange.

Even as progress was made on both fronts, in the evening of 30 August 1980, a two-hundredweight section of fibrous plaster broke away from Barry's roof without warning and crashed to the courtyard floor, providing a timely reminder to all concerned that action was required urgently.

Six months later, following detailed investigations which indicated serious overall dilapidation and leakage of the roof, the courtyard was closed to the public, and the structure made safe pending the outcome of the architects' deliberations, and the LIFFE negotiations.

GRE now decided to shelve their overall plans, as it emerged that, for the Gresham Committee, a financial futures market offered a solution which would restore the courtyard to its original function as an important centre of commerce in the City, while providing almost immediate revenue; the necessary accommodation could be carefully designed by Whinney McKay Lewis the architects, so as not to affect materially the fabric of the building.

The market was designed as an enclosed steel capsule, air-conditioned and fully serviced, covering the entire courtyard and ambulatory and rising to first floor sill height. Ancient Monument consent was granted, leasing arrangements agreed, and following its rapid construction and fitting out the market was soon in full cry, and it proved to be a resounding financial and technological success.

It was apparent, however, to GRE, their architects Fitzroy Robinson & Partners, structural and mechanical engineers Oscar Faber & Partners and quantity surveyors Henry Riley & Son, all of whom were reappointed by GRE in 1983, that the existence of LIFFE in the heart of the Exchange might prove an insurmountable obstacle to demolition and reconstruction above, below and adjacent a market turning over £26 billion of stock per day. Whilst it was implicit in LIFFE's leasing arrangements that development of the Exchange would be allowed and encouraged by the freeholders, GRE and their consultants were made equally aware that no disruption by noise, vibration, dust or dislocation of services could be tolerated which might interrupt the continuous functioning of the market, the electronic infrastructure or its personnel.

Undaunted, GRE drew up their detailed requirements which called for the architects to address all the fundamental inadequacies of the building. The exchange should be replanned with new entrance halls, lifts, staircases and corridors strategically located to improve access and circulation for both GRE and future tenants; it should incorporate raised platform floors and suspended ceilings for easy access to new services, and the building should be air-conditioned throughout. Two additional office floors were required, and the plethora of outmoded plant rooms, ducts and labyrinthine offices which had sprouted around Barry's courtyard roof since the end of the nineteenth century should be removed.

Within the Royal Exchange, the architects found that little tangible evidence of its illustrious past had survived a modernisation programme, carried out in 1929. Lloyd's palatial first floor Reading and Under-writing rooms were destroyed, and an additional, unlit, second floor level was constructed within the cavernous interior.

On the south side of the Exchange, however, also at first floor level, a fine suite of rooms which had been in almost continuous occupation by the Royal Exchange Assurance since 1844 remained substantially unscathed, and it would now be a requirement to restore and air-condition them, to form the core of GRE's executive accommodation.

Externally, the rejuvenation of the Exchange would be completed by repairing and repainting the fabric where necessary, cleaning the Portland stone façades and regilding Gresham's grasshopper wind vane, which for four hundred years had conspicuously represented the epicentre of commercial life in the City.

The architects' options for replanning the Royal Exchange were limited by the constraints imposed by Tite's rigorous plan form which, with the courtyard as its centre, would leave little room around the perimeter to insinuate the banks of high-speed lifts, escape stairs and vertical ducts necessary to service the building. Such difficulties are normal, however, when any venerable building requires comprehensive modernisation.

In the case of the Royal Exchange the unique and fundamental problem confronting the architects was

how to design two additional office floors on top of the Exchange, thus increasing its height by almost a third, whilst respecting and sympathising with Tite's concept and the orthodoxy of his composition.

Tite's description of his winning entry for the Royal Exchange indicates that his energies were concentrated on the imposing, west-facing portico, which he argued should present the character of grandeur, simplicity and usefulness.

At the opposite end of the building, the bell tower and cupola surmounted by Gresham's grasshopper provided a counterpoint, and the north and south elevations Tite described as exhibiting 'unbroken lines of entablature, with a repetition of arches of the same character for the shops, offices and entrances'.

Each element was an entity, and together formed an harmonious composition allowing little scope for further development. The courtyard elevations differ in style and scale from the exterior, however, with the lower arcade storey having a Doric order, and the upper fenestrated storey the Ionic, and it would be from this classically correct stacking of the orders that a solution to the seemingly intractable problem of adding two floors to the Royal Exchange would eventually emerge.

The obvious and conventional solution for increasing the floor space would have been to replace the hotchpotch of offices and plant rooms which littered the original roof at third floor level, with offices built up to form new third and fourth floors around the outside of Barry's courtyard roof, disguised externally to appear as a mansard roof behind Tite's parapet.

This concept, which had been given serious consideration some years earlier, merited conscientious re-examination since the approach, though pedestrian, offered the twin advantages of being low-key politically, and low in construction cost. For the architect, however, this inherited scheme appeared unworkable and inelegant in section, a somewhat subjective reaction perhaps, but confirmed by close analysis which revealed its shortcomings. Daylight into the offices would have been obscured on one side by the exterior of Barry's steeply rising barrel vault, springing from third floor level, and on the other side by the tall parapet surrounding the Royal Exchange. Views outwards would be dreary, Barry's roof being particularly offensive, having been designed on the outside with a certain 'agricultural' abandon, to be seen at a great distance, if at all.

In addition, the occupants of the new offices would be denied views of the mysterious and historic courtyard below them; they might almost be anywhere, and their isolated working environment would therefore compare badly with the accommodation enjoyed in the old part of the building. Finally the mansard roof enveloping the offices, rising above the external parapet of the existing building; a common enough sight on redeveloped buildings throughout the City, would in this instance contribute little to the stature of the Royal Exchange as a Listed Building and Ancient Monument.

Consequently a fresh and radical approach would be necessary to solve the deficiencies which a conventional redevelopment scheme would inherently embody.

In order to re-connect the tenants of the proposed third and fourth floors to the hub of the Royal Exchange, by providing views into the courtyard, it would be necessary to dismantle Barry's roof, add the two extra floors to Tite's courtyard façades, and reconstruct Barry's roof above the new fourth floor. This fundamentally different approach, at first a daunting proposition, led directly to the architectural solution.

Tite's formal arrangement of the classical orders in the courtyard — Doric which masked the ground and mezzanine floors, and Ionic the first and second floors — conveniently suggested that the courtyard elevations could now be 'completed' by the addition of the third great architectural order, the Corinthian, as a façade for the proposed third and fourth floors.

The solution seemed appropriate and authoritative, and by adding the Corinthian order to the Doric and Ionic orders bequeathed by Tite, thus completing the classical hierarchy, Tite's long shadow cast its influence on to the twentieth-century restoration and enlargement of the Royal Exchange. The decision to embark on a classical route for the extension of the courtyard would now inform all subsequent design considerations, and would wherever possible conform to the Gresham Committee's original design brief, which called for a building in the 'Greek, Roman or Italian style'.

On the outside of the Royal Exchange, the new floors would re-appear deferentially, as a classically detailed, double height attic, set well back from the existing parapet, offering no challenge to Tite's extravagantly detailed façades.

As the scheme developed on the drawing board, terraces were created, daylight admitted to areas long covered over, and as Tite's details, sometimes submerged beneath years of piecemeal alterations, were rediscovered, they were worked into the proposals.

The proposed scheme was not for the faint-hearted, given the strength of the conservation lobby who, it was anticipated correctly, would view the proposals with less than rapture, and a more timorous client than GRE and their project director, Mickola Wilson, might well have withdrawn support at this time in favour of a more modest option.

In the event, the scheme was approved by GREA, and in June 1984 by the Joint Grand Gresham Committee, and preparations were made to seek Planning, Listed Building and Ancient Monument Consent. The applications were short-lived when the Historic Monuments Commission considered that it would be inappropriate for the proposals to be subject to both Ancient Monument and Listed Building Controls, a judgment upheld by the Secretary of State for the Environment; and in February 1985 the Royal Exchange was peremptorily deleted from the Statutory Schedule of Ancient Monuments.

While GRE and their advisors considered the next move, a press conference was held and the scheme made public. Separate presentations were made by the architects to the Victorian Society, Georgian Group, SAVE Britain's Heritage and the Royal Fine Arts Commission, and discussion of details continued with the City and English Heritage.

Reactions to the scheme by the conservation groups and the press were generally hostile but guarded, in some cases recognising the validity of the architectural solution on its own terms, while remaining implacably opposed to its implementation, as a matter of principle.

In defence of the scheme, however, Anthony Blee of the Sir Basil Spence Partnership, appointed by the Gresham Committee as an independent Historic Buildings expert, noted that to some extent the courtyard proposals followed the precedent set by Michaelangelo, who, in 1545 following the death of Antonio da Sangallo the younger, finished the Palazzo Farnese in Rome by adding a Corinthian floor to the cortile. The differences in quality, style and details of the two buildings was recognised, but the scale and volume of the courtyards were to an extent comparable, giving rise to Blee's belief that the proposed courtyard would be 'elegant and nicely proportioned'. The Royal Fine Arts Commission and English Heritage seemed to concur with this opinion, and whilst expressing reservations on matters of detail, recorded their support for the scheme.

Raising Barry's roof to its new level over the proposed Corinthian order was another matter, however, and a ground swell of opinion seemed to agree with Clive Aslet, who in his critique in *Country Life* summarised that 'it will pop up like an urchin looking over a fence'.

Salvaging Barry's roof in the interests of conservation, already a bleak option structurally and economically, now gave way to the final radical decision to remove Barry's problematic roof once and for all, and design a new one, unobtrusive when viewed from afar, but compatible with the new courtyard elevations within.

While the architects addressed their new concerns, Oscar Faber, the structural and mechanical engineers, and Henry Riley & Son, the quantity surveyors, refined answers to three unique and complex problems which the critically narrow constraints of the design had imposed upon them.

The first question was whether, notwithstanding the fact that some of the old roof excrecencies would be removed, the considerable extra weight of additional office floors, new stonework façades, and roof-top plant rooms could be supported by the existing foundations and structure. Extensive studies were carried out by the engineers to determine the strength of the original 700 mm un-reinforced lime concrete and ballast foundation, the condition of twenty-four brick piers and vaults in the basement, and the composition of the 'Roman cement' mortar bonding. The ambulatory walls, external façade and retained cross walls would all be employed to support the new floors and were also subjected to intense scrutiny to establish their stability.

It was concluded that by strengthening the vaults and brick piers with heavily reinforced concrete surrounds and segments within the arches, the new work, which apart from the stonework cladding would be predominantly steelwork and lightweight concrete floor slabs, could safely bear upon the old foundations and load-bearing walls above. As a precaution, however, because of the complexity of the original structure and the difficulty of examining all areas prior to demolition, the engineers would need to monitor the patterns of load-bearing as work on the scheme progressed.

The incontrovertible rules of classical proportion which dictate the relationship in height between the Doric, Ionic and Corinthian orders would also dictate, with little room to manoeuvre, the height of the floors between the orders.

A further concomitant of this precept is that, once properly proportioned windows have been placed within the orders, the only space left for service trunking will be between the windows' heads and the underside of the floors above.

In a Grade I listed building it would be unacceptable for floors, ducts or false ceilings to obscure, even partially, window areas for the sake of technical expediency, and as a result the engineers faced their second problem, that of designing the services to fit diminished ceiling voids which had been determined by the proportions of the three orders in the courtyard.

Compounding the problem, it was also necessary for the engineers to install major plant elements into awkward spaces on the roof, in the unlit second floor and in the vaulted basement, and from these disparate sources, somehow feed air-conditioning trunking, telecom and data distribution services discreetly throughout the building and into the lavish, protected suite of boardrooms at first floor level.

After a careful analysis of the requirements and selection of suitable plant, including a fan-coil unit air-conditioning system which, unlike most commonly used systems, could fit into the restricted zone above the ceiling, the engineers demonstrated that they would be able to meet all the demands of their brief within the constraints imposed by the existing building, and the architects' solution for its extension and rehabilitation.

The third and perhaps most perplexing complication for Oscar Faber, GRE, and later the contractor, was the need to assure LIFFE, which occupied the whole courtyard, that during the demolition of Barry's iron and glass roof and subsequent construction of the Corinthian extension high above them, all their services would remain intact and there would be no interruption, for whatever reason, to the continuation of their daily activities.

The engineer's solution was direct. A weatherproof and impact-resistant deck was designed to cover the courtyard above LIFFE's roof, comprising no less than 5 kilometres of contiguous aluminium beams, supported on steel trusses which in turn would rest on the first floor window ledges. A 75 mm sandwich of polystyrene and plywood, incorporating a multi-layered waterproof membrane, would cover the 'crash deck'; and the entire edifice, requiring 500 tons of steel to construct, would provide LIFFE with the necessary noise, weather, dust and vibration free environment they required.

On completion of the method statement for the protection of LIFFE's market, the fundamental architectural, engineering and services disciplines had been drawn together, costings were prepared by the quantity surveyor Henry Riley & Son, and GRE's brief was substantially fulfilled.

Fresh applications for planning and listed building consent were drawn-up following the de-listing of the Royal Exchange as an Ancient Monument, and a submission for approval of the scheme was made to the City Corporation on 15 October 1985.

In all significant respects the submitted scheme remained as it had been conceived, but matters of detail had been addressed in response to observations often helpful or stimulating from the City Corporation and the Royal Fine Arts Commission.

By now opinion had polarised, and the lines had been drawn for a planning debate which would decide the fate of the Royal Exchange. The conservation groups and Amenity Societies maintained their publicly stated positions, SAVE holding firm to the view that the scheme '. . . threatens the character of the Exchange both internally and externally and is quite unacceptable for a historic building of such importance in the history and townscape of the City'. After reviewing the scheme, the Victorian Society

also re-asserted that it '. . . continues to feel that the alterations proposed are of far too radical a nature to be acceptable in the case of a Grade I Listed Building of major significance within the City'. By this time, the media, Amenity Societies and City Architect were generally agreed that, as a matter of principle, the Royal Exchange as a Grade I listed building should not be altered to this extent, and the scheme hung in the balance.

Six months after the submission, however, the first major hurdle was overcome when the London Division of the Historic Buildings and Monuments Commission decided that, notwithstanding the opposition of the Amenity Societies, it would be prepared to grant Listed Building Consent. Within the accompanying report, which significantly recognised the practical necessities which had led to the application, the Commission summarised its findings:

The existing character of the Royal Exchange is robust and assured, aimed at a measure of opulence. The proposals take their inspiration from that existing character and in some respects would increase the impact which the building at present makes on the observer. The Corinthian storey to the hall can be seen as adding to, rather than diminishing the imperial splendour at which Tite clearly aimed, while the change in proportion would increase the dramatic content of the interior.

On 8 July 1986 the Planning Committee met to resolve the issue. The City Architect, sharing the views of the Amenity Societies, recommended refusal of planning permission on the grounds that the Royal Exchange was one of the few Grade I Listed Buildings in the City and the extension would adversely affect the appearance of the building. Conversely the Committee felt that the main features of the building would maintain their prominence, the extension would barely be noticeable, and that the needs of a modern City financial institution should be met. Accordingly, by a majority of 18 to 1, the Committee resolved that the redevelopment of the Royal Exchange, with a new low profile courtyard roof, be approved in principle.

The Court of Common Council subsequently noted that,

The fact that a building is listed, as of special architectural or historical interest, does not mean that it will be preserved intact in all circumstances, but it does ensure that the case for its preservation is fully considered through the procedure for obtaining planning consent.

By January 1987, to the palpable relief of the promoters, Planning Permission and Listed Building Consent were received, and there began twenty-two months of intense activity in the preparation of working drawings, and, for the design team, absorbing and enlightening research into source material to ensure the authenticity of the classical details.

Bills of quantities were prepared, engineering solutions honed, and for GRE there would be the additional task of allaying the mounting fears expressed by LIFFE, for the safe and continuous operation of their market during the demolition and rebuilding programme.

During this period the architects turned their attention to the design for a new roof to replace Barry's crumbling structure. Initial thoughts were directed towards a simple steel and glass solution, similar in principle to the roof Sir Joseph Paxton had suggested for the Royal Exchange in 1851, a structure which appeared to have been derived from his transept in the Crystal Palace of the same year.

Unlike the structural austerity of the Crystal Palace, however, the Royal Exchange interior has always been a colourful and vibrant affair and, at its opening, all available surfaces in the ambulatory had been covered in frescos, competing in colour and intricacy with the tessellated courtyard floor, which owed its provenance to the mosaics of Ancient Rome.

Although the giant 'mosaic' had been removed early in its life as it had degenerated, and Sang's frescos later obliterated with plain paint, the initial intent was clear and it was therefore resolved to enliven the courtyard and hint at its colourful past by designing a gently curved glass roof, incorporating deeply coffered and richly coloured and decorated 'ceiling' panels.

The final design owed its origins to a monochrome illustration, published in *The Builder* in 1848, of a roof over the Museum of Economic Geology by Sir James Pennethorne, a contemporary of Tite, and provided an appropriate precedent, allowing scope for further development.

As the new roof begins two floors higher than Barry's, a shallow curved profile was adopted for the main structure, in order to conform with English Heritage's requirement that the new roof should be no higher at its apex than the top of Barry's original structure. Eight slender beams were designed by the engineers, using computer technology, to span the 18-metre courtyard, each springing from the new stone parapet reinstated from Tite's original drawings, and aligned with the Corinthian columns below.

The beams would support the double-glazed roof and fourteen 4-metre square coffered panels, ornamented with egg and dart, guilloche and other classical motifs to animate the roof design, provide solar shading within the courtyard, as well as walkways above for routine maintenance.

The entire roof was designed by the engineers to rest on sliding bearings, allowing the safe lateral movement of the structure caused by thermal expansion and the imposition of live and dead loads.

With the completion of the roof design, subsequently approved by the Planners and English Heritage, the last pre-eminent design hurdle had been cleared and the way was open for the twenty-seven-month contract to begin on site.

Laing London (of the John Laing Construction Group) were chosen as main contractors, responsible for running and programming their own work and that of myriad sub-contractors from the heavy demolition, concrete steel and stonework gangs to the specialist craftsmen.

Work began by scaffolding the outside walls, and a decorated plastic hoarding, with a full-size depiction of the Royal Exchange portico at its western end, thought at the time to be the largest architectural graphic in the world, was attached to the scaffolding to shroud the building.

On the inside, by craning steel girders through the first floor windows and into the courtyard, the massive 'crash deck' to protect LIFFE throughout the contract and ensure their continuity of trading was put into place.

Demolition and stripping out the interior would take forty-two weeks and begin in dramatic fashion by dismantling Barry's substantial but fragile courtyard roof. In a controlled sequence of operations, after making due allowance for the potentially destructive forces which would be released as segments of the giant barrel vault and dome were removed, the iron and glass edifice was carefully deconstructed. To ensure safety, most of the work was carried out at night after the LIFFE market below had closed down, but to the equal relief of the client, contractor and consultants as well as LIFFE, the objective was accomplished without incident, and an important milestone had been passed.

On completion of the full demolition programme more than 20,000 cubic metres of debris had been removed from the Royal Exchange, and the skills of the demolition contractor, T. E. Scudder, and Laing the main contractor, had combined to such effect that none of the LIFFE's 2,000 telephone lines had suffered during the controlled chaos around them, and the individual traders, for whom financial catastrophe loomed if demolition dust caused a momentary loss of vision, continued their frenetic activities unabated.

With demolition complete, all that remained of the Royal Exchange were the shops facing Cornhill and Threadneedle Street which continued their daily routine, the cocooned suite of preserved rooms on the first floor, the external and courtyard façades and the campanile, all of which were stabilised with a cat's cradle of scaffolding and bracing. The empty Exchange now echoed only to the muffled caterwauling of LIFFE's dealers ensconced in their protected shell.

Another milestone had been passed and the process of building accelerated rapidly with the arrival on site of the steelwork, some of which would be inserted with clinical precision through the walls and cavities of the preserved first floor rooms, and all swiftly assembled to form the framework and support of the new floors, light aggregate concrete walls and Portland stone façades.

Far away in Portland, the stone which would be required for the attic storeys and solid courtyard elevations was blasted from the Coombefield quarry and transported to Bath and Portland's Corsham works for processing.

In Corsham, computer modelling was employed to organise the planning, supply and fixing of 1,000 cubic metres of stone required for the scheme and assist its transformation into an 11,000-piece jigsaw, to be re-assembled on site within a fifteen-month timescale.

In contrast, traditional hand crafting skills of the highest order were employed to create the intricate Corinthian capitals, swags, scrolled keystones and anthemion embellishments for the courtyard, ensuring a quality equal to that of the craftsmen of Tite's day.

From his garden studio in the hamlet of Kilmerston near Bath, the sculptor and carver Mel Morris-Jones fashioned the first of twenty-four Corinthian capitals needed for the courtyard elevations.

Visiting the studio was a humbling experience for the architects and planning officers, there to 'approve' the work, who witnessed the sculptor, dust-covered from the material with which he was working and almost indistinguishable from it, undercutting luxuriant scrolls and foliage to wrest a Corinthian capital from one tonne of inert stone, his assistance being only the architect's drawing and the mallets and chisels bequeathed by tradition.

Each capital required six weeks to complete, and other skilled stone carvers, working from plaster casts of the original, were drafted in to achieve the work, with allowance being made for the individual 'handwriting' of each craftsman.

The first deliveries of stone reached the Royal Exchange in the autumn of 1989 and in December, with the second, third and fourth floors in skeletal form and roofed over, the building was topped out, in traditional manner, with suitable refreshment all round, by Sir Hugh Bidwell, Lord Mayor of London.

The year 1990 was heralded by the January hurricane which swept most of England, and stranded the three principal members of the architectural design team in Newhaven at Toggle Industries factory, where the vibrantly coloured and deeply coffered glass-reinforced plastic courtyard roof panels were nearing completion. In London the vast decorated hoarding was carried away as the hurricane blew itself out, but the scaffolding remained, as did the Exchange.

A more serious threat to the Exchange in the London of the 1980s was posed by terrorism, and in recognition of that fact, twenty-four-hour security had been maintained as a priority from the commencement of the contract. The wisdom of the decision was reinforced when, on 20 July 1990, Threadneedle Street was closed following an explosion which shook the neighbouring Stock Exchange, but the Royal Exchange was affected by no more than a temporary suspension of minor building activities.

Inside the Exchange, in more peaceful circumstances, attention had turned to the preserved rooms where services wee being installed, and decorative, open guilloche and lattice profiles, moulded in plaster from remnants of Tite's original details, were utilised as barely discernible ceiling grilles for air-conditioning in the oak-panelled Court Room, main corridor and adjoining Committee Rooms.

A plaster-domed dining room nearby, which in the past had been modelled on Sir John Soane's dining room in his Lincoln's Inn Square house, received special attention, and the marbled plastered walls and decorations were developed after studying Soane's drawings and the restored rooms in his country house, Pitzhanger Manor.

In a remote part of the first floor, three adjoining rooms formerly used by Lloyd's Sea Captains were also retained and decorated with stencilled patterns and borders in the style of the 1840s, following advice freely given by Dr Clive Wainwright of the Victoria and Albert Museum, who also directed the architects to the contemporary works of Owen Jones and later published source material by the Audsley Brothers. These valuable references resulted in the choice of Victorian colours which ensured a sympathetic relationship between the decorations of the Captains' rooms, the painted lantern over the eastern vestibule to the original Lloyd's entrance, and the coloured panels of the courtyard roof.

As the contract drew to a close with the completion of the courtyard roof and all the stonework façades, and while the scaffolding was being struck beneath Tite's cleaned and re-roofed portico, there remained one final act to be performed at the opposite end of the building, before the main contract could be properly concluded.

At the invitation of Ted Kier, Laing's imperturbable site manager, the architects, engineers and surveyors gingerly climbed the campanile scaffold, past the clock mechanism and carillon now restored by the original makers, to the top of the cupola; where, on a gently swaying platform 'for inspection purposes', they could admire the glistening, restored and regilded Gresham grasshopper, defending its space from the mere mortals around it and proclaiming its status high above the Royal Exchange, as the pre-eminent icon of commercial life in the City.

In April 1991, following the triumphant re-instatement of the golden grasshopper, the main contract was completed, but work continued as a separate contract to fit-out GRE's own offices to the exacting standards required for its International Headquarters.

When GRE returned to their traditional home, the retained first floor rooms which included the Chief Executive's Suite, the panelled Court Room and Committee Rooms had been lavishly redecorated, the second floor was equipped with audio-visual facilities with executive dining rooms nearby, and one area was specifically designed and carefully lit to display many of the historic artefacts associated with GRE's occupation of the second and third Exchanges.

In addition to GRE's headquarters, over 40,000 square feet of office space with de-mountable coffered ceilings incorporating air-conditioning, acoustic panels and lighting had been made available for letting.

Externally, five new shops were created, and not for the first time in its history, a public restaurant was re-introduced to the basement.

On completion of the scheme, fifty years of uncertainty concerning the future of the Royal Exchange had ended, and its redevelopment had assured its future for well into the twenty-first century, not as an anachronistic leftover from a bygone age, but as a vital living organisation capable of meeting current business demands as successfully as it had for the merchants and tenants for which it was built in 1844.

During the contract Laing London was awarded a 'Gold' under the City's Considerate Contractor Scheme, and the designers of the hoarding, Sampson Tyrrell, had received awards for improving the environment during the construction period.

Bath and Portland were highly commended for their stonework, and following the Royal opening by Queen Elizabeth II in October 1991, the Royal Exchange claimed the annual City Heritage Award for 'the best example of building conservation in the City of London'.

Final judgement must rest with Guardian Royal Exchange whose headquarters it remains, with the

Joint Grand Gresham Committee the freeholders, and with future occupants of the building, but it is hoped that the building and its restoration and enlargement accords with the sentiments expressed by Henry Russell-Hitchcock, a leading authority on Victorian architecture built between 1837 and 1851, who observed:

Architecture is, properly speaking, not collectible. Certain preservation programs amount to collecting buildings, however, and some museums collect — perhaps unwisely — what are called period rooms.

In general the more closely the attitudes of enthusiasts for the architecture for any period approach those of the collector, the more harm they do. Yet the monuments of any period of the past require intelligent understanding and respect from posterity if they are not all to be destroyed outright or else quite de-natured by unsympathetic renovation.

APPENDIX I

TRANSACTIONS OVER THE SITE OF THE EXCHANGE

The following extracts are from the Journals in the Corporation of London Record Office.
In 1839, they were transcribed and published by order of the Corporation. Here, we follow the text as printed.

Jor. Draper,
No. 19, fo. 12,
and
Letter Book V.
fo. 70b.

A Booke concernynge the newe Burse intended, which shall declare the charge that the cittie and citizens thereof susteyned and bare for th'obteynynge of the soyle thereof, and the names of every cittizen that contributed towardes that charge, and the somes that every of them haithe contributed, and other necessary matters worthie to be had in memory. Written the xiiij day of *September, Anno Domini* 1566, in the tyme of Sir *Richarde Champion*, Maior.

The Tenements late scituated on the Soyle of the Burse, purchased as foloweth:

Christs Church landes.
Purchased of the Deane and Chapter of *Christs* Churche in *Caunterburye*, xiij tenements, one storehowse, one garden and voide waye or soyle leadinge to a well, valewed at xxv*li. per ann.* There is to be paide for the same D.C*li.*, within six monethes next after request made for the same, and in the meane tyme and so longe as the said vj*C li.* is unpaide, they are to be paide xxx*li. per ann.* – – – – – – – – – – – – – – – – – – } 600*li.*

Travesses landes.
Item, of *John Traves*, marchaunttaylor, sixe tenements, and the moytie of one tenement, and one small cottage; and is paide for the same – – – – – – – – – – – – – – } 226*li.* 13*s.* 4*d.*

St. *Michaells* parish in *Cornehill* landes.
Item, of the Parson and Parishioners of the churche of St. *Michaell* in *Cornehill*, one tenement; and is paid for the same – – – – – – – – – – – – – – – – – – } 120*li.*

Mr. *Haywardes* landes.
Item, of *Rowlande Haywarde*, alderman, towe tenements; and is paide for the same – – } 340*li.*

Mr. *Pawnes* landes.
Item, of Mr. *Pawn*, of *Essex*, three tenements; and is paide for the same – – – – – – } 200*li.*

Sollam and *Meres* landes.
Item, of *John Sollam* and *Walter Meres*, towe tenements; and is paide for the same – – } 205*li.*

Mr. *Springhams* landes.
Item, of *Richarde Springham*, merecer, towe tenements; and is paide for the same – – – } 350*li.*

Mr. *Phillipps* lands.
Item, of *William Phillipps*, marchaunttaylor, vij cotages; and is paide for the same – – } 100*li.*

Jakes landes.
Item, of Mystres *Jakes* and her children, one small parte of a tenement; and is to be paide for the same lxvj*li.* xiii*s.* iv*d.*, which money is in the chamber of the cittye, and paide to th'andes of Mr. *Heton*, Chamberlyn of the cyttye, by *Thomas Rowe*, by the commaundement of the Lorde Maior and Courte of Aldermen – – – – – – – – } 66*li.* 13*s.* 4*d.*

Summa totalis of the Landes and Tenements purchased – – – – – – – – – – – – – – – – } 2208*li.* 6*s.* 8*d.*

The Leaces and Mens Interests of the Tenements aforesaide, bought and redemed as foloweth, and the gratefienge of other inhabitaunts, tenaunts at will inhabitinge there:

Bowghte of *Martyn Canne*, clotheworker, a leace of towe Tenements, parcell of *Christ's* Churche landes; and is paid for the same – 72*li.*

Item, of *William Bathewe*, clotheworker, one leace of a howse, parcell of *Christs* Churche landes; and is paide for the same – 60*li.*

Item, of *William Phillipps*, marchauntaylor, the lease of three howses, parcell of *Christs* Churche landes; and is paide for the same – 200*li.*

Item, of *Sampson Walkaden*, the leace of thre tenements, parcell of *Christs* Churche landes; and is paide for the same – 15*li.*

Item, of *Bateson*, clotheworker, for his interest of the said leace aforemencyoned; and is paide thereof iv*li.*　8*li.*

Item, of *Thomas Altham*, clotheworker, for one leace of a howse, parcell of *Christs* Churche landes; and is paide for the same – 100*li.*

Item, of *Anthony White* and *Henry Russhall*, towe leases of towe tenements, late the landes of *Sollam* and *Meres*; and is paide for the same – 120*li.*

Item, of *Phillipp Jones* one lease of three tenements, parcell of *Christs* Churche rents; and is paide for the same– 60*li.*

Item, of *John Traves*, one lease of one tenement, parcell of *Pawnes* landes; and is paide for the same– – 200*li.*

Item, of *Robert Dunkyn*, marchauntaylor, a leace of towe tenements, parcell of *Pawnes* landes; and is paide in hande xx*li.* by Mr. *Jackman*, and he is to be paide by the Chamberlyn Cxl*li.*; after, xx*li. per ann.* – – – 160*li.*

Item, of *Ralff Seymour*, clotheworker, one lease of one howse, parcell of *Phillipps* landes; and is paide for the same – 6*li.*

Item, of *Anthony Lamberdin*, draper, one leace of a howse, parcell of *Phillips* landes; and is paide for the same– 14*li.*

Item, of *William Prynne*, draper, one leace of a howse, parcell of *Phillipps* landes; and is paide for the same　20*li.*

Item, of *John Pickeringe*, barbor, a lease of one howse, parcell of *Phillipps* landes; and is paide for the same　16*li.*

Item, of *John Clarke*, tailor, a lease of one howse, parcell of *Phillips* landes; and is paide for the same　– – 14*li.*

Item, of *Thomas Lancaster*, a lease of one howse, parcell of *Phillips* landes; and is paide for the same– – – 15*li.*

Item, paide to *Humfrey Parrys*, barbor, for the redemption of his interest of one howse, late the landes of St *Michaell* in *Cornehill*– 33*li.* 6*s.* 8*d.*

Item, to *Blage*, clotheworker – 6*li.*

Item, to *Mathewe Heydon*, clotheworker – 8*li.*

Item, to the Inke wief – 20*s.*

Item, to goodwiffe *Hills*, for a lease, parcell of *Christs* Churche landes, whoe is to be paide by the Chamberlyn, by the order of the Maior and Courte – 29*li.* 9*s.*

Item, to *Kirbye* – 6*s.* 8*d.*

Item, to *Evan Appowell* – 5*s.*

Item, to goodwiffe *Roberts*– 30*s.*

Item, to goodwiffe *Spencer*– 6*s.* 8*d.*

Item, to *Atkyns*, shoemaker – 30*s.*

Item, to goodwiffe *Kinge* – 20*s.*

Item, there is to be paide yearelye, over and above the aforerecyted somes, 3*li.*, whiche is to be paide for obbett money to the Quene's Matie, goinge owte of the landes late Mr. *Pawnes*, wch beinge valewed after xx yeres purchase, maketh the some of – 60*li.*

Summa totalis of the Redempcõn of the landes and interests, with rewardes geven to the tenants at will – 1222*li.* 14*s.* 0*d.*

――――――

Charges necessarely spent and geven in rewarde for the procurement of the purchases aforesaid, and for th'assuraunces of the same, as followeth:

Geven in rewarde to the Prebendaries of *Caunterbury*, and to Mr. *Lovelaes*– – – – – – – – – – – – 20*li.*

Item, to the Register of *Caunterbury*, for the fees of the churche, and Mr. *Hides* fee, beinge Register– – – 4*li.* 10*s.*

Item, to the Rent-gatherer of *Christchurche* – 6*s.* 8*d.*

Item, to *Cox*, the Maiors officer, for his charges and the charges of the Register and others, towe tymes ridinge to *Caunterburye* – 4*li.* 6*s.* 8*d.*

Item, to the Chauncery men, for the licences procured under the greate seale for the churche of *Caunterbury* to passe there landes to the cytie, and for writting the saide licences– – – – – – – – – 10*li*. 9*s*. 6*d*.

Item, to Sir *William Hewett*, that he demaunded for his charges goinge downe to Mr. *Pawens* – – – – – 20*s*.

Item, to Mr. *Salvyn* and his clarkes, for councell drawinge and ingrossinge diverse bookes– – – – – – 54*s*.

Item, to Mr. *Hone* his clarkes, for writting of bookes – – – – – – – – – – – – – – – – – – 13*s*. 4*d*.

Item, to Mr. *Wilbram* his clarkes, for ingrossinge of bookes – – – – – – – – – – – – – – – – 6*s*. 8*d*.

Item, to *Stokes*, Mr. *Haywarde* his scrivenor, for ingrossinge a booke betwene the said Mr. *Haywarde* and the cittye – 6*s*. 8*d*.

Item, to M. Recorder his clarkes, for ingrossinge a greate booke betwene the cyttye and Sir *Thomas Gresham*, knight – 3*li*. 13*s*. 4*d*.

Item, to *Wallett* and *Willis*, for there attendaunce and paynes takinge – – – – – – – – – – – – 3*li*. 6*s*. 8*d*.

Item, to *Willis*, for his charges to *Tunbridge* to fetche up *Sollam* – – – – – – – – – – – – – – – 14*d*.

Item, to the Outroper, for his rewarde for sellinge the howses – – – – – – – – – – – – – – – 40*s*.

Item, to the Outroper's belman, for his paynes – 7*s*.

Item, for a chiest to laye the evidences in, and for writinge this booke, and the booke presented to Sir *Thomas Gresham*, knight – 44*s*.

Item, for the clensinge of the vawtes of the soyle, and is paide by Maister Chamberlyn of the cyttye – – 37*li*. 19*s*.

Item, for th'enrowlinge of the dedes and indentures passed by diverse of the sellers of the landes above mencyoned, and the fees therunto belonginge, which is to be paide by Mr. Chamberlyn, if it be reqwired 7*li*. 11*s*. 10*d*.

Summa of the pettye chargies – 101*li*. 16*s*. 6*d*.

Summa totalis of the hole chargies – 3532*li*. 17*s*. 2*d*.

Whereof the cittye oweth as followeth,
videlicet:

To the Deane and Chapter of *Caunterbury* 600*li*., and the cyttye is to pay yerely, duringe the tyme the same some is unpaide, 30*li*. *per ann*., and the same to be paide halfyerely – – – – – – – – – – 600*li*.

Item, to *Robert Dunkyn*, 140*li*., whiche is to be paid 20*li*. *per ann*, untill the same be full paide – – – – – 140*li*.

Item, to the Quene's Maistie, for an annuell rent of 3*l*. *per ann*. paiable owte of the landes late Mr. *Pawnes* 60*li*.

Item, to goodwiff *Hills*, 29*li*. 9*s*., whiche is to be paide half yerely, after 31*s*. *per ann*. – – – – – – – 29*li*. 9*s*.

Item, to *John Jakes* widdowe and his children, 66*li*. 13*s*. 4*d*., and is to be paide when the children come to there age; in the meane tyme M^ris. *Jakes* is to have 3*li*. 6*s*. 8*d*. paide to her yearely – – – – – – – – 66*li*. 13*s*. 4*d*.

Item, to Mr. *Haywarde*, alderman, for the rest due to him of the landes solde by him to the cyttye, of whiche some he shulde have bene paide by the late Alderman *Banckes* – – – – – – – – – – – – – 6*li*. 13*s*. 4*d*.

Item, to the Owtroper – 40*s*.

Item, to *John Gardener* – 13*s*. 4*d*.

Item, to *Batensonne*, clotheworker – 3*li*.

Item, there is owinge further to the companyes, which they have prested, *viz*., to the Drapers 60*li*., to the Mercers 70*li*., to the Grocers 60*li*., to the Marchaunt Taylors 60*li*., to the Goldsmithes 40*li*., to the Haberdashers 40*li*., to the Clotheworkers 30*li*., to the Fishemongers 40*li*., to the Iremongers 30*li*., to the Vinteners 20*li*., to the Sadlers 20*li*., to the Tallowechaundlers 10*li*., and to the Cutlers 10*li*., whiche are to be repaide at the Annunciacion of Our Ladye, in *anno Domini* 1567 – – – – – – – – – – – – – – – 490*li*.

Summa totalis of this Debt – 1399*li*. 9*s*. 0*d*.

A Releffe towardes the aunsweringe of the said Debte:

By 66*li*. 13*s*. 4*d*. paide in money into the Chamberlyns handes, to the use of *Jakes* his children – – – – 66*li*. 13*s*. 4*d*.

Item, by a frame of vij tenements, with the bricke tile leade and other stuf to the same appertaynynge, geven into the possession of the Chamberlyn, and valued at – – – – – – – – – – – – – – – – 100*li*.

Item, by these persones here named, which promysed to contribute towardes the charge aforesaid certen somes of money, as followeth, and hathe not paide the same, by reason whereof they are debters to the cittye, *viz. John Bull*, mercer, 3*li* 6*s*. 8*d*.; *John Foxall*, mercer, 30*s*.; *Robert Selman*, mercer, 20*s*.; *Thomas Heron*, grocer, for Mr. *Fowler*, 40*s*.; *Raffe Pinder*, grocer, 20*s*.; *William Chapman*, grocer, 26*s*. 8*d*.; Mr *Beswicke*, draper, 3*li*. 6*s*. 8*d*.; *Richarde Cragge*, draper, 20*s*.; *John Daniell*, draper, 20*s*.; *Thomas Eymes*, draper, 20*s*.; *William Gravener*, goldsmith, 4*li*.; Mr. *William Armorer*, clotheworker, 40*s*.; *William Ricksman*, clotheworker, 20*s*.; Mr. *Harrys*, letherseller, 20*s*.; Mr. Alderman *Bankes* his widdowe, 6*li*. 13*s*. 4*d*.; *John Marshall*, fishemonger, so muche as he shall have in rewarde for the forbearinge of his corne money – – – – – – 30*li*. 3*s*. 4*d*.

Item, John Braunche, draper, for the rest of towe howses sold him – – – – – – – – – – – – – – – 7*li*. 6*s*. 8*d*.

Summa of this Releaffe – 204*li*. 3*s*. 4*d*.

The howfinge lately scituated on the soile aforesaide, with the glasse leade bricke tyle tymbre and other stuff to the howses aforesaid apperteynynge, beinge solde to diverse persons, as followeth, contributed towardes the charge aforesaid, as foloweth:

The howfe latelye apperteynynge to St. *Michaells* churche, solde to Mr. *Braunche* – – – – – – – 67*li*. 6*s*. 8*d*.

Item, the lesser howse late Mr. *Haywardes*, solde to *Wright* the baker – – – – – – – – – – – 12*li*. 13*s*. 4*d*.

Item, the greater howse late Mr. *Haywardes*, solde to Mr. *Banister* – – – – – – – – – – – – – 45*li*.

Item, three howses late Mr. *Pawnes*, in one whereof Mr. *Traves* lately dwelled, and Mr. *Dunkyn* in an other, and the goodwiff *Roberts* in the other, and solde to Mr. *Beacher* – – – – – – – – – – – – 53*li*. 10*s*.

Item, one howse, late *Caunterbury* landes, whereof Mr. *Altham* dwelled, solde to *Evan Jones* – – – – – 40*li*.

Item, one howse, late *Meers* and *Sollames* landes, wherein *Rushall* dwelled, solde to Mr. *Braunche* – – – – 40*li*.

Item, the howse late *Meers* and *Sollames*, wherein *Anthony White* dwelled, solde to *Anthony Pryor* – – – – 27*li*.

Item, fyve howses, parcell of *Blackehorse* alley and late *Phillipps* lands, solde to *John Gardiner* – – – – – 20*li*.

Item, towe other howses of the said alley, and late *Phillipps* landes, solde to *John Browne* – – – – – – 8*li*. 13*s*. 4*d*.

Item, a litle howse in *Traves* landes, solde to *John Traves* – – – – – – – – – – – – – – – – – 16*li*.

Item, seven howses, late *Caunterburie* landes, in *Newe* alley, sold to Mr. *Allen* – – – – – – – – – 47*li*.

Item, fyve howses, late *Caunterburie* landes, in *Newe* alley, solde to Mr. *Mase* – – – – – – – – – 23*li*.

Item, towe howses, late *Springham* landes, sold to Mr. *Warner* – – – – – – – – – – – – – – – 50*li*.

Item, sex howses, late *Traves* landes, in *Swanne* alley, solde to *Richarde Dycher* – – – – – – – – – 9*li*. 10*s*.

Item, one litle howse, in the garden late *Caunterburie* landes, solde to *Kilbye* – – – – – – – – – – 40*s*.

Item, one litle store howse, late *Caunterbury* landes, solde to *Martyn Canne* – – – – – – – – – – 20*s*.

Item, the moytie of a howse, late *Traves* landes, solde to Mr. *Traves* – – – – – – – – – – – – – 4*li*. 10*s*.

Item, the brickes of *Caunterburie* garden and Mr. *Traves* garden, solde to Mr. *Springham* and Mr. *Beacher* – 11*li*.

Summa – 478*li*. 3*s*. 4*d*.

Hereafter shall appeare the names of all those persons as haith contributed towardes the chargies aforesaide, and haithe paide the same, with there severall somes that everye person haithe contributed and paide.

MERCERS.					
Sir Thomas Lighe	10*li*.	John Marsshe	5*li*.	Robert Wollman	3*li*.
Sir Richarde Malorye	10*li*.	Richarde Carrell	5*li*.	Thomas Revett	5*li*.
Roger Martyn, *Ald.*	10*li*.	Thomas Heton	5*li*.	Thomas Moore	4*li*.
Wm. Allen Allen, *Ald.*	10*li*.	William Chelsame	5*li*.	John Fitzwilliams	3*li*. 6*s*. 8*d*.
Lyonell Duckett, *Ald.*	10*li*.	John Greshame	6*li*. 13*s*. 4*d*	Thomas Egerton	3*li*.
Vincent Randall	5*li*.	Richarde Barnes	3*li*. 10*s*.	Henry Smythe	5*li*.
John Baker	3*li*.	John Bramston	20*s*.	Henry Champion	3*li*. 6*s*. 8*d*.
John Coseworthe	40*s*.	Richarde Springham	10*li*.	John Isham	5*li*.
		William Burde	5*li*.	Phillipp Cockeram	5*li*.

MERCERS.

Thomas Searle	–	3li. 6s. 8d.
William Lennarde	–	3li.
Matthew Fielde	–	4li.
Geffrey Duckett	–	4li.
Henry Vynar	–	5li.
Thomas Conney	–	50s.
Edwarde Castlyn	–	5li.
Thomas Bradshawe	–	50s.
Anth. Throgmorton	–	3li. 6s. 8d.
Anthony Calthropp	–	40s.
Edmonde Huggman	–	5li.
Edmunde Gressham	–	5li.
Richarde Hill	–	40s.
Richarde Graye	–	5li.
William Wrothe	–	40s.
Anthony Garrett	–	53s. 4d.
Thomas Hargrave	–	3li. 6s. 8d.
William Meredeth	–	4li.
Thomas Coranefield	–	3li. 6s. 8d.
Ambrose Smythe	–	3li. 6s. 8d.
Edwarde Worsope	–	4li.
Nicholas Lewsone	–	3li. 6s. 8d.
Henry Hungate	–	3li. 6s. 8d.
William Revett	–	3li. 6s. 8d.
Henry Ishame	–	3li.
Thomas Denhame	–	53s. 4d.
Robert Horewoode	–	53s. 4d.
William Lewsone	–	3li.
Dunstaine Walton	–	3li. 6s. 8d.
Ambrose Harrys	–	3li.
William Smythe	–	3li.
Walter Copinger	–	3li.
Roger Smythe	–	3li.
John Barfoote	–	3li.
John Conniers	–	3li. 6s. 8d.
Henry Russell	–	50s.
Thomas Bradley	–	20s.
Anthony Bucklowe	–	40s.
Thomas Griffith	–	30s.
Frauncis Kelke	–	40s.
William Elkyn	–	20s.
John Ceake	–	33s. 4d.
Richarde Painter	–	20s.
Richarde Hollyman	–	3li.
Henry Busshopp	–	40s.
Drewe Mompesson	–	40s.
William Dansey	–	30s.
Mathewe Gray	–	20s.
Richarde Mirthe	–	40s.
Anthony Walthall	–	20s.
Alexander Chisnall	–	40s.
Thomas Eadon	–	20s.
Hewgh Bradley	–	40s.
Edwarde Pickington	–	40s.
John Baker	–	40s.
Yonge Mr. Hare	–	20s.
Fuller, *th'elder*	–	20s.

Summa – 296li.6 s. 8d.

DRAPERS.

Sir Richard Champion, *Lorde Maior*	–	13li. 6s. 8d.
Sir William Chester	–	10li.
Mr. Quarles	–	5li.
Mr. Braunche	–	5li.
Mr. Brooke	–	40s.
Mr. Frauncis Barnam	–	5li.
Mr. Sadler	–	3li. 6s. 8d.
Mr. Wheler	–	5li.
Mr. Goslinge	–	20s.
Mr. Martyn Caltrope	–	6li. 13s. 4d.
Mr. Sutton	–	3li.
Mr. Lawrence	–	3li. 6s. 8d.
Brian Calverley	–	30s.
Mr. Warner	–	20s.
William Chester	–	30s.
George Braithwate	–	30s.
William Throogoode	–	30s.
James Penyngton	–	30s.
Mr. William Parker	–	40s.
Thomas Pullison	–	40s.
John Kempe	–	3li.
Thomas Barnam	–	30s.
Henry May	–	30s.
Mathewe Colclothe	–	40s.
John Totten	–	40s.
Walter Garrawey	–	40s.
William Vaughane	–	30s.
Anthony Prior	–	30s.
John White	–	20s.
John Noble	–	40s.
William Megge	–	30s.
Thomas Bulman	–	30s.
Laurence Goffe	–	40s.
John Marshe	–	30s.
Richarde Reynolds	–	30s.
Thomas Fisher	–	20s.
Nicholas Ager	–	20s.
William Tymes	–	20s.
John Trott	–	30s.
Thomas Chester	–	40s.
Henry Planckney	–	20s.
John Lowen	–	20s.
Humphrey Chaffyn	–	20s.
Richarde Bilham	–	20s.
Edwarde Boise	–	20s.
Symon Horsepole	–	20s.
Thomas Bye	–	20s.
Thomas Wiggan	–	20s.
John Gilbert	–	20s.
William Hobbs	–	20s.
Giles Lambert	–	20s.
Robert Chaundler	–	20s.
George Ulley	–	20s.
Abraham Veale	–	20s.
William Tempest	–	20s.
Thomas Walton	–	20s.
John Pawmer	–	20s.
William Wilkenson	–	30s.
Richarde Clarke	–	20s.

Anthony Webbe	–	20s.
William Gilbert	–	20s.
William Barnarde	–	20s.
William Garrawey	–	20s.
Richard Goddarde	–	20s.
William Lowe	–	20s.
Reignolde Hollingsworthe	–	20s.
Thomas Ellyot	–	20s.
Richard Champion	–	26s. 8d.
William Foxe	–	20s.
William Kelthridge	–	20s.
Richarde Sandall	–	10s.
William Coppinger	–	20s.
John Marshall	–	10s.
Thomas Duffelde	–	10s.
John Hale, and – Ricthorne		20s.
Roberte Coxe	–	10s.
Edmunde Moore	–	10s.
Vincent Painter	–	20s.

Summa – 144li.

GROCERS.

Sir John White, *Knt.*	–	13li. 6s. 8d.
Mr. Richarde Lambert, *Ald.*	–	10li.
Mr. Edwarde Jackman, *Ald.*	–	10li.
Mr. Jno. Ryvers, *Ald.*	–	10li.
Mr. Thomas Pickett	–	40s.
Mr. Richarde Thornell	–	5li.
Mr. Frauncis Bowyer	–	5li.
Mr. William Tuckar	–	20s.
Mr. Henry Mylles	–	6li.
Mr. William Boxe	–	4li.
Mr. Thomas Ramsey	–	4li.
Mr. Nicholas Luddington	–	53s. 4d.
Mr. Nicholas Revell	–	50s.
Mr. William Bodnam	–	5li.
Mr. William Coxe	–	20s.
Mr. Blase Saunders	–	20s.
Mr. Gregory Newman	–	3li. 6s. 8d.
Mr. Frauncis Robinsone		4li.
Mr. Wantone	–	40s.
George Stodderde	–	4lili.
Laurence Shereff	-	3li.
Thomas Gore	–	4li.
William Gibsone	–	4li.
Edwarde Elmere	–	4li.
Nicholas Backehouse	–	6li.
John Lambert	–	3li. 10s.
John Ritchie	–	3li.
Rauff Hitchecoke	–	30s.
Thomas Gunne	–	20s.
Robert Bassocke	–	40s.
William Smalewoode	–	40s.
John Blackman	–	3li.
William Yonge	–	53s. 4d.
George Stokmeade	–	40s.
John Moodie	–	40s.
Richarde Yonge	–	4s.

GROCERS.

William Armeshawe	—	3 *li.*
Rauff Woodcocke	—	3 *li.*
Richarde Colmer	—	40*s.*
Roger Wharfielde	—	3 *li.*
John Harte	—	3 *li.* 6*s.* 8*d.*
Hughe Morgan	—	5 *li.*
John Chapman	—	4 *li.*
William Cooke	—	3 *li.* 6*s.* 8*d.*
Humphrey Fairefaxe	—	3 *li.* 6*s.* 8*d.*
Richarde Chapman	—	20*s.*
Henry Cloke	—	30*s.*
John Turpyn	—	20*s.*
Thomas Hale	—	40*s.*
William Somerland	—	20*s.*
Walter Stonne	—	40*s.*
William Rowlandsonne	—	30*s.*
William Messe	—	33*s.* 4*d.*
Henry Foulkes	—	30*s.*
James Hewes	—	30*s.*
William Penningtonne	—	40*s.*
William Shackeltoune	—	30*s.*
Thomas Heatoune	—	13*s.* 4*d.*
John Thompsonne	—	40*s.*
Richarde Howlett	—	20*s.*
John Bull	—	53*s.* 4*d.*
Thomas Grey, *jun.*	—	30*s.*
William Horne	—	40*s.*
John Hudsonne	—	40*s.*
William Frende	—	3 *li.*
Robert Hardie	—	30*s.*
Edmunde Nedhame	—	30*s.*
Gabriell Colstoune	—	20*s.*
William Luddington	—	13*s.* 4*d.*
William Lare	—	20*s.*
William Smyth	—	30*s.*
Thomas Marten	—	40*s.*
Robert Winch	—	3 *li.*
Thomas Millingetone	—	30*s.*
John Gardener	—	3 *li.* 6*s.* 8*d.*
John Colmer	—	30*s.*
Richarde Cuttes	—	30*s.*
Richarde Denman	—	20*s.*
John Pelsaunte	—	30*s.*
William Massam and Robert Brooke	—	3 *li.* 6*s.* 8*d.*
Richarde Hale	—	40*s.*
Valentyne Cotten	—	30*s.*
William Salter	—	30*s.*
William Lovedaye	—	33*s.* 4*d.*
Marke Dingley	—	50*s.*
Ottwell Glydell	—	40*s.*
John Kirkby	—	40*s.*
Edwarde Mullynex	—	30*s.*
William Staines	—	20*s.*
John Jackman and John Bristowe	—	40*s.*
Gregory Yonge	—	30*s.*
William Cooles	—	20*s.*
George Southwicke	—	20*s.*
William Villers	—	40*s.*

John Lee	—	20*s.*
John Spencer	—	20*s.*
John Sturtyvant	—	40*s.*
Thomas Tyrrell	—	40*s.*
Thomas Hearne	—	20*s.*
Richarde Thomas	—	40*s.*
Edmunde Piggot and John Allen	—	40*s.*
John Wauton	—	40*s.*
John Rogers	—	40*s.*
Christopher Johnson	—	20*s.*
William Wauton	—	10*s.*
William Nowell	—	40*s.*
John Parker	—	53*s.* 4*d.*
Phelix Laurence	—	20*s.*
Dunstane Anys	—	40*s.*
Thomas Longstone	—	15*s.*

Summa – 281 li. 18s. 4d.

GOLDESMITHES.

Sir Martin Bowes, *Knt.*	—	13 *li.* 6*s.* 8*d.*
Mr. Stanley	—	40*s.*
Thomas Bowes	—	20*s.*
Thomas Gardyner	—	30*s.*
William Procter	—	20*s.*
Mr. Edward Gilbert	—	3 *li.*
John Langley	—	3 *li.*
John Harrysone	—	3 *li.*
Robert Browne	—	5 *li.*
Thomas Mustian	—	40*s.*
Marten Bowes	—	20*s.*
John Wetherall	—	30*s.*
Henry Sutton	—	20*s.*
John Mabb	—	20*s.*
Thomas Metcalf	—	20*s.*
Robert Fryar	—	20*s.*
William Holborne	—	20*s.*
Affabell Partridge	—	40*s.*
William Dixone	—	20*s.*
William Denhame	—	20*s.*
James Stoke	—	30*s.*
John Daniell	—	15*s.*
Richarde Rogers	—	40*s.*
Robert Wells	—	20*s.*
Frauncis Heaton	—	20*s.*
Richarde Marten	—	30*s.*
John Robinsone	—	20*s.*
Robert Brandone	—	40*s.*
Henry Gilbert	—	20*s.*
Robert Harrysone	—	20*s.*
William Calton	—	20*s.*
William Humfrey	—	20*s.*
Frauncis Trappis	—	20*s.*
Robert Askewe	—	20*s.*
John Foxe	—	20*s.*
Dericke Anthony	—	20*s.*
Frauncis Jacksone	—	20*s.*
John Paye	—	20*s.*
Thomas Clarke	—	20*s.*
Richarde Wickliffe	—	20*s.*
Richarde Handbury	—	20*s.*

John Eccleston	—	20*s.*
George Dalton, *jun.*	—	30*s.*
William Noke	—	20*s.*
Symon Brooke	—	20*s.*
John Waterscott	—	20*s.*
Henry Gainsford	—	20*s.*
Thomas Hartoppe	—	10*s.*

Summa – 78 li. 1s. 8d.

FISHEMONGERS.

Mr. Cowper, *Ald.*	—	3 *li.* 6*s.* 8*d.*
Christofer Bussher	—	40*s.*
Edmunde Warner	—	30*s.*
William Bulley	—	30*s.*
John Violett	—	40*s.*
Thomas Turnebulle	—	40*s.*
Thomas Jenings	—	3 *li.*
Thomas Sicclemore	—	40*s.*
Robert Yonge	—	4 *li.*
Robert Woode	—	20*s.*
Nicholas Hacker	—	30*s.*
Humfrey Wells	—	20*s.*
James Bacon	—	5 *li.*
Richarde Story	—	20*s.*
Henry Wallys	—	3 *li.*
Adrian Searell	—	20*s.*
John Pearse	—	4 *li.*
Richard Monse	—	30*s.*
Thomas Ware	—	50*s.*
Arthure Maltby	—	40*s.*
John Haines	—	40*s.*
John Turke	—	40*s.*s.
Owen Waller	—	20*s.*
Humfrey Keale	—	30*s.*
Richarde Violett	—	30*s.*
John Allott	—	40*s.*
Roger Hoole	—	20*s.*
Richarde Hopkyns	—	53*s.* 4*d.*
John Edmunds	—	26*s.* 8*d.*
Henry Hewarde	—	26*s.* 8*d.*
Edwarde Newborne	—	20*s.*
Simon Mawe	—	13*s.* 4*d.*
William Landishe	—	20*s.*
Henry Sleade	—	20*s.*
William heynes	—	30*s.*
Stephen Swinckfield	—	20*s.*
Thomas Bolnost	—	20*s.*

Summa – 67 li. 16s. 8d.

SKINNERS.

Mr. Gunter	—	3 *li.*
Mr. Fletcher	—	26*s.* 8*d.*
Mr. Walkaden	—	10 *li.*
Mr. George Allen	—	30*s.*
Mr. Starkey	—	4 *li.*
Mr. Franks	—	20*s.*
Mr. Anncell	—	3 *li.*
Mr. Forman	—	5 *li.*
Mr. Raybrown Bankes	—	20*s.*
Mr. Mawham	—	20*s.*
Mr. Banister	—	4 *li.*

SKINNERS.

Thomas Allen	—	3*li.*
Morgan Richards	—	40*s.*
William Banks	—	20*s.*
Mr. Dixe	—	3*li.*
Mr. Cocken	—	40*s.*
Mr. Slaney	—	40*s.*
Thomas Laurence	—	20*s.*
Richarde Salkinstall	—	40*s.*
Roger Bewe	—	20*s.*
Anthony Burbage	—	20*s.*
Awgustine Porter	—	20*s.*
Richarde Hewsone	—	20*s.*
Thomas Stone	—	20*s.*
William Towerson	—	40*s.*
George Lee	—	20*s.*
Nicholas Bucke	—	26*s.* 8*d.*
Thomas Pratt	—	30*s.*
John Middletone	—	40*s.*
Thomas Awdley	—	20*s.*
Foulke Heathe	—	20*s.*
Roger Mountague	—	20*s.*
Robert Colman	—	13*s.* 4*d.*
Barthilmewe Dabney	—	10*s.*
John Harrys	—	20*s.*
Blase Freeman	—	20*s.*
Thomas Gabb	—	26*s.* 8*d.*
Gryffyn Jones	—	20*s.*
Robert Springe	—	20*s.*
Richarde Bradshawe	—	26*s.* 8*d.*

Summa – 74*li.* 10*s.*

MARCHAUNTE TAYLORS.

Sir Thos. Offley, *Knt.*	—	10*li.*
Sir William Harper	—	5*li.*
Thomas Roe, *Alderman*	—	10*li.*
Sir John Yorke	—	6*li.* 13*s.* 4*d.*
John God	—	3*li.*
Emanuell Lucar	—	40*s.*
Richarde Hills	—	5*li.*
Robert Rose	—	50*s.*
John Offley	—	5*li.*
Rauff White	—	20*s.*
Thomas Browne	—	4*li.*
Frauncis Pope	—	40*s.*
William Sullyarde	—	3*li.*
Jerrard Gore	—	5*li.*
John Traves	—	5*li.*
Thomas Tomlynson	—	20*s.*
John Sparke	—	40*s.*
William Albanny	—	53*s.* 4*d.*
Robert Houlsonne	—	50*s.*
Christopher Merler	—	40*s.*
Nicholas Love	—	30*s.*
Thomas Shotteshame	—	3*li.*
William Kimpton	—	3*li.* 6*s.* 8*d.*
Richarde Johnsone	—	50*s.*
John Arthure	—	40*s.*
William Heton	—	40*s.*
Thomas Wilforde	—	50*s.*
William Hodsone	—	40*s.*

Nicholas Skeares	—	10*s.*
Richarde Ryall	—	10*s.*
Nicholas Spencer	—	30*s.*
Thomas Williamsone	—	30*s.*
George Willsdone	—	50*s.*
Richarde White	—	40*s.*
Arthure Dawbney	—	53*s.* 4*d.*
John Milner	—	3*li.*
Roberte Dove	—	5*li.*
Roberte Hawes	—	30*s.*
Richarde Offley	—	40*s.*
Thomas Smythe	—	30*s.*
John Mansbridge	—	30*s.*
Giles Jacobe	—	40*s.*
John Sleade	—	3*li.*
Charles Hoskyns	—	3*li.*
Richarde Bourne	—	30*s.*
William Phillips	—	3*li.* 6*s.* 8*d.*
Anthony Ratcliff	—	3*li.* 6*s.* 8*d.*
John Bragdon	—	30*s.*
Thomas Collett	—	40*s.*
Richarde Maye	—	30*s.*
Edwarde Bowen	—	20*s.*
Nicholas Clarkson	—	20*s.*
Rauff Spratt	—	30*s.*
Robert Brett	—	20*s.*
Mr. Thomas Offley	—	53*s.* 4*d.*
Mr. William Mericke	—	4*li.*
Mr. Wilkinsone	—	30*s.*
Mr. Sollame	—	40*s.*
Frauncis Warren	—	40*s.*
Richarde Williams	—	20*s.*
Richarde Hentone	—	20*s.*
Richarde Paramore	—	40*s.*
Thomas Pope	—	20*s.*
William Nedham	—	20*s.*
John Tappe and John Eadon	—	40*s.*
Edwarde Cruckston	—	20*s.*
George Saunders	—	40*s.*
Frauncis Withers	—	20*s.*
William Handforde	—	20*s.*
Nynyan Coxtone	—	20*s.*
Richarde Porter	—	20*s.*
Richarde Harrysone	—	20*s.*
Thomas Worledge	—	20*s.*
Richarde Nicolsone	—	20*s.*
Reynolde Barker	—	30*s.*
William Offley	—	10*s.*
Mr. Atkinson	—	10*s.*
Mr. Tolnage	—	20*s.*

Summa – 183*li.* 3*s.* 4*d.*

HABERDASSHERS.

Sir William Garrard, *Knt.*		10*li.*
Mr. Peacoke	—	40*s.*
Mr. Offley	—	4*li.*
Mr. Luntlowe	—	40*s.*
Mr. Beast	—	40*s.*
Mr. Hobsone	—	40*s.*
Mr. Beacher	—	5*li.*

Mr. Harbottell	—	20*s.*
Mr. Johnsone	—	20*s.*
Mr. Buckland	—	40*s.*
Mr. Awsten	—	20*s.*
Mr. Hawle	—	40*s.*
Mr. Blanke	—	4*li.*
Mr. William Bonde	—	5*li.*
Mr. Christofer Edwardes		40*s.*
Mr. Patricke	—	3*li.* 6*s.* 8*d.*
Mr. Petersone	—	40*s.*
Mr. Rigg	—	50*s.*
Mr. Smythe	—	3*li.* 6*s.* 8*d.*
Mr. Woodroff	—	3*li.* 10*s.*
Mr. Bancks	—	30*s.*
Mr. Cocke	—	40*s.*
George Barnes	—	4*li.*
Thomas Aldersey	—	4*li.*
Thomas Sares	—	40*s.*
John Barnes	—	4*li.*
Nicholas Culverwell	—	3*li.* 6*s.* 8*d.*
Frauncis Benesone	—	3*li.* 6*s.* 8*d.*
Henry Dale	—	40*s.*
William Sherringtone	—	40*s.*
Clement Kelcke	—	40*s.*
Thomas Bracey	—	40*s.*
Thomas Browne	—	30*s.*
Thomas Sanders	—	30*s.*
Launcelot Stringer	—	30*s.*
Edmonde Moyses	—	20*s.*
Roberte Appowell	—	40*s.*
Barthilmewe and Frauncis Dodd	—	5*li.*
John Abell		50*s.*
Ellis Wignall		40*s.*
Auncell Berket		50*s.*
Robert Gabbord		40*s.*
William Skott		50*s.*
Symon Smyth		30*s.*
George Bonde		3*li.*
Thomas Allen		30*s.*
William Stone		50*s.*
Christopher Hodsone	—	3*li.*
John White		40*s.*
— Candishe		20*s.*
John Tudball		50*s.*
Robert Stokes		50*s.*
Richarde Grangier		40*s.*
Richard Braborne		30*s.*
Humfrey Marbury		50*s.*
Stephen Woodrooffe		50*s.*
Richard Smythe		20*s.*
Henry Billingsley		20*s.*
John Darnelly		40*s.*
William Cowper		30*s.*
James Kayne		20*s.*
Thomas Marstone		40*s.*
John Hutton		20*s.*
John Hobson		13*s.* 4*d.*
William Armesley	—	20*s.*
Edmunde Calthropp	—	30*s.*
John Radall	—	20*s.*

HABERDASSHERS.

John Barwicke	–	20s.
Henry Averill	–	30s.
Edmunde Bowes	–	20s.
Thomas Bramley	–	30s.
Roberte Pheins	–	40s.
John Newton	–	30s.
Thomas Nevell	–	50s.
Phillipp Dodd	–	20s.
John Hotton	–	30s.
William Swayman	–	20s.
Richarde Gurney	–	20s.
John Stone	–	20s.

Summa – 175*li.*

CLOTHEWORKERS.

Sir William Hewett	–	10*li.*
Mr. Haywarde, *Ald.*	–	10*li.*
Mr. Hawes, *Ald.*	–	10*li.*
Mr. Fowlks	–	3*li.*
Mr. Luter	–	40s.
John Whithorne	–	40s.
Morrys Longe	–	3*li.* 6s. 8d.
Edwarde Ditcher	–	20s.
John Lacye *th'elder*	–	20s.
John Evans	–	40s.
William Franckleyn	–	40s.
Edwarde Burton	–	3*li.* 6s. 8d.
John Clarke	–	40s.
Roberte Howse	–	40s.
Richarde Lister	–	40s.
William Caree	–	40s.
Martyn Canne	–	5*li.*
Edwarde Osborne	–	4*li.*
William Hewett	–	3*li.* 6s. 8d.
John Whitbroke	–	3*li.* 6s. 8d.
Thomas Altham	–	40s.
Edwarde Altham	–	3*li.*
William Hardinge	–	20s.
Thomas Bayarde	–	40s.
Thomas Blackwaye	–	3*li.*
Adam Hutchenson	–	30s.
Nicholas Parkyns	–	3*li.* 6s. 8d.
Thomas Russell	–	20s.
John Farryngtone	–	20s.
John Lacye *the younger*	–	30s.
John Spencer	–	40s.
Richarde Staper	–	20s.
Richarde Howse	–	20s.
Thomas Skynner	–	30s.
Laurence Pawmer	–	20s.
Laurence Mellowe	–	20s.
Robert Cogham	–	13s. 4d.
John Simcotts	–	20s.

Summa – 101*li.* 16s. 8d.

IREMONGERS.

Mr. Draper, *Ald.*	–	10*li.*
Mr. Chamberlen, *Ald.*	–	10*li.*
Mr. Avenon, *Ald.*	–	10*li.*
Thomas Browne	–	4*li.*

John Caree	–	4*li.*
Edwarde Brighte	–	4*li.*
William Dane	–	5*li.*
James Harvye	–	4*li.*
Anthony Gamage	–	3*li.*
Richarde Morrys	–	3*li.*
William Page	–	30s.
John Hill	–	20s.
Roberte Cowche	–	20s.
William Pennyfather	–	20s.
John Style	–	20s.
William Plasdon	–	30s.
Olyver Fyssher	–	20s.
William Rowe	–	40s.
Robert East	–	20s.
Peter Whalley	–	20s.
William Chapman	–	20s.
William Skidmore	–	10s.
Richarde Vallans	–	20s.
Roberte Waynam	–	20s.
John Downe	–	20s.
Robert Gadyn	–	20s.
John Atkinsone	–	10s.

Summa – 75*li.*

SALTERS.

Mr. Andrewe Sares	–	40s.
Mr. Richarde Gaywoode	–	40s.
Mr. Lawrens Withers	–	40s.
Mr. John Skott	–	40s.
Mr. Robert Harding	–	3*li.* 6s. 8d.
Mr. Thomas Lytton	–	40s.
Mr. Edmond Kay	–	50s.
Mr. John Howlande	–	40s.
Mr. Ambrose Nicholas	–	5*li.*
Mr. Anthony Cage	–	4*li.*
Mr. Robert Sole	–	30s.
Mr. William Gibbons	–	40s.
Mr. Owen Cleydon	–	40s.
William Agar	–	20s.
Thomas Chambers	–	20s.
William Jeffes	–	20s.
John Hardinge	–	3*li.*
William Hitchcoke	–	40s.
Thomas Halle	–	30s.
James Ramscroft	–	20s.
Richarde Geares	–	20s.
Edmonde Bowdler	–	20s.
Richarde Packingtone	–	20s.
Roberte Lowsley	–	20s.
William Webbe	–	3*li.*
Robert Cage	–	30s.
Robert Browinge	–	30s.
George Howse	–	30s.
John Sackforde	–	20s.
John Kinge	–	20s.
John Withers	–	20s.
John Sutton	–	20s.
Edwarde Ditchfield	–	40s.
Robert Howe	–	20s.

Brian Gardner	–	10s.
John Irelande	–	10s.

Summa – 62*li.* 6s. 8d.

VINTENERS.

William Andrewe	–	30s.
William Abraham	–	30s.
George Calver	–	30s.
John Cater	–	30s.
Thomas Lowe	–	3*li.*
James Marston	–	20s.
Edwarde Lunne	–	20s.
Roberte Gibsone	–	30s.
Stephen Skidmore	–	20s.
Nicholas Crostwait	–	20s.
Stephen Crask	–	20s.
William Hamon	–	20s.
John Sandersone	–	20s.
Edwarde Bethame	–	30s.
Henry Panell	–	20s.
Cuthbert Buckell	–	30s.
Anthony Gregory	–	40s.

Summa – 23*li.* 10s.

LETHERSELLERS.

Thomas Kightley	–	5*li.*
Richarde Pope	–	4*li.*
Frauncis Kightley	–	26s. 8d.
John Borne	–	20s.
Charles Pratt	–	40s.
William Harte	–	40s.
Hughe Offley	–	40s.
John Boyleson	–	30s.
Edwarde Taylor	–	30s.
Richarde Cryar	–	20s.
John Brooke	–	20s.

Summa – 25*li.* 6s. 8d.

COWPERS.

Mr. John Heathe	–	5*li.*
Stephen Heathe	–	30s.
Mr. Wilsone	–	20s.
Mr. Edmonde Birde	–	20s.

Summa – 8*li.* 10s.

PEWTERERS.

Mr. Curteis	–	20s.
Thomas Allen	–	20s.
Thomas Hassell	–	20s.
John Catcher	–	20s.

Summa – 4*li.*

TALLOWCHANDELERS.

Olyver Daubney	–	3*li.* 6s. 8d.
John Kynge	–	20s.
John Chapman	–	30s.
Michaell Blage	–	33s. 4d.
Thomas Garrett	–	20s.
John Bayle	–	30s.
John Warren	–	20s.
Hughe Ingrame	–	20s.

TALLOWCHANDELERS.		
Walter Stone	—	20s.
Hughe Benney	—	50s.
John Shorte	—	20s.
Summa – 16*li.* 10*s.*		

SCRIVENERS.		
William Persone	—	20s.
John Lee *th'elder*	—	20s.
Thomas Piersone	—	20s.
Thomas Godfrey	—	20s.
Thomas Warett	—	20s.
John Nordon	—	20s.
Barthelmew Brokelsbey		20s.
Thomas Wytton	—	40s.
Peter Baker	—	30s.
Thomas Brende	—	30s.
Pawle Pope	—	20s.
Wilfride Lewtye	—	30s.
Summa – 14*li.* 10*s.*		

DYARS.		
Richarde Cowper	—	40s.
John Wilsone	—	20s.
Randall Thickins	—	20s.
Thomas Hackett	—	30s.
John Baylye	—	20s.
Summa – 6*li.* 10*s.*		

CUTLERS.		
Laurence Grene	—	40s.
John Dylland	—	20s.
Thomas Malledge	—	20s.
Richarde Mathewe	—	20s.
William Tedcastell	—	20s.
Summa – 6*li.*		

GIRDELERS.		
Robert Branche	—	40s.
Cuthbert Bestone	—	40s.
Thomas Jennyngs	—	20s.
John Stevenson	—	40s.
Thomas Moffit	—	20s.
Henry Callys	—	20s.
Thomas Damser	—	50s.

Humfrey Browne	—	20s.
Summa – 13*li.*		

The names of Forren Men contributinge towardes the chardges aforesaid, with there severall somes, *viz.*

Mr. Bodley	—	40s.
Mr. Killegrewe	—	40s.
Mr. Modesley	—	20s.
A litle Purse	—	6s. 6d.

The Benevolence of Companies, as foloweth, to the said chardge:

Salters	—	6*li.*
Skynners	—	4*li.*
Lethersellers	—	6*li.*
Pewterers	—	40s.
Dyars	—	40s.
Girdlers	—	3*li.* 6s. 8d.
Summa – 23*li.* 6s. 7d.		

Summa totalis of all the moneys contributed – 1685*li.* 9s. 7d.

The Lymettes of the Grounde taken in for the soyle of the Burse intended, and the owtbuyldings thereof, brought in ther severall parishes as heretofore the same did belonge.

The parishe of St. Michaell in Cornehill. The length of the soyle of that parishe on the streate side, from the half or channell of the late alley called *Swane* alley on the east parte, unto the further moste of the late alley called *Newe* alley on the west parte, conteyneth feete of assise Cxv foote.

The bredth from the late *Swane* alley abbuttinge on the strete on the southe parte, unto the grounde late *Richarde Springhams* on the northe parte, conteyeth the feete of assise Cviij foote.

And the bredth from the streate at the late *Newe* alley gate on the southe parte, unto the grounds late of *Christs* Churche in *Canterbury* on the northe parte, counteyneth lxij foote of assise.

The parishe of St. Christofer. The length of the soyle of that parishe on the streate side of *Cornehill*, from the late *Newe* alley gate on the easte parte, unto the howse late *John Jakes* on the west parte, conteyneth lxvi foote and vi inches of assise.

The bredth from the said streate on the southe parte unto the howse whereon on one *Scother* late dwelled, and the grounde late of *Christe* Churche in *Canterburye*, on the north parte, conteyneth lxxiij foote and vi inches of assise.

The parishe of St. Barthilmewes the litle, in the Warde of Brode streate. The length of that parishe on the streate side from the howse whereon *Thomas Bates* dwelleth on the east parte, unto the house late of *John Jakes* on the west parte, conteyneth Cxcviij foote and vi inches of assise.

The bredeth from the streate on the north parte of the said *Bates* his howse, unto the groundes late *John Traves* on the southe parte, conteyneth xc foote of assise.

The bredeth at *Jakes* his howse from the streate side on the north parte, unto the groundes late *Walter Meares* and *William Sollames* on the south parte, conteyneth lxxvi foote of assise.

The length of the soyle of the entended Burse and buildings thereof in *Cornehill* side from the easte to west, conteyneth a hundred threscore and one foote six inches of assise, large measure.

The length on the streate syde called *Broad* streete, easte and west, conteyneth a hundreth eightene foote and sixe inches of assise.

The bredeth begynnynge at the late *Swane* alley on the streate side of *Cornehill*, unto the streate called *Broad* streate southe and northe, conteyneth a hundreth fourescore eightene foote of assise.

The breadeth from the late *Newe* alley gate on the streate of *Cornehill*, unto the streate called *Broade* strete, sowthe and northe, conteyneth a hundreth forty-nyne foote and six inches of assise.

———

Tythes dewe heretofore to the severall Churches heretofore mencyoned:

St. *Michaell* in *Cornehill*.	Dewe to that Churche yerely for tythe paide by the inhabytaunts that inhabyted on the soyle aforemencyoned and apperteyninge to that parrishe — — — — — — — — — — — }	59*s*. 2*d*.
St. *Christophers*.	Dewe to that Churche yerely for the tythe paide by the inhabytaunts that inhabyted on the soile aforemencyoned and apperteyninge to that parrishe — — — — — — — — — }	26*s*.
St. *Barthilmewe* the littell.	Dewe to that Churche yerely for the tythe paide by th'inhabytaunts that inhabited on the soyle aforemencyoned and apperteynynge to that parrishe — — — — — — — — — }	4*li*. 1*s*. 10*d*.

Summa totalis of the yearely Tithes, the offeringe daies not accompted — — — — — — — — — — — — — — — — — — — } 8*l*. 7*s*. 0*d*.

The Salary and Wagies paid to the Clarke and Raker in there several parishes:

St. *Michaells* in *Cornehill*.	Paide by the inhabitaunts inhabitinge heretofore the soyle apperteynynge to that parrishe for the salary of the Raker yerely — — — — — — — — — — — — — — — — }	24*s*. 4*d*.
	Paide by the inhabitaunts afore recyted towardes the Clarkes wagies for that parrishe yerely — }	36*s*.
St. *Christofers*.	Paide by the inhabitaunts of that parrishe for the Rakers wagies yerely — — — — — —	6*s*.
	Item. Paide by the inhabitaunts as aforesaide towarde the Clarkes wagies of that parrishe yerely — }	9*s*. 4*d*.
St. *Barthilmewe* the litle.	Paide by the inhabitaunts inhabitinge heretofore the soyle apperteynynge to that parrishe for the salary of the Raker yearely — — — — — — — — — — — — — — — — }	15*s*. 4*d*.
	Item. Paide by the inhabitaunts afore resyted towardes the Clarkes wagies of that parrishe yerely — }	32*s*. 4*d*.

Summa totalis of the Rakers wagies for the hole soyle — — — — — 45*s*. 8*d*.

Summa of the Clarkes wagies for the hole soile — — — — — — — 3*li*. 16*s*. 8*d*.

The Bedells Wages.	The ordinarye wagies dewe to the Bedells of *Cornehill* Warde and *Broadstrete* Warde accustomably yerely paide by the inhabitaunts inhabitinge heretofore that soyle, over and besides there offerings at X͞pmmas, there night watchinge and extraordynary allowaunces, amounts to yerely — — — — — — — — — — — — — — — — — — }	15*s*. 4*d*.
Housholders in that soile.	There were inhabitinge in that soyle cõmonly called howsholders, bearinge scott and lotte in the cittye as freemen oughte to doe, the number of xlvi howsholders — — — — }	xlvi.

The coppie of the Bill mencyonynge the promys made by Sir *Thomas Gresham* to the cittie, over and besides the bargayne made by the said Sir *Thomas*, included in the greate booke, whereunto Sir *William Garrard*, Sir *William Chester*, Mr. *Lionell Duckett*, alderman, and diverse other are wittnesses.

Be it remembred that the ix^th day of *February* in *anno Domini* 1565, the right worshipfull Sir *Thomas Gresham*, knight, in the howse of Mr. *John Ryvers*, alderman, and in the presents of the worshipfull Sir *William Garrarde*, Sir *William Chester*, knights, *Thomas Rowe*, *Lyonell Duckett*, and the foresaid *John Ryvers*, aldermen, *German Ceolle* and *Thomas Banister*, merchaunts, did most franckly and lovingly graunte and promysse that w^thin one moneth next after the buildinge and fully fynisshinge of the Burse and Burse pawnes and other building intended, he wold assure to the citie for the citties use the moytie of all the said Burse, pawnes, and other buildings, aswell of those buildings planted within the circuite of the Burse as without; the proffitts thereof to come to the said citie, to the use of the mayor and cõminaltye of the said city, after the deceasse of the said Sir *Thomas Gressham* and of his wiffe, so that it happen that the said Sir *Thomas* doe dye without yssue of his body lawfully begotten: And the other moytye he haith likewise promysed to leave to the Marcerye, with like estate and like condicõn as aforesaid: and for the sewer performaunce of the premysses, the said Sir *Thomas*, in the presens of the parsons aforenamed, did give his hande to Sir *William Garrard*, and dranke a carouse to *Thomas Rowe*, the day and yere aforesaid. In wittnes whereof the persones aforenamed as wittnesses have set-to there handes.

WILLIAM GARRARD.   THOMAS ROWE.
WILLIAM CHESTER.   LIONELL DUCKETT.
JOHN RYVERS.
THOMAS BANISTER.

The Accomptauntes Charge:

Mr. *Jackman*, alderman, and *Thomas Rowe*, chargeth themselves to have come to there handes of the moneys made of the howses solde as aforesaid, the some of 490*li*. 16*s*. 8*d*. And of th'imprest money prested by certen companyes as afore mencyoned, 490*li*. And of the contribution money contributed by those persones in this booke recyted, the some of 1685*li*. 9*s*. 7*d*. whereof there came to the handes of Mr. *Jackman* the some of 2563*li*., and to the handes of *Thomas Rowe*, 83*li*. 6*s*. 6*d*., whiche maketh the some aforerecyted –   2646*li*.   6*s*.   3*d*.

The Accomptauntes Discharge:

Paide by the aforenamed accomptaunts of the moneys come to there handes as is aforesaide, aswell for the purchase made and paide for in this booke particulerly mencyoned, as also the redempcõn of mens leases and interests and other necessary expences likewise in this booke particulerly mencyoned and paide, the some of –   2645*li*.   4*s*.

Soe these Accomptauntes oweth to this Accompt – – – – – – – – – –   22*s*. 3*d*.

finis — By THOMAS ROWE.

APPENDIX II

In 1839 portions of the entries relating to the Exchange were abstracted from the City records and from the Gresham Repertories, and were printed. We here reprint the entries relating to the building of the Second Exchange.

AGREEMENTS WITH WORKMEN

6th *April, 1669*

THE committee also agreed with *John Tanner*, bricklayer, to doe all the brickworke for the incloseing the inner quadrangle of the Exchange according as Mr. *Cartwright* shall direct, untill new bricks are burned and common to bee had. And hee hereby promiseth to doe the same for 6*l.* 15*s. per* rodd.

In witnesse whereof I the said *John Tanner* have hereunto subscribed my hand, this   of *Aprill, anno Dom.* 1669.

They alsoe agreed with   *Doegood*, plaisterer, to doe all the plaine plaistering worke, which is to bee very well done, and floted; for which the committee are to give him twelve pence *per* yard, and fower pence *per* yard for rendring, if well done to theire content: and in case the city plaisterer bee content to worke upon these termes, than he to doe one moity of the worke.

In witnesse whereof, I the said   *Doegood* have hereunto subscribed my hand, this   day of *Aprill, anno Dom.* 1669.

They also agreed with *Matthew Sheppy*, glasier, to doe all the glasse worke, *viz.* that with quarryes att five pence *per* foote, and that with squares att six pence *per* foote. All his worke to bee well leaded and cemented to beare of the weather; and hee is to bring a patterne of his leade, according to which hee will performe the wholle.

In witnesse whereof, I the said *Matthew Sheppey* have hereunto subscribed my hand, this   day of *April, anno Dom.* 1669.

They also agreed with *Michaell Derby*, painter, to doe all the plaine oyle worke throughout the Exchange, three times over, and well stopped with putty, att nyne pence *per* yard square; and for all lights, they are either to bee measured or to bee valued by whome the committee shall appoynt.

In witnesse whereof, I the said *Michaell Derby* have hereunto sett my hand this seaven and twentith day of *Aprill, anno Dom.* 1669.

Upon treaty with *Roger Jerman* for the carpenter's worke, hee declared that the prizes following weare the lowest hee could descend to, *viz.*:

	l	*s.*	*d.*
For the roofeing, if hee weare held to cover itt with two ynch yellow deale plankes, as in the first agreement, nothing could bee abated of, *per* square, – – – – – – –	6	12	6
But if hee weare permitted to cover with good yellow dramdeale, then – – – – –	5	12	6
For floreing, *per* square – – – – – – –	7	12	6
For each modillion cornice, to bee four foote long, and twelve ynches one way and eight ynches the other, and two foote of it carved, – – – – – – – – – – – – –	0	18	0
For ceiling joysts, if done with oake, *per* square (one hundred squares in all) – – –	1	10	0
But if done with deale, then *per* square – –	1	5	0
For each lucerne window, there being tenne in all, for carpenter's worke onely,	20	0	0
For each square of guttering with oake –	3	0	0

7th *April,* 1669

The committee now agreed with *Thomas Cartwright*, mason, for stone and workemanshipp, by him to bee provided, wrought, and layd in the building the porticos on the outsides of the Royall Exchange, for the prizes following, *viz.*:

	s.	*d.*
For paveing with black marble and *Purbeck*	1	4
For black marble step, six ynches thick and one foote broad, within the quadrangle, *per* foote – – – – – – – – – – –	4	6
For marble step to lye betweene the colums, six ynches thick, and two foote nine inches broad, runing measure – – – –	18	0
But if done with *Porland* stone, then *per* foote – – – – – – – – – – – – – –	6	6
For the marble steps for the staires, six ynches thick and one foote broad, *per* foote, runing measure – – – – – –	5	0
For paveing the halfe paces with *Purbeck* and black marble *per* foote – – – – – –	1	4
For paveing the upper pawne with *Mitchells, per* foote – – – – – – – – –	0	8
For rustick peeres and arches, *per* foote –	5	0
Frontispeece worke, to bee measured cubically, the mason finding stone, { If upright, *per* foote – – – –	5	0
{ If mouldings, *per* foote – – – –	7	6
But if the committee find stone, then *per* foote – – – – – – – – – – – – – – –	5	9
For ashler, if itt bee of freestone – – – –	5	0

For the four great colums on the south side, thirty-five foote high and three and a half ynches diameter (the capitalls to bee carved), *per* foote – – – – – – – –   7   6

For *Purbeck* steps in the outward walke, six ynches thick and one foote broad, *per* foote   2   2

All upright worke that projects not forward, *per* foote – – – – – – – – – –   5   0

The Royal Exchange — A Chronology

Compiled by JOHN WATTS

For many years the meeting place of City merchants was in Lombard Street where they assembled twice a day in the open air exposed to all weathers. However, so opposed were they to any change, when in 1534 a letter was received from Henry VIII suggesting the use of Leadenhall for their meetings, the proposal was not accepted in Common Council.

In 1537 Sir Richard Gresham, Lord Mayor (and father of Sir Thomas), laid before Thomas Cromwell, then Lord Privy Seal, a design for a London bourse similar to that newly erected at Antwerp. Sir Richard wrote again to Cromwell on 25 July 1538 reminding him of the proposal.

Sir Thomas Gresham (1519–79) was admitted to Royal Service and in 1544 began trading in the Low Countries on King Henry VIII's behalf. In 1551 he was appointed to the ancient office of King's Merchant, which involved negotiating loans for the Crown from bankers in Antwerp and procuring supplies of military equipment for the State with credit earned from English cloth exports. Gresham remained in the Low Countries throughout much of the 1560s, raising loans and serving as a brilliant diplomat. By then acting for Queen Elizabeth I, he was rewarded with a knighthood and liberal grants of land. Stimulated by Antwerp's greatness, he offered to use his personal fortune to erect a London bourse.

A list of dates, events and people associated with the three buildings, follows.

14 May 1566	Common Council ordered that indentures should be sealed.
28 May 1566	Plans approved by the Court of Aldermen.
7 June 1566	Sir Thomas Gresham laid the first stone. Architect/Clerk of Works Hendryck van Paesschen (a Fleming); the design being a tolerably close imitation of the great Burse of Antwerp, the timber coming from the Gresham estates at Battisford and Ringshall in Suffolk and other building material from the Continent.
22 December 1568	Building opened.
23 January 1571	Visited by Queen Elizabeth I after dining with Sir Thomas Gresham at his house in Bishopsgate. She ordered that the bourse be called 'The Roiall Exchainge from thenceforth and not otherwise'.
21 November 1579	After the death of the founder, his widow contested the provisions in the will and petitioned the Aldermen and Lord Mayor to no avail.
23 November 1596	Lady Gresham died at Osterley Park.
17 March 1597	First meeting of the Joint Grand Gresham Committee.
3/4 September 1666	Building destroyed in the Great Fire.

FIRST ROYAL EXCHANGE

4 January 1564	At a Court of Aldermen, Sir Thomas Gresham said that he would be willing to erect a bourse if land could be provided.
8 January 1565	Court of Aldermen agreed to the building and arrangements were made to secure land fronting on to Cornhill (the total cost of the site was £3,532 17s. 10d. from 742 donations).
9 February 1566	Sir Thomas Gresham promised that within one month after the founding of the bourse he would make over the whole of the profits in equal parts to the City and to the Mercers' Company in case he should die childless and after the death of his wife.

SECOND ROYAL EXCHANGE

25 April 1667	Edward Jerman appointed architect.
6 May 1667	Foundation stone laid.
21 September 1667	King Charles II approved plans submitted by the Joint Grand Gresham Committee.
23 October 1667	Visit by Charles II to fix the first pillar on the west side of the north entrance.
31 October 1667	Visit by the Duke of York to fix the pillar on the east side of same.
18 November 1667	Visit by Prince Rupert to fix the pillar on the east side of the south entrance.
28 November 1668	Following the death of Edward Jerman, Thomas Cartwright, the mason, was appointed to complete Jerman's designs.

26 February 1669	In acknowledgement of his services, a presentation of plate was made to Cartwright by the Committee.
28 September 1669	Completed building (at a cost of £51,456 7s. 4d. plus £6,666 10s. 0d. spent on enlarging the site) opened by the Lord Mayor, Sir William Turner in place of the King.
9 March 1719	Mines Royal and Mineral and Battery Works (two charters of Elizabethan origin) were acquired and commenced insuring ships and merchandise in the Royal Exchange. Thomas Lord Onslow was appointed Governor (Capital £1,152,000).
22 June 1720	The above were succeeded by the granting of the first Royal Charter (Marine) incorporating The Royal Exchange Assurance.
29 April 1721	The second Royal Charter (Fire & Life) was granted to The Royal Exchange Assurance. (London Assurance which also received Royal Charters at the same time eventually moved into the Royal Exchange in 1845 and vacated in 1922 — see below).
10 April 1723	The Royal Exchange Assurance original grant of arms recorded at the College of Arms (grant later destroyed in the 1838 Fire).
7 March 1774	'Lloyd's Coffee-House' moved to the first floor in premises formerly occupied by the British Herring Fishery Society. (Lloyd's remained a tenant until 1928 — see below.)
1819–1824	The tower was taken down and rebuilt to the design of Mr George Smith, surveyor of the Gresham Estate, at a cost of £40,000 including other extensive repairs and alterations.
10 January 1838	Building destroyed by fire which began in Lloyd's rooms soon after 10 p.m.
28 March 1838	Royal Exchange Assurance paid £45,000 in settlement of the fire insurance claim (one half was paid to the Corporation of London and the other to the Mercers' Company).

THIRD ROYAL EXCHANGE

16 August 1838	Royal Assent given to the Act for rebuilding.
4 January 1839	Open design competition announced.
26 March 1839	Detailed instructions issued for a new building to be designed at a cost of £150,000.
1 August 1839	Deadline for delivery of designs — 38 submitted to be judged by Sir Robert Smirke, Mr Joseph Gwilt and Mr Philip Hardwick.
10 October 1839	Judges report submitted. No overall recommendation but the three prizes of £300, £200 and £100 were given to designs 36, 43 and 37 respectively.
19 November 1839	The Gresham Committee decided that eight designs should be referred to Mr George Smith and Mr William Tite.
29 November 1839	Mr Tite declined the reference.
31 January 1840	Mr Smith surveyor to the Committee reported that he considered all designs to be deficient. The Committee decided to ballot five eminent architects plus one of the original participants.
11 February 1840	Four declined to take part, leaving Mr Cockerell and Mr Tite to submit designs.
28 April 1840	Designs submitted by both architects.
4 May 1840	The Committee was addressed by each architect.
7 May 1840	The design by William Tite adopted.
29 September 1840	Approval given by the Lords Commissioners of Her Majesty's Treasury.
20 September 1841	The contract for the superstructure was awarded to Thomas Jackson in the sum of £137,600. The sculpture over the pediment was designed by Richard Westmacott, ARA (cost £3,150).
16 October 1841	Foundation contract awarded to Messrs Robert & George Webb in the sum of £8,124.
17 January 1842	Foundation stone laid by HRH Prince Albert.
18 June 1844	Statue of the Duke of Wellington by Sir Francis Chantry unveiled on the anniversary of the Battle of Waterloo in the presence of HM the King of Saxony and the Lord Mayor.
28 October 1844	The building opened by HM Queen Victoria and HRH Prince Albert.
28 October 1845	Marble statue of Queen Victoria by Mr T. G. Lough unveiled in centre of the Courtyard (cost £1,050).
19 July 1847	Marble statue of Prince Albert by Mr T. G. Lough unveiled in Lloyd's vestibule.

1883/84	Courtyard roofed after the desisn of Charles Barry (cost £12,000).
28 May 1895	First of a series of murals in the Ambulatory of the Courtyard unveiled by the Lord Mayor (see also 1921).
19 June 1896	Replacement statue of Queen Victoria by Hamo Thornycroft, RA, unveiled in the presence of the Lord Mayor.
6 April 1905	The Royal Exchange Assurance grant of arms re-exemplified at the College of Arms.
30 July 1918	Royal Exchange Assurance purchased London Assurance lease for £50,000 with possession in 1922.
23 February 1921	Unveiling by the Lord Mayor of the panel 'The Destruction of the second Royal Exchange in 1838' by Stanhope Forbes, ARA (presented by REA to commemorate its Bicentenary).
5 April 1922	Committee formed to decide alterations — Board Room, Committee Room, Soane Room and adjoining rooms built.
28 March 1923	First Court held following building work.
24 March 1928	Lloyd's moved to Leadenhall Street.
2 September 1928	Following purchase of Lloyd's lease for £97,800, work started on internal alterations at a cost of £145,000.
4 November 1929	Work completed.
17 February 1938	Visit by HM Queen Mary.
4 May 1953	Opening of the Mermaid Theatre by Bernard Miles in the Courtyard for Queen Elizabeth II's Coronation with performances of *As You Like It*, *Eastward, Ho!* and *Macbeth*. The three-month season also included Purcell's opera *Dido and Aeneas* in which Kirsten Flagstad gave her farewell stage performance on 5 June.
17 November 1953	Visit by HM Queen Elizabeth, the Queen Mother.
15 May 1968	The merger of The Royal Exchange Assurance and Guardian Assurance was incorporated under the Companies Act 1948–67.
1 November 1968	Guardian Royal Exchange plc acquired the shares of both companies and commenced trading.
3 August 1970	Guardian Royal Exchange Assurance Limited Armorial Bearing granted by Letters Patent at the College of Arms.

Early in 1980 deterioration of the cast iron dome caused by rain water penetrating resulted in sections of the internal cornice to fall and this lead to the closure of the courtyard.

In 1982 a roofed temporary trading floor was constructed for LIFFE (London International Financial Futures Exchange). Trading took place between 30 September 1982 and 13 December 1991 when LIFFE moved to larger premises at Cannon Bridge having become the second largest Exchange in the world and by far the largest in Europe.

Consideration of the proposed refurbishment took place over a number of years and due to the building's Grade I listing many conservation interests were involved before planning consent was granted to the designs prepared by the Fitzroy Robinson Partnership, in sympathy with Tite's original building.

19 November 1986	GRE Board approval was given to negotiate redevelopment without commitment (estimated cost £20–£30M).
16 December 1987	GRE Board discussed project costing in detail and agreed that the Life fund would acquire the General fund interest in the lease for £8M. Estimated cost including fees £45M plus a fit out cost of £5M.
18 January 1988	Executive, Secretary's Department, Finance and Investment Departments removed to 68 King William Street.
30 June 1988	GRE evacuation of the Royal Exchange completed.
28 September 1988	Contract enabling works started.
3 October 1988	John Laing Construction took over the building for the main contract.
4 October 1988	Building contract signed.
25 December 1990	GRE (UK) lease 43% of the total office area for £1.6M p.a. with 5 year rent reviews and a 6 month rent-free period. Other tenants include the State Street Bank and Trust Company, Fischer Francis Trees & Watts and Sidley & Austin.
23 October 1991	Visit by HM Queen Elizabeth II to re-open the refurbished building.
28 October 1994	150th anniversary of Queen Victoria's visit and the opening of the third Royal Exchange.
31 December 1996	LIFFE relinquish lease on the Courtyard.

Index

Compiled by HANA SAMBROOK, MA PhD

Note: Page numbers in italics refer to captions to Figures in the text